DICTIONARY
OF MISSION

The *American Society of Missiology Series,* in collaboration with Orbis Books, seeks to publish scholarly works of high merit and wide interest on numerous aspects of missiology — the study of mission. Able presentations on new and creative approaches to the practice and understanding of mission will receive close attention.

Previously published in
The American Society of Missiology Series

American Society of Missiology Series, No. 24

DICTIONARY OF MISSION

Theology, History, Perspectives

Edited by
Karl Müller, SVD
Theo Sundermeier
Stephen B. Bevans, SVD
Richard H. Bliese

ORBIS BOOKS

Maryknoll, New York 10545

This English translation and edition of *Dictionary of Mission* is copyright © 1997 by Stephen B. Bevans and Richard H. Bliese. This work is a translation and English-language revision of *Lexikon Missionstheologischer Grundbegriffe* (Dictionary of basic mission theology concepts), copyright © 1987 by Dr. Friedrich Kaufmann, edited by Karl Müller and Theo Sundermeier and published by Dietrich Reimer Verlag, Unter den Eichen, 57, 1000 Berlin 45, Germany. The initial translators of the German articles were Francis Mansfield, SVD, Eleonor Sakson, Klaus-Dieter Stoll, Vincent Twomey, SVD, and Michael Walpoe.

Published by Orbis Books, P.O. Box 308, Maryknoll, New York 10545-0308, U.S.A.
Manufactured in the United States of America.

Library of Congress Cataloging-in-Publication Data

Lexikon Missionstheologischer Grundbegriffe.   English
   Dictionary of mission : theology, history, perspectives / edited
by Karl Müller ... [et al.] ; foreword by Robert J. Schreiter.
     p.   cm.   (American Society of Missiology series ; no. 24)
   Includes bibliographical references.
   ISBN 1-57075-148-X
   1. Missions – Theory – Dictionaries.   2. Theology – Dictionaries.
I. Müller, Karl, 1918– .   II. Title.
BV2040.L4813   1997
266′.001 – dc21   97–23162
                                           CIP

Dedicated by
Stephen B. Bevans
to his confreres in
the Society of the Divine Word
Gary Riebe-Estrella
Roger Schroeder
Stanley Uroda

Dedicated by Richard H. Bliese
to his wife, Nina,
and to their children,
Aaron and Stephanie

Contents

FOREWORD

Robert J. Schreiter, CPPS

Theology of mission has undergone significant development in the latter half of the twentieth century. In the immediate period after the close of the colonial era in the late 1960s and early 1970s, mission itself came under profound questioning. It was indeed uncertain how or even if mission could continue, so inextricably linked it seemed to be with imperial expansion and a colonial mentality. Yet at the same time new impulses were emerging to rethink mission, marked especially by Vatican II on the Roman Catholic side and new thinking among the member churches of the World Council of Churches for Protestants and Orthodox. By the early 1980s that thinking was coming to fruition, perhaps most notably seen at the 1981 meeting of SEDOS (a research and service institute of Roman Catholic missionary orders), where mission was redefined under the fourfold heading of proclamation, dialogue, inculturation, and liberation. If mission in the previous period had been defined primarily in terms of expansion, this new approach, captured in this fourfold understanding, was marked by a sense of solidarity and accompaniment — walking with, rather than leading and guiding in evangelization.

Some would argue that mission is undergoing even further change as a result of the realignment of the world since the fall of the Berlin Wall in 1989 and the rapid advances in communications technology. Themes of solidarity and accompaniment persist in the missiological literature, but these approaches are now being exercised under different conditions. The world has been globalized — that is to say, made more radically into a single place — and at the same time particularized as the old communist-capitalist hegemony has given way to a multipolar and more unstable reality. In contrast to the earlier division of the world into East-West or North-South patterns, a pattern of inclusion-exclusion in the economy and in communications has become characteristic of the post-1989 era. There is also a great deal more localized conflict and overt violence than was permitted for most of the post–World War II period, and that has brought untold suffering to many nations and a migration of peoples unprecedented in history. At the same time, religious movements — Pentecostal and charismatic, as well as new religious and fundamentalist — respond to this turmoil and clearly mark the burgeoning religious scene in a way that is more profound than the response of the older, denominational churches. All of this makes for a deep churning of the social, cultural, and political matrix in which Christian mission finds itself at century's end.

Mission theology, because of its engagement with the world, thoroughly reflects the environment in which it takes place. It has been helped conceptually and theologically by its being moved from the periphery of the Christian church's concerns into the very ecclesial center in the last several decades. The ecumenical movement among the churches in that same period has also produced a more multifaceted and balanced approach to reflection on the single mission of the church catholic. The voices of the regional churches that were once the object of mission add new resonance to the whole as they have taken their places alongside (and sometimes ahead of) the North Atlantic churches that evangelized them. All of these developments make a reassessment of the state of mission in its theology, history, and multiple perspectives timely.

The volume you now have before you reflects these many changes that mission has undergone in the last half-century. Conceived and developed by two of Europe's most eminent missiologists, in the country where the scientific and sustained study of mission first took shape, it represents the finest of the chorus of voices that comprise contemporary missiology. It has now been updated and expanded by two North American missiologists who work together at one of the major centers for reflection on mission today. The choice of topics and the authors to address them reflects what Christian mission has become: a genuinely worldwide and ecumenical phenomenon. That there would be entries on regional theological developments is indicative of how the world church is developing. A host of other topics here explored show too how the landscape of mission is changing. Taken as a whole, then, the *Dictionary of Mission* is a road map through this exciting and challenging terrain.

Producing a dictionary of this scope and range, amid a field that continues to undergo development as the world it addresses also changes, is a prodigious accomplishment. The original editors, and now the North American editors who have expanded and updated it, are to be congratulated for having provided us with a benchmark by which to gauge missiology as we move into the third millennium.

PREFACE TO THE SERIES

The purpose of the American Society of Missiology (ASM) Series is to publish —
without regard for disciplinary, national, or denominational boundaries — scholarly works of high quality and wide interest on missiological themes from the
entire spectrum of scholarly pursuits relevant to Christian mission, which is
always the focus of books in the Series.

By "mission" is meant the effort to effect passage over the boundary between
faith in Jesus Christ and its absence. In this understanding of mission, the basic
functions of Christian proclamation, dialogue, witness, service, worship, liberation, and nurture are of special concern. And in that context questions arise,
including, How does the transition from one cultural context to another influence
the shape and interaction between these dynamic functions, especially in regard
to the cultural and religious plurality that comprise the global context of Christian
mission?

The promotion of scholarly dialogue among missiologists and among missiologists and scholars in other fields of inquiry may involve the publication of views
that some missiologists cannot accept, and with which members of the Editorial
Committee do not agree. Manuscripts published in the Series reflect the opinions
of their authors and are not understood to represent the position of the American
Society of Missiology or of the Editorial Committee. Selection is guided by such
criteria as intrinsic worth, readability, and accessibility to a range of interested
persons and not merely to experts or specialists.

The ASM Series Editorial Committee
James A. Scherer, Chair
Mary Motte, FMM
Charles Taber

PREFACE TO
THE ENGLISH EDITION

Stephen B. Bevans, SVD, and Richard H. Bliese

The 1987 publication of the *Lexikon Missionstheologischer Grundbegriffe,* under the joint editorship of Karl Müller and Theo Sundermeier, provided the German-speaking and scholarly world with a work that was judged "unparalleled in its presentation of basic concepts of mission theology"[1] and "a bonanza not only for the student of mission, but also for those working in the 'field.'"[2] The *Lexikon* contained 110 entries that spanned the breadth of contemporary missiological thought, providing the reader with ample bibliography at the end of each. Some ninety scholars, Catholic, Protestant, and Orthodox, contributed to the volume, among which were some of the most important thinkers in theology — and in particular mission theology — today. Besides the contributions of editors Karl Müller and Theo Sundermeier, entries came from such notables as Catalino G. Arévalo, David J. Bosch, Walbert Bühlmann, Arnulf Camps, Anscar J. Chupungco, Horst Rzepkowski, Hans-Werner Gensichen, Dietrich Ritschl, Leo Scheffczyk, M. M. Thomas, and Hans Waldenfels — to name but a few.

Reviewing the *Lexikon* in the journal *Missiology,* Robert J. Schreiter remarked that while it might be "too focused on the German-speaking world to warrant translation," it should nevertheless "inspire English-speaking missiologists to try to produce a similar work for use in their territory."[3] On the one hand, what we offer in this English edition of Müller and Sundermeier's work *is* a translation of the original German edition, and so in a certain sense we have not heeded our wise colleague's advice. On the other hand, what we have edited for English-speaking readers is, in many ways, quite a different book from the one that appeared in German a decade ago. We have worked over the last several years to produce a book that takes advantage of the richness of the original work, while at the same time attempting to produce a dictionary of mission theology that reflects the missiological currents of the 1990s and looks forward to some of the issues of the first years of the new century and millennium.

Readers of this volume will, hopefully, find a missiological dictionary that is even more complete and useful than the 1987 German edition. In many cases we have updated and revised the original articles, at times adding entire paragraphs to supplement the material or deleting sections which were outdated or which might have been of interest to only a limited readership. In other cases we have asked other authors to augment or even rewrite articles; in still other cases we

---

1. K. Piskaty, "An Encyclopedia of Mission Theology," review in *IRM* 77/311/312 (July/October 1989) 466.
2. F. Dierks, review in *Missionalia* 16/2 (August 1988) 112.
3. R. J. Schreiter, review in *Missiol* 17/4 (October 1989) 483.

have added articles, for example, "North American Mission Theology," "Common Witness," "Globalization," "Reconciliation," and "Ecology and Mission." Realizing that the German contributors were, in the main, men, we requested several more women to contribute articles. In addition, we have updated and anglicized the *Lexikon*'s extensive bibliographical entries and have provided some biographical data on all the contributors. This English edition has taken care to use, wherever possible, inclusive language both for human beings and for God. In some instances we have changed language that might have seemed to reflect a Western bias. For example, for the term "younger churches" we have often substituted terms like "Asian churches," "churches in India," or "churches in Latin America."

Abbreviations of periodicals, dictionaries, encyclopedias, and documents of the magisterium cited in the bibliographies and text have been listed (with some adaptations) according to the abbreviations given in the volume *Abkürzungsverzeichnis* in the 1976 edition of *Theologische Realenzyklopädie*. Where works were not included in this source, we invented our own abbreviations. A complete list of abbreviations is found on pp. xxi–xxvi.

Throughout the text, we have used the symbol → to indicate cross references.

We have entitled this English edition of Müller and Sundermeier's original work *Dictionary of Mission: Theology, History, Perspectives*. We hope that this title faithfully renders the German title in English and accurately captures the scope of the work. The volume is basically *theological* in content, but there are a number of articles that contain important historical information (e.g., the article "Rites Controversy") and provide perspectives on a number of current missiological issues (e.g., the articles "Fundamentalism" and "Common Witness"). As we worked on the English edition and began to add new articles to the original contents of the *Lexikon,* it became more and more apparent to us that many more topics could be treated in specific articles. While we realized, finally, that readers will not find specific articles on every aspect of mission and mission theology in this work, many more topics are treated in the context of the individual articles.

As we offer this volume to the missiological community, we are deeply aware of the debt we owe to Karl Müller, Theo Sundermeier, and the original contributors to the *Lexikon* for the careful scholarship and broad vision that marked the German edition. We hope that, in having made their efforts more available to the English-speaking world, we have been faithful to their spirit of ecumenical cooperation and theological substance. We are also aware that without the patience — and persistence — of the editorial staff at Orbis Books, and in particular of Bill Burrows, this English edition of the *Lexikon* would never have seen the light of day. Bill conceived the idea of this work in 1990, carefully shepherded it through the translation and editorial process, and even contributed two important articles. We need to express gratitude to Robert Schreiter as well. Bob has been involved in this project from the beginning and played an important role in the initial planning and design of this edition. We are further grateful to him not only for his fine contributions to the volume but for agreeing to write the foreword.

The last several years we have served as director (Bevans) and associate director (Bliese) of a new venture in ecumenical theological education: the Chicago Center for Global Ministries. The center was founded in 1993 by the Catholic Theological Union (CTU), the Lutheran School of Theology at Chicago (LSTC), and the McCormick Theological Seminary (MTS) and is a result of the kind of ecumenical commitment that is evident in the *Lexikon* and that is surely the future of the church's mission. We are grateful to the present presidents and deans of the three sponsoring schools of our center: President Bill Lesher and Dean Ralph Klein of LSTC, President Cynthia Campbell and Dean Heidi Hadsell of MTS, and President Donald Senior and Dean Gary Riebe-Estrella of CTU; we are also grateful to past acting-president Dan Little of MTS, past presisdent of CTU Norman Bevan, and former deans Kathleen Hughes and Leslie Hoppe of CTU. Their vision and support have made possible a number of Catholic/Lutheran ventures, including the present one.

We dedicate this book to people with whom we share our lives. Richard dedicates the book to his wife, Nina, and to his two children, Aaron and Stephanie. Steve dedicates his work to Gary Riebe-Estrella, Roger Schroeder, and Stan Uroda, fellow members of his religious congregation, the Society of the Divine Word. Mission, ultimately, is about relationships; it is about crossing boundaries, calling for conversion, and being converted ourselves. If we have succeeded in doing this in our own lives, it is in large part due to the love, challenge, and faithfulness of these people, whom we love and who — by God's amazing grace — love us.

PREFACE TO
THE GERMAN EDITION

Karl Müller, SVD, and Theo Sundermeier

In recent years, because of internal and external, theological and contextual reasons, it has become necessary to reflect anew on the subject of mission. The erosion of Christendom in traditional Christian countries, the end of the hegemony of the West and its culture, the growing self-confidence and political influence of the world's religions, the economic rift between North and South — all these things not only have had a dramatic impact on the peoples of the Third World but have also had an impact on churches worldwide. This is reflected in new exegetical insights, in the statements from Vatican II about the possibility of salvation in other religions, in the statements of world missionary conferences concerning the churches' social responsibility, and, finally, in the new orientations of mission theology emerging from the churches of the Third World. All aspects of the theology of mission need to be thought through once again. The concerns of mission theology are, in most theological dictionaries and encyclopedias, taken up only superficially. Furthermore, the time is long past when the riches of mission studies could be brought together by a single scholar in a way that is intellectually rigorous. It appeared necessary to us, therefore, to bring together and put into focus in one specific dictionary both technical information and current perspectives in mission theology.

With this idea in mind, we consciously avoided including mere reports about individual countries and their mission histories. We suggested to the contributors, rather, that they emphasize a systematic theological perspective and use models in approaching theological issues. This book, we hope, should quickly communicate to the reader a general overview of each topic that is treated. A relatively complete cross-reference system (cross references are indicated by the symbol →) should make it possible to cross-check individual topics and recognize personal opinions.

As we worked on this volume, it became increasingly apparent how close the churches are in the area of mission theology. The distribution of articles among Protestant and Catholic authors is relatively even. Unfortunately, there are only a few Orthodox authors included. Naturally, each author stresses particular aspects out of his or her own tradition. We recognized, however, that the differences that arose hardly touched upon any fundamentals of faith. The interconfessional aspect of our work brought us much joy.

We hope that this book will be a help to many: that it will provide stimulus for theologians for further research and provide direction for those who practice mission. For all, we hope that it might provide a deeper encounter with him who said, "Go, make disciples of all nations."

What is left to us is the honor of thanking all those who have made contributions from the very beginning of this project: Dr. Kaufmann of the Dietrich Reimer Verlag, for his unwavering interest in this undertaking; Dr. H. J. Findeis, for his important editorial work; our colleagues at the Missiological Institute at St. Augustin, in particular Ms. M. Ludwig. We also would like to thank the members of the Seminar in Theology at the University of Heidelberg, above all A. Grünschloß, T. Weiß, J. Anhegger, V. Küster, L. Schmidtke, and Ms. G. Rauscher, who saw to it that the entire manuscript was computerized and who, together with the friendly support of the data center of the University of Heidelberg, made sure that this volume came to press on time. Our thanks go as well to the contributors for their outstanding collaboration and — last but not least — to the German Society of Missiology, the Protestant Church of Westphalia, the International Association of Mission Studies, and the SVD Missiological Institute for their generous financial support.

ABBREVIATIONS OF PERIODICALS AND DOCUMENTS

AA	*Apostolicam Actuositatem* (Decree on the Apostolate of the Laity [Vatican II])
AAS	*Acta Apostolicae Sedis*
AbenR	*American Benedictine Review*
ACr	*Arte cristiana*
AfCS	*African Christian Studies*
AfER	*African Ecclesiastical Review*
AfStR	*African Studies Review*
AG	*Ad Gentes* (Decree on the Church's Missionary Activity [Vatican II])
AJIL	*American Journal of International Law*
AMS	*Americas: A Quarterly Review of Inter-American Cultural History*
AMZ	*Allgemeine Missionszeitschrift*
APQ	*American Philosophical Quarterly*
ARA	*Annual Review of Anthropology*
AsCS	*Asian Cultural Studies*
AThR	*Anglican Theological Review*
ATJ	*African Theological Journal*
AusBR	*Australian Biblical Review*
BEM	*Baptism, Eucharist, and Ministry*
BgMiss	*Bibliografia Missionaria*
BPCDR	*Bulletin Pontificum Consilium pro Dialogo inter Religiones*
BTA	*Bulletin de Théologie Africaine*
BTB	*Biblical Theological Bulletin*
BThA	*Bulletin de Théologie Africaine*
BThZ	*Biblische Theologische Zeitschrift*
BUC	*Bulletin de l'Union du Clergé*
CArtS	*Cahiers de l'art sacré*
CatMiss	*Catechesi Missionaria*
CBQ	*Catholic Biblical Quarterly*
CCGMpap	*CCGM Papers*
CD	*Church Dogmatics* (by Karl Barth)
CDCW	*Concise Dictionary of the Christian World Mission*
CF	*Culture et Foi / Cultures and Faith / Culturas y Fe*

ChD	*Christus Dominus* (Decree on the Bishops' Pastoral Office in the Church [Vatican II])
ChK	*Christliche Kunst*
ChrC	*Christianity and Crisis*
ChrTo	*Christianity Today*
CILJ	*Cornell International Law Journal*
CPDBT	*Collegeville Pastoral Dictionary of Biblical Theology*
CRA	*Cahiers des Religions Africaines*
CTM	*Currents in Theology and Mission*
CW	"Common Witness"
DBS	*Dictionary of the Bible* (ed. William Smith)
DBSup	*Dictionnaire de la Bible: Supplément*
DBV	*Dictionnaire de la Bible* (published by Fulcran Vigouroux)
DEM	*Dictionary of the Ecumenical Movement*
DH	*Dignitatis Humanae* (Declaration on Religious Freedom [Vatican II])
DictR	*Dictionnaire des Religions*
Dlg	*Dialog: A Journal of Theology*
DREA	*Dictionary of Religious Education*
DS	Denzinger-Schönmetzer
DV	*Dei Verbum* (Dogmatic Constitution on Divine Revelation [Vatican II])
EcD	"Ecumenical Directory"
ED	*Euntes Docete*
EglViv	*Église Vivante*
EHS	*Einleitung in die Heilige Schrift*
EK	*Evangelische Kommentare*
EKK	*Evangelische Katholischer Kommentar zum Neuen Testament*
EKL	*Evangelisches Kirchenlexikon*
EMM	*Evangelisches Missions-Magazin*
EMQ	*Evangelical Missions Quarterly*
EMS	*Informationsbrief Evangelischer Missionssendungsdienst*
EMW	*Informationen Evangelisches Missionswerk*
EMZ	*Evangelische Missionszeitschrift*
EN	*Evangelii Nuntiandi*
EncRel	*Encyclopedia of Religion*
ER	*Ecumenical Review*
EspM	*España Misionera*
EThL	*Ephemerides Theologicae Louvanienses*
EuA	*Erbe und Auftrag*
EvMiss	*Evangelikale Missiologie*
EvTh	*Evangelische Theologie*

EvW	*Evangelische Welt*
ExAud	*Ex Auditu*
Exch	*Exchange*
ExT	*Expository Times*
FZPhTh	*Freiburger Zeitschrift für Philosophie und Theologie*
GOTR	*Greek Orthodox Theological Review*
GS	*Gaudium et Spes* (Pastoral Constitution on the Church in the Modern World [Vatican II])
GuL	*Geist und Leben*
GWU	*Geschichte in Wissenschaft und Unterricht*
HCH(J)	*Handbook of Church History* (H. Jedin, ed.)
HERE	*Harper's Encyclopedia of Religious Education*
HerKor	*Herder-Korrespondenz*
HKG	*Handbuch der Kirchengeschichte für Studierende* (ed. Gustav Krüger)
HPTh	*Handbuch der Pastoraltheologie*
HR	*History of Religions*
HST	*Handbuch systematischer Theologie*
HthG	*Handbuch theologischer Grundbegriffe*
HThR	*Harvard Theological Review*
IBMR	*International Bulletin of Missionary Research*
IJAfHS	*International Journal of African Historical Studies*
IlRev	*Ilocos Review*
IndES	*Indian Ecclesiastical Studies*
IRM	*International Review of Mission(s)*
JAAR	*Journal of the American Academy of Religion*
JAEv	*Journal of the Academy for Evangelism*
JBI	*Journal of the Blaisdell Institute*
JBL	*Journal of Biblical Literature*
JBTSA	*Journal of Black Theology in South Africa*
JCQ	*Japan Christian Quarterly*
JES	*Journal of Ecumenical Studies*
JHLT	*Journal of Hispanic / Latino Theology*
JIAS	*Journal of Inter-American Studies*
JMB	*Japan Missionary Bulletin*
JMiss	*Jahrbuch Mission*
JRA	*Journal of Religion in Africa*
JSNT	*Journal for the Study of the New Testament*
JSO	*Journal de la Société des Océanistes*
JSSR	*Journal for the Scientific Study of Religion*
JTSA	*Journal of Theology for South Africa*

KGF	*Kulturgeschichtliche Forschungen*
KIG	*Kirche in ihrer Geschichte*
KuD	*Kerygma und Dogma*
KuKi	*Kunst und Kirche*
KW	*Kirchen der Welt*
KZRT	*Kairos: Zeitschrift für Religionswissenschaft und Theologie* (Salzburg)
LG	*Lumen Gentium* (Dogmatic Constitution on the Church [Vatican II])
LiArts	*Liturgical Arts*
LOCP	*Lausanne Occasional Papers*
LOP	*Lausanne Occasional Papers*
LouvStud	*Louvain Studies*
LR	*Lutherische Rundschau*
LThK	*Lexikon für Theologie und Kirche*
LV	*Lumen Vitae*
LW	*Lutheran World*
ME	"Ecumenical Affirmation: Mission and Evangelism"
MEKGR	*Monatshefte für Evangelische Kirchengeschichte des Rheinlandes*
MF	*Les Missions Franciscaines*
MissF	*Mission Focus*
Missiol	*Missiology: An International Review*
MissS	*Mission Studies*
ML	*Mysterium Liberationis*
MNeg	*Mundo Negro*
MSer	*Monumenta Serica*
MSOS	*Mitteilungen des Seminars für orientalische Sprachen an der (K.) Friedrich-Wilhelms-Universität zu Berlin*
MTh	*Modern Theology*
MySal	*Mysterium Salutis*
NA	*Nostra Aetate* (Declaration on the Relationship of the Church to Non-Christian Religions [Vatican II])
Namz	*Neue allgemeine Missionszeitschrift*
NCE	*New Catholic Encyclopedia*
NDSW	*New Dictionary of Sacramental Worship*
NDT	*New Dictionary of Theology*
NEAJT	*North East Asia Journal of Theology*
NedThT	*Nederlandse Theologisch Tijdschrift*
NRTh	*Nouvelle Revue Théologique*
NTR	*New Theology Review*
NTS	*New Testament Studies*
NZM	*Neue Zeitschrift für Missionswissenschaft*

NZSTh	Neue Zeitschrift für Systematische Theologie
OBMRL	Occasional Bulletin: Missionary Research Library
ÖEH1	Ökumenische Existenz Heute (vol. 1)
ÖL	Ökumene Lexikon
ÖR	Ökumenische Rundschau
OrChr	Oriens Christianus
PC	Perfectae Caritatis (Decree on the Appropriate Renewal of the Religious Life [Vatican II])
PCL	Promptuarium Canonico-Liturgicum
PM	Priester und Mission
PMV	Pro Mundi Vita
PMVB	Pro Mundi Vita Bulletin
PP	Populorum Progressio
PSB	Princeton Seminary Bulletin
PTh	Pastoral theologie
RCA	Revue Catholique d'Alsace
RCAfr	Revue du Clergé Africain
REB	Revista Eclesiástica Brasileira
RelSoc	Religion and Society
RevRel	Review for Religious
RGG	Religion in Geschichte und Gegenwart
RHMiss	Revue d'Histoire des Missions
RIL	Religion and Intellectual Life
RN	Revue Nouvelle
RM	Redemptoris Missio
RStR	Religious Studies Review
SC	Sacrosanctum Concilium (Constitution on the Sacred Liturgy [Vatican II])
SDGSTh	Studien zur Dogmengeschichte und systematischen Theologie
SEAJT	South East Asia Journal of Theology
SID	Studies in Interreligious Dialogue
SJTh	Scottish Journal of Theology
SJTh—OP	Scottish Journal of Theology — Occasional Papers
SM	Sacramentum Mundi
STh	Schriften zur Theologie
StLit	Studia Liturgica
StMiss	Studia Missionalia
StZ	Stimmen der Zeit
TBLNT	Theologisches Begriffslexikon zum Neuen Testament
TBT	The Bible Today
TD	Theology Digest

TDNT	*Theological Dictionary of the New Testament* (ed. Kittel)
TEd	*Theological Education*
Telema	*Revue de réflexion et créativité chretiénnes en Afrique*
TGA	*Theologie der Gegenwart in Auswahl*
ThB	*Theologische Berichte*
ThGl	*Theologie und Glaube*
ThPh	*Theologie und Philosophie*
ThpQ	*Theologisch-praktische Quartalschrift*
ThQ	*Theologische Quartalschrift* (Tübingen)
ThR	*Theologische Rundschau*
ThT	*Theologisch Tijdschrift*
ThTo	*Theology Today*
ThWNT	*Theologisches Wörterbuch zum Neuen Testament*
ThZ	*Theologische Zeitschrift* (Basel)
TI	*Theological Investigations* (Karl Rahner)
TRE	*Theologische Realenzyklopädie*
TS	*Theological Studies* (Woodstock, Md.)
TS(StL)	*Theological Studies* (St. Louis University)
TSJ	*Theological Studies in Japan*
UM	*Urban Mission*
UnSa	*Unam Sanctam*
UR	*Unitatis Redintegratio* (Decree on Ecumenism [Vatican II])
VF	*Verkündigung und Forschung*
VFTW	*Voices from the Third World (EATWOT)*
VidRel	*Vida Religiosa*
VigChr	*Vigiliae Christianae*
WBC	*The Women's Bible Commentary*
WDCE	*Westminster Dictionary of Christian Education*
WMANT	*Wissenschaftliche Monographien zum Alten und Neuen Testament*
WPKG	*Wissenschaft und Praxis in Kirche und Gesellschaft*
WZM	*Wege zum Menschen*
ZDTh	*Zeitschrift für Dialektische Theologie*
ZfM	*Zeitschrift für Musik*
ZM	*Zeitschrift für Missionswissenschaft*
ZMiss	*Zeitschrift für Mission*
ZMissR	*Zeitschrift für Missionswissenschaft und Religionswissenschaft*
ZMRW	*Zeitschrift für Missionskunde und Religionswissenschaft*
ZP	*Zeitschrift für Pädagogik*
ZPB	*Zeitschrift für Pädagogik-Beiheft*
ZRGG	*Zeitschrift für Religions- und Geistesgeschichte*
ZThK	*Zeitschrift für Theologie und Kirche*
ZZ	*Zwischen den Zeiten*

A

❧ THE ABSOLUTENESS OF CHRISTIANITY ❧

1. Terminology. 2. The Theological Issue at Stake. 3. Is the Term "Absoluteness" Necessary? 4. A Theological Interpretation.

1. The etymological roots of the English word "absoluteness" lie in the past participle of the Latin word *absolvere* ("to loosen" or "free"); the past participle is *absolutus* ("freed," "detached," or "disengaged," from which is derived the metaphorical use of the term in Latin: i.e., "perfect" or "complete"). The term was little used in philosophy and theology until the last decades of the eighteenth century and the turn of the nineteenth century, when F. W. J. Schelling (d. 1854) and G. W. F. Hegel (d. 1831) used *Absolutheit* and its cognates in discussions emanating from the idea of B. Spinoza (d. 1677) that God does not transcend the universe but is a kind of "universal substance" in which reality enjoys its being. Thus the present form of the argument about the absoluteness of Christianity enters Western theology through attempts to deal with historicism, romanticism, and pantheism.

One of the first observations one must make about the term, then, is that in choosing it as a standard of orthodoxy in →theology of mission and →theology of religions, Christian theologians should ask whether they are choosing a term that will bear all that is required of it. Nevertheless, out of the cultural and intellectual context that brought forth the modern use of the term did come the theological problems of "relativity," "evolution," and "development" that beset contemporary moral life and the struggle to formulate Christian identity in a pluralistic age.

In the New Testament, "absoluteness" is not a formal theme. Still, the adverb *ephapax* ("once for all" [Heb 9:12, echoing Jn 10:17–18]), although occurring in a text few theologians would care to base an entire christology on, exemplifies well the New Testament teaching that the salvation and revelation mediated by Jesus as the Christ have a final, unique, necessary, and universal character. It would be tempting to dismiss such terms as "finality," "uniqueness," "necessity," and "universality" concerning the Christ. But from the earliest strata of the New Testament onward, its christologies were missionary in origin and sought ways to state Christian belief in the definitiveness of Jesus for all humankind (see Bosch 1990; Legrand 1990).

2. While the term is philosophical, debates about whether and how Christianity is to be construed as absolute cut close to the core of Christian identity. In early strands of New Testament christology, for instance in Pauline literature, the title *Kyrios* (Lord) is routinely ascribed to Jesus as the Christ (see Romans and 1 Corinthians passim). *Kyrios* functionally relates Jesus to Yahweh's present and eschatological rule of the *kosmos*. In later strands of (deutero-)Pauline literature, this lordship is explicitly extended to include Christ's rule over everything (Eph 1:10); and the dwelling of the divine fullness in the Christ is taught (Col 1:19; 2:9). Even if one accepts the position of feminist theology that Jesus instituted a discipleship of equals and that the doctrine of "lordship" should be modified and understood in light of the female principle of *sophia* (wisdom), the relationship of

1

the Christ to the absoluteness of God needs to be taken into account — unless one wishes, for instance, to jettison such key texts as Romans 8, where Jesus as the Christ is envisaged as participating in the divine redemption of the entire cosmos.

At a second level, that of the political-theological implications of high christologies, as R. Cassidy shows, Johannine terminology was developed precisely to bring to the fore the Christian community's explicit belief that allegiance to Jesus as Christ was absolutely superior to Roman imperial theological claims on citizens. The unavoidable conclusion to be drawn from such texts is that, by the end of the first century of the Common Era, ontological and political interpretations of the person and office of the Christ — interpretations that would dominate Christian thinking virtually completely by the end of the sixth century — did, indeed, ascribe a "completeness" not unrelated to the etymological roots of the word "absolute."

If one agrees with B. Lonergan that the path from the concrete image-language of the early New Testament, through the self-consciously theological language of the later New Testament, to the abstract and formal dogmatic definitions of the early councils is not a deformation of primitive Christianity but an authentic development in understanding who and what Jesus was, the claim for the absoluteness of Jesus as the Christ and for Christianity is not merely speculative.

Discussions of Christianity as absolute have tended to be contentious and hard to contain, spilling over into questions of relativity and relativism. Nevertheless, there is no way to avoid these discussions, and to address them properly the name of E. Troeltsch (d. 1927) must be invoked. Given what we know from historical studies, in particular from the comparative and historical study of religions, Troeltsch judges that attempts to prove the absoluteness of Christianity have failed and both must and should fail, for theological, historical, and philosophical reasons. While he labored until the end of his life to erect a conceptual footing for the ultimate truth and value of Christianity, Troeltsch concluded that history would continually reveal the relativity of all human efforts to comprehend and transform the world.

Troeltsch's position has been characterized and sometimes caricatured as relativist ever since, although what he really showed was that both natural-scientific and historical studies (including studies of Christian origins) had revealed the interrelatedness of all that is (its relativity). He did this with such clarity that large segments of the Christian theological world have ever since tried to construct bulwarks around the notion that, if the Christ and Christianity are not absolute in a literal sense, then Christianity's most important truth — about the finality, uniqueness, necessity, and universality of the revelation and salvation offered in the Christ — rests on sand. The ultimate question concerning absoluteness, accordingly, is whether it is a matter of such essential importance or whether — in a way analogous to how the doctrine of creation was revised in dialogue with natural-scientific insights — the doctrine of the Christ's finality can be similarly revised.

3. Is the term "absoluteness" necessary? Without it, must Christianity fall victim to relativism? The issue for Christians and Christian mission seems to involve a twofold alternative and a clarification: (*a*) asserting biblical doctrines and later dogmas derived from them on the absoluteness and finality of Jesus as the Christ and Christianity as the normative and normal way God's saving grace reaches humankind; or (*b*) dealing dialogically with the problems posed by contemporary insights into the radical relativity, the rough parity, and the plurality of religious visions of the Whole; and (c) the need to distinguish between the absoluteness of Jesus as the Christ and Christianity, the movement that bears his name.

Judging that the first alternative leads to a fall into fideism and to an abandonment of dialogue, theologians influenced by contemporary hermeneutics and process thought are developing the second alternative, convinced that relativity does not necessarily entail relativism. As David Tracy has observed, "indifferentism" and its modern correlate, "lazy tolerance," are ideologies that, in effect, deny the ability to discern the relatively adequate and the relatively inadequate, degrees of good and bad or true and false, when, in fact, despite the complexity of dealing with the plurality of competing values and religious truths, we do succeed — if we work at it in genuine conversation — in attaining reliable "analogical" understanding of our own and the radically different truths of others. We do this even if issues often cannot be resolved finally because of the limited nature of religious language and experience. Still, it is a characteristic of human life that failures to resolve important issues finally do not lead people to doubt everything they believe. Life goes on, including religious life, after persons lose their first naïveté in the encounter with beauty in other religious truths and ways.

On the one hand, the Hebrew Testament (TANAK) means to teach the mysterious absoluteness of Yahweh. And the New Testament means analogously to ascribe that absoluteness to Jesus and (less explicitly) to the Spirit. (This is the essence of the Chalcedonian doctrine of consubstantiality of the Son and the Spirit.) On the other hand, practices derived from a literalist or a fundamentalist understanding of that doctrine lead intellectually to fideism and practically to zealotry. Given Christianity's history of fideism and zealotry, its assertion of its own absolute supernaturality seems to many a self-serving ideology at odds with the tender God revealed, for example, in Matthean and Lucan infancy narratives and unable to account for the paradoxical revelation of God in the death of Jesus. Asserting the absoluteness of "Christianity" and asserting the ultimacy of "revelation in Jesus" as the Christ are two quite different matters. That subtlety seems often to be missed.

Existential and crisis theologies use the term "decisive" to denote the stakes involved in the encounter with Jesus and the gospel, and that may show one way out of the conundrum posed by self-privileging fideism and uncritical relativism. R. Bultmann's theology, for instance, shunned such metaphysic-laden dogmatic terms as "absoluteness" in showing that the Christian kerygma was about representing a Jesus who even today challenges persons to choose between genuine and false existence. Few theologians would claim that Bultmann's theology does full justice to the richness of biblical traditions, but what does endure is the notion that the challenge of Jesus and the gospel is a fundamental choice of commitment to a vision and to a life-praxis consistent with that vision. This, it can be argued, is a better way to render the dynamics of the biblical narratives than the abstractness of the term "absoluteness." And if this is so, perhaps "absoluteness" is a term best relegated to historical handbooks, where experts can use it with the requisite nuance, rather than one to be used in present-day attempts to state the core of the Christian message.

4. There is in the Christian kerygma a vision of the character of reality as created by God that entails both divine sovereignty over creation and the goodness of creation. Creation and redemption are reciprocals, and when the New Testament ascribes redemptive significance to the death of Jesus and his resurrection by God, it also entails hope that the whole of the creation is related to God as is Jesus, the crucified and risen one. For the gospel to be truly good news, it must be news that God's healing, vivifying love knows no bounds, that the divine love, in other words, is absolute. Accordingly, constructions of the Christ and Christianity that interpret absoluteness *restrictively* or as a warrant for *superiority* are suspect. Two contemporary insights put flesh on the bones of this suspicion.

First, ideology critique makes one aware that human reason is often used self-servingly by individuals and institutions. Echoing R. Niebuhr's insight into the Christian doctrine of the fall, one can ask: Who gains from this construction of reality? And: Does this construction unfairly justify the dominant position of that group? In the case of Christianity, age-old interpretations of absoluteness have been used to warrant the supernatural status of the church and to diminish critiques. More importantly, they place certain dogmatic formulas in a privileged position quite out of keeping with the paradoxical structure of revelation in the death of Jesus. Such uses of absoluteness should raise questions whether this fundamentalist absoluteness is (*a*) what the New Testament meant to convey; or (*b*) true in any univocal sense.

Second, as astrophysics deepens insights into the age and breadth of the universe, the mystery of the divine as source of cosmic life appears ever less capable of being encapsulated by human abstractions. Thus, perhaps, Christian *hope* better embodies the Christic dynamic that the divine *cares* than does a strategy of drawing logical consequences of absoluteness from a doctrine such as divine lordship over creation and redemption. In the TANAK and the New Testament, the divine has two aspects: the one mighty and mysterious, the other personal and caring. For God, the source and future of all that exists, is imaged both as omnipotent creator, lawgiver, and judge and as the elder brother who accepts death rather than betray life. Equally central to that revelation, though lurking in the background to which she was relegated by patriarchal society, is the maternal Spirit in whose love humankind experiences hope despite the evident cruelty of reality. It may be that the most convincing way Christians can today witness the decisiveness of the means God offers to enjoy the ultimate victory of life is to incarnate the breath of life-giving hope offered at every moment by the Spirit. Such witness to the now and not-yet in the eschatological nature of Christian hope and love may ultimately be far more convincing than proclaiming belief in the absoluteness of Christianity.

The danger in asserting faith in the absoluteness of God and God's Christ as a key element in Christian identity is that this teaching can lead to arrogance and a sense of privilege. As one sees in texts such as Matthew 23, such attitudes on the part of Jesus' adversaries are what make the Jesus of the Gospels angry. Just as fundamentalist repetitions of literal doctrines of creation show a failure to appropriate earlier, more relaxed spiritual and allegorical interpretations of Genesis, it may be that literal interpretations of the doctrine of absoluteness betray a similar lack of imagination with similar consequences.

The issue ultimately raised by any doctrine is the question: What kind of "truth" is "evangelical" or "good news"? On the one hand, there is a correspondence view of truth that holds a religious truth to be like a statement of fact. An example is the doctrine that Jesus is both truly human and divine. In the face of reductionisms of every kind, holding fast to that proposition — even though it may not make one feel closer to God any more than the theory of thermodynamics makes one feel warm — keeps one from sliding into a variety of partial truths about Jesus of Nazareth. Positive in such views of truth is the way they counter subjectivism and relativism, which ultimately amount to the proposition that truth in matters transcendent is unattainable.

The drawback is that the character of such doctrinal truth is too narrow. It lies rooted in naive theories of correspondence between concepts and reality that embarrass when life is seen in its concrete complexity. Although religious truth *may* sometimes be about matters of fact reducible to certain propositions, it may be better to stress hope and love, virtues that reflect the totality of the revolution in consciousness entailed in the structure of Christian existence. Along with faith-as-trust, these virtues propel a transcendence that transforms individual hearts, communities, and cultures in ways that doctrines in which one "believes" do not.

On the other hand, an evangelical truth, in this connection, although not without a propositional component, has an "event" or "disclosure" character that leads to a stirring of a person's, a people's, and a culture's inner being. And here one enters a religious limit or boundary situation where experiences mediated by persons, symbols, sacraments, events, or texts disclose and engender a dynamic that enables the beholders of the mystery to peer beyond the limits of normal experience. Thus enlightened and empowered, they seek to realize in ordinary daily life a deeper reconciliation potential that penetrates, undergirds, and transcends the world of the everyday.

The existential absoluteness or decisiveness of Jesus as the Christ involves the claim that the Christ, in and through the movement bearing his name, has the capacity to mediate such experiences and to elicit in his and the movement's followers strong beliefs and motivations (*a*) that this is the way things *are* at their deepest level and (*b*) that individuals, groups, and cultures must strive to actualize the gospel's liberative imperative that the world be thus freed from bondage to sin and its enslaving consequences, both individual and social. In that process, mission is the participation of a community of disciples who become instruments of this grace in the divine mission, the so-called *missio Dei* of *Ad Gentes* (2–5) and sacrament of salvation of *Lumen Gentium* (1, 48). The absoluteness of the Christ, in other words, has its primary meaning as a decisive word addressed to prospective followers of Jesus, not as a foundation for an institution such as Christianity claiming superiority. In the dialectic of sin and grace is engendered in transforming love a freedom (Gal 5:13–14, 16, 18, 22–26) that will not yield the fruits of arrogance born of a sense of privilege (Gal 5:15, 17, 19–21).

Under the conditions of space and time, where the absolute is mediated by the relative (starting with the human nature of Jesus), every good is open to idolatry, abuse, and ambiguity. In the approach taken here to the presence of the absolute in the relative, however, one is at least involved in a process of self-critical spiritual discernment, dealing with spiritual matters — negative and positive — "spiritually." This, indeed, is the dynamic one finds Paul wrestling with in 1 Corinthians 9–13, Galatians 5, and Romans 14 — missionary texts that exude love for others, realism about human foibles, and joy at creation's richness, but not arrogance.

WILLIAM R. BURROWS

Bibliography

Aldwinckle, R., *Jesus: A Savior or the Savior?* (1982). Bosch, D., *Transforming Mission: Paradigm Shifts in the Theology of Mission* (1990). Bultmann, R., *Theology of the New Testament,* 2 vols. (1951–55). Cassidy, R. J., *John's Gospel in New Perspective: Christology and the Realities of Roman Power* (1992). Dupuis, J., *Jesus Christ at the Encounter of World Religions* (1991). Idem, *Toward a Christian Theology of Religious Pluralism* (1997). Fiorenza, E. Schüssler, *In Memory of Her: A Feminist Theological Reconstruction of Christian Origins* (1983). Gilkey, L., "Plurality in Its Theological Implications," in J. Hick and P. Knitter, eds., *The Myth of Christian Uniqueness* (1987). Gittins, A., *Bread for the Journey: The Mission of Transformation and the Transformation of Mission* (1993). Hegel, G., *The Phenomenology of Spirit* (1807; Eng. trans., 1977). Heim, S. M., *Salvations* (1995). Kasper, W., ed., *Absolutheit des Christentums* (1977). Knitter, P., *Jesus and the Other Names* (1996). Idem, *No Other Name?* (1985). Küng, H., *The Incarnation of God: An Introduction to Hegel's Thought as Prolegomenon to a Future Christology* (1987). Legrand, L., *Unity and Plurality: Mission in the Bible* (1990). Lonergan, B., *De Deo Trino,* 2 vols. (1964; vol. 1 partially translated as *The Way to Nicea* [1976]). Niebuhr, R., *The Nature and Destiny of Man,* 2 vols. (1941–43). Pannenberg, W., "Toward a Theology of the History of Religions," in *Basic Questions in Theology,* vol. 1 (1971). Ricoeur, P., *Essays on Biblical Interpretation* (1980). Ruether, R., *Sexism and God-Talk: Toward a Feminist Theology* (1983). Tracy, D., *The Analogical Imagination: Christian Theology and the Culture of Pluralism* (1980). Idem, *Plurality and Ambiguity; Hermeneutics, Religion, Hope* (1987). Troeltsch, E., *The Absoluteness of Christianity and the History of Religions* (1903; Eng. trans., 1971). Idem, *Der Historismus und seine Probleme* (1922).

❧ AFRICAN INDEPENDENT CHURCHES ❧

1. Definition. 2. Origin. 3. Distinguishing Characteristics.

1. Over a century ago a remarkable Christian movement began which has since gathered the momentum of an avalanche. South of the Sahara, 10 percent of the indigenous population (in South Africa as much as 30 percent of the blacks) belong to faith communities of this "African Reformation" (D. B. Barrett), a movement unique in mission history. These communities have developed such a strong missionary outreach that, according to the projections of futurologists, by the turn of the century the continent of Africa will be the most flourishing Christian area in the world.

The emergence of this new phenomenon has aroused the interest of many researchers who have attempted in recent decades to describe it in different ways. Political scientists speak of revolutionary cults, prophets in rebellion, and protonationalist movements. Psychologists speak of crisis or deprivation cults and of reform or revitalization movements. Sociologists call these groups separatist movements, sects, voluntary religious communities, or popular movements. Anthropologists see in them movements of accommodation or inculturation and label them nativist, revivalist, or transformation movements. Early missionaries branded them as heretical, syncretistic, or prophetic movements; eschatological, chiliastic, or messianic cults; and Pentecostal or visionary sects. All these labels represent only a partial description of particularly interesting characteristics. They are concerned with only a part of the movement, can be applied equally to other phenomena, and do not include the specific traits of this movement. Above all, they pay no attention to the self-awareness of the people involved. It is incumbent upon missiologists, therefore, to use the term by which these people designate themselves: "African Independent Churches" (AICs). Various kinds of groups, which can be recognized by their names and particular developments, and whose size can vary from a family grouping to a church with a million members, are called "communities" in order to distinguish them from the church bodies organized in the West. The use of this term, however, does not deny that they are churches in the New Testament sense.

2.   AICs emerged from the encounter between adherents of the original African religions and Christians from the West, who had come to Africa as missionaries, traders, settlers, and colonial administrators (→colonialism). In this encounter, an oral culture confronted a culture tied to the written word; small tribes saw themselves faced with Western, large-scale society; and tribal warriors bound by →tradition were confronted with enterprising representatives of a powerful civilization which thought and spoke differently from themselves. Initially the African religions reacted with hostility (a militant reversion to their traditional identity) or with submission (taking over Western forms of Christianity). It was only in a later phase that the interaction was developed in many areas of Africa — at the same time and without recognizable mutual influence. AICs evolved from such interaction, developing particular vitality in South Africa, Zaire, Nigeria, Ghana, and Kenya. The translations of the Bible into tribal languages by Protestant missionaries acted as catalysts in this process. AICs, therefore, are the result of Christian mission, even if not planned ones.

In 1862 the Methodist Society on the Gold Coast (present-day Ghana) became independent and formed the first AIC community. Others followed. Factors leading to separation were various conflicts with missionaries, natural catastrophes (e.g., cattle plagues and epidemics), the appearance of African charismatics, and increased pressure by the colonial powers. However, many AICs developed fully only after the political liberation of their countries. In essence they are something new which can be identified neither with the forms of traditional African religion nor with Western expressions of Christianity.

3.   As yet there is scarcely a literature on the AICs to be surveyed (see H. W. Turner), so no helpful typology has been established. B. Sundkler's division of the churches into Ethiopian and Zionist communities helps one to understand the early influences on the emergence of AICs, but not their present-day existence. Although many local variations exist, the AIC movement can be characterized by the following summary statements:

- AICs are expressions of a religious movement. They comprise a great number of communities and are the African response to the Christian message, a response which wishes to shape church life according to African forms and with African leadership.
- AICs reflect a holistic worldview which, according to the norms of African thought, links religion together with those dimensions of life which are designated secular in Western thought. AICs, therefore, have great social, economic, and political significance for their members as well as for their respective nations.
- AICs are differentiated from mission churches not by different doctrines but by their witness as African Christian communities which are concerned for the salvation of the whole person. Because of this, their healing work, on both an individual and a social level (a work not to be confused with that of faith healers), is, for Western observers, particularly striking.
- AICs are led by charismatic men and women whose divine calling is recognized by their communities on the basis of their extraordinary experiences

and holy lives. The leader appears to his or her congregation as the "mask of God" (Sundkler) and as "healer" (H. J. Becken); he or she is a type of African prophet, something peculiar to the AICs.

- AICs have developed their own symbolism of the holistic bestowal of salvation in elements, colors, and signs which are intelligible and meaningful for people in Africa but which significantly stop short of those used in the traditional religions of Africa.

- AICs are house churches which express their links with daily life and their surroundings by holding the overwhelming majority of their services in members' homes, on riverbanks and hills, or, more recently, on the seashore.

- AICs normally sing songs and choruses of their own composition and in their own native style. Although they come from a nonliterate culture, they assemble their own songbooks, some of which contain jewels of contemporary African poetry.

- Besides conversion and salvation, the AICs stress blessing and peace. Their prayers for preservation and their apotropaic rites merge easily into preventive health care. For them, death is not the declaration of the failure of their healing ministry but the entry into eternal peace.

- AICs are strict in many areas of ethical behavior (e.g., abstinence from tobacco and alcohol), and on the whole they are beneficial for the development of society in their emphasis on peacemaking, industry, and purity. In this they have recourse to the Bible, which they interpret literally and which is the basis of their theology.

- AICs address themselves to the needs which have resulted from rapid urbanization and industrialization in Africa. They concern themselves with unemployment and family separation and take up the questions of social and political liberation, even though in a different way from political parties.

- AICs are conscious of their ecumenical responsibility and cooperate with other AICs and with mission churches. They consider their contextual theology to be an example for the worldwide church.

- AICs have a strong missionary outreach across tribal and national boundaries, something which in the original religions of Africa, where community was identical with blood community, was inconceivable.

Christ has entered into the religions of Africa with the AIC movement, and some of those religions have been changed into Christian communities which carry on Christ's mission in a way relevant to their surroundings. The initial critical attitude of the mission churches toward the AICs has undergone a fundamental change in recent decades. A number of AICs belong today to national Christian councils, and some of the larger churches belong to the World Council of Churches, an example being the Church of Jesus Christ on Earth through the Prophet Simon Kimbangu, in Central Africa.

HANS-JÜRGEN BECKEN

Bibliography

Appiah-Kubi, K., and S. Torres, eds., *African Theology en Route* (1979). Barrett, D. B., *Schism and Renewal in Africa: An Analysis of Six Thousand Contemporary Movements* (1976). Becken, H. J., *Wo der Glaube noch jung ist. Afrikanische Unabhängige Kirchen im Südlichen Afrika* (1985). Daneel, M. L., "Missionary Outreach of African Independent Churches," *Missionalia* 8 (1980)

105–20. Idem, *Quest for Belonging: Introduction to a Study of African Independent Churches* (1987). Dickson, K., *Uncompleted Mission* (1991). Ekechi, F. K., "The Ordeal of an African Independent Church: The Nigerian Zion Methodist Mission, 1942–1970," *IJAfHS* 20 (1987) 691–720. Fashole-Luke, E., et al., eds., *Christianity in Independent Africa* (1978). Geffré, C., and B. Luneau, *The Churches of Africa: Future Prospects* (1977). Hood, R. E., *Must God Remain Greek?* (1990). Inkenga-Metuh, E., "The Revival of African Christian Spirituality: The Experience of African Independent Churches," *MissS* 7 (1990) 151–71. Kailing, J. B., "Inside, Outside, Upside Down: In Relationship with African Independent Churches," *IRM* 77 (1988) 38–58. Lamola, J. M., "Towards a Black Church: A Historical Investigation of the African Independent Churches as a Model," *JBTSA* 2/1 (1988) 5–14. Makhubu, P., *Who Are the Independent Churches?* (1988). Martin, M.-L., *Kimbangu: An African Prophet and His Church* (1975). Mwene-Batende, "Les perspectives spiritualistes dans les communautès messianiques africaines," in *L'Afrique et ses formes de vie spirituelle*, Actes du deuxième colloque internationale, *CRA* 24 (1990) 83–92. Nuñez, J. G., "¿Inculturación o sincretismo? Iglesias independientes en Africa," *MNeg* 32/343 (1991) 34–41. Oosthuizen, G. C., ed., *Religion Alive: Studies in the New Movements and Indigenous Churches in Southern Africa* (1986). Pato, L., "The African Independent Churches: A Socio-cultural Approach," *JTSA* 72 (1990) 24–35. Saah, R. B., "African Independent Church Movements," *AfCS* 7/3 (1991) 46–77. Sanneh, L., *West African Christianity* (1983). Shank, D. A., ed., *Ministry of Missions to African Independent Churches* (1987). Sundkler, B., *Bantupropheten in Südafrika* (1964). Idem, *Zulu Zion and Some Swazi Zionists* (1976). Tembe, B., *Integrationalismus und Afrikanismus: Zur Rolle der Kirchlichen Unabhängigkeitsbewegungen in der Auseinandersetzung um die Landfrage und Bildung der Afrikaner in Südafrika 1880–1960* (1985). Turner, H. W., *Bibliography of New Religious Movements in Primal Societies*, vol. 1, *Black Africa* (1977). Idem, *History of an African Independent Church: The Church of the Lord (Aladura)* (1967). Welbourn, F. B., and B. A. Ogot, *A Place to Feel at Home: A Study of Two Independent Churches in Western Kenya* (1966). Zvanka, S., "African Independent Church in Context," *Missiol* 25/1 (January 1997) 69–75.

✞ AFRICAN THEOLOGY ✞

1. Historical Overview. 2. Use of the Bible. 3. Christology. 4. Salvation. 5. Ecclesiology. 6. Marriage and Liturgy. 7. Conclusion.

African theology, or what some call African Christian theology, is that theology which reflects on the gospel, the Christian tradition, and the total African reality in an African manner and from the perspectives of the African worldview. The total African reality, of course, includes the ongoing changes in the culture. Some prefer to speak of theologies because they see much diversity in African culture and religion; others see a fundamental similarity in the religious experience and in the nature of the emergent issues. Discussion of African theology usually considers the scene in Sub-Saharan Africa, leaving aside the Coptic tradition in Egypt and Ethiopia. Until recently, it was usual to distinguish three currents of this theology: African theology, →black theology in South Africa, and liberation theology. African theology was seen as based on culture and as seeking to give African expression to the Christian faith. Black theology, influenced by a similar current in the United States, was viewed as focusing on politics and the issues of race and color. →Liberation theology, influenced by the Latin American model, was described as focusing on poverty. In recent times, however, there has been much merging of perspectives owing to the dialogical role of continental interchurch conferences and international symposia. Inculturation and liberation now tend to be tensions within the various camps themselves as theologians increasingly focus on the total reality of today's Africa. Besides, now that freedom has been gained in South Africa, new metaphors similar to those used in the rest of Africa are emerging, namely, →reconciliation and →liberation for full living and from the forces of death.

Theological writing in Africa has been circumstantial, focused on particular pastoral or moral problems. Very few of the writings are systematic treatises written with a view to developing a comprehensive theology. On the one hand, some voices, particularly C. Nyamiti, have been calling for a systematic treatment. On the other hand, theology need not always be systematic, and some are calling for an African narrative theology (e.g., J. Healey and D. Sybertz). There is little agreement as to how to characterize African reality theologically. Some, like B. Idowu, see the principal dialogue partner as African traditional religion, particularly the tradition of the living God. Others speak of a theology of life (T. Tshibangu) or a theology of fraternity (J. Agoussou). Still others argue that the fundamental element is the unitary vision of the universe and of life, or what J. Penoukou calls "cosmotheandric relation," in which being is shared between God, human beings, and the world. The 1986 meeting of the →Ecumenical Association of Third World Theologians (EATWOT) in Mexico suggested "anthropological poverty" as the theological locus for Africa. The recently concluded synod for Africa (1994) offered "the church as family of God" as a particularly apt model for African ecclesiology.

1. Since the fourth century, Christianity has existed in a fairly unbroken manner in the Coptic churches of Egypt and Ethiopia. In the rest of Africa, after a brief spell of mission on the coast of Ghana and in Angola in the fifteenth and sixteenth centuries, evangelization returned in earnest in the nineteenth century in the wake of the "scramble for Africa." The new wave of mission coincided with the ongoing Westernization of the continent and the social changes associated with it, mission itself being one of the agents of change. The period of mission was not a theological vacuum; implicit and inchoate African theology can surely be discerned in the lived experience of African Christians and the pastoral decisions of the church leaders. However, it is usual to begin the history of African theology around 1956, when many African voices began to call for what was variously termed "African theology," "Christian theology in Africa," and "African Christian theology." This was the period when many African nations were achieving independence from the colonial masters and African culture and self-determination were in the air. One of the voices was a group of French-speaking Catholic priests who published their open questions on what an African profile of Christianity might look like, thus giving religious expression to a century-old cultural movement associated with such names as E. W. Blyden (1832–1912) and W. E. B. Du Bois (1868–1963). It was not accidental that 1956 also saw the first Congress of Black Writers and Artists in Paris. On the Protestant side, the impetus came from the First Assembly of the All Africa Church Conference (AACC) in Ibadan, Nigeria, in 1958.

Vatican II (1962–65) (→Vatican Council II) and its theology of the local church proved a catalyst, as was the first meeting (in Uganda in 1963) of the AACC under its new name — the All Africa Conference of Churches. Both the change of name and the topic ("Theology of Nationalism") showed recognition of an emerging local church with its own theological agenda.

The first sketches of a would-be African theology appeared in 1965. They were written by B. Idowu and V. Mulago. The former based himself on traditional religion, and the latter adopted the philosophical background of "vital participation" as developed by P. Tempels. The following year the first consultation of African theologians met at Ibadan; the theme was "The Bible and Africa." The scholars compared and contrasted African beliefs and biblical concepts. Similar consultations at the Lutheran Missiological Institute, Natal, were published in 1974. The black consciousness movement in South Africa had in 1970 launched the Black Theology Project under the influence of J. Cone and his *Black Theology and Black Power*, which had been published in 1969. The first fruits of theologizing in the South African context were the work edited by M. Motlhabi in 1972, a work which was quickly banned by the apartheid government, and A. Boesak's widely read *Farewell to Innocence*.

Some of the works on African religiosity which proved fundamental to the reflection of theologians were those by J. V. Taylor, J. S. Mbiti, and D. Zahan. These had been preceded by G. Parrinder's classic *African Traditional Religion*. Since African religion is not a static reality, it is necessary to study it in its historical development. The beginnings of such study have been made in a work edited by T. O. Ranger and I. N. Kimambo and in another edited by K. Olupona.

Theological reflection in Africa received a powerful stimulus at the 1974 general synod of the Catholic Church on evangelization, and particularly from the statement of the African bishops present at that synod which called for mission based on African priorities and the African experience of God and Christ and which declared that "the bishops of Africa and Madagascar, considering as totally bypassed a certain theology of adaptation, opt for a theology of incarnation." The bishops viewed such a theology as emerging from the communities of faith as they reflect on the demands of faith in the context of culture and modern social changes. In the Catholic fold, this became the charter for efforts at African theology. Another step forward was taken at the 1977 Accra meeting of the Ecumenical Association of Third World Theologians (EATWOT), which founded the Ecumenical Association of African Theologians (EAAT) and which reached consensus on the five elements of a contextualized theology for Africa: the Bible and Christian heritage, African anthropology, African traditional religions, African independent churches, and other African realities.

Two parts of the African reality which need greater attention are the "oral theology" buried in sermons, songs, stories, and popular literature and the "practical theology" of the people as they strive to live the faith in context. Partly as a result of the international dialogues, the perspectives of the diverse approaches of inculturation, focused on culture, and liberation, focused on politics, began to merge. The African report at the 1986 EATWOT meeting at Oaxtepec, Mexico, presented jointly by theologians from South Africa and elsewhere in Africa, sought to further close the gap between the two approaches by suggesting "anthropological poverty" as the theological reality in which both culture and politics find a common ground. Such a poverty is both economic and cultural: it deprives one of history, personality, and self-determination. The year before, the "Kairos Document" had blazed the trail of what would be known as Kairos theology, which would find repercussions in various parts of the so-called Third World. Some significant works on African theology are those by J. Pobee, K. Dickson, T. Tshibangu, J. M. Éla, A. Ngindu Mushete, E. Martey, and the work edited by J. de Gruchy and C. Villa-Vicencio. The work by G. Setiloane considers certain concepts in African religion and thought which might form the basis for an African theology.

2. African independent churches generally use far more of the Old Testament than the "mission" churches and often interpret the New Testament from the perspective of the Old. That is because the worldview underlying the Old Testament is particularly similar to that of traditional Africa. A question is raised concerning the role of the Old Testament in Christian living and in the construction of an African theology. In much of African theology a sustained and internal encounter between the Bible, interpreted within its own context, and African culture is rare. There is need to examine the theology implicit in the popularity of certain texts and parts of the Bible. Since theology is, in a sense, a function of interpretation, an African hermeneutics of the Bible and Christian tradition has become an imperative. Generally speaking, theology in South Africa has paid closer attention to its basis in hermeneutics, although the perspective of social struggle as a heuristic tool offers little that is specifically African. The need to establish an interface between "trained" and "ordinary" readers and between the various interpretive approaches for liberation and the worldview of the "base" is shown especially in the work of G. O. West and the Institute for the Study of the Bible in South Africa.

3. Christology is the most developed area of African theology, and the various approaches to christology illustrate those in theology. There are at least four: the comparative, systematic, liberationist, and community-based approaches.

The *comparative* approach moves from the Bible to African culture or vice versa. It examines christological points with strong interest in Africa or how the person and work of Christ fit into the African conception of the universe. The →Jesus of these comparisons is the historical Jesus of the Gospels. The concepts of messiah, Christ, Son of Man, and Son of David are said to have little significance for Africa, whereas servant of God, Lord, savior, and Son of God are very relevant. The title "savior" has almost become a personal name for Jesus. As savior, Jesus acts with almighty power in the present to deliver the Christian who has committed himself or herself to him. While the West sees Jesus as savior on the cross, African Christians tend to focus on the present. The blood of the cross is a force which shields the Christian in the present against malevolent spirits and other evils.

The comparative method may also start from images or roles in African culture, investigating their value for christology. A book published in 1986 by some French-speaking African theologians (edited in English by R. J. Schreiter and entitled *Faces of Jesus in Africa*) did just this. The roles investigated were those of chief, ancestor, elder brother, master of initiation, and healer.

A Bantu chief is *mukalenge,* that is, one who has power. He is the protector and defender of his people in the battle against seen and unseen forces. He is "strong" in that he participates in the "vital force" of creation, hence guaranteeing abundance of life for his group. He is *mwene-muzi,* the very self of the village, since his person is the sum and substance of the whole community. In this sense he can easily symbolize the mediatorship of Jesus. This line of reasoning receives liturgical affirmation in some parts of Africa where the leopard skin, the symbol of the chief, is used to decorate the tabernacle or is laid out before people who are being ordained or who are making a profession.

In many African communities life is a process of continual initiation. Even death is an invitation into the form of life of ancestors. Such communities read the life of Christ from the vantage point of Heb 2:10, which presents him as the guide toward human perfection and salvation. His birth, growth, suffering, burial, and resurrection are seen as initiation moments which perfect him as a master of initiation able to lead us through life and death. A christology patterned on African initiation also views the church as the community of the initiated and the sacraments as instruments of initiation.

In Africa health is more a social and cultural concept than a biological one: a person's sickness is viewed as the result of her or his maladjustment to the social and cultural context. Healing (→healing and medical mission) in the traditional sense is a return to social harmony, physical health, and well-being under the eyes of God. To be healed is to recover lost harmony and to calm fear and anguish. In the African Christian view, healing in this sense is very much a function of Christ and the church. Many independent churches are almost uniquely dedicated to healing, and even the mainline churches are experiencing a resurgence of this ministry. In the christology of Christ the healer, he becomes the "medicine of life" in the Eucharist and in the sacraments.

The *systematic* approach is illustrated in the work of theologians such as V. Mulago, C. Nyamiti, and J. Penoukou, who generally speak of Christ as ancestor or elder brother. They have in common the search for a systematic and possibly scientific elaboration which would take account of the connection between the various mysteries of Christ and the church. Nyamiti explains his approach as an effort to elaborate and present the "deposit of faith" in an African manner by letting African themes enter internally into the elaboration of the revealed truths. He would first seek to bring African cultural elements to a scientific plane, something like an African metaphysics. It would seem that most of the theologians of this type function with some variation of the theory of "vital participation" (Penoukou refers to this as "cosmotheandric relation"). God, who has power and force in Godself, has the fullness of life; ancestors represent the concentration of life and vital energy necessary for the birth of all members of the lineage. To have life in abundance is to be properly related with the current of life emanating from God through the ancestors. In this view the life and death of Christ are seen as the process of accomplishment through which he became the "organic medium" of a family as *joto* (ancestor) in whom life and vital energy are concentrated. In such a christology the resurrection is constitutive of the work of redemption insofar as Jesus, who was "designated Son of God in power by resurrection from the dead" (Rom 1:4), "was handed over to death for our sins and raised to life for our justification" (Rom 4:25). In the phrasing of Nyamiti, the resurrection brought about the accomplishment of Jesus' ancestral qualities. Such a christology seeks a systematic link with the doctrine of the Trinity and of the church.

Dissenting voices have been raised, however. Does seeing Christ as ancestor limit his divinity? It would seem also that the African relation to the ancestors is more of a mutual entanglement than a living communion. A celibate, as Christ was, could hardly become an ancestor in the tradition; besides, the manner of Christ's death would not qualify him as an African ancestor. There may be issues of translation. It is not clear whether the people's faith associates Christ with the *muzimu,* the spirits of the dead toward whom the people entertain some ambivalent feelings. More seriously, one of the leading African theologians, J. S. Mbiti, has declared that the theory of "vital force" cannot be applied to other African peoples with whose life and ideas he is familiar. Is this a case where some African peoples have certain fundamental values not shared with others? Questions have also been posed concerning the method of dialoguing with "Catholic doctrine" instead of shaping a fresh perspective beginning with the Bible.

The *liberationist* approach is not as interested in a Christ for worship and spirituality as in a Christ who enables change and transformation. The focus is on the earthly Jesus and his commitment to the cause of the oppressed as the cause of God. Social struggle is adopted as a heuristic tool in interpreting both the gospel and the social situation. When Christianity transformed Jesus into the Christ, his social praxis became overwritten with a spiritual agenda. But for theology in South Africa, faith is concerned not with victorious struggle against doubts but with victorious struggle against conflicts in real-life existence. The powerful Christ is rejected because the people have risen against the powerful; the dead Christ of the processions of Holy Week is equally rejected because passivity defeats the struggle. Christ is black, where "black" symbolizes Africans and coloreds, that is, all nonwhites, hence all peoples under oppression. Christ suffers with them in the shanty towns, and as the Black Messiah he stands with them against oppression. With the advent of freedom, the perspective is shifting to Jesus as the reconciler whose inclusive meals symbolized universal reconciliation and Jesus as liberator for a full human life.

The *community-based* approach reflects on the community's actual experience of Christ. It seeks to discern portraits of Jesus which inform the people's actual Christian living and the parts of the Bible which speak more intimately to them. In other words, it seeks to discover the practical christology of the people. Research on the African independent churches shows their practical christology to be that of Christus Victor (the risen Lord of miracle power). It is a christology uniquely focused on the resurrection, the cross being only the symbol of completion whereby Jesus is invested with power on our behalf, a power which shields the believer from the mystical forces that people the African's world and is available in the fight to increase life in every sense. In many places, especially in eastern and central Africa, witchcraft is the evil from which deliverance is sought by the power of Christus Victor.

One thing remarkable about these christological elaborations is that they do not presume the Anselmian schema of "objective redemption" which continues to be the official doctrine in the mainline churches; the death of Jesus is not viewed as the sacrifice which brought our salvation but is rather linked with the resurrection in a dynamic process of initiation or perfecting of the risen Lord.

4. Both Christianity and African traditional religion are religions of →salvation, but whereas missionaries presented salvation as in the future, as individual, and as spiritual, Africans wish to experience it as present, as communal, and as holistic. Salvation is well-being and the possession of life in its fullest potency. But as nature, persons, ancestors, and the unseen are bound together in cosmic oneness, there can be no well-being unless one is in harmony with the cosmic totality. Life is physical: it is health, sufficient food, adequate housing, fertility, and offspring. Life is social and political. It is good neighborly relations, a good name, social justice, sharing, and solidarity with all in building the earthly city: "I am because we are; and since we are, I am." Life is mystical: "ontological balance" must be maintained between God and human beings, spirits and human beings, the departed and the living. When this balance is upset, people experience misfortunes and sufferings. Hence in many African independent churches "healing" is an integral part of church ministry, the priest being sacrificer, presider at prayer, healer, and psychiatrist.

Africa had no myths of the end-time, no concept of history moving forward to a future climax. Rather than myths of the fall of humanity, Africa had myths of the withdrawn God and no single myth suggesting a solution to or reversal of this loss. Encounter with the gospel has given Africa a concrete eschatological hope and a goal for human life which transcends this order of things.

5. When V. Donovan asked his Maasai converts to choose a name for themselves as a community in Christ, they quickly and instinctively settled on *orporor l'engai* (the age-group "brotherhood of God"). The African is a person-in-community. One of the deepest yearnings is to rediscover true community and solidarity amid the social changes of modern life. Africans see the only hope for this in the church. Hence in the submissions from the various dioceses in preparation for the 1994 African synod, most dioceses outlined their pastoral plan as that of "church as the family of God." The final document by the pope recalled that the synod took the church as family as its guiding idea for the evangelization of Africa. It was his hope that theologians would develop the theology of church as the family of God, showing its complementarity with other images of the church. In fact, considerable theological reflection has already accompanied the popular awareness of church as the family of God. There has also been considerable reflection on small Christian communities as the blocks for building this family of God, with Catholic bishops of AMECEA (Association of the Member Episcopal Conferences of Eastern Africa) adopting small Christian communities as the basis of their pastoral plan since 1976. It cannot, however, be said that an ecclesiology has emerged; what is in place is the conscious and ongoing practical articulation of church as family in the organization and administration of many dioceses.

6. Marriage, family, and liturgy are areas which are heavily subject to the impact of African culture, and so they have seen much pastoral adaptation and theological reflection. The traditional form of marriage differed from both the canonical form and the statute marriage of the colonial masters. Efforts have continued to integrate all these forms in one which would still be authentically African, truly Christian, and able to respond adequately to modern social changes. The basic study of marriage in African culture was a joint effort of the International African Institute, the International Missionary Council, and the British Social Science Research Council. It had three parts: "African Marriage and Social Change"; "Marriage Laws in Africa"; and "Christian Marriage in African Society." In 1973, J. S. Mbiti published a study of love and marriage in Africa, and A. Hastings authored a report commissioned by the Anglican bishops of eastern, central, and southern Africa. A project on behalf of sixteen Christian churches on marriage in eight countries of eastern and southern Africa (Kenya, Uganda, Tanzania, Zambia, Rhodesia, Lesotho, Malawi, and South Africa) was to follow in 1977. The Symposium of Episcopal Conferences of Africa and Madagascar (SECAM) studied African marriage and family life in its Nairobi (Kenya) meeting of 1978 and the Yaounde (Cameroon) meeting of 1981. It noted three fundamental aspects of African marriage which required integration in Christianity, namely, African marriage as at once a personal covenant and one between families; as celebrated in a process of dynamic stages; and as fundamentally oriented toward offspring. Various theologians are studying the challenges posed by the evolution of a truly African theology of marriage. Because of divergences in customs and practices, these studies (e.g., that of J.-B. Bigangara) tend to focus on particular groups. The African synod called on episcopal conferences, in cooperation with universities and Catholic institutes, to set up study commissions to continue the study of the cultural and theological aspects of marriage.

The Roman missal for the dioceses of Zaire (Democratic Republic of Congo) and its presentation volume contain one of the best examples of pastoral and theological reflection on the liturgy in the African context. The Zairean rite nevertheless illustrates one of the handicaps of theologizing in context within the Catholic tradition: the sometimes unsympathetic control from above. What set out as an original effort when presented in December 1973 took on certain contours of the Roman rite when approved fifteen years later. The Ndzon-Melen Mass of Yaounde is based on the cultural model of the African *palaver:* shared word and meal in an assembly convoked by one who has a problem. The Zairean and Ndzon-Melen rites are examples of the dynamic liturgical thinking in much of Sub-Saharan Africa. Some theologians have reflected on the need to make the Eucharist (→Eucharist [Lord's Supper]) from local foodstuffs so it may truly be a meal at home among people in Africa.

7. Unfortunately, the African voice is scarcely being heard because of the dearth of African publishing houses and the comparatively prohibitive cost of books within the African context of weak economies. Thousands of theses and papers continue to gather dust and may never see publication. African periodicals sometimes circulate more in Europe and America than within Africa itself. The result is that researchers are often not acquainted with similar research elsewhere in Africa. Further, greater attention needs to be paid to the biblical foundations of the emerging theology as well as to its anchoring in the experience of the people. Theology in Africa should become a force for liberation tending at once toward spiritual salvation and human liberation. In this manner it will respond to the African concept of salvation, which is holistic. Increasingly, this is being verified as cultural and spiritual aspects receive greater attention in South Africa and the liberative aspect garners more notice in other parts of Africa. With such vibrant theological activity in progress a truly African theology is well on its way.

JAMES C. OKOYE, CSSP

Bibliography

Abega, P., "Liturgical Adaptation," in E. Fashole-Luke, ed., *Christianity in Independent Africa* (1978) 597–605. African Peace and Justice Network, ed., *The African Synod: Documents, Reflections, Perspectives* (1996). Appiah-Kubi, K., and S. Torres, eds., *African Theology en Route* (1979). Becken, H.-J., *Relevant Theology for Africa* (1974). Bigangara, J.-B., *Mariage chrétien et mariage traditionell burundais: Divergences, convergences et perspectives* (1989). Boesak, A., *Farewell to Innocence: A Socio-ethical Study of Black Theology and Power* (1977). De Gruchy, J., and C. Villa-Vicencio, eds., *Doing Theology in Context: South African Perspectives* (1994). Dickson, K., *Theology in Africa* (1984). Dickson, K., and P. Ellingworth, eds., *Biblical Revelation and African Beliefs* (1969). Donovan, V. J., *Christianity Rediscovered* (1982). Éla, J.-M., *African Cry* (1980). Idem, *My Faith as an African* (1988). Ennang, K., *Salvation in a Nigerian Background: Its Concepts and Articulation in the Annang Independent Churches* (1979). Fashole-Luke, E. W., "The Quest for African Christian Theologies," in *Mission Trends* 3 (1976) 135ff. Healey, J., and D. Sybertz, *Towards an African Narrative Theology* (1996). John Paul II, *Ecclesia in Africa* (postsynodal apostolic exhortation) (1995). *Kairos Document: Challenge to the Church: A Theological Comment on the Political Situation in South Africa* (1995). Kalilombe, P., *From Outstation to Small Christian Communities* (1984). Kweshi, O. B., "Religions africaines: Un 'lieu' de la théologie africaine," *CRA* 12 (1978). Martey, E., *African Theology: Inculturation and Liberation* (1993). Maurier, H., "La théologie africaine francophone," *Spiritus* 88 (1982). Mbiti, J. S., *African Religions and Philosophy* (1969). Idem, *Concepts of God in Africa* (1970). Idem, *New Testament Eschatology in a New Testament Background* (1978). Idem, "Some African Concepts of Christology," in G. F. Vicedom, ed., *Christ and the Younger Churches* (1972) 51–62. Idem, "Some Currents of African Theology," *ExT*

87 (1976). Moloney, R., "African Christology," *TS* (1987) 505–15. Idem, "The Zairean Mass and Inculturation," *Worship* 62 (1988) 433–42. Mosala, I., *Biblical Hermeneutics and Black Theology in South Africa* (1989). Motlhabi, M., ed., *Essays on Black Theology* (1972). Mpolo, M. M., "Witchcraft and Dreams Analysis: Perspectives in African Pastoral Psychology," *BTA* 7 (1985). Mpongo, L., "Le rite zairois de la messe," *Spiritus* 73 (1978) 436–41. Mugambi, J. N. K., and L. Magesa, eds., *The Church in African Christianity: Innovative Essays in Ecclesiology* (1990). Mulago, V., *Un visage africain du christianisme* (1965). Muzorewa, G., *The Origins and Development of African Theology* (1991). Mushete, A. N., *Les themes majeurs de la théologie africaine* (1989). Ntreh, B. A., "Towards an African Biblical Hermeneutics," *ATJ* 19 (1990) 247–54. Nyamiti, C., "African Christologies Today," in J. N. K. Mugambi and L. Magesa, eds., *Jesus in African Christianity: Experimentation and Diversity in African Christology* (1989) 17–39. Idem, *African Theology: Its Nature, Problems, and Methods* (1971). Idem, *Christ Our Ancestor: Christology from an African Perspective* (1984). Idem, *The Scope of African Theology* (1973). Oduyoye, M. A., *The Sons of God and the Daughters of Men: An Afro-Asian Interpretation of Genesis 1–11* (1984). Okolo, B., "Emmanuel: An African Inquiry," *AfER* 20 (1978) 135. Okoye, J. C., "The Eucharist and African Culture," *AfER* 34 (1992) 277–78. Idem, "The Special Assembly for Africa and Inculturation," *StMiss* 44 (1995) 275–85. Olupona, J. K., *African Traditional Religions in Contemporary Society* (1991). Parrat, J., "African Theology and Biblical Hermeneutics," *ATJ* 12 (1983) 88–94. Parrinder, G., *African Traditional Religion* (1954). Penoukou, E. J., "Realité africaine et salut en Jesus Christ," *Spiritus* 89 (1982). Pobee, J., *Towards an African Theology* (1979). Ranger, T. O., and I. N. Kimambo, *The Historical Study of African Religion* (1972). Sankey, P., "The Church as Clan: Critical Reflections on African Ecclesiology," *IRM* 83 (1994) 437–49. Schreiter, R. J., *Faces of Jesus in Africa* (1991). Setiloane, G., *African Theology: An Introduction* (1986). Shorter, A., "Ancestor Veneration Revisited," *AfER* 25 (1983). Idem, "Folk Christianity and Functional Christology," *AfER* 24 (1982). Idem, *Jesus and the Witchdoctor: An Approach to Healing and Wholeness* (1985). Shorter, A., L. Magesa, and K. Benezeri, eds., *African Christian Marriage* (1977). Taylor, J. V., *The Primal Vision: Christian Presence amid African Religion* (1963). Tempels, P., *La philosophie bantou* (1948). Tshibangu, T., *La théologie africaine* (1987). Ukpong, J., *African Theologies Now* (1984). Uzukwu, E., "Food and Drink in Africa and the Christian Eucharist," *AfER* 22 (1980) 370–85. Idem, *Liturgy Truly Christian, Truly African* (1982). Idem, "Le salut du point de vue congolais," *Spiritus* 23 (1982) 251–53. Wambudta, D. N., "Hermeneutics and the Search for a Theologia Africana," *ATJ* 9 (1980) 27–39. West, G., *Biblical Hermeneutics of Liberation: Modes of Reading the Bible in the South African Context* (1991). Idem, "Two Modes of Reading the Bible in the South African Context of Liberation," *JTSA* 73 (1990). Zahan, D., *The Religion, Spirituality, and Thought of Traditional Africa* (1979). Zairean Episcopal Conference, *Misel Romain pour les dioceses du Zaire: Presentation de la liturgie de la Messe* (1973).

❧ ANCESTOR WORSHIP I (GENERAL) ❧

1. Theological Relevance.   2. Attempts at Solutions.

Ancestor worship, a constant factor in the history of religions, is a complex phenomenon that is very common among the peoples of Africa, Asia, and Oceania. It can pervade the whole of religious, social, and private life and epitomize all that is holy to a particular society. It presupposes faith in life after death.

1.   Since ancestor worship implies ideas and practices concerning the link between the living and the dead, it is of immediate theological importance for the church wherever it occurs. Catholic missiology regards the Christianization (contextualization) of ancestor worship as vital, but up to now no satisfactory and comprehensive treatment or solution of the question has been found.

In the Old Testament, ancestor worship was irreconcilable with faith in Yahweh. Any cult of ancestors was strictly forbidden (Lv 19:28; Dt 14:1). In accordance with this tradition, missionaries rejected ancestor worship and condemned it as magic, idolatry, and polytheism. (There were some exceptions to this — e.g., the Jesuits in China.) Belief in ancestors was wrongly identified with belief in spirits. On a dogmatic level, ancestor worship was judged in the light of the First Commandment; on a moral level, it was contrasted with the Fourth Commandment and considered an obstacle to conversion. But neither attempts to abolish ancestor worship nor increasing urbanization has managed to shake it. Nor will it be shaken, for ancestor worship is the most important instrument of →tradition in many cultures.

The official stand of the Catholic Church on ancestor worship can be seen in the Roman decisions concerning the Chinese, Japanese, and Malabar rites and concerning the reverence shown to Confucius. In this connection the Chinese →rites controversy has become a paradigm. Clement XI (*Ex illa die,* 1715) and Benedict XIV (*Ex quo singulari,* 1742) forbade the Chinese rites (including ancestor worship). It was not until 1935–36 that the Congregation for the Propagation of the Faith allowed the erection of ancestor tablets and, under certain conditions, obeisance before them. Nowadays, on the occasion of the Chinese New Year, special church ceremonies in honor of heaven and the ancestors are held and even encouraged. In Africa and Oceania on important feasts the ancestors are included in the ceremonies and prayers, for example, at funerals and on the feast of All Souls. The rites controversies in the Catholic Church have made it possible to draw up principles and norms of behavior, but there is hardly any reference to these in the African literature on the subject (→ancestor worship II [in Africa]). The Roman Catholic Church distinguishes between acts which have as their object the observance of a religious cult and the veneration given to persons (ancestors) which is regarded simply as part and parcel of a specific culture. But here we see the gap between the interpretation of ancestor worship by anthropology and comparative religion, on the one hand, and theology, on the other. It is hard to draw a line between veneration and cult, and there is a real danger of misunderstanding and compromising the content of faith. The church must always bear in mind how the acts in connection with ancestor worship are understood in various contexts. If the link with the ancestors is understood as the maintenance of the family bonds even beyond death, there is nothing in this that militates against the Christian faith. The general attitude of the Catholic Church toward the non-Christian religions according to Vatican II and subsequent magisterial teaching (*Nostra Aetate, Ad Gentes, Evangelii Nuntiandi, Africae Terrarum, Redemptoris Missio, Dialogue and Proclamation*) applies here as well.

2. But different kinds of ancestor worship express themselves in complex forms and also contain elements irreconcilable with the faith of the church. Theology and →liturgy are attempting in the spirit of dialogue to reconcile ancestor worship with the Christian faith. These basic *approaches* concerning ancestor worship can be distinguished as follows.

2.1. A theological-biblical solution can be constructed on the basis of 2 Mc 12:44f.; Wis 3:1–9; Lk 16:19–31; Jn 11:26; 14:1–14; 1 Cor 15:15–52; 1 Th 4:13f., 18; Heb 11:39–12:29; 1 Jn 3:2f.

2.2. An ecclesiological answer, not universally accepted, however, is based on the concept of "vitally necessary participation." Ancestor worship is rooted in the relationship between the living and the dead; this is manifested also in the veneration of the saints. In this way ancestor worship is reconciled with the Catholic teaching regarding the community of saints (*LG* 49–51). The living and the dead form a close *communio,* and the community of saints includes community with the ancestors (Eph 1:10).

2.3. A christological interpretation treats ancestor worship within the context of redemption. Ancestor worship can describe a "memorative-narrative soteriology" (B. Bujo); Jesus, after all, showed solidarity with the ancestors of goodwill (*descensus ad inferos*) so that they would find their raison d'être and fullness of life only in him. That means that although righteous ancestors have never heard of him, they have died in Christ and share community with him. All righteous ancestors are secure in Christ, and the vitality passed on to their descendants flows from him alone. According to this view, the ancestor worshiper can pray only to his ancestors and ask for their intercession through Christ. Hence ancestor worship is an expression of solidarity within the *corpus mysticum* of that Christ who alone constitutes the future (→christology).

Another christological attempt is based on the principle that Christ, through the incarnation and the work of redemption, is the only true brother and ancestor. Here the community of saints, who are also ancestors, pneumatologically speaking, and the human community with the redeemer are regarded as the foundation of Christian ancestor worship. The →Eucharist (Lord's Supper) is celebrated as an "ancestor ritual." The possibility of a certain pluralism in theology and liturgy granted to the young churches by Vatican II allows experiments in the contextualization of ancestor worship, and every attempt at Christianizing ancestor worship should take the context into account. It is the task of the missiologists and missionaries to investigate the whole spectrum of perspectives revealed by ancestor worship.

ROMAN MALEK, SVD

Bibliography

AAS 28 (1936) 406–9 (*Pluries Instanterque*); 32 (1940) 24–26 (*Plane Copertum*); 59 (1967) 1073–97 (*Africae Terrarum*). Ahern, E., *The Cult of the Dead in a Chinese Village* (1973). "Ahnen, Heranwachsende und das Absolute: Eine Einübung in die Kontextualisierung," *PMVB* 68 (September-October, 1977). Bujo, B., *African Theology in Its Social Context* (1992). Idem, "Der afrikanische Ahnenkult und die christliche Verkündigung," *ZMRW* 64 (1980) 193–306. Idem, "Nos ancêtres, les saintes inconnus," *BTA* 1–2 (1979) 165–78. Bureau, R., and J.-P. Eschelmann, "Ancêtre en Afrique noir," in *DictR* (1984) 40–45. *Collectanea S. Congr. de Prop. Fide Romae* 1 (1839–41) 130–41 (*Ex quo singulari*). Daneel, M. L., "The Christian Gospel and the Ancestor Cult," *Missionalia* 1 (1973) 46–73. Éla, J. M., "Ancestors and Christian Faith: An African Problem," *Concilium* 102 (1977) 34–50. Hardacre, H., "Ancestor Worship," *ER* (1987) 263–68. Hsu, F. L. K., *Under the Ancestors' Shadow* (1948). Huonder, A., *Der chinesische Ritenstreit* (1921). Hwang, B., "Ancestor Cult Today," *Missiol* 5 (1977) 339–66. Ishola, A. A., "Ancestors or Saints?" *ED* 36 (1983) 267–82. Janelli, D. Y., and R. L. Janelli, *Ancestor Worship in Korean Society* (1982). Janssen, H., "Ancestor Veneration in Melanesia: A Problem of Syncretism in Pastoral Work," *NZM* 31 (1975) 181–91. Jordan, D. K., *Gods, Ghosts, and Ancestors: The Folk Religion of a Taiwanese Village* (1969). Kabasélé, F., "Christ as Ancestor and Elder Brother," in R. J. Schreiter, ed., *Faces of Jesus in Africa* (1991) 116–27. Kollbrunner, F., "Auf dem Weg zu einer christlichen Ahnenverchrung?" *NZM* 31 (1975) 19–29, 110–23. Kopytoff, I., "Ancestors as Elders in Africa," *Africa* 41 (1971) 129–42. Larre, C., "Ancêtres en Chine," in *DictR* (1984) 45. Meggitt, M., and P. Lawrence, eds., *Gods, Ghosts, and Men in Melanesia* (1965). Metzler, J., *Die Synoden in Indochina 1625–1934* (1984). Idem, *Die Synoden in China, Japan und Korea 1570–1931* (1980). Minamiki, G., *The Chinese Rites Controversy: From Its Beginning to Modern Times* (1985). Mulago, V., "Die lebensnotwendige Teilhabe," in *Theologie und Kirche in Afrika,* ed. H. Bürkle, 54–72 (1968). Idem, *La religion traditionnelle des Bantu et leur conception du monde* (1973). Newell, W. H., *Ancestors* (1976). Nyamiti, C., *Christ as Our Ancestor: Christology from an African Perspective* (1984). Ohm, T., "Ahnenglaube und Mission in Afrika," *ZMR* 24, (1934) 324–35. Idem, *Ex Contemplatione Loqui* (1961) 257–71. Reinhard, P., "Jésus fête la pâque au séjour des ancêtres," *Spiritus* 22 (1981) 424–30. Ross, A. C., *A Vision Betrayed: The Jesuits in Japan and China, 1542–1742* (1994). Rükker, H., *Afrikanische Theologie: Darstellung und Dialog* (1984). Schatz, K., "Inkulturationsproblem im ostasiatischen Ritenstreit des 1718, Jahrhunderts," *StZ* 197 (1979)

593–608. Schreiter, R. J., "Ancêtres in Océanie," in *DictR* (1984) 45–46. Yang, D. K., *Religion in Chinese Society* (1961).

✥ ANCESTOR WORSHIP II (IN AFRICA) ✥

1. Veneration or Worship? 2. The Place of the Ancestors in Traditional Religion. 3. Recent Anthropological Interpretation. 4. Missiological Interpretation. 5. Ancestor Worship and African Churches.

1. The term "ancestor worship" in its conventional English form has been contested by Africans for some time. This contestation has focused upon two misconceptions. First, to some the traditional African relationship to the dead usually simply implies one's relation to one's forebears in the narrowest sense — that is, to the fathers and mothers from whom one is descended by blood. Because this is misleading, J. S. Mbiti replaces the term "ancestors" with "the living dead." The living dead do not have to be one's own ancestors but are distinguished from the nameless dead more than five generations back — the latter are no longer remembered by name and are no longer worshiped. Second, the cultural and emotional attitude of the living to their dead in pre-Christian Africa is even more controversial: Was it really "worship"? That is, did they really pray to their ancestors, as the classic animistic theory of E. B. Tylor and H. Spencer assumed and as the Christian missions accepted? Did they turn the ancestors into gods? The more recent scholarly explanations of traditional religion, at least those given by educated Africans influenced by Christianity, contest this assertion radically and see in it a tendentious Western misunderstanding. "Honoring" one's father and mother, as in the Fourth Commandment, was never in conflict on the human level with "worshiping" the one God, a worship prescribed in the First Commandment and known all over Africa at all times. Thus, as J. Kenyatta pointed out, it is not only Catholics who make a distinction between *adoratio,* which is rendered to God alone, and *veneratio,* which is given to the ancestors and to those still alive who merit it, just as the saints are venerated in the West.

Ancestor worship in this limited sense is naturally connected to death rituals and mourning customs, these two not being identical. Between the physical death of a person and the beginning of his or her veneration as the newest and youngest ancestor there lies a ritually determined fixed interval. While at a feast for the ancestors joyful trust and desire for the participation of the dead in the good fortune of the living predominate, in their own death rituals fear and protection against the spirit of the dead, who has not yet been given a ceremonial farewell, are more strongly felt. The highly developed death and mourning rituals are as widely practiced as ever, even where traditional ancestor worship has long since become a thing of the past, through Christian and secular influence.

2. In all discussions of whether "worship" or "veneration" of the ancestors is the correct term, educated Africans agree that ancestors played an important, even a central, role in traditional religion. The living can understand themselves as human beings only in relation to their past. The ancestors were more important than sorcery, magic, and powerful objects. Although graves and, to some extent, skulls play a certain role, artistic representations of ancestors known by name are relatively rare: the relationship to them — like the relationship to the one

God, of whom there are also no pictures or statues — is nonmaterial and spiritual. However, one addressed God only in exceptional circumstances; one addressed the ancestors regularly. In many West African languages the word for God is the singular form of the word used for the ancestors. Two Nigerians, E. B. Idowu and V. Uchendo, draw attention to a general tendency among the Yoruba and the Ibos. As well as veneration of the ancestors as human beings, there existed and still does exist worship of them as deities. Similarly, as Uchendo has indicated, Mbiti's limiting of the ancestors known by name to a maximum of five generations is not applicable there. The ancestors are in general *intermediaries* between the divine and the human, transmitting God's gifts to the living and to their guardian angels, without themselves being creators or absolute lords of the world. Their tribal limitation is an aspect of their humanity; only God is universal. The ancestors are peculiar to each group. This, according to Mbiti, is the fundamental reason why a stranger — whether a slave or a woman entering into a patrilineal family by marriage — can never genuinely convert to an African traditional religion, unlike a world religion.

In practical terms, worship of the ancestors can take place on an individual or a family level or — according to the political order of a particular traditional society — on a village, tribal, or national level. (There are regularly recurring festivals at the graves of chiefs and kings in Nigeria, Ghana, and South Africa.) At times of crisis and transition (puberty, contracting a marriage, illness, and even crises in young people's school or professional lives), individuals seek the blessing and assistance of their close ancestors, in order to survive in the competitive struggles of society. Offerings of food and wine, especially libations of palm wine sprinkled on the ground, are as indispensable as verbal invocation. One can negotiate with the ancestors, but not with God. Occasionally the ancestors are covetous or angry and must be propitiated; but generally they are benevolent in their relations with their living descendants. Evil and vindictive spirits, whom one must fend off with magic, are rarely counted among the ancestors.

3.   More recent anthropological interpretation of ancestors in Africa is taking a sociological and psychological direction. J. Goody (1962) has set out the fundamentals of the essential relationship between "ancestors and property" in Ghana as follows: those ancestors — female as well as male — from whom one has inherited property and status and who thus have claims on the living who have taken their place are accorded veneration by the family. Ancestor veneration is thus, at the very least, a social ideology, a symbolic superstructure of actual relationships based on possessions and power. M. Fortes has traced the Oedipus complex in the psychologically ambivalent relationship of the living to the dead in Africa, as part of the general tension between generations in all human societies. Aspiring young men may not desire the death of their fathers, who control the relationship between them, but must at the same time want it in order to ensure their own external self-realization — limited and mortal though it is. Like all human mourning for the dead, ancestor worship includes, as well as piety, an indirect admission of guilt for this death wish.

At the present time, more stumbling blocks in the way of investigations in Asia (→ancestor worship I [general]) arise from research into ancestor worship in Africa than the other way round. In Africa the basic principles can be grasped more directly: there is no bureaucratization of the ancestors by written codification; the cycle of their festivals is organized according to the calendar and in accordance with the limited memory of an illiterate culture.

4. Western missiology today recognizes, as do Africans' own Christian theological interpretations, that the struggle against ancestor worship as "idolatry" was an error, comparable to reducing African religion to "nothing but ancestors." Equally certain, however, is that ancestors, as P. Beyerhaus has noted, represent a temptation toward syncretism (in its negative sense of a betrayal of the substance of the Christian faith) in the African churches. Many forms of *veneratio* are in conflict with the profound understanding of Jesus Christ as the only mediator. It must be admitted that ancestors may prove to be less of a problem of faith for African Christians today than fear of sorcerers and witches or active recourse to magical forms of protection. For its part, Western theology must not only advise Africans on the correct approach to the dead but also learn from them at the same time: that is, in their understanding of personal resurrection (see H. Häselbarth); in the therapeutic value of their death rites (T. Sundermeier); and in African ancestors as a possible entry to new "symbolic" thought (H. Rücker).

5. For the African churches, ancestors are a pastoral and liturgical issue before they become a theological theme (→African theology). Reactions to the problem take different forms, varying with denomination and type of church. The Zionist independent churches, while expressly rejecting "heathen" ancestor cults, allow the commemoration of their founders, their graves, and the places where they were active. This is done for cultural and also partly doctrinal reasons, and it gives fresh life to the helpful and powerful nearness of the good and pious ancestors in a new form. In Catholic missions a parallel was drawn early on between the African ancestors and the saints, but more recent experience has thrown greater light upon the intrinsic difference between ancestors and saints. According to J. M. Éla, the ordering of society for the sake of the living depends directly upon the public worship of village ancestors, who cannot in any way be replaced by Western saints imported into Africa and the people's festivals. The social function of the ancestors in giving the individual an identity over and against society is also being rethought in African Catholic terms: only the adult person who has a personal spiritual relationship with his or her dead father can have a similar relationship with Jesus Christ (see P. Tchouanga). Protestant African theologians (e.g., J. S. Mbiti, E. B. Idowu, K. Dickson, and E. Fashole-Luke) typically find themselves confronted with the dogmatic problem of "scripture and tradition" in making ancestor worship "Christian." Although the New Testament says nothing about a Christian duty of venerating one's ancestors, for Africans it remains an imperative arising from the innermost parts of the human soul, partly in the expectation of the help from those who died in the faith and equally out of concern and intercession for the salvation of one's forebears, who did not know the gospel.

HORST BALZ

Bibliography

Diangienda Kuntima, *Histoire du Kimbanguisme* (1984). Goody, J., *Death, Property and the Ancestors* (1962). Häselbarth, H., *Die Auferstehung der Toten in Afrika* (1972). Idowu, E. B., *African Traditional Religion* (1973). Kenyatta, J., *Facing Mount Kenya* (1938). Mbiti, J. S., *African Religions and Philosophy* (1969). Idem, *Bible and Theology in African Christianity* (1986). Newell, H., *Ancestors* (1976). Pobee, J. S., "Ahnen und Heilige und die Kirche in Afrika," *UnSa* 43 (1988) 309–15. Pula, A. L., "Balimo (Ancestor) Veneration and Christianity," *AfER* 32 (1990) 330–45.

Rücker, H., *Afrikanische Theologie* (1985). Rukamba, I., "Le culte des ancêtres dans la tradition rwandaise et le culte des saints dans la doctrine Chrétienne: Essai d'inculturation," *Urunana* 24/71 and 72 (1991) 3–36; 37–63. Idem, "Le rite du culte des ancêtres: Guterekera: Prélude à la communion chrétienne," *Urunana* 22/66 (1989) 1–26. Tertrais, M., "La foi et la croyance dans le culte des ancêtres," *BPCDR* 24 (1989) 83–88. See also the bibliography for "Ancestor Worship I (General)."

❧ ANTHROPOLOGY ❧

1. The Discipline of Anthropology. 2. Anthropology and Mission.

1. Broadly speaking, anthropology studies people and their relations to one another and to the environment in which they live. Adjectives like "cultural" and "social" have characteristically been associated with anthropology in order to differentiate certain aspects of the study from other kinds of anthropological endeavor, like the analysis of somatic types (physical anthropology) or the study of historical antecedents (archaeology/paleontology).

Though "social" and "cultural" anthropology are not adequate descriptions of, respectively, British and North American approaches, and though the term "sociocultural" is sometimes used, there remains a discernibly different approach to the subject according to whether one focuses on social relationships as features of a consistently changing network or on culture conceived of as a bounded, discrete entity. "Social" at least serves to emphasize that more than purely personal meanings are the subject of anthropological inquiry. But the very concept of "culture" has been so impugned in academic debate that "cultural anthropology" is judged by many an inadequate title for a discipline that attempts to understand a world marked by change and pluralism, not to say unpredictability and fluidity. If the differences between American and British anthropology were formerly more marked, now the similarities are more apparent; but names, once attached to different schools of thought, sometimes outlive their usefulness.

Anthropology's historical endeavor to establish itself as respectable took place within the context of two dominant intellectual theories of the time. It was struggling to come of age in a world almost mesmerized by the paradigm of (biological) evolutionism, and notions of "equilibrium" underpinned academic models of the world.

First, applied to living species, Darwinian evolutionism was strongly deterministic. As a tool for understanding human societies, it proved both reductionistic and ethnocentrically skewed: reductionistic because it blinded anthropologists, committing them to placing every society on a developmental curve of human cultures; ethnocentric because inevitably the idealized culture of the anthropologist (Victorian European) was deemed to mark the end point of the curve.

Second, though anthropology examined the human subject as a creative agent and choice-maker (thus not easily reducible to "rules" or "laws"), there was real tension between attempts to understand human behavior as truly creative and its reduction to instinctive, behavioral, or unfree responses. The putative creativity of the subject became bogged down by the weight of the contemporary "homeostatic" or "equilibrium" models of society. "Functionalist" anthropology, though presenting behavior and belief as all of a piece, or composed of interlocking, rational, and "functional" components, was fatally flawed. For if everything in human organization should be understood as so interconnected and interdependent, human organization must indeed be tending toward stasis. But if this was the case, how could one account for aberrant or pathological behavior, much less explain social change, culture-clash, or the "translation" of sociocultural behavior and belief?

Anthropology sought models and method yet struggled against the tendency to be dominated by them. It proved relatively easy to describe behavior or phenomena. But to compare such things cross-culturally; to identify real similarities and not merely superficial resemblances; to create analytical and explanatory schemata; and to move beyond impressionistic responses and ensure replicability or interpretation of social data — these proved to be the formative tasks of anthropology. As regards models, early "Darwinian" social evolutionism gradually lost ground to a "Newtonian" diffusionism which postulated single "centers" from which cultural ideas and social institutions somehow "radiated," thus explaining rather better than linear evolutionism the existence of similar expressions of human ingenuity in widely separated areas.

Another explanation of social life, the "functionalism" of B. Malinowski (d. 1942), based on a biological theory of needs, was superseded by the more sophisticated "structural functionalism" of A. R. Radcliffe-Brown (d. 1959), which shifted the anthropological gaze away from specific individuals, seeing "social structure" as an arrangement not of individuals in this sense but of "moral persons" understood as clusters of social statuses and roles. Anthropology was not interested in an individual's particularity and uniqueness but qua "wife," "mother," blacksmith," or "shaman." Such study was deemed to throw more light on the dynamics of society as a whole and social values and mores.

After a burst of energy between the two world wars, many of the perceived tasks of British anthropology were becoming clearer. Meanwhile, the transatlantic school, associated with names such as A. L. Kroeber, F. Boas, and R. Benedict, showed interest not only in the material culture of Native American peoples but in rather abstract ideas and values, perceived to be incarnated in discrete and bounded "cultures": whence "cultural anthropology." Fascination with the history of culture and the comparative study called ethnology served, for a while, to distinguish the American from the British schools; but there was always curiosity, communication, competition, and a measure of convergence. Today the actual difference between the two is often minimal or even nonexistent.

In the mid–twentieth century, French intellectual C. Lévi-Strauss became identified with the development of "structuralism," a theory concerned not with actual, embodied behavior but with the purported underlying structures of the human "mind-as-such." Lévi-Strauss's study focused on the myths (the imaginative and coded statements, rarely written, of truths often buried beneath consciousness) of different social groups in Amazonia and on the wonderful "transformations" of these narratives through time and space. These transformations, said Lévi-Strauss, occurred through the unconscious application of sophisticated and entirely rational "rules." It must be humanly possible to learn the rules, and so even an anthropologist might come to interpret some of the belief and behavior of otherwise inscrutable people!

The value of this approach and associated insights should not be underestimated: any attempt to establish scientifically the unity of humanity not only is a potential antidote to theories of "superior races" but provides a point of departure for addressing the rationality, meaning, or translatability of such human social institutions as belief in spirits, witchcraft, and other standardized modes of behavior. Individuals are different, and if some are credulous or simpleminded, peoples as such — groups which have survived over generations and succeeded in providing for present and future needs — are neither stupid nor irrational.

It is possible to argue for either losses or gains in the field of anthropology: there have been proliferation and fragmentation. "Poststructural" and "postmodern" movements have led some people to a virtual deconstruction of the whole anthropological enterprise and others to a pervasive and stultifying relativism. But there are anthropologists who have espoused a reengagement with the-other-as-subject. Theirs, however, is an anthropology that no longer chases spurious objectivity or a purely dispassionate study but acclaims the "reflexivity" of the anthropologist, making a virtue of his or her embodied and engaged involvement with the people and dramas studied, admitting that the presence of the anthropologist is sometimes less "fly-on-the-wall" than "fly-in-the-ointment"!

There have also been casualties. "Culture" itself, a cornerstone of the original edifice, survives, but scarred and pockmarked by academic sniping. To some it is merely a facade: unnecessary, unwarrantably "essentialized" or "reified," and unable to bear any weight. Others, who respect it as a foundation of anthropology, feel obliged to state that it is only a part and not the whole, that it is not immutable, that it weathers, and that cornerstones sometimes collapse unless sustained by radical engineering feats.

What of anthropological method? Initially, comparative or "cross-cultural" information on human groups came largely from missionaries, colonial agents, and a few travelers and traders; some of the finest "amateur" anthropologists were in fact missionaries. But the self-appointed professional anthropologist received and interpreted this contrasting, confusing, and qualitatively varied material in the comfort of the library or the study. Asked whether he had actually encountered any of the "primitive people" he wrote about so magisterially, Sir James Frazer, author of the daunting, encyclopedic *Golden Bough,* expostulated, "God forbid!" The epithet "armchair" anthropologist was appropriate. But with improved communications, and with more "scientific" expeditions to faraway places, things began to change.

Today, and for almost a century, the most important methodological tool of the anthropologist (which has been continuously refined) has been the "participant observation" fashioned by B. Malinowski. He mentored a generation of students through this "rite of passage," which takes many months and often many years and which continues as the formal initiation for anthropologists. Participant observation offers an unequaled vantage point for reflection on human variety and its meaning, despite the changing theoretical perspectives which mark anthropology itself. And though the end of the twentieth century sees a discipline very different from its younger self — less grandiose in its claims, less universalizing in the "laws" it discerns, more inclined to repudiate the crude seduction of generalizations for the more subtle satisfaction of insights — nevertheless there continues to be both a fascination for and an increasing engagement with people and with the meaning they make. This makes the relevance of anthropology for mission studies, and the potential for mutual enrichment, probably greater than it has ever been.

2. *Participant observation.* Even an anthropology with inflated claims would have relevance to those ambassadors of Christ who seek to respect and understand human variety and who believe Christianity must express itself as more than simply a universal monoculture. But anthropology has moderated some earlier assumptions about human development and predictability and seems more interested in dialogue with other people likewise interested in humanity and human values.

Participant observation is much more complex and demanding than it sounds, requiring not merely a genuine interest in people and a respectful curiosity about their behavior and associated belief-system but serious and honest scholarship which would provide comparative and contextualized data as a hermeneutical key. Attention and intuition are inadequate without some intellectual depth. If goodwill is a necessary but insufficient tool for learning languages, the same is true of learning "culture." Shortsighted and perhaps foolish is the missioner who does not stand upon the shoulders of anthropologists in order to view what lies ahead and on all sides. Participant observation may be the best vantage point.

Once situated close to an unfamiliar group of people, the enthusiastic student must, by trial and error but with serious respect for the hosts, both discover and create a role which will allow for the optimal production of comprehensible and translatable interaction with local people. A successful (effective, but deferential and trusting) participant observer is not one who unilaterally decides when to participate and when to observe but one who can read cues and negotiate appropriate behavior. In some cases the desire to participate — or merely to observe — must be modified, resisted, or even stifled.

Like all processes, participant observation unfolds over time. The anthropologist characteristically undergoes some real bonding with local people, which contributes to the mutual building of trust. Missioners are ideally suited for such bonding, since they commit themselves to people for extensive periods of time. But they do need to be aware that little can be accomplished by someone in too much of a hurry. Without mutual trust there will be little chance of effective evangelization.

Karl Rahner said that all good theology must be good anthropology. For Christians venturing beyond familiar cultural boundaries, this is a wise saying. Much remains to be done if missioners are to be trustworthy in relation to other people and effective ministers of a gospel which calls all parties to radical conversion. Anthropology has no magical solutions, but it has accumulated a great store of experience about human nature.

Inculturation. Anthropology is likely to be useful only for those who accept that grace builds on nature. If human nature is seen as irreversibly evil, then simply approaching another culture on its own terms and learning about its meaning-system will be no better than an interesting diversion, for the missioner will continue to believe that destruction of local cultures is a prerequisite for evangelization. This, tragically, is not unknown within Christian history. But cultures are more widely understood today as expressions of the marvelous and rich diversity of human life: contexts in which grace may abound. People are called to conversion in the context of their culture and not simply after their culture has been destroyed. To destroy people's culture is to demean and mutilate human beings.

Inculturation is impossible to bring to realization unless theology and anthropology engage in some kind of covenantal relationship. Inculturation is the process whereby the gospel becomes culturally comprehensible and assimilable in whatever environment it may be preached. That is not to say it becomes "palatable" like bland or mashed food. Rather it is translated into the languages and culture of local people and must sustain them for the long haul. It will always constitute a challenge, but a gospel that is incomprehensible, or which appears to call people to betray the very foundations of their own culture, can hardly be said to ennoble or liberate. If we believe that grace builds on nature, we can then forge theological/missiological links with anthropology.

Further applications. Any undertaking which refuses to face constructive criticism or fails to take advantage of other people's insights must be judged bigoted, arrogant, and narrow. The practical insights and methodological procedures gained by anthropology are particularly germane to a missiology seeking real understanding and engagement with people. Interdisciplinary collaboration is now actively sought by practitioners of both anthropology and theology. If anthropologists have had to face criticism for their professional detachment and lack of moral responsibility toward the people they study, missioners have not been immune from charges that they rode roughshod over people's cultures, values, and social relationships. But both have learned a great deal about social organization, meaning-in-culture, social change, exploitation of peoples and resources, ecology and environment, and so forth. Their disciplines can complement each other and are finding creative ways of doing so.

There is no universal language, nor a universal theology. All theology is local. But anthropology may help, better than other disciplines, to interpret the local and to facilitate translation across a wider world. Anthropology may suggest how missioners, as strangers and outsiders — though participant observers — may share resources very creatively and avoid being exploitative tourists or hostile judges. Anthropology has discovered the authenticity of a phenomenological, embodied, committed engagement with others and has learned that intellectual understanding is only partial and inevitably warped. Some missioners already know this, implicitly, just as they know that terms such as "illiterate" and "primitive" may obscure a people's oral sophistication and creativity. Anthropology may contribute to their making explicit what they only sense and to their using their intuitive wisdom to fortify people who have been oppressed and ridiculed.

Not everyone, though, can transcend ethnocentrism and become anthropologically and ethnographically sophisticated. Anthropology may be a bridle to lead people to water; but it cannot force them to drink.

Unwritten and informal rules lie beneath people's behavior and mythology. Missioners can capitalize on this knowledge as they continue the search for meaning and for the convergence between the gospel and people's hearts and minds. And poststructural anthropology, in a move which echoes a development in theology, is pursuing a "return to the subject." Such serious attention to people's inherited wisdom and embodied experience exemplifies the attitude of Jesus himself.

ANTHONY J. GITTINS, CSSP

Bibliography

"Anthropology," in *The International Encyclopedia of the Social Sciences,* vol. 1 (1968) 304–44. Boon, J. A., "Anthropology, Ethnology, and Religion," in M. Eliade, ed., *EncRel,* vol. 1 (1987) 308–16. Carrithers, M., *Why Humans Have Cultures* (1992). Conn, H., *Eternal Word and Changing Worlds: Theology, Anthropology, and Mission in Trialogue* (1984). Geertz, C., *The Interpretation of Cultures* (1973). Gittins, A. J., *Bread for the Journey: The Mission of Transformation and the Transformation of Mission* (1993). Idem, *Gifts and Strangers: Meeting the Challenge of Inculturation* (1989). Hiebert, P., *Anthropological Insights for Missionaries* (1985). Idem, *Anthropological Reflections on Missiological Issues* (1994). Idem, *Cultural Anthropology* (1983). Jackson, M., *Paths toward a Clearing* (1989). Jorgensen, D., *Participant Observation* (1989). Leach, E., *Rethinking*

Anthropology (1961). Lett, J. *The Human Enterprise: A Critical Introduction to Anthropological Theory* (1987). Luzbetak, L., *The Church and Cultures* (1988). Pannenberg, W., *Anthropology in Theological Perspective* (1985). Rogerson, J. W., "Social Sciences and the Bible," in B. Metzger and D. Coogan, eds., *The Oxford Companion to the Bible* (1993). Schreiter, R. J., "Anthropology and Faith: Challenges to Missiology," *Missiol* 19/3 (July 1991) 283–94. Idem, "Faith and Cultures: Challenges to a World Church." *TS* 50 (1989) 744–60. Shorter, A., *Towards a Theology of Inculturation* (1989). Taylor, M. K., *Beyond Explanation: Religious Dimensions of Cultural Anthropology* (1986).

✎ ANTHROPOLOGY AND MISSION ✎

1. The Nature of Missiological Anthropology. 2. History. 3. Current Trends.

1. Missiological anthropology might best be regarded as a specialized form of applied anthropology. Its specific aim is missiological, while the perspective and approach taken are anthropological. Missiology provides the theological issues and goals; anthropology provides the scientific processes and standards. More specifically, missiological anthropology seeks (*a*) to bring together the various concepts, insights, principles, theories, methods, and techniques of anthropology that are relevant to the mission of the church; and, (*b*) to show how such a body of knowledge might be employed for a better understanding and realization of that mission. The basic anthropological fields applied are ethnology and ethnography, but other branches of anthropology are useful as well, for example, ethnohistory, psychological anthropology, and sociolinguistics.

Ethnological theory is useful especially for cross-cultural missionary work but is no less pertinent and applicable to all local churches of the world, including those of the West, for example, for the development of local liturgies and religious educational programs and for the solution of social problems.

2. From the earliest times ethnographical information was employed by the church for communicational and adaptational purposes. Thus, the Apostle Paul strongly opposed the Judaizing trends of the infant church. Directives from Pope Gregory the Great (d. 604) and many other popes have shown an empathetic appreciation of local political, social, and cultural peculiarities of peoples. Even during the most ethnocentric periods of church history there have always been great champions of indigenization, such as Saints Cyril and Methodius (the ninth-century apostles to the Slavic peoples), R. Lull (d. 1316), M. Ricci (d. 1610), R. de Nobili (d. 1566), B. de las Casas (d. 1566), and J.-F. Lafitau (d. 1740); and, when Protestants became engaged in missionary work, there were such thinkers and leaders as B. Ziegenbalg (d. 1719), H. Venn (d. 1873), and R. Anderson (d. 1855). The main ethnographers and folklorists throughout the Middle Ages and the Age of the Great Discoveries were invariably missionaries, some of whom are appreciated to this day, for example, B. Shagún (d. 1590) and Lafitau. In fact, anthropology itself is sometimes said to have its origin in missionaries.

Ethnography, which has always appeared at various levels of sophistication and reliability, assumed new missiological relevance with the birth of modern Catholic missiology and its emphasis on missionary accommodation. A further milestone was the direct involvement of missionaries in ethnology under the leadership of W. Schmidt, SVD, and his journal *Anthropos*.

The first handbooks and guides for cross-cultural mission work of more recent times were modest in scope (mainly small ethnographic and linguistic aids) until the appearance of Eugene A. Nida's works, especially his *Customs and Cultures: Anthropology for Christian Missions* (1954) and *Message and Mission: The Communication of the Christian Faith* (1960). In 1958, anthropologist M. Gusinde, SVD, published his mission anthropological compendium *Die völkerkundliche Ausrüstung des Missionars*. Important, too, was the journal *Practical Anthropology* (1952–72 [now called *Missiology: An International Review*]), published expressly for missionaries. *The Church and Cultures: An Applied Anthropology for the Religious Worker,* a systematic introduction to applied mission anthropology by L. J. Luzbetak, SVD, appeared in 1963 and was thoroughly revised in an edition which appeared in 1989.

3. The post–World War II years witnessed a sudden rise of national pride and a hunger for equality and self-determination on the part of the Third World and so-called mission countries, which, in turn, gave birth to a general cultural sensitivity never witnessed in the world or in the Christian churches before. Important in this regard were the international gatherings of the World Council of Churches and of the Lausanne Covenant denominations and, especially, Vatican II, a turning point in Catholic history, when the church declared itself a *world church* not merely as heretofore, only theoretically, geographically, and potentially, but in essence and in fact, as Asian and African as European. It is now broadly recognized by Christian churches that mere accommodation is not enough: Christ has to be incarnated, inculturated, contextualized — not merely transplanted or translated. This new self-understanding called for a new interpretation of mission and a correspondingly new job description for missiological anthropology.

A missiological anthropology *as a fully developed discipline* does not yet exist, although present-day anthropological concepts, theories, principles, and field techniques are being used in both theoretical and practical missiology. What is still needed today is a missiological anthropology in the strict sense of the term. This would be an *organized* body of ethnological concepts, principles, theories, methods, and techniques, organized in such a way that this body of scientific knowledge could be constantly tested and retested as it grew, clarifying more and more the cultural implications of mission action and becoming an ever more reliable tool for mission experimentation, control, and prediction.

The primary concerns of missiological anthropology today are: (*a*) cross-cultural communication; (*b*) social action; and (*c*) what missiologists variously refer to as *inculturation, contextualization, incarnation, evangelization of cultures,* and *the construction of local theologies.* The specific contribution expected of anthropology today is the clarification of the sociocultural context in which the gospel must be viewed.

LOUIS J. LUZBETAK, SVD

Bibliography

Arbuckle, G. A., *Earthing the Gospel* (1990). Chupungco, A., *Cultural Adaptation of Liturgy* (1982). Conn, H., *Eternal Word and Changing Worlds: Theology, Anthropology, and Mission in Trialogue* (1984). Engel, J. F., *Contemporary Christian Communications: Its Theory and Practice* (1979). Gittins, A. J., *Bread for the Journey: The Mission of Transformation and the Transformation of Mission* (1993). Idem, *Gifts and Strangers: Meeting the Challenge of Inculturation* (1989). Gusinde, M., *Die völkerkundliche Ausrüstung des Missionars* (1958). Hesselgrave, D. J., *Communicating Christ Cross-culturally: An Introduction to Missionary Communication* (1978). Hesselgrave, D. J., and E. Rommen, *Contextualization: Meanings, Methods and Models* (1989). Hiebert, P., *Anthropological Insights for Missionaries* (1985). Idem, *Anthropological Reflections* on *Missiological Issues* (1994). Holland, J., and P. Henriot, *Social Analysis: Linking Faith and Justice* (1983). Kirby, J. P., "The Anthropology of Knowledge and the Christian Dialogue with African Traditional Religions," *Missiol* 20/3 (July 1992) 323–41. Kirby, J. P., and S. van der Geest, "The Absence of the Missionary in African Ethnography," *AfStR* 35/3 (1992) 59–103. Kraft, C. H., *Christianity in Culture: Dynamic Biblical Theologizing in Cross-cultural Perspective* (1979). Idem, *Communication Theory for Christian Witness* (1983). Luzbetak, L. J., *The Church and Cultures* (1989). Idem, "Cross-cultural Missionary Preparation," *Trends and Issues* (1985) 61–79. Idem, "'Inculturation': A Call for Greater Precision," in K. Piskaty and H. Rzepkowski, eds., *Verbi Praecones: Festschrift für P. Karl Müller, SVD zum 75. Geburtstag* (1993) 43–50. Luzbetak, L. J., and D. L. Whiteman, "Selected Annotated Bibliography on Missiology: Missiological Anthropology," *Missiol* 21/2 (April 1993) 241–44. Mayers, M. K., *Christianity Confronts Culture: A Strategy for Cross-cultural Evangelism* (1974). Nida, E. A., *Customs and Cultures: Anthropology for Christian Missions* (1954). Idem, *Message and Mission: The Communication of the Christian Faith* (1960). Rahner, Karl, "Towards a Fundamental Theological Interpretation of Vatican II," *TS* (1979) 716–27. Salamone, F. A., ed., *Missionaries and Anthropologists,* pt. 2, Studies in Third World Societies 26 (1985). Schreiter, R. J., "Anthropology and Faith: Challenges to Missiology," *Missiol* 19/3 (July 1991) 283–94. Idem, *Constructing Local Theologies* (1985). Idem, "Faith and Cultures: Challenges to a World Church," *TS* 50/4 (December 1989) 744–60. Shorter, A., *Toward a Theology of Inculturation* (1988). Stott, J., and R. T. Coote, eds., *Gospel and Culture* (1979). Whiteman, D. L., ed., *Missionaries, Anthropologists and Cultural Change,* Studies in Third World Societies 25 (1985).

❧ APOCALYPTIC AND MISSION ❧

1. Definition. 2. Influence of Apocalyptic in Paul and the Synoptic Gospels. 3. The Authority of Apocalyptic and Innovation in Religion and Church History. 4. Apocalyptic and Innovation in Contemporary Christianity. 5. Apocalyptic as a Spur to the Mission of the Church and Change.

1. Apocalyptic is that religious outlook which roots perception of the divine purpose in the manifestation of divine knowledge through revelation by vision, hearing, or dream. This knowledge includes anything concerning human destiny and the nature of the divine purpose, whether of the past, present, or future, and could extend to knowledge of the divinity and the origin of the world. (This is particularly the case with the Jewish apocalyptic and mystical tradition.) Apocalyptic is represented particularly in apocalypses (literary works which purport to offer direct information of God's purposes) but also is evident as a form of religion where understanding of God and the world is rooted in the claim to a superior knowledge in which divine insight transcends the wisdom which human reason alone could offer.

2. Apocalyptic is linked with mission at the fundamental moment of the Christian understanding of the task of the church: Paul's mission to the Gentiles. In this Paul takes upon himself the role of agent of God's eschatological promise to allow Gentiles to share in Israel's ultimate salvation, not through the conventional process of conversion and circumcision as proselytes but through faith in the Messiah. The perception of the divine will, vouchsafed to the elect by means of revelation, undergirds Paul's understanding of his central role in salvation history as one directly commissioned by God as apostle to the Gentiles (Gal 1:12, 16). Galatians has implications for an understanding of mission in two areas: certainty about God's purposes, particularly the applicability of scripture to human experience, and the use of apocalyptic imagery as a vehicle of eschatological promise. In the New Testament, however, Paul's writings do not stand alone in their testimony to the significant part played by apocalyptic. In the Synoptic Gospels the baptism of Jesus (→Jesus) plays a key role in determining Jesus' understanding of his mission (see Mt 3:13–17; Mk 1:9–11; Lk 3:21–22). In addition, Peter's vision depicted in Acts 10:1–11:18 helped in the transition from a Jewish-based messianism to one more universal in scope. The basic New Testament understanding of the church's mission, therefore, is inextricably linked with apocalyptic rather simply sanctioned by those who could claim apostolic authority because of their close links with Jesus of Nazareth.

3. The church's mission is rooted in the conviction that the presence of the eschatological Spirit enables those in Christ to bear witness to the ultimate fulfillment of the divine purpose in the coming reign of God. Such an uncontroversial statement about the basis of the church's mission does, however, conceal the problem of how the specific working out of that mission is articulated in various times and places. The specific problem is the extent to which an initiative in mission can be taken without the *consensus fidelium*. On the whole, that may not be an insuperable problem when a development does not mark a large departure in doctrine or ethics. The problem does become acute, however, when, as is the case with Paul, the development marks a significant departure from current practice and attracts adverse reactions. This is particularly true when its authorization is claimed to come from divine revelation. A claim to be the recipient of an apocalypse may (as was often the case in the apocalyptic literature of →Judaism) lead to some uncertainty over the precise meaning of the contents of the revelation. What could not be questioned, except by outright denial, was the certitude of the recipient of that revelation that a direct communication had come from God. What is clearly the case with Paul (and various significant movements in the history of religion marked by apocalyptic revelation — most notably Islam) is that a very unstable situation is engendered when the claim to apocalyptic revelation has as its content an innovation in belief or practice. The abandonment of circumcision as an initiation rite by Paul is a case in point. Although Paul does attempt to justify it on scriptural grounds, the initial impetus is rooted in apocalyptic revelation. Similar instances may be cited in the history of the church where resort to that absolute certainty which apocalyptic and mysticism (viewed as the understanding of matters beyond normal human perception) offer can be used to justify unscrupulous and dehumanizing behavior in the pursuit of some higher goal. Whatever other merits might be found in the theology of T. Müntzer (d. 1525), such prophetic certainty enabled him to espouse a theology of holy war as a constitutive element in the mission of the elect (→prophecy). He considered that he had complete clarity of thought and perception to identify the children of light and the children of darkness. The results in the Peasants' Revolt of 1525 were catastrophic.

The history of Christianity is littered with the deviations of that idiosyncratic kind of behavior backed up by an appeal to apocalyptic. Mission, therefore, which is not rooted in the dialectic between consensus and charisma and marked by the recognition that the church lives "between the times" — between this age and the age to come — has always the capacity for distortion. Equally, the foundational documents of Christianity indicate that a community which refuses to allow the disturbing breeze of the apocalyptic spirit to open up new and unexpected areas of activity is in danger of becoming a petrified shell.

4. In contemporary Christianity the privileged status presupposed by apocalyptic revelation can be found in contrasting wings of Christian faith and practice. Evangelical Christianity is rooted in the conviction that God's ultimate revelation is to be found in scripture and that scripture demands that believers proclaim the gospel to all creatures. The gospel that is preached demands both a change of heart as well as an acceptance of a certain fixed pattern of belief. →Liberation theology, in contrast, does not explicitly use the language of apocalyptic directly to support its claim to privileged knowledge, yet running through its distinct perspective is the view that the perspective of the poor must be determinative of the mission of the church. It is with them that God is particularly present, and action done to and with them is activity directed toward God. In other respects also, liberation theology draws on the theological perspective of the apocalyptic tradition: reading the signs of the times (a feature of the papal encyclical *Populorum Progressio*), the critique of ideology, and prophetic theology. In examining the role of apocalyptic in determining mission we saw how often a sense of certainty undergirded courses of action. Some of that outlook is evident in liberation theology's conviction that the prophetic critique of social arrangements can be done via a mixture of Christian insight and socioeconomic analysis. Such an assessment, however sophisticated, is supported by the view that insight into the true nature of history and institutions is a present possibility. Accordingly, ambiguity is resisted and the possibility of real knowledge opened up, which in turn can lead to particular and often controversial forms of action. Thus, for example, in South Africa, the Kairos Document, on the one hand, attempted to read the signs of the times by offering a searching critique of state manipulation of religion and the promotion of politically painless trends in theology and, on the other hand, called for an outspoken prophetic theology which would criticize the status quo from the perspective of the oppressed and would engage in action for justice. For the Kairos theologians this was of the essence of the church's mission.

5. The apocalyptic literature of the Bible has proved to be a fertile ground for understandings of Christian mission. Thus, in contemporary religion committed to premillennialism, a particular sketch of biblical eschatology based on Daniel, Ezekiel, Revelation, and 1 Thessalonians offers a scenario which links the present activity of the church with the imminent expectation of the end of the world in a divinely ordained nuclear catastrophe. In view of that prospect the only safe course of action is to be born again and thereby guarantee an escape from the terrors of the end-time by means of the Rapture (1 Thes 4:17), when Christ mysteriously draws the elect to himself. In light of this, the most appropriate course of action is to engage in a mission which will draw as many as possible into that privileged circle. Such use of the apocalyptic passages is by no means a recent phenomenon, however. Although Augustine loosened the ties which bound the mission of the church to the this-worldly coming of the kingdom, there was a far-reaching challenge to that view by Joachim of Fiore, a Calabrian abbot and commentator on Revelation. His writings are significant for two reasons. First, his complex interpretation of the Book of Revelation resulted in a theology of history based on a form of dispensationalism. Second, and more importantly, he maintained a close link between the future age of perfection and human history and agency. Joachim saw the emergence of two monastic orders as fulfilling the apocalyptic prophecies. The Franciscans (the Dominicans were the other order) in particular attached great significance to Joachim's interpretation of apocalyptic tradition and identified their movement with that kind of decisive eschatological moment. The apocalyptic legacy had a long history in the Franciscan movement (where it undergirded the convictions of some more extreme elements) and contributed to an ongoing story of radical dissent in the Hussite and later movements of the Radical Reformation.

What is remarkable about the Joachite tradition is that it helped to provoke an attitude to eschatology in which human agency had a full part. This contrasts with a determinist apocalyptic theology which would render humanity powerless in the face of the cosmic forces. Yet even those movements which have used apocalyptic as a detailed timetable of the course of human history have never totally excluded the need for human activity in mission, if only to rescue the elect in the short space of time before the parousia. It might not be to engage with the structures of a world which is passing away, but it does involve enabling those who wish to respond to Christ.

The apocalyptic tradition in mission, therefore, can be seen partly as a result of an attitude which is an indispensable motivator of human activity in effecting change, whether in the religious or political sphere. The belief that absolute certainty is possible can have disastrous consequences when it leads to the anathematizing of persons or positions. What the apocalyptic tradition does guarantee, however, is that inactivity because of ambiguity cannot forever characterize the mission of the church. Questions may be raised about the wisdom of particular courses of action. Nevertheless, the profound sense of conviction which the apocalyptic tradition offers enables those who espouse it to engage in a fearless critique or dangerous activities, fortified by the knowledge that what they are engaged in is not merely the product of human whim but rooted in the ultimate purposes of God for humanity.

CHRISTOPHER ROWLAND

Bibliography

Becker, C., *Paul's Apocalyptic Gospel: The Coming Triumph of God* (1984). Bosch, D. J., *Transforming Mission* (1991) 131–54. Carriker, C. T., "Missiological Hermeneutic and Pauline Apocalyptic Eschatology," in C. van Engen, D. Gilliland, and P. Pierson, eds., *The Good News of the Kingdom* (1991) 45–55. "Challenge to the Churches" (the Kairos Document) (1985). Cohn, N., *The Pursuit of the Millennium* (1957). Collins, J. J., *The Apocalyptic Imagination: An Introduction to the Jewish Matrix of Christianity* (1984). Firth, K., *The Apocalyptic Tradition in Reformation Britain* (1975). Hellholm, D., ed., *Apocalypticism in the Mediterranean World and the Near East,* Proceedings of the International Colloquium on Apocalypticism (1979). Kinkel, G. S., *Our Dear Mother Spirit: An Investigation of Zinzendorf's Theology and Praxis* (1990). Lindsey, H., *The Late Great Planet Earth* (1972). McGinn, B., *Apocalypticism in the Western Tradition* (1994). Idem, *The Calabrian Abbot: Joachim of Fiore in the History of Western Thought* (1985). Reeves, M., *Joachim of Fiore and the Prophetic Future* (1976). Rowland, C., *The Open Heaven: A Study of Apocalyptic in Judaism and Early Christianity* (1982). Idem, *Radical Christianity: A Reading of Recovery* (1988). Schattschneider, D. A., "The Missionary Theologies of Zinzendorf and Spangenberg," in *Transactions of the Moravian Historical Society* 22:213–33. Scholem, G., *Major Trends in Jewish Mysticism* (1955). Scott, T., *Thomas Müntzer* (1989). Smith, J. Z., "Wisdom and Apocalyptic," in B. A. Pearson, ed., *Religious Syncretism in Antiquity: Essays in Conversation with G. Widengren* (1975) 131–56. Widengren, G., *The Ascent of the Apostle and the Heavenly Book* (1950). Williams, G., *The Radical Reformation* (1962). Wilson, B. R., *Magic and the Millennium: A Sociological Study of Religious Movements of Protest among Tribal and Third-World Peoples* (1973).

❧ ART ❧

1. Concept. 2. Interplay of Art and Early Christianity. 3. From "Christian" to "Sacred" Art. 4. Contemporary Perspectives.

1. In this entry art is broadly defined as that which is produced through the application of skill and taste, such as music, painting, literature, sculpture, and so on. As such, it is a basic human activity, some form of which is apparent throughout human history and in every known culture. A work of art can be classified in a variety of ways, for example, according to (a) the geographic area in which it appears (Japanese art); (b) the historical era in which it emerges (Renaissance art); (c) an identifiable style, movement or school whose principles it embodies (e.g., impressionism); (d) perceived levels of sophistication in the art (e.g., the fine arts); (e) the media of the artistic expression (e.g., the visual arts); (f) the theme or topic of the work (e.g., seascape painting); (g) the way it is used (e.g., liturgical art); or (h) the group of people, not necessarily living in the same geographic area, who employ an identifiable art or art form (e.g., Islamic architecture). Such classifications are not mutually exclusive and sometimes are most effective when employed in combinations, for example, early twentieth-century French impressionism or medieval Jewish folk music.

This ambiguity regarding the classification of art underscores the difficulty with the term "Christian art," which could refer to art produced by Christians, art employed by Christians, art dealing with Christian themes, and so on. All of these can be legitimate uses of the term.

2. Throughout the history of Christianity, believers have employed the arts, broadly speaking, in the proclamation of the gospel and the establishment of the church. Originally this meant borrowing art forms already in existence, such as Jewish or Greek musical forms (see the allusion in Eph 5:19) or Jewish poetry (the probable origin of the Magnificat [Lk 1:46–55]). Sometimes these forms were borrowed without change; other times borrowed forms were applied to specifically Christian themes or subjects. Thus frescoes of the Christian catacombs are in Late Antique (Greco-Roman) style but treat subjects such as the Good Shepherd. Although this process of borrowing artistic forms from "non-Christian" sources continued throughout the history of Christianity, it is virtually the only basis for speaking of pre-Constantinian Christian art. One of the few exceptions is the literary form known as the Gospel, which appears to be an original contribution of the emerging Christian community.

After the alliance between Christianity and the empire under Constantine (d. 337), the relationship between art and Christianity shifted. As the Greco-Roman Empire wed itself to Christianity, and then became eclipsed by Christianity, so were the art forms of the empire enveloped and transformed by Christianity. The imperial audience hall (one type of basilica) was adapted to worship and transformed in the process (e.g., old St. Peter's in Rome). Classical rhetoric was borrowed and transformed in the growing number of fixed liturgical texts (e.g., the Roman canon). Greek metrical poetry provided the inspiration and then gave way to Christian hymnody, properly speaking.

Emerging Christian art — now defined not simply as art employed by Christians but as art produced by Christians — was hybridal, that is, a composite of "non-Christian" styles, forms, or techniques adapted to Christian themes and usage and transformed in the process. However, with the rise of Christianity in European and Middle Eastern civilizations, and its alliance with the dominant culture — including the acceptance of the Neoplatonic linkage between the beautiful and the good — artistic perceptions within Christianity changed. As Christianity grew in social and political influence in the Middle Ages, the beautiful or artistically acceptable was increasingly defined in terms of the philosophical tenets, artistic canons, and taste of the dominant culture and not, as previously, according to what may simply have served the proclamation of the gospel. Thus the pagan (or better, indigenous) roots of many Christian art forms were downplayed or forgotten. Furthermore, art forms sanctioned by Christian society increasingly were more acceptable than indigenous art forms of those groups or societies evangelized by the church.

3. The emergence of "sacred art" as art thought to embody and properly reflect the principles of Christianity is detectable in the instructions and legislation outlining which art forms are and are not acceptable for Christians. Already in the third century, and more in the fourth century, writers like Novatian (d. ca. 258) considered dance and musical instruments "pagan" and unacceptable to Christians (*De spectaculis* 3.2–3). Augustine of Hippo (d. 430) knew the tension between the arts and worship and the danger of being moved more by the singing than by what is sung (*Confessiones* 10.33). This tension is part of the reason why certain types of music or other art forms eventually were considered more acceptable than others. Thus, as part of the mission to the English church, the musical usage of Rome was imported (Bede, *Historia* 2.20) if not imposed (4.18) — a tradition which Bede (d. 735) refers to as "sacred music" (4.2), apparently in distinction from the musical traditions of the English people, which Bede considers "religious" or "devotional" music (4.24). At least for one part of the English mission, receiving the Catholic faith was also linked to a request for architects so that a church could be built "in the Roman style" (5.21).

The same phenomena marked the reform of the Gallican church under Charlemagne (d. 814) and his successors. Here Roman books, Roman usage, and even Roman chant were imposed upon churches in the realm (*Admonitio Generalis* 79). While Roman forms actually intermingled with Gallican forms in architecture, music, and rite so that new hybrids of music, architecture, and worship evolved, these were not considered hybrids at the time but "Roman." This was consonant with a growing trend in the medieval West to idealize the Roman way in all things ecclesiastical, so that to be Christian often meant conforming to Roman usage, including the perceived artistic tastes of the Roman church. There were multiple non-Roman artistic influences afoot in the late medieval church (e.g., Burgundian musical forms, Parisian architecture, and Florentine painting). Despite such artistic richness and diversity, one important axiom in Christian missionary efforts was the primacy of the art forms of the official church. A celebrated example was the music of Palestrina (d. 1594), which seemed to fulfill certain requirements of the Council of Trent: that is, the texts were relatively clear and the music avoided techniques considered "impure."

In the West this primacy of sanctioned ecclesiastical art forms, first linked with the churches in union with Rome, included the other Christian churches after the sixteenth-century Reformation — all of which were intimately linked to European culture and tastes. Thus missionary efforts down to our own day were often marked by the tendency to import traditional, European art forms and less inclined to employ indigenous art forms in the proclamation of the gospel. M. Ricci (d. 1610), a Jesuit missionary to China, exemplifies the exception to this trend. Although an enthusiastic admirer of the Italian Renaissance, he campaigned for the Sinicizing of Christian objects so that the Chinese could better grasp the Christian message.

Despite the vision of people like Ricci, the Christian churches of the West contributed to and supported an intrinsic link between artistic forms which were produced according to the artistic canons of the dominant culture and the proclamation of the gospel. Unfortunately, however, this relationship was not always cast in cultural or aesthetic terms. Under the influence of Neoplatonism, which recognized a link between the beautiful and the good, Christianity asserted a relationship between the beautiful and the holy. Consequently, what on face value were issues of form, style, and taste, Christianity often translated in terms of morality and sacrality.

An explicit affirmation of this perspective is found in the work of the Roman philosopher Boethius (d. 524), who became the most influential authority on music in the Christian West during the Middle Ages. Heavily influenced by the writing of Pythagoras and Plato, Boethius taught that "music is related not only to speculation but to morality as well" (*De institutione musica libri quinque,* introduction). Through the work of Boethius, and to a lesser extent the monk Cassiodorus (d. 583), the belief that music embodied the essence of virtue or vice was perpetuated in the church. One effect of this perspective was a tendency to legislate music, and to a lesser extent the other arts, as though in themselves they could be virtuous or immoral. For John XXII (d. 1334), this meant banning certain dissonant intervals which were thought to be capable of weakening the soul. More recently, Pius X (d. 1914) required that music must be holy and "exclude all profanity not only in itself but also in the manner in which it is presented" (*Tra le sollecitudini* 2). It is in this context that music and the other arts considered appropriate for the proclamation of the gospel, especially through the liturgy, were considered not simply Christian but "sacred" arts.

4. Over the past century there have been profound changes in the thinking about art, especially in the West, and these changes have challenged the traditional wisdom about the link between the artistic canons of the dominant culture and the proclamation of the gospel. This shift has occurred, in large part, because of conversations about art in non-Christian contexts, across a wide spectrum of artistic and nonartistic disciplines. For example, developments in archaeology, art history, and musicology have provided a richer historical frame for understanding the indigenous influences upon those various works considered Christian art throughout the centuries. Social sciences such as anthropology and ethnology have rendered baseless the a priori claims of superiority by one culture over another. Out of the historical fields, social sciences, and traditional artistic disciplines have emerged new areas of specialization such as ethnoart and ethnomusicology, which study the relationship between art and society, especially in nondominant cultures. It is under the scrutiny of such disciplines that traditional concepts of beauty and sacrality — and the belief that certain styles or forms are inherently better for the proclamation of the gospel — disintegrate.

Sacrosanctum Concilium (SC) reflects this shift when it notes: "The church has not adopted any particular style of art as her very own; she has admitted styles from every period according to the natural talents and circumstances of peoples, and the needs of the various rites" (123). Despite this apparent disavowal of Neoplatonic principles as the framework for judging art, and a move to what might be considered an emic basis for evaluating art — at least for Roman Catholics — problems remain. Chief among these is the intimate relationship between certain dogmatic tenets or ecclesiological perspectives and the arts which have given them voice. For example, while most Christians live in the Southern Hemisphere, the traditional art forms of the Northern Hemisphere — like the representatives of the cultures who produced them — continue to hold a place of priority in the Christian churches. Furthermore, certain Western artistic forms (e.g., the chorale for Lutherans, the basilica for Roman Catholics, Wesleyan hymn-texts for Methodists) are so deeply rooted in the self-identity of the churches that the various cultural manifestations of these traditions often seem incapable of abandoning or even radically altering such forms. An authentic emic approach to the arts in Christianity is a challenge not only to artistic taste but also to deep-seated ecclesiastical perspectives and doctrinal formulations. Principles for resolving this tension are yet to be articulated adequately.

EDWARD FOLEY, OFM CAP

Bibliography

Althaus, P., "Die Illustration der Bibel als theologisches Problem," *NZSTh* 1 (1959) 314–26. Aufhause, J. B., "Christliche einheimische Kunst in nichtchristlichen Ländern," *ChK* 25 (1925) 161–74. Idem, "Eingeborene christliche Kunst in nichtchristlichen Ländern," *ChK* 31 (1935). Beckmann, J., "Die Stellung der katholischen Mission zur bildenden Kunst der Eingeborenen," *Acta Tropica* 2 (1945) 211–32. Beckwith, J., *Early Christian and Byzantine Art,* 2d ed. (1979). Berg, L., *Die katholische Heidenmission als Kulturträger* (1927) 104–204. Bernhard, H., "L'art chrétien en Chine du temps du P. Matthieu Ricci," *RHMiss* 12 (1935). Bodo, J. R., "The Artist in the Local Church," *ThTo* 34 (1977) 40–44. Bornemann, F., *Ars Sacra Pekinensis: Die chinesische-christliche Malerei an der Katholischen Universität (Fu-Jen) in Peking* (1959). Bouveignes, O. de, "L'art indigène baptisé," *EglViv* 2 (1950) 28–38. Butler, J. F., "The New Factors in Christian Art outside the West: Developments since 1950," *JES* 10 (1973–74) 94–120. *Catalogue (illustr.) of the Vatican Exhibition of Missionary Art* (1950). Constantini, C., *L'Art chrétien dans les missions* (1949). Idem, "Arte cristiana negra," *ARc* 26 (1938) 1–32. Idem, *L'arte cristiana nelle missioni: Manuale d'arte per i missionari* (1940). Idem, "L'arte sacra nei paesi di missione," in *Problemi missionari del nostro tempo: Conferenze tenute all'Università Cattolica del Sacro Cuore dal 25 Novembre al 6 Dicembre 1933* (1934) 99–128. Idem, *L'istruzione del S. Uffizio sull'arte sacra* (1952). Idem, "Missionary Art," *LiArts* 4/1 (1935) 11–31. Idem, "Il problema dell'arte missionaria," *ARc* 22 (1934) 33–62. Corbin, S., *L'église à la conquête de sa musique* (1960). Decker, R. B. de, "L'adaptation de l'art religieux en Afrique," in *Mission et cultures non-chrétiennes, XXIXe semaine de missiologie* (1959) 272–89. Deichgräber, R., *Gotteshymnus und Christushymnus in der frühen Christenheit* (1967). Dussel, E., "Christian Art of the Oppressed in Latin America (Towards an Aesthetics of Liberation)," in *Symbol and Art in Worship,* vol. 132 of *Concilium* (1980) 40–52. *Exposição de arte sacra missionária: Edição commemorativa* (1952). Fleming, D. J., *Each with His Own Brush: Contemporary Christian Art in Asia and Africa* (1938). Foley, E., *Foundations of Christian Music: The Music of Pre-Constantinian Christianity* (1992). Hadjinicolau, N., *Histoire de l'art et lutte des classes* (1973). Havelock, E., *Preface to Plato* (1963). Kain, T., *The Dancing Church* (1992). Kowalsky, N., "Actualidad del arte cristiano en los paises de misión y posibilidades que ofrece para el porvenir," in *La Adaptación Misionera X. und XI. Mission Study Weeks at Burgos 1957 and 1958.* Krautheimer, R., *Early Christian and Byzantine Architecture,* 4th, rev. ed. (1986). Laufer, B., "L'art chrétien dans les pays de missions," *MF* 28 (1950) 67–94. Idem, "Christian Art in China," *MSOS* 13 (1910). Idem, "Le douloureux problème des arts missionaries," *CArtS* 7/8 (1951). Lehmann, A., *Afroasiatische christliche Kunst* (1967). Idem, *Die Kunst der jungen Kirchen* (1955). Mariani, G., *La legislazione ecclesiastica in materia d'arte sacra* (1945). McKinnon, J., *Church Fathers and Musical Instruments* (1965). Perbal, A., "Enquête 1938 sur l'art sacré indigène," *AfER* 12 (1938) 139–51. Quasten, J., *Music and Worship in Pagan and Christian Antiquity* (1983). Romita, F., *Ius musicae liturgicae: Dissertatio historico-iuridica* (1947). Schlunk, M., "Mission und Kunst," *NAMZ* 7 (1930) 26–32; 40–51. Schüller, S., "Christliche Eingeborenenkunst in nichtchristlichen Ländern," *ChK* 32 (1935–36) 193–215. Idem, *Christliche Kunst aus fernen Ländern: Christliche Kunst aus Afrika, Südamerika, Indien, Java, Indochina, China und Japan* (1939). Silver, D., "Ethnoart," *Annual Review of Anthropology* 8 (1979) 267–307. Sundermeier, T., *Südafrikanische Passion: Linolschnitte von Azariah Mbatha* (1977). Swiderski, S., *Art et louange: Les symbols de l'art sacré populaire dans l'adaptation chrétienne* (1982). Ten Berge, J., "La nécessité d'art chrétien indigène en pays de mission," in *Compt rendu de la quatrième semaine de missiologie de Louvaine* (1926) 213–31. Thiel, J. F., ed., *Christliches Afrika:*

Kunst und Kunsthandwerk in Schwarzafrika, 2d ed. (1980). Idem, "Entstehungsprobleme einer christlichen Kunst in Afrika," *KuKi* 4 (1981) 202–5. Thiel, J. F., and H. Helf, *Christliche Kunst in Afrika* (1984). Toscana, G., "Arte cristiana nei paesi di missione," *Fede e Civiltà* (1960) 411–36. Walls, A., "The Western Discovery of Non-Western Christian Art," in *The Missionary Movement in Christian History* (1996) 173–86.

B

❧ BAPTISM ❧

1. The Meaning of Baptism. 2. Biblical Foundations. 3. Baptism and the Spirit. 4. Catechumenal Ministry. 5. Infant Baptism. 6. Ecumenism, Evangelization, and Culture.

Baptism is the Christian symbolic action involving a pouring or immersion in water and the invocation of the Trinity that makes an individual a member of the church. Since the reforms of Vatican II, baptism, confirmation, and Eucharist once again constitute the three "sacraments of initiation" in the Roman Catholic Church: rites that celebrate conversion to Christ and full incorporation into God's people (*General Introduction to Christian Initiation* 2). For this reason, from the perspective of many of the liturgical churches (Roman Catholic, Lutheran, Anglican), it is impossible to deal adequately with baptism without speaking of the complement of rites that leads to the Eucharist and that celebrates initiation (→initiation in diverse contexts) into the Body of Christ. *Baptism, Eucharist, and Ministry (BEM)*, the so-called Lima Document of the World Council of Churches (1982), also emphasizes this initiatory character of baptism as "the sign of new life in Jesus Christ. It unites the one baptized with Christ and with his people" (*BEM* 2).

1. The meaning of baptism is complex. It includes God's call to share divine life, the personal conversion of the candidate for baptism, union with Christ, the beginning of a new life lived in Christ, reception of the Spirit, and admittance to the community of the church. Theological reflection and adequate pastoral practice must keep in mind the interrelation of all these meanings. God calls us in and through Christ, and we respond in faith. The grace-filled moment when this call-response is ritualized takes place at baptism.

It must be emphasized, however, that this call is freely made by God — no one "deserves" to be baptized since baptism is at core the celebration of God's gift of faith. Baptism is the church's announcement of the movement of God in Christ in the particular context of a person's life — a movement that cannot be earned but is experienced as gift. It is God who calls and we who respond with faith — for this reason baptism has been called the "sacrament of faith" par excellence. Appropriately from the beginning of the church, a renunciation of evil and a proclamation of faith in Christ have been intrinsic parts of the baptismal rite and are, in fact, the origin of formulas such as the Apostles' Creed.

Because of the church's outreach in mission lands and the need for a renewed evangelization of countries heretofore regarded as Christian, the way by which an adult is prepared for baptism has become an increasingly important object of study during the past fifty years. Historical research, theological reflection, and insights from the social sciences, such as anthropology, sociology, and psychology, influenced the churches' new approaches to the ministry of initiation. Much of the impetus for this reexamination came from mission lands where initiation into the church using the traditional convert-class model was becoming increasingly less satisfying and more problematic.

Thus, many of the churches — especially those with a high sacramental tradition — have reevaluated the importance of the personal and social context for the effective celebration of a sacrament. The sacraments celebrate faith; they do not create it (*SC* 59). A responsible pastoral approach to baptism will always take into account the gradual nature of this conversion of adults rather than simply focus on the correct performance of the rite. For this reason, several churches have recovered early Christianity's catechumenal approach to initiation in order to respect the various stages or moments of a person's journey of conversion to God in Christ in the midst of the church. A review of the origins and development of baptism in the scriptures and in the church's early history will help situate the renewed catechumenate and the normative nature of the Adult Rite of Christian Initiation.

2. The fact that John the Baptist used water as a sign of repentance and conversion to God should not be surprising — the ritual manipulation of water was a sign used throughout the ancient world for cleansing and purification. Ritual ablutions, lustrations, and baths are to be found in many religions bordering the biblical world. The use of water was especially important in many of the Hellenistic mystery religions, such as those devoted to Isis and Mithras, both of which used a form of baptism. These actions often signified purification, but also death and rebirth. The books of the Old Testament also recognize the life-giving power of water (see Is 41:17–20; Ez 47:1–2). The destructive power of water finds its primary reference in the primordial flood which washed the world free of human sin. But the theological *locus classicus* in the Bible for the image of water that deals both life and death, and also manifests God's power and desire to liberate God's people from slavery, is the water of the Red Sea depicted in Exodus 14.

The baptismal symbolism of the New Testament, therefore, grows out of a rich Old Testament tradition which cannot, of course, be separated entirely from the ritual practices of the surrounding religions of the Mediterranean Basin — although modern scholarship has discounted the direct development of Christian baptism from either the mystery religions or Jewish proselyte baptism. Rather, Christian baptism is in continuity with the baptism of repentance for the forgiveness of sins (Mk 1:4) practiced by John the Baptist. The New Testament also explores the rich symbolism of water in the Old Testament by using these various images which shed light on baptism. Purification, sanctification, giving life, dealing death — the water used during the celebration of baptism evokes all of those images in the writings of the New Testament.

The Greek word *baptein* originally signified "to sink," "to drown." Paul is familiar with the same symbolism, now applied to the manner in which we participate in the death and resurrection of Jesus: the paschal mystery. This is the primary optic through which he views baptism in Rom 6:1–11, which is not a treatise on the sacrament of baptism so much as an exposition of why Christians are empowered to live a new ethical life in Christ. Paul's understanding of baptism as being crucified with Christ by dying to sin and death in the waters of baptism and sharing in Christ's resurrection is one of the most important sacramental metaphors used by the church.

Baptism is also seen as rebirth. The most obvious example of this is advanced in Jn 3:1–7, in the dialogue between Jesus and Nicodemus in which Jesus assures the learned Pharisee that no one can see the reign of God without being born from above (or "again" — the adverb *anothen* has both meanings). This image is reinforced by the other Johannine writing of the New Testament as well as by the image of baptism as the "water (or bath) of rebirth" (*loutron paliggenesia*) found in Ti 3:5.

Both of these images — those of dying and rising with Christ and being born again — are reflected in the later patristic description of the baptismal font as *taphos kai meter* (both "tomb and mother"). After the initial period when baptism was administered out-of-doors in running streams or lakes (see Acts 8:38; *Didache* 8), and once the Christian community started building formal places of worship, baptisteries were constructed that evoked both death and rebirth. The usage of the early period is reflected in the cross-like shape of some early baptismal fonts or their design in the form of hexagons illustrating the passion (since Christ died on the sixth day of the week) or octagons (representing rebirth and re-creation, since the resurrection took place on the "eighth day," the day of cosmic re-creation in Christ — the day out of time itself).

3. The New Testament does not consistently present the action of the Holy Spirit in relationship to baptism. In some of the descriptions in the Acts of the Apostles, the reception of the Spirit and the water bath are closely related, such as in 1:5 and 11:16. Chapter 8 of Acts, however, distinguishes Philip's baptism of the Samaritans done in the name of the Lord Jesus (v. 16) from the reception of the Holy Spirit when Peter and John lay hands on them later. This incident is often used as the biblical warrant for the conferral of a separate sacrament of the giving of the Spirit as somehow "completing" what was accomplished at baptism. We also see, however, the reception of the Spirit before the water bath. Such is the case with Cornelius in Acts 10:47. Considering that there is very little evidence to suggest that the church practiced a rite of the giving of the Spirit completely separated from baptism during the first several centuries, an appeal to the Samaritans' "confirmation" appears as a rather questionable warrant for current pastoral practice.

Due to confirmation's rather "checkered" past, its link with baptism has been variously observed or downplayed. What can be stated with some certainty is that the Spirit is active in baptism, and some of the churches believe that there is no need for a sacramental pneumatic "completion of baptism." Some of the churches issuing from the Reform, while questioning the sacramentality of confirmation, have maintained a repeatable celebration of affirmation of baptismal faith for those baptized as infants. The Eastern churches — both the Orthodox and those in union with Rome — have maintained the ancient practice of conferring all of the sacraments of initiation (baptism, chrismation, and Eucharist) at the same celebration regardless of the age of the candidate. It is significant that the new Roman Catholic discipline governing adult initiation is that confirmation be celebrated immediately after baptism, unless there are serious reasons to prevent its conferral.

4. As the church moved into the Greco-Roman world it was confronted with not only indifference but outright hostility and persecution. In order to prepare those who had to face suffering for the name of Christ, the catechumenate was developed in the first several centuries of the Common Era in order to prepare the new Christians adequately for the rigors of the controversial life they had chosen. Documents for the subapostolic period, such as a catechetical instruction like the

Didache (ca. 110) or poetic material such as the *Odes of Solomon* (ca. 120), speak to Christian formation before baptism and to the meaning of baptism itself.

It was in light of the need for formation in, rather than simple information about, the faith that the catechumenate developed in the various parts of the Roman Empire both before and after the legalization of Christianity in 313 C.E. The *Apostolic Tradition* (ca. 215), attributed to Hippolytus (d. ca. 235), is the most comprehensive witness to the early church's approach to the catechumenate. According to this invaluable source, the catechumenate was not a time to attend "convert classes" but a period of holistic preparation of candidates for baptism. For a number of years, the catechumens "heard God's word," learned to pray, and practiced works of charity. In short, they learned how to lead a Christian life.

The ancient catechumenate thus became a model for modern church practice. *Ad Gentes* (*AG*) of Vatican II sums up the catechumenal process well in its article calling for its reinstitution: "Those who have received from God the gift of faith in Christ, through the Church, should be admitted with liturgical rites to the catechumenate which is not a mere exposition of dogmatic truths and norms of morality, but a period of formation in the whole Christian life, an apprenticeship of sufficient duration, during which the disciples will be joined to Christ their teacher" (*AG* 14).

5. While the norm for baptism — that is, the way in which the meaning of the sacrament is most fully and eloquently expressed — is the baptism of adults, in much of the world, and in the majority of the churches, infant baptism is still the usual practice. Although questioned by churches from the Radical Reformation (Mennonites, Amish, Baptists) because of the impossibility of the infant confessing a personal faith, this practice has known a very long history. Although it is impossible to prove whether or not the church of the New Testament baptized infants, second-century evidence attests to this practice. But infant baptism, at least in the West, is very much influenced by Augustine's appeal to the practice in his argument against the Pelagians and in support of the developing doctrine of original sin.

The modern rationale for continuing infant baptism is based on the serious consideration given the context in which the child is raised: the family, the wider church, and the culture. It is in the faith of the church that the child is baptized, and according to Roman Catholic canon law (§868), the minister who is reasonably sure the child will be raised in the faith is to baptize. For this reason, in the Rite of Baptism for Children, both parents and godparents profess that faith in order for the baptism to proceed. This also accentuates the need to be pastorally sensitive and supportive of the traditions of *compadrazco* (godparentage) in many traditionally Christian cultures.

6. The celebration of baptism is not a monopoly of any one ecclesial communion. Since the controversy between Cyprian of Carthage (d. 258) and Pope Stephen I (d. 257) in the third century, the validity of baptism administered by those not in communion with the great church has not been seriously challenged. It is significant that the irrepeatable character of this sacrament — the conviction that there is indeed one baptism for the forgiveness of sins and that baptism celebrates the believer's participation in the paschal mystery of Jesus Christ — has led to a remarkable amount of ecumenical convergence. Of all of the sections of *Baptism,*

Eucharist, and Ministry (*BEM*), the part treating baptism has received the widest support among the churches.

Baptism also establishes a new relationship between the believer and the surrounding non-Christian world in apparently contradictory ways. On the one hand, it separates the baptized from the world in which they live and brings them into conflict with it. →Jesus himself foresaw the opposition between his disciples and the world. The discussion of the catechumenate in *AG* 13 points to the transformation in "outlooks and morals" that is to take place; *Baptism, Eucharist, and Ministry* speaks of "a new ethical orientation under the guidance of the Holy Spirit" that is part of the experichen of baptism (*BEM* 4). Each Christian suffers from the opposition which Jesus' message provokes. On the other hand, the baptized are bound anew to their surroundings due to the bonds of cultural and social solidarity and responsibility. Christians live in a new community among their fellow human beings with esteem and love (see *AG* 12). Baptism in fact signifies insertion into the reign of God, which begins to manifest itself in the renewal of the earthly human society (*AG* 11, 12; *BEM* 7, 10).

The meaning of baptism was sometimes compromised due to an uncritical understanding of the church's relationship to the world. In the Middle Ages, Christianity identified itself with European culture — especially western European culture. As a result of this myopic perspective, it seemed natural to demand that non-Western converts adopt European names and customs in order to be baptized. Baptism was thus largely perceived as a denial of the indigenous culture and as a betrayal of one's ancestors. For this reason, the *General Introduction to Christian Initiation* of the Roman liturgical books, in keeping with the spirit of *Sacrosanctum Concilium* (37–40), encourages local adaptation and inculturation of the various rites of the catechumenate so that they may speak more eloquently the message of Christ to people of diverse cultures. Bishops' conferences are called upon "to carefully and prudently weigh what elements of a people's distinctive traditions and culture may suitably be admitted into divine worship" (*SC* 30.2); they are also called upon to judge "whether the elements of initiation in use among some peoples can be adapted for the rite of Christian baptism and [to decide] which elements are to be incorporated into the rite" (*SC* 32).

Initial attempts at inculturation have begun around the world. But inculturation without grounding in the renewed understanding of baptism will ultimately be superficial and ineffective. For our ministry of initiation to be effective, baptism must again be understood as a deeper insertion into and commitment to human society with the duty of proclaiming, living, and making the reign of God a reality in our society and among all people.

MARK R. FRANCIS, CSV

Bibliography

This article is based on J. Neuner, "Taufe," in K. Müller and T. Sundermeier, eds., *Lexikon Missionstheologischer Grundbegriffe* (1987) 456–61. Beasley-Murray, G. R., *Baptism in the New Testament* (1962). Covino, P., "The Postconciliar Infant Baptism Debate in the American Catholic Church," *Worship* 56 (1982) 240–59. Kavanagh, A., *The Shape of Baptism: The Rite of Christian Initiation* (1978). Kriegisch, R., "Christian Initiation and Inculturation," *AfER* 30 (1988) 29–39. Lohfink, G., "Der Ursprung der christlichen Taufe," *ThQ* 156 (1976) 35–54. Lorenzen, T., "Baptism and Church Membership: Some Baptist Positions and the Ecumenical Implications," *JES* 18 (1981) 561–74. Mitchell, L., *Initiation and the Churches* (1991). Morris, T., *The RCIA: Transforming the Church: A Resource for Pastoral Implementation* (1989). Murphy Center for Liturgical Research, University of Notre Dame, *Made Not Born: New Perspectives on Christian Initiation and the Catechumenate* (1976). Office of Evangelism Ministries, the Episcopal Church Center, *The Catechumenal Process: Adult Initiation and Formation for Christian Life and Ministry* (1990). Scheer, A., "The Influence of Culture on the Liturgy as Shown in the History of the Christian Initiation Rite," *Concilium* 122 (1979) 14–25. Searle, M., "Infant Baptism Reconsidered," in *Alternative Futures for Worship,* vol. 2, *Baptism and Confirmation* (1987) 15–54. Stevick, D. B., *Baptismal Moments, Baptismal Meanings* (1987). Turner, P., *Confirmation: The Baby in Solomon's Court* (1993). Vorgrimler, H., *Sacramental Theology* (1992) 102–21. Wagner, G., "Baptism from Accra to Lima," in Max Thurian, ed., *Ecumenical Perspectives on Baptism, Eucharist, and Ministry,* Faith and Order Paper 116 (1983) 12–32. World Council of Churches, *Baptism, Eucharist, and Ministry* (the Lima Document), Faith and Order Paper 111 (1982). Yarnold, E., "Baptism, Theology of," in P. Fink, ed., *The New Dictionary of Sacramental Worship* (1990) 115–22.

✌ BIBLE ✌

1. Fundamental Assumptions.   2. The Biblical Foundations for Mission. 3. Contextual Interpretation of the Bible.

1.   The word of God is the source and norm of Christian faith and action. This general Christian principle is also valid for the theology and practice of mission (→theology of mission). While recognizing that the Bible and the word of God are connected, there are significantly different ways of understanding this relationship in modern theology. The spectrum stretches from the acceptance of a virtual identification between the two to the view that there is a wide chasm between the word of God and the Bible, a chasm that can be bridged only by a particular interpretive process. Some exegetes avoid this theological issue as insoluble or even irrelevant and tend to concentrate on historical or literary aspects of the Bible rather than its relevance for faith and action. Another issue is whether nonbiblical sacred texts can mediate the word of God, as is affirmed, for example, by certain Indian theologians concerning the Upanishads (→theology of religions). Any particular theological perspective on all of this is influenced by one's understanding of the nature and modes of revelation and of how the scriptures relate to tradition and the life of the church.

In any event, an authentic Christian theology of mission should take its inspiration and validation from the word of God expressed in the scriptures.

2.   Most recent attempts to articulate a theology of mission begin with a biblical basis. In addition to one's understanding of the normative role of scripture there is also the issue of what one understands by mission. If mission is understood predominantly as conversion to the gospel and proselytizing, then this can dictate one's appeal to the Bible for support for this approach. If one has a more dialogical approach and values sensitivity to the cultural and religious heritage of non-Christian peoples, one will emphasize the role of "witness," and other aspects of the Bible will be appealed to. In some instances, particularly but not exclusively in evangelical circles, the Bible is considered as dogmatic proof for the necessity of mission as proclamation and conversion. In this perspective, mission is based on the biblically revealed creation of the world by God, by the divine choice of an elect people, and, ultimately, by the fact that the unique mode of redemption for all peoples is through Jesus Christ. The eschatological perspective of some New Testament traditions, such as Romans 9–11, links the church's mission to the expected end of the world. Proclamation of the gospel to all peoples therefore becomes an urgent Christian responsibility. The "Great Commission" of Mt 28:18f. is, understandably, a prominent text in this type of deductive approach. Other specific texts can be appealed to as support for one or other mission issue: for example, 1 Tm 2:4 is valued not only as a justification for mission but, in the view of some, as an opening for other ways of salvation. Pauline texts such as Rom 10:14–15 and 15:1–21 have also served as the starting points for biblical theologies of mission or as biblically warranted strategies for mission work such as Paul's itinerant missionary style (see, e.g., the work of R. Allen).

More recent attempts to build a biblical theology of mission have taken a dialectical approach, finding major motifs or dynamics of the Bible as both inspiration and illumination of the church's mission responsibility but recognizing the need to take into account contemporary experience as also instructive for what form mission is to take. Salvation history has been used as such an overarching biblical theme, for example, in the reflections of the World Council of Churches. The drama of salvation between God and Israel is seen as preparatory for the universal scope of the gospel and its concomitant mission in the New Testament. In many circles, however, this type of motif has fallen into disfavor because it tends to make the Hebrew scriptures too ancillary to the New Testament and risks forcing the biblical materials into an arbitrary format. Similar overarching themes might be the notion of "call" or the motif of liberation. The latter has found particular resonance in Christian communities who suffer oppression. The Old Testament paradigm of exodus and the liberating dimensions of Jesus' ministry of the reign of God are considered essential elements of the Christian sense of mission that entails confronting oppressive structures and bringing the gospel's redemptive power to those in need. While all of these are fundamental biblical currents and certainly contribute to a theology of mission, it is not certain that any single motif can stand as the definitive biblical foundation for the church's mission.

More recent works have emphasized the diversity of the biblical witness as the foundation for a pluralistic approach to mission. This coincides with a strong emphasis in contemporary biblical hermeneutics which stresses that the Bible is capable of multiple valid readings. D. Senior and C. Stuhlmueller, for example, trace the various interactions of Israel with its wider environment through the Old Testament traditions and the analogous struggle of the early church with the Gentile issue reflected in the New Testament as illustrative of the onward movement of the Bible and the ultimate source of mission theology. Both Israel and the early church developed their self-identity as a religious community in relation to a multicultural context. The various approaches taken in different biblical traditions help ground a pluralistic theology of mission in dialogue with contemporary experience. L. Legrand, too, searches for fundamental dynamics within the biblical drama as a framework for contemporary mission theology. He notes a "bipolar" dynamic in the Old Testament, encompassing, on the one hand, a theology of election whereby Israel realized its identity as a people before God and, on the other, a theology of witness that attempted to understand Israel's relationship to the nations. The same dynamic, although in a different key, can be found in the New Testament. The early church, inspired by the mission of Jesus, also attempted to understand itself as a community of God's people, but at the same time it was also caught up in a vigorous outreach beyond the church to the Jewish community and the Gentiles. Legrand emphasizes the necessity of a dialectic between these fundamental biblical movements and contemporary experience.

Attempts to approach the entire biblical witness from the vantage point of mission have been relatively rare in modern biblical studies. Some authors have concentrated on key biblical texts or specific dimensions of the biblical perspective. D. J. Bosch, for example, views primitive Christianity as the first instance of a missionary "paradigm" that takes different forms in the history of Christianity. The Old Testament prepares for this paradigm, but a true sense of mission develops only in Jesus' own ministry and the early church. Bosch studies dynamics of Jesus' mission within Israel (with its apocalyptic emphasis on the coming rule of God), his outreach to sinners and the marginalized, and his empowerment of the disciples as key elements of what will become the early Christian notion of mission. The theologies of Matthew, Luke-Acts, and Paul illustrate that a sense of mission was constitutive of early Christian consciousness. B. F. Meyer asks why a sense of world mission becomes an essential part of the self-identity of a community whose origins are Jewish. He emphasizes not only the centrifugal movement of Jesus' ministry but the important dynamic of culture. A key influence in the development of early Christian self-identity was the Greek-speaking, Hellenistic, Jewish-Christian community that, in effect, mediated the gospel between its Palestinian origins and that community's sense of mission to the Greco-Roman Gentile world.

In many of these studies the concern is not simply to articulate a biblical basis for mission but to develop a "spirituality" of mission that has biblical roots.

3. The multicultural nature of the worldwide Christian community coincides with another emphasis of contemporary biblical interpretation, namely, that any reading of the biblical text — and indeed the biblical text itself — is culturally conditioned. The Bible includes traditions that came from the diverse and evolving economic, political, and cultural circumstances of Israel. The New Testament traditions reflect the struggle of the early church to bridge both economic and cultural boundaries as it moved out into the Mediterranean world. Just as the church's theology and practice of mission have been influenced by political and cultural assumptions, so too is one's interpretation of the biblical text. One has to apply a "hermeneutic of suspicion" to traditional readings of the Bible. The emergence of theologians and exegetes in non-Western cultures is having a strong impact on biblical interpretation, including a biblical theology of mission. Readers from traditional cultures, for example, can be more sensitive to the communitarian nature of the Bible, to the New Testament emphasis on charismatic healing, and to the role of spirits and exorcism as integral to the church's "mission." Interpreters from societies that suffer economic and political oppression can be more alert to the Bible's concern with economic and political liberation and to issues of abusive power. Theologians immersed in cultures influenced by non-Christian religious traditions have also attempted to read the biblical materials from the vantage point of their native religious and cultural context. Without doubt this ferment will lead over time to a renewal of the contemporary biblical theology of mission, which, to this point, has been formulated primarily by Western theologians.

DONALD SENIOR, CP

Bibliography

Allen, R., *Missionary Methods: St. Paul's or Ours?* (1956). Amaladoss, M., "Other Scriptures and the Christian," in *Making All Things New: Dialogue, Pluralism, and Evangelization in Asia* (1990) 31–43. Anderson, G. H., *Bibliography of the Theology of Missions in the Twentieth Century* (1966). Bevans, S., "The Biblical Basis of the Mission of the Church in *Redemptoris Missio,*" in C. van Engen, D. S. Gilliland, and P. Pierson, eds., *The Good News of the Kingdom: Mission Theol-*

ogy for the Third Millennium (1993) 37–44. Blauw, J., Gottes Werk in dieser Welt: Grundzüge einer biblischen Theologie der Mission (1961). Bosch, D. J., "Reflections on Biblical Models of Mission," in J. M. Phillips and R. T. Coote, eds., Toward the 21st Century in Christian Mission (1993). Idem, Transforming Mission: Paradigm Shifts in Theology of Mission (1991). Brown, R. M., Unexpected News: Reading the Bible with Third World Eyes (1984). Brueggemann, W., "The Bible and Mission: Some Interdisciplinary Implications for Teaching," Missiol 10/4 (October 1982) 397–411. DuBose, F. M., God Who Sends: A Fresh Quest for Biblical Mission (1983). Fiorenza, E. Schüssler, ed., Aspects of Religious Propaganda in Judaism and Early Christianity (1976). Gnanakan, K. R., Kingdom Concerns: A Biblical Exploration toward a Theology of Mission (1989). Gutiérrez, G., A Theology of Liberation, rev. ed. (1988). Hahn, F., Mission in the New Testament (1966). Hengel, M., "The Origins of the Christian Mission," in Between Jesus and Paul: Studies in the Earliest History of Christianity (1983) 48–64, 166–79. Kelsey, D., The Uses of Scripture in Recent Theology (1975). Kertelge, K., ed., Mission in Neuen Testament (1982). Legrand, L., Unity and Plurality: Mission in the Bible (1990). Meyer, B. F., The Early Christians: Their World Mission and Self-Discovery (1986). Nomenyo, S., "L'Afrique à l'écoute du message biblique," Flambeau 36 (November 1972) 202–19. Perkins, P., "The Missionary Character of the Church in the New Testament," in N. Greinacher and A. Muller, eds., Evangelization in the Word Today (1979) 1–71. Pontifical Biblical Commission, "The Interpretation of the Bible in the Church," Origins 23/29 (January 6, 1994) 498–524. Schreiter, R. J., "The Bible and Mission: A Response to Walter Brueggemann and Beverly Gaventa," Missiol 10/4 (October 1982) 427–34. Senior, D., "Correlating Images of the Church in the New Testament," Missiol 23/1 (January 1995) 3–16. Idem, "The Struggle to Be Universal: Mission as Vantage Point for New Testament Investigation," CBQ 46 (1984) 63–81. Senior, D., and C. Stuhlmueller, Biblical Foundations for Mission (1983). Soards, M. L., "Key Issues in Biblical Studies and Their Bearing on Mission Studies," Missiol 24/1 (January 1996) 93–109. Spindler, M., "Bibel," in K. Müller and T. Sondermeier, eds., Lexikon Missionstheologischer Grundbegriffe (1987) 50–53. Idem, "The Biblical Factor in Asian Theology," Exch 11/32–33 (1982) 77–101. Idem, "Bijbelse fundering en oriëntatie van zending," in A. Camps et al., eds., Oecumenische inleiding in de Missiologie (1988) 137–54. Spindler, M., and P. R. Middlekoop, Bible and Mission: A Partially Annotated Bibliography 1960–1980 (1981). Tamez, E., Bible of the Oppressed (1982). Van Engen, C., "The Relation of Bible and Mission in Mission Theology," in C. van Engen, D. Gilliland, and P. Pierson, eds., The Good News of the Kingdom: Mission Theology for the Third Millennium (1993) 27–36.

❧ BLACK THEOLOGY ❧

1. Social Context. 2. Origins. 3. The Name. 4. Major Themes.

Black theology is an aspect of the rather recent theological genre known as liberation theology. The latter, a worldwide theological phenomenon, encompasses a variety of related but nuanced and distinctive theologies, including: Latin American theology of liberation, which wrestles with class domination and oppression; black theology, which deals with problems of racial domination and oppression in North America and South Africa; feminist/womanist/mujerista theology, which calls the attention of the church to the perennial problem of male domination and exploitation of women in all societies. What characterizes these types of liberation theology is that they arise from the experience of one or another form of human oppression. They thus focus attention on the concrete, particular broken relationships in society that manifest themselves in a variety of types of alienation, and they try to find ways of resolving that alienation in the light of the gospel so that people can at last break out of oppression and bondage and come to liberation and freedom.

1.   Black theology owes its origin to the unique experience of the people of color (especially of African descent) in North America and South Africa, where people's blackness was enough justification to subject them to a life of pain, humiliation, degradation, exploitation, and oppression. Black theology, therefore, is a particular theological response to a unique situation of racial domination and oppression.

The term "racial domination" refers to a conscious or unconscious belief in the inherent superiority of all people of European ancestry, a superiority which entitles whites to a position of power, dominance, and privilege and which justifies their systemic subordination and exploitation of people of color, who are regarded as inferior and doomed to servitude.

In North America, racial domination has revolved around the history of slavery, which was brutal and degrading and had a shattering effect on black personhood. After being captured, millions of Africans were driven like animals, treated as beasts of burden, shipped across the seas, and stripped of their language and culture. Not only did racism determine the most basic institutions of American society; it also ensured that blacks were to remain on the fringe of society, deprived, dependent, humiliated, and depersonalized — without justice, freedom, or a share in the political, economic, and cultural spheres. In South Africa, blacks were victims of racial oppression not because of slavery per se but because of European settler →colonialism, which used its cultural, scientific, economic, and military power to subjugate the people of color, to rob them of their dignity by subjecting them to a systematic destruction of their personhood through physical and spiritual torture, intimidation, degradation, and denial of basic human rights.

Black theology, in other words, owes its origin to a painful racial situation in which the color of one's skin had enormous sociopolitical significance. Here one's color determined one's fate and quality of life. One's entire life was determined by whether one was black or white. Where one could live or work; what bus or train one could use; which schools or churches one could attend; which restaurant or restroom one could use; whom one could love — all these were determined by whether a person was black or white.

2. It is out of this painful social context of oppression, dehumanization, and destruction of black personhood that black theology was born, as a theological protest against racial domination and humanity's inhumanity. Black theology can thus be defined as a conscious, systematic, theological reflection on black experience, an experience characterized by oppression, humiliation, and suffering in white racist societies.

The foundations of black theology were laid when black church leaders broke away from white churches for racial, political, and theological reasons. Indeed, in racist societies where the Christian faith was co-opted and used to justify the enslavement and colonial domination of one racial group by another, it was only natural that the oppressed blacks, reflecting on their situation in the light of the gospel, would reject the brand of Christianity that was being presented and would affirm their own humanity. In this way the gospel was transformed into an instrument for resisting the extreme demands of racial oppression, and thus the foundations were laid for a theology which sought to interpret such oppressive conditions in the light of the biblical God, whose justice demands that the oppressed and downtrodden be set free. Black theology, as a response to a white theology which sanctifies racist social institutions, is thus a passionate call to freedom; it invites all people of color in God's name to authentic human existence and freedom.

3. Black theology derives its name from the unique black experience in racist societies, societies in which the concept "black" has always had a negative connotation while the concept "white" has always had a positive connotation. Even the

Bible tended to reinforce that outlook by teaching that God would wash our hearts whiter than snow (Is 1:18; Ps 51:9), while darkness or blackness boded disaster or signified evil (Zep 1:15; Jb 10:22; Jn 1:5; 1 Jn 1:5–7). In Western culture, black became symbolic of mourning while white became symbolic of joy. People speak of a "black day" or a "black mood." In situations in which skin color plays a decisive role and people are divided into white and black, the very blackness of some people is often spontaneously understood to refer to something that is dirty, bad, inferior, shameful, and therefore something to be rejected. Indeed, because racism has radically undermined and called into question the humanity of people of color, it has caused blacks to despise themselves and feel ashamed of their God-given black humanity, because it is difficult for them to understand why their *blackness* should call forth such contempt, hatred, and wanton violence from white people.

Against this background it is to be expected that — if it is to have any positive message to proclaim to black people, so that blacks can once again affirm and seek to realize their God-given true humanity — black theology cannot identify itself with white theology, which tends to reinforce the myth that *whiteness* is the norm of what is authentically human. Black theology, rather, must speak positively about blackness as the legitimate form of human existence, authorized by God the creator. It has to declare unequivocally that humanity means black humanity and that, if God became truly human in →Jesus to liberate humanity, Jesus Christ was a black liberator from white racist oppression. In other words, to talk about *blackness* is to make both theological and philosophical statements: on the one hand, it means declaring that blackness is a gift from God about which blacks need not feel ashamed or apologize; on the other, it means proclaiming that because to be black is *not* to be a nonperson, a no-thing, a person without a past worth knowing about, *black is beautiful and is something to be valued and to feel good about.*

The fact that blacks stood up and affirmed black humanity in the midst of racist societies, where black personhood was questioned and denied, was nothing short of miraculous. It involved a qualitative leap, a radical transformation of the heart and mind of the black person; it amounted to a rebirth and total conversion (*metanoia*) that enabled blacks to participate in the creation of their new humanity in Christ, the black liberator.

In order to avoid misunderstanding about the term "black theology," it needs to be borne in mind that the concept blackness has a twofold meaning in black theological rhetoric: first, blackness is a *physiological trait* of particular people who are black-skinned and are historically the victims of white racism; second, blackness is an *ontological symbol,* referring to a situation of oppression as well as to an attitude, a state of mind, that works with and alongside God, who always sides with the oppressed in order to liberate them into the freedom for which they were created. The latter aspect of blackness is the universal note of black theology, pointing to human solidarity in suffering and struggle on behalf of and together with all the oppressed peoples.

4. Two of the dominant themes in black theology are the conflict between the oppressed and the oppressor and the divine preferential option for the oppressed.

4.1. Blacks cannot help but become conscientized to the fact that they are poor, powerless, and dominated neither by accident nor by divine design. Rather they are *made* poor and impotent by another class of people, the white dominant group that denies blacks the right to shape their lives. And this awareness of being made poor and rendered powerless leads blacks to opt for a radical change which often involves them in a confrontation with white racists who want to maintain the present, unequal material relationships. Thus, reflecting theologically on the inhumanity to which white racism has subjected them, blacks find themselves thrown into a situation in which they cannot avoid seeing the world as a battleground between white oppressors and oppressed blacks. Indeed, the fact that white racism encourages blacks to accept the already established and patently unjust social order is evidence that, far from being serene and normal, the world is in a state of conflict. It is polarized between two groups, the powerful and dominant whites, who benefit from the oppressive sociopolitical conditions, and the exploited and dominated blacks, who are victims of racism.

In view of this conflict between dominant whites and oppressed blacks, black theology insists that the reality of such a world should become a subject, a datum for theological reflection. This constitutes a major departure from traditional theology, which, done from the point of view of the privileged, well-fed, and rich whites, tries to close the eyes of many Christians to the reality of conflict between whites and blacks, who are unable to live and work together in harmony. By focusing on the conflict that is endemic to racist societies, black theology is able to confront more realistically and concretely the reality of the sinful alienation between whites and blacks. It thus highlights the fact that the conflictive nature of our world is symptomatic of human fallenness and sin; it underscores the fact that racism is one of the fundamental breaches of fellowship between God and human beings and between human beings themselves. Racism is understood as the sinful refusal to love, to have fellowship with, and to be available for the well-being of one's neighbor who happens to have a different skin color. This fundamental sin of alienation is the cause of injustice, oppression, and the will to dominate others, resulting in conflict and polarization between white oppressors and oppressed blacks. In order to confront this sin of racism, black theology calls for the radical transformation of individuals and social structures, because the gospel message proclaims that in Christ the alienation between God and humanity, and between human beings themselves, has been overcome. Indeed, the gospel as a free gift of God holds the promise that reconciliation and fellowship between the oppressor and the oppressed could become palpable realities in this world of conflict. The gospel, therefore, has the power to bring a total conversion from past oppressive tendencies, thus creating a profound solidarity between white oppressors and oppressed blacks. Black theology contends that when people face candidly the racial factors that breed alienation and conflict, they will be open to the transformative power of the gospel, which will lead whites and blacks to acquire qualitatively new ways of becoming human in their relationships to one another.

4.2. Given the fact that the racist world is characterized by conflict between white oppressors and oppressed blacks, it follows that any theology which acknowledges this conflict can no longer afford to remain socially and politically neutral. The struggle between the oppressor and the oppressed is ultimately one of life and death; in the midst of such a struggle, the church and its theology must take sides out of the conviction that the demands of the gospel are incompatible with the unjust, alienating, and polarizing social order of racist societies. In consequence, black theology, as a thoroughgoing incarnational theology, places a high premium on the fact that in becoming human in Jesus, God, the king of kings, was not born in the sumptuous palaces of kings. Rather, the almighty and transcendent God chose to empty the Godhead of divine power and glory in order to take on the nature of a slave. God descended the throne and chose to be born to poor parents, to live and die as a poor and oppressed human being so as to give the oppressed new life and hope. In doing so, our creator chose to identify with and to share in human suffering and pain so that God might win freedom and life in its fullness for the downtrodden. This, as black theology points out with insight, is what lies at the core of the lowly birth of Jesus in a manger. There was no room in the inn for God-incarnate. In his ministry Jesus is numbered among those who are despised and rejected by society, thus demonstrating that God is a thoroughly biased God and takes the side of the oppressed, the weak, the exploited, the hungry, the homeless, and the scum of society.

Black theologians are persuaded that the motif of God's preferential option for the poor and oppressed runs through the Bible like a red thread. It is discernible in the Exodus event in which God took the side of the oppressed Israelites against the oppressive Pharaoh and his underlings. God sided with the Israelites not because they deserved to be delivered. The issue was not that a particular people was sinless, lovable, and therefore savable; rather, the issue was the concrete evil of oppression, injustice, and suffering to which the enslaved and exploited Israelites were subjected. It is in an encounter with these manifestations of evil that God cannot help but feel constrained to come down on the side of the poor, the oppressed, and the downtrodden. Similarly, this divine partiality in defense of the interests of the poor was made known when Jesus identified himself with the marginalized in his birth, his life, and his death. As a consequence, Jesus was numbered among those who were rejected by society. For he deliberately chose as friends not the priests, Sadduccees, Pharisees, and scribes but sinners, prostitutes, traitors, and the others on the bottom of society. In short, Jesus' companions were the sick ones who desperately needed a physician — and knew it (see Mt 9:11–13). The others thought they were whole. And in opting to side with the oppressed and downtrodden, God declared that the divine self is not prepared to put up with social situations in which the poor and the powerless are oppressed and humiliated on the grounds of color, religion, or class. Consequently, black theologians argue that just as God liberated Israel not only from spiritual sin and guilt but also from oppressive sociopolitical and economic deprivation, God will again liberate the oppressed blacks both from their personal sins and guilt and from historical structures of evil, exploitation, and oppression that are embodied in racist societies.

In conclusion, black theologians are fully aware that God's preferential option for the poor, one that takes sides with the powerless in situations of injustice and oppression, may sound ruthless and harsh to those who are well placed and privileged in society. For it now appears that God is no longer neutral, that God has favorites and does not love masters and slaves in the same way. However, it is important to understand that black theology shuns a sentimentalism that sees poor and oppressed groups as sinless. Rather, in their arguments for the preferential option for the poor, black theologians are proposing a sophisticated hermeneutical approach to the Bible. This hermeneutical approach provides black theology with a principle whose sole aim, when it draws theological reflection from those who are powerless, defenseless, and disadvantaged, is the building of a more human society. This critical principle, rooted as it is in the divine principle and concern for the disadvantaged who cannot enforce their rights and defend their personal dignity in racially dominated society, aims to provide guidance for Christians working for justice for everyone *before, during,* and *after* social revolution. In this way, new rulers might be prevented from becoming oppressors themselves in the newly created social order.

SIMON S. MAIMELA

Bibliography

"Bekenntnis und Widerstand: Kirchen Südafrikas im Konflikt mit dem Staat, Dokumente zur Untersuchung des Südafrikanischen Kirchenrats durch die Eloff-Kommission," *EMW* (1983). Blaser, K., *Wenn Gott schwarz wäre... Das Problem des Rassismus in Theologie und christlicher Praxis* (1972). Boesak, A. A., *Black and Reformed: Apartheid, Liberation, and the Calvinist Tradition* (1984). Idem, *Black Theology, Black Power* (1978). Idem, *Comfort and Protest* (1987). Idem, *The Finger of God: Sermons on Faith and Responsibility* (1982). Idem, *Walking on Thorns* (1984). Buthelezi, M., "Einheit der Kirche in der Zerrissenheit der Menschheit durch Rassismus," in E. Lorenz, ed., *Politik als Glaubenssache? Beiträge zur Klärung des Status Confessionis im südlichen Afrika und in anderen soziopolitischen Kontexten* (1983) 13–23. Cone, J. H., *Black Theology and Black Power* (1969). Idem, *A Black Theology of Liberation*, 3d ed. (1990). Idem, *For My People: Black Theology and the Black Church* (1984). Idem, *God of the Oppressed* (1979). Idem, "Theology as the Expression of God's Liberating Activity for the Poor," in T. W. Jennings, ed., *The Vocation of the Theologian* (1985) 120–34. Cone, J. H., and G. S. Wilmore, eds., *Black Theology: A Documentary History*, 2 vols. (1993). Crawford, R. G., "Black Liberation Theology in South Africa and Liberation Theology in Latin America," *ExT* 101 (1990) 329–33. Farisani, T. S., *... In der Hölle, siehe, so bist du auch da: Ein Tagebuch aus südafrikanischen Gefängnissen* (1985). Goba, B., *An Agenda for Black Theology: Hermeneutics for Social Change* (1988). Hopkins, D. N., *Black Theology USA and South Africa* (1989). *The Kairos Document: Challenge to the Church: A Theological Comment on the Political Crisis in South Africa* (1986). Kamphausen, E., "Schwarze Theologie: Allan Aubrey Boesak, Südafrika," in H. Waldenfels, ed., *Theologen der Dritten Welt: Elf biographische Skizzen aus Afrika, Asien und Lateinamerika* (1982) 95–114. Khumalo, B., "Schwarze Theologie (Black Theology)," in *Ökumene-Lexikon* (1983) 1077–80. Kretzschmar, L., *The Voice of Black Theology in South Africa* (1986). Maimela, S. S., "Man in 'White' Theology," *Missionalia* 9 (1981) 64–78. Maimela, S. S., and D. N. Hopkins, eds., *We Are One Voice* (1989). Mofokeng, T. A., *The Crucified among the Crossbearers: Towards a Black Christology* (1983). Moore, B., *Black Theology: The South African Voice* (1973). Idem, *The Challenge of Black Theology in South Africa* (1974). Mosala, I. J., *Biblical Hermeneutics and Black Theology in South Africa* (1989). Mosothoane, E., "Toward a Theology for South Africa," *Missionalia* 9 (1981) 98–107. Pero, A., and A. Moyo, eds., *Theology and Black Experience: The Lutheran Heritage Interpreted by African and African American Theologians* (1988). Scherzberg, L., *Schwarze Theologie in Südafrika* (1982). Sundermeier, T., "Das Kreuz in afrikanischer Interpretation," in *Das Kreuz als Befreiung: Kreuzesinterpretationen in Asien und Afrika* (1985) 45–72. Idem, *Zwischen Kultur und Politik: Texte zur afrikanischen und schwarzen Theologie, Zur Sache — Kirchliche Aspekte Heute* 15 (1978). Sundermeier, T., ed., *Christus, der schwarze Befreier: Aufsätze zum Schwarzen Bewußtsein und zur Schwarzen Theologie*, 3d ed. (1981). "Teología negra y cultura afro-americana y caribeña," *Misiones Extranjeras* (1989) 573–80. Tödt, I., ed., "Theologie im Konfliktfeld Südafrikas: Dialog mit Manas Buthelezi," *Studien zur Friedensforschung* 15 (1976). Tutu, D. M. B., *Hope and Suffering: Sermons and Speeches* (1984). Villa-Vicencio, C., and J. W. de Gruchy, eds., *Resistance and Hope: South African Essays in Honour of Beyers Naudé* (1985). William, J., "Towards a Womanist Theology of Liberation in South Africa: Black Domestic Workers as a Case Study," *JBTSA* 4/2 (1990) 24–35. Young, J. U., *Black and African Theologies: Siblings or Distant Cousins?* (1986).

❧ CHILDREN AND MISSION ❧

1. New Testament Perspectives. 2. Missionary Activity on Behalf of Children. 3. Children's Participation in Missionary Activity. 4. Mission Education. 5. Current Trends.

1. New Testament sources provide solid foundations for understanding the centrality of children in the mission of Jesus (Müller 1992). Jesus Christ, through his infancy and childhood (Matthew 2; Luke 2), affirms the full humanity of all children. In a similar fashion, his announcement of the reign of God offers insight into the importance of children in the *missio Dei* (Mk 9:36–37; Lk 10:21). Discipleship and adherence to the will of God are demonstrated through solicitude for children (Mk 9:37). Jesus is quick to admonish the disciples for their disregard for children (Mk 10:13–16; Mt 19:13–15). In several narratives about healing (Mt 9:18, 23–25; Mk 5:21–23, 35–43; 7:24–30; 9:13–26; Jn 4:46–53), Jesus demonstrates his particular concern for all children, regardless of their parentage. He is unequivocal in his teaching about safeguarding children from harm and corruption (Mk 9:42; Mt 18:6; Lk 17:2).

2. Following the example and teachings of Jesus, the legacy of missionary concern and care for the temporal well-being of infants and children can be traced throughout the history of Christianity (Boswell 1988; Wood 1994). This concern is equaled and at times surpassed by concern for their eternal salvation. Beginning with the early church, diverse and dissenting opinions on the necessity and appropriateness of infant baptism reflect the range of theologies and anthropologies that inform and influence the beliefs and actions of the Christian community (Aland 1963). Though the Christian tradition identifies parents as the primary evangelizers of their children, the reception and incorporation of infants and children into the life and mission of the church pose numerous theoretical and practical challenges to missionaries. This is especially true in circumstances where the exigencies of the gospel are unknown or ignored and the heightened vulnerability of infants and children is further exacerbated by indifference or injustice. In the modern era, many missionary efforts on behalf of children have led to the establishment of mission schools, hospitals, orphanages, and nutrition centers. Though criticism of various missionary strategies for building up the Christian community has drawn attention to the actual and potential problems associated with such efforts (e.g., Westernization, neocolonialism, institutionalization, financial dependency, forced conversions, alienation, and abuse), the fact remains that many of these efforts have served the best interests of children by safeguarding their human dignity and upholding their value as children of God. Whether scrutinized or acclaimed, the adequacy and appropriateness of missionary responses to the spiritual and material needs of infants and children remain criteria for evaluating Christian missionary activity inasmuch as many people become Christians during their youth.

3. Over the course of centuries, the participation of children in the missionary activity of the church has taken several forms. Narratives, legends, and devotions memorializing the holy childhood of Jesus (Houselander 1948), the slaughter of the Holy Innocents (Mt 2:16), and the phenomenon of the Children's Crusade of 1212 (Gray 1972) remind the church of the place of children as martyrs and witnesses for the faith. In various Christian traditions, individual children have been raised up as models of holiness, exemplars of virtue, and defenders of the faith. They also have been recognized as gifted evangelists and healers. In this regard, it is important to underscore the significance of missionary children who have shared in the life and commitment of their parents from an early age. Though historical research on the scope and significance of these children's power and influence remains for the most part a lacuna in the history of Christian missions, efforts to remedy this are underway due to growing interest in the study of missionary memoirs, local church histories, and the annals of missionary societies of the nineteenth and twentieth centuries. Along this line, it is also important to recognize the part which children have played in offering substantial financial resources in response to missionary appeals, lest such efforts be overlooked or underestimated.

4. Traditionally, mission education has served to foster missionary vocations and encourage personal responsibility for supporting the missionary activity of the church through prayer and almsgiving. In recent years, world realities and shifts in ecclesial consciousness have required mission educators to do more than update the language of their appeals from "ransoming pagan babies" to "saving the children" (Meagher 1991). Currently, efforts to broaden the horizons of mission education for children have resulted in programs designed to create faith-based experiences of solidarity with children around the world, to educate for peace and justice in light of the gospel message, to foster respect for all peoples, and to cultivate reverence for all creation (McGinnis 1988).

5. At the present time, participation in the mission of Jesus Christ requires Christians of all ages and persuasions to take account of the state of infants and children throughout the world (UNICEF 1995; Van Bueren 1993; Vittachi 1989). It is a matter of conscience that calls for a recommitment to what B. Myers refers to as mission's neglected priority. At the conclusion of the twentieth century, children under the age of fifteen constitute more than one-third of the earth's inhabitants. The majority of these children dwell in the cities of Asia, Africa, and Latin America. Misery and violence undermine their existence. Growing numbers are abandoned, unwanted, orphaned, and killed (Kilbourn 1995). They are exploited as child laborers and juvenile sex workers. Consistently, girls are more vulnerable than boys. They receive less food, less health care, and less education. As the third millennium of Christianity approaches, these findings alert missionaries not only to the hopes and struggles of children (Coles 1990) but to the challenges and implications of these hopes and struggles for the church and the world (Brierley 1988; Leach 1994).

MARGARET E. GUIDER, OSF

Bibliography

Aland, K., *Did the Early Church Baptize Infants?* (1963). Amnesty International U.S.A., *Children, the Youngest Victims: Compilation of Amnesty International Documents and Articles concerning Human Rights Abuses of Children* (1990). Anderson, H., and S. Johnson, *Regarding Children* (1994). Ariès, P., *Centuries of Childhood* (1962). Boswell, J., *The Kindness of Strangers* (1988). Brierley, P., *Children and the Church* (1988). Cohn, I., and G. Goodwin-Gill, *Child Soldiers: The*

Role of Children in Armed Conflict (1994). Coles, R., *Moral Life of Children* (1986). Idem, *Political Life of Children* (1986). Idem, *Spiritual Life of Children* (1990). Ennew, J., and B. Milne, *The Next Generation: Lives of Third World Children* (1990). Frank, P., *Children and Evangelism* (1994). Gray, G. Z., *The Children's Crusade* (1972). Houselander, C., *The Passion of the Infant Jesus* (1948). Irvine, G., *Best Things in the Worst Times* (1995). Kilbourn, P., *Children in Crisis* (1995). Idem, *Healing the Children of War* (1995). Leach, P., *Children First: What Society Must Do — and Is Not Doing — for Children Today* (1994). Lester, A., ed., *When Children Suffer: A Sourcebook for Ministry with Children in Crisis* (1987). McGinnis, K., and J. McGinnis, *Parenting for Peace and Justice* (1988). Meagher, L., *Teaching Children about Global Awareness* (1991). Müller, P., *In der Mitte der Gemeinde: Kinder im Neuen Testament* (1992). Myers, B., "State of the World's Children: Critical Challenge to Christian Mission," *IBMR* 18/3 (1994) 98–102. UNICEF, *Report on the State of the World's Children: 1995* (1995). Van Bueren, G., *International Documents on Children* (1993). Vittachi, A., *Stolen Childhood: In Search of the Rights of the Child* (1989). Walters, D., *An Assessment of Reentry Issues of the Children of Missionaries* (1991). Wood, D., *The Church and Childhood* (1994).

❧ CHINESE THEOLOGY ❧

1. Fixing the Position of Chinese Theology. 2. The Panorama of Modern Chinese Theology. 3. A Theological Potential Still Untapped. 4. Possible Lines of Development and Priorities in the Near Future.

Chinese theology is both a goal for the future and an already emerging reality. The word "Chinese" here suggests more an ethnic quantity (Chinese people) than a geographical unity (Chinese territory). The concept "Chinese theology" is understood in this article, first, in the broader sense of "a theology in Chinese," that is, a theology which, at least in its linguistic form, has liberated itself from the foreign idiom (Latin, English, etc.) and tries to express the ideas of current international theology in the Chinese language. Second, in a narrower sense, "Chinese theology" refers to various forms of a growing indigenous theology which is inspired by the Chinese world of ideas and life.

1. Christian theology is only one of the many factors in the general growth process of the church in China. A four-phase model enables us to see Chinese theology in this greater living context. The four phases overlap and should not be strictly separated in a chronological order.

In the first phase Christianity with its non-Chinese forms enters China. The whole range of Western theology is expounded in the Chinese language. In this phase the Chinese idiom with its own modes of thought tries to give intelligible expression to theological ideas which are not of autochthonous origin. Sometimes Chinese theologians (teachers and students) feel like "foreigners" in their own country.

The second phase brings increased contacts between Christianity and Chinese thought. For that reason comparative studies appear on concepts like "heaven" (*tian*), "sin" (*zui*), and "life" (*sheng*). On closer inspection one discovers a double-pronged thrust in this process. On the one hand, the Christian theologians use Chinese concepts, interpreting and integrating them into the total framework of the original (not genuinely Chinese) Christian thinking. Some native concepts or categories appear unacceptable and are (at least in this phase) rejected — for example, the ambiguous concept "reincarnation." On the other hand, an intellectual countermovement with a distinct Chinese stamp emerges even in this phase: certain Christian concepts (at least in their traditional presentation) seem to contradict the deepest Chinese feelings about the world: for example, the explanation of original sin as the sin of Adam and Eve through which human nature was corrupted. The ancient Chinese understanding of the goodness of human nature is opposed to this.

The intercultural dialogue of these comparative studies of concepts logically leads to the third phase in which theology becomes more radically rooted in the real context of the Chinese people. Theology now looks for the fundamental elements of the worldview and elemental philosophy of the Chinese which underlie all concepts and categories. The theologians then discover that whereas Christian thought was profoundly stamped by the category of "person," because of the special revelation of God as three persons, the Chinese understanding of humankind and the world is primarily sensitive to the totality of the universe. At this juncture not only different concepts but different kinds of worldviews clash: on the one hand, basically a *monism* which ultimately sees all things in one rather apersonal, homogenous totality; on the other, a *theism* which, in the light of a historical revelation, emphasizes the personal, free, creative, loving activity of God and through this explains the free, personal, contingent cooperation of creatures.

In the field of →eschatology, to mention another example, Western theologians preferably present the eschatological reality in a temporal framework in which the linear movement toward a future goal constitutes the basic idea. Chinese philosophy, which emphasizes the here and now of salvation in a clearly articulated anthropocentrism, raises the following question: Is the biblical time frame essential for a genuine understanding of the core of Christian eschatology, or can the same message be also understood in concepts of the growing intensity or quality of the human participation and integration in the absolute and all-embracing mystery of love? Chinese eschatology does not use so much the model of extended time, of the personal I-thou encounter, or of an actual judgment but rather concepts like fullness of life, becoming one, quality, harmony of the whole individual, and the voice of conscience as present eschatological judgment.

The theological reflection of the first three phases will take decades and centuries. The goal of the whole development might be the fourth phase: an inculturated, native church rooted in the context of the Chinese people and with it a Chinese theology which is open to the world, that is, which attempts to have an overall view from the perspective and life of its own cultural context and also maintains a dialogue with non-Christian religions and worldviews. The goal sheds light on the present.

2. Because of the varied missionary history and complex cultural situation of China today, five kinds of Chinese theology can be distinguished. Taken together they form one dynamic, pluralistic process of theological reflection in the Chinese local church.

2.1. *The theology of the theological faculties in China.* The whole spectrum of theology that is taught and published in the Catholic and Protestant theological faculties of the West is also found both in the People's Republic of China and in Hong Kong and Taiwan. The Catholic Chinese theology on the Chinese mainland is still rather influenced by the Scholastic tradition, whereas the theology in Hong Kong and Taiwan is more colored by the modern theology of the West. The liberation theology of Latin America and other countries of the Third World does not appeal too much to the Chinese theological mind, but nevertheless it is gradually getting more and more of a hearing both in the People's Republic and in Hong Kong and Taiwan (→liberation theology).

2.2. *Theological reflection in the People's Republic of China.* Little is known about theological reflection in the People's Republic of China because of the atheistic-communist system. But it must exist: otherwise the heroic witness of Christian faith in the course of decades of persecution would have been unthinkable. This contextual reflection on the faith is quite rudimentary; it is rarely written down, concentrates on the essential questions of survival in a milieu hostile to the faith, and reads theological literature from Hong Kong and Taiwan. The encounter with the ideology of Marxism-Leninism also has an effect on its theological curricula. On the level of philosophy of science, this theology has still an enormous amount of work to do.

2.3. *Theology in the context of the traditional culture, especially of Confucianism.* In the context of the traditional Chinese culture, especially of Confucianism, theology begins with attempts to reflect on the core of the Christian message with the help of one of the key concepts of Chinese philosophy, for example, with root terms like "filial piety" (*xiao*/hsiao), "humanity" (*ren*/jen), "way" (*dao*/tao), and "life" (*sheng*). But Chinese theology ought not to stop at these groping attempts that sometimes want to impose a synthesis. At a more radical level it takes up the basic question about Chinese thought categories as a whole. Here emerges the category of unity (*i-ti*), which, as a complement to the Christian personalistic point of view, can open a way to an autonomous and integrated self-understanding for the Chinese Christian and create a solid basis for Christian meditation in the Chinese cultural sphere. The concrete application of the category of unity to the cosmic Christ — as the universal human being, the *Homo nobilis,* in whom the harmony of the whole cosmos reaches its peak and who is simultaneously the unique point in which the unspeakable divine mystery becomes visible and enters into the universal rhythm "of all things under heaven" — may be of great interest. One reason for this is that P. Teilhard de Chardin lived for many years in China and was much inspired by Chinese thought. The category of unity in the sphere of sacramental theology also leads to very favorable results: the whole life of the community is reflected in the celebration of the sacraments. Here the aspect of minister and recipient as individuals is not denied, but more important are the theological reasons for the active participation of the whole believing community. Closely allied to the category of unity — so to speak, as a glance into the dynamic, innermost core of this all-encompassing unity — is a second element, the *qi* (*ch'i*): energy, mysterious field of force on all levels of the universe, élan vital, all-pervading power of inspiration (i.e., in theological terms, the →Holy Spirit).

This kind of theology will continue to be of value as long as the classical culture influences the Chinese people. But it cannot claim to be the only form of Chinese theology; it hardly considers the contexts of Chinese subcultures: for instance, the concrete, sociopolitical questions of modern Taiwan.

2.4. *The "homeland theology" among the Taiwanese.* In the "homeland theology," the life-experience of the Taiwanese (Chinese who have had their homeland in Taiwan for centuries) is theologically articulated. This theology speaks about the people, the exodus of Israel, the ancestors (from mainland China), the search for a land, the longing for a strong national identity, the experience of being crushed by the great powers, and the final self-discovery in the Christ of the paschal mystery. In this theological searching a kind of "Taiwanese liberation theology" is gradually being developed.

2.5. *The theology of an integral quality of life.* The theology of an integral quality of life works in an interdisciplinary fashion, ecumenically, according to an integrated work rhythm. It reflects on the total context of Taiwanese society. From the perspective of theological anthropology — which understands the individual as relation, structure, and developing process — all important spheres of human life (economic, social, political, intellectual, spiritual, psychological, aesthetic, moral, and religious) are questioned as to their inner coherence and integration as a *mystery of life*. At the very center of this mystery is Jesus Christ and in him the triune God.

This theology too has — like the forms mentioned above — much hard work ahead of it. Chinese thought and experience offer a rich untapped potential for theological reflection.

3. From the wealth of Chinese thought and experience we will sketch three sources not yet theologically utilized.

The *bipolarity* in the unity of yin and yang pervades the whole of creation. "Yang" means strength, activity, giving, heaven, sun, fire, and the male. "Yin" means softness, grace, receiving, earth, moon, water, and the female. This precious insight into the very center of life's mystery could be analogically applied to the mystery of the Blessed Trinity. The Father appears in the face of the yang, the Son in the face of the yin, and the Holy Spirit as the mysterious unifying power of love. In this way the Chinese yin-yang philosophy is incorporated in a very positive way into a Christian theology.

The Dao-de-jing (Tao-te-ching) peers deeply into the mystery of weakness and power, of death and new life. Chapter 78 says: "The weak conquers the strong. The soft conquers the hard.... Whoever takes upon himself the dirt of the country,... whoever takes upon himself the disaster of the country, is destined to be the king of the earth." The face of the Suffering Servant of God appears to the Christian reader. The countenance of Jesus bears the features of water, noninterference, humility, emptiness, and weakness (unto the cross) but also precisely in that the traits of the overwhelming love of God. Through Jesus the darkness of death is absorbed into the mysterious strength of the life-creating love of God. The resurrected Lord wants, like the tao, to be very near, but not obtrusively so.

The human being as *ens ethicum* (in contrast to the Western idea of the human being as *ens rationale*) assigns theology the complex problem of the relationship between theory and praxis. As a logical consequence, Chinese theology as a theology of the Chinese has to try to develop a more integral view of theory (vision) and praxis (action).

4. On a methodological level there is urgent need for a differentiated reflection on the relationship between theory and praxis. Chinese theology must confront the reality of Marxism and the problems it poses (especially in the form of neo-Marxism). It must articulate more intensively the basic structures of Chinese thought patterns and philosophy. Chinese theology will slowly learn — like all other theologies — to tackle in teamwork the incalculable wealth of modern thinking today and tomorrow.

Since the totality and praxis of Christian existence in community and private life are crucial for the Chinese mentality, the *spiritual* dimension will play an important part. This is a question of personal achievement and grace, rationally founded morality and religious foundation, immanence and transcendence, anthropocentric and implicit religiosity and theocentric and explicit experience of God, and, finally, the status of the great wise men of China (Confucius, Lao-tzu, Mencius) in the context of salvation history and Jesus Christ.

Chinese theology will take more seriously the *dialogue* with the Christian traditions outside the Catholic sphere (→ecumenism) and the dialogue with non-Christian religions (→theology of religions), because the basic conviction that the living God has stored up valuable insights in the individual religions in the course of salvation history necessarily leads to a more radical encounter with these religions; they cannot be ignored. Chinese theology will — we can seriously hope — also make a constructive contribution toward *finding the identity* of the Chinese of tomorrow.

Once the local Chinese church has expressed its wisdom and thought patterns in an authentic Chinese theology there will also be the possibility of formulating the *creed* in a more Chinese way. Then themes like "yang-yin," life, *qi* (*ch'i*), harmony, way (*tao*), and unity will probably become relevant. The universal church seems to be approaching in the individual local churches a new hermeneutical situation in which the individual specific formulas of the faith are no longer fully congruent. Here we see the important role of the church's magisterium (universal and local). Should not the teaching church as a preparation for the future situation exercise a more noble style of listening and discreet choice of language? In this situation the linguistic norms laid down by the magisterium of the church would have as their primary task not maintaining a uniform dogmatic language but rather opening the individual local churches and their theologies in relation to the different creeds and theological models by means of a constant return (*metanoia*) to the saving mystery of Christ.

LOUIS GUTHEINZ, SJ

Bibliography

Capra, F., *The Tao of Physics: An Exploration of the Parallels between Modern Physics and Eastern Mysticism* (1983). Chang Ch'un-shen, A. B., "Chinese Church and Christology," in *Collectanea Theologica Universitatis Fujen* 37 (October 1978) (in Chinese) 435–51. Idem, "Dann sind Himmel und Mensch in Einheit: Bausteine chinesischer Theologie," *Theologie der Dritten Welt* 5 (1985). Ch'eng Shih-kuang, *Zwischen Himmel und Menschen* (1974) (in Chinese). Fang Chih-jung, M., "A Comparison between the Confucian Concept of Heaven and the Biblical Notion of God," In *Collectanea Theologica Universitatis Fujen* 31 (April 1977) (in Chinese) 15–40. Idem, "An Essay Interpreting Matthew 5:45, 48 through the I Ching (the Book of Changes), Chapter I: On Heaven," in *Collectanea Theologica Universitatis Fujen* 29 (September 1976) (in Chinese) 329–46. Gutheinz, L., "China im Wandel: Das chinesische Denken im Umbruch seit dem 19 Jahrhundert," *Fragen einer neuen Weltkultur* 1 (1985). Idem, "Chinesische Weltanschauung und christliche Eschatogie," *NZM* 39 (1983) 241–66. Idem, "Theologie im chinesischen Kontext: Internationale Missionsstudientagung 'Kirche auf eigenen Füßen,' Theologie im Kontext," *Ordensnachrichten* 19/6 (1980) 367–79. Lam, Wing-hung, *Chinese Theology in Construction* (1983). Lau, M. G., and J. Tong, "Theological Tendencies in the Chinese Church," *Indian Theological Studies* 19 (1982) 339–50. LIRT (Research Team on Quality of Life in the Bioregion of Taiwan), *Quality of Life in the Bioregion of Taiwan* (1994). Lokuang, "Sin in Chinese Culture," in *Collectanea Theologica Universitatis Fujen* 8 (June 1971) (in Chinese) 265–85. Missionswissenschaftliches Institut Missio. e. V., *Theologie im Kontext: Informationen über Theologische Beiträge aus Afrika, Asien, Ozeania und Lateinamerika* (published since 1979). Pui-lan, K., *Discovering the Bible in the Non-Biblical World* (1995). Sin-Jan, C., *Wu Leichuan: A Confucian-Christian in Republican China* (1995). Song, C. S., *The Compassionate God* (1982). Idem, *The Tears of Lady Meng: A Parable of People's Political*

Theology (1982). Idem, *Theology from the Womb of Asia* (1986). Idem, *Third Eye Theology: Theology in Formation in Asian Settings* (1979). Standaert, N., *The Fascinating God* (1995). Welte, P., "Schwerpunkte des theologischen Denkens im Kontext der chinesischen Kultur." *ZMR* 65 (1981) 161–72.

❦ CHRISTOLOGY ❧

1. In Latin America.   2. In Asia.   3. In Africa.   4. In the West.

The churches of the Third World today are becoming more acutely aware of their autonomy in relation to the churches of Europe and North America and their inner connection with the cultural and socioeconomic reality of their various countries and continents. Because of the claims of the world religions (→theology of religions) and confronted with the challenges of economic exploitation and social oppression on all continents, autonomous but seldom systematically worked out theological studies (→contextual theology) are gradually emerging. These theological efforts see themselves as reflections of ecclesiastical praxis in various contexts and understand Jesus Christ as the foundation and criterion of a Christian way of life which responds to specific, concrete situations. Originally, these theological outlines and consequently also the christological studies were expressed with different accents: generally speaking, in Latin America the goal was the *social* liberation of society (→liberation theology); in Asia the focus was on the →inculturation of what have remained mostly small, Europeanized churches and — through dialogue with the various Asian religious traditions — the accomplishment of what could be called *religious* liberation; in Africa, in the context of colonial oppression and cultural disparagement, theology concentrated on *cultural* liberation. In recent years — particularly with the help of the Ecumenical Association of Third World Theologians (EATWOT) — both cultural/religious and sociopolitical questions have been taken up by all the Third World churches as indispensable theological sources and starting points.

1.   In Latin America (→Latin American theology) the decisive impulses for an original liberation theology and christology were given by the General Conference of the Catholic Bishops at Medellín (1968). Then and afterwards, as a result of the analysis of the Latin American reality, the liberating struggle against every kind of personal and structural oppression, rooted in the option for the poor, has increasingly emerged as the most urgent Christian ethical and theological task. The gradually developing →liberation theology (some of the figures being G. Gutiérrez, J. L. Segundo, S. Galilea, E. Tamez, J. Sobrino, and J. M. Bonino) emphasizes the primacy of praxis and understands theology as the critical reflection on praxis in the light of the revelation of Jesus Christ. From this starting point it is understandable that christological contributions have emerged mainly within the informal framework of small and intimate *comunidades de base* (base communities), as well as out of unstructured situations like workshops, meditation groups, Bible study groups, and so on. There are a number of shorter christological reflections that have been published (G. Gutiérrez, H. Assmann, I. Ellacuría, S. Galilea, etc.), but there exist as of yet only a few comprehensive studies (L. Boff, H. Echegaray, and J. Sobrino). Hermeneutically, in all these different christological outlines, the Latin American situation of oppression and liberation is interpreted from the perspective of Jesus Christ. Conversely, the incarnation, death, and resurrection of Christ are interpreted from the situation of the liberating praxis. Consequently, corresponding to the different evaluations of the Latin American reality, there is a different *christological interest* for these theologians: for instance, questions are asked about the theological meaning of self-abandonment (even to death) in the praxis of liberation (H. Assmann); about the political behavior of Christians in Latin America; about the relationship between struggle against sin, the message of the reign of God, and the human struggle for liberation (G. Gutiérrez); and about the relatedness of contemplation and commitment (S. Galilea). The second generation of liberation theologians is not primarily interested in the transformation of Latin American society but rather in the transformation of the church (e.g., in popular piety and a more holistic liberation). Thus, L. Boff demands the following features for a Latin American christology: the anthropological element (the humanity of Jesus) before the ecclesiological, the utopian element (the realization of a reconciled world in Christ) before the factual, the critical element (the relevance of the message of Jesus) as opposed to fossilized dogmatic positions, the social (the solidarity of Jesus with the deprived) before the personal, and orthopraxis (discipleship, in imitation of the way Jesus acted) before orthodoxy. In the first part of his voluminous christology, Boff shows from the perspective of modern experience of oppression that Jesus' basic concern was the comprehensive liberation of all people. In the second part, Jesus' death on the cross is shown to be the consequence of his liberating praxis. In this sense Jesus' death is the consequence of his incarnation and hence is the most powerful expression of divine solidarity with the crucified poor of this world. In the resurrection Jesus Christ is revealed as the archetype of authentic humanity, the very image of what God desires women and men to become. Like Boff, other liberation theologians focus on the historical Jesus and his liberating praxis. Key passages for these studies are the sermon of Jesus in Nazareth (Lk 4:16–30), the Sermon on the Mount (Matthew 5–7), and the parable about the final judgment (Mt 25:31–46). The focal point of their reflections, however, is the death and resurrection of Jesus, together with his message of the reign of God, anticipated and universalized in Jesus.

2.   In Asia the circumstances in the Philippines (→Filipino theology), the only "Christian" country in Asia, resemble most of all those of the people of Latin America. Hence it is not surprising that, along with efforts to connect christology to Philippine popular religiosity and cultural values (see, e.g., B. Beltran and J. M. de Mesa and L. L. Wostyn), several christological themes from Latin America are taken up as well. In other Asian countries, however, the great religions of Asia provide the primary contexts for theological reflection. But the examples of India, Korea, and Japan show how different the christological contributions can be.

2.1.   In India, christological models (→Indian theology) until the beginning of the 1970s were mostly contributions to the inculturation of Indian theology within the context of Hinduism. Since the nineteenth century, Christian theologians have been challenged by the christological impulses of Hindu reformers who presented Jesus Christ as a great prophet and moral teacher, as an avatar, a yogi, a mystic, and a universal principle, all in the context of the social decline and colonial oppression of India and in the confrontation with European social and religious influences (see R. Roy, K. C. Sen, Vivekananda; later M. Gandhi, S. Radhakrishnan, and, drawing on Vivekananda, Akhilananda, and Abhedananda). On the Christian side, the first autonomous christological treatises in the context of Hinduism were presented by South Indians: J. J. Appasamy (Christ in the context of the *bhakti* tradition), V. Chakkarai (Jesus as avatar), and P. Chenchiah (Christ as the beginning of a new cosmos — drawing on Aurobindo). It was not until the 1960s that a more thorough confrontation with the Hindu philosophical tradition in terms of the Christ-event began (R. Panikkar); more recently, Indian-Hindu history and its relation to Jesus Christ (S. Samartha, M. M. Thomas, and important impulses from S. Devanandan) have been addressed. Faced with the universal orientation of both religions (in Christianity, Christ as the mystery of God for the whole world; in Hinduism, the fundamental equality of all religions as ways to the one *brahman*), Panikkar inquires about the possibility of a Hindu-Christian dialogue. Since only God and not the individual understanding of God can be the meeting place of religions, the question is the discovery of this meeting place in God, who is present in the concrete history of humanity under different names: "Christ" is then the Christian category of this presence of God. (Similar approaches of a "cosmic christology" can be found also in Sri Lanka in the context of Buddhism.) The more sociopolitical perspective of Samartha and Thomas is different from this approach. The context of christology is not Hinduism as a religious experience but the concrete Indian situation at the present time as a religious, social, and political task of Hinduism. Up to today both the changing Indian society and Hinduism — mainly in the form of Advaita-Vedanta (see Abhishiktananda and B. Griffiths) — are seen as promising contexts of a future christology and more recently have also been combined (see, e.g., D. S. Amalorpavadass, G. M. Soares-Prabhu, F. X. D'Sa, and M. Amaladoss). Drawing on the liberation theology of Latin America in recent years, theologians (see, e.g., M. M. Thomas, S. Rayan, J. Desrochers, and S. Kappen) have increasingly elaborated a christological basis of a holistic liberation of the poor and marginalized (against caste Hinduism) of Indian society. In this connection a Jesuan theology — one emphasizing the solidarity and sympathy of Jesus with the oppressed — stands in the foreground (see especially S. Kappen).

2.2. Minjung theology arose in the 1970s from the context of the political oppression of the Korean people and from the struggle for survival of Korean church groups (→Korean theology). Through it an attempt is made — especially by participating in the suffering of the people — to discover the essential identity of the Korean people and their culture (e.g., the importance of shamanism) and to make their suffering theologically fruitful. There has not yet appeared a comprehensive Korean christology, but several theologians have developed some historical sketches. Enslaved and deprived people (as subjects of their own destiny) achieve their theological importance through the collective-corporative interpretation of the passion of Jesus (see, e.g., Byung-Mu Ahn). Jesus' unconditional acceptance of the people (*ochlos,* not *laos*) is fundamental. The death of Jesus is not *for* the people but is *participation* in the destiny of the people. And the way Jesus endured his suffering and death is recognized as an act of God overcoming hatred and violence. Because of Jesus' resurrection, his disciples are urged to go "outside the camp" (Heb 13:13ff.) to encounter oppressed people and to set forth on an exodus from every form of domination and oppression. In the course of history, the church of Christ must fight, hope, and suffer for liberation until the fulfillment of the messianic reign (see Yong-Bock Kim).

2.3. In Japan (→Japanese theology) christological studies are an important factor in the indigenization of the Christian churches. Beyond this, however, they make use of fundamental Shinto, Confucian, and Buddhist ideas to open up, for Japan and the whole world, a new approach to the message of Christ, a message more profound than that offered by Western theologies. Ultimately, this message is always one about experience of the *im*-mediateness of God to people and between people. In K. Kitamori's work (drawing on Buddhist ideas and the attitudes of the samurai), this reveals itself as "the pain of God" in which the love of God overcomes the divine anger over human opposition. Christ's cross reveals that the all-determining love of God is always suffering love and pain stemming from the hopeless pain of the world. In contrast to Kitamori's christology "from above," the Catholic author S. Endo is concerned with the experience of the immeasurability of the compassionate love of Jesus. In his novel *Silence,* the persecution of Japanese Christians and even the betrayal of the cross by the missionaries are still surrounded by the love of Christ. The moment the priest apostatizes, steps on the cross, and so abandons his last support, he experiences within himself the liberating love of Christ. Endo emphasizes the motherly love of God, the *com*passionate Christ (not the Christ who liberates from suffering), and a Christ-experience that can be fully understood only by drawing on Zen Buddhist *satori* experience. In the case of other Japanese christologies which are influenced by Buddhist ideas, the key issue is the experience of the self-emptying of the redeeming God in Christ so that men and women really become fully human. K. Koyama reminds us of the risen Christ who died on the cross with "no handle" and who "did not handle us." The theologian and philosopher K. Takizawa emphasizes the enlightening experience of Immanuel, the God who from eternity is a fundamental fact of existence, a "God for humanity" who *is* intimately *with* each creature of this creation and whose call Jesus has answered in a perfect way by losing his life, thus becoming the standard for all human answers. Naturally the christological impulses in economically successful Japan have not arisen out of the experience of social and economic oppression of the people; the question of poverty and suffering has been dealt with within the context of self-emptying.

3. In Africa, after the physical destruction of the people by slavery, European colonialism suppressed African culture and with it African self-esteem. Within the framework of this "anthropological poverty" (E. Mveng), →African theology attempts to inculturate Christianity and Christ by having recourse to authentic African culture and ways of thinking. Hence, corresponding to African ideas, Christ is presented as tribal chief (see the works of P. de Fueter and J. Pobee); as initiation leader (E. Mveng; →initiation); as elder brother, corresponding to his protecting and mediating role in the extended family (H. Sawyerr and J. W. Z. Kurewa); as clan ancestor who sees to the welfare of the community and individuals and who protects and instills courage for the struggle for peace (D. Lwasa, C. Nyamiti, and J. W. Z. Kurewa); and, finally, in harmony with ideas of the African independent churches, as healer and revealer whose "Holy Spirit" is sometimes understood as "medicine" (B. Kibongi and A. Shorter). In all these views the soteriological function of Christ is of the greatest importance. The victorious Christ, not the suffering Christ, is emphasized. These are all valuable christological impulses; a comprehensive christology, however, has still to be elaborated. In the opinion of some African critics (e.g., J. S. Ukpong), many of these impulses are adaptations of Western elements of systematic christology to African conditions and will hardly lead to an original African christology.

Apart from this African theology, in South Africa, as a result of the struggle for liberation from white domination and racist oppression, →black theology has emerged (see M. Buthelezi, B. Goba, T. A. Mofokeng, A. Boesak, S. Dwane, and others). The starting position for this liberation theology was the creation of a positive "black consciousness" in the situation of total exploitation and alienation. In the context of these experiences and by falling back on the biblical Jesus of the poor, the white Jesus of the missionaries was unmasked as one who was basically on the side of the white oppressors and had sanctioned the subservience of the blacks. Since Christ is a God of the deprived and enslaved, Christ must be black (A. Boesak); thus black theology reverses the previous theological understanding. This Jesus Christ participates in the lot of all sufferers in his suffering. In it all these sufferers are loved and, from being passive victims, are re-created as "cross-bearers" (T. A. Mofokeng) who fight for a full human existence. Many of these christological ideas can also be found in the theology of the black Christ depicted by J. H. Cone, whose U.S. black theology is closely linked with black theology in South Africa. In West and East Africa, apart from a christology one-sidedly oriented to African culture, the opposition against the modern forms of socioeconomic oppression is theologically articulated and is sometimes linked to the liberation theology of Latin America (see C. B. Okolo, Z. Nthamburi, L. Magesa, K. Appiah-Kubi, and others). The poverty and humiliation of Jesus are identified with the poverty and humiliation of Africans. The resurrection of Jesus is release from all reality in which justice and equality are denied.

4. In nearly all christologies from the Third World, the traditional Western theologies are attacked, at least indirectly (→European theology). The basis of such an attack is the realization that local socioeconomic forms of exploitation which make up the respective contexts of the Third World theologies are inseparably linked with Western ambitions for hegemony and economic power. These matters, however, have only recently been identified as a context of Western theology in general and of the christology elaborated in the West. Because of its lack of contextual consciousness, Western theology has falsely universalized Christ and his act of reconciliation and so neutralized Jesus' option for the poor in his concrete participation in the destiny of the oppressed. In this way the incarnation event was made idealized and abstract. At the same time this theology has failed to see that the universalized Christ of the West itself stems from a context-linked Western understanding, and consequently one particular, historically developed theology has been made the standard of all theological developments of the world. The consequence of the ahistorical consciousness of traditional Western christology has been the view of the redemptive act of Jesus as an individualistic, isolated act of obedience toward God, and this has resulted in a correspondingly individualistic Christian piety. From the opposite perspective, European theologians have pointed out the danger of most christologies of the Third World: identifying the act of God in history today with particular historical processes.

In the last two decades, Western theology has become increasingly conscious of its context and has produced a number of important christological studies. E. Schillebeeckx has produced a three-volume work on christology, grace, and ecclesiology which focuses on the historical Jesus and his healing, holistic, and reconciling message of the coming of God's reign. J. D. Crossan has made use of contemporary biblical exegesis, historical studies, and the social sciences to sketch a picture of the historical Jesus and his deeply countercultural vision of an "unbrokered kingdom," and P. F. Knitter has raised the question of a religious pluralism which would acknowledge Jesus as one among several saviors that God has provided for humankind in the context of the world's religions. Finally, feminist theology, in particular the work of E. Schüssler Fiorenza, has emphasized the radical equality that was present in the original circle of disciples around Jesus and has challenged not only Western theology but Third World theology as well to reevaluate the place of women in church and society. As is evident in the work of R. J. Schreiter, First and Third World christologies are now engaged in a fruitful and mutually critical dialogue.

NORBERT KLAES

Bibliography

Ahn, B. M., "The Korean Church's Understanding of Jesus," *VFTW* 8 (1985) 49–58. Balasuriya, T., "Third World's Rediscovery of Jesus Christ," *VFTW* 8 (1985) 1–8, 116. Beltran, B., *The Christology of the Inarticulate* (1985). Bettscheider, H., ed., *Das asiatische Gesicht Christi* (1976). Boff, L., *Jesus Christ Liberator* (1978). Boshoff, C., "Christ in Black Theology," *Missionalia* 9 (1981) 107–25. Boyd, R., *An Introduction to Indian Christian Theology,* 3d ed. (1979). Bravo, C., "Jesus of Nazareth, Christ the Liberator," in I. Ellacuría and J. Sobrino, eds., *Mysterium Liberationis* (1993) 420–39. Bujo, B., *African Theology in Its Social Context* (1992). Bussmann, C., *Befreiung durch Jesus? Die Christologie der lateinamerikanischen Befreiungstheologie* (1980). Chikane, F., "The Incarnation in the Life of the People in Southern Africa," *JTSA* 51 (1985) 37–50. Chung, H. E., *Das koreanische Minjung und seine Bedeutung für eine ökumenische Theologie* (1984). Commission on Theological Concerns of the Christian Council of Asia, *Minjung Theology: The People as Subjects of History* (1983). Cone, J. H., *A Black Theology of Liberation,* 3d ed. (1990). Idem, *God of the Oppressed* (1975). Crossan, J. D., *The Historical Jesus: The Life of a Mediterranean Peasant* (1991). Dehn, U., *Indische Christen in der gesellschaftlichen Verantwortung* (1985). De Mesa, J. M., and L. L. Wostyn, *Doing Christology: The Re-appropriation of a Tradition* (1989). Desrochers, J., *Christ the Liberator* (1977). Dickson, K., *Theology in Africa* (1984). Echegaray, H., *The Practice of Jesus* (1984). Elwood, D. J., ed., *Asian Christian Theology: Emerging Themes* (1980). Endo, S., *A Life of Jesus,* 2d ed. (1980). Idem, *Silence* (1979). Fabella, V., "Christology from an Asian Woman's Perspective," in V. Fabella and S. A. L. Park, eds., *We Dare to Dream: Doing Theology as Asian Women* (1990) 3–14. Fiorenza, E. Schüssler, *In Memory of Her: A Feminist Reconstruction of Christian Origins* (1983). Goldstein, H., *Brasilianische Christologie: Jesus, der Severino heisst* (1982). Gutiérrez, G., *A Theology of Liberation,* rev. ed. (1988). Keenan, J. P., *The Meaning of Christ: A Mahayana Theology* (1989). Kitamori, K., *Theology of the Pain of God* (1965). Knitter, P. F., *No Other Name?* (1985). "Kontextuelle Theologie der Dritten Welt," *VF* 30/1 (1985). Koyama, K., *No Handle on the Cross: An Asian Meditation on the Crucified Mind* (1977). Lefebure, L. D., *The Buddha and the Christ* (1993). Melanchton, M., "Christology and Women," in V. Fabella and S. A. L. Park, eds., *We Dare to Dream: Doing Theology as Asian Women* (1990) 15–23. Mofokeng, T. A., *The Crucified among the Crossbearers: Towards a Black Christology* (1983). Mugambi, J. N. K., and L. Magesa, eds., *Jesus in African Christianity: Experimentation and Diversity in African Christology* (1989). Nyamiti, C., *Christ as Our Ancestor: Christology from an African Perspective* (1984). Panikkar, R., *Salvation in Christ: Concreteness and Universality, the Supername* (1972). Idem, *The Unknown Christ of Hinduism,* rev. ed. (1981). Pieris, A., *An Asian Theology of Liberation* (1988). Pobee, J. S., *Toward an African Theology* (1979). Pope-Levison, P., and J. Levison, *Jesus in Global Contexts* (1992). Rayan, S., *The Anger of God* (1982). Ritschl, D., "Christologie in der Dritten Welt," in E. Fahlbusch et al., eds., *Evangelisches Kirchenlexikon,* vol. 1 (1986) 732–35. Rücker, H., *Afrikanische Theologie* (1985). Schillebeeckx, E., *Christ: The Experience of Jesus as Lord* (1981). Idem, *Church: The Human Story of God* (1990). Idem, *Jesus: An Experiment in Christology* (1979). Schreiter, R. J., "Teaching Theology from an Intercultural Perspective," *TEd* 26 (autumn 1989) 13–34. Idem, ed., *Faces of Jesus in Africa* (1991). Sobrino, J., *Christology at the Crossroads* (1984). Idem, "Systematic Christology: Jesus Christ, the Absolute Mediator of the Reign," in I. Ellacuría and J. Sobrino, eds., *Mysterium Liberationis* (1993) 440–61. Sugirtharajah, R. S., ed., *Asian Faces of Jesus* (1993). Sundermeier, T., *Das Kreuz als Befreiung: Kreuzesinterpretationen in Asien und Afrika* (1985). Idem, *Zwischen Kultur und Politik* (1978). Takayanagi, H. S., "Christologie in der japanischen Theologie der Gegenwart," in J. Pfammatter and F. Furger, eds., *Theologische Berichte,* vol. 2 (1973) 121–33.

❧ CHURCH GROWTH MOVEMENT ❧

1. Origins. 2. Methods. 3. Theological Tenets. 4. Critique.

1. The Church Growth movement had its historical starting point in the American Institute of Church Growth, founded in 1960 by D. A. McGavran (1897–1990). Since 1965 the movement, sometimes known as the Church Growth school, has had its center at the School of World Mission at Fuller Theological Seminary in Pasadena, California. McGavran himself founded the School of World Mission and recruited the largest missiological faculty in the United States. Closely associated with the Church Growth school were McGavran's colleagues at Fuller, most notably C. P. Wagner, A. F. Glasser, and P. Hiebert.

McGavran worked for seventeen years as a missionary of the Disciples of Christ in India and based his academic work on experiences gained there. McGavran's book *The Bridges of God* appeared in 1955 and was the "literary prelude" to the Church Growth movement. The book was followed in later years by an astonishingly large number of publications about the movement. As C. P. Wagner has observed, scores of books have been published in almost every part of the world; a number of journals have devoted whole issues to the ideas and practices of the Church Growth movement; periodicals devoted to the subject (e.g., *Church Growth Digest* and *Global Church Growth Bulletin*) appeared; and over 350 theses have been written on the subject at Fuller Seminary alone (Wagner 1981, xi).

2. The Church Growth movement sees itself as embodying the modern missiology of the evangelical wing of the Protestant churches and as very far removed from the missionary understanding of J. Hoekendijk and the Geneva staff of the World Council of Churches (WCC). McGavran placed the church and the question of its visible growth at the center of his thought. The methods of the social sciences and, in particular, the study of culture provided him with facts for his strategy for a successful mission and evangelization of particular groups and regions. With regard to missionary methods, McGavran distinguished between "discipling" (the elementary preaching of the faith and the quick integration of those reached into the church or congregation) and "perfecting" (the subsequent and more thorough teaching of the faith). McGavran even considered the possibility of continuing old social structures (e.g., segregation) in newly created congregations (so-called homogeneous units), especially during the stage of "discipling," where there is rapid and convincing "winning of the winnable." The growth of the new community which overcomes the old distinctions (as per Gal 3:28) is reserved for the second stage, that of "perfecting."

3. McGavran and, in his footsteps, the whole Church Growth school of thought display a pragmatic, methodical approach and an outspoken, optimistic vision. They have proposed that the two billion still-unreached people in the world can be reached for Christ. McGavran charged the missiologists and ecumenical strategists in Geneva with pointed lack of interest in world evangelization, however it might be disguised. The Church Growth movement has remained conservative evangelical, even if its research methods are unconventionally open to empirical academic disciplines, even to the point of using modern electronic databases in the service of the preaching of the gospel. C. P. Wagner lists five theological assumptions which undergird the movement: (1) the glory of God as the chief end of human life; (2) the lordship of Jesus Christ; (3) the Bible as the one norm of truth and human behavior; (4) the conviction that not all will be saved, for salvation depends on accepting the gospel; and (5) the belief that the Spirit is at work in the lives of all believers in all cultures (Wagner 1981, xiii).

4. On the one hand, theological criticism of the Church Growth school is concerned especially with the scarcely considered empirical description of the church and the interest that arises from it in the numerical growth of churches and congregations. Theological difficulties result also from the unclear distinction between the stages of "discipling" and "perfecting" in the act of mission — in the first stage, the social and political dimensions of conversion and new life in the community seem to disappear. Often the scarcely restrained strategic optimism and enthusiasm for world mission run up against great skepticism.

On the other hand, the solid study and research program of the Institute for Church Growth receive general recognition and admiration, and missiologists will acknowledge that the Church Growth movement has been one of the most important developments in missiological thought and practice in the twentieth century.

The Church Growth movement has had little impact among Roman Catholics, although its influence can be felt in the writings of V. J. Donovan.

HERWIG WAGNER

Bibliography

Chaney, C. L., *Design for Church Growth* (1977). Donovan, V. J., *Christianity Rediscovered* (1982). DuBose, F. M., *How Churches Grow in an Urban World* (1978). Gibbs, E., *I Believe in Church Growth* (1982). Glasser, A. F., "An Introduction to the Church Growth Perspectives of Donald Anderson McGavran," in H. M. Conn, ed., *Theological Perspectives on Church Growth* (1976) 21–42. Hunter, G. G., III, *To Spread the Power: Church Growth in the Wesleyan Spirit* (1987). McGavran, D. A., *The Bridges of God: A Study in the Strategy of Missions* (1981 [1955]). Idem, *How Churches Grow: The New Frontiers of Mission* (1970). Idem, "Missiology Faces the Lion," *Missiol* 17/3 (July 1989) 335–41, 352–55 (with responses by R. J. Schreiter, J. A. Scherer, D. J. Hesselgrave, and S. Escobar: 342–52). Idem, *Understanding Church Growth* (1980). McGavran, D. A., ed., *Church Growth and Christian Mission* (1965). Idem, *Eye of the Storm: The Great Debate in Mission* (1972). Peters, G. L., *A Theology of Church Growth* (1981). Petersen, J. R., "Church Growth: A Limitation in Numbers?" *ChrTo* 25/6 (March 27, 1981) 18–23. Reeves, R. D., and R. Jenson, *Always Advancing: Modern Strategies for Church Growth* (1984). Shenk, W. R., ed., *The Challenge of Church Growth: A Symposium* (1973). Tippett, A. R., ed., *God, Man and Church Growth* (1973). Van Engen, C., *God's Missionary People: Rethinking the Purpose of the Local Church* (1991). Wagner, C. P., "Aiming at Church Growth in the Eighties," *ChrTo* (November 24, 1980) 24–27. Idem, *Church Growth and the Whole Gospel: A Biblical Mandate* (1981).

~ COLONIALISM ~

1. Colonial Rule in Historical Perspective. 2. Motives for Colonial Expansion and Colonial Ideology. 3. Forms of Rule and Economic Structures in the Colonial System. 4. Decolonization. 5. Neocolonialism and Critical Evaluation.

1. From a historical point of view, colonialism is that process of Western expansion which began in the fifteenth century with the explorations by the Portuguese and Spaniards and which resulted in the extension of European rule over more than half of the land surface of the earth and over a third of the world's population. In the perspective of world history, the spread of European colonial domination over a great part of the earth must be understood in the broader context of migrations, colonial undertakings, and empire-building throughout history (e.g., the expansion of Hellenism under Alexander or the colonization policies of Rome). Ultimately, however, no colonization process has released such enormous economic, military, and intellectual forces as has the expansion of the Western world in the modern period, culminating in the nineteenth century and only ending in the second half of the twentieth century. This process of "Europeanizing the earth" forced indigenous societies to undergo profound social and cultural changes; some of these changes are still going on, and the long-term effects of others are still being felt. Even though most of the countries once under Western rule have achieved political independence, the fact remains that they are often still economically dependent on the countries that colonized them.

2. Without overlooking such factors as the spirit of adventure and the urge to discover and conquer new territories, in a systematic consideration of colonialism four levels of motivation can be distinguished:

- *Settlement, "overpopulation."* Beginning with the Spanish conquest of Central and South America, dissatisfaction with existing religious, political, and economic conditions, as well as the hope for a better life, was one of the central motives of Western colonial expansion. Moreover, in the nineteenth century the Malthusian nightmare about the tendency of the population to grow in a geometrical progression while the nourishment base grows only in an arithmetical progression fostered collective fears that made the population-and-emigration argument an important factor of colonial propaganda. On the one hand, the result of this type of colonialism was, as a matter of fact, meager; only a small number of incomplete settler colonies developed (e.g., South Africa, Algeria, Rhodesia, Kenya, Southwest Africa). On the other hand, precisely in these settlements a strongly racist master-mentality developed.

- *Economic and socioeconomic impulses.* From the beginning, economic profit and wealth constituted a decisive factor in colonial expansion. For instance, the dynamism of the growing commercial capitalism must be seen as the primary cause of European colonialism in Latin America. Whereas, in the mercantile system, the colonies had to contribute to the enrichment of the homeland, in the nineteenth century the search for raw materials and new markets became particularly important because the acquisition of colonies — according to the socioideological argumentation for colonialism — was also interpreted as a solution for the inherent economic and social disparities of the modern industrial society. In some cases at least, it is questionable whether the colonial empires really brought their owners economic profit: in a number of short-lived colonies (e.g., those of Germany between 1884 and 1918) the investments were undoubtedly higher than the returns.

- *Power, prestige.* Apart from political and strategic reasons, national rivalry was also an important motive. In an age of nationalism and imperialism, the colonial movement met the need for national prestige felt in a large section of the population; hesitating governments were often pushed into acquiring colonies by the pressure of nationalism.

- *Mission, civilization.* From the very beginning, the spread of the gospel played a decisive role in Western expansionism. It is a historical fact that, despite different starting positions and goals, mission was aligned with colonialism. In the sphere of sociocultural transformation of indigenous societies in particular, historians attach considerable importance to the "mission" factor. In a secularized form, and out of an undiminished Christian Western feeling of superiority, the spread of European civilization and the establishment of a "modern" society became part of the colonial program. This is true even if the degeneration of this "cultural mission" into egoistic national ideologies is just as obvious as the fundamental tendency of colonialism toward ideological justification.

3. Three more or less interrelated processes enforced and consolidated colonial rule and were typical of the "colonial system": (*a*) the subjection of *foreign* peoples forced to remain as such, thus safeguarding European rule by means of the military and administrative apparatus of the colonial powers, along with a legal and social system establishing racial inequality — a system in which all important decisions were made in the mother country; (*b*) the economic valorization of the territories acquired in conjunction with the economic exploitation of the conquered peoples; and (*c*) the cultural and missionary penetration of these areas and the simultaneous loss of the cultural autonomy of the peoples brought into *direct* dependence. However, the forms of domination — which ranged from a formal and direct territorial domination or the conservative stabilizing system of "indirect rule" to a mere nominal control over the territories claimed — were as varied in the intensity of their control and their consequences as the economic structures of the different colonies and the sociocultural transformation processes that developed. Consequently, colonized peoples have experienced colonialism in a wide variety of ways.

4. The period after World War I is characterized as the heyday of colonialism and, simultaneously, as the period of the incipient decay of formal colonial empires. The notion that understood (or merely justified) the colonial claim to power as an obligation to develop the colonies as a preparation for their independence increasingly asserted itself. This was reflected, for instance, in the mandate and trusteeship system of the League of Nations/United Nations. But most of all it was the change in the "international system" that was colonialism's demise: the Cold War, the emerging national consciousness of the colonized peoples along with the development of resistance and liberation movements, as well as the erosion caused by two world wars were all factors which hastened the process of decolonization.

5. Whereas the left-wing liberal and socialist criticism of the peak colonial phase had rejected colonialism as inhuman, economically inefficient, and a continuing source of conflicts, the radical criticism of the late colonial and postcolonial periods pointed out especially the psychologically deforming and socioculturally disintegrating effects of colonial practice as well as the economic dependencies it created (see the works of F. Fanon). In political debate, "neocolonialism" is used today to describe the active policy of the rich industrial countries of safeguarding the structures of domination created in colonialism and informal imperialism so as to maintain the present world economy — one based on an international division of labor — to their own advantage (this analysis is often referred to as "dependency theory"). In contrast to K. Marx, who conceded that colonialism *also* had some positive, modernizing effects, modern, especially Marxist, theorists go so far as to claim that colonialism, by integrating precapitalist societies into the capitalist (economic) system, radically interrupted the (supposed) process of independent development and in fact turned it into "underdevelopment" — or, at best, caused mere "growth without development" (see Rodney 1972). In this way not only is the poverty of the former colonies seen as the result of colonialism, but the wealth of the industrial countries is made directly responsible for the backwardness and underdevelopment of the poor countries.

Colonial rule undoubtedly means that subject peoples are exploited and denied an identity; colonial structures are, in varying degrees, responsible for such problems as artificial national boundaries, one-sided export structures, delayed or insufficient industrialization, and political and economic dependencies. It must be questioned, though, whether the causes of insufficient industrialization and diversification — factors generally considered fundamental for colonial economies — do not lie deeper and whether the thesis that the integration of the colonial territories into the economic process has per se brought about underdevelopment is not too simplistic. Important preconditions totally or largely independent of colonialism are often overlooked: the influence of climate and soil composition, the pressure of a rapidly growing population, deforestation and overgrazing, but especially obstacles in the political, social, and cultural structures and patterns of behavior. Even less tenable are those theories of colonialism which make the development of the First World dependent on the marginalization or underdevelopment of the rest of the world in a capitalistic system or see the profits from colonialism as the financial precondition of the Industrial Revolution. Not only does the "drain-of-wealth theory" proceed from the hardly justifiable premise that the wealth of one necessarily means the poverty of the other, but it also overlooks the fact that internal processes within Europe were probably more important for the breakthrough to the modern industrial nation than the "forced contributions" of the Third World. But most of all, that theory is blind to the complexity of economic development and nondevelopment. In general, factors such as the standards of technology, work productivity, the structure of a national economy, trade relations, and so on, probably play a much more important role. The decisive impulse, however, has to be attributed to the sociocultural context (work ethic, organizational efficiency, etc.). It was the sociocultural context of Europe and North America which created the conditions for the Industrial Revolution, and it was the Industrial Revolution which pushed colonized and poor noncolonized countries alike to the periphery.

Colonial "dictated development" was geared to the interests of the mother countries and tuned exclusively to the Western model of modernization. This, nevertheless, created the conditions and instruments for the political struggle for emancipation and for the integration of the newly independent nations into the one world. Likewise, Western culture and traditional values and beliefs have combined to form new cultural identities. Hence, in the perspective of world history the age of colonialism — in spite of immense social cost for those affected and long-term consequences — has contributed to an ultimately inevitable process of "modernization" which cannot be undone by either complete or temporary withdrawal from the world economy.

In this connection we should not ignore the role and consequences of Christian missionary activity. Even if missionaries often acted and reacted very conservatively with regard to the colonial situation, their institutions — for example, the school systems that were almost totally in their hands — not only created the possibility of social mobility in the colonial society but through the spread of the Christian teaching unleashed a yearning for liberation and emancipation based on religion and natural law. These yearnings thus promoted the creation and development of protonationalist groups and movements, and so, in the last analysis, the mission schools became catalysts of national emancipation and social progress (→youth and mission). In this way the revolutionary, modernizing, and emancipatory effects of Christian missionary activity have made decisive contributions to the dissolution of colonial rule.

HORST GRÜNDER

Bibliography

Albertini, R., "Colonialism and Underdevelopment: Critical Remarks on the Theory of Dependency," in L. Blussé et al., eds., *History and Underdevelopment: Essays on Underdevelopment and European Expansion in Asia and Africa* (1980) 42–52. Idem, *Dekolonisation: Die Diskussion über die Verwaltung und Zukunft der Kolonien 1919–1960* (1966). Idem, *Europäische Kolonialherrschaft 1880–1940* (1976). Ansprenger, F., *Auflösung der Kolonialreiche* (1981). Bade, J., ed., *Imperialismus und Kolonialmission: Kaiserliches Deutschland und koloniales Imperium* (1982). Balandier, G., "Die Koloniale Situation: Ein theoretischer Ansatz," in R. Albertini, ed., *Moderne Kolonialgeschichte* (1970) 105–24. Baumgart, W., *Der Imperialismus: Idee und Wirklichkeit der englischen und französischen Kolonialexpansion 1880–1914* (1975). Bosch, D. J., *Transforming Mission: Paradigm Shifts in Theology of Mission* (1991) 298–313. Boxer, C. R., *Women in Iberian Expansion Overseas, 1415–1815: Some Facts, Fancies and Personalities* (1975). Cady, J. F., *The Roots of French Imperialism in Eastern Asia* (1954). Carrington, C. E., *The British Overseas: Exploits of a Nation of Shopkeepers* (1968). Christensen, T., and W. R. Hutchison, eds., *Missionary Ideologies in the Imperialist Era: 1880–1920* (1982). Dussel, E., ed., *The Church in Latin America 1492–1992* (1992). Easton, S. L., *The Rise and Fall of Western Colonialism* (1964). Emerson, R., *From Empire to Nation: The Rise to Self-assertion of Asian and African Peoples* (1960). Fanon, F., *The Wretched of the Earth* (1976 [1961]). Fieldhouse, D. K., *Black Africa, 1945–80: Economic Decolonization and Arrested Development* (1986). Idem, *The Colonial Empires: A Comparative Survey from the Eighteenth Century* (1982). Idem, *Colonialism 1870–1945: An Introduction* (1981). Fischer, W., "Wie Europa reich wurde und die Dritte Welt arm blieb," *GWU* 32 (1981) 37–46, 297. Gensichen, H. W., "Die deutsche Mission und der Kolonialismus," *KuD* 8 (1962) 136–49. Idem, "Mission, Kolonialismus und Entwicklungshilfe — Eine kritisch-geschichtliche Würdigung," in J. Baur et al., eds., *Die Verantwortung der Kirche in der Gesellschaft: Eine Studienarbeit des Ökumenischen Ausschusses der Vereinigten Evangelisch-Lutherischen Kirche Deutschlands* (1973) 195–212. Idem, "Missionsgeschichte in der neueren Zeit," *KIG* 4 (1976). Gheddo, P., *Why Is the Third World Poor?* (1973). Gollwitzer, H., *Europe in the Age of Imperialism, 1880–1914* (1979). Gründer, H., "Christianizierung und Kolonialismus — Bemerkungen zur Rolle der Religion im westlichen Expansionismus der Neuheit," *Zeitschrift für Kulturaustausch* (1984) 257–66. Idem, *Christliche Mission und deutscher Imperialismus: Eine politische Geschichte ihrer Beziehungen während der deutschen Kolonialzeit (1884–1914) unter besonderer Berüchsichtigung Afrikas und Chinas* (1982). Idem, "Kolonialpolitik und christliche Mission im Zeitalter des Imperialismus: Entwicklungslinien und Forschungsperspektiven," in *Geschichte der deutschen Kolonien* (1985) 33–40. Hammer, K., *Weltmission und Kolonialismus: Sendungsideen des 19. Jahrhunderts im Konflikt* (1978). Hoffner, J., *Kolonialismus und Evangelium: Spanische Kolonialethik im Goldenen Zeitalter* (1972). Jedin, H., ed., *Handbook of Church History*, 10 vols. (1965–1980). Konetzke, R., *Süd- und Mittelamerika*, vol. 1, *Die Indianerkulturen Altamerikas und die spanisch-portugiesische Kolonialherrschaft* (1956). McAlister, L. N., *Spain and Portugal in the New World, 1492–1700* (1984). Metzler, J., ed., *Sacrae Congregationis de Propaganda Fide Memoria Rerum 1622–1972*, 3 vols. (1971–76). Mommsen, J., *Imperialismustheorien: Ein Überblick über die neueren Imperialismustheorien* (1980). Müller, K., "Christliche Mission und Kolonialismus im 19. und 20. Jahrhundert," *ZMRW* 64 (1980) 192–207. Neill, S., *Colonialism and Christian Missions* (1966). Parry, J. H., *The Spanish Seaborne Empire* (1990). Prien, H.-J., *Die Geschichte des Christentums in Lateinamerika 1492–1977* (1977). Raven, S., *Rome in Africa* (1993). Reinhard, W., "Geschichte der europäischen Expansion," 2 Vols. (1985 [1983]). Rodney, W., *How Europe Underdeveloped Africa* (1972). Taylor, A. J. P., *Germany's First Bid for Colonies, 1884–1885: A Move in Bismarck's European Policy* (1967). Thomson, D., *England in the Nineteenth Century* (1985 [1950]) 203–20.

∾ COMMON WITNESS ⁓

1. Terminology. 2. Some Important Documents. 3. Reasons for Common Witness. 4. Possibilities for Common Witness.

1. In its New Testament context, "witness" (*martyria*) refers in the first place to eyewitness accounts in faith of Jesus' life, ministry, and meaning for human life (e.g., Lk 24:48; Acts 1:8); more generally, "witness" refers to the account of faith in Jesus that all Christians give to others, an account which comes from "their personal experience of him, and in response to his commission." When the term "common witness" is used, however, in contemporary ecumenical thought and practice, it refers to a variety of Christian activity by which Christians point to Christ by living, working, studying, or praying together (see Meeking and Stott 1986, 83). Common witness has been recognized as particularly important in contemporary understandings of the church's missionary activity, and this article will focus on the missionary value of witnessing together.

2. In the last several decades numerous official church documents and joint statements — Roman Catholic, conciliar (Protestant and Orthodox), and evangelical — have called for common witness, the most important of which are the 1984 (unofficial) report of the Evangelical–Roman Catholic Dialogue on Mission (ERCDOM); the two joint statements of the World Council of Churches and the Roman Catholic Church, "Common Witness and Proselytism" (1970) and "Common Witness" (CW; 1980); and the statement of the Fifth World Conference on Faith and Order in 1993. In April 1994, a major conference was held in Atlanta entitled "Common Witness in a Changing World Order: An Urgent Challenge for U.S. Churches"; and earlier the same year a number of U.S. evangelicals and Roman Catholics issued a statement entitled "Evangelicals and Roman Catholics Together," in which they too called for joint witness to the gospel in the contemporary world, in the United States and beyond.

3. A survey of what these various statements say about common witness reveals that — in addition to the reasons that lack of unity is against the express will of the Lord (Jn 17:21) and that the refusal to witness together to the gospel is in fact a counterwitness — two principal theological reasons are given as to why common witness is an essential part of (is "constitutive of," as one document ["Final Report of CWME Consultation" 1989] has it) authentic missionary activity. First, Christians are *already* one by virtue of their baptism and so are called to witness together to the gospel. Although it is readily acknowledged that this unity "is not yet realized perfectly," it is also acknowledged that such unity "is real and operative," and so "this unmerited gift requires that witness be borne in common as an act of gratitude" as well as a "means of expressing and deepening" it (see CW 15). Second, Christians are called to common witness because of the connection between community and mission in God as such: Mystery, Word, and Spirit equal to one another, coinhering in one another, witnessing to one another, inviting humanity to join them in their community and their mission. As a 1986 statement insists, the church's mission suffers, is seriously distorted, or disappears altogether "whenever it is not possible to point to a community in history that reflects this trinitarian existence of communion" (Bria 1986). The 1993 Roman Catholic "Ecumenical Directory" gives one other reason; it is not a theological one, but nevertheless important. Especially in areas where the church has been newly established, says the directory, Christianity has a chance to make a new start, and missionaries and peoples of new churches should work together to "ensure that the human, cultural and political factors that were involved in the original divisions between churches and have marked the historical tradition of separation will not be transplanted into areas where the Gospel is being preached and churches are being founded" (EcD 207).

4. The possibilities of common witness in Christian mission are manifold. The church documents of the last three decades mention opportunities for common prayer and worship, common work for justice (D. Tutu has said that "apartheid is too strong for a divided church" [*Koinonia* 4.5]), common prophetic countercultural witness, common material and spiritual support, common artistic ventures, exchange of professors and common theological education and theological research, common efforts of inculturation, common witness to the gospel in the midst of persecution and support of those persecuted, common participation in interfaith dialogue, common efforts at Bible translation, common reconciliation efforts in situations of conflict, common use of the media, and — with some reservation — common efforts at evangelism.

While there remain scandalous rivalries and shameful "sheep-stealing" in many parts of the world, it is clear that such activity is neither gospel-inspired nor church-sanctioned. As the *Manila Manifesto* has pointedly insisted: "If the task of world evangelization is ever to be accomplished, we must engage in it together."

Stephen B. Bevans, SVD

Bibliography

Bevans, S. B., C. W. Forman, and J. A. Scherer, eds., *Common Witness in a Changing World Order: An Urgent Challenge for U.S. Churches: Preparatory Materials* (1994). Bria, Jon, comp. and ed., *Go Forth in Peace: Orthodox Perspectives on Mission*, WCC Mission Series 7 (1986) 3–9. "Common Witness" (CW) (1980). *Evangelicals and Catholics Together: The Christian Mission in the Third Millennium*, in K. A. Fournier with W. D. Watkins, *A House United?* (1993) 337–49. Fifth World Conference on Faith and Order, "Towards *Koinonia*/Communion in Faith, Life and Witness," *Ecumenical Trends* 22/6 (June 1993) 2–24. "Final Report of CWME Consultation of Eastern Orthodox and Oriental Orthodox Churches," in *Mission from Three Perspectives* (1989) 32–47. "Final Statement: A Call to Common Witness" (available from the United States Catholic Mission Association) (1994). John Paul II, "Ut Unum Sint: On Commitment to Ecumenism," *Origins* 25/4 (June 8, 1995) 49–72. Meeking, B., and J. Stott, eds., *The Evangelical–Roman Catholic Dialogue on Mission 1977–1984* (1986). Pontifical Christian Unity Council, "The 1993 Directory for Ecumenism," *Origins* 23/9 (July 29, 1993) 130–60. Scherer, J. A., and S. B. Bevans, *New Directions in Mission and Evangelization*, 1, *Basic Statements 1974–1991* (1992). *Verbum SVD* 28/1 (1987) (entire issue on common witness).

✎ COMMUNICATION ✎

1. Basic Concepts. 2. Theological Foundations. 3. Missiological Approaches. 4. Mission Method and Use of Communications. 5. Intercultural Communication as Missionary Demand.

1. In its broadest sense, "communication" covers everything which brings people closer together, unites and binds them in one way or another. The Latin root *communis* means "common," "to have something in common." Everything which leads to being together, to having something in common, can thus be called communication. The road and transport system of a country is a means of communication and so is the latest in information transfer technology. Very often "communication" is understood in the sense of mass communication or mass media, especially referring to the technical means and instruments of mass production and mass distribution of messages. The preparatory commission for Vatican II's document on communication, *Inter Mirifica,* introduced in an explanatory note at the beginning of the document the expression "social communication." The commission explains that for the church's understanding, "communication" must refer to more than the mass media. The church's concern should be all communication in human society. "Social communication" thus includes all means, ways, and processes of the communication of human beings in society. This makes mass media only one — not the exclusive — aspect of communication in human society. For the church, "communication" thus also includes traditional means like rituals, drama, and all forms of group communication which have a special bearing on the missionary mandate of the church. Most church documents, including those expressing the canon law, now use the expression "social communication." In professional circles beyond the church, the expression is also becoming more and more accepted.

2. Theologically, "communication" should be understood much as Vatican II's *Ad Gentes* understands mission: "The pilgrim Church is missionary by its very nature. For it is from the mission of the Son and the mission of the Holy Spirit that it takes its origin, in accordance with the decree of God the Father" (*AG* 2). The church is by its "very nature" also communication. The Holy Trinity exists in the inner communication between the three persons. The human capacity for communication, the ability to express ourselves, rests on this trinitarian basis since God has created us in God's image and likeness (Gn 1:26). God, however, communicates not only within God's self but also to creatures. The whole of revelation is a practice in God's communication to God's creatures, a practice which Pope John Paul II sees occurring on the two levels of creation and grace (*Dominum et Vivificantem* 50). God's self-communication extends to us: "By Divine Revelation God wished to manifest and communicate both Himself and the eternal decrees of His will concerning the salvation of mankind" (*DV* 6). Mission is concerned with the continuation and deepening of this revelation. The high point of God's revealing communication is God's incarnation through Jesus Christ: "In the past God communicated to our forefathers through the prophets at many times and in various ways. But in his last days he has spoken to us by his Son whom he appointed heir of all things and through whom he made the universe. The Son is the radiance of God's glory and the exact representation of his being, sustaining all things in his powerful word" (Heb 1:1–3). The way Jesus communicated his "mission method," so to say, is described by the Pastoral Instruction on Social Communication (*Communio et Progressio,* 1971) in the following way: "While he was on earth, Christ revealed himself as the perfect communicator. Through his 'incarnation' he utterly identified himself with those who were to receive his communication, and he gave his message not only in words but in the whole manner of his life.... He preached the divine message without fear of compromise. He adjusted to his people's way of talking and their patterns of thought. And he spoke out of the predicament of their time." In this perspective, A. Dulles concludes "that theology is, at every point, concerned with the realities of communication," and Christianity is "preeminently a religion of communication, for God in his inmost essence is a mystery of self-communication" (1992, 22). In this sense, *communication* is a theological principle and basis which is especially realized in the missionary sending of the church (kerygma). Thus, mission means the prolongation of God's self-communication into the here and now of a given culture. Incarnation and evangelization are communication activities which rest on the Holy Trinity and the sending of the incarnate Son of God (Mt 28:16–20).

3. Missiological approaches to communication date back, at least, to H. Kraemer's Laidlaw Lectures at Knox College, Toronto (January–February 1956), published as *The Communication of the Christian Faith* (1957). Kraemer distinguishes between "communication of" and "communication between," which are closely connected in Jesus Christ. "Communication between" refers to communication as a "fundamental human act," a horizontal happening between people; it refers to true evangelism as "communication, transmitting the creative spark of the regenerating and converting word by witnessing to it" (11). "Communication of" refers to "the Christian message which by its very nature aims at the deepest communications,...the togetherness in the communion with Christ" (12). "Communication of" and "communication between" must be kept together. H. Burkle sees "communication of" and "communication between" as two aspects of one and the same happening: "What happens between God and the human being, and between person and person, does not fall apart but is one and the same communication process where always both happen together. It is not God's communication happening first which has to be brought to people. A missionary is always one who receives and shares at the same time. Mission is never 'monologue' but dialogue and a challenge to total openness" (1979, 85ff.). Missionary communication is not confined to verbal proclamation but rather reflects and uses the whole life of people with all their communicative possibilities and dimensions. E. Nida, linguist and translation secretary of the American Bible Society, is especially interested in the basics of communication to be applied in transcultural missionary situations. His *Message and Mission* (1960; rev. ed. 1990) is an introduction to the principles and procedures of communication and is the most comprehensive attempt by a missiologist in this field. Nida argues that the message of God's word has to be placed into the dynamics of communication in given cultures and societies. C. Kraft (1979) follows Nida in his concern for language and culture and focuses especially on the person of the sender in the communication process. In Catholic theology, B. Lonergan views research, interpretation, history, dialectics, foundations, doctrines, systematics, and communications as eight "functional" specialties. "It is a major concern in this final stage [communications] that the theological reflection bears fruit. Without the [first] seven stages,...there is no fruit to be borne. But without the last, the first seven are in vain for they fail to mature" (Lonergan 1971, 355). Similarly to C. Kraft, who distinguishes between the "extractionist" and "identificational" approach of the communicator, Lonergan sees the Christian communicator and missionary as either a classicist or a pluralist. The classicist "would feel it was perfectly legitimate...to impose his culture on others, for he conceives his own to be the norm. Accordingly, for him to preach both the Gospel and his own culture is for him to confer the double benefit of both, the true religion and the true culture" (ibid., 363). The pluralist, in contrast, "acknowledges a multiplicity of cultural traditions. In any tradition, he envisages the possibility of diverse differentiations of consciousness, but he does not consider it his task either to promote the differentiation of consciousness or to ask people to renounce their own culture. Rather he would proceed from within their culture and he would seek ways and means for making it into a vehicle of communicating the Christian message" (ibid.). A. Dulles has analyzed different communication models of the church on the basis of Vatican II texts. In addition to the hierarchical, the sacramental, and the communion or community models he sees also a herald, or kerygmatic, model which builds very much on *Dei Verbum, Ad Gentes,* and a secular-dialogic model based mainly on *Gaudium et Spes.* In the latter, the non-Christian world is not simply seen as "raw material for the church to convert to its own purposes, nor as a mere object of missionary zeal, but as a realm in which the creative and redemptive will of God is mysteriously at work" (Dulles 1988, 118).

4. In the beginning of the church, the oral tradition of the apostles was written down and became available to all in the form of a book. The Bible became the basis for all theology and all proclamation. God's word was communicated in the ways and with the means of the respective times and cultures through preaching, Christian art, music, drama, customs, rituals, and so on. After the invention of printing with movable letters around 1450 the missionary church began to use this "modern" means of communication. In 1626, four years after its foundation, the Congregation for the Propagation of the Faith in Rome started its own printing press. The need for this, however, had to be defended by Francesco Ingoli, the first secretary of the congregation, in at least five different speeches before the cardinals. His main arguments were the following: (*a*) The missionaries in Rome needed specialized books about language study. (*b*) The production expenses of a self-owned press were one-third lower than if the books were sent to other printers. (*c*) Only the congregation's press was specialized in different languages, including Indian languages like Malayalam. Within its first twenty years, the press acquired the capability of printing in twenty-three languages. (*d*) If the Protestants printed and distributed many Bibles, the Catholics must follow them. (*e*) The mission of Jesus obliges us to use books for mission work: missionaries cannot fulfill their mandate without books, and books also reach where missionaries are not able to go. (*f*) For the spreading of God's word, no investment can be too high. Ingoli believed the most important needs for mission work in those days were missionary personnel, schoolwork, local clergy, and printing presses. The congregation's press existed as a separate enterprise until 1909, when it was incorporated into the Vatican press, thus becoming the Polyglotta Vaticana, which still exists.

Later, different popes stressed, mainly in their encyclical letters on mission, the need for using modern means of communication. Pope Pius XII in his *Evangelii Praecones* (1951) underlines the importance of the press and publishing. He calls the "dissemination of timely publications a useful service" and further elaborates: "It is scarcely necessary for us to dwell at length on this point, for everyone knows how effectively newspapers, magazines and reviews can be employed." In his encyclical *Fidei Donum* (1957) on Africa, he further writes that "the Catholic press must be developed in all its forms. Modern techniques for the diffusion of culture must be studied, for it is known in our day how important well-formed and enlightened public opinion is." Pope John XXIII in *Princeps Pastorum* (1959) quotes this text and extends it geographically beyond Africa to the whole world and to the media beyond the press, into electronic means. In a similar vein, Pope John Paul II says in his *Redemptoris Missio* (1990) that "it is necessary to spread information through missionary publications and audiovisual aids. These play an important role in making known the life of the universal church and in voicing the experiences of missionaries and of local churches in which they work. In those younger churches, which are still not able to have a press or other means of their own, it is important that missionary institutes devote personnel and resources to these undertakings." Earlier, Vatican II's mission document, *Ad Gentes,* called on the Congregation for the Propagation of the Faith to "furnish genuine and adequate information about missionary work" (29) and in general "information to foster missionary awareness" (36). This document also demands the training of experts "in the use of technical instruments and in social communications" (26). All the "means of evangelization" mentioned in Pope Paul VI's *Evangelii Nuntiandi* (40–48), like witness of life, preaching, liturgy, catechesis, mass media, personal contact, sacraments, and popular piety, must also be considered means of social communication. Specifically for the mass media, he stresses that "the Church would feel guilty before the Lord if she did not utilize these powerful means that human skill is daily rendering more perfect. It is through them that she proclaims from the housetops the message of which she is the depository" (45).

In *Redemptoris Missio,* Pope John Paul II goes beyond a mere instrumental approach and sees the world of communication as the first modern "Areopagus" of our time. "The means of social communication have become so important as to be for many the chief means of information and education, of guidance and inspiration in their behavior as individuals, families and within the society at large. In particular the younger generation is growing up in a world conditioned by the mass media" (RM 37). With these considerations Pope John Paul II goes further than all other church documents. He not only admits "to some degree, perhaps, this Areopagus has been neglected" but asserts, for the mission of the church, that "involvement of the mass media, however, is not meant merely to strengthen the preaching of the Gospel. There is a deeper reality involved here: Since the very evangelization of modern culture depends to a great extent on the influence of the media, it is not enough to use the media to simply spread the Christian message and the Church's authentic teaching. It is also necessary to integrate that message into the 'new culture' created by modern communications. This is a complex issue, since the 'new culture' originates not just from whatever content is eventually expressed, but from the very fact that there exist new ways of communicating, with new languages, new techniques and a new psychology. Pope Paul VI said that 'the split between the Gospel and culture is undoubtedly the tragedy of our time' (*Evangelii Nuntiandi* 20), and the field of communications fully confirms this judgment" (37).

The role of communication in mission has been very clearly expressed by a document of the 1995 General Congregation of the Jesuits, "Dimensions and Particular Sectors of Our Mission — Communication: A New Culture." The document says that communication "has usually been considered as a section of apostolic activity," but one has "to acknowledge that communication is not a domain restricted to a few...professionals but a major apostolic dimension for all apostolates" (4.1). It also states that "not all [Jesuits] should engage in media, but every Jesuit, in order to be effective, must be aware of and well-versed in the language, symbols and strength and weaknesses of the modern communication culture. [They must] realize that this new communication is a milieu in which large numbers of people can be reached and enriched, where literacy, knowledge and solidarity can be fostered."

5. Mission is especially concerned about the "communication between cultures." The Christian message was first lived and expressed in the ways and means of Mediterranean cultures but had and has to be "translated," or rather "incarnated," into other cultures. E. Nida (1960, 46; 1990, 52f.) thus has proposed a "three-language model of communication," which was extended by D. J. Hesselgrave to a three-culture model of missionary communication (1978, 72ff.). The first level of this communication is the message of the Bible; the second level is the missionaries' culture; and the third level is the respondent culture.

Pentecost (Acts 2; 5:9) showed how the foundation of the church was an intercultural happening: representatives of all cultures of those days were present at the preaching of the apostles in Jerusalem. The Acts of the Apostles is full of attempts by the primitive church at intercultural communication. In fact, the history of the church is but one testimony of the attempts to communicate Christ's message interculturally in many ways.

Intercultural communication is defined as interaction between members of different cultures or the exchange of thoughts and meanings between people of different cultures. It is a field of growing concern to businesspeople and interculturalists. The *International Journal of Intercultural Relations* of the Society for Intercultural Education, Training, and Research has been published since 1976 and reflects some of these concerns. Areas like cross-cultural psychology and counseling have received growing attention. For intercultural and missionary communication, one needs not only to know the respondent culture in general terms but also to have a solid knowledge and experience of the means, structures, processes, effects and contexts of communication of a given cultural group. This totality has been called "ethnocommunication" (Eilers 1992, 137–43). Only if one is familiar with communication *in* culture can one be able to also communicate *between* cultures. This is a basic condition for any serious dialogue and missionary communication.

Franz-Josef Eilers, SVD

Bibliography

Burkle, H., *Missionstheologie* (1979). Dulles, A., *The Craft of Theology: From Symbol to System* (1992). Idem, *Reshaping Catholicism: Current Challenges in the Theology of the Church* (1988). Eilers, F.-J., *Church and Social Communication: Basic Documents* (1993). Idem, *Communicating between Cultures: An Introduction to Intercultural Communication,* enlarged ed. (1992). Idem, *Communicating in Community: An Introduction to Social Communication* (1994). Hall, E. T., *Beyond Culture* (1977). Idem, *The Dance of Life* (1983). Idem, *The Hidden Dimension* (1969). Idem, *The Silent Language* (1959). Hesselgrave, D. J., *Communicating Christ Cross-culturally: An Introduction to Missionary Communication* (1978). Idem, *Counselling Cross-culturally: An Introduction to Theory and Practice for Christians* (1984). Kraemer, H., *The Communication of the Christian Faith* (1957). Kraft, C., *Christianity in Culture: A Study in Dynamic Biblical Theologizing in Cross-cultural Perspective* (1979). Idem, *Communication for Christian Witness,* rev. ed. (1991). Lonergan, B., *Method in Theology* (1971). Nida, E., *Message and Mission: The Communication of the Christian Faith* (1990 [1960]). Samovar, L. A., and R. F. Porter, *Intercultural Communication: A Reader,* 5th ed. (1988). Schreiter, R. J., *Constructing Local Theologies* (1985).

❧ CONFESSION ❧

1. European Confessions and Contextual Declarations of Faith. 2. Confession and Identity. 3. Confession, Unity, and Discipleship. 4. Genuine Confession as the Work of the Spirit.

A confession of faith is a formal, usually brief, summary of a church's central principles and doctrinal beliefs. Alongside the task of embracing the essential content of the faith, a confession also has the function of demarcating that faith in relationship to other religions and heretical tendencies. A confession makes positive assertions about what God has told God's people and negative statements that demarcate God's truth from human perversion and error. Furthermore, the role of a confession can be expanded to include not only the functions of self-definition and demarcation but also those of establishing and preserving the community of faith, of proclaiming and sharing its message, and of praise and worship. A Christian confession is spoken to God publicly in order to honor God. It is faith moving into life and speech, word and deed (Acts 3:20; 1 Cor 12:3).

The roots of Christian confession extend back to the praise of Yahweh in the Old Testament as well as to the New Testament testimony that Jesus of Nazareth was God in the flesh, was crucified, and rose from the dead. From the early confessions that "Jesus is Lord and Christ" (Acts 2:36), through the creeds of the patristic period and medieval conciliar decrees, the church always expressed its faith publicly, echoing the earlier confession of faith and always anchoring its confession with scripture. Important was not only the content of the confession (*Bekenntnis*) but the act of confessing (*bekennen*); for example, the heroic confessions of martyrs.

The perspective of viewing churches as "confessional groups" arose out of the Reformation and the Catholic reform which followed. First among these sixteenth-century movements were the Lutherans, who submitted their confession to the emperor at Augsburg in 1530. Numerous Protestant confessions followed. In Europe, the word "confession" soon came to denote what North Americans call a denomination — that is, a church or body of Christians having a particular confession of faith, administrative consolidation, and legal identity.

In those Protestant churches of Africa, Asia, and Latin America founded upon Western mission traditions, the drawing up of a confession of faith was the occasion for the clarification of a church's doctrinal, administrative, and legal position in regard to its context as well as its confessional and/or denominational tradition. As a rule, the development of these churches' confessions and their identities as churches leaned heavily upon the Reformation and post-Reformation doctrines. These same churches followed different practices in regard to written confessions.

1. Preambles of church constitutions contain statements of doctrine and confessional positions of identity. Most churches in Africa, Asia, and Latin America accept, within the framework of a basic formula designed for use within their particular contexts, the Apostles' Creed, the Bible, a catechism of one of the Reformers, and, frequently, the Nicene Creed. In the 1947 Declaration of Faith of the Federation of Evangelical Lutheran Churches in India, the European missionaries attempted to pass on to the Indian church, in addition to the biblical doctrine, their own Western confessional tradition reformulated to accommodate Indian culture. Since the 1950s it has been recognized by mission personnel that a church starting out on its own must also develop its own creed within its own context. In this phase, in which many churches still find themselves, churches make decisions about accepting historical confessions. Whereas ecumenical creeds are usually adopted, the denomination-specific confessions of faith (e.g., those sixteenth-century confessions like the Augsburg Confession) are not always used. These churches' concern to find their own ecclesial identities is linked to the insight concerning the regional and historical limitations of the Reformation statements. What is worth emphasizing in this regard is the acknowledgment by these churches that "tradition" cannot be merely accepted without being confessed anew in a particular time and context. It is also true for cross-cultural transmission of faith that nothing can become new without the old passing away (2 Cor 5:17). Churches and mission sponsors in the West have arrived only hesitantly at the understanding that churches with other cultural backgrounds must abandon a historical confession of faith from Europe on the grounds of its "foreign" character. The critical question of "old" and "new" turns upon Christ's presence. Moreover, when European confessional traditions are themselves put into question in this way by churches of other cultural backgrounds, a promising reversal emerges. The older churches are confronted with the question of whether they want to entrust themselves to Christ anew and whether, for their part, they want to confess him anew decisively within their own context (→contextual theology).

2. As churches have searched for identity, more and various forms of confessions of faith have emerged. The basis of union for the Church of South India (1947) unites the traditions of the member churches, the confession of the universal church in India, and the reality of Indian culture. The confession of the Batak Church in Indonesia (1951) is characterized by the basic Reformation position as well as some elements dismissed due to contextual considerations. This confession takes the form of a catechism accepted by the Lutheran World Federation. It transcends Western denominational boundaries, as the Assembly of the East Asian Christian Conference (EACC) in Bangkok confirmed in 1964. The confession of the Church of Jesus Christ in Madagascar (1958) is also a document of church union based on the church's independence and self-sufficiency over against missionary bodies and denominational barriers. In the Kyodan Church in Japan (1954) a minimal consensus was endorsed with an explanation of the apostolic creeds. The "Confession of Faith of the Presbyterian Church in Taiwan" (1985) refers expressly to culture in the anthropological sense and to the sociopolitical context of the church. Challenged by the system of apartheid, the Presbyterian Church in South Africa adopted a declaration of faith which describes apartheid as an "ideological heresy." The confession of faith of the Presbyterian-Reformed Church in Cuba (1977) is to be understood in its socialist context.

3. The pressure for the unity of Christians and the unity of the churches (→unification of churches) is significant as a motivation for the development of creedal statements. It has an effect not only on the convergences of doctrine but also and above all on the basic structure of the formation of confessions and on the actual "confession of faith" against the background of other faiths. It is precisely the experience of Christianity being divided and in the minority that calls the churches to overcome factional divisions in a common confession. The EACC study "Confessing the Faith Today" (1963–66), as well as the developments in South Africa, shows the heavy emphasis on existential confession as the emerging and vital form of confession today. This is connected to the fact that unity has not been sought primarily through a doctrinal consensus. The context for the development of a confession of faith is, in non-Western cultural milieus, the totality of witness in the face of other faiths. Such a confession is informative, enriching, and missionary and proves its concreteness through a lived-out discipleship. Put more succinctly: it is not so much the doctrine of different theological and denominational positions but the witness of Christian existence which is the context for the formation of confessions in these churches.

4. A similar impetus for a common confession of the apostolic faith comes from East Asia. In his introduction to Faith and Order Paper 104 (1980), C. S. Song distinguishes between (a) the "preconfessional," the objective, historical, and logical declaration about Jesus (Mt 16:13–14), and (b) "confessing," the existential response to the question of Jesus (Mt 16:16). The change from factual statement to decisive witness indicates the authentic confession as the work of the Spirit (Mt 16:7). Confessing the faith and the presence of the Spirit belong together. Therefore true confession is not a matter of human "works." According to Song, true confession breaks down in the third stage, the "postconfessional situation" of human ways of arguing, as Peter's dispute with Christ makes clear (Mt 16:22). Postconfessional situations misunderstand the consequences of suffering with Christ. Christian churches should recognize "their confessing situation" and give it priority over against a preconfessional and postconfessional confessing. Because God acts in the "confessing situation" (see Mt 16:17), is this not therefore the best place where Christians and churches can regain their unity?

LOTHAR SCHREINER AND RICHARD H. BLIESE

Bibliography

Bolewski, H., "Bekenntnisbildung und Unionstendenzen in den Jungen Kirchen," LR 3 (1953) 316–17. Confessing Our Faith around the World, vol. 1, Faith and Order Paper 104 (1980). Confessing the Faith in Asia Today: Statement of EACC (1966). Dankbaar, W. F., "De ontwikkeling van de belijdenis in de jonge Kerken," NedThT 2 (1947–48). "Declaration of Faith Approved for Use in the Presbyterian Church of Southern Africa," ExT 83 (1974). "Erklärung bezüglich des gemeinsamen Verständnis des christlichen Glaubens in Indonesien," Informationsbrief, EMS 2 (1986). Estborn, S., "Das Bekenntnis in den lutherischen Kirchen Indien," Das Bekenntnis im Leben der Kirche (1963) 170–71. Fleming, J., ed., Confessing the Faith in Asia Today, special EACCb Faith and Order Issue, SEAJT 8/1/2 (1966). Freytag, J., and H. J. Margull, Junge Kirchen auf eigenen Wegen (1972). Heron, A. I. C., ed., The Westminster Confession in the Church Today (1982). Hofmann, J. C. K., "Über das Verhältnis der Mission zur Kirche," in Die confessionelle Frage innerhalb der Norddeutschen Missions-Gesellschaft und die allgemeine Versammlung Mecklenburgischer Missionsfreunde zu Rostock (1844). Hüffmeier, W., and M. Stöhr, "Glaubensbekenntnis der Presbyterianischen Kirche in Taiwan," Barmer Theologische Erklärung (1984) 207. Kellerhals, E., Die Bekenntnisfrage auf dem Missionsfeld (1940). Kolb, R., Confessing the Faith: Reformers Define the Church, 1530–1580 (1991). Lindbeck, G. A., "The Confessions as Ideology and Witness in the History of Lutheranism," LW 7 (1961) 388–401. Lislerud, G., "Das Bekenntnis in den lutherischen Kirche Südafrikas," in Das Bekenntnisbindung und Bekenntnisbildung in Jungen Kirchen (1953). Idem, "Randbemerkungen zur Entwicklung des Bekenntnisses in asiastischen und afrikanischen Kirchen," Basileia (1959) 271–77. Maletzke, G., "Intercultural and International Communication," in H. D. Fischer and J. C. Merill, eds., International and Intercultural Communication (1976) 409–16. Oosthuizen, G. C., Theological Discussions and Confessional Developments in the Churches of Asia and Africa (1958). Scherer, J. A., Mission and Unity in Lutheranism (1969). Schreiner, L., Das Bekenntnis der Batak-Kirche (1966) Idem, "Wie wird in den Kirchen Asiens und Afrikas mit Autorität gelehrt? Lehren der Kirche Heute," ÖR 33 (1978) 60ff. Simatupang, R. B., "The Confessing Church in Contemporary Asia," SEAJT 8 (1967) 53ff. Sitaram, K. S., and R. T. Cogdell, Foundations of Intercultural Communications (1976). Spindler, M. R., "Creeds and Credibility: The New Statement of Faith of the Church of Jesus Christ in Madagascar," Missiol 7 (1979) 112–13. Steubing, H., Bekenntnisse der Kirche: Bekenntnistexte aus zwanzig Jahrhundert (1970). Stock, L., Cubanisches Glaubensbekenntnis (1980). Vischer, L., Reformed Witness Today (1982).

❧ CONTEXTUAL THEOLOGY ❧

1. Concept. 2. Text and Context. 3. Social Analysis. 4. Contextual Perspectives. 5. Local Theologies. 6. Contextuality and Universality.

1. Contextual theology is a form of Christian theology necessary today in view of the increasing consciousness of plurality of religions, worldviews, philosophies, cultures, and sociopolitical systems. Such consciousness obliges theology to adapt its form and language to various historical and social milieus. As long as the Christian faith and Christian theology realized themselves primarily in a milieu which Christianity had itself helped shape, the dominant understanding of Christianity and its context were so interwoven that the tension between them was hardly noticed or reflected upon, and deviations from the prevailing understanding of Christianity were punished as heresy. The concept "context" developed from work with literary texts, that is, in the fields of epistemology, hermeneutics, and logic. It is becoming increasingly important in verbal and nonverbal translation processes in the intercultural and interreligious sphere. Reflection on contexts, with regard not only to verbal texts but also to society and life, constitutes for Christianity today the precondition for an evangelization (→evangelism, evangelization) which aims at effectively indigenizing the message of the gospel and rooting it in foreign cultures (→inculturation).

2. The relationship between text and context is of fundamental importance in modern study of the basic text of Christianity, the →Bible, that is, in biblical hermeneutics. The problem of understanding scripture today involves both the original *Sitz im Leben* of the first Christian community and modern contexts.

2.1. To rediscover the original understanding of holy scripture we can make use of the knowledge of the original contexts deduced by the historical-critical method; the method pays attention to literary forms and asks which meaning "the sacred writer, in a determined situation and given the circumstances of his time and culture, intended to express and did in fact express through the medium of a contemporary literary form," in the "customary and characteristic patterns of perception, speech and narrative which prevailed at the age of the sacred writer," and in "the conventions which the people of his time followed in their dealings with one another" (*DV* 12). Although individual New Testament texts admittedly had specific Christian communities or individuals as addressees, it is in their totality and total context that they have become the fundamental document of the Christian faith and self-understanding. Because of this, the history of tradition, the history of the church, and the history of Christian theology remain important for the understanding of holy scripture. Furthermore, this process of tradition provides examples and models since the translation of the Christian message was realized in the various stages of Christian history (e.g., Jewish-Greek, Roman, European [including the Reformation and Enlightenment epochs, nineteenth-century colonialism, etc.]) and among various peoples (Jewish-Greek, Romans, Germans, Slavs, etc.).

2.2. According to *GS* 4, the church has the duty of "reading the signs of the time and of interpreting them in the light of the Gospel" in order to carry out its task. The polarity of "signs of the time" and "light of the Gospel" points beyond the tension between proclamation and holy scripture to the tension between society/

world/time and the gospel. This focuses attention on the *present* context of the gospel or its nontheological milieu because it is in society, in culture, and in history that the proclamation of the gospel takes place and where we find the addressees of the message. The understanding of scripture in the *Sitz im Leben* of modern people is essentially stamped not only by their questions, problems, and interests, their forms of behavior and patterns of thought and speech, but also by the structures of the world in which they are living. Consequently the translation of the gospel is not to be understood in the sense of a word-for-word translation but requires an encounter of the various horizons of comprehension. This can, properly understood, be called "a merging of horizons" (H. G. Gadamer) since in the question-answer encounter of modern men and women with scripture a new situation arises both for the receiver of the message and, in a certain sense, for the message itself, in which neither the hearer of the word nor the word itself remains quite the same. Indeed, it is a part of the Christian self-understanding that the gospel has properly touched hearers only when they allow it to be master over them and do not, conversely, try to manipulate it.

3. In order to study the "signs of the time," Christian theology — the scientific and methodological reflection on what we say about God and what God says with respect to Jesus Christ — must examine the sociohistorical context of the faith and its transmission. This context is also important because individuals not only live with a definite language (with its structures and forms of expression) and as members of a definite people (with particular sociopolitical structures, history, level of civilization, and culture) but also live within the greater contexts of national and world history in the spheres of economics, politics, the history of culture and thought, worldviews, and religions. In reference to the present situation, *Gaudium et Spes* says: "Nowadays when things change so rapidly and thought patterns differ so widely, the church needs to step up this exchange by calling upon the help of people who are living in the world, who are expert in its organizations and its forms of training, and who understand its mentality, in the case of believers and nonbelievers alike. With the help of the Holy Spirit, it is the task of the whole people of God, particularly of its pastors and theologians, to listen to and distinguish the many voices of our times and to interpret them in the light of the divine word, in order that the revealed truth may be more deeply penetrated, better understood, and more suitably presented" (44). From this it follows that: (*a*) Theology must engage in interdisciplinary cooperation, especially with the social sciences, cultural anthropology, ethnology, comparative religion, and philosophy. (*b*) Theology must take account of the results of social analysis, examine its premises, and influence its ethical consequences, inasmuch as theology, in view of the proclamation of salvation, always has a therapeutic intention. (*c*) Theology must pay attention to those nontheological factors which influence it, the languages it has to use and into which it is to be translated, the interests connected with its work, and the methods it uses. (*d*) The diversity of thought patterns and languages results in a diversity of theological languages. The legitimacy of the individual language is manifested in its basic communicability and convertibility into other theological languages and their basic unity.

The determination of the context through social analysis has two fundamental aspects: first, the material or perspectives of social analysis; second, the method and apparatus of determining the context.

4. In more recent times, basically three aspects of the social context of a time and/or a region have been considered: (*a*) the socioeconomic and political conditions and developments, (*b*) the cultural situation, and (*c*) the ideological and religious situation. The process leads via the cultural consequences to a reevaluation of religious relevance. The question to be clarified in each individual case is whether behind the factual behavior there lies a moral decision which degrades the spiritual realm to an epiphenomenon of material developments and, at least by implication, makes an atheistic option for the primacy of matter over spirit.

4.1. *The socioeconomic and political context.* Theology has concerned itself with questions about the socioeconomic and political context at least since the emergence of Christian social teaching at the end of the nineteenth century. This body of church teaching developed after the sociopolitical structures of Europe had begun to change under the influence of the emerging industrial society, tensions between capital and labor, shifts of emphasis from country to town, and the political focus on the new bourgeoisie; further, Christianity had to take up the challenge posed by the ideologies of liberalism and socialism and find its own answer. Within the framework of theology in general, Christian social teaching, important as it is, has functioned up to now as a type of smoke screen: theology as a whole did not see the need to change into a contextual theology related to the social context. The situation has become more acute since the middle of the twentieth century due to the communication and information revolution, which now makes possible immediate and widespread exchange between nearly all parts of the world. Additional factors have been the tensions in international economics and politics and the fact that colonialism has had to give way to new forms of nationalism and internationalism. It is true that power struggles today are determined by a great variety of factors and consequently cannot be explained simplistically, but they are generally described in terms of polarities which suggest a compulsion to decide pro or con: rich-poor, capitalism-socialism, liberalism-conservatism, East-West, North-South, developed-underdeveloped, dominating-oppressed, dictatorships-democracies. The problem comes to a head in the Third World's struggle for its place and identity between the First and Second Worlds (→development; liberation theology).

In this connection, two factors have to be taken into account (*a*) The premises of the economic and political theories applied to social analysis or of the sociological methodology have to be examined, especially if, like classical Marxism, they proceed beyond the economic and political sphere to a comprehensive interpretation of culture and history. (*b*) Theology for its part should not overlook the fact that the social form of religion, including Christianity, stands in a continuous interrelationship with all social factors and consequently is subject to the influence of conflicting interests; accordingly, theology has to refine its own critical sense by continuous discernment of spirits, and it cannot escape criticism from the outside either.

4.2. *Cultural context.* The experience of cultural pluralism is part and parcel of the experience of the contemporary world. Consequently, one's own cultural context changes. All cultures are, albeit in different ways, part of the context of one's own culture. But where one's own cultural context is relativized in the encounter of different cultures, it loses its normative power; the concept of culture itself becomes an empirical, descriptive category. Even if the socioeconomic conditions form an important substratum in the development of cultures, additional factors have to be taken into account for the determination of the cultural milieu, such as the different ways of using things in science and technology, art and literature, the social institutions, ethics and law, philosophies, worldviews, and religions (see *GS* 53). There are, in addition to those tensions mentioned in the preceding section, further tensions which mark the transition from a descriptive social analysis to the sphere of norms: nature-culture, humanity-nature, individual-society, language-behavior, spirit-matter, autonomy-heteronomy, culture-cultures. A very important question is whether and to what extent cultural analysis puts the cultures in the context of the history of ideas. This has consequences for theology: (*a*) The interest in the cultural context and its study with the aid of the historical sciences, linguistics, anthropology, archaeology, and so on, change theology itself from a mainly deductive-speculative to a mainly inductive-empirical science which, moreover, recognizes the pivotal importance and responsibility of the subject of science. (*b*) Cultural pluralism leads to a theological pluralism which makes the traditional theology of the West reflect both on its regional importance (→European theology) and on its universal importance or its role within a "cross-cultural" theology (→intercultural theology). (*c*) The emphasis on the human subject in modern science forces theology to reinterpret the role of humanity in the tension between cosmocentrism and anthropocentrism, on the one hand, and anthropocentrism and theocentrism, on the other. This interpretation also provides an opportunity for Christianity inasmuch as the atheistic inversion of Western anthropology from a conception of humanity based on theology of creation to one stamped by a "God complex" is increasingly reaching its limits and is condemned to failure. At the same time this proves immanentistic secularism to be an ideology.

4.3. *The ideological and religious context.* Worldwide the experience of religious pluralism goes hand in hand with this cultural pluralism. For Western culture the ideological and religious context can be characterized as follows: (*a*) Christianity is split into a variety of Christian churches and communities, but within the Christian churches there is an increasing consciousness of what Christians have in common (→ecumenism). (*b*) The Western world is stamped to a great degree by a process of de-Christianization and secularization, of life without faith in God, and of practical atheism, agnosticism, and atheistic humanism. Accordingly, in many forms of Western philosophy, God plays no significant role. (*c*) In spite of all this there is an increasing awareness of a pluralism of religions, the spreading influence of an esotericism, and interest in new religious movements. The determination of the religious milieu begins with a phenomenological-historical description and goes on to question the relationship between religion and society, religion and culture. In this connection the problem of the concept of religion, the relationship between a descriptive understanding (i.e., that produced by comparative religion) and a normative understanding (i.e., that generated by philosophy of religion or theology) of religion (→religion, religions) has to be taken into account.

The consequences for Christian theology are twofold. First, in the encounter with the other religions the claims of Christianity should not be compromised. Second, through dialogue and collaboration with adherents of other religions and in witnessing to the Christian faith and way of life, Christians acknowledge, preserve, and foster the spiritual, moral, and sociocultural values found in non-Christian religions and cultures (*NA* 2) (→theology of mission; theology of religions).

5. In order to bring theology into contextual perspective (→black theology; liberation theology) it has become regionalized into local theologies (→African theology; Chinese theology; European theology; Indian theology; Japanese theology; Korean theology; Latin American theology; Filipino theology). Latin American liberation theology, which, in its concrete implementation, embraces a variety of liberation theologies, has become the paradigm of a local contextual theology — with all its possibilities but also with all its risks. Important elements are (*a*) social analysis which strongly emphasizes socioeconomic conditions; (*b*) a biblical hermeneutics going back to the immediacy of the original Gospel texts; and (*c*) the articulation of a theology which, in contrast to the traditional academic theology, aims at including the ordinary people (→"people" [*Volk*], "nation") as the subjects of theology. Among the peoples and churches of Africa the emphasis has shifted to a process of liberation in which Christianity empties itself so much that it can liberate Africans from cultural impoverishment and give them a new identity. Asian Christianity and theology face the task of proclaiming the Christian message as the true, transcultural, universal message of salvation not only in cultures molded by living world religions but also in countries influenced by modern civilization: it must claim to be a message that liberates without destroying all that is good in Asian society. On the one hand, a European contextual theology leads to a new learning process in dealing with foreign cultures and religions which relativizes the European-Western theology; on the other hand, in the future this theology will have to bring its inherited aptitude for critical discernment into the international-intercultural or intercultural-theological dialogue. In North America, theology faces the daunting task of dialoguing with, critiquing, and being affected by a desacralized, highly technological, and individualistic culture while at the same time allowing itself to be cross-fertilized by the theologies emerging from various cultural and political minorities — African-Americans, Latinos, Native Americans, gays, and lesbians. In addition to the attempts to develop closer interdisciplinary cooperation between theology, philosophy, and other branches of learning and to foster context-conscious cooperation between the theological disciplines, there is also the special task of paying attention to the proper relationship between contextuality and universality.

6. The postulate of a contextual theology is not to be misunderstood as the denial of the universal claim of Christianity; it means rather the determination to reach all potential "hearers of the Word" (K. Rahner) in the most varied sociocultural situations and to defend such a claim meaningfully even within the framework of religious pluralism. Such a theological attitude is the consequence of the realization that not every language, including theological language, can be understood everywhere. All the more important, therefore, is the determination to maintain a fundamental unity which will be guaranteed if the various languages and forms of theology from the different regions and times remain intertranslatable and so mutually intelligible. For a contextual fundamental theology this not only means the obligation of understanding theology as apologetics *ad intra* and *ad extra* (or as hermeneutics) but above all means developing fundamental theology as "dialogics," that is, as a theory of behavior based on dialogue and partnership which takes into account the conditions of an all-embracing, communications-oriented society. In the long run, only on the foundation of such behavior can the message of the gospel be expressed in the diversity of languages, thought, and behavior patterns of the world without losing its universal claim.

HANS WALDENFELS, SJ

Bibliography

Anderson, G. H., and T. F. Stransky, *Third World Theologies* (1984). Arbuckle, G. A., *Earthing the Gospel: An Inculturation Handbook for the Pastoral Worker* (1990). Bevans, S., *Models of Contextual Theology* (1992). Idem, "Seeing Mission through Images," *Missiol* 19/1 (January 1991) 45–57. Biser, E., *Religiöse Sprachbarrieren* (1980). Boff, C., *Theology and Praxis: Epistemological Foundations* (1987). Carrier, H., *Gospel Message and Human Cultures: From Leo XIII to John Paul II* (1989). Connor, J. H., "When Culture Leaves Contextualized Christianity Behind," *Missiol* 19/1 (January 1991) 21–29. Crollius, A., and A. Roest, *Inculturation: Working Papers on Living Faith and Cultures* (1982). Friedli, R., *Fremdheit als Heimat* (1974). Gadamer, H.-G., *Truth and Method* (1960). Gensichen, H. W., *Mission und Kultur* (1985). Gilliland, D. S., *The Word among Us: Contextualizing Theology for Mission Today* (1989). Hall, D. J., *Thinking the Faith: Christian Theology in a North American Context* (1989). Hesselgrave, D. J., and E. Rommen, *Contextualization: Meanings, Methods, and Models* (1989). Hick, J., *Truth and Dialogue* (1974). Hiebert, P. G., "Critical Contextualization," *IBMR* 11/3 (July 1987) 104–12. International Theological Commission, "Faith and Inculturation," *Irish Theological Quarterly* 55/2 (1989) 142–61. Koyama, K., *Waterbuffalo Theology* (1976). May, J. D., *Meaning, Consensus and Dialogue in Buddhist-Christian Communication* (1984). Pannenberg, W., *Theology and the Philosophy of Science* (1976). Pater, W. de, *Theologische Sprachlogik* (1971). Paus, A., *Kultur als christlicher Auftrag Heute* (1981). Rolston, H., III, *Religious Inquiry — Participation and Detachment* (1985). Schineller, P., *A Handbook on Inculturation* (1990). Schreiter, R. J., "Communication and Interpretation across Cultures," *IRM* 85 (1995) 227–39. Idem, *Constructing Local Theologies* (1985). Idem, "Faith and Cultures: Challenges to a World Church," *TS* 50/4 (1989) 744–60. Shorter, A., *Toward a Theology of Inculturation* (1988). Smith, W. C., *Towards a World Theology* (1981). Stackhouse, M. L., *Apologia: Contextualization, Globalization, and Mission in Theological Education* (1988). Waldenfels, H., *Kontextuelle Fundamentaltheologie* (1985). Idem, "Von der Weltmission zur Kirche in allen Kulturen," *Die Kirche Christi* (1982) 303–50.

❧ CONVERSION ❧

1. Conversion in Context. 2. Characteristics of Conversion. 3. Conversion as a Radical Experience.

The understanding of Christian conversion derives from ideas associated with the Hebrew *teshuvah* (implying "turning" and rooted in *shub*, "to return home") and the Greek *metanoia* (involving a marked change of mind and direction). It has been defined both as a change of religion and as formal recommitment to Christianity — as event and process, and in terms of a break from or continuity with the past. On the relationship of "first" and "ongoing" conversion, and the status of group conversions relative to individual conversion, discussions continue. Conversion, then, is complex and multifaceted. This article concentrates on aspects of conversion related to mission and deriving from comparative and cross-cultural studies.

1. If conversion is understood as a religious experience, this still begs the question of what it actually entails, especially where "religion" is not institutionalized as it is among the so-called world religions. For many peoples, religion is inextricable from life, embedded within its very fabric. "Religious" experiences are thus not entirely or always separable from what is conventionally labeled "economic" or "political" or "social" activity. Nor should one consider "popular religiosity" or "syncretism" only as pejorative terms; they identify the existential situation for many a true conversion.

Human behavior can only be interpreted through a careful consideration of its context. Socialization is the process whereby a person becomes a member of a particular social group. It comprises both formal and informal learning, the assimilation of social values, a system (not necessarily codified) of belief(s), and an understanding of relevant sanctions. "Religious" behavior and belief are assimilated during socialization. Yet once imbued with society's norms and values, human beings are not deprived of strategic choices or insulated from all risk. Worldwide, people perceive themselves to enjoy a degree of free will.

2. Viewed as action, conversion assumes responsibility and maturity (Jung suggested that the second half of life was particularly appropriate for conversion: one has erred, perhaps grown wiser, and is more able to confront death). As response, conversion assumes an ongoing relationship between the convert and God. But such maturity need not be expressed as individualism or pure autonomy.

Conversion requires a free human response: forced conversion is an oxymoron. Yet choice or freedom may be validly expressed communally. If autonomy is a feature of individualism or independence, heteronomy describes relatedness or interdependence. Conversion is as much about the latter as about the former. People in social groups frequently act precisely *as* a group, and the exercise of individual choice is subsumed into the group choice, as discerned or decided by appropriate authority.

The (Western) view that only personal and individual choices are true choices sits very uneasily with the suggestion that there may be authentic conversion of whole groups of people. This view may also imply that conversion must be an instantaneous, if not a dramatic, event. Both these intuitions need to be challenged if one is to grasp the dynamics of conversion in cross-cultural perspective.

A virtually instantaneous "turning" does not of itself mark true conversion, especially if it should prove temporary. Whimsical or purely pragmatic changes of mind are not conversion experiences, while recidivism describes "backsliding" or the abandonment of what might initially have seemed a conversion. It is far better, as modern studies in psychology, anthropology, and spirituality have indicated, to investigate conversion as a process, sometimes almost imperceptible. But to qualify as religious, it must at least be expressive of a relationship with God.

Paul's conversion (Acts 9:3ff.; 22:4–21; 26:12–18; Gal 1:11–24) is often taken as typical, exemplifying a dramatic, instantaneous "turning." Certainly it illustrates personal, autonomous decision making, based on the discovery of a new relationship with God, an act of pure grace. But Paul's undoubted transformation is far from instantaneous; it takes place over a period of time and is marked by several incidents (call, debilitation, blindness, the laying on of hands, baptism, recovery of strength). Moreover, it is by no means the only authentic expression of Christian conversion.

3. Conversion's fruit is the transformation by grace of a life, but often by gradual blossoming and ripening rather than spontaneous fructification. Conversion would then be a process rather than an event, part of life's unfolding. Yet such a "fruiting" cannot be merely cosmetic; it must be the consequence of a "rooting" in grace. True conversion is a radical affair, touching life's very roots; and the fruit depends on the roots' vitality.

Radical is not necessarily dramatic; conversion occurs through continuity as well as by discontinuity with earlier life. Radical disjunction certainly marks the lives of some individuals, particularly men, but does not necessarily characterize all communities, or many women. Communities (whether nuclear family or village) may realign values and aims so that over time a clear change (conversion) is noticeable, though perhaps with little drama. Likewise, many women's experience is that lives may be lived authentically through commitment to daily routine, rather than by blazing new trails like explorers or pioneers. But critical for authentic conversion is that it be radical.

If radical does not mean sensational, it does mean profound, and the conversion process represents the ultimate transformation of the community (and its members) in Christ. Missioners, especially, must discern the "seeds of the word" or "gospel values," or simply the presence of God, among people long before the arrival of Christian ministers. Since people are made in God's image (and what God makes is good) and are redeemed in Jesus, God's grace is not beyond the reach of any people. The call to conversion is God's invitation to a radical and explicit commitment to values of the reign of God, but God calls within particular social contexts, not only through outsiders. The normal channels of conversion are local cultures.

Both cultures and persons, however, are called to "turn," to conversion. Though culture is people's point of departure, the breaking through of God's reign into the entire world will always entail the relativization of every culture and the bending of every knee. But a radical response is not incompatible with the continuity of many cultural forms and certainly does not imply the destruction of every culture. And though there are many dramatic responses to grace, many examples of clean breaks with the past, and numerous instances of individuals standing against a group, these are not absolute criteria of conversion. The support of a community can legitimately endorse an individual's conversion and offer positive and negative sanctions to help it continue over time.

ANTHONY J. GITTINS, CSSP

Bibliography

Bynum, C., "Women's Stories, Women's Symbols: A Critique of Victor Turner's Theory of Liminality," in R. Moore and F. Reynolds, eds., *Anthropology and the Study of Religion* (1984) 105–25. Conn, W., *Christian Conversion* (1986). Conn, W. ed., *Conversion: Perspectives on Personal and Social Transformation* (1978). Costas, O., "Conversion as a Complex Experience," in J. Stott and R. Coote, eds., *Down to Earth: Studies in Christianity and Culture* (1980). Fragomeni, R., "Conversion," in M. Downey, ed., *The New Dictionary of Catholic Spirituality* (1993) 230–35. Gillespie, V. B., *The Dynamics of Religious Conversion* (1991). Griffin, E., *Turning: Reflections on the Experience of Conversion* (1982). Hefner, R. E., *Conversion to Christianity: Historical and Anthropological Perspectives on a Great Transformation* (1993). Houlden, J. L., "Conversion," in B. Metzger and M. Coogan, eds., *The Oxford Companion to the Bible* (1993) 132–34. Kasdorf, H., *Christian Conversion in Context* (1980). Nock, A. D., *Conversion: The Old and New in Religion from Alexander the Great to Augustine of Hippo* (1933). O'Rourke, D. K., *A Process Called Conversion* (1985). Rambo, L. R., "Conversion," in M. Eliade, ed., *EncRel*, vol. 4 (1987) 73–79. "Current Research on Religious Conversion," *RStR* 8 (April 1982) 146–59. Idem, *Understanding Religious Conversion* (1993). Sanneh, L., *West African Christianity* (1983). Singleton, M., "Let the People Be: Popular Religion and the Religion of the People," *PMVB* 61 (1976). Tippett, A. R., "Conversion as a Dynamic Process in Christian Mission," *Missiol* 5 (1977) 203–21.

❧ CREATION THEOLOGY AND MISSIOLOGY ❧

1. Relevance of Creation Theology for Missiology. 2. Some Important Aspects.

1. In recent missiological discussion, K. Hartenstein draws attention to the importance of creation theology for missiology — without, however, pursuing the matter in any great detail. He asserts that the first chapters of Genesis are of special relevance for the clarification of the relationship between "heathenism" and the community of Christ.

In the theology of the Middle Ages, a link was established between the creation-event and "the peoples of the world" (or "heathens"), but creation and the order of creation could not be described as "revelation" but just "teachings" — wisdom or philosophy according to Hugh of Saint-Victor (or see Aquinas, *Summa contra Gentiles* 2. 2–4).

In the writings of the early mission theorists and in the discussions and controversies after the "discovery" and evangelization of Latin America the theology of creation was quite extensively considered (by B. de Las Casas, J. Zumárraga, J. Garcés).

The Book of Genesis was very important in the theology and missiological approach of Martin Luther, who proposed that the message of the creation of all life and the goodness of God must be incorporated into the idea of mission and help to justify it. In the course of the early development of missiology, creation theology was at times referred to in passing, but its relation to missiology was not worked out in any depth (see G. Warneck; G. Grendel).

J. Blauw's missiological discussion paper (Blauw 1961) for the World Council of Churches did not confine itself to a few biblical "mission" texts but made the whole Old Testament an essential reference for mission theology. Since the Old Testament is meant for the whole world and has validity for all people, Blauw emphasizes its universal message. Taking Genesis 1–11 as a starting point, Blauw argues that from the very beginning the "peoples" were the focus of attention: God's message and action aim at universality.

Creation theology provides a unifying approach and the key to a theological interpretation of modern mission theology (→theology of mission) and its discussion about the relationship between church and world, Christianity and the religions, and, consequently, the theological status of history (→history of mission), religions, and cultures.

2. The attention of mission theology is directed to creation theology by questions of importance for the universal church and new departures in contextual and local theologies (→contextual theology). Creation theology can offer a common basis and reveal the theological direction for the mission of the church.

The theological classification of the religions (→theology of religions) and the openness of Christianity to dialogue become comprehensible in the light of creation theology. It is not the theology of redemption which provides a direct access and an appropriate theological interpretation of these questions, since essential areas of Christianity are excluded. Christian theology and the theology of evangelization — as proclamation and responsibility for the world — need creation theology in order to fully understand the message of the redemption. Creation challenges Christians and all human beings as *homines religiosi* to experience and understand themselves and all people as creatures of the common Father, sons and daughters who all have a share in the created world.

Creation theology constitutes the foundation and provides the background to the series of statements of →Vatican Council II on the religions and their relationship to Christianity and to the common questions and searchings of humanity. The assumption that all women and men constitute one community only becomes apparent from the perspective of the origin and goal of humanity as provided by salvation history. The divine will to save is universal since it corresponds to the universality of the act of creation. The order of creation and the theological statement about God as the one and all-embracing creator become the common root of the order of salvation for all. The religions also belong to this order of creation. Hence we see the urgency of taking the idea of creation as a point of departure for missiology.

The observations of the World Council of Churches about interreligious dialogue are rooted in the biblical statements on creation. The basis of the encounter with the religions is the one world created by God and the nature of humanity oriented to God. It is of vital importance for evangelization to emphasize the unity of the whole creation in the light of the Christian understanding of humankind. In order to do justice to the religions, missiology must start with the biblical understanding of humanity and creation theology.

The creation-theology approach offers a theological foundation and a religious anchoring for →development and human →liberation. An increasing emancipation and humanization of the world are in accordance with the creative will of God. A similar understanding of creation forms the background for the statements of Vatican II in *Gaudium et Spes* (*GS*). The commitment to development and liberation has its roots in the plan of creation and cannot be separated from the plan of redemption (*EN* 31). The order of creation demands solidarity with all people and provides the theological background for the statements on Christian responsibility for the world (*GS* 69). Creaturehood establishes equality among human beings and is the fundamental reason for the task and mission of the church to promote development, liberation, and justice. By the fact of being created, the economic, political, and social orders exist and are anchored in society and God (*GS* 36). The economic and political contribution of the church to modern development is expressly and repeatedly founded in creation theology. God created all of reality and women and men in God's image. Therefore, in "personhood" humanity possesses a reference point for solidarity with and responsibility to others.

It follows that the infringement of human dignity, and consequently the order of creation, is described as sin. Certain structures are sinful because they constitute a "no" to creation and to human beings. A system which sets itself against human beings — making them dependent and subjecting them to oppression — also sets itself against creation and against the will of the creator. Because of the relationship of God to humanity created in God's image, crimes against human beings are tantamount to a rejection of God and the order of creation. The "situation of injustice" is identical with the denial of the order of creation and God's saving plan.

Paul interprets the theology of creation from the perspective of the saving event in Christ (→Paul the Apostle as Missionary). The expectation of a new creation, of a new heaven and a new earth, leads to participation in solidarity with human beings living in poverty and with the misery of the whole of creation. This theology of sym-pathy with the misery of the world is understood as an element of the following of Christ. The participation in the history of Christ is expressed in the sym-pathy with suffering creation and the wretchedness of humanity. Even if the solidarity with the whole of creation is linked to Christ, it has strong roots in creation theology. This solidarity and sym-pathy are not ethical demands but a basic part of Christian praxis and Christian life.

Within the present sociopolitical context of more recent theology there is a shift from the biblical theology of the New Testament to that of the Old Testament. Creation theology constitutes the link. It is not a means of making statements about God, the world, and humankind; rather it tries to throw light on the meaning of the world and of being human. The dignity of human beings and their liberty are grounded in creation theology.

Liberation theology appeals to creation theology in connection with the exodus. It determines its image of humanity from the idea of creation, and this is necessarily linked with the "new creation." Conducting women and men to liberation, to the "new humanity," and to the "new world" is a continuation of the work of creation.

Creation theology is expressly used as the basis of the theology of the Ecumenical Association of Third World Theologians (EATWOT). Contextual theology uses the sociocultural milieu as one of its bases for theological reflection and hence also the statements on the reality of creation.

Since the beginning of creation, God has been present in the world. Creation is the first saving act on a course over which humanity is led to the new creation.

There is a tension between the teaching on creation and soteriology and also between the two concepts of the world. Distinct from a concept of the world opposed to God, a world which is to be "brought home" into the church through mission, there is the notion of the "world in the making," oriented to God by creation and redemption. This latter is a holistic worldview, an integral model, that from the very beginning interprets salvation with reference to the world. Christians' responsibility for the world and their social commitment are ethical consequences not of the faith but of life in conjunction with faith. The "salvation of the world" exists only in concrete, worldly — that is, created — reality. Even if only fragmentary and provisional, salvation reveals itself in faith and the hope for the fulfillment of the world.

Creation and →salvation (redemption) as the action of God on the world converge and unite in the incarnation of God in the world. And because God lays claim to the world as divine creation, Paul carries the message into the world. For him the "new creation" is nearly always creation as a whole. The creator's concern for the world is one of the main themes of the Gospel of Luke (F. Hahn). For Luke, as for Paul, God is the creator of the world and remains so for all eternity. The unreconciled world is the creation of God, just as the reconciled world remains the creation of God.

Nevertheless, we must admit that a duality exists in theological reflection and in the history of theology: between creation and redemption, nature and grace, necessity and freedom. But this dualistic way of thinking does not embrace the whole of reality since the contrasting concepts are embraced by a third. From the very beginning the goal of creation is the "new creation"; it is initiated in the sacrifice and resurrection of Jesus Christ. The goal of creation is not the incarnation of God, the coming of Jesus, but the reign of God, for which Jesus came; this is the "basic reason of creation" (K. Barth). Creation is not oriented to the creation of men and women as images of God but to the establishment of humanity's original purpose. Thus the incarnation is related as well to the original creation of humanity as image of God. Creation is oriented to the establishment of the original destiny of humanity with its future in a "human world community."

In the New Testament, creation or a mediating role in creation is expressly attributed to Christ (1 Cor 8:6; Col 1:16; Heb 3:4; see Jn 1:3). The Christian dimension is decisive for creation. The central unifying idea is the covenant, which is also the decisive element for creation. Creation and covenant originate in God. Creation is not a presupposition; it is a "first beginning" of salvation, and consequently there is no essential difference between covenant and creation. The creation account has a kind of "logical" priority above the rest of tradition. Both statements are internally related. Creation must be understood from the perspective of the covenant and salvation; as a consequence, the message of the saving work of Jesus must include the teaching on creation. Since Jesus Christ is the only mediator of salvation, creation as the first step of salvation must inevitably be related to Christ. Hence the new creation in Christ is not an unforeseen event but the determining and primary fact which makes creation meaningful and through which it is realized. It constitutes "the real goal of creation" (K. Rahner).

The language of religion employs two main approaches. According to one, "manifestation" is more prominent; according to the other, the emphasis is on "proclamation." This differentiation is often used to substantiate a contrast between preverbal and verbal forms of religious language (P. Ricoeur). But religious language cannot be categorized in this strict form. Each type uses the categories of the other form; that is, both forms of religious language are related. The difference between them lies in the type of human participation. The preverbal form is mediated by ritual; the verbal form gives precedence to the word, to proclamation. Creation theology establishes a relationship between both models of interpretation. Creation is not only the reality which needs mediation through symbol and word but is also the very basis of language. Here space and time are structured; here we find material for proclamation. Creation as a symbol mediates between the two forms of religious comprehension because it is present in both. Consequently creation and its theology are also important for theological mediation in missionary proclamation.

HORST RZEPKOWSKI, SVD

Bibliography

Altner, G., *Schöpfung am Abgrund* (1974). Bindermann, W., *Die Hoffnung der Schöpfung: Romer 8, 18–28 und die Frage einer Theologie der Befreiung von Mensch und Natur* (1983). Blauw, J., *Gottes Wort in dieser Welt: Grundzüge einer biblischen Theologie der Mission* (1961). Bonnard, P. L., "La sagesse en personne annoncée et venue," in *Jésus Christ* (1966) 133–44. Borges, P., *Métodos misionales en la cristianización de América siglo XVI* (1960). Bürkle, H., *Einführung in die Theologie der Religionen* (1977). Clifford, A. M., "Creation," in F. Schüssler Fiorenza and J. Galvin, eds., *Systematic Theology: Roman Catholic Perspectives* (1991) 195–248. Cloes, H., "La systématisation théologique pendant la premiére moitié du XIIe siècle," *EThL* 34 (1958) 277–329. Daly, G., *Creation and Redemption* (1989). Ganoczy, A., "Die Bedeutung des christlichen Schöpfungsglaubens für die Einheit der Menschheit," in A. Ganoczy and H.-W. Gensichen, eds., *Christliche Grundlagen des Dialogs mit den Weltreligionen* (1983) 127–50. Idem, *Der Schöpferische Mensch und die Schöpfung Gottes* (1976). Idem, "Schöpfung im Christentum — Versuch einer Neuformulierung im Hinblick auf den Dialog in der abrahamitischen Ökumene," in H. Waldenfels, ed., "...denn Ich bin bei Euch," *Perspektiven im christlichen Missionsbewußtsein heute* (1978) 351–62. Grendel, J., "Die zentrale Stellung des Missionsgedankens im ewigen Heilsplan Gottes," *ZMRW* 1 (1911) 281–93. Hall, D. J., *Professing the Faith: Christian Theology in a North American Context* (1993) 187–359. Hayes, Z., *What Are They Saying about Creation?* (1980). Lash, N., *Believing Three Ways in One God* (1992) 35–42. Moltmann, J., *God in Creation: A New Theology of Creation and the Spirit* (1985). *Monde nouveau, création nouvelle,* vol. 34/131 of *Spiritus* (May 1993). Oberg, J., "Mission und Heilsgeschichte bei Luther und in den Bekenntnisschriften," in *Lutherische Beiträge zur Missio Dei* (1982) 25–42. Perlitt, L., "Auslegung der Schrift — Auslegung der Welt," in T. Kendtorff, ed., *Europäische Theologie: Versuch einer Ortsbestimmung* (1980) 27–71. Peters, T., "God and the Continuing Creation," in *God: The World's Future* (1992) 122–39. Rahner, K., "The Order of Redemption within the Order of Creation," in

The Christian Commitment (1963) 38–74. Ricoeur, P., "Manifestation and Proclamation," *JBI* (1978) 13–21. Rosenkranz, G., *Die christliche Mission* (1977). Rzepkowski, H., "Ganzheitliches Heil — Entwicklung — Frieden," in H. Fries, F. Köster, and F. Wolfinger, eds., *Warum Mission? Theologische Motive in der Missionsgeschichte der Neuzeit: Ereignisse und Themen der Gegenwart* (1984) 223–63. Schmid, H. H., "Schöpfung, Gerechtigkeit und Heil: Schöpfungstheologie als Gesamthorizont biblischer Theologie," *ZThK* 70 (1973) 1–19. Schoonenberg, P., *Covenant and Creation* (1969). Idem, *God's World in the Making* (1967). Smart, N., and S. Konstantine, "Divine Creativity," in *Christian Systematic Theology in a World Context* (1991) 201–48. Strolz, W., "Das Schöpfungswort im Anfang (Gen 1,1–31) und das fleischgewordene Wort (Joh 1,14): Eine sprachtheologische Besinnung," in A. Ganoczy and H.-W. Gensichen, eds., *Christliche Grundlagen des Dialogs mit den Weltreligionen* (1983) 98–126. Thiel, J. F., "Die Bedeutung von Raum und Zeit als religiöse Dimensionen," *Verbum SVD* 22 (1981) 19–38. Thuren, J., "Mission und Heilsgeschichte aus biblischer Sicht," in *Lutherische Beiträge zur Missio Dei* (1982) 17–24. Tracy, D., *The Analogical Imagination: Christian Theology and the Culture of Pluralism* (1981). Tracy, D., and N. Lash, eds., *Cosmology and Theology,* vol. 166 of *Concilium* (June 1983). Trigo, P., *Creation and History* (1991). Ukpong, J. S., "Christian Mission and the Recreation of the Earth in Power and Faith: A Biblical-Christological Perspective," *MissS* 9/2/18 (1992) 134–47.

❧ CULTURE ❧

1. Concept of Culture.   2. Variety of Cultures.   3. Mission and Culture.

Missiologists need a concept of culture that possesses sufficient semantic dynamism to help in the translation of missiological reflections into missionary guidelines.

1. Despite the fact that culture exists everywhere, "culture" does not mean the same thing everywhere or for all writers. Especially in languages that distinguish between "civilization" and "culture," certain semantic differences can arise. In fact, the two terms can have very different, even contrary, meanings. In these cases, the former term refers to a more refined style of life and artistic, academic, and spiritual achievement. The latter is reserved for the more material, technological, and socially organized sphere of life.

A consideration of the original meaning of the word "culture" gives us an approximation of the meaning which is decisive for missiology. Etymologically "culture" (from the Latin *colere* = cultivate, to modify nature creatively) refers to the activity through which women and men influence the environment in which they live with their physical and spiritual powers, at least partially change it, but at the same time develop themselves as individuals and members of a community. In this way men and women establish a suitable environment for themselves which is more than mere nature. Consequently, culture can be described as an essential characteristic of human existence: where there are human beings, there is culture, because the human being is naturally a cultural being. Or again: what distinguishes human nature from all other living creatures is human culture.

2. The universal phenomenon of culture can be analyzed conceptually with reference to its diverse parts. In its living reality, culture allows an almost endless variety of possibilities of combinations, forming an amazing wealth of different individual cultures. No combination, however, reaches such perfect integration that it can ever manifest itself as an absolutely closed system which is unresponsive to internal development or external influences. All cultures are subject to continuous change, which can sometimes be rapid or sometimes extremely slow; consequently, cultures can be understood only from a dynamic and diachronic perspective. Every graduated categorization of cultures is to a certain extent problematic since it depends on the relativity and limited validity of the criteria of selection. When studies use heavily biased terms like "primitive" and "high" to refer to cultures, their comparisons of value should be avoided as meaningless and only their comparison of facts should be taken into consideration.

Our knowledge of culture is a product of research work over the last 150 years. Cultural →anthropology and sociology have made the most noteworthy professional contributions. Pioneering ideas are associated with famous names: for example, E. Tylor, R. Linton, A. L. Kroeber, and C. Kluckhohn struggled for clear definitions; and B. Malinowski and C. Lévi-Strauss developed the theories of functionalism and structuralism. There are hundreds of definitions of culture, and not one of them can claim to be exclusively correct. For most purposes, however, a general definition of culture and a summary listing of basic individual factors or greater units of composition are sufficient. For our purposes, then, we might say that culture is a system that gives meaning to life, that embraces human existence in all its dimensions, and that is learned and realized in the respective social group; or, in other words, it is the typical value-world and way of life of a jointly organized group of persons in their material and interpersonal environment. To this belong traditions, norms, language, mentality, worldview, kinship, social relationships, forms of government, types of economy, artistic achievement, technologies, science, tools, ways of feeling, attitudes, activities, behavior patterns, convictions, symbol systems, customs, and so on.

Generally speaking, there are qualitative differences in the adhesive strength of such components: around an almost irremovable core (e.g., religious traditions), there are peripheral phenomena (e.g., technology) which are more amenable to possible change. There have always been cultural contacts and conflicts, that is, contact and exchange in a positive as well as negative sense. Nevertheless, all cultures today find themselves in a more or less marked crisis situation: all are somehow confronted — because of the possibilities of global communications and transportation — with numerous aspects of a modern scientific-technological supercivilization with globally expanding tendencies and several concrete crises in consequence.

On a completely different level, namely, that of ideologies and religions, some similar worldwide movements are becoming more and more obvious. One of these is Christianity, which has been making its claim to universality for nearly two thousand years but in the meantime has only partially realized it. Consequently, a confrontation with culture and cultures is something built into Christianity as such, and the missionary as messenger of the faith to the non-Christian world expects the assistance of theologians to shed some light on the situation.

3.   Theological problems arise not only because of typically religious or other related questions (e.g., non-Christian or atheistic ideologies) but also from the global human context of those cultures where missionary activity is carried on. Sociocultural factors and various situation-determined elements of a particular milieu form the decisive background for acceptance or rejection, interpretation or transformation of the message in the evangelization process. The attentive consideration of such points influences to a great extent both the degree of effectiveness of the presentation of Christianity by the "missionizers" and the possibility of a meaningful transmission in relevant, coherent forms of expression and suitable social ways of behavior on the part of the "missionized."

Because of these obviously important missionary implications, the determination of the theological status of "culture" has to be taken very seriously. Especially in more recent times, Protestant thinkers from various churches have done pioneering and exemplary work in this field, and their discussion of culture has proved in many respects quite stimulating and fruitful. Because of diverse confessional, organizational, and regional alignments, however, the Protestant discussion has been rather convoluted and not always very consistent.

H. R. Niebuhr describes five types of relationship between Christianity and culture; in the course of church history, all these types are demonstrable, though they sometimes overlap. The five basic models are: (*a*) Christ *against* culture; (*b*) Christ *of* culture; (*c*) Christ *above* culture; (*d*) Christ and culture *in paradox;* and (*e*) Christ the *transformer* of culture. For our purposes, the terms of these typologies might be changed to better describe missionary situations. We may speak of the Christianity/culture relationship in terms of (*a*) *conflict* (because of opposing values, vigilance is necessary); (*b*) *association* (culture virtually serves as a vehicle of expansion of Christianity); (*c*) *value difference* (Christianity is far superior to the world); (*d*) *coexistence* (normally little friction, with occasional tensions); or (*e*) Christianity as *agent and changer of culture* (here, of course, there are both positive and negative possibilities of interpretation).

Generally speaking, Lutheran theology, with its deliberately sharp distinction between law and freedom, has had a large role in the formation of a Protestant understanding of culture. Consequently, culture is regarded as a situation of tension not only between Christians and non-Christians but also among Christians themselves and, by no means least, within their own hearts.

Behind such an interpretation there are different views of "culture": for example, as a counterconcept to the word of God, that is, as "world" with characteristics inimical to the faith in a Johannine sense; as a degenerate group-characteristic of a specific kind (personality cult, racism, etc.) which is in need of prophetic witness; as a social expression of hopes and ideals, especially spiritual and religious expectations; as a geographically and historically determined milieu that must be changed by Christianizing; finally, in a neutral anthropological sense, as the totality of values, habits, relationships, life patterns, and so on, in a specific group. In spite of all the criticism of the world — which indeed stands under the judgment of God but which also experiences God's love and grace — the latter-mentioned views of culture seem to be gaining currency. Missionaries who are involved in "first proclamation" especially realize the importance of intercultural contacts and attribute — regardless of the metaempirical aspect of divine activity — fitting importance to solid anthropological and sociological insights in the service of Christian evangelization. Even a glance over confessional boundaries confirms this.

Within Catholic thought, the most important formal "breakthrough" with the aid of relatively modern terminology occurred at Vatican II. A passage in *Gaudium et Spes* can be regarded as a basis and model for numerous later statements: "The word 'culture' in the general sense refers to all those things which go to refining and developing humanity's diverse mental and physical endowments. Men and women strive to subdue the earth by their knowledge and labor; they humanize social life both in the family and in the whole civic community through the improvement of customs and institutions; they express through their works the great spiritual experiences and aspirations of peoples throughout the ages; they communicate and preserve them to be an inspiration for the progress of many, even of all humanity" (*GS* 53). The historical and social dimension of culture and cultures is unmistakable in this formulation; an ethnocentrically narrow or even "aristocratic" view of culture seems to be clearly overcome, and there is no place for "cultureless" peoples anymore — a fact that is supported by other passages in the document (e.g., *GS* 58).

Ad Gentes (*AG*), the council's decree on missionary activity, also has very significant things to say about culture and about Christianity's relation to it. Here, however, we can only glance at the most important points. Topics range from the positive evaluation of the cultures (*AG* 9, 15) to the implantation of the →local church (19, 22, 40); from the training and readiness of missionaries to adapt (25–26) to the striving of the clergy and laity for the Christian encounter with cultures (16, 20–21, 34, 40–41). One of the main statements of interest to us is in paragraph 10, where we encounter not only remarkable elements of an anthropologically valid paraphrase of human society but also a decisive theological principle. The text here speaks in a sociological sense of "large and distinct groups united by enduring cultural ties, ancient religious traditions, and strong social relationships." The church must encounter them with the same incarnational dynamism with which "Christ by his incarnation committed himself to the particular social and cultural circumstances of the men among who he lived."

The 1975 apostolic exhortation *Evangelii Nuntiandi* (*EN*) is one of the most important statements of the postconciliar period in regard to the relation between Christianity and culture. The passage about the evangelization of cultures (20) expressly states that the concept of culture is used according to its comprehensive meaning in *GS* 53, that is, in the general understanding of human "culture" as well as in the various particular forms of different "cultures." The proper evangelization of culture and cultures is not a question of a decorative veneer for Christianity but a continuing process of vital dialogue between the spirit and message of the gospel and the structures and values of culture/cultures, a process which aims to reach down to a culture's very roots. The sociological aspect is also strongly emphasized in this passage: evangelization takes its starting point from the human person and advances to interpersonal relationships and the relationship with God.

Evangelii Nuntiandi 20 makes some other fundamental points. The gospel and its transmission in evangelization are not identifiable with any particular culture and remain per se conceptually and objectively independent in relation to all cultures, even if in their expression they are of necessity linked with numerous cultural phenomena. Culture is the human foundation on which, and with the help of which, evangelization is realized; although the good news may in principle seem independent from the cultures into which it is supposed to penetrate, in practice it is not irreconcilable with them. Thus cultural encounter is of crucial importance for the church in every missionary approach; the church, in consequence, must grapple with social macrostructures, with all their ideological, historical, economic, and anthropological underpinnings.

Subsequent ecclesiastical documents (e.g., Pope John Paul's 1990 encyclical *Redemptoris Missio;* the 1991 joint statement of the Pontifical Council for Interreligious Dialogue and the Congregation for the Evangelization of Peoples, *Dialogue and Proclamation;* and the 1987 statement of the International Theological Commission, *Faith and Inculturation*) take a tack similar to that of *Evangelii*

Nuntiandi. In the encounter with culture, says John Paul II, "the universal Church herself is enriched with forms of expression and values in the various sectors of Christian life, such as evangelization, worship, theology, and charitable works. She comes to know and to express better the mystery of Christ, all the while being motivated to continual renewal" (*RM* 52). It must be noted, however, that John Paul II's 1995 encyclical *Evangelium Vitae* approaches culture somewhat more critically, speaking of "the culture of death" as opposed to the "gospel of life."

EUGEN NUNNENMACHER, SVD

Bibliography

Arbuckle, G. A., *Earthing the Gospel* (1990). Bevans, S. B., *Cultural Expressions of Faith: Church Teachings and Pastoral Responses* (1993). Idem, *Models of Contextual Theology* (1992). Boer, W. de, *Das Problem des Menschen und die Kultur* (1958). Breton, S., P. Colin, and E. Dussel, *Theologié et choc des cultures* (1984). Burrows, W. R., ed., *Redemption and Dialogue: Reading "Redemptoris Missio" and "Dialogue and Proclamation"* (1994). Danckwortt, D., *Probleme der Anpassung an eine fremde Kultur* (1959). Filbeck, D., *Social Context and Proclamation* (1985). Fischer, H., *Theorie der Kultur* (1965). Gignon, O., *Die antike Kultur und das Christentum* (1966). Gittins, A. J., *Gifts and Strangers: Meeting the Challenge of Inculturation* (1989). Haas, W., *Östliches und westliches Denken* (1967). Hall, E. T., *Beyond Culture* (1976). Idem, *The Silent Language* (1959). Henke, P., *Sprache, Denken, Kultur* (1975). Hiebert, P. G., *Anthropological Insights for Missionaries* (1985). Idem, *Anthropological Reflections on Missiological Issues* (1994). Idem, *Cultural Anthropology* (1983). Inch, M. A., *Doing Theology across Cultures* (1982). Kraft, C., *Christianity in Culture* (1979). Kroeber, A. L., *The Nature of Culture* (1952). Lett, J., *The Human Enterprise* (1987). Kroeber, A. L., and C. Kluckhohn, *Culture: A Critical Review of Concepts and Definitions* (1952). Luepfert, E., *Die Einheit der Kultur* (1954). Luzbetak, L. J., *The Church and Cultures* (1988). Niebuhr, H. R., *Christ and Culture* (1951). Scherer, J. A., and S. B. Bevans, eds., *New Directions in Mission and Evangelization* 1, *Basic Statements, 1974–1991* (1992). Schreiter, R. J., *Constructing Local Theologies* (1985). Idem, "Defining Syncretism: An Interim Report," *IBMR* 17/2 (April 1993) 50–53. Idem, "Faith and Cultures: Challenges to a World Church," *TS* 50 (1989) 744–60. Idem, *The New Catholicity* (1997). Shorter, A., *Toward a Theology of Inculturation* (1988). Singer, M., "Culture," in *International Encyclopedia of the Social Sciences*, vol. 3 (1968) 527–43. Stott, J., and R. Coote, *Down to Earth: Studies in Christianity and Culture* (1981). Tillich, P., *Theology and Culture* (1959).

❧ CULTURE OF MODERNITY ❧

1. A Vital but Neglected Area of Missiology. 2. Neglect Due to Western Syncretism. 3. Unique Responsibility of Western Churches. 4. Distinctive Elements in Western Culture. 5. Necessary Elements in a Missionary Approach. 6. A Concrete Start.

1. The foreign missionary enterprise has, during the past three hundred years, been almost entirely directed from the nations of Europe and North America to the peoples of Asia, Africa, Latin America, and the Pacific. As the fruit, under God, of these missionary labors, large and rapidly growing churches have come into existence and are — in many places — shaping the development of national life. At the same time, the churches of the old Christendom are on the defensive or in decline. There are, therefore, good reasons for the view that the most urgent task facing the universal church at this time is presented by the culture which now dominates its old heartland. Three such reasons may be suggested.

1.1. The Western culture of modernity, which has developed in Europe and its cultural offshoots since the eighteenth century, has more worldwide influence than any other culture, including that of Islam. Thus, under the name of "modernization," the nations of the Third World are eager to adopt the distinctive elements of Western culture.

1.2.   Although this culture has deep Christian roots, it has rejected Christianity as public doctrine, has relegated it to the sphere of purely private opinion, and has developed powerful defenses against the thrust of the gospel. What W. Lippmann called "the acids of modernity" have proved powerful enough to dissolve ancient structures of religious belief wherever they have penetrated.

1.3.   Missions have themselves been among the primary agents of modernization in the areas where they have worked. Through schools and colleges, hospitals, technological training, and projects for "development," they have inculturated great numbers of people, especially of the Christians under their guidance, into assumptions and lifestyles of modernity.

2.   The significance of what was taking place was hidden from the eyes of Western missionaries because of the extent to which the Western churches were living in a symbiotic alliance with their culture. Christianity and "civilization" were seen as parts of one reality, and missions were seen as having a "civilizing" role in the rest of the world. Ever since the emergence of the modern worldview during the eighteenth-century Enlightenment, Christian apologists have sought to defend the Christian faith by showing that it is compatible with the new view. The effort was made to demonstrate the "reasonableness" of Christianity. There was no effective move to bring the "reason" which dictated the parameters for religion under the scrutiny of the gospel. The missionaries sent out from the Western churches thus took with them a message which was already syncretistic, an amalgam of Christian and modern elements in which the absolute supremacy and decisiveness of Christ were not adequately secured. Insofar as the churches of the Third World are deeply committed to and involved in the process of modernization, there is no reason for thinking that they will be exempt from the corrosive power which it has exercised with such devastating results in the churches of the old Christendom.

Missionaries and missiologists have been much exercised during recent decades with questions concerning the relation of the gospel to the variety of human cultures, questions which are discussed under such titles as "indigenization" and "contextualization" (→contextual theology; inculturation). Unfortunately, these discussions have been almost entirely concerned with the impact of missions from churches culturally embedded in the West to the peoples of the East and South. Missiologists have been alert to the dangers of syncretism which arise when the gospel is communicated in the language and idiom of a people nurtured in a non-Christian worldview. They have generally failed to recognize the extent to which Christianity has been so deeply involved in modern culture that it has been unable to stand over against it where dissent is required.

3.   It is now widely accepted that missions in the modern world must be multidirectional, that every church has a responsibility for world mission, and that there is a mission field in every land. Churches in the old Christendom, struggling against the apathy or hostility of their cultures, have been refreshed and encouraged by the witness of missionaries from the vigorously growing churches of the Third World. But such missionaries are inevitably those who have been given a long general and theological training in a European language and in institutions modeled on the educational system of the West and North. It is as difficult for them as it is for native Europeans to find a stance from which "modern" culture can be critically assessed, because they are already part of that culture. The major responsibility for initiating a critical dialogue with, and a missionary approach to, Western culture has to be taken by the churches which are part of that culture.

4. The most distinctive feature of modern culture is its sharp division of human affairs into a public world of "facts" and a private world of "values." The former is the world of public doctrine. It determines what may and what may not be taught in the state schools and universities. The latter is the world of free personal choice. "Religious freedom" means the freedom of each to have "a faith of one's own," because "faith" does not refer to any objective reality which might govern public doctrine. Within this framework, Christian churches are free to develop and enlarge their membership. Under certain conditions, they do so. But they are, and increasingly are seen to be, marginal in the life of society.

Within this radically bifurcated culture, the area of science and technology provides the main dynamic for public life. The area which is concerned with "values" tends increasingly to degenerate into subjectivism and relativism. The claim for human autonomy over against the claims of religious tradition has led to the erosion of belief that there can be objective reality in a moral order. The program of systematic doubt generally associated with the name of Descartes proves increasingly self-destructive since the enterprise of doubt itself depends upon presuppositions which are not doubted. The resulting situation has been summarized by the Chinese writer Carver T. Yu in the phrase "technological optimism and literary despair." There are many signs of a tendency to abandon the Western tradition in favor of an Eastern type of monism as represented in such phenomena as the New Age movement.

5. A missionary approach to modernity has to include at least the following four elements. First, there must be an effort to examine and analyze the assumptions which underlie current theory and practice in the different sectors of public life, this analysis to be done in the conceptual framework provided by the Bible. This, it would seem, is best done by inviting people who are committed Christians and who are highly competent in the several fields of public life to work in their particular fields along with theologians and biblical scholars. This can be expected to lead into a program of publication challenging the other practitioners in these fields to take seriously the critical questions which are put to them in the light of the gospel.

Second, theologians and biblical scholars need to clarify the nature of the authority of the gospel. This involves taking up the familiar questions of the role of scripture, tradition, reason, and experience in authorizing the Christian proclamation (→theology of mission). In particular, there is an urgent need for a fresh effort to overcome the disastrous split between "conservatives" and "liberals" in the interpretation of scripture and to inquire how far this split is merely one manifestation of the more fundamental split in modern culture between the public world of facts and the private world of values.

Third, there is a need at the same time to raise these questions at other levels — at the level of ministerial training, of pastoral ministry, and of popular reading and discussion in congregations.

Fourth, there is a need for the development of a program for training a new type of missionary who can exercise leadership in the enterprise as a whole.

6. A modest attempt is being made by the British Council of Churches to address the problem of mission to Western culture. Following the very widespread publication and discussion of a booklet entitled *The Other Side of 1984: Questions to the Churches* (1983), a program was initiated under the title "The Gospel and Our Culture." Seminars have been established dealing with the following issues: the authority of the gospel, epistemology, history, science, economics, education, health and healing, the media, and the arts. A program of publications is under way, and a program of study and discussion for use in congregations is being published entitled "Another Way of Looking at Things." A quarterly newsletter is circulated, and corresponding groups are at work in North America, Australia, and New Zealand.

LESSLIE NEWBIGIN

Bibliography

Bosch, D. J., *Believing in the Future: Toward a Missiology of Western Culture* (1995). Brown, G., et al., "Selected Annotated Bibliography on Missiology: The Gospel and Our North American Culture," *Missiol* 19/4 (October 1991) 495–98. Burnham, F. B., ed., *Postmodern Theology: Christian Faith in a Pluralist World* (1989). Dulles, A., "Catholicism and American Culture: The Uneasy Dialogue," *America* 162/3 (January 27, 1990) 54–59. George, F., "Evangelizing American Culture," in K. Boyak, ed., *The New Catholic Evangelization* (1992) 42–55. Hauerwas, S., and W. H. Willimon, *Resident Aliens* (1989). Hunsberger, G. R., ed., *The Gospel and Our Culture*, special issue of *Missiol* 19/4 (October 1991). Hunsberger, G. R., and C. van Gelder, eds., *The Church between Gospel and Culture: The Emerging Mission in North America* (1996). Newbigin, J. E. L., *Foolishness to the Greeks* (1988). Idem, *The Gospel in a Pluralist Society* (1989). Idem, *The Other Side of 1984* (1983). Shenk, W. R., "Missionary Encounter with Culture," *IBMR* 15/3 (July 1991) 104–9. Idem, *Write the Vision: The Church Renewed* (1995). Taber, C. R., "God vs. Idols: A Model of Conversion," *JAEv* 3 (1988) 20–32. Tamney, J. B., *The Resilience of Christianity in the Modern World* (1992). Van Engen, C., "Evangelism in the North American Context," *JAEv* 4 (1989) 45–55. Yu, C. T., *Being and Relation: A Theological Critique of Western Dualism and Individualism* (1987).

D

❧ DEVELOPMENT ❧

1. Concept. 2. Theories. 3. Goals. 4. Development Thought in and Action by the Churches. 5. Development and Mission. 6. Theology of Development? 7. The International Debt Crisis.

1. Development is a normative concept with a relative meaning in practice. Broadly, it denotes desired social and economic progress — and opinions will always differ on what is desired. Development is thus not static but depends on the given values prevailing in a certain time and place. Like the social, economic, and cultural conditions to which it refers, this concept is subject to constant change.

Since the end of the eighteenth century, the word has designated the development of individuals, groups, peoples, and societies. M. Weber placed the development of human beings in the context of culture, religion, and economy, seeing the development of rational, economic ways of life as being determined by the respective religion. In 1912, J. A. Schumpeter defined as "development" any innovative technological phenomenon breaking the capitalist "cycle" and initiating a new process. In 1940, C. Clark spoke of progress as the road to prosperity, a road the poor countries had to take through industrialization. Since about 1950, development has been the economic and cultural gauge of the civilization, capitalization, and industrialization of former colonies, when they followed the pattern of European and North American society. This restrictive interpretation has made the concept of development increasingly questionable since the 1960s, when it began to be doubted whether the course taken by some societies should be normative for others. Third World representatives have spoken of "alternative development," denoting the recourse of each culture and society to its own traditions, which once were labeled "underdeveloped." The refusal to adopt Western models uncritically has initiated — or strengthened — intellectual and political decolonization. Less Western, more person-centered development stresses "human" development as the goal of economic growth. J. Nyerere, for example, claims that people cannot "be developed" but can only develop themselves. Pyramids, even highways, can be built on command; agricultural and industrial production can be raised at will. None of this, however, necessarily leads to the development of human beings. Humanity and self-reliance are interrelated and point to the ambivalence of economic growth as the essence of development.

2. Today there are two groups of relatively incompatible development theories. The first is a group of modernization theories that accepts the development paradigms of Western capitalist societies. Under such visions, the underdeveloped countries are said to be backward, needing to "catch up" in the phases of transition from tradition to modernity in order to become economically competitive (see W. W. Rostow). Institutions are set up to suit an industrialized, urban infrastructure; the urban middle classes are fostered as the prime representatives of a modern way of life. Traditional arrangements and economic sectors have to recede. This leads to the infrastructure of a society with a compulsion to modernize. The modernization theories also include the "dualism" theory, according to which an underdeveloped, feudal, and "precapitalist" sector, with a largely subsistence economy, contrasts with a developed sector, with capitalist means of production. Economic prosperity is supposed to "trickle down" into the underdeveloped regions. The basic inter-dependence between the sectors in respect of labor and movement of goods is disregarded. The "Alliance for Progress," founded in 1962 by J. F. Kennedy, pro-moted modernization in Latin America through *desarrollismo,* the ideology of rapid economic growth. An industrial upturn through entrepreneurial initiative by indigenous interests is supposed to speed up autonomous development and gradually replace foreign interests. *Desarrollismo* has failed in both the democra-cies and the totalitarian regimes of Latin America. The result has been increasing marginalization and oppression of more and more of the population.

The second group of theories criticizes modern imperialism and the dependency that grew from it. These theories arose in the mid-1960s in reaction to the modern-ization theories. They claim that underdevelopment is not an earlier stage in the history of Third World countries and refute the notion that such countries are on the "periphery" or are "satellites" of dominant industrialized states (the supposed "centers" or "metropolises") (see A. G. Frank). J. Galtung's theory of "structural imperialism" points out the structural violence between the center and the pe-riphery. The countries of the South that are rich in raw materials are exploited by the industrialized centers of the North. In the Third World countries there are "subcenters" in the cities and agglomerations — also called "development islands" (Strahm 1985, 27) — which favor industrialization at the expense of the rural pe-riphery and dominate the respective society by their access to communications and Western culture. The hinterland supplies the city with cheap labor and raw materials; country dwellers have to buy expensive goods from the cities. Margin-alization is the negative consequence of this "structural heterogeneity" typical of peripheral capitalism in the Third World: the mass of the population has to do without political participation, just payment, and security. Casual work, day labor, and sheer struggle for survival are the result. This process leads to national disin-tegration. Some Third World countries (e.g., China) have responded to structural dependence with "dissociation," that is, with delinkage in selected areas of the economy (see D. Senghaas). As far as possible, these countries try to set up an in-ternal market for low-cost consumer goods, particularly for staple foods. Relations with industrialized countries are maintained only if they serve the self-sufficiency of the internal economy.

3. Because of increasing hunger and growing mass poverty in the Third World, it is undisputed that development must start with satisfying basic material needs — for food, clothing, and housing. Otherwise there is no point in fulfilling social needs: education, social security, meaningful work, a healthy environment, cul-tural identity, and political participation. Several groups and institutions have proposed this strategy of basic-needs as a critique of the ideology of rapid economic growth, a policy which has only deepened the material hardship of the poorest of the poor. The basic-needs strategy was raised by the Cocoyo (Mexico) declaration of the 1974 United Nations Conference on Trade and Development (UNCTAD); the United Nations Environment Programme (UNEP); the 1975 report "What Now" by the Dag Hammarskjöld Foundation (in Sweden); the proposal "Catastrophe or New Society" put forward in 1975 by the Bariloch Foundation, an Argentinean group that confronts the Club of Rome's "limits to growth" with "limits to misery";

and, finally, the action program Employment, Growth and Basic Needs adopted by the World Employment Conference in 1976. The Cocoyo declaration stated that a growth process that served only to widen the gap between and within countries was not development but exploitation.

The discussion of basic-needs objectives must include the causes of poverty, hunger, and mass starvation. A distinction between short- and long-term goals would too easily conceal the fact that mass death will continue unabated unless the root causes are tackled. Only socially just structures based on equality in political decision making will enable a country to satisfy the material and social basic needs of its population in a lasting way. Growth, work, equality/justice, participation, and independence are all interrelated. There is no growth unless the poor have been given work, allowed their fair share of affluence, and enabled to contribute to the country's independence. Both UNCTAD (founded in 1964) and the World Bank's "Pearson Report" of 1969 described the means to this end and called on the industrialized countries to abolish discrimination against the Third World in international trade. The report urges the industrialized nations (a) to adapt commodity prices to those of industrial products and thus improve the terms of trade; (b) to help reduce the debt burden by loans on favorable terms; and (c) to raise public aid to 0.7 percent of the GNP.

In 1983, UNCTAD IV in Belgrade did not succeed in convincing the creditor countries to remit the overall debt (in 1984, $895 million) or to pay compensation for loss of export earnings from raw materials. The Group of 77 (now 130 developing countries, constituted in 1967) has not managed to achieve fixed prices and guarantees for commodities, which would reduce the dominant influence of large transnational companies on the commodity markets. The Lomé agreements between the European Community and the ACP states are also designed to promote this end, although it is arguable whether they actually do enhance the economic equality of the sixty-five signatory states from Africa, the Caribbean, and the Pacific. There is little hope of a "new international economic order" while the industrialized countries still put pressure on the Third World: 26 percent of the world's population accounts for 78 percent of production, 81 percent of energy consumption, 70 percent of use of chemical fertilizer, and 87 percent of arms spending. Three-quarters of humankind are left with one-fifth of production and natural resources.

4. In the mid-1960s both the Catholic and the Protestant churches declared their rejection of the strategy of catching up in economic terms, focusing on striving for justice in their thinking, developmental education, and practical assistance ("helping them to help themselves"). The Roman Catholic Church contributed to this with *Gaudium et Spes (GS)* of Vatican II (1965) and with the encyclical *Populorum Progressio* (On the Progress of Peoples [1967]). The Second Latin American Bishops' Conference in Medellín, Colombia, in 1968 also opened the eyes of the churches to the ecclesiological consequences of the struggle for justice. The church as the new people of God changes and takes on the form of a base community when it witnesses to the unity of the history of salvation and humanity, thus centering its proclamation on the yearning of the poor for liberation. At the World Conference for Church and Society in 1966 and at the fourth assembly of the →World Council of Churches (WCC) in Uppsala in 1968, the phrase "responsible society," coined in Amsterdam in 1948, was taken up, and focus was on justice as such a society's constitutive element. Uppsala called on the churches to allocate 5 percent of their budgets for development. The papal commission Justitia et Pax and the WCC in 1967 founded a committee called Society, Development, and Peace (SODEPAX), which held a conference in Beirut in 1968, taking up the calls of Third World countries to open up the world market to (semi-)finished products. The conference called for the just distribution of talents, resources, and wealth as the practical sign of human love. Through the Commission on the Churches' Participation in Development (CCPD), founded in 1970, the WCC tries to promote the initiatives of the rural poor: day laborers, landless laborers, migrant workers in Africa, campesinos in Latin America, and untouchables in India. At the first WCC development conference in Montreux, Switzerland, in 1970, Indian economist S. Parmar named three interdependent conditions for development from below: self-reliance of those involved; social justice in respect to work, property, education, and political participation; and economic growth to raise the standard of living of the poorest, with justice taking priority. All of this also had an impact on relations between northern and southern churches. The newly gained independence of many Third World churches was radicalized at the Bangkok World Mission Conference in 1973 into a call for a moratorium on the sending of missionaries and financial aid from the West. Churches in the South wanted to gain a wholeness through being both receivers and givers, thereby spiritually strengthening ecumenical relations — "so that money is no longer the only axis around which mission turns" (J. Gatu). While the moratorium did not materialize, it made the rich churches rethink their interchurch relations. For the Third World churches and their societies it is important that the rich churches and countries "get off their backs," leaving them the right to define who they are and where they want to go, without being told by anyone else (Cox 1970). At the second WCC development conference in Montreux in 1974 the Argentinean theologian J. Míguez Bonino claimed that church life worldwide depended on the church's taking sides. The church had to be the church of the poor, or it was risking its very nature. Since Montreux II the struggle of the poor for →liberation from oppression has been the new name for development and has become an integral part of ecumenical ecclesiology. The Western churches are thus no longer asked what they can do for the poor but whether they are participating in the struggle of the poor. At the fifth assembly of the WCC in Nairobi in 1975 the Indian theologian M. M. Thomas stated that a holistic "spirituality of struggle" was essential to the unity of the church and humankind. Nairobi's call for a "just, participatory and sustainable society" was an attempt to give the member churches social-ethical criteria for assessing power in their societies — particularly in view of new technological potential — and calling it to account. The sixth WCC assembly in Vancouver in 1983 integrated justice into an ecumenical covenant for "justice, peace and the integrity of creation," which is also meant to help overcome the division between theology and development ethics. South African theologian A. Boesak deplored this division: "We have not yet understood that every act of inhumanity, every unjust law, every untimely death, every utterance of faith in weapons of mass destruction, every justification of violence and oppression is a sacrifice on the altar of the false Gods of death; it is a denial of the Lord of life." A genuine theological contribution to this has been made by the CCPD in its attempts to study the social consequences of transnational corporations in low-wage countries and to take the side of the victims.

In Germany, Catholic and Protestant churches have participated in the fight against hunger, poverty, and injustice since 1959 through their relief agencies Misereor and Brot für die Welt (Bread for the World), as well as through their state-aided special agencies. These assist rural cooperatives, contributing to emancipation from feudal dependence, and other self-help initiatives of indigenous populations. It may well be asked to what extent Western churches show their Third World partners the trust appropriate between sisters and brothers and extend ecumenical sharing to decision-making processes. In synodal decisions between 1968 and 1975, and particularly in the 1973 Protestant memorandum on church development services, there was a call for decisive political, economic, and structural measures to be taken in the industrialized countries. The Joint Development Policy Congress in 1979 and the joint declarations of UNCTAD reflect their concern for "the social question of our century" (declaration of the third UNCTAD conference in 1972).

5. Just as mission cannot remain an empirical "sending" event subject to unhistorical and uncritical human initiative, development and church development services cannot serve a blind, technocratic belief in progress. The mission command of Mt 28:18–20 corrects both; "go" and "therefore" cannot be separated. The spirit of the going is the "crucified spirit" which eschews both the progressive solutions and the institutionalized *missio gloriae*. The manner of going is defined by the spirit of the One who suffers for the world, with and through it, because he suffers it uniquely. The centers of mission and development are the places on the fringe, the sides of the road where he suffered and showed compassion, the inconspicuous places where he calls on the disciples to stop. He gave new life to the people on the fringe and rose up against the deaths they died there. If only the "go" counts, the spirit of Christian mission becomes a spirit against the spirit of Christ (K. Koyama). Sending out and changing, developing and shaping in his spirit mean accepting our history as Jesus Christ does (Rom 5:8). Christ's saving act is directly related to the world, and this is fundamental to both development and mission. In him is manifest God's standing by humanity as a whole and the whole person (Jn 3:16); in him salvation and healing, reconciliation and liberation are inseparable. In the person and work of Jesus, God proclaims sovereignty over the whole of life and not just over a religious sector of it. Likewise, the church is concerned with all areas of life: and so it is not the church development services that bring salvation but the reverse. Israel was freed from Egypt; Jesus came to save the world; and so it is salvation that sets the church moving. The church witnesses to the love and justice of God inherent in this salvation in its liberating action no less than in its word of intercession and solidarity, thus giving a holistic account of the burning hope of the coming kingdom. Church development services will thus be wary of idealizing the powers-that-be in the world. Church mission will thus not identify the Western civilization process with Christ's saving act, as occurred during colonial times. If God's workings are not confined to the church and God's rule is understood universally, then signs of the coming kingdom and symbols of God's spirit will be sighted in times and places still closed to Christianity. God will regain the once good creation, and where this happens it is not persons, missions, and development agencies but God alone who promises the despised and downtrodden that they will break their boundaries "to the right and to the left" (Is 54:3). The 1980 World Mission Conference in Melbourne called the rich churches to repent: "The crucified and risen Christ is a judge of shallow lifestyles and invites the churches to repentance and new life.... Judgment must begin at the household of God." The salvation the church offers is judged by its concern for the welfare of the poor. Anyone seeking separation from the poor is cut off from salvation in Christ.

6. It is difficult to interpret development theologically not only because of the ambiguity of the term, its association with growth theory, and its process character but also because of all kinds of misleading theological legitimation of development processes by those in power at a given time. "Peace," "social justice" (S. Parmar), and "liberation" (J. Míguez Bonino) are policy-related, contextual synonyms for development and are also conditions for it. While they are more accessible to theological interpretation than development, they do not leave the field of concepts. For the people affected by structural dependence and underdevelopment, it is essential to know who is legitimizing which concept and why. The truth of spoken words will become clear only in their political and economic forms. Grassroots groups and community initiatives in Asia, members of the ecumenical network of the Urban Industrial Mission, saw, in 1973, the concept of "development" abused by political leaders who trampled on the human rights of the poorest classes. For these groups, development became a synonym for the idols of "national security," idols to which thousands of people were sacrificed on the pretext of an alleged external threat. Churches and theologians in Asia have replaced a "theology of development" with a "theology of the people of God" in order to express the fact that the dispossessed — small farmers without land, fishermen without water, workers without wages, families without housing — bear God's promise and are active in a just development. Only a development which accepts them as "God's favorites" (C. Avila) is worthy of the name and prepares the way toward understanding divine election (1 Cor 1:27–28). This does not mean identifying "the people" (→"people" [*Volk*], "nation") and "the people of God" with each other; this would ideologize the suffering people and subjugate them again to the interests of certain power groups. The "people of God" is, above all, the movement of those who follow Christ, see the "signs of the times" (Mt 16:3; Lk 19:42), and confront their societies with the truth which disarms all powers and which can stand before God and God's judgment. Then a society will not remain apathetic and content with "development projects" which are an alibi of the powerful for unjust conditions. Then the rich will be freed from godless bonds and the stultifying captivity of Mammon and will look to a future which God holds ready for them (M. M. Thomas). A Christianity concerned with unity will not overlook the rift in its own body due to the division into powerful and powerless, rich and poor. Indeed, its unity will not be restored until it is accountable to God in its ecclesiological form and as the "people of God" (Lv 26:12; Is 55:3–5) recognizes the reasons for this rift, changes its own structures, and works for the transformation of the world economy. A "theology of the people of God" can contribute constructively to the unity of humankind and the church if it questions the social form of the church and relates it to its responsibility for a sustainable community worldwide (see U. Duchrow).

7. The churches began to be aware of the international debt crisis in the 1980s. In 1988 the external debt of Third World countries was 1.2 billion dollars. They find it hard enough to pay the interest, let alone the principal, as debt servicing can constitute 46 to 60 percent of annual export earnings. In the case of Ghana, for example, interest payments in 1987 were 57 percent of such earnings. The papal commission Justitia et Pax and the CCPD have perceived the ambivalence of church aid if the churches do not take a clear stand on the growing pauperization of the Third World caused by the debt crisis. They presuppose that the latter is not a purely practical or technical problem to be left to the credit institutions: private banks, the IMF, and the World Bank. Ultimately the experts cannot cope, hence the churches' view that the debt problem is fundamental to human survival and international justice. It can be resolved only through debt remission by the industrialized countries in a common spirit of solidarity.

The churches have publicly declared their advocacy for the victims of the debt crisis (the CCPD/WCC in November 1984 and the Vatican in January 1987). With their institutional weight and their influence on development policy, the churches are now called upon to create a hearing for criticism of the Western development model of rapid growth at the expense of the Third World and its raw materials. They will have to contribute to the construction of an alternative development paradigm based on justice and self-reliance. Otherwise, it would be farcical to go on giving aid.

In a study on Jesus' driving the money changers out of the temple (Mk 11:15–19), Philippine theologian F. Cariño uses the term "thieves" for companies that make money for its own sake, without regard for the basic needs of people. He adds: "We are literally being bled to death by this debt burden and the economic system and powers that control and run today's economic machinery." Referring to Martin Luther's catechism, he makes it a faith issue: "Your God is where your heart is. Those who possess wealth at the expense of others commit, in this sense, a crime not only against humanity but also against God. Their wealth has become their God, and they worship Mammon and no longer the God and Father of our Lord Jesus Christ."

Wolfgang Gern

Bibliography

Agbasiere, J. T., and B. Zabajungu, eds., *Church Contribution to Integral Development,* African Theology in Progress 2 (1989). Blaser, K., "Die erste Barmer These im aktuellen theologischen Kontext," in *Barmen und die Ökumene* (1984) 5–18. Bosch, D. J., *Transforming Mission: Paradigm Shifts in Theology of Mission* (1991) 432–47. Brandt Commission, *Common Crisis, North-South: Co-operation for World Recovery* (1983). Idem, *North-South: A Program for Survival* (1980). Cariño, F., *The Sacrifice of the Innocent: Themes on Christian Participation in the Philippine Struggle* (1984). Idem, *Theology, Modernization and Ideological Politics* (1974). CELAM, *The Church in the Present-day Transformation of Latin America in the Light of the Council: Second General Conference of Latin American Bishops* (1970). Christian Conference of Asia, *Report of an Asian Ecumenical Consultation on Development, Priorities and Guidelines* (1974). Club of Rome, *Reshaping the International Order* (RIO Report) (1976). Conference on Society, Development, and Peace, *World Development: Challenge to the Churches* (1969). Cordova, A., *Strukturelle Heterogenität und wirtschaftliches Wachstum* (1973). Cordova-Michelena, H. S., *Die wirtschaftliche Struktur Lateinamerikas* (1979). Cox, H. G., "Barbie Doll and the Spectre of Cultural Imperialism," *ChrC* 27/4 (1970) 81–82. Dams, T., ed., *Entwicklungshilfe — Hilfe zur Unterentwicklung?* (1974). Datta, A., *Ursachen der Unterentwicklung* (1982). Dejung, K. H., *Der Entwicklungsdienst der Kirche — ein Beitrag für Frieden und Gerechtigkeit in der Welt,* Denkschrift der EKD-Kammer für Kirchl. Entwicklungsdienst (1973). Idem, *Die ökumenische Bewegung im Entwicklungskonflikt 1910–1968* (1973). Dhavamony, M., ed., *Evangelization, Dialogue, and Development* (1972). Dickinson, R. D. N., "Entwicklung in ökumenischer Sicht," Texte zum kirchlichen Entwicklungsdienst 12 (1975). Idem, *Poor, yet Making Many Rich: The Poor as Agents of Creative Justice* (1983). Idem, *Richtschnur und Waage* (1968). Duchrow, U., "EKD und kirchliche Entwicklungsdienst," *Epd-Dokumentation* 9 (1973). Idem, *Entwicklung-Gerechtigkeit-Frieden, Kongreß der Kirchen in*

Bonn 1979 (1979). Idem, *Weltwirtschaft heute — ein Feld für Bekennende Kirche?* (1986). Eagleson, J., and P. Scharper, eds., *Puebla and Beyond* (1979). Eppler, E., *Wenig Zeit für die Dritte Welt* (1971). Erler, B., "Ermutigung zum Leben: Kirchliche Hilfe in der Dritten Welt," *EPD-Dokumentation* 17 (1977). Idem, *Tödliche Hilfe* (1985). Fanon, F., *The Wretched of the Earth* (1976 [1961]). Ferré, F., and R. H. Mataragnon, eds., *God and Global Justice: Religion and Poverty in an Unequal World* (1985). Frank, A. G., "Für eine mit den Armen solidarische Kirche," *EPD-Dokumentation* 25a (1980). Idem, *Kapitalismus und Unterentwicklung in Lateinamerika* (1969). Galtung, J., *Strukturelle Gewalt* (1975). Gensichen, H. W., *Mission und Kultur* (1985). Gern, W., "Dritte Welt," *EKL* 1:923–41. *Global 2000: Der Bericht Präsidenten* (1980). Gollwitzer, H., "Grundlagen einer gerechten, partizipatorischen und verantwortbaren Gesellschaft: Vorlage der ÖRK-Zentralausschusssitzung in Jamaica 1979," *Epd-Dokumentation* 7 (1979) 35–54. "Die Weltverantwortung der Kirche in einem revolutionären Zeitalter," in *Die Zukunft der Kirche und die Zukunft der Welt: Die Synode der EKD 1968* (1968) 69–96. Goodall, N., ed., *The Uppsala Report* (1968). Gremillion, J., ed., *The Gospel of Peace and Justice: Catholic Social Teaching since Pope John* (1976). Guitard, O., *Bandoung et le réveil des peuples colonisés* (1961). Gutiérrez, G., *A Theology of Liberation*, rev. ed. (1988). Herrera, A. O., et al., *Grenzen des Elends: Das Bariloche-Modell: So kann die Menschheit überleben* (1977). Horowitz, I. L., *Three Worlds of Development: The Theory and Practice of International Stratification* (1966). Hürni, B., *Der Beitrag des Ökumenischen Rates der Kirchen zur Entwicklungshilfe* (1973). Illich, I., *The Church: Change and Development* (1970). Idem, *Retooling Society* (1973). Jonas, R., and M. Tietzel, eds., *Die Neuordnung der Weltwirtschaft* (1976). Koyama, K., *No Handle on the Cross: An Asian Meditation on the Crucified Mind* (1977). Kunst, H., and H. Tenhumberg, eds., *Leere Hände: Eine Herausforderung für die Kirchen: Arbeitsheft zum ökumenischen Austausch von Ressourcen* (1980). Idem, *Soziale Gerechtigkeit und internationale Wirtschaftsordnung* (1976). Lindquist, M., *Economic Growth and the Quality of Life: An Analysis of the Debate within the World Council of Churches, 1966–1974* (1975). McDonagh, S., *Passion for the Earth* (1994). Meadows, D. H., *The Limits to Growth* (1972). Müller, K., *Mission Theology: An Introduction* (1987) 126–41, 184–88. Myrdal, G., *Against the Stream: Critical Essays on Economics* (1973). Idem, *Asian Drama: An Inquiry into the Poverty of Nations* (1968). Idem, *The Political Element in the Development of Economic Theory* (1990). Nohlen, D., and F. Nuscheler, eds., *Handbuch der Dritten Welt*, 8 vols. (1982–83). Nürnberger, K., *Die Relevanz des Wortes im Entwicklungsprozeß* (1982). Nyerere, J., *Freedom and Development* (1974). Idem, *Man and Development* (1974). O'Brien, D. J., and T. A. Shannon, eds., *Catholic Social Thought: The Documentary Heritage* (1992). Potter, P., ed., *Das Heil der Welt Heute* (1973). Prebisch, R., *Hacia un dinámica del desarrollo latinoamericano* (1963). Rossel, J., "Teilen in der ökumenischen Gemeinschaft," *Texte zum kirchlichen Entwicklungsdienst* 32 (1983). Rostow, W. W., *The Stages of Economic Growth* (1960). Rudersdorf, K. H., *Das Entwicklungskonzept des Weltkirchenrates* (1975). Santa Ana, J. de, *Good News for the Poor: The Challenge of the Poor in the History of the Church* (1979). Schober, T., et al., eds., *Ökumene — Gemeinschaft einer dienenden Kirche* (1983). Schumpeter, J. A., *Theorie der wirschaftlichen Entwicklung* (1912). Senghaas, D., *Weltwirtschaftsordnung und Entwicklungspolitik: Plädoyer für Dissoziation* (1977). *SODEPAX: In Search of a Theology of Development: A SODEPAX-Report* (1969). Song, C. S., *The Tears of Lady Meng: A Parable of People's Political Theology* (1982). Spae, J. J., "SODEPAX: An Ecumenical and Experimental Approach to World Needs," *ER* 26/1 (1974) 88–99. Steidlmeier, P., *The Paradox of Poverty: A Reappraisal of Economic Development* (1987). Strahm, R. H., *Warum sie so arm sind* (1985). Thimme, H., and W. Wöste, eds., *Im Dienst für Entwicklung und Frieden* (1982). Wöhlcke, M., *Die neuere entwicklungstheoretische Diskussion* (1977). World Conference on Mission and Evangelism, Melbourne, 1980, "Your Kingdom Come," in J. A. Scherer and S. B. Bevans, eds., *New Directions in Mission and Evangelization*, vol. 1, *Basic Statements 1974–1991* (1992) 27–35. World Council of Churches, Central Committee, *Nairobi to Vancouver, 1975–1983* (1983).

❧ DIALOGUE ❧

1. Clarifications. 2. Reasons for Dialogue. 3. Challenges. 4. Obstacles.

1. Interfaith dialogue is a mutual opening of persons to each other, arising from the desire to learn from another faith and to be enriched by it. Dialogue of this kind must be differentiated from testimony to the convictions which an individual or a community adheres to in faith. Dialogue and witness are not mutually exclusive, however; both are necessary for the fullness of life of a religious community. Because neither side can abandon its testimony, dialogue becomes a kind of reciprocal testimony, in which a phase of "witnessing" or proclamation alternates with a phase of respectful listening. Such fearless giving up of oneself is possible for those who feel that witnessing to the true light does not presuppose that darkness must reign everywhere else, and who therefore do not exclude the possibility that "God" — in theistic terms — has left signs pointing to the divine outside the area of the positive revelation of the single traditions (Christianity, Judaism, and Islam, for example). It is significant that in Islam the verses of the Qur'an are called "signs" (*ayat*). This indicates their relationship to other signs that God places "outside" the Qur'an for the believer to remember God by. Such testimony includes repeated moments for the partners in dialogue to give themselves up to God, especially when God meets them in the form of a testimony which is normally expressed in a form excluded by their own community of faith. And, although we use here the language of theistic traditions in referring to "God" as the ground of religious experience, it is important to remember that many follow nontheistic traditions, yet find in dialogue that there is much to converse with others (including theists) about. Dialogue brings together the entire history of reciprocal relationships of two faith communities. Kenneth Cragg describes such an experience with the image of taking off one's Christian shoes in front of a mosque, so that one can go inside to let oneself become a Muslim for a time. (The title of one of Cragg's books is *Sandals at the Mosque: Christian Presence amid Islam.*)

2. The motives for dialogue are multiple. First, dialogue helps dissolve centuries-old misunderstandings and polemical clichés. It brings to light true similarities and authentic differences which unite and divide the two communities. Dialogue promotes real understanding.

Second, dialogue serves to improve relationships between people. Dialogue puts a stop to all who misuse →religion in order to justify large or small wars, the causes of which have nothing to do with the core of a given religious tradition. Dialogue refines our perception of →God, who does not desire such conflicts, and unmasks those who hide their own motives for conflict behind what they allege to be divine authorization.

Third, dialogue frees people from fear of one another. The person who dialogues dares to enter into strange territory and discovers others in their humanity. Dialogue can break the vicious circle of fear and siege mentality. It encourages people not to put up with a religiously polarized world. Through dialogue one sees the practicability of working together with those of other faiths in humanitarian, economic, political, intellectual, and spiritual matters.

In the fourth place, dialogue can contribute to the deepening of one's own faith. "The word of my Muslim brother can become for me the Word of God" (H. Tessier). Someone of another faith can become an icon through which "my" God comes to me in a strange form and so leads my faith to its full potential. The "lights" from outside, then, belong to the "light" which I know from "my" revelation. Karl Barth says in *CD* IV/3.2 (see pp. 779–80) that it is not only permissible for the church to seek Christ outside itself, but a duty which, when one fulfills it, frees one from provincialism and the danger of obduracy.

Finally, whenever dialogue brings believers nearer to each other, they become the authors of unity, because believers are the firstborn of a world which should become as much a unity in the last things (Omega) as it was in the first things (Alpha).

3. The challenges of dialogue are both real and diverse, and they should not be underestimated. Anyone who lives in today's world, which is characterized by the interpenetration of different social groups, first of all should *live* a life of dialogue (→theology of mission). Still, fear of what is strange is grist for the mill of suspicion operated by guardians of "pure" faith and "true" doctrine. Such attitudes separate people and compartmentalize the earth. This is what has happened to Jews, Muslims, and Christians in the Middle East, and between Hindus and Muslims in India. The examples are multiple. It may, indeed, be that the contemporary world, despite all its means of communication, lives less harmoniously than Jews, Christians, and Muslims in medieval Spain, or even fifty years ago in the Arabic-Islamic world. The failure of wealthy industrial nations to protect immigrants from non-Western lands (most of whom are not Christian) is a part of this sad chapter of history. Nevertheless, the commingling of followers of the various faiths of humanity seems unstoppable. It finds expression, for example, in mixed marriages which de facto create people with double religious loyalties. In the "dialogue of life," an oral testimony takes the form of people explaining their motivations to those with whom they have lived, or to those with whom they have been engaged in joint action (the "dialogue of action").

We may speak, too, of theological and philosophical dialogue. The necessary complement to the "dialogue of life" and the "dialogue of action" is opening of oneself to the ideas, the culture, and the philosophy of the other's world. In this process one can discover that problems known from the history of one's own theology or philosophy have also been tackled (and still are being tackled) by the other tradition with which one has entered into dialogue, even if those problems are expressed in different ways and with different terminology. In such an academic dialogue, one can see comparisons between Christian disputes over christological doctrines and discussions in Islam over whether the Qur'an is created or uncreated. Organized meetings sponsored by such organizations as the WCC unit on Dialogue with People of Living Faiths or the Pontifical Council for Inter-religious Dialogue are examples of such encounters. In universities academics attempt to clarify conceptual foundations and to study religion using "scientific" methods. Often these academic encounters become fruitful as *loci* for dialogue, even when that is not the original goal.

Because the core of religion lies in the mysterious depths of human persons in their communities, its full reality remains unknown to the outsider who does not share its faith. Thus so-called objective or scientific knowledge of religions often seems superficial to the followers of living religious traditions. It is important to realize too that believers of one tradition who study the history of other traditions know their own religion from the inside, but others only from the outside. When this limitation is not recognized, the comparisons made between religions are often shallow. This is why we must recognize the primacy of religious experience and spirituality and seek to learn whether the results of "objective" studies of religions seem fair to those who participate in a religious worldview from the inside. The need to speak clearly and objectively about a given tradition to "outsiders" in language that "insiders" judge to be adequate is one of the greatest challenges to interreligious dialogue. We have hardly begun to accomplish it.

The World Day of Prayer for Peace, held at Assisi on October 27, 1986, might be cited as an example of a dialogic moment at which religious differences were respected and yet unity was felt. At Assisi, spiritual leaders from all over the world

gathered to pray together — each representative following his or her own tradition — for world peace. More such experiences may increase the fruitfulness of
dialogue and lessen the possibility that what we call "dialogue" is actually (in the
words of J. Kitagawa) "mutual monologue."

4. Among the obstacles to dialogue is the elemental fact that human beings
as individuals and as persons in community seem to regard themselves as self-
sufficient (see Qur'an, Sura 96:6), and to consider themselves to be the center of
their world. It is perhaps no accident that the great historian of religion Mircea
Eliade found that one of the central functions of each religion is to give its followers a sense of an *axis mundi,* the still point around which all revolves and
which confers meaning on all else. As necessary as this function is psychologically,
it brings religions and their followers into conflict with the beliefs of other communities that also know the "true" *axis mundi.* Westerners smiled at the belief
that China was the "Middle Empire," but every cultural and religious group has
some functional equivalent, whether it be Israel as "the Chosen People" or Islam
as those who have fully submitted to God. In parallel with this is the tendency
of each religious tradition to subsume those who follow other traditions under
its own belief system's categories, or, what is worse, to relegate them to "outer
darkness." Albert Camus describes this process graphically in *The Fall* (1956).

The 1991 Vatican document "Dialogue and Proclamation" outlines eleven obstacles to dialogue, among which some of the most important are (*a*) insufficient
grounding in one's own faith; (*b*) insufficient knowledge of other religions; (*c*) cultural and language differences; (*d*) political differences, or relationships that are
burdened by past injustice; (*e*) suspicion about the other's motives in dialogue;
and (*f*) materialism, religious indifference, and the multiplication of religious sects
which create confusion and raise a number of new problems. Nevertheless, the
document insists, obstacles "should not lead us to underestimate the possibilities
of dialogue or to overlook the results already achieved.... So despite the difficulties, the Church's commitment to dialogue remains firm and irreversible" (54; see
Burrows 1993, 107). The anomaly of this position, from the point of view of persons
in other traditions, is that dialogue is also professed to be an aspect of Christian
mission, and so is feared as a "reconnaissance exercise" on the part of Christians.

In this regard, what is called "progress" in dialogue and welcomed enthusiastically in mainline Protestant and Roman Catholic worlds seems less positive in
other religious traditions. Instead of being accorded the dignity of being worthy
"others" entering into conversation as equals, followers of these traditions have,
for example, been called "anonymous Christians." One doubts that Christians or
Hindus would feel complimented if they were called "anonymous Muslims." Yet
for a number of years, Christians felt good calling others anonymous Christians,
instead of letting them speak about who they really are. The issue of "incommen-
surability" needs to be constantly kept in mind when dialogue is advocated, for it
is difficult to discover criteria of truth that enable one to judge fairly the "truth"
of a tradition that lies outside one's own system of reference. It should be understood from the outset, therefore, that misunderstanding will accompany both the
invitation to dialogue and its results. To many the invitation to dialogue comes
from those who till recently were trying to convert them. To many others dialogue
seems a Trojan horse that threatens to bring in dangerous, relativizing, and secularizing ideas. And so, at the close of the second Christian millennium and the

start of the third, it becomes apparent that those who would enter into dialogue need to be persons of infinite humility. The path of dialogue is not an easy one.

ULRICH SCHOEN

Bibliography

Amaladoss, M., *Making All Things New: Dialogue, Pluralism and Evangelization in Asia* (1990). Barth, K., *CD* IV/3.2 (1962). Beyerhaus, P., *The Authority of the Gospel and Interreligious Dialogue* (1996). Bosch, D. J., *Transforming Mission: Paradigm Shifts in Theology of Mission* (1991) 474–89. Burrows, W. R., ed., *Redemption and Dialogue: Reading* Redemptoris Missio *and* Dialogue and Proclamation (1993). Cragg, K., *Sandals at the Mosque: Christian Presence amid Islam* (1959). Eck, D. L., *Encountering God: A Spiritual Journey from Bozeman to Banaras* (1993). Gioia, F., ed., *Interreligious Dialogue: The Official Teaching of the Catholic Church (1963–1995)* (1997). Jenkinson, W., and H. O'Sullivan, eds., *Trends in Mission: Toward the 3rd Millennium* (1991) 263–91. Klos, F. W., C. L. Nakamura, and D. F. Martensen, eds., *Lutherans and the Challenge of Religious Pluralism*. Knitter, P. F., *Many Religions, One Earth* (1995). Mercado, L. N., and J. J. Knight, eds., *Mission and Dialogue: Theory and Practice* (1989). Rosales, G. G., and C. G. Arévalo, eds., *For All the Peoples of Asia: Federation of Asian Bishops' Conferences: Documents from 1970 to 1991* (1992). Scherer, J. A., and S. B. Bevans, eds., *New Directions in Mission and Evangelization 1: Basic Statements 1974–1991* (1992). Schoen, U., *Das Ereignis und die Antworten* (1984). Tessier, H., *Église en Islam* (1984). Tillich, P., *The Future of Religions* (1966). Tracy, D., *Dialogue with the Other: The Inter-Religious Dialogue* (1990). Idem, *Plurality and Ambiguity: Hermeneutics, Religion and Hope* (1987).

✎ ECOLOGY AND MISSION ✑

1. Emphasis on the Whole Person. 2. Dialogue and Mutuality. 3. Faithfulness to Christian Values.

Reflection on the purpose and methods of Christian mission has in one way or another always paid attention to the social environments in which mission activity has sought to accomplish its tasks. Each particular social environment varies, but all include political, religious, linguistic, economic, and other cultural elements. In fact, whether implicit or explicit, distinct understandings of these elements, their interrelationships, and their relative importance can be closely correlated to distinct approaches to mission philosophy, efforts, and goals. Unlike, for example, many nineteenth-century mission attitudes, much of contemporary mission thought seeks not only to understand social and historical environments but to be sensitive and open to the specificities of given environments. Such an understanding builds upon at least some social and cultural elements in specific contexts, in the construction of an appropriate contextual (→contextual theology) approach to mission.

This deepened contextual sensitivity to the human social environment is of critical importance to successful and thoughtful mission activity. Happily, such sensitivity to the human social environment is also an important part of and a first step toward a growing sensitivity to the natural environment in which human life is embedded and without which human life cannot be sustained. Slowly, Western Christians are coming to understand the central fact that has too often been ignored: that the human social environment is itself intricately related to, even dependent upon, the natural environment. Like it or not, this is the wider context in which human history unfolds. Indeed, today it is becoming less and less possible, or even less and less sensible, to talk about the human social world as if it were separate from rather than intricately related to the larger realm of creation, that is, the natural world.

As this awareness of the natural world penetrates contemporary Christian thought and Christian identity, it becomes impossible to use and to share with others Christian theological, biblical, ethical, and historical sources without including the growing body of literature in these and other fields which are rethinking and reexamining Christian assumptions about and activity within the natural world.

A number of interests and themes of contemporary mission thought lend themselves to the inclusion of the natural environment as an area of focus and concern. Three are of particular importance: (1) emphasis on the whole person; (2) interest in dialogue and mutuality; and (3) faithfulness to Christian tradition and values.

1. In the mission field, perhaps as nowhere else, it is important to comprehend that the human spirit and the human physical self are in some ways essentially inseparable. It is neither possible nor morally justifiable to address the human spirit while the human physical self suffers hunger, disease, or physical oppression. It is the recognition of this inseparability of body and spirit that has led missionaries to be involved in education, health care, and economic development. It is but a short step, therefore, to extend this interest to a concern for the natural environment.

Such concern fits particularly well with involvement in the areas of health and development. It is virtually impossible today to be unaware of the effects of the natural environment on the health of the human body. The effects extend from diseases specific to climates and regions, to nutritional deprivation and starvation due to climate change, to effects of the depletion of the ozone layer or acid rain. Mission work has often focused on the effects of the natural environment on the human body and spirit. Today it is important to tend not only to the effects of nature on human health but also to the effects of human activity on nature — effects which, ironically, often help create the natural dynamics which eventually harm humanity.

The environmental effects of development projects aimed at the well-being of humans must also be an area of critical concern for the mission field. This is a special concern since in many parts of the world mission workers are often directly involved in such development projects. The polemic about development projects aimed at short-term human well-being at the expense of long-term environmental damage is well publicized. It is critically important for mission workers to understand the elements of this polemic and participate in the debate and in the development of coherent and informed Christian thought about it.

The complexity of the interactions of the human social world and the natural world are such that the need for education is constant. Mission workers must not only educate themselves about these dynamics; they must also include these themes as intricate parts of mission education and reflection, both in the field and at home.

2. Much of contemporary mission thought demonstrates a growing ability to be self-critical. The capacity for self-critical thought lays the foundation for relationships that are characterized by dialogue and mutuality. Part of the self-critical capacity of Christian thought involves awareness and critique of values, practices, and assumptions in one's own culture which disregard or harm the other. Such values and practices, often communicated inadvertently by Christian thought and practice, are destructive of dialogue and mutuality and create a dynamic which much of contemporary mission thought struggles to understand and to overcome.

Today, given the environmental challenges that we have created, it is important that Christians critique not only habits and assumptions that impede genuine cross-cultural encounters but also the structural elements of one's own cultural, political, and economic contexts. This is important because these assumptions and structural elements not only wreak havoc on other peoples and cultures but also endanger the natural environment. It is critically important, therefore, that Christians at home and abroad learn to scrutinize the elements of their cultures which are destructive of the natural environment and wasteful of nature's bounty given by God to all.

In the West, a part of such self-scrutiny will involve the assessment of the extent to which the spread of Christianity through mission efforts has been accompanied by an economic model — industrial, consumer-oriented, and growth dependent — which is intrinsically destructive of the natural world. The West must ask itself not only about the desirability and feasibility of spreading this model around the world, thus encouraging an early and dramatic encounter with global natural limits, but also whether to continue this model at home. In this self-questioning dialogue, partners across the globe will be especially valuable. Western Christianity can and must learn, from Christians and non-Christians alike, habits, practices, traditions, and values that respect, protect, and foster the flourishing of the natural environment. This should be a dominant theme in the mission conversations and encounters in the years ahead. It is also a theme on which the simplest, most humble among us will often be our leaders.

3. In some circles it has been popular to blame Christianity for the environmental danger in which humanity finds itself. In other circles this is hotly contested. It is neither accurate nor helpful for Christians to either accept or reject blame for the massive environmental destruction we witness today. Rather, Christians must learn to think and act responsively. They must ask whether the environmental crisis is not providing the necessary occasion to reread the biblical texts, to rethink what appear to be historical certainties, and to reflect on traditional values and practices. In this way the occasion is provided to reevaluate Christian faith and faithfulness.

The dominant understanding of the biblical texts and Christian traditions in the West has in recent centuries been marked by excessive attention to the drama between humanity and God. As a consequence, little attention has been given to the all-enveloping natural stage on which the drama unfolds. When one looks carefully, this natural stage itself is also an integral part of the divine-human drama and is thus to be included in the human understanding of God's creation, of human sin, and of human responsibility.

Not only are scholars exploring the views of nature in the biblical texts; similar research is being done with regard to Christian traditions and the histories of Christian communities. Scholars are rediscovering and exploring values within Christianity which serve to critique excessive materialism and advocate simplicity and sufficiency. Such values and habits carry new meaning and new urgency within the context of Christian mission today. Biblical study, ethical discernment, and historical critique, therefore, uncover long-forgotten values and virtues which nurture humanity in its proper relationship with the natural world.

Mission thought and practice can contribute depth and breadth to this renaissance of Christian self-understanding. Enriched in turn, it can better contribute to the cultures and communities, the social and the natural environments, in which its own mission activity unfolds.

HEIDI HADSELL

Bibliography

Beversluis, J., *A Source Book for Earth's Community of Religions* (1995) 195–218. Boff, L., *Ecology and Liberation* (1995). Bradshaw, B., *Bridging the Gap: Evangelism, Development, and Shalom* (1993). Brown, R. M., *Making Peace in the Global Village* (1981). Duchrow, U., and G. Leidke, *Shalom: Biblical Perspectives on Creation, Justice, and Peace* (1989). Hall, D. J., *Christian Mission: The Stewardship of Life in the Kingdom of Death* (1985). Idem, *The Steward: A Biblical Symbol Come of Age* (1990). Hiebert, T., *The Yahwist's Landscape: Nature and Religion in Early Israel* (1996). McDaniel, J., *With Roots and Wings* (1995). Murray, R., *The Cosmic Covenant: Biblical Themes of Justice, Peace, and the Integrity of Creation* (1992). Reid, B., "Paul for an Ecozoaic Age," in *The Ecological Challenge: Ethical, Liturgical, and Spiritual Responses* (1994). Rhoads, D., *The Challenge of Diversity: The Witness of Paul and the Gospels* (1996). Roberts, W. D., *Patching God's Garment: Environment and Mission in the 21st Century* (1994). Sittler, J., "Called to Unity." *ER* 14 (1962) 177–87. Wilkinson, L., "Christ as Creator and Redeemer," in *The Environment and the Christian: What We Can Learn from the New Testament* (1991). Wink, W., "Eco-Bible: The Bible and Ecojustice," *ThTo* 49 (1993) 465–77.

❧ ECUMENICAL ASSOCIATION OF ❧ THIRD WORLD THEOLOGIANS (EATWOT)

1. Historical Background. 2. Self-understanding. 3. Achievements and Challenges. 4. Organizational Structure and Activities.

The Ecumenical Association of Third World Theologians (EATWOT) is composed of men and women whose aim is the "continuing development of Third World Christian theologies which will serve the church's mission in the world and witness to the new humanity in Christ expressed in the struggle for a just society" (art. 2, EATWOT constitution). The association is committed to foster "new models of theology which would interpret the gospel in a more meaningful way to the peoples of the Third World and promote their struggle for liberation" (preamble, constitution). Among these new models are Latin American →liberation theology, →black theology of liberation, minjung theology in Korea (→Korean theology), *dalit* theology in India (→Indian theology), and the theology of struggle in the Philippines (→Filipino theology).

1. EATWOT was born in Dar-es-Salaam, Tanzania, in 1976. The decades before its birth were a time of awakening for the Third World, the so-called underdeveloped (or, more euphemistically, "developing") countries of Africa, Asia, and Latin America. People in the Third World had become conscious of the fact that their countries were not "underdeveloped" by virtue of limited natural or human resources but were forced into such a condition as a result of years of exploitation and domination — economical, political, and cultural. First by colonization and then by neocolonialism, they had been driven to the periphery, made to depend on, and serve the interests of, a powerful center which consisted mostly of the affluent nations of the West in collaboration with local elite groups. At this time, too, Third World Christians had become aware that the "universal" theology they had inherited from the West was not pertinent to their context of poverty and marginalization; traditional theology had to be reformulated to make it meaningful to peoples struggling for a more just and egalitarian world. This was the backdrop of EATWOT's foundation.

In August 1976, twenty-two representatives from Africa, Asia, and Latin America, and one black theologian from the United States, met in Dar-es-Salaam for an "ecumenical dialogue of Third World theologians," to share with one another theological efforts in their respective areas. The participants came from the main Christian denominations — Catholic, Protestant, and Orthodox. The dialogue consisted of: (*a*) an analysis of the socioeconomic, political, and cultural realities of each continent; (*b*) an evaluation of the presence of the church on each continent; and (*c*) a survey of efforts toward forging appropriate theological approaches in the Third World. Despite differences in their racial and cultural backgrounds, religious affiliations, and theological orientations (which at times led to disputes and tensions), the participants unanimously rejected the dominant theology of the West as irrelevant to their contexts. In the end, they found the dialogue so worthwhile that they agreed to have similar exchanges in the future and to form an association.

2. EATWOT's founding members had their own understanding of what it meant to be Third World theologians. For them "Third World" describes a social condition rather than a strictly geographic location, as attested by the participation in their dialogue of a black theologian from the United States. The term, therefore, refers to a quality of life characterized by poverty and different forms of oppression and includes any marginalized group of people in other parts of the world (called the "diaspora" in the original EATWOT constitution). Third World theologians, then, are not simply those who live in a Third World country, but those who take the Third World context seriously and do theology from the vantage point of the poor and oppressed who seek justice and liberation. Similarly, not all theologies produced in the Third World are Third World theologies, but only those which offer an alternative voice. While the use of the term "Third World" has been questioned by some, EATWOT maintains it as constitutive of its theological identity.

3. EATWOT has become an important forum for exchange and mutual challenge and enrichment for Third World theologians who previously worked in isolation and knew little of attempts to contextualize theology outside their own areas. EATWOT has thus enabled Third World theologians to speak with a concerted voice. A number of EATWOT members are authors of important books on Third World theology. By doing theology from a Third World perspective and making an option for the poor and oppressed fundamental to theological method, EATWOT has contributed to breaking theology from its exclusively Western moorings. The primacy of liberation praxis, the move from a philosophical/metaphysical approach to a more sociological approach, the departure from traditional epistemology, and the use of critical analysis of economic, political, and religio-cultural contexts as integral to theology are elements pointing to a paradigm shift in theological thinking and a reversal of the conventional academic model of theologizing predominant in the West. Without an in-depth analysis of Third World realities, EATWOT theologians insist, it is not possible for societies in the Third World to interpret God's will and saving activity in a meaningful way.

In the course of promoting new theological models, EATWOT faces a number of long-standing challenges. Foremost among these are the incorporation of Third World women's liberationist perspectives and the emancipating theological insights of racial and ethnic groups, indigenous communities, *dalits,* and other marginalized peoples; a reinterpretation of scripture that takes into account gender, racial, cultural, and religious differences; the inclusion of the ecological and cosmic dimensions in liberation theology and spirituality; and, very importantly, the recognition of the theologian's own sexist and racist biases in reformulating theology. EATWOT also faces newer challenges, such as those resulting from the impact of high technology and the problems ensuing from new ethical and moral issues. But the most pressing among the newer challenges arises from the worldwide phenomenon of →globalization, the push of affluent nations and multicultural corporations for an integrated global market that entails a global culture. As Third World theologies are contextual, no serious theologizing can be done without taking into consideration the destructive consequences of economic and cultural globalization on Third World peoples, their resources, and their environment. At the same time, this demands a political vision which can be translated into action to bring about a just world. One perennial challenge to EATWOT persists: to assist the church in redefining its mission in the light of Third World realities and experience, so that the fullness of life of the gospel will truly be available for all.

4. EATWOT has a constitution and an executive committee, but no permanent secretariat. It holds a general assembly every five years. To facilitate its work, EATWOT has divided itself into four regions: Africa, Asia, Latin America, and other areas where oppressed groups live. Membership is limited to those who come from these four regions but is not restricted to professional theologians. As an ecumenical association, its membership is further limited to members of Christian churches who confess faith in Jesus Christ.

To accomplish its aims, EATWOT employs three main means: conferences, commissions, and publications. EATWOT conferences are organized on three levels — national, regional, and intercontinental — with themes that reveal EATWOT's theological priorities. After the initial dialogue in Dar-es-Salaam, EATWOT organized other intercontinental conferences. The next three were patterned after the original dialogue but highlighted the continent where the meeting was held. Thus the conference which took place in Accra, Ghana, in 1977 focused on the African reality and was entitled "The Christian Commitment in Africa Today: Concerns of Emerging Christian Theologies." The third conference was held in Wennappuwa, Sri Lanka, in 1979. Its theme was "Asia's Struggle for Full Humanity: Towards a Relevant Theology." In São Paulo, Brazil, in 1980, the conference theme was "Ecclesiology of Basic Christian Communities," focusing on the basic communities of Latin America. EATWOT held its fifth intercontinental conference in New Delhi, India, in 1981. Entitled "Irruption of the Third World," its goal was to synthesize EATWOT's work of the previous five years as well as to serve as its first general assembly. It became clear during the conference, however, that the proposed synthesis was not viable. Each region had its own emphasis and needs. While Latin America, for example, stressed class analysis, Africa accented culture and indigenization, and Asia focused on religious plurality. If Third World theology was to be both contextual and liberationist, it needs to be plural as well. There was a consequent shift to regional efforts.

Despite recognizing and affirming the principle of regionalization, EATWOT did not abandon intercontinental conferences. In Geneva, Switzerland, in 1983, EATWOT deviated from its usual intra-Third World conference pattern to hold an intercontinental dialogue with progressive theologians from Europe and North America, and arrived at a new methodology for doing theology based on commitment.

In Oaxtepec, Mexico, in 1986, the theme was "Commonalities and Divergences in Third World Theologies." In Nairobi, Kenya, in 1992, the theme was "A Cry for Life: The Spirituality of the Third World," with three subthemes dealing with christology, spirituality, and commitment. The conference in Tagaytay City, Philippines, in 1996 addressed the phenomenon of globalization and its effects on Third World theologies and was entitled "The Search for a New Just World Order: Challenges to Theology." These last three meetings also functioned as the association's second, third, and fourth general assemblies.

EATWOT organizes other meetings through its commissions, which are created to respond to specific interests of members. The first commission was the Working Commission on Church History in the Third World. Established in 1981, it produced in separate volumes the historia minima of the Christian churches in Africa,

Asia, and Latin America. The second commission was the Commission on Theology from Third World Women's Perspective. It was initiated in 1983 by the women members who wanted space within EATWOT to set an agenda that would ensure the inclusion of their experience and liberating theological insights. The women's commission reworks classical theological themes and reflects on critical issues affecting women's lives. In 1995 in Costa Rica, it organized a dialogue between EATWOT women and Western feminist theologians on crucial issues of violence against women. The third EATWOT commission, the Intercontinental Theological Commission, was formed in 1986 to address vital theological concerns in small intercontinental groupings. Its first three meetings treated methodology, christology, and popular religion, as well as women's experience of the sacred.

Publishing the results of its meetings is a third way that EATWOT achieves its goal. The principal papers from the intercontinental meetings have been published in several volumes by Orbis Books. Orbis has also published volumes representing one regional work, some of the commissions' work, and works by Latin American, Asian and African women. All these are cited in the bibliography of this article. EATWOT also has its own biannual journal, entitled *Voices from the Third World;* the journal is largely composed of papers prepared for the various commissions and essays written by individual EATWOT members.

Virginia Fabella, MM

Bibliography

Abraham, K. C., *Third World Theologies: Commonalities and Divergences* (1990). Abraham, K. C., and B. Mbuy-Beya, eds., *Spirituality of the Third World* (1994). Appiah-Kubi, K., and S. Torres, eds., *African Theology en Route* (1979). Fabella, V., ed., *Asia's Struggle for Full Humanity* (1980). Idem, *Beyond Bonding: A Third World Woman's Theological Journey* (1993). Fabella, V., P. K. H. Lee, and D. Kwang-sun Suh, eds., *Asian Christian Spirituality: Reclaiming Traditions* (1992). Fabella, V., and M. A. Oduyoye, eds., *With Passion and Compassion: Third World Women Doing Theology* (1989). Fabella, V., and S. Ai Lee Park, eds., *We Dare to Dream: Doing Theology as Asian Women* (1990). Fabella, V., and S. Torres, eds., *Doing Theology in a Divided World* (1985). Idem, *The Emergent Gospel: Theology from the Underside of History* (1978). Idem, *Irruption of the Third World: Challenge to Theology* (1983). Mananzan, M. J., et al., eds., *Women Resisting Violence: Spirituality for Life* (1996). Oduyoye, M. A., and M. R. A. Kanyoro, eds., *The Will to Arise: Women, Tradition, and the Church in Africa* (1992). Tamez, E., ed., *Through Her Eyes: Theology from Latin America* (1989). Torres, S., and J. Eagleson, eds., *The Challenge of Basic Christian Communities* (1981).

✎ ECUMENISM ✎

1. The Concept. 2. Historical Survey of the Ecumenical Movement. 3. Theology of Ecumenism. 4. Contemporary Models of Unity. 5. Contemporary Problems and Tasks.

1. The term "ecumenical" in theology today generally refers to the movement which seeks to achieve external unity among the world's denominationally divided churches. The original meaning of the word (from *oikeo:* to dwell, inhabit; and *oikos:* house, household; *oikoumene:* the whole inhabited earth [Lk 4:5]) has lapsed into disuse, as did the later development of the sense of a common basic attitude or doctrinal consensus by the "inhabitants" of the surface of the earth or the members of the church. A more modern, comprehensive meaning has since been developed: "ecumenical" means the entirety of the church, which, looking back to its common original tradition and looking forward to its hope, seeks a commonality in doctrine and in the life of faith. The ecumenical movement consists of those churches which "together seek to know Christ." Such a cooperative attitude includes at the outset several features: (a) the limitation of ecumenism to Christians or to Christian churches; (b) the recourse to a tradition (which at least in the beginning was a common one) of the apostolic witness and its basic interpretation in the primitive church; (c) a principled openness toward the insight that one does not possess the whole truth in all its aspects — that is, an openness toward changes in one's own doctrine and way of life; and (d) the conviction and the hope that the efforts for exchange between, and finally the unity of, the parts of the church are God's will and are even presaged in the unity of God the Father, Jesus Christ, and the Holy Spirit.

The concept of ecumenism described in this general way immediately poses at least three problems: (a) by concentrating on *Christian* churches, there is a failure to relate to the ecumenical problem par excellence, the separation between Jews and Gentiles (Christians); (b) for the same reason, the relation to other religious traditions is excluded; and (c) the Roman Catholic understanding of truth (and to date, the doctrine of the Orthodox churches) is opposed to the postulated view that ecumenical endeavor includes openness to changes in doctrine. Because of these immediate problems, the danger is that the understanding of ecumenism sketched out above is limited to certain Reformation churches — a contradiction in itself.

2. Ecumenism first became a "movement" in the period of evident disruption of the church, especially in the nineteenth and twentieth centuries. Since the beginning of the apostolic period, however, responsible leaders of the church have struggled to overcome differences over doctrine (e.g., Paul in Galatians, Irenaeus against the Gnostics, Athanasius against Arius, Augustine against Pelagius) and to clarify questions of Christian life (e.g., Paul in 1 and 2 Corinthians) and questions of constitution and law in the church (e.g., the treatment of apostates in persecution, standardization of the date of Easter, recognition of decisions of synods and councils). For various reasons, emperors and patriarchs wanted councils. Finally, one can understand all controversies over the primacy of the pope, the Eucharist, the limitation of the freedom to establish new monastic foundations, and even the suppression of reform movements, as being ultimately "ecumenical" in intent. One can say, in other words, that the church action in such controversies attempted to safeguard church unity, even though the methods used in the defense of unity might appear strange today. The search for the unity of the church of Christ was strongly impressed on the churches of the Reformation in the sixteenth century, as the Augsburg Confession and the ecumenical activities of Calvin clearly demonstrate.

With few exceptions, the Jews stand entirely outside the field of vision in all these ecumenical endeavors. The Hebrew Bible was usurped completely by Christians, and the promises to Israel were reinterpreted in a Christian way. Even ecumenical endeavors in the eighteenth century (with the exception of occasional rays of hope in Zinzendorf) and in the nineteenth century (the time of the great missionary activity of the Protestant churches) lacked insights into the links between Jews and Christians. Except in the work of some Enlightenment philosophers, the world religions were also outside the purview of the Christian West (→religion, religions).

Toward the end of the nineteenth century, the ecumenical movement gained impetus from three sources: from the division of the churches on the mission field; from insight into the social needs of industrialized nations; and from concern for world peace in the years before 1914. The following can be given as important dates: missionary conferences in London in 1878 and 1888; the Ecumenical Missionary Conference in New York in 1900, which led to the Edinburgh World Missionary Conference (→world missionary conferences) in 1910. The founding of the YMCA in 1844 and the YWCA in 1855 — which led to the founding of the World Alliance of YMCAs in 1892, the World Alliance of YWCAs in 1893, and the World Student Christian Federation in 1895 — was also essential in the movement's development. Social work in big cities such as London and Berlin led eventually to the Life and Work movement (Stockholm, 1925), whose creation was contributed to by the peace and friendship work of the German and British, and also the French, churches (the founding of the World Alliance for Friendship between the Churches occurred in 1914).

In Edinburgh in 1910, the dogmatic/theological problems were deliberately pushed into the background, and even more significantly so in Stockholm in 1925 (their motto: "Doctrine divides, service unites"). Inspired first of all by Bishop C. Brent of the Protestant Episcopal Church of America's mission to the Philippines, and R. Gardiner, a New England lawyer, the Faith and Order movement (by "order" is meant polity and constitution of the various churches) sought from the beginning to work out the theological differences between the churches. The history of the Faith and Order conferences from Lausanne (1927), through Edinburgh (1937), Lund (1952), Montreal (1963), and Accra (1974) to the most recent conferences in Lima (1982), Stavanger (1985), and Campostella (1993) reflects very clearly the various stages of their work in addressing those differences.

Paralleling the series of great world conferences (of the International Missionary Council [IMC], the Life and Work movement, and the Faith and Order movement [the union of the latter two movements in 1948 at Amsterdam and the addition of the IMC in 1961 in New Delhi led together to the founding of the →World Council of Churches (WCC)]), the denominational world alliances offered Christian churches hindrances and stimuli to the movement in equal measure. The oldest is the Lambeth Conference of the churches of the Anglican Communion (1867). There followed the founding of the World Alliance of Reformed Churches (1875); the establishment of the world alliances of Methodist churches (1881), the Congregationalists (1891), and the Baptists (1905), as well as the World Lutheran Federation (1923), came later. The existence of these joint efforts provided a plurality of opportunities for so-called bilateral negotiations and unions in the ecumenical movement, both of which can create problems as well as point out new paths. For example, there would be problems if, in unions with the Roman Catholic Church or Orthodox churches, historically related sister churches were left out. There are new paths, if new insights are achieved in individual negotiations rather than in the general discussion of multilateral bodies.

Finally, it is worth naming the different national ecumenical bodies: the National Council of Churches of Christ (formerly the Federal Council) in the USA; the British Council of Churches (which became the Inter-church Process in 1991); and the Co-partnership of Christian Churches in Switzerland and the Federal German Republic. Around 1960, the East Asia Conference of Churches, the All-Africa Council of Churches, the Melanesian Council of Churches, and the Conference of European Churches came into existence. The constitutions, functions, and competence of these bodies vary considerably from country to country. The Orthodox churches are fully represented in all of them, the Roman Catholic Church in most of them, and representatives of Jewish bodies are present as guests in a few of them.

3. The historical process of the formation of the ecumenical movement must be distinguished from the basic theological problems of ecumenism. These problems are for their part tied up in a complex way with the so-called nontheological factors, which can be systematically described in sociological, psychological, or economic terms. Hardly any of the theologically defined differences — for example, the principal attitude toward the Johannine scriptures (Orthodoxy), the attitude toward the Pauline texts (Protestantism), the tension between a sacramental-sacerdotal understanding of the church and a Reformation one, or controversies over a new form of liberation theology — are to be understood or resolved in exclusively theological terms. There are always other components of the problems involved. This should be borne in mind in surveying the following list of the principal theological problems of the ecumenical movement.

3.1. The creation of denominational churches goes back to the possibility of drawing different inferences from biblical texts or theological topics. Deductions which have not been strictly drawn from biblical texts and tradition are the logical reason for the multiplicity of theological opinions and lifestyles. No matter how much false exegesis there is, it is generally not worthwhile to challenge sister churches on points of difference, "false deductions" from the Bible, and the tradition of the early church. Particularly because of the lack of a clear distinction between, for example, genuine biblical and early Catholic doctrines, both the sacramental High Church and the classical Reformation models of the church and ecclesiastical offices can be justified more or less legitimately. Different denominations can be explained, on the one hand, by the different selections and interpretations of the ancient texts that are possible and, on the other hand, by the phenomenon that a freely flowing river of far-reaching consequences for church order and unity will generally be "stopped." Denominations are consequently presentations of "acquired" doctrinal opinions and attitudes to life.

3.2. Was there a "five-centuries consensus"? The phenomena sketched out in 3.1. led after the Reformation (e.g., in G. Calixt) and again in the Oxford movement (J. H. Newman) to the hope that the existence of unity of doctrine and life in the church in the first five centuries could be proved historically and utilized theologically for today. The lines of demarcation of the biblical canon were then, so to speak, brought forward from the end of the first century to the end of the fifth. Historical research in the nineteenth and twentieth centuries showed, however, that complete consensus in the early church did not exist at all. Nevertheless, it is still worthwhile today to consider afresh that, even if there were no historical consensus in the first five centuries, the churches actively engaged in the ecumenical movement today should find common ground by looking back to the early church, rather than in more direct contact with their present-day teachings. The widely neglected study of patristics should therefore receive new attention.

3.3. The maintenance of denominational identity is another problem. Instead of blaming the theological programs which first understand faith as the gift of God and second ascribe to the faithful a high degree of shared responsibility in the church ("the priesthood of all believers"), one could well say that the church leaders and clergy are the ones above all who persist in maintaining specific denominational identity. For many of the faithful, the identity received through tradition is only important in moral questions of daily life (marriage, education, social ethics); in the field of doctrine it is often irrelevant. In the United States, church members not infrequently change their denomination after moving or marriage, as do refugees in Africa.

3.4. Is the unity of the church "a pretense"? In countless ecumenical publications, one reads of the unity of the church which is already given and willed by God. Because the gift already given cannot be understood historically, there remain only two possible ways to distinguish this axiom from a meaningless, empty formula: the trinitarian interpretation (God's innermost reality is a prototype of unity) and the reference to God's promise to make unity a reality in the future. The door to an understanding of ecumenism is opened in both alternatives, which makes overcoming the schism between Jew and Christian a matter of importance as an example and also creates a link between "the unity of the church" and "the unity of humanity," without the ecumenical movement remaining a self-contained hope of one of the world's great religions.

4. The Roman Catholic understanding of ecumenism is contained more dynamically in Vatican II's *Unitatis Redintegratio (UR;* 1964) than in statements issued before the council, but it sometimes presents a model with the implicit and partly explicit expectation that other Christian churches should reintegrate into the Roman Catholic Church, a model which differs in character from the various conceptions of the churches represented in the WCC. Nevertheless, among the member churches, the group of Orthodox churches (members of the WCC since 1961) maintains a concept which, with all variables on the theme of the immutability of the teaching of the ecumenical councils of the early church, holds firm to the view that, in this respect also, a "reintegration" of the later doctrines of other churches into the dogmatically fixed treasure of truth of the ecumenical councils appears to be an absolute condition. Ecclesiology and the understanding of the claims to truth of the classical early church are the great problematic areas today of the ecumenical movement. In this problematic situation, the Roman Catholic Church occupies a special place only very vaguely, since, in accordance with its understanding of its own position, it is not a member of the WCC — although it is fully represented in Faith and Order and in many other ecumenical organizations. Moreover, on the practical and personal level, relations between Catholic and Protestant theologians, ministers, and congregations are to a great extent very close and exude confidence. Often the differences within a denominational tradition are de facto greater than between groups and different individual denominations. In this way, the questions mentioned above in section 3.3 concern the upholders of denominational identity. The following models of ecumenism stand out:

- An attempt to achieve a full union of all churches, through relativizing doctrinal differences (mainly Protestant inspired). This is a model which today finds very little support.
- The so-called Roman Catholic model of reintegration, in which changes (e.g., extensions) of its own teaching are seen as possible. (There are already observable differences within the Roman Catholic Church today in this respect.)

- The understanding of ecumenism in the Orthodox churches, which totally excludes changes in the basic body of doctrine.

- The model of "conciliar unity" which was reflected in the world assemblies in New Delhi (1961), Uppsala (1968), and Nairobi (1975). This model is widely supported. The "New Delhi formula," which is not dissimilar from the Catholic decree in some respects, strives for mutual recognition of ministries and emphasizes the mutual responsibility of all believers in each place in witness and service, in contradistinction to the universal church.

- A model that emphasizes the differences between the above models and fiercer preservation of denominational identities under the slogan, "Unity in reconciled diversity." One sees in this the importance of the insight that the churches are equally guilty in their relations with one another, and that their mutual trust must be based on forgiveness and shared hope, not simply on tolerance.

The contemporary worldwide project "Justice, Peace, and the Integrity of Creation" and attempts at a "common expression of apostolic faith" (in light of the Nicene Creed) and common witness in mission should be viewed from the perspective of this last-mentioned model. One cannot predict which conflicts will arise with other models.

5. The following problems are coming to light in the ecumenical movement:

- The dominant role of Euro-American theology in the ecumenical movement and the difficulty of expressing the piety and theological articulation to be found in churches of the Third World, the result being that discourse and exchange are problematic.

- The cerebral, verbal nature of many ecumenical activities and, at the same time, the oftentimes superficiality of theological analysis (conditioned by the lack of common life — "conviviality" — and by ecclesiastical anti-intellectualism).

- The division of the churches of the ecumenical movement into, on the one hand, altar-sacrament and priest churches and, on the other hand, minister-teacher and counselor-oriented churches ("high" churches and "low" churches).

- The continual and recently intensified outbreak of ecclesiastical and national provincialism among ministers and church members in all parts of the world, partly connected to regionalism, which is to be welcomed on other grounds.

- The asymmetry in relation to the dominant role of ecclesiastical law as opposed to theology in some denominations.

- The cautiousness of some established churches toward planned unions with others, at the cost of undermining already existing consensus or chances of convergence (e.g., the retarding effect of caution vis-à-vis the Orthodox on the part of Catholics in questions of ordained ministry).

- Hesitancy before the problem of Jews and Christians and uncertainty as to how to relate with non-Christians.

In light of these problems and in recognition of the danger to the continuing existence of humanity, under pressure from war, famine, and destruction of the necessary conditions for life for present-day and future generations, major practical issues become part of the work of fulfillment for the ecumenical movement (strengthening peace, consoling the perplexed, clarifying problems, development work in joint mission). There is also the important matter of setting an example for others (i.e., offering a prototype for conciliar decisions in parliaments, in the United Nations, in communities, and in families; for relations with minorities and foreigners; of forgiveness and reconciliation; of therapy and aid).

Theology has as much of an analytical as a visionary role in all this: analytical in research into the basis for the existence of specific and differing traditions and in concern for the translation of the language of one tradition into that of another; visionary in readiness for new concepts, the setting of tasks and insights, which are more than a selection, reevaluation, or combination of already known traditions and positions. The realization of ecumenism is, however, not the task of theology as such; rather, living together, building trust, joint action, and joint worship must both *precede* and *follow* any theological activity.

DIETRICH RITSCHL

Bibliography

Association of the Member Episcopal Conferences of Eastern Africa, *Ecumenical Initiatives in Eastern Africa: Bibliography* (1982). Bell, G. A. K., *Documents on Christian Unity,* 4 vols. (1924–58). Bellini, A., *Il movimento ecumenico* (1960). Bosch, D. J., *Transforming Mission: Paradigm Shifts in Theology of Mission* (1991) 457–67. Brown, R. M., "Ecumenical Movement," in *EncRel* 5 (1987) 17–27. Cavatassi, N., *The Ecumenical Movement Today* (1991). *Doing the Truth in Charity: Statements of Pope Paul VI, Pope John Paul I, John Paul II, and the Secretariat for Promoting Christian Unity, 1964–1980* (1982). Fey, H. E., ed., *The Ecumenical Advance: A History of the Ecumenical Movement,* vol. 2 (1970). Fifth World Conference on Faith and Order, "Towards Koinonia/Communion in Faith, Life and Witness," *Ecumenical Trends* 22/6 (June 1993) 2/82–24/104. Fink, B. E., *Der Weg zur Bewegung für Praktisches Christentum, "Life and Work"* (1985). Fries, H., and K. Rahner, *Unity of the Churches: An Actual Possibility* (1985). Gassmann, G., "Einheit der Kirche," in *EKL* 1:1002–7. Goodall, N., *The Ecumenical Movement: What It Is and What It Does* (1966). Hastings, C. B., *Harmony among Christians: A Model Other Than Structural Union* (1992). Iguarta, J. M., *La esperanza ecuménica de la iglesia: Un rebaño y un pastor: Textos y estudios* (1970). Jenkinson, W., and H. O'Sullivan, eds., *Trends in Mission: Toward the 3rd Millennium* (1991) 292–302. John Paul II, "Ut Unum Sint: On Commitment to Ecumenism," *Origins* 25/4 (June 8, 1995) 49k–72. Lange, E., *Die ökumenische Utopie oder Was bewegt die ökumenische Bewegung?* (1986 [1972]). Lescrauwaet, J. F., *Critical Bibliography of Ecumenical Literature* (1965). Lossky, N., ed., *Dictionary of the Ecumenical Movement* (1991). Lowery, M. D., *Ecumenism: Striving for Unity amid Diversity* (1985). Maron, G., ed., *Evangelisch und Ökumenisch* (1986). McDonnell, J. J., *The World Council of Churches and the Catholic Church* (1985). Neuner, P., *Kleines Handbuch der Ökumene* (1984). Nissiotis, N., "Towards a New Ecumenical Era," *ER* 37/3 (1985) 326–35. O'Niell, C. A., ed., *Ecumenism and Vatican II* (1964). Papandreou, D., *Orthodoxie und Ökumene: Gesammelte Aufsätze* (1983). Potter, P., *Life in All Its Fullness* (1981). Raiser, K., "Beyond Tradition and Context: In Search of an Ecumenical Framework of Hermeneutics," *IRM* 80 (July–October 1991) 347–54. Idem, "Einheit der Kirche — Einheit der Menschheit," *ÖR* 1 (1986) 18–38. Idem, "The Holy Spirit in Modern Ecumenical Thought," *ER* 41 (July 1989) 375–87. Rouse, R., and S. Neill, *A History of the Ecumenical Movement, 1517–1948* (1967). Scherer, J. A., and S. B. Bevans, eds., *New Directions in Mission and Evangelization,* vol. 1, *Basic Statements 1974–1991* (1992). Tavard, G. H., *Two Centuries of Ecumenism* (1960). Utuk, E. S., *From New York to Ibadan: The Impact of African Questions on the Making of Ecumenical Mission Mandates 1900–1958* (1991). Villain, M., *Introduction a l'oecumenisme* (1961).

❧ ESCHATOLOGY ❧

1. Unrelated Eschatological Themes. 2. Intertheological Structuring. 3. Existential Reference to Praxis. 4. Differentiated Integration.

The recent change in eschatological thinking has been to a considerable degree determined by the missionary situation and the mission of faith in the world. Previously, eschatology was only one of the *objects* of missionary proclamation and praxis. Today, however, mission is increasingly becoming a constitutive *subject* of Christian hope and eschatology, which is the practical and theological form of such hope.

1. Before systematic eschatology was renewed by giving it a biblical basis and an existential-practical reference, eschatology consisted of a rather unrelated collection of different tracts: on death, judgment, heaven, purgatory, hell, resurrection from the dead, last judgment, fulfillment of the cosmos, and so on. All these stood side by side in a poorly structured catalogue and combined the most varied ideas, images, and mythological embellishments which were not harmonized by a methodological interpretation (the hermeneutics of eschatological statements). The intertheological structuring with reference to the mystery of Christ was quite weak, as was the rootedness of the objectivized contents in the praxis of Christian hope of the individual and of the believing community. Mission, as witness and active transmission of Christian hope, was scarcely a topic of eschatology. Conversely, the proclamation of the "last things" was an integral part of missionary preaching and catechesis, particularly urgent in view of the situation of salvation or damnation of the heathen. Consequently, the prospect of "eternity" as punishment or reward was particularly stressed as a motive for conversion; mission was not yet understood as a factor of the fulfillment of salvation and history.

2. As soon as the mystery of Christ (the proclamation of the reign of God and of Jesus' death, resurrection, and parousia) exercised a systematizing effect, the interrelationship of the scattered fragments began to be seen. The fragments formed "magnetic fields": eschatological fulfillment has indeed begun with God's salvific turning to humanity, but it still has to come to historical fruition in the human history of faith and hope. By the death and resurrection of Christ, the clear decision of God for the eternal salvation of humanity and the world has been actualized within history. This central and unsurpassable decision concerns all and everything: humanity, history, and the cosmos. Conversely, this eschatological perspective lends wholeness and universality to the Christ-event and to the essence and action of the church. The church and its preaching, liturgical, and charitable activity assume an eschatological dimension. In this way a heretofore individualized and otherworldly mission is transformed into a social and universal sign-event within this world and history: mission now is not only concerned with eschatology but is itself an essential element of eschatology. The proclamation of Jesus Christ is announcement and inauguration of the reign of God; motivated by it and oriented to it, mission is, in a literal sense, relative, derivative, anticipatory. The reign of God lies at the root of and at the same time delimits the church and its missionary activity; it is the announcement of fulfillment — but no more than its inauguration. This theological rootedness in the mystery of Christ and this opening to the world bring about a decisive transformation from a neutral and indifferent "doomsday mood" to an unambiguous emphasis on salvation. In the place of fear, hope returns — but without losing sight of challenge and decision.

3. In its scattered and disintegrated form, eschatology became an appendage to this world as "the hereafter," without clear reference to human existence and history. The questions treated by eschatology concerned the time after death and the end of history; the only link with these postmortal processes and "places" consisted in the reward-and-punishment equation for this-worldly and premortal behavior. The bestowal of the beatific vision, judgment, bliss or damnation, eternal life, and resurrection stood in a qualitative discontinuity with this world and history. In this world the human being operated, but in the otherworld God operated alone, in pure gratuitousness, without the cooperation of human beings. Just as the *eschata* or the *eschaton* are unrelated to the world, so too all action within the world and history was unrelated and meaningless with reference to the hereafter. The meaning of earthly and inner-worldly life did not transcend the juridical meritoriousness or punishability in the next world; it did not constitute an internal and lasting contribution to the *eschaton*. Nevertheless, this theoretical dualism was, by reason of fortunate inconsequence, often mitigated by integrating praxis.

The rapprochement began from both sides, spurred on by the biblical renewal but just as much by the conscious constellation of eschatological hopes around the believing subject and around the personal and social existence of humanity and its history. As a central idea and crystallization of the fulfillment of salvation the biblical symbol of the →reign of God is more relevant than the abstract and private idea of the "beatific vision" because it includes the physical and spiritual wholeness of the individual and the social and cosmic dimension of salvific fulfillment — without losing the personal communication between God and human beings. The link between the present decision of faith and conversion and the awaited fulfillment by God is assured by the proclamation of Jesus in the parables of the reign of God. The similarly holistic and integrating Old Testament concept of *shalom* — in which the relationship to God and that between individuals and groups form an indissoluble unity — is being rediscovered above all in the missionary church and the growing world church. These and other eschatologically integrating nuclei grow beyond the limits traced between this world and the next, and open themselves to contemporary human history, to the whole of humanity and its social complexities.

Conversely, the this-worldly and interhistorical human praxis oriented toward the future is enhanced by the specifically Christian hope and the "anonymous" human and social responsibility for the future. The eschatological quality of such praxis is founded in the history of Jesus, in the gift of the Spirit, and in the new pneumatic reality of the redeemed individual and the saving community of the church. The redeemed and redeeming activity of humanity has the same eschatological value; and the "objectivizations" of this activity also constitute an integrating part of the redeemed world.

Significantly, it was European theology that produced the vision of P. Teilhard de Chardin as representative and model of such a universal and historical eschatology: incarnation, transformation of matter by human technological activity, increasing socialization of humanity, and so on, harmonize with an evolutionary — and at the same time eschatological — dynamism in creation, which *through* incarnation and resurrection moves toward the same indivisible fulfillment (Omega).

However, the more obvious and more pressing concretization of hope for the removal of the great social and political evils in the world is primarily represented by the churches of the Third World. In so doing they take up what is true in the very secularized (and previously condemned) Marxist eschatology which was originally formulated to spearhead the critique of religion. Though the utopia of the reign of God and the promise of *shalom* do not yet mediate conceptual or practical statements about the precise meaning of the future and fulfillment, they nevertheless provide strong structures for crystallization and integration. Such ideas introduce an eschatology in which the dualisms which characterize, polarize, and paralyze the traditional Western eschatolgy are overcome: we must speak not only of material and spiritual →salvation — of resurrection of the body as well as immortality of the soul, of individual and personal bliss — but also of reconciliation of all society and humanity, of ethical responsibility for the future that is linked indissolubly with fulfillment in grace. A further result is the opening of ecclesiocentric narrowness and the location of eschatological symbolism of the church within the universal horizon of the world (see L. Rütti). In this context the status of mission is enhanced: mission is now no longer a subject accidental to eschatology; it is that realization of the church in which it most intensively expresses its eschato-practical and eschato-logical existence. This might lead temporarily to partial deficiencies in ecclesial practice or to exaggerated claims that the spiritual nature of the gospel has been compromised — as was the case with the charge of the magisterium that →liberation theology is Marxist. Nevertheless, the positive aspects of holistic evangelization and integral liberation greatly outweigh what are certainly genuine risks.

4. The critique and correction of this type of integrated eschatology have come not only from within theology. Just as the euphoric or optimistic eschatologies of the 1960s and 1970s were results not only of the stimuli coming from within theology but also of the sense of a new awakening in the history of ideas and social development, of scientific and technical progress, and the incipient global consciousness of a world society, a more sober and chastened attitude toward the future has had an effect on eschatology as well. The acceleration of technical progress has begun to flag, producing virtually insoluble problems that damage and threaten the ecological balance and other conditions essential for human life on the earth. The increased availability of energy by means of atomic technology has rather suddenly turned into the apocalyptic possibility of total destruction by the new weapons. In addition, global society has been confronted with unsolved problems of similar proportions: economic and social discrepancies between North and South; famines and supply problems; crushing indebtedness and impoverishment of the Third World (→development); abrupt and violent substitution of the last traces of colonialism by new conflicts and tensions including civil wars; racial unrest with simultaneous international polarization. The cessation of the Cold War has not only failed to ease many of these problems; in many cases it has made them more urgent and more complex. In this rather revisionary climate, therefore, the euphoric eschatology of Teilhard de Chardin or the messianic *shalom* visions of liberation theologies and Third World churches are no longer possible. On top of this have come the terrifying knowledge and almost daily vision of indescribable suffering because of political, economic, racial, and gender oppression, with its results of abject poverty, exploitation, and loss of dignity. The euphoric eschatology of the recent past has been blamed not only for having neglected the death of individuals and their eternal future beyond the grave but also for having repressed and kept silent about unrequited suffering and the denial of the rights of countless individuals and groups (→human rights). As a result of self-criticism proceeding from the center of the Christian faith and in the context of a more sober public opinion, other models of eschatology have emerged which give contemporary expression to the biblical apocalyptic visions, the reality of the theology of the cross, and the tragedy of the marginalized multitudes unjustly and often violently deprived of their rights. The concern about the preciousness of the individual, about the weak, the suffering, and the broken has once again, but from a different angle, become an indispensable theme of a Christian eschatology which does not want to lose its identity (see J. B. Metz). The closer limits of the development of world and history and of the shaping of the future direct our gaze again to the horizon of a transcendental fulfillment which, while not dispensing with human responsibility, always remains dependent on the free, unpossessable, and gratuitous power of the God who raises from the dead. Unredeemed history (also called the "eschatological reservation"), as the macroscopic stamp of the cross and Good Friday, is only balanced in a small measure by foretastes and prerealizations of paschal salvation. The task now is to maintain Christian hope — stripped of all naive expectations of the future — in the face of the contradictory and challenging head wind of fear and powerlessness. In its praxis and witness in the missionary situation, Christian hope must not abandon solidarity with all individuals of goodwill and good hope; within this cooperation for a just future, however, it must find its own voice and identity. Without abandoning human wholeness and solidarity, it must promise each individual an irrevocable, personal hope. Without watering down material, even materialistic, salvation, it must maintain the qualitative transcendence of human personhood ("soul"); without falling back on pious consolations about the hereafter and with full commitment to historical changes and improvements, it must face the barrier of death and, in so doing, bear witness to hope; without abandoning ethical responsibility and the active struggle for justice and solidarity, it must confess its own and others' failure, incapacity, and hope for God's free and gratuitous fulfillment; without abandoning the efforts to actualize publicly the claim of the gospel by prophetic critique, it must leave the judgment and the establishment of final justice to the Day of the Lord (→theology of mission). Thus the church's witness to hope, even though it can never fully "belong to the world," is always realized — not by lapsing into otherworldliness but by giving an account of the hope that is in us (see 1 Pt 3:15) for God's salvation of the world in solidarity and co-responsibility.

DIETRICH WIEDERKEHR

Bibliography

Alfaro, J., *Esperanza cristiana y liberación del hombre* (1971). Beyerhaus, F., "Eschatology: Does It Make a Difference in Missions?" *EMQ* 26 (1990) 366–76. Bosch, D. J., *Transforming Mission* (1991) 498–510. Breuning, W., and R. Friedli, eds., *Seele: Problembegriff christlicher Eschatologie* (1986). Collet, G., *Das Missionsverständnis der Kirche in der gegenwärtigen Diskussion* (1984). Congar, Y., *Une peuple messianique: Salut et liberation* (1975). Dexinger, F., ed., *Tod-Hoffnung-Jenseits: Dimensionen und Konsequenzen biblisch verankerter Eschatologie* (1983). Eagleson, J., and P. Scharper, *Puebla and Beyond: Documentation and Commentary* (1979). Greinacher, N., ed., *Konflikt um die Theologie der Befreiung: Diskussion und Dokumentation* (1985). Greshake, G., and G. Lohfink, *Naherwartung-Auferstehung-Unsterblichkeit* (1975). Gutiérrez, G., *A Theology of Liberation*, rev. ed. (1988). Hayes, Z., *Visions of a Future* (1989). Idem, *What Are They Saying about the End of the World?* (1983). Hellwig, M. K., "Eschatology," in F. Schüssler Fiorenza and J. Galvin, eds., *Systematic Theology: Roman Catholic Perspectives*, vol. 2 (1991) 349–72. Idem, *What Are They Saying about Death and Christian Hope?* (1978). Kehl, M., *Eschatologie* (1986). Knörzer, W., *Reich Gottes: Traun-Hoffnung-Wirklichkeit* (1969). Kramm, T., *Analyse und Bewärung theologischer Modelle zur Begründung der Mission: Entscheidungskriterien in der aktuellen: Auseinandersetzung zwischen einem heilsgeschichtlich-ekkelesiologischern und einem geschichtlich-eschatologischen Missionsverständnis* (1979). Küng, H., *Eternal Life? Life after Death as a Medical, Philosophical, and Theological Problem* (1984). Lakeland, P., "Providence and Political Responsibility: The Nature of Praxis in an Age of Apocalypse," *MTh* 7 (July 1991)

351–62. Lohfink, G., *Death Is Not the Final Word* (1977). Metz, J. B., *Faith in History and Society* (1980). Moltmann, J., *Theology of Hope* (1967). Mußner, F., *Christus vor uns: Studien zur christlichen Eschatologie* (1966). Pannenberg, W., "Constructive and Critical Functions of Christian Eschatology," *HThR* 77 (April 1984) 119–39. Idem, *Theology and the Kingdom of God* (1969). Peters, T., *God: The World's Future* (1992) 306–31. Phan, P., *Eternity in Time: A Study of Karl Rahner's Eschatology* (1988). Rahner, K., *Foundations of Christian Faith* (1978) 431–47. Idem, "The Hermeneutics of Eschatological Assertions," *TI* 4 (1966) 323–46. Idem, "Ideas for a Theology of Death," *TI* 13 (1975) 169–86. Idem, "The Inexhaustible Transcendence of God and Our Concern for the Future," in *Concern for the Church* (1981) 173–86. Ratzinger, J., *Eschatology, Death, and Eternal Life* (1988). Rütti, L., *Zur Theologie der Mission: Kritische Analysen und neue Orientierungen* (1972). Rzepkowski, H., *Der Welt verpflichtet: Text und Kommentar des Apostolischen Schreibens Evangelii Nuntiandi — Über die Evangelisierung in der Welt von heute* (1976). Sauter, G., *Zukunft und Verheissung: Das Problem der Zukunft in der gegenwärtigen theologischen und philosophischen Diskussion* (1973). Scherer, J. A., "Why Mission Theology Cannot Do without Eschatological Urgency," *Missiol* 18/4 (October 1990) 395–413. Schillebeeckx, E., and B. Willems, eds., *The Problem of Eschatology*, vol. 41 of *Concilium* (1969). Schwartz, H., "Eschatology," in C. E. Braaten and R. W. Jensen, eds., *Christian Dogmatics*, vol. 2 (1984) 473–587. Idem, *On the Way to the Future* (1972). Shaull, R., *Befreiung durch Veränderung: Herausforderungen an Kirche, Theologie und Gesellschaft* (1970). Shaull, R., with G. Gutiérrez, *Liberation and Change* (1977). Skydsgaard, K. E., "The Kingdom of God and the Church," *SJTh* 4 (1951) 383–97. Smart, N., and S. Konstantine, *Christian Systematic Theology in a World Context* (1991) 388–428. Snyder, H. A., *Models of the Kingdom* (1991). Suchocki, M., *The End of Evil: Process Eschatology in Historical Context* (1988). Tiryakian, E. A., "Modernity as an Eschatological Setting: A New Vista for the Study of Religions," *HR* 25 (May 1986) 378–86. Vorgrimler, H., *Hoffnung auf Vollendung: Aufriss der Eschatologie* (1984). Walle, A. R. van de, *From Darkness to the Dawn* (1985). Weigert, A. J., "Christian Eschatological Identities and the Nuclear Context," *JSSR* 27 (June 1988) 175–91. Wiedenmann, L., *Mission und Eschatologie: Eine Analyse der neueren Deutschen Evangelischen Missionstheologie* (1965). *Your Kingdom Come: Mission Perspectives,* Report on the World Conference on Mission and Evangelism, Melbourne, Australia, May 12–25, 1980 (1980). Zwi Weblowsky, R. J., "Eschatology," in *EncRel,* vol. 5 (1987) 149–51.

❧ ETHICS ❧

1. A Variety of Approaches. 2. Values and Norms. 3. Culture: Historical Change as a Factor. 4. Culture: Social Pluralism as a Factor. 5. The Question of Christian Ethics. 6. Ethics and Mission.

1. The very definition of ethics is tied up with the way one conceives its function or purpose, determines its content, and responds to its main themes. Within a cognitive map of traditional concerns in ethics and a corresponding family tree of schools of thought, we could restate some definitions as follows.

Some define the purpose of ethics as the encompassing, systematic, and rigorous study of the meaning and application of evaluative intelligence. As the analysis of the good (or similar predicates) and its realization in human action, study can operate at various levels. At the morals level, ethics studies commonsense opinions and convictions about what is ultimately good and worthwhile, moral rights and obligations, and commendable conduct or character. At the ethics level, ethics is conceived as a systematic, rigorous, and critical inquiry into the implicit postulates, premises, or theories of morals. At the metaethical level, ethical theory itself is critiqued, and it is asked what meaning normative ethical statements have, whether they can be known to be true and whether they can be justified at all.

Although the concrete focus is on intelligent and voluntary human action, the real content of ethics spans the whole range of human experience, inclusive of implicit views regarding, for example, one's self-image, one's location within the secular world, and one's relation to ultimate reality, always from the viewpoint of the good, right, and proper and at the varying levels described above. Crucial differences of judgments occur, for example, if human nature is seen as basically good (Aquinas, Rousseau) or corrupt (Luther, Hobbes), concrete or universal, static or transformable, earthly or graced.

Themes can and have been variously grouped into, for example, critical, performative, or normative theories. An important question is: What moves one to act at all? This has led to various speculative responses from the fields of psychology of motivation, phenomenology of human experience, theories of moral anthropology, and comparative ethics in social anthropology. A second critical issue is: What is the good to be pursued? Teleological or axiological theories attempt to answer why things are good in themselves and therefore to be pursued. A third serious issue is twofold: How ought I to pursue this good, or how ought I to live? In the former, normative ethical theory or deontology grapples with when conduct is right or wrong and hence with issues of principles, norms, standards, rules, and so on. In the latter, the focus is on what kind of character is commendable or reprehensible, channeling into the discussion of virtues. Although they are held to be interrelated, proposals often divide into separate developments.

Accordingly, and in the broadest sense, ethics is the science of the motives and ends, the goodness or badness, the rightness or wrongness, the virtue or vice of human behavior. Approaches will differ according to the articulation of questions, arrangements of priority, urgency of response, use of vocabulary, and so on. More narrowly described, ethics is a practical and normative science, based on reason, which examines human behavior and provides norms for human goodness or badness.

2. Historically, moral theology has tended to focus on the personal significations of human praxis as good or bad (virtues) while philosophical ethics has tended to concentrate on objective references for praxis as right or wrong (norms). Thus, from a systematic point of view, the ethical question has been reduced very often to the practical and normative: What ought I to do? One way of understanding the answers to this is to focus on theories regarding the main components of moral action, which are acts, motives, and consequences. The history of ethics chronicles those attempts to provide accounts for one or the other; it also shows that none has succeeded in providing a comprehensive and satisfactory theory which would account for all of them altogether. Each is a product of a philosophical commitment, grounded on postulates or convictions.

Prior to What ought I to do? one must address two interrelated issues: What is the good to be sought? and How does one formulate universal norms?

First, what does human action intend? Historically, some of the principal answers to this question have included *sophia* (Socrates), ideal models (Plato), contemplative *eudaemonia* (Aristotle), pleasure (Aristippus and J. Locke), temperance (Epicurus), apathy (Epictetus), power (Thrasymachus), supremacy (N. Machiavelli, F. Nietzsche), utility as hedonistic (J. Bentham, J. and J. S. Mill) or nonhedonistic (G. E. Moore), duty (I. Kant), and authenticity (M. Heidegger) — to name but a few. In a certain sense all seem to agree on an essential human well-being without restricting this to self-realization.

Second, the most difficult yet critical issue of ethics concerns moral norms. The question is not only How does one judge an act as good or evil? but also Is there a universal set of norms transcending differences of individuality, historicity, or social belonging? Historically, again, one can note different stresses on the human faculty for determining such norms.

a. Norms are established by logical reason, although reason-centered accounts differ. Examples are Plato's knowledge of the Forms or Aristotle's principle of the Mean. Aquinas's natural law is practically equivalent to reason, insofar as the good is that which is in accord with human nature as it ought to be. Among modern forms are rationalist nonnaturalism (A. C. Ewing, C. D. Broad) or that emphasizing human rights (e.g., W. K. Frankena).

b. Norms are determined by a kind of "feeling," of which the variants are moral sense, intuition, interest, conviction, desire, and so on. Examples are D. Hume's view of moral passions; I. Kant's sense of duty in the categorical imperative; eighteenth-century British theory; Fletcher's sense of what constitutes Christian loving in a particular situation; Scheler's intuition of value, which is a priori, preceding moral obligation and even motive. A similar emotive intuition can be found in N. Hartmann or D. von Hildebrand; G. E. Moore, H. A. Prichard, and W. D. Ross are also included in feeling-centered views.

c. Norms are fixed by practical reason, interpreted as, for example, temperance, moderation, discipline, realism, resignation, power. In different ways D. Scotus, William of Ockham, T. Hobbes, A. Schopenhauer, S. Kierkegaard, and J.-P. Sartre appealed to some kind of fiat. Since there are as many standards as there are societies, some relativists deny universal principles, arguing that one set of principles is as good as the other; others hold that supracultural norms are not impossible. Utilitarianism (such as individual hedonism or social eudaimonism) accents not the type of action or motive of action but the effects of action. Proportionalism and certain performative theories urge acting according to the more urgent duty and larger benefits for all.

3. The logical analysis of the field sometimes obscures the fact that ethics has had a relatively long history. From Homeric times to G. F. Hegel, Western ethics was built up by generations of philosophizing; it spanned centuries of articulation of the fundamental questions, sifting the numerous sides to every issue, before settling into the major groupings as exemplified above. The moral agent is not "timeless," and neither are the concepts which theorists employ for comprehending; the types of action people do, the ends they pursue, the consequences of their acts — all these occur in the concrete; they are determined by history and culture.

The ethical thinker does not raise questions *in vacuo;* the ethical theorist does not construct systems *in abstracto;* the moralist responds to questions posed by human activity in history: those unresolved by previous theories, those raised by new experiences, those pressed by allied sciences. Because ethics and culture are intrinsically rather than only contingently related to each other, modern theories tend to shift emphasis from the essential forms of the ethical questions to other contingent aspects derived from new sciences or concerns.

It is not denied that there are constant themes across historical periods; they do not differ in essential moral concerns; generalizations are not impossible, although they can be spoken of only in the most formal and abstract senses (Baron Montesquieu, D. Diderot). The accent on cultural history has sometimes issued in relativism but need not be construed as its equivalent; it simply argues that periods differ about the scale, accents, and contents of ethical concerns, even if such concerns are acknowledged to remain universal.

Even the distinction between first-order discourse about lived conduct (morality) and second-order discourse (ethics) cannot be understood ahistorically. It is morals which provides content for the ethics which organizes it. This is evident in any moral language, the specific nuances of which are tied to the periods in which they were born. Because a people's history and moral concepts are imbedded in each other, evolve together, and mutually influence each other, moral language indexes its historical contexts; they are inseparable and unintelligible apart from each other.

Another example of cultural change attendant to historical change is the disintegration of the unified and integrated cosmic order, differentiating into natural order, social order, and metaphysical order. Such transitions from *mythos* to *chronos,* or from social *Historie* to existentialist *Geschichte,* provided occasions for vastly different responses. Concern for *bonum* alternated between analysis and realization, structure and evolution, justification and critique.

The most serious issue is how philosophical thought relates ethically to historical change (C. Darwin, S. Freud, K. Marx). In the concrete, ethics can be used consciously or unconsciously to preserve the dying order (e.g., moral conservatism from Aristotle to D. Hume) or to justify the birth of the new (e.g., Buddha, Jesus, or Mao Tse-tung and China's Cultural Revolution).

4. Just as there is an intrinsic relationship between ethics and culture with regard to history, so there is one between ethics and society. This nexus, all but ignored in the past when society was more integrated, has acquired prominence in view of the fragmentation and heterogeneity of modern culture. As societies change, so do their ethics (as in the Industrial Revolution); equally, as values and norms change, so too do social arrangements (as with revolutionary ethics).

Moral agents are not detached from their social groups; the ideals they pursue, the values they hold, and the norms they follow are influenced by society in general and particular ways. There is no morally neutral activity insofar as society is concerned, and a socially solipsist ethics is a myth. As morality does not exist stripped of all specific social forms, ethical reflection itself cannot be understood apart from its insertion into some kind of social life. The rationality of an ethical system is intelligible only in the historical period and social order in which it is imbedded. Thus the connections in ethics between convictions and interest, bias or prejudice (B. Lonergan), become important.

The insight that ethical theory must be referred to the matrix of human relationships in which the questions were phrased and answered has several implications. One implication is that society is not merely a neutral context in which people behave ethically according to some supracultural, universally applicable norms; ethics is bound up with social structure and is socially conditioned. Views of the human must include theories of society, for example, Is society only a group of individuals, or is it more than that? The view of nature conceived as natural (presocial) and a view of society concomitant to nature because it inheres in social relations bring back issues of natural law with distinct implications for private and public issues of morality. Hegel, F. H. Bradley, and T. H. Green typify the critique of asocial and individualist views of morality.

Society implies vertical pluralism. "Comparative ethics" is the descriptive study by social scientists of actual beliefs and values; ethics in the strict sense studies the justifications for those beliefs and values. Although it has always been recognized that ethical theory is foundational to other theories — for example, parts of political theory, economic theory, jurisprudence — it is clearer today that these are not formulated in the same way by different participants in the social process. Class considerations (e.g., elite, bourgeois, and proletariat) give rise to ethics which are heterogeneous, factually and evaluatively. One has only to contrast the aristocratic views of Plato and Aristotle with the egalitarianism of rights advocates. Kant's formalism and the stress on transcendental values did not abstract from society as they claimed to; in fact, they legitimized values and norms of social conformism. In the opposite direction, Hegel, Marx, the English idealists, and many others proposed values and norms which subverted consciously or unconsciously manipulative sociopolitical, economic, cultural, and religious systems.

Society implies horizontal pluralism. Comparative ethics also shows how different societies hold different ethics. At its broadest, for example, the West emphasizes the normative before the comparative (descriptive or phenomenological). The Western emphasis is on the self-subsistent and individual, or self-contained and private morality. A major shift in the history of ethics is the stress on the individual, giving rise to theories of natural rights, self-love, and so on. But this modern discovery, no matter how valuable, has not dissolved issues related to human community, for example, problems of benevolence and altruism. The polarities between modern individualism and traditional communitarianism manifest two aspects of human nature as such. Ethics must face the issues of ethnocentrism and internationality, with its related issues of variable values and relative norms.

5. Two of the basic postulates of ethics are human freedom and the immortality of the human soul. The former is necessary for responsibility; the latter as justification for doing good and avoiding evil at all. This notion can also be found in some Eastern ethics where reward and punishment are considered as immanent in the deeds themselves, in virtue of, for example, natural law (e.g., karma). Other views are only slowly asserting themselves.

The linkage of ethics to a wider context of significance brings it just a step away from ideas of religion. For ethics includes the person's perception of self in relation to worldview and, in that context, the determination of the *summum bonum,* no matter what content it may have. In that light, most forms of Western ethics include religion as a third postulate. Despite or because of the evident moral injustice and evil in the world, there must be an ultimate power who rewards and punishes in the end. For Christian ethics in particular, God is a necessary postulate.

Ethics has often limited the polarities of moral reality to good and bad, right or wrong. At other times it has focused on the commendable and reprehensible, the uniqueness of the individual and the indispensability of community. Christianity has been known to be open to a variety of conceptual frameworks, but it is debated whether it also introduces moral content previously unknown to human experience or reason. Some have suggested that its ideas of salvation, the virtues of meekness and humility, self-sacrificial altruism, and love of enemies are specific to Christianity; but not all are convinced. Most Christian versions of ethics have refused to dissolve the polarities mentioned above and have even heightened a preference for one or the other side of the polarity under debate. Thus, while insisting that the biblical ideal is oriented to new persons or new beings born of a new creation, Christianity is also aware that historical reality forces us to turn to philosophy, the concern of which is with new systems and theories of human action.

6. Christianity is premised on religious ideals embodied in the notion of the reign of God; its ethics is normed by its theology, which in turn is grounded on revelation. Traditional Roman Catholicism is unique in having fused theology and metaphysics in natural law and in having its normative ethics cleared by a moral authority which issues definitive resolutions. Christianity, however, does not escape the sometimes divergent movements of conscience and faith, and even if today most traditions occupy a middle ground between extreme fundamentalist and radically liberal views, the Protestant Reformation and the Catholic Counter-Reformation are painful reminders of how bitter such breaks can be.

Beyond ecumenism, the churches continue to be challenged by human experience as such, new explanations from the sciences, the convictions of alternative systems antedating Christianity, and the inherently critical nature of philosophy. Modern Christianity faces serious challenges today from social pluralism and historical modernity. The church, a minority in some cultures (Asia) and a majority in others (Latin America), includes the poorest of the poor in Asia but also the privileged elite of the North Atlantic. History looks backward in Africa and forward in Latin America. Technology and humanism clash in every development movement. Older churches must contend with ones more recently established; the dominant West and North must be open to the richness of the churches of the East and South.

Evangelization today must find ways to accommodate all these changes and has correspondingly emphasized justice and peace, missionary dialogue, inculturation, secularization, and so on. Clearly the challenges of culture imply a review of dogmatism, acknowledgment of pluralism, recognition of a limited relativism, acceptance of tolerance, and a tempering of absolutism. The challenges of history have implications for critical conservation but also for syncretism, for realism but also for idealism, for responsibility but also for liberation, for truth but also for ambiguity, for principle but also for compassion. This evangelization agenda was fulfilled in Jesus, whose moral choices exemplify how one can be part of a cultural milieu and yet transcend it, how one can truly be part of a social environment and yet embrace others. The church, conscious of its historical and social anchorage, can do no less as it proclaims God's reign.

DIONISIO MIRANDA, SVD

Bibliography

Brandt, R., *A Theory of the Good and the Right* (1979). Crawford, S. C., ed., *The Evolution of Hindu Ethical Ideals* (1982). Idem, *World Religions and Global Ethics* (1989). Cua, A., *Ethical Argumentation: A Study in Hsun-Tzu's Moral Epistemology* (1985). Idem, *The Unity of Knowledge and Action: A Case Study in Wang Yang-Ming's Moral Psychology* (1982). Danto, A., *Mysticism and Morality: Oriental Thought and Moral Philosophy* (1972). Fakhry, M., *Ethical Theories in Islam* (1991). Foot, P., *Theories of Ethics* (1979). Green, R., *Religion and Moral Reason: A New Method for Comparative Study* (1988). Idem, *Religious Reason* (1978). Gula, R., *Reason Informed by Faith: Foundations of Catholic Morality* (1989). Gustafson, J., *Can Ethics Be Christian?* (1975). Hauerwas, S., *A Community of Character: Toward a Constructive Christian Social Ethic* (1981). Idem, *Truthfulness and Tragedy: Further Investigations in Christian Ethics* (1977). Idem, *Vision and Virtue: Essays in Christian Ethical Reflection* (1981). Hovanissian, R., ed., *Ethics in Islam* (1983). Jhingran, S., *Aspects of Hindu Morality* (1989). Jules-Rosette, B., ed., *The New Religions of Africa* (1979). King, N., *African Cosmos* (1986). Kitagawa, J., and M. Cummings, eds.,

Buddhism and Asian History (1989). Little, D., and S. Twiss, *Comparative Religious Ethics: A New Method* (1978). Lovin, R., and F. Reynolds, eds., *Cosmogony and Ethical Order: New Studies in Comparative Ethics* (1985). MacIntyre, A., *Three Rival Versions of Moral Enquiry* (1990). Mantovani, E., *Traditional and Present-day Melanesian Values and Ethics* (1991) Mbiti, J., *African Religions and Philosophy* (1969). McCormick, R. A., *Notes on Moral Theology* (1965–1980; 1981–1984) (1981, 1984). Míguez-Bonino, J., *Toward a Christian Political Ethics* (1983). Miranda, D. M., *Buting Pinoy: Probe Essays on Value as Filipino* (1992). Misra, G. S. P., *Development of Buddhist Ethics* (1984). Moreno, F., *Moral Theology from the Poor* (1988). Peters, T., *God: The World's Future* (1992) 357–77. Quintos, L., *The Moral System of Buddhism* (1977). Rescher, N., *Moral Absoluteness: An Essay on the Nature and Rationality of Morality* (1989). Sempebwa, J., *African Traditional Moral Norms and Their Implications for Christianity: A Case Study of Ganda Ethics* (1983). Sigwick, H., *The Methods of Ethics* (1966). Smart, N., and S. Konstantine, *Christian Systematic Theology in a World Context* (1991) 359–87. Tachibana, S., *The Ethics of Buddhism* (1926). Wadell, P., *Friendship and the Moral Life* (1989). Idem, *The Primacy of Love: An Introduction to the Ethics of Thomas Aquinas* (1992). Zahan, D., *The Religions, Spirituality, and Thought of Traditional Africa* (1979).

❧ EUCHARIST (LORD'S SUPPER) ◆

1. Terminology. 2. Lord's Supper in the Bible. 3. Lord's Supper in Systematic Theology.

1. "Lord's Supper" (= Eucharist) is the common Christian designation for the central liturgical and sacramental event called by Vatican II "the source and summit of the Christian life" (*LG* 11; *SC* 10) "from which the Church ever derives its life and on which it thrives" (*LG* 26). In the Catholic Church synonymous expressions from the early church ("breaking of bread" [1 Cor 10:16; Acts 2:46]; "sacrifice" [in the works of Cyprian and Augustine]; gathering = *collecta*) yielded to the term "sacrifice of the Mass." After the Council of Trent (1545–63), "Eucharist," which was used for the first time by Justin, came to be preferred as a designation for the thanksgiving, praise, and sacrifice which are at the heart of the action. The term "Lord's Supper" has the advantage of elucidating the direct connection of the ecclesiastical cultic event with the last meal of Jesus Christ and hence identifying this sacrament as an immediate institution of Christ.

2. Even if the nature of Jesus' meal as paschal is exegetically a matter for discussion, its connection with the paschal rite (especially in the words spoken over the gifts) cannot be disputed. Similarly, neither can its creative recasting be overlooked. For Jesus interprets the gifts to mean himself ("This is my body" and "This is the cup of my blood") and in this way declares that he vicariously dies for the disciples (as for the whole of humanity). At the same time it is evident that the narratives describing the institution of the Lord's Supper differ from one another in some details. Thus in the (probably older) Pauline (Antiochian) version the emphasis is on the meal as such (1 Cor 11:23–24; Lk 22:19–20), whereas in the so-called Petrine form (Mt 26:26–28; Mk 14:22–24) it is the elements of the meal that are accentuated, in particular the blood as sacrificial material (→sacrifice). Nevertheless, it is not a question here of contradictory or incompatible concepts. Both streams of tradition show that on the night before his passion Jesus did not simply celebrate a farewell meal (like the farewell meals of the patriarchs in the Old Testament); rather, with the words spoken over the gifts and the accompanying actions, he performed the act of self-abandonment which reached its highest expression on the cross and which (in analogy to Ex 24:8) sealed the new covenant. Protestant exegesis too (in spite of some problems posed by historical-critical investigation) concedes that Jesus describes himself (in the words of the Last Supper) as a sacrifice, more precisely as the eschatological paschal lamb (cf. 1 Cor 5:7), whose death inaugurates the new covenant prefigured in the covenant on Sinai and prophesied for the time of salvation (Jer 31:31–34). Jesus' death, says J. Jeremias, is a vicarious death.

Just as Jesus' death was no private religious event, neither was the Lord's Supper. The essential and temporal universality of this event is expressed especially in the command to recall the event (anamnesis) "Do this in memory of me" (Lk 22:19; 1 Cor 11:24, 25b). Hence the remembrance or recollection becomes the comprehensive structure of the Lord's Supper, in the sense not only of a memory open merely to the past but also, as the so-called eschatological view shows ("until it is fulfilled in the Kingdom of God" [Lk 22:15f.]), of a meaning open to a perspective directed toward the heavenly banquet in the reign of God.

3. Through the anamnesis or words of institution Jesus obliged and empowered the church, invested with his authority, to repeat his action in the sacrament of the Eucharist in a manner essentially corresponding to the original event: a sacrifice offered in the form of a meal. In spite of the considerable change to which the Eucharist as a liturgical ritual event was subjected in the course of history, ranging from the simple domestic community celebrations of the early church to the solemn pontifical liturgies of the Middle Ages and finally to the more simple celebrations of the modern liturgy (a diversity still mirrored today in the variety of recognized rites), the church has always been conscious of the obligation to preserve the original essence of the Lord's Supper and has tried to consolidate this identity in particular in its dogmatic teaching. In this way the paramount position of the Eucharist among the sacraments has become more pronounced, for in the Eucharist the whole work of salvation, culminating in the cross and resurrection, takes place sacramentally together with its agent and subject, Jesus Christ.

Hence the Eucharist is oriented in a special way toward the presence and the present, but not in a simple and uniform way. Whereas traditional theology focused on the presence of Christ under the elements of bread and wine, deeper reflection on the biblical and theological contexts has broadened the insight into the differentiation of modes of presence. Accordingly, Christ is present as the (heavenly) Lord and main actor (principal real presence). As such he makes the sacrificial event on the cross present (memorial real presence which, by the mediation of the minister, takes place in words and signs). He also surrenders himself as a gift in this act identical with the sacrifice of the cross (substantial somatic presence).

The various kinds of presence which exist side by side indicate the richness of a saving event which is so mysterious that it cannot be fathomed completely by the human mind. It is nevertheless comprehensible to faith that the *scopus* of the Eucharist and its *proprium* consist in making present the body and blood (and hence the whole person) of Christ under the elements of bread and wine, that is, in the so-called somatic presence. For the presence of the *minister principalis* is a factor in all sacraments. In each sacrament there is also (even if not in the same way) a reenactment of the saving action of Christ. It is only in the Eucharist that the reenactment of the perfected work of salvation, the victorious cross-event, is present together with the sacrificial gift on the cross, the *Christus passus*.

In this event lies the most profound, most challenging mystery of the Lord's

Supper. In an attempt to bring it home to Christians in the early church, theologians used the concept of transformation (metabolism), and, since the Middle Ages and the Council of Trent, the concept of a change of substance (transubstantiation) has been employed. Accordingly, after the change of the substance of bread and wine (even if the external appearances remain), Christ is present "truly, really, and essentially."

The term "transubstantiation," because of its close connection to past cosmological and ideological ideas, has been the subject of some recent criticism. As modern substitutes, "transsignification" (change of signs) or "transfinalization" (change of meaning) have been suggested, but these do not express the full meaning of the original term, which can also suggest "change of essence." For the ecumenical debate concerning the Eucharist, it is important that Luther (in spite of rejecting transubstantiation) insisted on the somatic real presence of Christ. From this point of departure there arise further possibilities of convergence concerning the sacrificial character of this sacrament. Calvin, however, saw the relationship of the signs of bread and wine to the body of Christ in the sense not of an identity but rather of a dynamic participation of the believing receiver in the body of Christ. Zwingli stood for a purely symbolic, figurative interpretation of the bread and wine.

Even if it is impossible to give a comprehensive conceptual explanation for the nature of the presence of Christ, its meaning and goal are quite clear. They do not consist in the "miracle" of the presence as such but rather consist in the application of the saving work of Christ to the faithful, in their "taking" of the gifts, and in the acceptance of the sacrifice. Such an acceptance cannot happen in a purely passive way and must involve a personal appropriation of the event. For this reason "the sacrifice of Christ" has always been regarded as also "the sacrifice of the church." This does not mean that the church can add something to the sacrifice of Christ. Rather, by taking up the sacrifice of Christ, so to speak, the church associates itself internally and externally with it and presents it "through him, with him, and in him" to the Father. In this way the whole Christian existence is absorbed into Christ's movement to the Father. The eucharistic transformation, then, happens not only to the material bread and wine but in a certain way also to the faithful. Through the Eucharist the faithful are enabled and obliged to transform the world in Christ. Consequently, as the greatest sign of unity the Eucharist not only mediates essential energy for uniting the church but also provides incentive for the Christian commission to evangelize the world.

LEO SCHEFFCZYK

Bibliography

Averbeck, W., *Der Opfercharakter des Abendmahls in der neueren evangelischen Theologie* (1966). Cambridge Conference on the Eucharist, *One Loaf, One Cup: Ecumenical Studies of I Cor. 11 and Other Eucharistic Texts* (1993). Chilton, B., *A Feast of Meanings: Eucharistic Theologies from Jesus through Johannine Circles* (1994). Davies, H., *Bread of Life and Cup of Joy: Newer Ecumenical Perspectives on the Eucharist* (1993). Fahey, M., *Catholic Perspectives on Baptism, Eucharist, and Ministry* (1986). Jeremias, J., *Eucharistic Words of Jesus* (1977). Jones, P. H., *Christ's Eucharistic Presence: A History of the Doctrine* (1994). Kinnamon, M., *Why It Matters: A Popular Introduction to the Baptism, Eucharist, and Ministry Text* (1985). Larere, P., *The Lord's Supper: Towards an Ecumenical Understanding of the Eucharist* (1993). Lazareth, W. H., *Growing Together in Baptism, Eucharist, and Ministry: A Study Guide* (1982). Limouris, G., *Orthodox Perspectives on Baptism, Eucharist, and Ministry* (1985). Moloney, F. J., *A Body Broken for a Broken People: Eucharist in the New Testament* (1990). *Oxford Dictionary of the Christian Church*

(1988). Piepkorn, A. C., "Digests of Recent American and European Discussions of the Sacrament of the Altar," in *Lutherans and Catholics in Dialogue,* vol. 1/3 (1974) 125–48. Reumann, J. H. P., *The Supper of the Lord: The New Testament, Ecumenical Dialogues, and Faith and Order on Eucharist* (1985). Seybold, M., and A. Glaser, *Das "Lima Paper"* (1985). Stromberg, J., *Sharing One Bread, Sharing One Mission: The Eucharist as Missionary Event* (1972). Thurian, M., *Churches Respond to Baptism, Eucharist, and Ministry (BEM)* (1986). Idem, *Ecumenical Perspectives on Baptism, Eucharist, and Ministry (BEM)* (1983). World Council of Churches, *Baptism, Eucharist, and Ministry* (1982).

❧ EUROPEAN THEOLOGY ❧

1. The Concept of Theology in European Thought. 2. Characteristics of European Theology. 3. Biblical Theology. 4. Systematic Theology (Protestant, Catholic). 5. Summary.

1. The concept "theology" as it has developed in Europe is derived from the Greek word *theologia*. Plato understood it as the interpretation of the myths from the perspective of civic behavior; for Aristotle it was the summit of reflection on being, *noesis noeseos,* or God. The Stoics understood theology as the teaching about civic duties; at the same time it was a critical judgment on the mythical stories about the gods. In early Christianity the word was not used at first, the subject being sometimes referred to as *vera philosophia.* It was not long, however, before the word "theology" was reserved for christology, with salvation history coming under the heading of *oikonomia.* By the sixth century, "theology" was uniformly used and distinguished according to different types: for instance, philosophical and mystical, affirmative (cataphatic) and negative (apophatic) — according to whether it referred to God with human categories or one's experience of the divine as totally other. For Augustine, theology was philosophizing about God; Christian doctrine, in contrast, was *doctrina sacra* or *doctrina christiana.* The whole epoch up to that time was characterized by a zealous search for truth stamped and formed by contemporary ideas from Stoicism and Neoplatonism. The modern concept of theology as responsible or scientific reflection from and about the faith dates from the High Middle Ages; it was then that the Aristotelian concept of science began to be applied. With Thomas Aquinas this reflection on faith reached a previously unattained level. Aquinas linked the truths attained by the light of faith in a discursive method, related them with undisputed truths of reason, and arranged them into a systematic summary or *summa.* Parallel to this we have the Franciscan school (especially under Bonaventure) which was influenced by the Neoplatonic illuminism of Augustine and saw in Christ the medium of our knowledge about God. Centuries later the Reformers, especially Luther, took as a theological starting point a deep mistrust of the *ratio* of the sinner and developed a theology which was nourished purely from faith — with special reference to the foolishness of the cross. In the seventeenth and eighteenth centuries, separate theological disciplines began to emerge: biblical theology, dogmatics or systematic theology, moral theology or ethics, apologetics or fundamental theology, church history and liturgy. In our own day we notice the emergence of a number of special theologies (theology of hope, liberation, environment, women, etc.) which are concerned more with orthopraxis than with orthodoxy. Neither should we forget the theologies which were rooted in a certain time or cultural development, for example, the liberal, fundamentalist, pietistic, neo-Scholastic, and political theologies.

The "death of God" theology of the 1960s was a phenomenon which arose as a consequence of linguistic and social analysis.

2. A typical characteristic of European theology, including that of the Orthodox, is its claim to *universalism;* it wants to make statements valid for all, since God, about whom it claims to speak, is Lord and Master of all, whose Son has come to save us all, and the reign of God and its eschatological goal are meant for everybody. In addition, there is the Aristotelian model of science, according to which there is no real knowledge of the particular and individual. Only universals which are distilled from the accidental and historical can mediate statements with general validity. In this way an *abstract* theology emerges which is applicable to all in the same way. The nominalism of the Late Middle Ages tried to solve the problems which thus arose (e.g., through the *Devotio Moderna*). But Luther was the first to expose the insufficiency of the traditional theology and to introduce historicity. Contemporary theology is characterized by *topicality.* The statements of the faith not only refer to their past importance but in each situation must be experienced afresh. Consequently, they must be related to the historical circumstances, the cultural context, and the needs and justified expectations of the faithful. Systematic presentations in the manner of the medieval *summae* are no longer possible. Such relevance also calls for contact and dialogue with the sciences, especially the social sciences. Much effort has been put into the conversation with secularization, sociology, and Marxism of various types. In the last analysis it is a question of elaborating a theologically acceptable anthropology. A further characteristic of European theology is its search for *foundations.* It concerns itself with the historicity of the life of Jesus, with biblical language and forms of speech (symbols, myths, parables), and with adequate hermeneutics. As a result, it regards the scriptures as normative books of faith which bear witness to and promote the faith but have no intention of imparting any other kind of knowledge. In this way rationalism in exegesis is effectively combated. Because the Bible is the *norma non normata,* biblical theology is of special importance.

3. Biblical theology does not want to come between the believing reader and the scriptures, since God reveals Godself just as God pleases. Consequently, Vatican II advised Catholics to read and reflect on the holy scriptures frequently (see *DV* 22ff.). For Protestants this has been taken for granted. In Europe the results of the council can be seen in Bible services and meditations; but in order to avoid as far as possible the dangers of a subjectivist interpretation, modern exegesis developed. The historical-critical method (analysis of the cultural context of the biblical text) is helpful not only for word and sentence analysis but also for showing comprehensive connections between the individual statements and the totality of the book in question or other books. Even in patristic times, of course, and especially in the Middle Ages, attempts were made to identify the triple (or quadruple) meaning of the individual passage. This means that the literal meaning of the text was not left in isolation; it was transcended in the direction of christology, Christian life, and eschatology. This art of transcending is a gift of the Spirit and of the *sensus fidei,* a gift which the faithful receive and without which the theologian cannot carry out his or her task. In our time the special relationship of the Old and New Testaments has been recognized; it is much more profound than was generally supposed. Systematic theology takes over the findings of biblical theology and asks questions of the biblical text resulting from the concrete Christian life and its context. It must be careful not to follow fashionable trends which falsify the original kerygma.

4. World War I exposed the failure of nineteenth-century Protestant liberal theology, and as a consequence there was a radical return to biblical revelation. K. Barth (1886–1968) was the spokesman for a group of theologians who represented a theological trend called "dialectical theology," for which the second edition of *Epistle to the Romans* (1922) acted as a catalyst. In this work Barth carries the Reformation teaching of the one and only God who revealed himself in Jesus Christ to its logical conclusion. This God is and remains unattainable for the human *ratio* and for religious feelings. We find God in the word of the Bible, where there is communicated both anger because of our sin and mercy because of God's grace. Whoever surrenders to this word experiences both God's no and God's yes. Hence the individual finds himself or herself in a dialectical tension between this God and his or her own worldliness. Theology attempts to express this tension and courageously champion God's claim to the world. While being critical toward society and the world, in its own sphere theology has to take *theologia crucis* (negative theology) seriously. R. Bultmann (1884–1976) was a fellow traveler of Barth at the time of the latter's study on the Epistle to the Romans but modified the basic Reformation theme in the spirit of the existential analysis of M. Heidegger. Bultmann wanted to emphasize the indispensable factor of history, essential for our saying yes to God. E. Brunner (1889–1966) is another representative of this dialectical theology. He too had to separate himself from Barth because he was preoccupied by the question how God's word can reach people, especially those of the working class. In this search Brunner discovered the philosophy of M. Buber, whose reflections about dialogue ("I-thou" relationships) became Brunner's key experience in his theological investigations. For when the divine "I" speaks to us it always meets a "thou" which (because of reason or being God's image) is of the same kind and so can and must respond (in gratuitously bestowed freedom). Since humanity constantly tries to show how important it is and to deny allegiance to God, there is a dialectical tension between God's word and our response. Consequently, theology should not (primarily) teach dogmas but point out ways in which God's word can become an event for us. What results from this is "responsive relevance" or "personal co-respondence." The intention of these and other theologians is to show that God gives a new direction to people and motivates them so that they can better cope with the great challenges of the times. Important also is P. Tillich (1886–1965), who tried to speak to the modern person suffering from alienation and despair; J. Moltmann (b. 1926), whose anthropology is particularly concerned with the future of humankind, suffering, and ecology; W. Pannenberg (b. 1928), whose efforts to throw light on the meaning of history through the cross and resurrection of Jesus have attracted attention; and, finally, G. Ebeling (b. 1912), a follower of D. Bonhoeffer, who tries to make the gospel effective in today's secularized world.

In the Catholic Church the new theological approach, already prepared for since the turn of the century by intensive patristic and liturgical studies, was given decisive impulses by Vatican II. It was concerned essentially with the transcending of the neo-Scholastic methods and the reinterpretation of the traditional doctrinal formulas. In this respect, K. Rahner (1904–1984), whose theological career began with the exercises of St. Ignatius, particularly distinguished himself. Despite language difficulties, his works have probably contributed more than any others to the *aggiornamento* and have given him worldwide recognition. He uses the transcendental method (from Kant's *Critique of Pure Reason*) and accordingly inquires about the conditions which must be fulfilled if God would be revealed and communicated in absolute freedom, and so Rahner discovers the unlimited openness of the human spirit, which he (following Heidegger) calls the "supernatural existential." Rahner finds further support for his thesis in the teaching of High Scholasticism about the preapprehension of the totality of being. According to this, human beings are by their very existence on the way to God, the supreme being; more importantly, God belongs to the very definition of being human. From this perspective light is thrown on the incarnation of God's Son. For when it pleases God to empty Godself and to go into the "other," God can only become a human being. God-become-human is then the supreme form of being human, and every person is the possible brother or sister of Jesus Christ. The divine in Jesus does not suppress the human but assists it toward fulfillment. With reference to theological anthropology it should be noted that the human person as empty form is a creature that always points away from self, is "ex-sistent," dependent on communication with other human beings and the world. H. U. von Balthasar (b. 1904), a former companion of Rahner and later his untiring admonisher, took another direction. He attempted to use the phenomenological method and tried in all his works to point out the glory of the self-communicating and sacrificial love of God. We do not have to be determined by (Greek) tragedy or by the way of illusion (as in Buddhism) but should let ourselves be seized by the divine love which alone can tear down our prison walls and bestow on us the real freedom of the children of God. For this the cross is a sure signpost. Other theologians have devoted themselves to the question of being Christian in very different ways, for example, H. Küng (b. 1928), E. Schillebeeckx (b. 1914), and J. B. Metz (b. 1928). The latter, in particular, stresses the social dimension of theology. In his "political theology" he never tires of criticizing bourgeois self-assertion and its preoccupation with security. Just as important for him is the *memoria passionis,* by virtue of which there must never be another Auschwitz or any other such act of inhumanity. In spite of such horrors, we, confident in God's promises, seek a more human world, even if the "eschatological reservation" must always be kept in mind. Metz, whose ideas are very close to liberation theology, has tried to elucidate this new way of doing theology for Europeans.

5. In Europe there have always been different theologies. What united them was reflection on the one God who redeemed us in Jesus Christ through the Spirit. All other reflections are based on a definite context which has always been conditioned by history, society, and culture. As a result of the continuous cultural exchange on the small continent of Europe, a kind of cultural synthesis has developed which is different from other continents and which can be called Europeanism (E. Troeltsch, T. Rendtorff). It tends toward individualism and to taking itself as the absolute norm. It is precisely because of this latter factor, among other things, that many Third World theologians reject and disparage every kind of European theology. There are, however, others (e.g., L. Boff) who recognize that their theology cannot exist without European theology. Both are interdependent and must learn from each other (K. Rahner).

HEINRICH DUMONT, SVD

Bibliography

Balthasar, H. U. von, *The Theology of Karl Barth* (1971). Idem, *The von Balthasar Reader* (1987). Barth, K., *Evangelical Theology* (1963). Bauer, B., *Entwürfe der Theologie* (1985). Beinert, W., *Wenn Gott zu Wort Kommt: Eine Einführung in die Theologie* (1978). Congar, Y., *A History of Theology* (1968). Dillenberger, J., and C. Welch, *Protestant Christianity* (1954). Ebeling, G., *The Study of Theology* (1978). Eicher, P., *Die anthropologische Wende* (1970). Idem, *Theologie: Eine Einführung in das Studium* (1980). Eicher, P., ed., *Neues Handbuch theologischer Grundbegriffe*, 5 vols. (1984). González, J. L., *Christian Thought Revisited: Three Types of Theology* (1989). Idem, *A History of Christian Thought*, 3 vols. (1986). Kasper, W., *Theology and Church* (1989). Kaufmann, G., *Tendenzen der katholischen Theologie nach dem 2. Vatikanischen Konzil* (1979). Klinger, E., and K. Wittstadt, *Glaube im Prozess* (1984). Luther, M., *Selected Writings of Martin Luther 1520–1523,* ed. T. G. Tappert (1967). Nichols, A., *The Shape of Catholic Theology* (1991). O'Donovan, L., ed., *A World of Grace: An Introduction to the Themes and Foundations of Karl Rahner's Theology* (1980). Rahner, K., "Aspects of European Theology," in *TI* 21 (1988) 78–98. Idem, *Foundations of Christian Faith* (1978). Rendtorff, T., "Gott im alten Kontinent, Europäismus als geschichtlicher Kontext der Theologie," *EK* 12 (1979) 327–30. Rendtorff, T., ed., *Europäishe Theologie: Versuche einer Ortsbestimmung* (1980). Schleiermacher, F. E., *Brief Outline on the Study of Theology,* trans. T. Tice (1977). Idem, *The Christian Faith,* ed. H. R. Mackintosh and J. S. Stewart (1976). Schoof, T. M., *A Survey of Catholic Theology, 1800–1970* (1970). Schulz, H. J., *Tendenzen der Theologie im 20. Jahrhundert* (1966). Seckler, M., *Im Spannungsfeld von Wissenschaft und Kirche* (1980). Sölle, D., *Thinking about God: An Introduction to Theology* (1990). Tarnas, R., *The Passion of the Western Mind* (1991). Tillich, P., *Systematic Theology* (1967).

🔑 EVANGELICAL MISSION THEOLOGY I 🔑

1. Evangelical Mission. 2. Basis and Historical Roots. 3. Understanding of Unity. 4. Lines of Demarcation and Organizations.

1. Since the 1940s in North America and the 1960s in Europe, there has existed a specific evangelical theology of mission which lays claim to the missiological heritage of the "Great Century" (K. Latourette), just as the more ecumenically minded "conciliar" theology of mission does. However, the evangelical tradition interprets this heritage somewhat differently.

In spite of the pluriform expressions of the evangelical theology of mission, and in spite of the fluid transitions to the conciliar theology of mission, the evangelical theology of mission is distinguished by certain common features: (*a*) a close relationship to holy scripture, which is regarded as inspired and all-sufficient for life and doctrine; (*b*) emphasis on the atoning and redemptive work of Christ; (*c*) emphasis on the necessity of a personal decision of faith (→conversion); and (*d*) the priority of evangelization and the building up of congregations over all other work (e.g., social justice and interreligious dialogue) in the field of mission.

2. The historical roots of evangelical theology lie in the revival movements of the second half of the nineteenth century, while the conciliar missions have their roots more in the revival movements of the first half of the nineteenth century. The revivals of the second half of the nineteenth century were mainly interdenominational (D. L. Moody founded the first significant interdenominational congregation in Chicago in 1864) or undenominational (like the Brethren movement), and, as far as world mission is concerned, they found their typical expression in the →faith missions. The strong soteriology and the weak ecclesiology of the evangelical theology of mission can be explained by this historical background. The soteriology is mainly Calvinistic, but strongly influenced in the direction of Arminianism by the Holiness movement which emerged from Methodism.

Besides the basic convictions named above, two points play an essential role, both of which justify the need for worldwide mission and continual new advances to people unreached by the gospel: (*a*) the conviction that all who do not believe in Christ are lost eternally; and (*b*) the actual expectation of the imminent return of Christ, before which event the gospel must be preached to all nations. One can easily deduce from these basic convictions that much (but not all!) evangelical theology of mission is opposed to historical criticism in methods of exegesis, liberal theology, the social gospel, liberation theology, and every idea of there being many ways to salvation. Evangelical theology of mission tends to be individualistic; its strong social commitment, therefore, takes a concrete personal form rather than a sociopolitical form. Parallel to this, one finds the local congregation emphasized more than the church as a whole.

3. The understanding of unity in the evangelical theology of mission is personal (the common faith *is* primary; structural unity is secondary); continuity is understood as continuity of the same faith and doctrine, not as continuity of the same church structure, whose faith and doctrine may change.

4. There are graduated shades of opinion about separation in the evangelical theology of mission. Even when a growing percentage of evangelical missionaries, especially in the United States, come from local congregations not linked to a denomination or from evangelical denominations, the majority still belong to churches with a theological pluralism and do not consider separation even over serious theological differences. (In this they differ from fundamentalists.)

The position of the Pentecostal movement differs from country to country. Whereas the Pentecostals represent the strongest element of the evangelical missionary movement in Scandinavia, it is a matter of dispute in Germany as to whether they belong to it at all. It is an open question whether the charismatic movement will develop an independent theology of mission.

In Germany and Switzerland, the majority of evangelical missions belong to the relevant organization, the Arbeitsgemeinschaft Evangelikaler Missionen (AEM), in Britain to the Evangelical Missionary Alliance, in the United States to the Evangelical Federation of Missionary Associations (EFMA) and the International Federation of Missionary Associations (IFMA). The evangelical theology of mission has found expression in various declarations, including those which resulted from meetings in Wheaton, Illinois, and in Berlin, both held in 1966. The most significant statement of evangelical mission theology, however, is the Lausanne Covenant, the result of the International Congress on World Evangelization in 1974. At Lausanne, the Lausanne Committee for World Evangelization (LCWE) was founded. The LCWE held consultations on "the homogeneous unit principle" in 1977 and on "the gospel and culture" in 1978, and in 1980 a major consultation was held in Pattaya, Thailand on world evangelization. With the World Evangelical Fellowship (WEF), the LCWE cosponsored a consultation in England in 1980 on living a simple lifestyle and another in the United States in 1982 on evangelism and social responsibility. In 1989, the LCWE held its Second World Congress on World Evangelization in Manila and published a document entitled the *Manila Manifesto*. As the introduction to this document explains, the manifesto "takes up the two congress themes, 'Proclaim Christ until He Comes' and 'Calling the Whole Church to Take the Whole Gospel to the Whole World.'" Its first part is a series of twenty-one succinct affirmations. Its second part elaborates these in twelve sections, which are commended to churches, alongside the Lausanne Covenant, for study and action.

Between 1977 and 1984, three sessions of the Evangelical–Roman Catholic Dialogue on Mission (ERCDOM) took place. While the participants discovered major differences of opinion in several areas — particularly in ecclesiology and theological anthropology — they also found that their traditions agreed in many other areas, for example, the universal need for revelation, the urgency of missionary work, and the centrality of the mystery of Christ.

KLAUS FIEDLER

Bibliography

Bassham, R. C., *Mission Theology, 1948–1975: Years of Worldwide Creative Tension — Ecumenical, Evangelical, and Roman Catholic* (1979). Bevans, S., "What Catholics Can Learn from Evangelical Mission Theology," *Missiol* 23/2 (April 1995) 155–64. Beyerhaus, P., "Evangelikale Missionen," in *EKL,* 1191–94. Bloesch, D. G., *The Future of Evangelical Christianity* (1983). Bosch, D. G., *Transforming Mission: Paradigm Shifts in Theology of Mission* (1991) 400–420. Burnett, D., *God's Mission: Healing the Nations* (1986). Douglas, J. D., ed., *Let the Earth Hear His Voice* (1975). Flood, R., *The Story of the Moody Church* (1985). Geldbach, E., "Evangelikale Bewegung," *EKL* 1186–91. Gensichen, H.-W., "Erwartungen an eine evangelikale Missionswissenschaft," *EvMiss* 3 (1985) 7–11. Glasser, A. F., "Evangelical Missions," in J. M. Phillips and R. T. Coote, eds., *Toward the 21st Century in Christian Mission* (1993) 9–20. Idem, "The Evolution of Evangelical Mission Theology since World War II," *IBMR* 9 (1985) 9–13. Hauzenberger, H., *Einheit auf evangelischer Grundlage: Vom Werden und Wesen der Evangelischen Allianz* (1986). Hay, I., *Unity and Purity: Keeping the Balance* (1983). Keyes, L., *The Last Age of Mission: A Study of Third World Mission Societies* (1983). McGavran, D. A., ed., *The Conciliar–Evangelical Debate: The Crucial Documents (1964–1976)* (1977). McQuilkin, R., *The Great Omission* (1984). Meeking, B., and J. Stott, eds., *The Evangelical Roman Catholic Dialogue on Mission 1977–1984* (1986). Nicholls, B. J., ed., *In Word and Deed: Evangelism and Social Responsibility* (1985). Padilla, C. R., "Evangelische Missionswissenschaft," *EvMiss* 1 (1985) 3–8. Idem, *Mission between the Times: The Essays of C. René Padilla* (1985). Padilla, C. R., ed., *The New Face of Evangelicalism: An International Symposium on the Lausanne Covenant* (1976). Peters, G. W., *A Biblical Theology of Missions* (1975). Idem, *Saturation Evangelism* (1970). Idem, *A Theology of Church Growth* (1981). Pommerville, P., *The Third Force in Mission* (1984). Quebedeaux, R., *The Young Evangelicals* (1983). Rommen, E., *Die Notwendigkeit der Umkehr: Missionsstrategie und Gemeindeaufbau in der Sicht evangelikaler Missionswissenschaftler Nordamerikas* (1987). Samuel, V., and C. Sugden, eds., *Sharing Jesus in the Two Thirds World* (1983). Sauter, G., *Heilsgeschichte und Mission* (1985). Scherer, J. A., *Gospel, Church and Kingdom: Comparative Studies in World Mission Theology* (1987). Scherer, J. A., and S. B. Bevans, *New Directions in Mission and Evangelization,* vol. 1, *Basic Statements 1974–1991* (1992) xvi–xix, 253–314. Stott, J. W., *Christian Mission in the Modern World* (1986). Stransky, T., "Evangelical–Roman Catholic Dialogue on Mission," in N. Lossky, eds., *Dictionary of the Ecumenical Movement* (1991) 393. Van Engen, C., *God's Missionary People: Rethinking the Purpose of the Local Church* (1991). Van Engen, C., D. S. Gilliland, and P. Pierson, eds., *The Good News of the Kingdom: Mission Theology for the Third Millennium* (1993).

❧ EVANGELICAL MISSION THEOLOGY II ❧ (LAUSANNE MOVEMENT)

1. Introduction to Evangelicalism.   2. World Evangelical Fellowship. 3. The Lausanne Movement.   4. Evangelicals and Catholics.

1. Evangelicalism is a complex and significant phenomenon. Its predominant features, which reach across denominational lines, are confidence in the power of the gospel and the authority of scripture, coupled with a passionate desire to reach out and share the good news with others. Its roots extend back to the Reformation, and it came into its own in nineteenth-century evangelical movements, above all the Evangelical Alliance (established 1846). These nineteenth-century movements, in turn, stand on the shoulders of earlier post-Reformation evangelical movements, such as Pietism, Moravianism, Methodism, the Free Church movements in Europe, and similar awakening movements of the eighteenth and nineteenth centuries. Evangelicalism lays strong emphasis on mission, spiritual unity among Christians, and prayer for the advance of the reign of God.

Evangelicalism is characterized not only by what it wishes *to affirm* (the mandates of scripture and the power of the gospel) but certainly also by what it wishes *to reject*. It could not follow liberal Protestantism in embracing (*a*) the kinds of biblical criticism which undermined the deity of Christ and the authority of scripture, (*b*) evolutionary theory, or (*c*) a social gospel separated from the life-changing power of the proclaimed gospel. It sought to distance itself from fundamentalist divisiveness and polemics and to avoid unnecessary breaches in fellowship. Evangelicalism retains many supporters and followers within mainline denominations affiliated with the conciliar ecumenical movement. At the same time, it numbers countless others related to conservative evangelical denominations and some missionary agencies which view the ecumenical movement with suspicion. There is very wide diversity in the ways evangelicals understand and appreciate the Catholic Church, a spectrum that ranges between openness and being relatively closed.

Generally speaking, evangelicals wish to promote unity and fellowship among Christians for more effective witness of the gospel. Their preferred approach to unity is to foster interpersonal relationships of common faith, trust, and prayer, rather than relying on organizational or hierarchical structures. Evangelicals possess a common creedal stance grounded in the essentials of Christian faith as proclaimed in the scriptures. Yet they are likely to allow some liberty when it comes to interpreting the essentials of faith and doctrine and are less likely than fundamentalists to break off fellowship over points of doctrinal interpretation.

2.   Especially since World War II, evangelicalism has shown a "new face" and has attempted to shed some undesirable baggage from the past. During the past two decades, it has carefully presented its missiological stance and goals and has shown considerable vigor in responding to the new, postmodern missionary paradigm. Two organizations in particular which have defined the missiological agenda of evangelicals are the World Evangelical Fellowship (WEF, founded 1951) and the Lausanne Committee for World Evangelization (LCWE, founded 1974), often simply referred to as the Lausanne movement. Both organizations, while primarily North American in background and support, are seeking to develop a worldwide following and a global program. The two bodies have maintained close and cooperative relationships with each other, and many evangelicals identify with both.

In 1943 the National Association of Evangelicals was formally organized (in Chicago), which led ultimately to an international gathering in Boston (in 1950). The NAE Commission on International Relations became the Commission for the World Evangelical Fellowship, and in 1951 (in Zeist, the Netherlands) the WEF became an official reality. The WEF is an alliance of some sixty national and regional evangelical bodies, open to national fellowships of evangelical believers all over the world. Since its inception, the WEF has given special emphasis to evangelism, prayer life, spiritual retreats and conferences, scholarship programs for Third World students, books for seminaries, and Bible training institutes. Its important contributions to evangelical missiology have come through consultations devoted to special topics, some of them jointly convened with units of the Lausanne Committee. Among these have been consultations entitled "The Theology of Development" (1980), "Evangelical Commitment to Simple Life-Style" (1980), "The Relations of Evangelism and Social Responsibility" (1982), "The Church in Response to Human Need" (1983), "The Work of the Holy Spirit and Evangelization" (1985), and "Conversion" (1988). In the mid-1970s, a clearly defined women's movement was identified, and in 1980 the International Forum of Evangelical Women was formed, with representatives from each of the continents.

3. The Lausanne Committee for World Evangelization (LCWE), formally constituted at the International Congress on World Evangelization (ICOWE) held at Lausanne, Switzerland, in July 1974, is in reality the continuation committee for the Lausanne movement. Organized under the personal initiative and leadership of Billy Graham, with major assistance from the evangelical journal *Christianity Today* and various evangelistic agencies and missionary associations, the ICOWE carried forward the momentum of two earlier congresses held in 1966: the Wheaton Congress on the Church's Worldwide Mission and the Berlin World Congress on Evangelism. Employing the newer term "evangelization," the Lausanne Congress sought to forge a bond between evangelicals concerned with world mission and those primarily interested in evangelism. The LCWE, as its name suggests, is not a council of churches or religious organizations but rather a loose coalition of individual persons, mission and evangelism agencies, and institutions sharing a common theological position and with a common missionary and evangelistic purpose. It is governed by an international committee of seventy evangelical leaders. Identification with the LCWE is made by signing the Lausanne Covenant and thereby covenanting with others "to pray, plan, and work together for the evangelization of the whole world."

The official report of the ICOWE's 1974 meeting is entitled *Let the Earth Hear His Voice.* The spirit and purpose of Lausanne were well expressed in Billy Graham's opening address, "Why Lausanne?" Graham said that the common characteristics of earlier great movements for evangelism were that they all took their stand on the basis of the scriptures, held a definite view of the need of salvation and the lostness of humans apart from Christ, strongly believed in conversion, and were convinced that evangelism was not an option but an imperative. The conciliar ecumenical movement, Graham believed, had departed from its earlier evangelistic vision and commitment after Edinburgh 1910. Evangelicals gathered at Lausanne were thus being challenged to take the lead in restoring world evangelization to its rightful place. Participants and observers have noted the intentionality of cultural reflection and the need for integrating evangelical distinctive elements with the realities of national, political, and social needs.

One of the most enduring achievements of the ICOWE was the drafting and formal adoption of the fifteen-paragraph declaration known as the Lausanne Covenant. It was to become the ongoing basis for evangelical cooperation and a further catalyst to evangelical unity. The covenant, prepared under the leadership of Anglican evangelical J. R. Stott, attempts to define sensitive issues of evangelical missiology: the authority of the Bible, the uniqueness of Jesus Christ, the relation between evangelism and dialogue, the relative priority of evangelization and social concern, the centrality of the church in evangelism, the necessity of partnership and cooperation, and many others. Despite the warm reception given the Lausanne Covenant, some issues were not settled by the ICOWE, and groups such as the "radical evangelicals" and the WEF commissions pressed for further clarifications and refinements. The struggle with the complexities of cultural interaction provided opportunities for strenuous dialogue among evangelical leaders and resulted in a series of smaller consultations with accompanying summary documents (entitled "The Lausanne Occasional Papers"). Even so, Lausanne 1974 "marks the high point in the development of evangelical mission theology," and the Lausanne Covenant remains "the most mature and comprehensive statement produced by evangelicals" (Bassham 1979).

Between 1974 and 1989, the LCWE carried on its work by means of working groups on theology, mission strategy, intercession, and communication. The LCWE's Strategy Working Group cooperated closely with MARC–World Vision in relation to the "unreached peoples" project and in designing evangelism strategies. The largest single LCWE effort in this early period was expended on the planning of the 1980 Pattaya (Thailand) Consultation on World Evangelization.

The most vital LCWE document in recent years comes from the Second International Congress on World Evangelization (Manila, 1989, often referred to as Lausanne II) and is entitled the *Manila Manifesto: An Elaboration of the Lausanne Covenant Fifteen Years Later*. The full report of Lausanne II is found in *Proclaim Christ until He Comes: Calling the Whole Church to Take the Whole Gospel to the Whole World*. The *Manila Manifesto,* again prepared under the leadership of J. R. Stott, is in some ways an updating of the Lausanne Covenant, but without departing from the covenant's essential affirmations. The *Manila Manifesto* may be seen as evangelicalism's response to the postmodern missionary paradigm, with special regard for the challenges of the year 2000 and beyond. Together with the covenant, the manifesto will provide authoritative guidance and inspiration to evangelical workers and set the tone for evangelical missiology into the future. While possessing no official authority, these two documents embody a broad consensus of evangelical opinion and conviction about mission and evangelization.

4. The most recent development of evangelical missiology is emerging from dialogues with Roman Catholicism. In a series of three meetings from 1977 to 1984, theologians and missiologists named by the Vatican Secretariat for Promoting Christian Unity and evangelical participants from many denominations took part in the Evangelical–Roman Catholic Dialogue on Mission (ERCDOM). The evangelicals did not officially represent any international body, although all were associated with the LCWE. The convener of the ERCDOM evangelicals was J. R. Stott. The focal point of all discussion was Christian mission.

One of the most striking recent statements from another unofficial, yet influential, evangelical-Catholic consultation is the 1994 document *Evangelicals and Catholics Together: The Christian Mission in the Third Millennium*. This statement intends to speak not "officially for . . . but responsibly from our communities and to our communities." The document suggests, as did the consultations from 1977 to 1984, that the commonalities between evangelicalism and Roman Catholicism are substantial, particularly when viewed against the background of the present "post-Christian" age. Both are major presences in the modern Christian world; both are alarmed at the growth in secularism and materialism in Western society; both see dangers posed to Christians throughout the world by the rise of Islamic fundamentalism; and both are concerned about the increasing moral chaos in the West, at both the individual and social levels.

The true impetus behind this document, as well as most evangelical-Catholic dialogues, is the present reality of and the planning for Christian mission within the third millennium. Recognized is the fact that "the two communities [evangelicals and Roman Catholics] are the most evangelistically assertive and most rapidly growing [Christian fellowships] in the world." Today there are approximately 1.7 billion Christians in the world. About a billion of these Christians are Catholics, and more than 300 million are evangelical Protestants. Although evangelicals and Catholics constitute the growing edge of missionary expansion, their relationship also represents many ongoing conflicts and tensions (e.g., in Latin America, in eastern Europe, and, also, in the United States). These tensions necessitate asking the question: How will the missionary endeavor started within the greatest century of missionary expansion in Christian history proceed into the next millennium? The growing consensus that appears to be emerging among younger evangelicals is a pragmatic one: they agree to collaborate with Roman Catholics on a limited range of issues, while acknowledging that differences remain on others. Given the dangers in the world, they argue, Christians need to set their differences aside and support and defend their common ideas, values, and mission without compromising the distinctive elements, for that compromise would result in a lack of integrity and a denial of the very heart and essence of the gospel.

Many suggest that evangelicalism and Roman Catholicism may grow closer in the years that lie ahead while still maintaining a degree of distance between them, especially in regard to certain fundamental doctrinal differences. Without denying or underplaying these differences, the possibility that the two groups could form a coalition working for doctrinal orthodoxy, missional cooperation, and moral renewal at every level of the global society is a powerful one. The missional potential of such an alliance remains to be worked out and tested at all levels of the church: grassroots, congregational, national, and global.

JAMES A. SCHERER, RICHARD H. BLIESE, AND JOHN W. NYQUIST

Bibliography

Bassett, P. M., "Evangelicals," in *DEM* (1991) 393–95. Bassham, R. C., *Mission Theology, 1948–1975: Years of Worldwide Creative Tension — Ecumenical, Evangelical, and Roman Catholic* (1979). Bloesch, D. G., *The Future of Evangelical Christianity: A Call for Unity amid Diversity* (1983). Colson, C., and R. J. Neuhaus, eds., *Evangelicals and Catholics Together: Toward a Common Mission*. Coote, R. T., "Evangelical Missions," in *DEM* (1991) 392. Dayton, E., "Ten Historic Years," in *The Future of World Evangelization: The Lausanne Movement* (1984) 47–57. Idem, *That Everyone May Hear: Reaching the Unreached* (1979). Dayton, E., and A. F. Glasser, *Planning Strategies for World Evangelization* (1980). *Evangelicals and Catholics Together: The Christian Mission in the Third Millennium* (1994). Geisler, N. L., and R. E. MacKenzie, *Roman Catholics and Evangelicals: Agreements and Differences* (1995). Glasser, A. F., "Evangelical Missions," in *Toward the 21st Century in Christian Mission* (1993) 9–20. Glasser, A. F., and D. A. McGavran, *Comtemporary Theologies of Mission* (1983). Graham, B., "Why Lausanne?" in *Let the Earth Hear His Voice: International Congress of World Evangelization* (1975). Henry, C. F., and W. S. Mooneyham, eds., *One Race, One Gospel, One Task: World Congress on Evangelism, Berlin 1966* (1967). Howard, D. M., *The Dream That Would Not Die: The Birth and Growth of the World Evangelical Fellowship, 1846–1986* (1986). Lindsell, H., *The Church's Worldwide Mission: An Analysis of the Current State of Evangelical Missions and a Strategy for Future Activity* (1966). LOP, *An Evangelical Commitment to Simple Life-style: Exposition and Commentary by Alan Nichols*, LOP no. 20 (1980). Idem, *Grand Rapids Report: Evangelism and Social Responsibility: An Evangelical Commitment*, LOP no. 21 (1982). Idem, *The Pasadena Consultation — Homogeneous Unit Principle*, LOP no. 1 (1978). Idem, *The Willowbank Report: Report of a Consultation on Gospel and Culture Held at Willowbank, Somerset Bridge, Bermuda, from 6–13th January 1978*, LOP no. 2 (1978). Padilla, C. R., *The New Face of Evangelicalism: An International Symposium on the Lausanne Covenant* (1976). Pate, L. D., *From Every People: A Handbook of*

Two-Thirds World Missions (1989). Phillips, J. M., and R. T. Coote, *Toward the 21st Century in Christian Mission* (1993). Piper, J., *Let the Nations Be Glad! The Supremacy of God in Missions* (1993). Rausch, T. P., "Catholic-Evangelical Relations: Signs of Progress," *One in Christ* 32/1: 40–52. Scherer, J. A., *Gospel, Church and Kingdom* (1987) 164–95. Scherer, J. A., and S. B. Bevans, *New Directions in Mission and Evangelization,* vol. 1, *Basic Statements, 1974–1991* (1992) 253–314. Stransky, T., "Evangelical–Roman Catholic Dialogue on Mission," in *DEM* (1991) 392–93. Webber, R. E., *Common Roots: A Call to Evangelical Maturity* (1978).

✎ EVANGELISM, EVANGELIZATION ≈

1. Definitions. 2. Evangelism within the Mission of the Church.

1. Evangelism and evangelization are derived from the Greek verb *euanglizein / euangelizesthai,* the most basic New Testament meaning of which is the proclamation of the inauguration of the reign of God in the person and ministry of Jesus and a call to repentance and faith (Mk 1:15). *Euangelizesthai,* commonly used by Luke, is in essence to be regarded as a synonym for *keryssein* (Matthew, Mark) and *martyrein* (John). It is preferable to understand "evangelism" as referring to (*a*) the activities involved in spreading the gospel (however defined; see below) and (*b*) the theological reflection on these activities, whereas "evangelization" may be used to refer to (*a*) the process of spreading the gospel or (*b*) the extent to which it has been spread (e.g., "The evangelization of Africa has been completed").

Definitions of evangelism abound (see Barrett 1987). Currently, however, there are several different and even conflicting interpretations of evangelism (and, by implication, of evangelization).

a. Evangelism is sometimes defined according to *method* and *style.* It is then primarily understood as public preaching of a revivalistic nature to large (often outdoor, or television) audiences by specially gifted (often itinerant) "evangelists." It aims at the exposure of the sinner's rebellion against God's rightful claim on individuals, calls for a "decision for Christ," and manifests itself in a personal spiritual experience of forgiveness and new life. The date of this event is often regarded as of the greatest importance. The salvation imparted through this kind of evangelism is usually understood in terms of (the guarantee of) future eternal bliss or the "saving of the soul."

To define evangelism primarily in terms of method and its aim solely in personal, spiritual, and otherworldly categories is, however, dangerous reductionism.

b. Some define evangelism in terms of its results: evangelism is communicating the gospel effectively; it is producing converts. The most famous example of this understanding of evangelism is the formulation in "Toward the Conversion of England" (a report of a commission on evangelism appointed by the archbishops of Canterbury and York, 1919): "To evangelize is so to present Christ Jesus in the power of the Holy Spirit, that men shall come to put their trust in God."

This definition, subsequently adopted by various bodies and still in use, particularly in evangelical circles, tends, however, to confuse evangelism with its aims (or one of its aims). In this definition the ministry of presenting Christ only becomes evangelism when it achieves positive results. This is unacceptable. The ministry of evangelism is evangelism whether in fact people respond positively to it or not.

c. More often evangelism is defined in terms of its "objects"; where this happens, evangelism is usually distinguished from mission. Mission then has to do with people who are not yet Christians (particularly in the Third World), evangelism with people who are no longer Christians (particularly in the West). Mission is concerned with first conversion, Christianization, beginning, *vocare,* the stranger; evangelism has to do with calling back, re-Christianization, new beginning, *re-vocare,* the estranged (T. Ohm; K. Barth; less absolute also H. J. Margull). A constituent factor in this distinction is the *corpus Christianum* thinking and the idea of the indelible character of baptism: within Western Christendom, evangelism should be carried out, not mission. Against this background, home missions are judged to be theologically distinct from foreign mission. The "object" of home mission (= evangelism) is every member of the church who, even if baptized, still has to *become* a believer.

d. The above distinctions — even though still widely held today, in both Protestant and Roman Catholic circles (*Ad Gentes* is ambiguous on this point) — have since World War II increasingly come under attack. At the inaugural meeting of the World Council of Churches (WCC) (Amsterdam, 1948), due to the influence, among others, of H. Kraemer, the delegates recognized that the problems of the proclamation of the gospel in the East and the West are essentially the same and that the old distinctions have become redundant. The International Missionary Council meeting at Willingen (1952) endorsed the Amsterdam position. This view has, by and large, been sustained ever since. P. Potter, past general secretary of the WCC, was, therefore, correct when he said, in 1968, that ecumenical literature since Amsterdam (1948) has used "mission," "witness," and "evangelism" interchangeably.

The same has been happening in evangelical circles, except that mission-evangelism has been defined more narrowly there than in ecumenical circles. In the words of A. Johnston: "Historically the mission of the church is evangelism alone" (1978, 18), where mission-evangelism is understood almost exclusively as "soul-winning." The ecumenical understanding of mission-evangelism, by contrast, is that of "the whole church taking the whole gospel to the whole world," in other words: the total Christian ministry to the world outside the church.

e. Margull (and, to some extent, also J. Verkuyl) supports a view somewhere between positions *c* and *d.* Margull distinguishes between "missionary proclamation" (a term he prefers to "evangelism"), which takes place in the West, and "foreign evangelism" or "mission," the distinctive feature of which is "to proclaim the gospel where no church as yet exists, where the Lordship of God has never yet — historically — been proclaimed, where *pagans* are the object of concern." Even so, Margull affirms the necessity of "*synchronizing* to a degree these two missionary activities in such a way that evangelism is subsumed within foreign evangelism," and he adds, in parentheses, "(It is best to speak of interdependence)" (1962, 274–75).

2. It is indeed advisable to distinguish between evangelism and mission, not, however, along the lines suggested by Margull (position *e* above) but rather in such a way that *mission* is understood as the total task God has set the church for the salvation of the world or as the church's ministry of stepping out of itself, into the wider world, in this process crossing geographical, social, political, ethnic, cultural, religious, ideological, and other frontiers or barriers. *Evangelism,* in contrast, may then be regarded as one of several dimensions of the wider mission of the church, indeed the core, heart, or center of mission.

Seen against the background of mission as the "whole church bringing the whole gospel to the whole world," the distinctive feature of evangelism may then, among other things, consist in the following.

a. Evangelism as the proclamation of salvation in Christ to all who do not believe in him, announcing forgiveness of sins, calling people to repentance and faith and to a new life in the power of the Holy Spirit. "As kernel and center of the Good News, Christ proclaims salvation, this great gift of God which is liberation from everything that oppresses people but which is, above all, liberation from sin and the Evil One, in the joy of knowing God and being known by him, of seeing him and of being turned over to him" (*EN* 9; see *AG* 13). Evangelism is, however, more than "soul-winning," for the ultimate concern of the latter is only the salvation of souls that must endure when all the world has perished. Evangelism is concerned with the salvation of people (not just "souls") in terms of all their relationships.

b. Evangelism as aimed at people being brought into the visible community of believers (see *AG* 13). "It is at the heart of the Christian mission to foster the multiplication of local congregations in every human community" (*Ecumenical Affirmation: Mission and Evangelism,* 25 [see Scherer and Bevans 1992, 44]). Evangelism is, however, never to be confused with proselytism. Evangelism is not a form of ecclesiastical propaganda and may never have as its primary objective the enlarging of the membership of a particular church or the promoting of particular doctrines. Such an enterprise is not evangelism, but propaganda.

c. Evangelism as involving witnessing to what God has done, is doing, and will do. Christians do this by word and deed, proclamation and presence, explication and example.

d. Evangelism as invitation. It should never deteriorate into coaxing, much less into threat. It is not the same as: (1) offering a psychological panacea for people's frustrations and disappointments; (2) inculcating guilt feelings so that people (in despair, as it were) may turn to Christ; or, (3) scaring people into repentance and conversion with stories about the horror of hell. People should turn to God because they are drawn by God's love, not because they are pushed to God for fear of hell.

Evangelism is only possible when the community that evangelizes — the church — is a radiant manifestation of the Christian faith and has a vibrant lifestyle. "The medium is the message" (M. McLuhan). If the church is to impart to the world a message of hope and love, of faith, justice, and peace, something of this should become visible, audible, and tangible in the church itself (see Acts 2:42–47; 4:32–35). H. W. Gensichen mentions five criteria for a church involved in evangelism: (1) it should be able to make outsiders feel at home; (2) it should not merely be an object of pastoral care with the pastor having the monopoly; (3) through its members it should be involved in society; (4) it should be structurally flexible and adaptable; and (5) it should not defend the interests of a select group of people (1971, 170–72).

Evangelism offers people salvation as a present gift and with it assurance of eternal bliss. However, if the offer of all of this gets center-stage attention in our evangelism, the gospel is degraded to a consumer product. Evangelism then fosters the pursuit of pious self-centeredness. It has to be emphasized, rather, that the personal enjoyment of salvation never becomes the central theme in biblical conversion stories (K. Barth). The enjoyment of salvation is not wrong, unimportant, or unbiblical, but it is almost incidental and secondary. It is not simply to receive life that people are called to become Christians, but rather to give life. Therefore, to be called means to receive a commission (see Gensichen); put differently: evangelism is calling people to become followers of Jesus; it is enlisting people for involvement in mission (in the comprehensive sense of the word, as outlined above).

Evangelism should always be contextual. It involves a "dialogue" between the situation in which people find themselves and the evangelist's particular understanding of scripture (Costas 1989). It is a witness that takes place in a given social and historical context and addresses socially and historically situated human beings. It involves not only individuals but also particular communities and life-situations. The offer of new life in Christ is never made "in general."

In summary, then, evangelism may be defined as that dimension and activity of the church's mission which, by word and deed and in the light of particular conditions, offer every person, everywhere, a valid opportunity to be directly challenged to a radical reorientation of her or his life, which involves, among other things, deliverance from slavery to the world and its powers; embracing Christ as savior and Lord; becoming a living member of his community, the church; being incorporated into his service of reconciliation, peace, and justice on earth; and being integrated into God's purpose of placing all things under the rule of Christ.

DAVID J. BOSCH

Bibliography

Anderson, G. H., and T. F. Stransky, eds., *Mission Trends*, vol. 2 *Evangelization* (1975). Armstrong, J., *From the Underside: Evangelism from a Third World Vantage Point* (1981). Barrett, D. B., *Evangelize! A Historical Survey of the Concept* (1987). Barth, K., *Church Dogmatics*, IV/3 (1962). Bevans, S., and R. Schroeder, eds., *Word Remembered, Word Proclaimed* (1997). Bohr, D., *Evangelization in America* (1977). Bosch, D. J., *Transforming Mission: Paradigm Shifts in Theology of Mission* (1991) 409–20. Boyac, K., ed., *The New Catholic Evangelization* (1992). Castro, E., *Freedom in Mission: The Perspective of the Kingdom* (1985). Costas, O. E., *Liberating News: A Theology of Contextual Evangelization* (1989). Dhavamony, M., ed., *Evangelization, Dialogue, and Development* (1972). Dulles, A., "John Paul II and the New Evangelization," *America* 166/3 (February 1, 1992) 52–59, 69–72. Gensichen, H. W., *Glaube für die Welt* (1971). Greinacher, N., and A. Müller, eds., *Evangelization in the World Today*, vol. 114 of *Concilium* (1979). Hollenweger, W. J., *Evangelism Today: Good News or Bone of Contention?* (1976). Hunter, G. G., *How to Reach Secular People* (1992). Johnston, A., *The Battle for World Evangelism* (1978). Krass, A. C., *Evangelizing Neo-pagan North America* (1982). Margull, H. J., *Hope in Action: The Church's Task in the World* (1962). Müller, K., *Mission Theology: An Introduction* (1987). Nationwide Initiative in Evangelism, *Evangelism: Convergence and Divergence* (1980). Newbigin, L., *The Gospel in a Pluralist Society* (1989). Ohm, T., *Machet zu Jüngern alle Völker!* (1962). Poetsch, H. L., *Theologie der Evangelisation* (1967). Pope-Levison, P., "Evangelism in the WCC," in J. A. Scherer and S. B. Bevans, eds., *New Directions in Mission and Evangelization*, vol. 2, *Theological Foundations* (1994) 126–40. Rosales, G., and C. G. Arévalo, eds., *For All the Peoples of Asia: Federation of Asian Bishops' Conferences, Documents from 1970 to 1991* (1992). Scherer, J. A., and S. B. Bevans, *New Directions in Mission and Evangelization*, vol. 1, *Basic Statements 1974–1991* (1992). Shivute, T., *The Theology of Mission and Evangelism in the International Missionary Council from Edinburgh to New Delhi* (1980). Stevenson, W. T., ed., *Evangelism: A Consultation*, supplementary series 8 of *ATR* (March 1979). Verkuyl, J., *Contemporary Missiology: An Introduction* (1978).

❦ FAITH ❧

1. Faith in the History of Theology. 2. Various Models of Faith.

1.   According to holy scripture, faith is the total and integral response of a human being to God. In the Old Testament it concerns the attitude to the God of the covenant and in the New Testament to God revealed in Jesus Christ. This attitude of the whole person implies various elements, especially that of trust — a person totally builds his or her life on God and God's word — but also the element of the recognition of truths of the faith.

In the course of history the church has articulated its understanding of faith in different situations. The Fathers of the Church had to protect the *regula fidei* against the first heresies. In this way the dogmatic aspect of the faith came to the fore. Augustine treated the subject in the context of the understanding of Roman authority and his personal experience. He tried to solve the problem of the relationship between faith and reason: *credo ut intelligam.* From the beginning of Scholasticism this problem of faith and reason came increasingly to the foreground of theological and philosophical interest. It should suffice to recall here the formula of Anselm of Canterbury, *fides quaerens intellectum,* and his method of looking for necessary reasons within the context of faith; also to be recalled is the struggle between dialecticians and antidialecticians, along with the solution of the question by Thomas Aquinas, who linked faith and reason far more harmoniously. Finally, one must remember the dissolving of the synthesis of faith and reason in nominalism.

At the time of the Reformation the understanding of faith had to do mainly with the relationship between faith and justification (fiducial faith). The understanding of faith in the modern era is colored by the Catholic/Protestant split and by the relationship of faith to modern philosophy and to the natural sciences and historical consciousness. Catholic theology has been more interested in certain aspects of the demonstrability of the faith, whereas Protestant theology has developed further its understanding of fiducial faith.

2.   Nowadays the attempts at understanding faith are demonstrated in various models.

One type of model takes up problems that were already discussed in the nineteenth century. An example is the *neo-Scholastic model*. The exposition of Thomas Aquinas in his *quaestio disputata* entitled *De Veritate* is taken as a starting point, and the nature of the act of faith is determined deductively. Faith does not lie on the first level of rational activity but on the second level, on the level of judgment. It is understood as an act of reason without evidence; it is not determined by its own formal object of reason but by the will which determines the reason. Furthermore, much thought is given to the origin of faith. Hence, faith is defined as an act of reason which assents to a certain article of the faith, not because of an inner understanding but because of the authority of the self-revealing God.

It must be asserted as a criticism against this theory that faith is almost exclusively regarded as an act of reason, while the other elements of this integral act are somewhat neglected. But the main problem is that the personal aspect of faith is not sufficiently considered: in comparison with other acts of reason based on evidence, faith seems to be an act of lesser knowledge. It is too much measured against the ideal of impersonal knowledge. According to holy scripture, however, faith is a personal act, an act of the whole person.

This criticism is taken up by the *personal model* of faith (E. Brunner, G. Ebeling, P. Tillich, B. Welte, etc.). This model proceeds from a phenomenology of one person believing another. In this case the fundamental formula is: I believe you. Secondary to this is the formula: I believe something. As an analogy to this interpersonal belief, an attempt is now made to understand the Christian faith. Here the fundamental formula is: I believe God. As a consequence of this personal belief, the truths of the faith are accepted, but such truths are not indifferent pieces of information but the self-giving of God as such. The problem of the certitude of faith can be properly solved only when we consider the personal structure of faith. In the last analysis, certitude depends on the divine person and not on the previous recognition of the reasons for credibility. These are rather in the nature of signs. The structure of personal faith also shows that it is wrong to separate personal faith from dogmatic faith (the "I believe you" from the "I believe that"). Personal faith and dogmatic faith are closely connected because of this structure. From what we said it also follows that it is not enough to define faith merely in opposition to knowledge and reason, as happens in the Scholastic analysis. For there its personal structure and the special value of faith are not sufficiently recognized. Faith seems rather to be a lesser kind of knowledge.

K. Rahner introduced a *transcendental-theological model* of faith which is helpful in demonstrating the salvific meaning of faith in various religions (→theology of religions). First, Rahner investigates the conditions of the possibility of our categorical knowledge. The basic condition is the openness of our spirit to the unlimited horizon of being. In this openness of our spirit we also implicitly know God: *Desiderium naturale videndi Deum.* It is this nonconceptual knowledge of God that makes all conceptual statements about God possible. If the created spirit was not constitutively in an a priori relation with the Absolute, it could never find the Absolute, would not even have the problem of the Absolute. This presence of God is the condition for the human statement about God.

All this is decisive in order to understand how the God of revelation makes religious faith possible. No new categorical objects enter our consciousness through grace, but the transcendental movement of our spirit is modified supernaturally by grace and oriented to God as God truly is. Our cognitive faculty is, as such, elevated by grace. The formal aspect of our cognitive faculty consists in its orientation on being. This orientation is now supernaturally elevated to an orientation on God per se. This means that the triune God enters into the deepest recesses of the human spirit, addresses it, and invites it to community.

From the perspective of this understanding of faith we can now address the question about faith in the religions (→religion, religions). Because of God's general intention to save all, we must presuppose that grace is actually offered to humanity and that men and women are able to accept it or reject it. This real offer of grace is now explained as a supernatural modification of human transcendence. Because of this supernatural modification which touches the consciousness of humanity in the depths of the soul, in a broad sense we can speak already about a supernatural revelation of God to human beings. Here it is a question not of the categorical revelation of a definite object but of the nonconceptual modification of human transcendence which nevertheless brings with it a real communication of God as a real offer to human freedom. Hence supernatural revelation is coextensive with the history of humanity. But Christian theology must not only reflect theoretically about faith in the religions; it must also come to grips with faith in the actual religions. H. Waldenfels speaks about the meditative or mystical contemplation coming from Asia which invites many people in the West to self-discovery and self-realization. This Asian religiosity often takes the place of Christian faith and gives those molded by the natural sciences an answer to questions which science cannot give. The dialogue of the Christian faith with authentic faith in other religions has only just begun.

The *model of correlation* draws on ideas of the Protestant theologian P. Tillich. Among Catholic theologians it was K. Rahner in particular who used this model in his anthropocentric orientation of theology. It attempts to make faith possible for contemporary men and women. Consequently, this model places great value on subjective reason. The problem is to make the meaning of the Christian mystery in its totality comprehensible for the modern person. The word of God always begins with human experience and involves a new understanding of humanity. Hence an attempt is made to develop a dialectic between human existence and Christian faith, a dialectic in which the former comes to meaning and fulfillment through the latter (transcendental anthropology). Hence this method of finding a basis for the faith consists in reflecting on the relationship between the Christian faith and the human experience of the self. All too often the modern person has difficulties with faith, and the statements of faith seem to be mythical because no connection is seen between faith and experience. But there is a danger here of reducing faith to human proportions and of human experience determining faith. For this reason, Rahner emphasizes in this context the radically "theocentric" nature of revelation and so expressly distances himself from a new form of modernism. Faith must not be emptied of meaning and reduced to the way humanity sees itself. The theocentric nature of faith points out that God's revelation judges, changes, and deepens human self-understanding. This possible danger should not, however, lead to the neglect of the anthropological orientation of modern philosophy and the failure to base faith on the anthropocentric horizon of understanding.

The anthropocentric model of faith focuses too much on the individual person. As a criticism and development, the *political model* (developed by J. B. Metz, J. Moltmann, and the liberation theologians) tries to bring the social dimension into play. Faith has to render an account by critically analyzing the Christian faith and its relationship to the world. Vatican II in *Gaudium et Spes (GS)* emphasized that this is the most important task of the faith today in the face of the pressing problems of humanity, especially the social questions, peace, disarmament, and preservation of creation. Hence today it is not so much a question of faith and reason as of faith and praxis. Latin American →liberation theology plays a special role here. Faith flows from concrete praxis of faith. To the degree that Christianity reflects on these "political" implications of the faith and puts them into practice, it will appeal to people of today as a very appropriate form of living. In this way the present will be oriented to the future from the perspective of the "dangerous remembrance" of the life, death, and resurrection of Jesus.

HERIBERT BETTSCHEIDER, SVD

Bibliography

Alfaro, J., "Faith," *SM* 2 (1968) 313–22. Aubert, R., *Le problème de l'acte de foi* (1969). Balthasar, H. U. von, *Theological Anthropology* (1968). Brunner, E., *The Divine-Human Encounter* (1980) Idem, *Revelation and Reason: The Christian Doctrine of Faith and Knowledge* (1946). Buber, M., *Two Types of Faith* (1951). Cirne-Lima, C., *Personal Faith* (1965). Dewart, L., *The Foundations of Belief* (1969). Dulles, A., *The Assurance of Things Hoped For* (1990). Idem, "Faith and Revelation," in F. Schüssler Fiorenza and J. P. Galvin, eds., *Systematic Theology: Roman Catholic Perspectives,* vol. 1 (1991) 89–128. Ebeling, G., *The Nature of Faith* (1961). Idem, *Word and Faith* (1963). Eschweiler, K., *Die zwei Wege der neueren Theologie* (1926). Gerber, U., *Katholischer Glaubensbegriff: Die Frage nach dem Glaubensbegriff vom Vatikanum I bis zur Gegenwart* (1966). Gerrish, B. A., *Grace and Reason* (1979). Gilkey, L., *Message and Existence* (1979) 23–38. Goba, B., "What Is Faith?" in S. B. Thistlethwaite and M. P. Engels, eds., *Lift Every Voice: Constructing Christian Theologies from the Underside* (1990). Gries, H., *Glaube und Kirche auf dem Prüfstand* (1970). Idem, *Herausgeforderter Glaube* (1968). Haight, R., *An Alternative Vision: An Interpretation of Liberation Theology* (1985) 64–82. Kerstiens, F., *Die Hoffnungsstruktur des Glaubens* (1969). Knauer, P., *Verantwortung des Glaubes: Ein Gespräch mit G. Ebeling aus katholischer Sicht* (1969). Löhrer, M., *Der Glaubensbegriff des hl. Augustinus in seinen ersten Schriften bis zu den Confessiones* (1955). Mercado, L., *Elements of Filipino Theology* (1975) 115–24. Newman, J. H., *An Essay in Aid of a Grammar of Assent* (1979). Idem, *Newman's University Sermons* (1970). Metz, J. B., *Faith in History and Society* (1980). Moltmann, J., *Theology of Hope* (1967). Oman, J. W., *The Natural and the Supernatural* (1931). Pieper, J., *Belief and Faith: A Philosophical Tract* (1963). Rahner, K., "The Acceptance in Faith of the Truth of God," *TI* 16 (1979) 169–76. Idem, "The Act of Faith and the Content of Faith," *TI* 21 (1988) 151–62. Idem, "Anonymous and Explicit Faith," *TI* 16 (1979) 52–59. Idem, "Atheism and Implicit Christianity," *TI* 9 (1972) 145–64. Idem, "Faith as Courage," *TI* 28 (1983) 211–25. Idem, "The Foundation of Belief Today," *TI* 16 (1979) 3–23. Idem, *Foundations of Christian Faith* (1978). Idem, *Hearers of the Word* (1969). Idem, "Theology and Anthropology," *TI* 9 (1972) 28–45. Ratzinger, J., *Introduction to Christianity* (1969). Seckler, M., *Instinkt und Glaubenswille nach Thomas von Aquin* (1961). Tillich, P., *Dynamics of Faith* (1967). Trütsch, J., and L. Pfammater, "Der Glaube," in *MySal* 1:791–903. Türk, H. J., ed., *Glaube-Unglaube* (1971). Waldenfels, H., *Kontextuelle Fundamentaltheologie* (1985). Welte, B., *Religionsphilosophie* (1978). Idem, *Was ist Glauben?* (1982).

❧ FAITH MISSIONS ❧

1. Definition and Characteristics. 2. Historical Examples. 3. Theology. 4. Present-day Expansion.

1. "Faith missions" describes a large number of mainly nondenominational and often international evangelical missions whose theology of mission and missionary methods go back to H. Taylor (1832–1905), the founder of the China Inland Mission in 1865 (known today as the Overseas Missionary Fellowship). The term "faith missions" refers to the means of financing these missions. The missionaries are not employees of the mission, but members. They do not receive a salary, but ask God for the means necessary for their living and are convinced that "God's work done in God's way will not lack God's supply" (Taylor). In practical terms, there are very different ways of understanding this view which is shared by all. In the formative period there was more stress on the importance of a "general fund" for all missionaries; today the tendency is to place importance on "individual support." But in all cases, differences of missionary income are not due to the kind of job done or seniority of position.

More significant than the financial angle, even when it is not mentioned by name, is the ecclesiological aspect of faith missions, which are nondenominational and founders of churches at the same time. "Nondenominational" means that their missionaries can come from widely different Protestant denominations, as long as they agree on the basic principles of faith (ecclesiology is not one of these). Faith missions have an individualistic concept of unity: churches do not cooperate to form a faith mission; individuals who happen to be members of various churches can unite to form a faith mission, but they do so as individuals, not as representatives of their respective churches. It thus comes about that missionaries from churches with incompatible beliefs belong to the same faith missions. These conflicting ecclesiologies become most visible in the issue of infant or believers' baptism and in the issue of church government. The mission work tends to create churches with the practice of adult baptism and presbyterian forms of church government, but churches which practice infant baptism are also created (e.g., the Churches of Christ in Nigeria and the Sudan United Mission). Even a few Anglican dioceses trace their origin back to faith missions (China Inland Mission; Africa Inland Mission).

2. Faith missions have mainly geographical names, indicating their field of work, often with a rider expressing the desire that through their work untapped areas would be reached: Central America Mission; Africa Inland Mission; Sudan Pioneer Mission. Others have more general names: Regions Beyond Missionary Union; Unevangelized Fields Mission; and so on. After the faith missions' beginnings in China, their main field of work became Central Africa, because it was largely untouched by previous missionary efforts. All the older faith missions have close connections with F. and G. Guinness (1832–98 and 1835–1910, respectively) and the East London Training Institute founded by them (1873–1910): Livingstone Inland Mission (F. Guinness, London, 1873); Christian and Missionary Alliance (A. B. Simpson, New York, 1882–87); South Africa General Mission (S. Walton and Mrs. O. Howe, London, 1889–91); Evangelical Alliance Mission (F. Franson, Chicago, 1890); Africa Inland Mission (J. Scott, Philadelphia, 1895); Sudan Interior Mission (R. Bingham, Toronto, 1893–1900); Sudan United Mission (L. and K. Kum, Sheffield, 1904); Worldwide Evangelization Crusade (C. T. and P. Studd, London, 1913).

Since the 1930s the number of faith missions specializing in a definite commission has increased, for example, Wycliffe Bible Translators (1935), Christian Literature Crusade (1942), Christian Nationals Evangelism Commission (1943), and Trans-world Radio (1952). The faith missions are theologically on the conservative side.

3. The Bible is primarily understood as a personal call (commission and promise) of the triune God, then as the presentation of God's saving work for all people, and then as the basis of Christian doctrine. In doctrine it is possible to have wide variations, especially in ecclesiology, eschatology, and pneumatology. The eschatology of faith missions is not speculative but applied: before the Lord comes, all nations must be reached with the gospel (Mt 24:14) (→apocalyptic and mission; eschatology).

Faith missions were the first large missionary movement after the Moravians and the voluntary society movements; most of the opposition to them came from long-established missions and their proponents, which perceived the new missions as competition and a challenge. It was not the intention of the faith missions, however, to be competitive in any way, since they worked almost exclusively in areas not reached by established missionary effort. But they were a theological and organizational challenge for established missions because they originated from a different religious background and employed some different principles in their missionary methods.

Next to the nondenominational character and the "faith principle" of financial provision, an important innovation in faith missions was the full equality of ordained and lay missionaries. Equally important was the employment of both women (single and married) and men in pioneering missionary work. H. Taylor was the first to entrust a single woman with an entire province of independent work, and in faith missions generally women have often developed pioneering evangelistic work (e.g., M. Moe, South Africa; J. Veenstra, Nigeria; A. Doering, Zaire; A. Carmichael, Japan; D. Tinnevelly, South India; G. Aylward, China). These opportunities have been taken by women in many faith missions since 1900.

Because the understanding of the sacraments is not much emphasized, laypeople have more opportunities for spiritual work than in many denominational missions, and less well-educated missionaries are also given the opportunity to take part in mission work in the faith missions. The majority of missionaries of the faith missions are educated in nondenominational Bible colleges, whose academic level is relatively low.

The novelty of the faith missions is that they go back to another movement for spiritual renewal. While the long-established missions have their roots in the Great Revival around the end of the eighteenth century, the faith missions were born from the next revival, which started in 1858 (United States) and 1859 (United Kingdom), in which the evangelist D. L. Moody played a leading role after 1873. This revival incorporated three new spiritual movements which greatly influenced the faith missions: the Brethren movement (ca. 1829), which did not recognize ordination and strongly stressed individual and congregational independence; the Holiness movement (ca. 1835), which understood holiness as "power for service" and sanctification as a second crisis-experience after conversion; and the Prophetic movement (ca. 1813), which expected Christ's return before the beginning of the millennium and held that the primary task of the church was to evangelize the whole world "to hasten the return of the King."

4. Until the beginning of the twentieth century, the faith missions were mainly an Anglo-Saxon phenomenon; since then they have gained firmer footing on the European mainland, and for the last twenty years they have grown increasingly in the Third World (e.g., Indonesian Missionary Fellowship [Batu, 1961]; African Enterprise [Pietermaritzburg/Nairobi, 1962]; Indian Evangelical Mission [Bangalore, South India, 1965]; Calvary Ministries [Gana Ropp, Nigeria, 1974]; Japan Antioch Mission [1977]; or other independent branches of faith missions: e.g., WEC Brazil or SIM Singapore). For faith missions the final stage in mission work is not "two-way traffic" but the development of new missions (denominational and nondenominational) in the field of non-Western churches.

KLAUS FIEDLER

Bibliography

Bacon, D., *From Faith to Faith: The Influence of Hudson Taylor on the Faith Missions Movement* (1984). Broomhall, A. J., *Hudson Taylor and China's Open Century*, 5 vols. (1981). Chatelin, A., *Héli Chatelin: L'ami de l'Angola: Fondateur de la mission philafriaine* (1918). Cowan, G., *The Word That Kindles* (1979). Fiedler, K., *Das Kirchenverständnis der Glaubensmissionen und ihrer Kirchen in Afrika* (1989). Gration, J. A., *The Relationship of the Africa Inland Mission and Its National Church in Kenya between 1895 and 1971* (1974). Hartzfeld, D., and C. Nienkirchen, *The Birth of a Vision* (1986). Keyes, L. E., *The Last Age of Missions: A Study of Third World Mission Societies* (1983). Keyes, L. E., and L. D. Pate, "Two-Thirds World Missions: The Next 100 Years," *Missiol* 21/2 (April 1993) 187–206. McKay, M., *Faith and Facts in the History of the*

China Inland Mission 1832–1905 (1981). Niklaus, R., J. Sawin, and S. Stoesz, *All for Jesus* (1986). Nilsen, M., and P. Sheetz, *Malla Moe* (1980). Pate, L. D., *From Every People: A Handbook of Two-Thirds World Missions* (1989). Schirrmacher, B., *Baumeister is der Herr* (1978). Spartialis, P., *To the Nile and Beyond: The Birth and Growth of the Sudanese Church of Christ* (1981). Steele, F., *Not in Vain: The Story of North Africa Mission* (1981). Taylor, H., *Retrospect* (1900). Taylor, H., and G. Taylor, *Biography of James Hudson Taylor* (1965). Idem, *Hudson Taylor's Spiritual Secret* (1932). Torjesen, E., *A Study of Fredrik Franson* (1984). Wilson, S., and J. Siewert, eds., *Mission Handbook: North American Protestant Ministries Overseas* (1986).

❧ FILIPINO THEOLOGY ❧

1. Spanish Period. 2. American Period. 3. Vatican II and Subsequent Period. 4. Areas of Particular Contemporary Interest.

1. The Spanish period of Filipino theology extended from 1521/65 to 1898. Obviously, the first theological horizon of the church in the Spanish period (the Philippines was "discovered" by Magellan in 1521; the first settlement of Manila, by Legaspi, was in 1565) was the Counter-Reformation. The instruction in Christian doctrine which we know of was excellent in its pedagogical methods but inevitably reflected the concerns of the Counter-Reformation. A number of catechisms were published, either translations of Bellarmine or inspired by his method and approach. Works of devotion (novena booklets, sermons) can be said to contain "implicit" theological thought. Very significant among catechetical and devotional writing is the *Pasyon Mahal*, a narrative, in metered verse, of the entire biblical history, but developing especially the passion and death of Christ. Versions in various local dialects exist. The *Pasyon* makes use of symbols and narrative to communicate doctrine. It makes the passion and death of Christ a key reference point for Christian life.

In general, the writings of missionaries during the Spanish period concentrated on the positive exposition of the gospel and church teaching, in catechetical works, sermons, devotional manuals, and moral treatises. Works on apologetics were few (A. Lopez, SJ, is an exception). This changed only in the twentieth century. P. Fernandez (1979, 418–25) gives a fairly complete survey that includes also "more formal theological work."

Some thought might be given to the influence of the Salamanca school (Francisco de Vitoria, OP) and its thought on colonization and the attendant factors. This is reflected in particular in Bishop Domingo Salazar, OP, and the Synod of Manila (1582–86).

2. The American period lasted from 1898 to 1946. In seminaries (Sto. Tomas, San Jose, Vigan, and others), Latin texts, mostly of Roman and Spanish provenance, continued to be used. English texts were largely translations and summaries of "classic" Scholastic textbooks. On a smaller scale, booklets produced during this period largely emulated the pamphlet apostolate quite widespread in the U.S. church.

There was a significant increase in works on apologetics, reflective of the concerns of the U.S. church. These answer difficulties posed by the modern mentality and scientific progress (see, e.g., Fr. MacCarthy and later Fr. J. P. Delaney at the University of the Philippines).

New was the accent on Christian/Catholic social teaching (e.g., at the Ateneo de Manila, in the work of Fr. J. A. Mulry, at the Chesterton Evidence Guild, on the *Catholic Hour* [a radio show], and in the catechism on social teaching). The Jesuit periodical *Cultural Social* served as a channel for some of this information. These developments had an influence on the formation of lay Catholics, especially in the field of political action, which was, later, to produce people like S. Rodrigo, M. Manahan, and R. Manglapus.

Finally, Filipino writers entered the scene with writings on Catholic philosophical and theological themes (e.g., H. de la Costa, SJ, and his popular theological writings in *Commonweal*).

3. Vatican II (1962–65) really started things moving in Filipino theology. But it was at first only a very hesitant "thawing" of the theological climate. The editorial of a special issue of *Philippine Studies* (July 1965) noted:

> Not even the present Ecumenical Council, which has stirred up so remarkable a theological ferment in most countries, has succeeded in bringing about a theological awakening within our Catholic community. The appearance of a theological work...is regrettably a real rarity on local publication lists. There is no appreciable demand for such items locally, and the theologians we may have in our midst ordinarily reach only the students in our major seminaries and are usually so involved in administrative and pastoral concerns that they simply do not have the time necessary for the serious pursuit of their craft. And so no theological work of any genuine quality or value is being "locally produced," — or — if it is — the general lack of interest successfully prevents it from coming to the surface here.

As far as the Protestant scene is concerned, R. Tano (1981, 10–12) characterizes the situation as an overall lack of significant theological writing, due to immediate practical concerns (pastoral work, church extension) and to a certain isolation from public involvement in sociopolitical and similar issues.

But the movement initiated by Vatican II did gradually gain ground and momentum. Instrumental in this were renewal programs for priests and sisters and lecture series for the public. Much of this concentrated on commentaries on Vatican II, but through these, trends of contemporary European philosophy and theology, especially liberal European theology, began to influence the Philippine theological scene. Nevertheless, these conferences and series also addressed issues of local interest and significance. They constituted an awakening of sorts in the theological field.

During this period, scholars began first steps toward relating the results of social science to theology (e.g., F. Lynch, SJ, and H. de la Costa, SJ). Others translated or transposed newer, mostly Western "liberal" theology onto the local religious education scene. A good example of this is V. Gorospe and R. L. Deats, *The Filipino in the Seventies: An Ecumenical Perspective*. Among Protestant theologians in the 1960s and 1970s, E. Nacpil was the most articulate and forceful theological writer.

It was at this point that what we might call "historical theology" was brought to bear on some events and movements in the general or church history of the Philippines and on some phenomena studied by sociology and anthropology. The following may be mentioned by name: H. de la Costa, SJ, and his pioneering work in Philippine church history, especially his studies on the Filipino clergy, continued and extended by J. Schumacher, SJ; G. Anderson's work in Philippine church history; P. de Achútegui, SJ, and his massive volumes on Aglipay (the founder of the Philippine Independent Church); studies on the Iglesia ni Kristo by J. Sanders, J. J. Kavanagh, and F. Elesterio; D. Elwood's writing on christology; and research into popular piety and folk Catholicism by V. Marasigan, SJ. Much of the work in "historical theology" remains unpublished, hidden away in scores of theses at seminaries and universities. No survey of this vast body of literature has been done.

The general pattern followed in these theses would seem to be the following: first, social-scientific or historical research on a given situation or topic; second, an analysis of this research (e.g., causes of the situation, genesis of the phenomenon); and, third, a theological reflection on this material with the aim of evaluating its place and significance in the life and history of the church in the Philippines.

One significant factor in the thawing of the theological climate in the Philippines in the 1960s was the emergence of Marxist-Maoist thought as dialogue partner of theological reflection. This was the case particularly in activist circles, for example, in student organizations, farmers' groups, and social-analysis seminars. Latin American liberation theology in the wake of Medellín (1968) also began to exercise influence in the late 1960s.

The 1970s were marked by a sudden explosion of theological reflection, a "blooming of a thousand flowers." Most of this was in oral or mimeographed form or, if published, in writings that were rather unsystematic. That explosion, however, had effects still powerfully felt today. Rather than give a chronological survey of these decades, since we are covering only a short span, it would seem better to attempt a classification by areas of interest. For want of a more careful analysis, this has to be rather rough and preliminary. Present-day theological thinking in the Philippines would seem to gravitate around three areas of interest. The first is theologies taking the magisterium as base. The mainstream theology which has developed in the church in the Philippines since Vatican II might be said, with positive (rather than pejorative) connotations, to be based in the magisterium. This does not mean, by and large, a mere parroting of magisterium texts but — especially in better speaking, teaching, and writing — a considerably creative and forward-looking use of the texts of Vatican II and other magisterium documents and their application to the Philippine (and Asian) settings.

The texts of the Federation of Asian Bishops' Conferences (FABC) have been a really creative source of influential — perhaps decisively influential — theological thinking (along highly "pastoral and missionary" lines) for episcopal texts and theological writings in the Philippines (and in other regions of Asia). A particularly influential example is the celebrated final document of the first plenary assembly of the FABC (Taipei, 1974).

J. H. Kroeger, MM, sees the Philippine bishops responding to the sociopolitical realities by way of the methodology of "the signs of the times." This response has been focused on "human promotion" understood as the fostering of the total welfare of the-human-being-in-society from a Christian faith perspective. Kroeger argues that "human promotion" is an integral dimension of the Philippine church's operative vision of its mission. This approach is that of *integral evangelization*. "Integrality" is an interpretative key unlocking the core of the Philippine local church during the post–Vatican II decades (see Kroeger 1985).

Although usually a distinction is made between texts of the magisterium and general theology, it can be said that in the case of the Philippines the statements from the FABC have been in fact a "mainstream theology" of the post–Vatican II period. They have given the overall direction to the life and work of the church in those areas of its mission which might be seen as new or as responses to new challenges — the "growing points" of history — in the Philippines and in Asia.

Among the writers on the Philippine scene who might be listed in this "mainstream," but with different concerns and emphases, are: Bishop T. Bacani, Bishop F. Claver, S. Vengco, C. G. Arévalo, A. B. Lambino, J. H. Kroeger, J. Schumacher, P. S. de Achútegui, R. Intengan, V. Gorospe, A. Balchand, F. Clark, F. Gomez, G. W. Healy, and others.

The following Philippine writers have done work on theological textbooks, which in the 1970s began to appear again, especially for a seminary audience. Fr. Pedro Sevilla has distinguished himself in writing several textbooks in the Filipino language; Bishop L. Legaspi has written on ecclesiology; and Fr. B. Pena has done work in christology. Fr. C. H. Peschke, SVD, has written a complete course on Christian ethics, which has enjoyed dissemination and use on several continents.

The second major area of theologizing may be characterized as attempts at dealing with inculturation or indigenization. Here the aim is to construct a Filipino theology. A conscious effort is made to "radicate" theological thought in Filipino meanings and values as found, principally, in traditional culture; in traditional Filipino religiosity and popular piety; in traditional and contemporary belief and value patterns (as manifested in local customs, practices, popular aphorisms, and relationship patterns); in the structure, patterns, and vocabulary of the native languages.

The methodology employed consists roughly of the following: an analysis of cultural life-patterns with the help of sociology and anthropology (the work of F. Lynch, M. Hollsteiner, and J. Bulatao has been particularly influential in this regard); an attempt at a conceptual systematization and the synthesis of a worldview of sorts from the data; then a confrontation of Filipino culture thus articulated with biblical and dogmatic church teaching in order to find points of convergence and divergence. The ultimate goal is to develop a theological vision with distinctive Filipino emphases and concerns.

In a way, the most explicitly developed approach has been that which focuses on language, especially on word-usage, etymology, and the like. Here the key words of the given language (e.g., Tagalog) lead to an understanding of key concepts, key themes, and key values, which in turn open up to the Filipino mind and heart. Thus, the notion of *loob,* a word or combining form used with others to form a cluster of meanings, is seen as a rich channel of expression of a particular perspective on self, relationships, life, society, and world. Theologians who are working along these lines include R. Villote, L. Mercado, B. Beltran, J. de Mesa, V. Gorospe, V. Marasigan, R. Ferriols, and D. Miranda. Their work is connected with the historical theology mentioned earlier.

The third major area of reflection is that which revolves around the liberation problematic. Over recent years, the liberation problematic has been an important, maybe even *the* most important, focus of attention. Given the Third World situation in which the country has found itself, consciously so understood since the late 1960s, serious theological work by all concerned theological writers has touched — in lesser or greater, less or more intense degrees — the nagging problem of the poverty of 70 percent of the Filipino people and the questions it raises.

Bishop F. Claver has said that the Philippine church has been groping for a theological stance on the issues of "poverty, deprivation, and oppression" for some decades and that the coming of Latin American liberation theology provided a framework for a reflection that had been going on for some time. Then, too, the wide dissemination of Marxist-Maoist thought in intellectual and student circles, in the late 1960s especially, with its slogan words "imperialism," "feudalism," and "bureaucrat capitalism" and its analysis of Philippine society, called for a theological response perhaps not much different from Latin American liberation theology. Paul VI's *Populorum Progressio* (1967), taken as the theme of the first meeting of Asian bishops during the first papal visit to Asia (1970), focused concern on the causes of poverty, the issues of development, and the relationship of the church's mission to justice within Philippine society and within the international global community.

The theological reflection which emerged from the confluence of the above (and other) currents can rightly be called "liberation theology," understanding the term in its broader meaning and keeping in mind that there are various forms. A classification of various kinds of liberation theology can be made on the basis of the depth and extent of the influence of Marxist analysis and Marxist prescriptions for social transformation. It must be remembered that theological reflection done on these issues was directed to action, that is, to concrete involvement in action-groups or movements and even to direct political and revolutionary action.

The Philippine group in EATWOT (→Ecumenical Association of Third World Theologians) and the Christians for National Liberation (CNL) generally show close affinity with the analysis of the situation and the prescriptions for action given by political groups of the far left and the National Democratic Front (NDF). The following are representative of this position: E. de la Torre, C. Abesamis, M. J. Mananzan, L. Hechanova, K. Gaspar, and V. Fabella. Because of a network of international contacts, this group has had greater international exposure than others, and its work has been given wider distribution internationally.

A second group comprises those theological writers who consciously and explicitly link their work with the documents of the official ecclesial magisterium (documents of Vatican II, CELAM, the FABC, and so on). They try to discern a stance for Filipino Catholics and other Christians in light of the church's social teaching. The Catholic Bishops' Conference of the Philippines (CBCP) has tended to rely more frequently on the advice and presentation of this more centrist group. It includes Bishop F. Claver, Bishop T. Bacani, C. G. Arévalo, A. Lambino, and J. Blanco.

A third type of liberation theology is found in the more simplified writing done in and for meetings of basic ecclesial communities (BECs) or basic Christian communities (BCCs). Positions here vary from far left to somewhat left of center. It would be impossible to give a more accurate classification of the various strands of thought within BECs and BCCs. J. Carroll and F. Claver have said that BECs and BCCs range from "purely worship-oriented" to "highly socially and politically committed." Little of this thinking is available in writing, except in mimeographed or Xeroxed form. This category has been included here because it has had much influence, especially among the grassroots strata of the church, both in rural and urban settings.

4. The sociopolitical scene remains the main focus of interest among theologians who work on immediately relevant issues. A good example of such work is the theological reflection on the "EDSA Revolution" of February 1986 (see de Achútegui 1986). The ideological stance of the present government, its commitment to democracy and nonviolence, is the subject of ongoing reflection on faith and ideology (see Elwood 1985).

The theology of nonviolence emerged largely after the assassination (1983) of Philippine martyr B. Aquino. It was especially promoted by J. Blanco and had an extraordinary influence on the events which led to the February revolution (1986). A centrist group of theological writers has tended to move toward a position of active nonviolence which has influenced more moderate groups within Philippine society.

Other areas in which there is considerable theological interest are religious education and catechesis; BECs; and, perhaps more than any other concern, the emergence and articulation of an authentic Filipino spirituality for our time. Institutes and workshops on this latter theme have been multiplying since the 1980s.

In the area of "inculturation," the following perhaps deserve to be noted. Work on texts from the Spanish period, both in Spanish and the vernaculars, has either been begun or is being carried forward. There is special interest in the relation of these texts to the sociopolitical aspirations of the people (see Ileto 1979). Similarly, indigenous religious texts and nonchurch sources and forms of popular piety are being investigated (see Marasigan). Most recently, ecological concerns have been developed in relation to inculturation (see Lovett 1986).

CATALINO G. ARÉVALO, SJ

Bibliography

Anderson, G. H., *Asian Voices in Christian Theology* (1976). Beltran, B., *Christology of the Inarticulate* (1985). Claver, F., et al., *In the Philippines: Christian Faith and Ideologies,* Loyola Papers 10. De Achútegui, P. S., ed., *The Miracle of the Philippine Revolution,* Loyola Papers 15 (1986). De la Costa, H., A. Lambino, and C. G. Arévalo, *On Faith, Ideologies and Christian Options,* Loyola Papers 7/8. De la Costa, H., and J. Schumacher, *Church and State: The Philippine Experience,* Loyola Papers 3. Idem, *The Filipino Clergy: Historical Studies and Future Perspectives,* Loyola Papers 12 (1979). De la Costa, H., et al., *On Faith and Justice,* Loyola Papers 5 (1977). De la Torre, E., *Touching Ground, Taking Roots* (1986). De Mesa, J., *And God Said "Bahala Na": The Theme of Providence in the Lowland Filipino Context* (1979). Idem, *In Solidarity with the Culture: Studies in Theological Re-rooting* (1987). Idem, *Isang Maiksing Katekismo para sa mga Bata: A Study in Indigenous Catechesis* (1984). De Mesa, J., and L. Wostyn, *Doing Christology: The Reappropriation of a Tradition* (1989). Idem, *Doing Theology: Basic Realities and Processes* (1982). Elwood, D., *Asian Christian Theology: Emerging Themes* (1980). Idem, *Faith Encounters Ideology: Christian Discernment and Social Change* (1985). Elwood, D., and P. Magdamo, *Christ in Philippine Context* (1971). Fabella, V., "Christology from an Asian Woman's Perspective," in V. Fabella and S. Ai Lee Park, eds., *We Dare to Dream: Doing Theology as Asian Women* (1989). Fernandez, P., *History of the Church in the Philippines 1521–1898* (1979). *The Filipino Face of Christ,* special issue of *DIWA* 6/1 (October 1981). *Filipino Patterns in Adult Catechesis,* special issue of *DIWA* 2/1 (October 1977). Gorospe, V., *Church and Society: Challenges for Tomorrow,* Budhi Papers 5 (1983). Idem, *The Filipino Search for Meaning* (1974). Gorospe, V., ed., *Faith, Justice and the Filipino Christian* (1976). Idem, *Filipino Theology Today,* Budhi Papers 3. Gorospe, V., and R. L. Deats, eds., *The Filipino in the Seventies: An Ecumenical Perspective* (1973). Gresh, T., ed., *Basic Christian Communities in the Philippines* (1977). Hardy, R. P., ed., *Ating Mga Kapatid: A Spirituality of the CBCP* (1984). Idem, *The Philippine Bishops Speak (1963–1983)* (1984). Ileto, R., *Pasyon and Revolution: Popular Movements in the Philippines: 1840–1910* (1979). *International Colloquium on Contextual Theology,* vol. 14/40 of *Philippiniana Sacra* (January–April 1979). Kroeger, J., *The Philippine Church and Evangelization, 1965–1984* (1985). Labayen, J., *To Be the Church of the Poor* (1986). Lambino, A., E. Martinez, and C. G. Arévalo, *Towards Doing Theology in the Philippine Context,* Loyola Papers 9 (1977). Lovett, B., *Life before Death* (1986). Lynch, F., et al., eds., *Modernization: Its Impact in the Philippines* (1971). Marasigan, V., W. Ysaac, et al., *Inculturation, Faith and Christian Life,* Loyola Papers 6. Mercado, L., *Elements of Filipino Theol-*

ogy (1975). Idem, ed., *Doing Filipino Theology* (1997). Miranda, D., *Buting Pinoy: Probe Essays on Value as Filipino* (1993). Idem, *Pagkamakatao: Reflections on the Theological Virtues in the Philippine Context* (1987). Nacpil, E., and D. Elwood, eds., *The Human and the Holy* (1978). *Philippine Priests' Forum* (1969–1981). Rosales, G., and C. G. Arévalo, *For All the Peoples of Asia* (1992). *Some Aspects of Contemporary Theology,* special issue of *Philippine Studies* 13/3 (July 1965). Tano, R. D., *Theology in the Philippine Setting: A Case Study in the Contextualization of Theology* (1981).

❧ FUNDAMENTALISM ❧

1. Characteristics. 2. Principal Themes. 3. Fundamentalism outside the United States.

Fundamentalism is a twentieth-century development within American evangelical Protestantism. Its most distinguishing feature is its militant opposition to modernist, liberal theology and the cultural change associated with it. In particular, fundamentalism opposes biblical criticism, the social gospel movement, and the secularization of social and political institutions.

Until the beginning of the twentieth century, most American Protestants were evangelicals. As such, they accepted the atoning work of Jesus Christ for their salvation, professed complete confidence in the Bible, and sought to lead others to accept Jesus as their savior. Mass meetings called "revivals" were the practical means used to lead people to Christ.

1. Two characteristics of evangelical revivalism became hallmarks of fundamentalism: biblicism and religious individualism. Biblicism is the belief that the Bible alone is the believer's guide to faith and life. Essential to this belief is inerrancy, the doctrine that the Bible is free from any error, scientific, historical, or religious. Fundamentalism assumes that divine revelation could not come by way of a book that contained any errors. The Bible, therefore, must be inerrant. The fundamentalist doctrine of inerrancy was a response to historical criticism of the Bible that rejected the Bible as a source for the reconstruction of ancient Israel's history or the life of Jesus.

Fundamentalism was also a response to a profound spiritual and cultural crisis that many evangelicals experienced at the beginning of the twentieth century. They were certain that the dominant culture in America was openly turning away from God. What made this crisis even more acute for fundamentalists was their conviction that Christian denominations were cooperating in the death of Christian civilization. The fundamentalists spurned liberalism and modernism, which they saw as misguided attempts to adapt religious ideas to secular humanist values. In particular, fundamentalism rejected the social gospel movement that arose at this time.

Proponents of the social gospel wanted to enlist Christians in the transformation of society which would bring about the reign of God. Fundamentalists repudiated the identification of human progress with the coming of God's reign. The myth of human progress prevented people from seeing their true state before God. Fundamentalism also rejected the modernist assertions that the only test of truth was action and that faith in Christ was irrelevant except as an inspiration to moral action — more specifically, social action.

Fundamentalists are individualist, soul-saving evangelists. What they regard as crucial is the regenerating work of Christ that saves souls. Compared to this, the aims of the social gospel movement were inconsequential. The goal of every Christian is to lead people to Christ through witnessing to the power of salvation. Trying to reform society diverts believers' time and energies from confronting people with the gospel. In any case, this world is passing away. Why bother trying to reform it?

The theory of evolution appeared to provide a scientific basis for liberalism's belief in the myth of human progress. Also, fundamentalists saw the theory of evolution as contradicting biblical teaching in the Book of Genesis. Opposition to this theory became a symbol of the fundamentalist rejection of modernism and liberalism.

It is important to note that fundamentalism did not emerge as a rural, southern phenomenon. It was the result of philosophical and theological debates that occurred within mainline churches in major urban areas. The rejection of biblical criticism was made by conservative theological faculties of major universities. The conflict between the evangelicals and the modernists was played out as they contended for control of major Protestant denominations.

Fundamentalism lost the battle against evolution and, more importantly, the battle for control of the Protestant churches in America. Fundamentalists then developed their own educational institutions such as Bible colleges, publishing houses, and missionary boards. These were independent of mainline denominational control. Fundamentalists gathered in their own local congregations and developed a religious subculture with distinctive mores and social connections. They consciously separated themselves from the dominant religious and secular ethos that they deemed to be anti-Christian.

2. Fundamentalism derived its name from a series of booklets called *The Fundamentals* written between 1910 and 1915. Conceived and financed by a wealthy layperson, these booklets were a compendium of conservative, evangelical beliefs. To ensure the widest possible distribution the booklets were sent free of charge to Protestant religious leaders throughout the English-speaking world.

The publication of *The Fundamentals* had little immediate impact. Neither theological journals nor popular religious periodicals gave the booklets more than a passing notice. But the project did have some long-term effects. *The Fundamentals* became a reference identifying the doctrines of the emerging fundamentalist movement. It is important to note that this work was moderate in its approach and represented a transitional stage from evangelicalism to full-blown fundamentalism.

At the same time, another important fundamentalist work appeared: the *Scofield Reference Bible*. The interpretive notes in this Bible were the work of C. I. Scofield. He popularized *dispensationalism,* the most distinguishing doctrine of fundamentalist biblical interpretation. Dispensationalism divides history into seven distinct epochs. Each of these represents a different "dispensation" through which God governs the world and tests human obedience.

The current dispensation is the "dispensation of grace" or the "dispensation of the church." In this dispensation that began with Jesus' death, God requires only one act of obedience from human beings: the confession of sin and acceptance of the atoning death of Jesus. Nothing else can merit salvation. That is why it is essential to confront people with the gospel — so that they can make a decision for Christ.

One effect of dispensationalism is to deny that the moral teaching of Jesus has any relevance to salvation. Jesus lived in the dispensation of the law. His words were directed to Jews whose salvation depended on the observance of this law, but this dispensation has passed. That is why the letters of Paul are more decisive in formulating fundamentalist theology than the Gospels.

Fundamentalists are not certain how long the present dispensation will last. They believe that the Second Coming of Christ is imminent and look forward to the final dispensation — that of the reign of God. It will begin with "the rapture" in which all those who have accepted Christ go to heaven. There they will escape seven years of tribulation that will conclude with the battle of Armageddon. Following the defeat of the powers of evil, the thousand-year reign of Christ on earth will begin. At the conclusion of the millennium, the final judgment will occur. Those who have accepted Jesus will go to heaven. All others will be condemned to eternal hellfire. This scenario developed from a fundamentalist reading of biblical texts about the eschaton, principally Ezekiel, Daniel, and Revelation.

These books are particularly attractive to fundamentalists because of their pessimism about the possibilities of the present. Fundamentalists see themselves as a misunderstood and persecuted minority. They also believe that this world carries the seeds of its own destruction. Circumstances will get worse until Jesus returns. When he does return, however, true Christians will be vindicated. In contrast, liberalism's view of this world is optimistic. Christians can transform this world and inaugurate the kingdom of God on earth.

Fundamentalism, in part, arose as a reaction against the optimism of theological liberalism, but the crisis went deeper. At the beginning of the twentieth century, conservative, evangelical Christianity was no longer the dominant influence in American society as it once was. Fundamentalists were horrified by what they considered the secularization of American culture. What appalled them even more was that the churches themselves were abetting this secularization through the social gospel movement and their acceptance of modern biblical criticism. The secularization of American culture was another stimulus for fundamentalism's basic pessimism.

In the last twenty years, evangelicals and fundamentalists have made significant attempts to reverse the process of secularization. Strengthened by their growth in numbers and their political power, fundamentalists have developed a political agenda that opposes what they call "secular humanism." Among items in this agenda is the inclusion of "scientific creationism" in public school curricula, the defeat of the Equal Rights Amendment, passage of an antiabortion amendment, and the enacting of laws to allow prayer in schools.

Except for the defeat of the Equal Rights Amendment, the fundamentalists have not been successful in promoting their agenda. Some fundamentalist leaders have decided to leave the political arena and return to the pulpit. Still, fundamentalists and religious conservatives have had a significant impact on the American political scene. Courting the evangelical and fundamentalist voting bloc caused a serious rift within the conservative political movement in the United States.

3.   Fundamentalism, then, is one religious response to a major change in society: the secularization of American culture. Similar changes have taken place in other cultures, and these have occasioned similar religious responses. This has led to

the application of the term "fundamentalism" to movements in other cultures that attempt to reverse secularization.

The secular character of modern Israeli society has been a shock to many religious immigrants to Israel. These pious Jews expect to come to a country where observance of Jewish law will be universal. Instead they find that about 80 percent of Israeli Jews are nonobservant. The label "Jewish fundamentalism" has been applied to the *haredi* movement, which rejects the values of secular Israeli society and attempts to impose its patterns of religious observance on modern Israeli society.

A similar phenomenon is going on in the Islamic world. Colonialism and the oil economy led to the introduction of Western values and the development of secular political and social institutions in Islamic countries. Islamic fundamentalism is a reaffirmation of the foundational principles of Islam and an effort to reshape society in terms of those principles. This movement is marked by a literalist interpretation of Islam and a rigid and even violent pursuit of social and moral reconstruction.

By law, India is a secular state, but its Hindu majority has produced religious activists who are not satisfied with the traditional Hinduism of temple priests and ritual. Hindu fundamentalists want to replace the secular state with a nation based on Hindu law and traditions. This has led to violent clashes with the Muslim and Sikh minorities that threaten the institutions of Indian democracy.

Fundamentalist movements have risen within the Sikh, Buddhist, Confucian, and Shinto traditions. The fundamentalist impulse has emerged every time traditional religions have encountered the social and political movements of the twentieth century. Fundamentalists of any religious stripe are not at home in the twentieth century. They live by the myth of a "golden age" when religious perspectives supposedly shaped the institutions and values of a people.

For American Protestant fundamentalists that golden age was the eighteenth and nineteenth centuries, when Christian values shaped America. For the Hindu fundamentalists, it was the legendary rule of Ram, the perfect king who upheld Hindu law on earth. Each fundamentalism has its own golden age.

The fundamentalist impulse is not satisfied with a nostalgic gaze at the past. Every fundamentalism is committed to the restoration of its golden age. Fundamentalists are ready to take militant action to accomplish that restoration. Forms of militancy vary from the bombing of an abortion clinic in the United States to the stoning of cars being driven on the Sabbath in Israel. Political assassinations and armed battles have also been tools of some fundamentalisms. Fundamentalism's most characteristic and dangerous feature is its militancy in its program of religious restoration.

In the United States, the militancy of Protestant fundamentalism expresses itself primarily in energetic proselytizing. Converts are sought not only among non-Christians but also from mainline churches. Fundamentalists have been so successful that in the last twenty years the only Protestant denominations that have experienced growth are those with a conservative or fundamentalist bent. Simultaneously, mainline denominations have lost membership. In a typical fundamentalist congregation converts comprise about 50 percent of the community. Fundamentalist congregations also engage in missionary endeavors outside the United States; in those places their aggressive proselytizing and the simplicity of their message combine with great success.

LESLIE J. HOPPE, OFM

Bibliography

Ammerman, N. T., *Bible Believers: Fundamentalists in the Modern World* (1987). Averill, L. J., *Religious Right, Religious Wrong: A Critique of the Fundamentalist Phenomenon* (1989). Balmer, R., *Mine Eyes Have Seen the Glory* (1989). Barr, J., *Beyond Fundamentalism* (1984). Idem, *Fundamentalism* (1977). Boone, K. C., *The Bible Tells Them So: The Discourse of Protestant Fundamentalism* (1989). Caplan, L., ed., *Studies in Religious Fundamentalism* (1987). Clabaugh, G. K., *Thunder on the Right: The Protestant Fundamentalists* (1975). Cohen, N. J., *The Fundamentalist Phenomenon* (1990). Cohn, N., *The Pursuit of the Millennium* (1961). Dixon, A. C., L. Meyer, and R. A. Torrey, eds., *The Fundamentals: A Testimony to the Truth,* 12 vols. (1910–15). Dollar, G. W., *A History of Fundamentalism in America* (1973). Evans, R. L., and I. M. Berent, *Fundamentalism: Hazards and Heartbreaks* (1988). Falwell, J., ed., *The Fundamentalist Phenomenon* (1981). Fracke, G., *The Religious Right and Christian Faith* (1982). Furniss, N. F., *The Fundamentalist Controversy, 1918–1931* (1954). Gasper, L., *The Fundamentalist Movement* (1963). Gatewood, W. B., ed., *Controversy in the Twenties: Fundamentalism, Modernism, and Evolution* (1969). Halsell, G., *Prophecy and Politics: Militant Evangelists on the Road to Nuclear War* (1986). Henry, C. F. H., *The Uneasy Conscience of Modern Fundamentalism* (1947). Hill, S. S., Jr., and D. E. Owen, *The New Religious Political Right in America* (1982). Hutchinson, W., *The Modernist Impulse in American Protestantism* (1976). Kraus, C. N., *Dispensationalism in America: Its Rise and Development* (1958). Lawrence, B. B., *Defenders of God: The Fundamentalist Revolt against the Modern Age* (1989). Loetscher, L. A., *The Broadening Church* (1954). Marsden, G. M., *Fundamentalism and American Culture* (1980). Idem, *Reforming Fundamentalism: Fuller Seminary and the New Evangelicalism* (1987). Idem, *Understanding Fundamentalism and Evangelicalism* (1991). Marty, M. E., and R. S. Appleby, eds., *Fundamentalisms Observed* (1981). O'Meara, T. F., *Fundamentalism: A Catholic Perspective* (1990). Packer, J. I., *"Fundamentalism" and the Word of God: Some Evangelical Principles* (1974). Peterson, P. D., ed., *Evangelicalism and Fundamentalism: A Bibliography Selected from the ATLA Religion Database* (1983). Piepkorn, A. C., *Profiles in Belief,* vols. 3 and 4 (1979). Poythress, V. S., *Understanding Dispensationalists* (1987). Russell, W., C. A., *Voices of American Fundamentalism* (1976). Ryrie, C. C., *Dispensationalism Today* (1965). Sandeen, E. R., *The Origins of Fundamentalism* (1968). Idem, *The Roots of Fundamentalism* (1970). *Scofield Reference Bible* (1909). Selvidge, M. J., ed., *Fundamentalism Today* (1984). Stevick, D. B., *Beyond Fundamentalism* (1964). Szasz, F. M., *The Divided Mind of Protestant America, 1880–1930* (1982).

G

❧ GLOBALIZATION ❧

1. Definition.   2. Globalization and Sociology.   3. Globalization and Religion.   4. Globalization and Mission.

1.   Just as postmodernism was *the* concept of the 1980s, globalization may be *the* concept of the 1990s, a concept which tries to express and analyze human development and change at the inauguration of the third millennium. "Globalization" has been used as a business concept since the early 1960s. By the 1970s its popularity expanded into many disciplines so that it began to replace the term "internationalization" not only in business but in the areas of education and politics. The use of the terms "global" or "globalization" today is ubiquitous both inside and outside the academic community. This is true despite the curious fact that within the academic community, there is still no agreed upon definition of globalization.

Although the formation of a theory around the phenomena of globalization is still very much in its infancy stage, some consensus is beginning to form among sociologists, philosophers, and theologians about its reality, dynamics, and social impact. First, globalization is seen as an outgrowth and continuation of the modernization process in the West. This process, embedded in a capitalistic economy, frees the individual from some of the constraints of society. Because of its expansionist nature, globalization, like modernization, values progress and innovation. Its ethos for the individual is embodied in the French Revolution's "liberty, equality, fraternity" or in the American Revolution's "life, liberty, and the pursuit of happiness."

Second, although some measure of globalization has always occurred (the same can be said of modernization), recent advancements in technology have accelerated the process so that today, globalization is creating a worldwide uniform cultural reality; that is, globalization describes the process of the world becoming more and more "a single place" (R. Robertson). Globalization as a concept refers both to the compression of the world into a single place and the intensification of consciousness of the world as a whole (R. Robertson). The former "natural" constraints of geography and time are being quickly erased. The onrush of economic, technological, ecological, scientific, material, and political forces is demanding integration and uniformity, thus rapidly creating a homogeneous culture across the globe. The emerging global culture — sometimes whimsically referred to as McWorld (B. Barber) while the process of global culture's formation is dubbed "the Coca-colonization of the world" — is tied together by technology, communications, and commerce. Its icons include T-shirts, baseball caps, denim jeans, athletic shoes, MTV, Macintosh, and McDonald's. The deeper processes and actions to which the concept of globalization now refers have been proceeding, with some interruptions, for many centuries, but the main focus of the discussion of globalization is on relatively recent times. The increasing interconnectedness of the world as a single place, and the consequences and dynamics of this growing interconnectedness, is at the heart of theories on globalization. Consequently, the world as a global system and not some subunit of it (such as the nation, the state, or the region) is the primary focus of attention in globalization studies.

Third, despite its connection with modernization, globalization as a movement is not simply another form of Western imperialism (although non-Western scholars and theologians often disagree with this point). Modernization has been changing as it has been exported around the globe because its receiving cultures have not been passive but active. As modernization has interacted with local cultures, it has experienced a "ripple-back" effect. This effect is sometimes referred to as "reflexivity" (S. Lash, J. Urry). The result is that with globalization, modernization has taken on a new form. The West is no longer simply colonizing the world; the West itself is being "colonized" and changed in the process.

Finally, although the formidable power of globalization tends to flatten and corrode local values, leading to a greater uniformity and a self-conscious orientation to the world as a global whole, it also leads toward various kinds of global protests. R. Robertson (1995) and J. Friedman (1994) have described these acts of protest against the powerful homogenizing force of globalization. Robertson coined the phrase "glocalization" to express the reassertion of the local. Friedman analyzed a spectrum of acts of resistance ranging from fundamentalism through cultural revitalization to a new ethnification of local culture. These antisystemic global protests, which R. J. Schreiter calls "global flows," take shape as strong reactions both to what is viewed as the hegemony of Western imperialism (whether political, economic, or cultural) and to the failure of global systems to live up to their promised benefits. The result is that multifaceted battles are declared locally against every kind of cultural, religious, economic, and national interdependence; against every kind of artificial social cooperation; or against any move toward cultural homogeneity from outside. This retribalization or reassertion of the local is, however, not antiglobal but antisystemic in nature. Its protest is very much included within the overall movement of globalization.

In summary, globalization is a recent, complex, worldwide social phenomenon which encompasses the opposing forces of "particularism" and "homogeneity," forces which B. Barber labels "Jihad and McWorld." These forces are working simultaneously all over the world in the same places and at the same times. In short, the planet is falling precipitately apart and coming reluctantly together at the very same moment. Both forces represent the dialectical dynamics of globalization: the one re-creating various kinds of local borders through parochial concerns from within, the other making borders porous by universalizing markets, ideas, and technology from without.

Globalization can thus be briefly defined as "a social process in which the constraints of geography on social and cultural arrangements recede and in which people become increasingly aware that they are receding" (Waters 1995, 3). Globalization is the compression of the world into a single place and culture and the intensification of our consciousness of this compression (R. Robertson). Or more succinctly, "Globalization is the compression of time and space under the forces of reflexive modernity" (Schreiter 1996, 2).

2. Curiously, "globalization" is being treated as less controversial in sociological circles than "postmodernism." This may be because sociological theories of change have almost always implied the universalization of the processes that they explain.

P. Beyer states that the "social and scientific development of globalization as a specific theoretical and empirical theme" only began to appear consistently in sociological literature in the late 1970s, "although significant seminal contributions date from the decade previous" (Beyer 1994, 14). R. Robertson was the first sociologist to use the term "globalization" in an article title (1985), although he had used the concept earlier. The use of the noun "globalization," therefore, has been developing rapidly since the mid-1980s. During this period, its use increased enormously, so much so that it is virtually impossible to trace the patterns of its contemporary diffusion across a large number of disciplines. The *Oxford Dictionary of New Words* includes "global" in its 1991 edition. It defines "global consciousness" as "receptiveness to [an understanding] of cultures other than one's own, often as part of an appreciation of world socio-economic and ecological issues." The dictionary maintains that this usage was influenced by M. McLuhan's idea of "the global village," explored in *Explorations in Communication* (1960).

Globalization theory distinguishes itself from longer established world perspectives in that it takes as its primary unit of social analysis the entire globe, which it treats as a single social system. Five sociologists in particular have been critical in the early analyses of globalization: J. Friedman, A. Wallerstein, J. Meyer, R. Robertson, and N. Luhmann (see Beyer 1994).

For sociologists, two chief results of using the "global whole" as an analytical tool have emerged. First, the recognition of global culture has resulted in a new social unit whose dynamics must be described as more than a simple expansion of Western modernity. It is true that sociologists recognize that globalization begins in all parts of the globe except the West as an exogenous process, that is, as Western economic, political, technological, or broadly cultural imperialism. Nevertheless, global culture points to a new social process which is more than the spread of one historically existing culture at the expense of others (as was the case with the British Empire and American imperialism). It is the creation of a new culture with definite structures and a broad social context which sociologists have found so compelling. In addition, this "global whole" is more than a collection of juxtaposed particularities. Rather, this new and distinct universal whole contextualizes the many particularities over against itself, that is, "the global." This shift in the unit of analysis is the root difference between the globalization perspective and others that look at the whole world, such as international relations, whether political or economic.

Second, the recognition of the rapidly emerging global culture raises questions about the future of this social development worldwide. For example: What will be the effect of this global movement on local cultures, their extinction or reassertion? Consequently, two fundamental questions for sociologists are: (*a*) Does globalization mean a progressive homogenization of all cultures so that, two or three centuries from now, only "global culture" will exist? or (*b*) Does globalization merely change the context in which particular cultures exist, implying transformation but not the disappearance of separate and recognizable identities (see Beyer 1994)?

3. If particular cultures are changing in response to globalization, so too is religion. Like culture, religious traditions face serious challenges in the wake of global culture. Three such challenges are: the fragmentation of globalized society, religious relativism, and the increasing individualization of religion.

In his book *Religion and Globalization,* P. Beyer suggests that globalized culture brings to every society not only homogenization but an ever-increasing functional differentiation at every level. Thus, as any society becomes more complex and differentiated, it likewise becomes more fragmented. The specificity of this fragmentation, which functions in the same way as stations on a factory assembly line, has advantages in regard to the efficiency, development, and management of each system within global culture, e.g., the economy, business, politics, education, science, and so on. Globalized culture's greatest disadvantage in regard to specificity is, ironically, the isolation of the systems it creates. Each of the systems tends to function autonomously, independent of any overarching schema or *telos.* What, then, holds all the independent systems functioning together as a whole in society? What ties together the systems as far as meaning and purpose? And how should society respond to and judge among all the divergent "global" claims made by each of its systems (e.g., economy vs. politics; economy vs. science)?

Religion can make three general responses to the fragmentation of globalized culture: a traditional, a prophetic, or a revisionist response. Religion can play the traditional role of "giving meaning" to the whole — that is, of being that social system which describes a culture's overarching *telos.* In a globalized society, where fragmentation between systems (science, technology, education, politics) becomes more evident, religion can try to play its traditional role by giving universal meaning to all of the global systems and, in general, "tying life together." Second, religion can accept a prophetic critical role, exposing society's ills or its lack of *telos.* As prophet, religion addresses the problems created by global culture and the questions the global systems cannot or will not resolve (that is the role played by, e.g., liberation theology and ecological theology). Religion can also try to humble other systems (e.g., politics, science, or economics) which elevate themselves within global society and are made to stand for the whole. Third, as a revisionist force, religion can completely reject global culture and return society, or at least a remnant of society, to a preglobalized ideal state of existence (the role played by, e.g., fundamentalists).

Religion's response to globalized society, whether traditional, prophetic, or revisionist, faces the additional hurdles of religious individualism and religious relativism. These forces are particularly debilitating because they have a direct effect on religion's public influence within global culture. Because globalization is a form of the modernization process, its effects on religion are that of modernization: both a continuing relegation of religion to the private and voluntary sphere and the relativism of religious values and beliefs. As religion becomes more privatized and individualized, its ability to function as a public discourse between global systems becomes weakened (see Beyer 1994). Religion's public power is further diminished when its values and beliefs are viewed over against the backdrop of all of the world's religions and value systems. Religion in general, or any particular religion, becomes just one voice among many, instead of a common voice uniting all. Under the impact of globalization, therefore, religion as system tends to be diminished and relegated to the margins, and its responses to global movements and problems (traditional, prophetic, and revisionist) can be reduced merely to local movements and to private spheres of influence.

How, then, should religion function in a global world which is becoming increasingly homogeneous but is marked by religious individualism, relativism, and an increasing fragmentation in society?

4. On the one hand, the church in a sense has outpaced modern society in response to globalization. The church has had a global vision of its essence and work because of Jesus' Great Commission in Matthew 28. The missionary expansion of the church in the nineteenth century and the ecumenical orientation of Protestant, Catholic, and Orthodox churches in the twentieth century are further evidences of this growing global posture. In addition, most churches today embrace the global cultural values of progress, equality, and inclusion as well as the global system-values of progress, efficiency, technical rationality, and functional differentiation (e.g., specialization and professionalization of ministry). In response to globalization, the six missional areas of the church can be summarized as: mission and evangelism; ecumenism; interfaith dialogue; urban ministry; cross-cultural ministry; and peace, justice, and ecology.

On the other hand, the church, especially the church in the West, must increasingly learn how to be the church within a worldwide global process which is radically changing the context for mission at home and abroad. How can the church balance the vitality of new, emerging local theologies (e.g., the particularities of →liberation theology, feminist theology, minjung theology, eco-spirituality) with the classical claims to universal truths in church dogma (doctrinal homogeneity)? Can Christian worldwide mission and evangelism, as widely practiced until the mid–twentieth century, be sustained in an unaltered form when constantly challenged by the truth-claims of all the world's religions? And given the crisis in global economy, global ecology, and global politics, can the religions of the world unite to create a global ethic? As a part of a massive recontextualization of church and mission under the impact of globalization (referred to by D. Bosch as a "paradigm shift" for mission), a few important themes will surely emerge as central to Christian mission. These themes are not so much new theological categories as a rethinking of traditional ones. These broad themes are listed under the subheadings of: catholicity (the missional goal); global anthropology and global crises (the malady); global gods and the triune God (the means to achieve God's mission); and global responsibility: dialogue, witness, evangelism, justice, and mission (the admonition to missional responsibility).

4.1. *Catholicity (the missional goal).* R. J. Schreiter suggests that the universalizing (homogenizing) and particularizing tendencies felt within the churches as part of global culture may make the term "catholicity" the theological equivalent of "globalization." In terms of the four marks of the church confessed in the Nicene-Constantinopolitan Creed, different ones have been especially significant at different points in church history: oneness in times of schism, holiness in the Donatist controversy, apostolicity at the time of the Reformation. Perhaps the time has come to reexamine and expand our understanding of catholicity, in view both of what Christianity has become and of the world in which globalization is taking place (see Schreiter 1994; 1996; 1997).

4.2. *Global anthropology and global crises (the malady).* As we approach the year 2000, many are increasingly aware of the relentless changes to our world and the challenges they bring. With these changes have come both local and global crises. One cannot easily escape the awareness that global crises have the potential to cause enormous trauma and social conflict both at home and abroad. One is also conscious that crises contain not only danger but also opportunities. So as the problems of ecology, sexuality, gender inequality, race, the sustainability of life, nuclear power, world order, and poverty are debated, one must likewise question the definition of humanity, the *humanum,* which is being sought as the global community approaches these problems. Just as the new insights into the individual dramatically influenced the theologies of the sixteenth century, globalization is today raising important theological questions such as: How will globalization's effect on the present anthropological sensitivities mold theological responses to both local and global definitions of the human situation?

4.3. *Global gods and the triune God (the means to achieve God's mission).* Eighty-five out of every hundred people on earth are adherents of a religion. As the twentieth century merges into the twenty-first, the global village includes more than five billion religious people. The religions are not dying out in global culture; they are pervasive, powerful, influential, and growing. This sets the scene for dialogue about God and salvation. How will God and God's work of salvation be imaged in global culture, or even reimagined? How will this imaging take place not only within Christianity itself (e.g., in the feminist critique of God) but also in dialogue with all the world's religions? Religious pluralism and the parallel issues of contextualization pose the greatest challenge to Christian mission in the area of translating the name of God and God's salvific work. Can Christianity's exclusive affirmation of salvation "in no other name" be balanced with its inclusive desire to discover the *logos spermatikos* everywhere (i.e., God's presence and saving truth in every culture, religion, and place)? The naming of God in global culture will certainly be linked to the theological discourse about soteriology. As we speak of God, we will simultaneously speak about and interpret God's work of salvation. The power for salvation will be tied together with the power of God's name. The doctrine of the triune God will certainly take more prominence in Christian mission theology as the unity and diversity of God's persons are more closely reviewed in reference to God's mission in the world.

4.4. *Global responsibility: dialogue, witness, evangelism, justice, and mission (the admonition to missional responsibility).* Globalization will certainly foster global protests by local Christian churches against the movements and injustices of global culture. Such protest might tempt the church to "flee the world." However, globalization must also foster an acceptance by churches of global responsibility. Instead of fleeing, the church must become more enmeshed in the world. In particular, this will demand that the church practice solidarity with those persons and entities that suffer under the forces of globalization: that is, the poor and the environment. Ultimately, Christian mission can never flee the world for long. Churches must embrace both antiglobal protests as well as global culture as such in order to serve the world and reflect Christ's missional presence in it. The world often sets the agenda into which the church enters preaching God's salvation in Christ and for which it performs works of love and service. Acceptance of global responsibility requires the church to define mission as broadly as possible without prioritizing, marginalizing, or rejecting certain aspects of it.

To be the church in mission has always meant to be engaged with the world. The world, however, is radically changing under the influence of globalization. So too must the church reexamine its call to mission in response to this new "global village." The challenge for the church is to respond to the forces of globalization while being faithful to its own identity and witness. This "call to responsibility" is likewise a call to be faithful to the triune God's mission in the world.

RICHARD H. BLIESE

Bibliography

Amaladoss, M., "Mission and Missioners in Today's Global Context," in *United States Catholic Mission Association Occasional Papers* (1993). Appadurai, A., *Modernity at Large: Cultural Dimensions of Globalization* (1996). Barber, B., *Jihad vs. McWorld* (1995). Idem, "Jihad vs. McWorld," in *The Atlantic Monthly* (March 1992) 53–65. Bevans, S., "Partner and Prophet: The Church and Globalization," *CCGMpap* 2 (1996). Beyer, P., *Religion and Globalization* (1994). Bliese, R., "Globalization: A Challenge for Lutheran Missiology in the 21st Century," *CTM* 24/3 (1997) 201–9. Bosch, D., *Transforming Mission* (1991). Budde, M., *The Two Churches: Catholicism and Capitalism in the World System* (1992). Featherstone, M., *Global Culture* (1990). Featherstone, M., S. Lash, R. Roberton, *Global Modernities* (1995). Foster, R., "Making National Culture in the Global Ecumene," *ARA* 20 (1991) 235–60. Friedman, J., *Cultural Identity and Global Process* (1994). Küng, H., *A Global Ethic* (1993). Lash, S., and J. Urry, *Economies of Signs and Space* (1994). Lechner, F., "Religion, Law, and Global Order," in *Religion and Global Order* (1991) 263–80. Luhmann, N., *Essays on Self-Reference* (1990). Idem, *Funktion der Religion* (1977). Idem, *Soziale Systeme: Grundriß einer allgemeinen Theorie* (1984). McLuhan, M., and B. R. Powers, *The Global Village: Transformations in World Life and Media in the 21st Century* (1989). Moore, W., "Global Sociology: The World as a Singular System," *American Journal of Sociology* 71/5 (1966) 475–82. Organization for Economic Cooperation and Development (OECD), *Globalization of Industrial Activities* (1992). Pittman, D. A., R. L. F. Habito, and T. C. Muck, *Ministry and Theology in Global Perspective* (1996). Ritzer, G., *The McDonaldization of Society* (1993). Robbins, T., *Cults, Converts, and Charisma: The Sociology of New Religious Movements* (1988). Robertson, R., *Globalization: Global Theory and Global Culture* (1992). Idem, "Globalization: Time-Space and Homogeneity-Heterogeneity," in *Global Modernities* (1995). Idem, "Interpreting Globality," in *World Realities and International Studies* (1983). Idem, "The Relativization of Societies: Modern Religion and Globalization," in *Cults, Culture, and the Law* (1985). Robertson, R., and W. Garrett, eds., *Religion and Global Order* (1991). Roozen, D. A., A. F. Evans, and R. A. Evans, *Changing the Way Seminaries Teach: Globalization and Theological Education* (1996). Schreiter, R. J., "The Concept of God in Global Dialogue," *CCGMpap* 3 (1996). Idem, "Globalization, Religion, and Theological Education: Challenges to the Chicago Center for Global Ministries," *CCGMpap* 1 (1994). Idem, *The New Catholicity* (1997). Smart, B., *Postmodernity* (1993). Smith, C., *The Emergence of Liberation Theology: Radical Religion and Social Movement Theory* (1991). Turner, B., "Politics and Culture in Islamic Globalism," in R. Robertson and W. Garrett, eds., *Religion and Global Order* (1991) 161–82. Wallerstein, I., *The Modern World-System*, vols. 1 and 2 (1974, 1980). Waters, M., *Globalization* (1995).

❧ GOD ❧

1. Interreligious Hermeneutics of the Word "God." 2. "God" in the Nonbiblical Religions. 3. "God" in Judaism. 4. "God" in Christianity. 5. The Monotheistic Task of Uniting Humanity.

1. The plurality of concepts of God encountered in the religions shows that the meaning of the word "God" (or "the divine") cannot be found through definition or be classified within the realm of the finite, for the event of an encounter bursting open human finiteness precedes all theology. God's parousia is experienced as a relativization of the finiteness of human existence. To report such an event is to name the God-experience. Hence the word "God" — and its diverse parallels — is a code standing for the original names, expressing the power over life and death one has experienced and before which the whole person (body and spirit) and the person's whole world (thinking and being) are mortal. The fundamental, primeval event of the encounter with the *theos* is the unsurpassable relativization of the human world in human death — irrational but real.

Around this "knowledge" revolve the classical religions (→religion, religions): it also constitutes the background of the theologies of the churches outside the First World (→liberation theology) where it determines key themes such as "symbol," "experience," "praxis," and →"liberation."

Consequently, one of the concerns of theology is the basic problem of speaking of the divine in its unconditionality with the concepts of human interpretation of reality even though it does not fall into the categories of the mortal world. In modern interreligious and theological dialogue we must learn to deal with the relativity of the classical ontological horizon, because the *theos* is the relativizing principle which, becoming an event, can be expressed only as a contradiction to the ontological principles.

The relativity of the ontological horizon before "God" means neither negation nor simply that *semper maior* of God which Western theology has always held. "God" relativizing the ontological horizon means the unrestrictedness of God in relation to the universal truth of onto-logic, which in the principle of contradiction not only prevents its own relativity and at the same time also the discursive access to consciousness of the divine (i.e., to religion) but also limits the creatures of God to the horizon of being and proscribes the spirits and gods of the religions. The universal ontological principles or criteria of truth then claim to be guardians of monotheism and implicitly legitimize (colonial) power. This loss of the idea of "God" — veiling, as it does, the repression of death — appears logically as the "death of God"; and the narrow classification of the image of God in the religions as "pantheism," "dualism," "polytheism," "anthropomorphism," "worldliness," and many more, and the problems associated with them in interreligious dialogue, correspond to the absolute validity of the ontological horizon. If the divine is expressed as an encounter with the Unutterable — but fundamentally according to the condition of the human consciousness — there is a difference between the divine producing and relativizing the human consciousness, on the one hand, and the divine testified to by the human consciousness, on the other. This corresponds to the difference between the "creator of the world" and the world as object of human experience. No matter what our concept of the world is, the world is a "symbol": its finite conditions give utterance to the divine, and the consciousness of this is the structural principle of "religion"; this, therefore, is the visible shape of its god.

Such a view of reality based on the "bursting open" of human finiteness interprets this event not as an error of knowledge but as relativization of the metaphysically or transcendentally interpreted epistemological criteria of truth; and so the subjective human experience preserves its freedom with regard to the criteria of the objective or ontological. Since the latter emerge only as the result of reflection, they cannot lay claim to validity when contrasted with the encounter with the divine. Accordingly, the divine is encountered in components of experience which do not belong to the scientific concept of experience but rather contradict it (e.g., "miracle," "spirits," "gods"). In this way the divine differs fundamentally from the result of reflection, religiosity from philosophy and science. Because of this encounter with the all-relativizing divine, the world of experience of the religious human being is greater than the world of scientific rationality and metaphysical reason.

For the divine to be expressed the total experience of the human being is decisive and indispensable. Since the narration of an encounter with the divine is expressed in *concrete* terms, it confronts theoretical thinking either with contradictions or with "pure" historical facts; as a consequence a judgment demanding objective criteria on the being or existence of the divine must be decided in the negative.

But from a religious perspective the concrete *is* the very being of the divine. This "is" signifies no real identification but points out that place in the ontological horizon of objective statement which the Unutterable has chosen as its decisive presence and consequently "utterance." Since the "is" implies a relativity of the ontological horizon there exists a contradiction which indicates from a religious perspective that the divine cannot be grasped by reason. Smoothing out this contradiction means renouncing talk about God. Hence such renunciation exists in all those interpretations that, following Aristotle, do not accept the divine as a relativization of the ontological horizon; that must begin, therefore, with a Neoplatonic dualism (quite unlike Plato!) and then either mix, change, or divide; signify, represent, or, indeed, identify.

Since the human experience of finiteness deprives the onto-logic of its exclusivity, the experience of the world becomes Janus-headed: the experience of what is life-promoting ("good") or life-negating ("evil"). From the veneration of a power over life and death proceeding from the experience of finiteness follows logically the presence of this divine power in a yes to life ("Father," "Mother," "Parent"), which demands a reinterpretation of the contrary experiences. The divine is known from the past as transmission of life; the necessity of continuing to allow the divine to be experienced as life-promoting becomes the basic principle of →ethics. Cult and sacrifice serve this purpose on a functional basis; this makes them prone to ideology. The basic ambivalence of the religious interpretation of reality always finds a human expression connected with the individual or the group's interests which, in the last analysis, remains evolutive-egocentric.

2.　In *Hinduism* we find the assessment of the pluriform world as an ontological form of the divine (*brahman*) determined by human beings and disrupted by their egoism (*maya*); correspondingly, it is not the empirical human being but the soul (the self: *atman*) that is one (not two) with the divine. To the extent that the individual reaches the goal to become the ontological form of the *real* self, a person helps humanity and the world to mature toward the unity of the *brahman*. The soul has the opportunity to come nearer to this unity in the cycle of reincarnations (*samsara*).

Criticizing the ideological manipulation of the communication about the divine, *Buddha* preaches the way of a liberation from "suffering" (*dukkha*) as a release from captivity in the limitedness of mortal human beings, that is, in the "great death," in the nonduality of *atman* and *brahman*. By silencing even the will by contemplation, the subjection to categories disappears and with it the ambivalent ontological form of the divine. Consequently, Nirvana, also called "nothingness" or "emptiness," arrived at by thus conquering the death barrier, is, in its redeeming unconditionality, in no sense an object of reason. Since Nirvana is not a concept, has neither name nor being, Buddhism is often called an "atheistic religion."

Muhammad preaches the Lord as judge and merciful God of all; his unconditionality, transcendence, unity, and reality stand in the hermeneutical horizon of the religious perspective which relativizes the ontological. But since the symbolic principle is of no importance in the Koran, this latter is proclaimed revelation.

Allah (only "God is God") does not reveal himself as historically experienced (symbolic) presence but as his word in the form of "clear" sentences to which unconditional submission (Islam) is due, since laying down conditions would be idolatry (*shirk*). Hence Islamic monotheism understands itself as a liberating criticism of all gods (because this criticism, not being symbolic, is necessarily "fundamentalist"). Since Allah's power correlates to nobody's power, he is "person" and the precondition of unity and peace.

3.   With the precondition of *Judaism* that God has revealed Godself, the meaning of the word "God" changes: YHWH is the one who, according to biblical tradition, has been revealed as the one whom Israel experiences at various times (in its history) (Ex 3:14f.), so that Yahweh is not one of the gods deduced from the human experience of finiteness; these gods, rather, are Yahweh's modes of presence for a holy people.

Yahweh's name is (according to the symbolic principle) the event which liberated the enslaved people of Israel from catastrophes from the time of the patriarchs onward. The past liberating event (*facta bruta*) becomes known as an act of *Yahweh* by the fact that a present and comprehensively committed liberating way of life becomes a symbol; that is, it is experienced as the presence (shekinah) of a liberating divine being — of a God who is announced as the *one and only* God, since absolutely no other value (e.g., survival) is preferred to liberation (*zkr*/anamnesis). Such absoluteness logically implies the unlimited universality of liberation/love, which is the identity of Yahweh; and for this reason monotheism is the particular mandate (to Israel) in a universal perspective: "Hear, O Israel, Yahweh is our God, Yahweh alone" (Dt 6:4). Human behavior — that is, every individual's act of decision for Yahweh (life according to the Torah) — is constitutive for each statement about Yahweh, whose turning to humanity is laid down in tradition. Such a decision (i.e., love of God) allows men and women to *know God* and not a concept, the fixed identity of which could be argued about. Here an ontological concept of God (opposed to which ethics is trivialized into an ultimately unimportant consequence) would be just as false as an existentialist-subjective interpretation. The Bible contains no ontological statement that God exists but rather the affirmation that we can rely on the promise: "Listen to my voice, then I will be your God [Elohim!], and you shall be my people" (Jer 7:23).

The Bible distinguishes between Yahweh, the God of the patriarchs, and Elohim, the form in which Yahweh can be experienced by all. Whenever people respect the universal laws of life, whenever religions venerate their God as the God of all humanity, they honor the work of Yahweh under particular names — even when they do not know this. Accordingly, the biblical God demands not that such gods be disregarded but that they be relativized; since even if they too are God's activity, they are nothing in themselves when they are venerated in God's place. Yahweh cannot be experienced except through the Elohim, but the Elohim remain a pantheon of gods if human decision does not come into play, relativizing the gods with regard to the one and only God: only by the act of faith does Yahweh come into the world.

4.   With the good news that this happened before the eyes of Jesus' disciples, the New Testament tradition begins: "Jesus is the Christ." In the opinion of the disciples, Jesus had lived the love of Yahweh in such an exclusive manner that he had to die; for only the sacrifice of one's own life for the life of others rela-

tivizes all (symbolically present) gods or goals of life with reference to Yahweh. This act testifies to a trust in Yahweh in the face of death (hence understood as powerlessness), and in this way Yahweh is revealed as the truly one and only God. Consequently, death (the way of the cross) is the basis of salvation (the resurrection); otherwise by preferring life against the mind of Yahweh the message of the biblical God dies away behind the various particular gods, one's own and others', for example, Mammon (sin).

Confessing Jesus Christ, the God-become-flesh (incarnation), involves as a basis and normative claim the general religious principle of symbol (Hypostatic Union). Here, however, the criterion of the divine is not the human will to live but the all-embracing love of the one God. Consequently, it relativizes the symbol oriented to human life by its orientation to Yahweh. This corresponds to the unity of the gods/religions, being relativized by the one God. The "principle of unity" that comes into play here is the symbolic "bursting open" of the human intellect by its orientation to monotheism: the Holy Spirit, the Spirit of freedom. By leading the way of the cross, this Spirit is to be distinguished from "the spirits." If the religious (symbolic) perspective in the encounter with Jesus of Nazareth (→Jesus) allows itself to be drawn into the orientation of the Hebrew Bible and so into the ultimate relativization of self in faith, it is faced with the God of the New Testament proclamation. If this believing relationship is questioned as to the nature of God, we find that Jesus is the presence of the God who is already known from the past history of the world who, bursting open human limitedness, again and again lovingly approaches men and women (Holy Spirit). In this confessional tradition Jesus is "the Christ," and so *is* God. In this trinitarian statement about God it must be especially emphasized that the biblical God cannot be expressed if one of the three "persons" is not mentioned. God *is*, indeed, trinitarian. The divine unity is, nevertheless, not ontological — for the Spirit transcends the ontological horizon (as well as symbolic hermeneutics) — but comes about in the event of the way of the cross: the existence of the biblical God. Thus, the Christian God is known only in God's saving activity or "mission."

Since God has no existence apart from that of witnesses, the message of the savior God on the cross is handed down in no other way than by consistently proceeding along this way toward the unity and peace of humanity, a "suffering for the sake of justice." Hence the act of following Christ, the only ontological promise of salvation which the faith knows, is constitutive of and a constant corrective for the new people of God, the church. As experienced presence of God among humanity, the church bears the name of its God; it is Christ's "sacrament," his body in the world. Only if the church continually re-presents God's saving activity in the world can it have the right to call itself God's church: the church is missionary therefore by its very nature (*AG* 2).

5. Since a *comparison* of the gods would have to be based on a generic term which would also represent the *unity* of the gods or the "highest God," it fails; the divine relativizes all theory. The particularity of the gods cannot be overcome by reflection. Accordingly, the mode of being of the divine in dialogue or in competition with another model cannot be sacrificed since the divine has no voice beyond its form. Religion must preserve itself in the interest of its truth (fanaticism): because the gods themselves are human, they do not enable humankind to achieve unity.

Only the Bible testifies to a nonhuman, divine perspective entrusted to humanity, expressing this as well as the relationship of creator and creature. This is at the same time the foundation of the so-called claim to →the absoluteness of Christianity, a claim which is based not on the (death) experience of humanity but on the inconceivable event of God addressing human beings; this is the basis of the specific meaning of the concept of person applied to the biblical God. This personal God can only be encountered in the risky way of enabling life and mediating peace between the particular interests (universality); otherwise there is only a pantheon. It is true that with regard to the latter's ultimate unity the myth of religions knows metatheories (e.g., Bhagavad Gita 9:23f.), but myth (even the biblical) can be reduced to anthropology. Furthermore, myth is relativized before the God of biblical faith insofar as confessing the unity of the pantheon religiously (not only theoretically) implies an act of decision for monotheism. In other words, while the way of the cross is open to all, the way of commitment for the unity of humanity is exclusively dependent on God. By appealing to the new name of Yahweh, Jesus — who is for this reason the Christ, the essence of the personal God — is shown to be not self-preservation but commitment to the welfare of all humanity. This involves a basic continuity of the worldwide Elohim experiences with Israel's knowledge of Yahweh — that is, the recognition of the experiences, the preservation of the cultural individuality, and respect for the wisdom of the religions, especially their efforts for justice and peace. Because God's very own name is liberating love, this harmony with human longing for peace does not lead to a functionalization of God but shows the biblical unity of Elohim and Yahweh.

HERIBERT RÜCKER

Bibliography

Armstrong, K., *A History of God* (1993). Boff, L., *Trinity and Society* (1988). Bönhnke, M., and H. Heinz, eds., *In Gespräch mit dem dreieinen Gott* (1985). Bosch, D. J., *Transforming Mission: Paradigm Shifts in Theology of Mission* (1991) 389–93. Bracken, J. A., *The Divine Matrix: Creativity as Link between East and West* (1995). Breuning, W., ed., *Trinität* (1984). Bsteh, A., ed., *Der Gott des Christentums und des Islams* (1978). Casper, B., ed., *Gott nennen* (1981). Cone, J. H., *A Black Theology of Liberation* (1986) 55–81. Dalferth, I. U., *Religiöse Rede von Gott* (1981). Eck, D., *Encountering God* (1993). Eicher, P., *Offenbarung* (1977). Falaturi, A., et al., eds., *Drei Wege zu dem einen Gott* (1980). González, J. L., *Mañana: Christian Theology from a Hispanic Perspective* (1990) 89–115. Greshake, G., *Tottes Heil — Glück der Menschen* (1983). Gutiérrez, G., *On Job: God-Talk and the Suffering of the Innocent* (1987). Hall, D. J., *Professing the Faith: Christian Theology in a North American Context* (1993) 43–183. Heschel, A., *God in Search of Man* (1955). Hill, W., *The Three-Personed God* (1983). Hood, R. E., *Must God Remain Greek? Afro Cultures and God-Talk* (1990). Johnson, E., *She Who Is: The Mystery of God in Feminist Theological Discourse* (1992). Jüngel, E., *God as the Mystery of the World* (1983). Kasper, W., *The God of Jesus Christ* (1984). LaCugna, C. M., *God for Us: The Trinity and Christian Life* (1991). Idem, "The Trinitarian Mystery of God," in F. Schüssler Fiorenza and J. Galvin, eds., *Systematic Theology: Roman Catholic Perspectives* (1991) 149–92. Laube, J., *Dialektik der absoluten Vermittlung* (1984). Lee, J. Y., *The Trinity in Asian Perspective* (1996). Mbiti, J. S., *Concepts of God in Africa* (1970). McFague, S., *Models of God: Theology for an Ecological, Nuclear Age* (1987). Moltmann, J., *The Trinity and the Kingdom* (1981). Muñoz, R., *The God of Christians* (1991). Oman, J. W., *Grace and Personality* (1928). Peters, T., *God — The World's Future* (1992) 82–121. Idem, *God as Trinity: Relationality and Temporality in Divine Life* (1993). Rahner, K., *Foundations of Christian Faith* (1978). Idem, *The Trinity* (1974). Richard, P., *The Idols of Death and the God of Life* (1983). Schaeffler, R., *Fähigkeit zur Erfahrung* (1982). Seebass, H., *Der Gott der ganzen Bibel* (1982). Smart, N., and S. Konstantine, *Christian Systematic Theology in a World Context* (1991) 149–99. Song, C. S., *The Compassionate God* (1982). Strolz, W., and H. Waldenfels, eds., *Christliche Grundlagen des Dialogs mit den Weltreligionen* (1983). Thoma, C., and M. Wyschogrod, eds., *Das Reden vom einen Gott bei Juden und Christen* (1984). Tracy, D., "Approaching the Christian Understanding of God," in F. Schüssler Fiorenza and J. Galvin, eds., *Systematic Theology: Roman Catholic Perspectives* (1991) 131–48. Will, J. E., *The Universal God: Justice, Love and Peace in the Global Village* (1994). Yagi, S., and U. Luz, eds., *Gott in Japan* (1973).

H

ᔈ HEALING AND MEDICAL MISSIONS ᔈ

1. Definition. 2. Healing and Mission. 3. Healing and Medical Missions in a Systematic Theology of Mission.

1. The fact that the key word "healing" receives hardly any mention in general reference works and medical dictionaries in comparison with theological works points to the peculiar character of "healing" as an observable physical experience — one, however, rendered only partly objective — with an essentially religious dimension. Linguistically also, the concept defies an abstract formal definition because as a gerund it not only shares in the transitive and intransitive use of the verb "to heal" but also does so in its different meanings (deliverance from suffering in body and soul, means of salvation, redemption from sin, rescue from danger and adverse circumstances). Originally used only in connection with physical, bodily occurrences, "healing" today means, in the broader sense of the word, a course of events: for example, healing as the (complete) victory over a defect or injury of an individual; or healing in a more collective sense — through recovery, or through organic, mental, spiritual, or social compensation.

"Medical mission/Medical missions" (in German, *ärtzliche Mission*), when used in the singular, originally meant one of the medical posts supported by a Christian congregation (dispensary for the poor, clinic, etc.). In the middle of the nineteenth century, the meaning was broadened to describe the almost exclusively Protestant medical branch of overseas mission, which paralleled the development of medical science in its rapid growth. This reached its apogee in the 1920s, in terms of the number of staff involved (as shown in "The Place of Medical Missions in the Work of the Church," the statement of the International Missionary Council Meeting, Jerusalem, 1928). Although this terminology has largely disappeared from use today, except in the names of certain institutions and their publications, as well as in occasional references in the context of the whole design of the theology of mission, the concern of the Christian Medical Commission (CMC), founded by the →World Council of Churches in 1968, continues today. This intense concern has to do with the search to determine the correct understanding of the Christian commission to heal, a search conducted by the international study process of the CMC.

2. In the process of healing, a profound, indescribable, life-giving power is often experienced as a "miraculous" recovering of the usual energy for life after a period of sickness and weakness. Totally secularized, high-performance medicine also views this power as the decisive factor in the success of therapy. This power is the basis not only of the religious dimension of "healing" but even more so of its pluriform cultural and religious interpretation in the course of human history. Since New Testament times, the Christian community, independently of Jesus' miracles of healing, saw itself confronted by the phenomenon of "healing" (see Mk 9:38–40; Acts 19:13–14; etc.), above all because of its proclamation of Jesus of Nazareth as the one not only who himself heals or saves but who is declared to be the "savior of the world." This declaration led to a prolonged dispute with the Asclepius cult and found an echo in the use of the healing theme by the apologists and Church

Fathers, as well as in their image of *Christus medicus.* Today the Christian theology of mission sees itself challenged by groups and movements that place great emphasis on healing: for example, the African independent churches, the Brazilian Afro-American Umbanda movement, the Fifohazana in Madagascar, and the "modern religions" in Japan. The resignation of Archbishop Milingo of Lusaka is another part of this challenge. It is not possible to treat here in detail the different circumstances in which "healing" can take place (Which illnesses are healed? Which therapies or rituals take place? Is the healing effected through a healing object or by the person performing it? etc.), even though precise knowledge is very important for the success of indigenization. In general, the more strongly a culture emphasizes the mysterious (religious) character of "healing," the less secularized it is, and medical practitioners in heavily religious cultures generally are aware of their definite priestly functions.

In more secularized cultures, in contrast, most successful treatments for illnesses which were previously apparently incurable, as well as the prevention of epidemics, have become possible through objective insight into physiological and pathological processes and their sociohygienic connections. The process of healing itself has remained, however, puzzling and unfathomable to medical knowledge. In these cultures there is talk of "miracle" or "faith healing" only in extreme cases. With increasing secularization, the unity of the healer-priest's functions disintegrates into the separate professional roles of medical and pastoral-spiritual-priestly vocations. Because of this, the proclamation of the gospel and the meeting of physical needs can become virtually distinct. At the study conference convened by the LWF and the WCC in Tübingen in 1964 on the issues of medical mission, very basic questions of the Christian duty to heal were taken up on a broad basis and were then considered more thoroughly at a follow-up conference held in the same place in 1967. Fundamental to these conferences was the knowledge that there is a special task for the Christian church in the field of healing and that this "healing activity . . . [is] in the first place laid upon the congregation as a whole, and only subsequently on those who are specially trained for it."

3. The command to heal (Mt 10:8ff.; Lk 10:9; also Mk 16:15–18) is the unfolding of the Great Commission (Mt 28:18f.) in tangible form. This hinders the interpretation of medical missions as a means to an end and as a diaconal activity of mission service. In 1928 this was already formulated in the Jerusalem statement (cited above): "Medical work should be regarded as in itself an expression of the spirit of the Master, and should not be thought of as only a pioneer of evangelism or as merely a philanthropic agency." Medical mission is a special expression of the *verbum visibile* for the congregation and the church which listen to the →word of God. It is thus different from other medical practice because it realizes the eschatological dimension of all healing. This affects not only the method of dealing with sick people, derived from the background of biblical anthropology, but even more the recourse to medical knowledge and skill, the understanding of sickness and health, and the choice of areas and types of work. In this respect it can be legitimately understood as *imitatio Christi;* and healing, either strongly christologically or pneumatologically accentuated, can be made theologically understandable in the wider connection of the *missio Dei* by coordinating it with soteriology. Such an understanding opens up a new view of salvation and the role of the sacraments and sacramentals in a time of strong psychological self-understanding; it also casts new light on confession, the knowledge of sin, and the forgiveness of sins. While the Anglican Church has long integrated the "healing ministry" as an officially recognized church office and is a member of the Churches' Council for Health and Healing, and while the Roman Catholic Church since Vatican II has given new respect to the sacrament of extreme unction as the anointing of the sick, such recognition of the healing ministry is lacking in Protestant mainline circles. But those circles are being challenged on this point by many of the churches of the Third World.

The universality of the experience of healing indicates the universality of the experience of sickness, suffering, and death as physical manifestations of (new) creation and the fall. The universality of thinking and knowledge as human expressions of life embodies the same point, to which the universality of the ambiguity of all things, with the momentous history of misunderstandings, corresponds (Rom 1:18). From here onward, individual religions, cultures, means of salvation, secular-scientific medicine, and healing practice must be subjected to critical questioning. This concerns not only interpretations but also the experience of salvation, which, fragmentary as ever, is potentially present in every act of healing and every social reconciliation. This potential is fully bound up with the word and with the message of resurrection and the promise implied therein of eternal life willed by God. The relationship of medical to evangelistic work in mission is therefore dialectical: the ministry of healing needs the proclamation of the revelation of salvation in order to express its true identity; and the proclamation of salvation needs the actual concrete experience of healing, as it also seeks to make the ministry of healing possible, in order to give expression to its own intention. In any case, this can be convincingly perceived only when the congregation as a whole accepts that it is charged with the healing commission, does not allow it to be delegated to particular professional groups, and undertakes this work. This was emphasized by the 1964 Tübingen conference and also by Vatican II's decrees on the apostolate of the laity (*Apostolicam Actuositatem* [*AA*]) and on the missionary responsibility of the church (*Ad Gentes* [*AG*]), together with certain subsequent postconciliar documents. In some overseas, Christian, community-health services (e.g., the Jamkhed and Health for One Million programs of the Syrian Malankara Church, both in India), this is seen in model form.

CHRISTOFFER GRUNDMANN

Bibliography

Ahern, S. M., *Innovative Models of Healing and Health Ministry* (1984). Appiah-Kubi, K., *Man Cures — God Heals — Religion and Medical Practice among the Akans of Ghana* (1981). Bate, S. I., *Inculturation and Healing* (1995). Beth, K., "Heilung, religiöse," in *RGG* 3/3:194. Boston Pastoral Institute, *To Heal the Sick: A Look at the Medical Apostolate* (1970). Erk, W., and M. Scheel, *Ärztlicher Dienst weltweit* (1974). Grundmann, C., "Healing as a Missiological Challenge," *MissS* 6 (1986) 57–62. Idem, "The Role of Medical Missions in the Missionary Enterprise," *MissS* 2 (1985) 39–48. Häring, B., *The Healing Ministry of the Church in the Coming Decades* (1982). *Health and Healing: Report of the Makumira Consultation on the Healing Ministry of the Church* (1967). *Health Is Wholeness: Report of the Limuru Conference on the Healing Ministry of the Church* (1970). Katz, R., et al., eds., *Boiling Energy — Community Healing among the Kalahari Kung* (1982). Kelsey, M. T., *Healing and Christianity* (1973). Lagerwerf, L., "Witchcraft, Sorcery and Spirit Possession — Pastoral Responses in Africa," *Exch* 14 (1985) 1–62. Lambourne, R. A., *Community, Church and Healing* (1963). Idem, *Explorations in Health and Salvation* (1983). Larty, E., "Healing: Tradition and Pentecostalism in Africa Today," *IRM* (1986) 75–81. Maddocks, M., *The Christian Healing Ministry* (1981). Marty, M. E., and K. L. Vaux, *Health / Medicine and the Faith Traditions — an Inquiry into Religion and Medicine* (1982). McGilvray, J., *The Quest for Health and Wholeness* (1982). "Medicine, Healing and Mission," *Missiol* 21/3 (July 1993). Milingo, E., *The World in Between: Christian Healing and the Struggle for Spiritual Survival* (1984). Moyers, B., *Healing and the Mind* (1993). Numbers, R. L., and D. W. Amundsen, eds., *Caring and Curing — Health and Medicine in the Western Religious Traditions* (1986). Nzunga, M., *Some Implications of Indigenous Healing for the Christian Church in Zaire* (1980). Offner, C. B., and H. Van Straelen, *Modern Japanese Religions — with Special Emphasis upon Their Doctrines of Healing* (1963). Peelman, A., ed., "Medicine Challenging the Mission of the Church: Le médecine autochtone: Un défi pour la mission," *Kerygma* 46/20 (1986). Sheils, W. J., ed., *The Church and Healing* (1982). Singer, P., *Traditional Healing: New Science or New Colonialism?* (1977). Sullivan, L. E., "Healing," in *EncRel* 6 (1987) 226–34. Tillich, P., *The Meaning of Health: Essays in Existentialism, Psychoanalysis, and Religion,* ed. P. LeFevre (1984). Wilkinson, J. W., *Health and Healing — Studies in New Testament Principles and Practice* (1980). World Council of Churches, *The Healing Church* (1965). Idem, "The Search for a Christian Understanding of Health, Healing and Wholeness," summary report of the study program of the CMC and WCC (1976). Yoder, P. S., *African Health and Healing Systems* (1982).

∽ HISTORY OF MISSION ∝

1. Mission and History. 2. The History of Mission as Church History. 3. Church History as the History of Mission.

1. The relation of mission to history is already included in the broader, multifaceted understanding of mission as the "dynamic orientation of the message" toward the world. The fundamental biblical witnesses to the eschatological saving action of God in Jesus' cross and resurrection are not merely reports of past events but instruments in the transmission of the present history of God with the world. Just as it is certain that the gospel cannot be derived from the world and history, it is equally certain that they are both essential elements in its proclamation. The dialectical relationship between mission and history is also sometimes manifested, and particularly so, in the intentional execution of mission. This is done in two ways. One the one hand, mission cannot operate as mission in and to the world in only one of the demarcated areas of history, that is, "salvation history"; it must rather allow itself to be continually involved with new historical contexts, with cultures and languages in which the gospel should "pitch its tent" (Jn 1:14), without being subject to their frailty or transitoriness. On the other hand, mission cannot identify itself permanently with any of its historical contexts or sanction their circumstances, as they are at any one time. The freedom of the Spirit in the face of history is seen in the fact that, through mission, both the contextualization of the gospel in all cultures and the proclamation of the transforming power of the gospel are effected. Under these twin aspects, the task and function of writing the history of mission are also defined in relation to writing church history.

2. S. Neill, one of the few masters of the historiography of mission, has described mission history as "a very dull subject" unless, as Neill himself has done for India, it "surveys the whole history" of the geographic area under consideration "in relation to the presence and growth of the Christian community"; that is, it must see mission as a part of the country's life (Neill 1984, xi). According to him, mission history should no longer be written as the history of the events in mission, its agents, and its methods, that is, a mere extension of Western church history; rather — and primarily — mission history is the record of the coming into being and development of indigenous Christianity within its own context. This is a method which is taken seriously by W. Freytag: "With proclamation, something new always comes into being.... Another church always arises" (1961, 121). The writing of mission history fails in its purpose if it ranks the external expansion of a Western church higher than the inner growth of faith in another environment and so remains a prisoner in the provincialism of its own past. The grand old man of the discipline, K. S. Latourette (1884–1968), was the first historian of mission to take up consciously and expressly, in his principles of writing history, the question of the effect of Christianity on its surroundings and of the surroundings on Christianity. He takes this into consideration throughout his seven-volume work *A History of the Expansion of Christianity*.

One cannot say the same of other colleagues of his in this field, although the reasons for this may differ from case to case. The fact that the sources for the history of the church in the Third World lie mainly in Western archives cannot serve as an excuse for neglecting the contextual factors in historiography. It is an untenable fiction to say that basically only Western historians can bring objectivity and neutrality to the writing of the history of "mission churches." Recourse to this fiction is completely forbidden if the Western missionary, as a historian, is under the influence of his or her own ideas of contextuality, ideas which, either consciously or unconsciously, he or she makes binding on the indigenous congregation or church members.

Should contextual church history be written, therefore, exclusively by indigenous authors? Is it true that — as is often stressed by West African church historians — only the objects of evangelization themselves can understand the inner life of the African church in its interaction with African society? The demand of F. M. Zahn, the Bremen Mission inspector, was pointing somewhat in this direction over a hundred years ago when he insisted that the writing of mission history must also "attempt to show the revolution which happens through the preaching of native Christians." Such a history of missionary efforts will, in fact, fully come into existence only when it knows that it is free of all foreign demands for control and supervision and when it becomes itself part of the process of emancipation through which such churches become aware of their own identity.

3. Theological education is the place where "doing church history," that is, one's own church history, can be practiced in the Third World. Provided imagination and the understanding of facts are available, models of church history practice can be developed which stream out into the church in the region. With the help of the Theological Education Fund, projects of this kind were introduced in West and East Africa a quarter-century ago. Meanwhile, immense projects devoted to writing indigenous church history are being carried out mainly by local researchers. For example, in 1973 the Church History Association of India conceived the idea of the six-volume *History of Christianity in India*. The volumes that have so far appeared make two things clear: as the program had indicated, the emphasis is firmly on "Indian Christians, as they were and as they saw themselves, on their relations to society, culture, religion, politics in India, on the changes which these relations made on them, on their acceptance of the Gospel, and also within the culture and society to which they belonged." At the same time, the perspective is truly ecumenical, so that Indian Christendom and its history are always seen and described in the light of the whole of Christianity and its worldwide mission. F. M. Zahn had demanded from the writing of church history, among other things, that it reflect the process of "awaking and revival," which had often been the trigger of missionary action in the past. In addition it would be desirable today that feedback from the writing of contextual church history goes out to the whole Christian world; this would strengthen awareness of the missionary dimension of all Christian history. Mission is "the one Church of God in its movement," the "self-fulfillment of the Church" as a whole (K. Rahner), not as an end in itself, but only in fulfillment of the universal apostolic service. Finally, in this way, all those triumphalistic demands which only too often afflicted the older missionary historiography would be taken care of, corrected, and abolished by the concept of "mission as dialogue" (W. Ustorf).

Hans-Werner Gensichen

Bibliography

Bosch, D. J., *Transforming Mission: Paradigm Shifts in Theology of Mission* (1991). Dries, A., "The Hero-Martyr Myth in United States Catholic Mission Literature 1893–1925," *Missiol* 19/3 (April 1991) 305–14. Dussel, E., ed., *The Church in Latin America: 1492–1992* (1992). Freytag, W., *Reden und Sätze,* vol. 2 (1961). Frohnes, H., H. W. Gensichen, and G. Kreschmar, eds., *Kirchengeschichte als Missionsgeschichte,* 2 vols. (1974, 1978). Gensichen, H. W., "Kirchengeschichte im Kontext: Die Historiographie der jungen Kirchen auf neuen Wegen," *LR* 26 (1976) 301–13. Latourette, K. S., *A History of the Expansion of Christianity* 7 vols. (1937–45). Neill, S., *Colonialism and Christian Missions* (1966a). Idem, *A History of Christianity in India,* vol. 1 (1984). Idem, *A History of Christian Missions* (1966b). Nemer, L., *Anglican and Roman Catholic Attitudes on Missions: An Historical Study of Two English Missionary Societies in the Late Nineteenth Century (1865–1885)* (1982). Ross, A. C., *A Vision Betrayed: The Jesuits in Japan and China 1542–1742* (1994). Sanneh, L., *Translating the Message: The Missionary Impact on Culture* (1989). Ustorf, W., "Missionsgeschichte als theologisches Problem," *ZMiss* 9 (1983) 19–29. Vischer, L., "Kirchengeschichte in ökumenischer Perspektive," *ThZ* 38 (1982) 367–472. Yates, T., *Christian Mission in the Twentieth Century* (1994).

❧ HOLY SPIRIT ❧

1. Terminology. 2. Biblical Foundations. 3. Immediate Perspectives.

Western philosophical-theological tradition has made it rather difficult to find an approach which would lead to an understanding of that reality which the Bible calls "spirit" (*ruach/pneuma*). That tradition considers spirit almost exclusively as the opposite of matter and body and thus almost exclusively associates it with soul, intelligence, mind, as well as with ideas and theories. Resonances of other, more primal, experiences can still be found only in such related terms as "spirited" or "inspiration." In addition, while we do indeed possess a doctrine of the Spirit, we have few if any of those "Spirit-experiences" which are presupposed in the biblical statements concerning the Spirit. In this regard, non-European peoples may be endowed with much more favorable prerequisites.

1. Both the Hebrew *ruach* and the Greek *pneuma* originally denoted agitating and agitated tumult, wind, or storm, as well as the breath (of life), breathing (Latin: *spiritus*). Accordingly, the notion of a transforming, life-giving, or even destructive force is predominant. (The German *Geist,* akin to English "ghastly," indicates etymologically a condition of being excited, shocked, and horrified.) Derived meanings include: the inner self, heart, soul, intellect. And finally, *ruach* and *pneuma* also stand for (impure) spirits, demons, and celestial beings. Only on two occasions does the Old Testament speak of the "Holy Spirit" (Ps 51:13; Is 63:10). Its affinity with God is thereby indicated (otherwise expressed by "Spirit of Yahweh," "Spirit of the Lord").

2. *Old Testament.* A sharp distinction between a profane and a theological usage of the term is not to be found in the Old Testament. Where the Bible speaks about God's activity and the experience of same, this is often done by referring precisely to God's *ruach.* For the biblical writers the term "spirit" does not primarily conjure up something spiritual (as we would put it) but rather images of power, energy, dynamism. Power is almost a synonym for the Spirit (see Lk 1:35; 1 Cor 2:2–4; among others). The Spirit is experienced in the tumult of the storm, in the howling of the wind (Gn 1:2; 8:1; Ez 37:1–4; see Jn 3:8). Spirit is the breath of God, God's quickening breath (Jb 33:4; Ps 104:29–30; Is 40:7; Ex 15:8–9). Thus, it is somewhat incomprehensible, mysterious, surprising. This unintelligible, alien force manifests itself also in its ecstatic effects on humans (e.g., on groups of prophets [see 1 Sm 10:5–12; 19:19–24]) and in the Spirit-endowments of charismatic leaders of Israel, who are thereby made capable of performing extraordinary feats (see Nm 11:15–16). Characteristic of the effect of the Spirit is not being spiritual but rather being enthused or inspired. Even the verbs used to describe endowments of the Spirit indicate its vigorous and incalculable nature. The Spirit "falls on" a person, "lays hold" of him/her, "impels," "seizes," "overcomes."

An extraordinary and lasting endowment of the Spirit is attributed to the Servant of God and messianic ruler. Due to this gift the servant will be able to exercise the office as ruler in accordance with the will of God (see Is 11:1–9; 42:1; 61:1). At the time of the exile and after, the expectation of an eschatological endowment of the Spirit on the entire people was developed, which would lead the people to conversion and renewal (Ez 36:25–28; Jl 3:1–5).

New Testament. In the New Testament, the Spirit is the gift of the risen and exalted Lord (see Lk 24:49; Jn 7:39; 20:22; Acts 2:33). It is the distinguishing mark of the community of Jesus and characteristic of the new, eschatological era (Acts 2:17–18). Before Easter, only Jesus was considered filled with the Spirit. Admittedly the Gospels speak remarkably seldom about Jesus' endowment with the Spirit. However, apart from the "infancy narratives," the descent of the Spirit on the occasion of the baptism of Jesus makes it unambiguously clear that his entire work was accomplished in the power of the Spirit (see Mk 1:10 and par.; Jn 1:32–33; 3:34; Lk 4:1, 14, 18). In Mt 12:28 the healing of the sick by Jesus is explicitly attributed to the Spirit (Lk 11:20 has "finger of God," an expression for God's power). Special signs of the Spirit's presence in Jesus are his unique relationship with God, his authority in word and deed (See Mk 1:21–28), and his unusual, fearless dealings with men and women and with traditions, breaking loose from all limitations and conventions. All of this characterizes →Jesus as a man filled with and led by the Spirit.

For the period after Easter, the Holy Spirit is promised to believers as advocate before the courts. Not they but rather the Spirit will then speak and take on their defense (Mk 13:10–11 pars.). This aspect is more clearly expounded by John, probably due to the special situation of the community he addresses. Such is already indicated by the use of the unusual term *parakletos,* that is, the counsel or advocate summoned (to help). As the "other Paraclete," the Spirit will bear witness to Jesus and come to the assistance of the afflicted disciples (15:26–27). The Spirit will "convict the world," disclose unbelief, and demonstrate that Jesus is victorious over the world (16:7–11). Here the Spirit is seen as the advocate who resumes the pre-Easter debate between Jesus and the (unbelieving) world in the manner of a judicial review. As the "Spirit of truth," the Spirit also continues the revelatory activity of Jesus after Easter and is the guarantor of the unadulterated (Johannine) Jesus tradition in that the Spirit "teaches all" and "reminds of all" that Jesus has said (14:26). In this way believers are led into an ever deeper knowledge of the truth, and thereby the revelatory activity of Jesus is kept alive in the community (16:12–15). In the activity of the Spirit, the post-Easter community experiences the presence of the risen Lord in their midst. Thus, the Spirit's activity is also understood as glorifying Jesus (16:15).

Apart from these christological and ecclesiological aspects, John also recognizes (as does Paul) an activity of the Spirit that is directed to the awakening of faith. Through being "born of the Spirit," the "fleshly" human being, that is, one who is purely worldly and self-seeking, is transformed into a believer open to the word of God (3:3–4; 6:63). In John, moreover, the Spirit very clearly bears personal traits (especially by paralleling the Spirit's activity with that of Jesus).

In the Acts of the Apostles, the Spirit is also seen as the one who continues Jesus' work after Easter (see esp. 1:6–8). As the ministry of Jesus began with the descent of the Holy Spirit, so also does the ministry of the church (2:1–13). Afterward the Spirit impels the Jewish-Christian community to open itself also to non-Jews (8:29; 10) and accompanies the developing church even further on its way by sending out missionaries (13:2–4), giving instructions (16:7; 19:21), and occasioning extraordinary actions (10:44–45; 19:6). The entire alternative lifestyle of the young community is understood in Acts as the consequence of the descent of the Holy Spirit (see 2:42–47; 4:32–35; 5:12–16).

Pauline pneumatology is, likewise, primarily Christocentric. By means of the resurrection, Jesus has become "life-giving Spirit" (1 Cor 15:45), so that in the activity of the Spirit, Jesus' presence is experienced as *Kyrios,* Lord. Thus Paul (→Paul the apostle as missionary) can also say without hesitation: "The Lord is the Spirit" (2 Cor 3:17; see Rom 1:3–4). "To be in Christ" and "to be in the Spirit" are almost identical (see Rom 8:9–11; 15:18–19; 2 Cor 13:3–5). Only "in the Spirit" can one, therefore, recognize and confess Jesus as Lord (1 Cor 12:3). In Paul, however, the Spirit is also viewed in terms of Jesus' supreme significance for the church, which is, indeed, the living, pneumatic body of the risen Lord. The Spirit is the church's principle of life (1 Cor 12:13). One can, without exaggeration, in analogy with the Son's "becoming human," speak of the Spirit's "becoming Church" (P. Knauer). The Spirit provides this community/body with a multiplicity of gifts (charisms) so that it may be a living organism. For it is not uniformity but diversity which characterizes the Spirit (Rom 12:3–8; 1 Cor 12–14). The Spirit liberates from isolation, deploys the abilities of the individual person with regard to the building up of the community, and establishes a living relationship between the individual believers. In fact, the Spirit *is* this relationship, or is, as it were, the "we" of the community. The "life-giving Spirit" (2 Cor 3:6) transforms the "old person" into a "new creation," in that the Spirit liberates him/her from enslaving, harmful powers of the old world: from the power of sin, the letter that kills, egoism, death. Thus, the new human being is able to produce "the fruits of the Spirit" (see Gal 5:22). By means of the Spirit, the human being is changed from a slave into a liberated child of God, who, without fear and full of confidence, may call God "Father" — "Abba" (see Gal 4:6; Rom 8:14–16; also 5:5). Finally, the Spirit is also the cause of hope, the eschatological "first part-payment," the "firstfruits" of the definitive liberation and perfection of the entire creation (Rom 8:23; 2 Cor 1:22; 5:5).

3. In theological discussion concerning the Spirit, the main issue has been about the Spirit's personal nature and place within the Trinity (namely, the Spirit's "procession" from the Father and the Son; in this regard the First Council of Constantinople [381 c.e.] was epoch-making). In line with Augustine's trinitarian theology, the view prevailed more and more in the West that the Spirit "proceeds from the Father and the Son" (*filioque*). Unfortunately, as a consequence of these doctrinal disputes, the Holy Spirit became more and more a specialty of theological debate and the "unknown God" of believers. Despite the Spirit's "rediscovery" after Vatican II, the Spirit still leads a shadowy existence in the normal, everyday life of believers and in the parishes. For them the word "Spirit" is an empty term without any corresponding experiences on their part (outside of "Pentecostal groups" and "charismatic prayer groups").

The Bible indicates that the characteristic effect of the Spirit consists in liberating the individual person from being locked up in him/herself, so that he/she can, in an act of self-transcendence, enter into relationship with →God and with other people. Thus the Spirit's primary operations — faith, love, hope — are characteristic of a new "ec-static" and dialogical existence. According to the New Testament (and as one's own experience teaches), it is precisely this which one cannot achieve oneself. For that, one needs the opening and liberating power of God which is the Spirit.

Experience of the Spirit is always the experience of being endowed, of unmerited gifts, of effects beyond one's own ability. The activity of the Spirit manifests itself above all in the experience of that which is unexpected, surprising, and superabundant. This includes diversity in unity and the orientation toward what is to come.

If it is characteristic of the Spirit to join what is old with what is new; what is past with what is to come; diversity with unity; freedom and development of the individual with responsibility for the whole of the community; if the Spirit is God's power and does not allow Godself to be limited or confined within any barriers or patterns — then it is immediately evident that the Spirit is truly the power we need in order to be able to continue the worldwide work of liberation which Jesus began in the power of the same Spirit.

A number of authors (e.g., Y. Congar, L. Boff) have proposed that feminine or female characteristics should be attributed to the Spirit and that the Spirit should be referred to with feminine pronouns. As E. Johnson points out, however, one must be careful not to subordinate the Spirit to the "Father" and "Son" in this way, and one must be conscious of the fact that all language about God is tentative, metaphorical, or at best symbolic and is never to be understood literally or univocally.

Other theologians (e.g., R. Hood) have attempted to speak of the Holy Spirit in the context of popular belief in spirits within certain cultural contexts (notably Africa). More reflection, however, needs to be done in this area, although such work holds much promise for the future in terms of developing an understanding of God the Spirit in more inculturated ways.

FELIX PORSCH, CSSP

Bibliography

Boer, H., *Pentecost and Missions* (1964). Boff, L., "An Alternative View: The Church as Sacrament of the Holy Spirit," in *Church: Charism and Power* (1985) 144–53. Idem, *Trinity and Society*

(1988). Comblin, J., "The Holy Spirit," in *Mysterium Liberationis* (1993) 462–82. Idem, *The Holy Spirit and Liberation* (1989). Congar, Y., *I Believe in the Holy Spirit,* 3 vols. (1983). Idem, *The Word and the Spirit* (1986). De la Potterie, I., *La vie selon l'ésprit: Condition du chrétien* (1965). Fee, G. D., *God's Empowering Presence: The Holy Spirit in the Letters of Paul* (1994). Gelpi, D. L., *God Breathes the Spirit in the World* (1988). Haughey, J. C., *The Conspiracy of God: The Holy Spirit in Us* (1976). Hawthorne, G. F., *The Presence and the Power: The Significance of the Holy Spirit in the Life of Jesus* (1991). Heitmann, C., and H. Mühlen, eds., *Erfahrung und Theologie des Heiligen Geistes* (1974). "The Holy Spirit in Mission," *Missiol* 16/4 (October 1988). Hood, R. E., *Must God Remain Greek? Afro Cultures and God-Talk* (1990). John Paul II, Pope, *Lord and Giver of Life: Encyclical Letter "Dominum et Vivificantem" of the Supreme Pontiff John Paul II on the Holy Spirit* (1986). Johnson, E. A., *She Who Is* (1992). Idem, *Women, Earth, and Creator Spirit* (1993). Kasper, W., *The God of Jesus Christ* (1984). Lodahl, M. E., *Shekhinah / Spirit: Divine Presence in Jewish and Christian Religion* (1991). Mainville, O., *L'ésprit dans l'oeuvre de Luc* (1991). Menzies, R. P., *The Development of Early Christian Pneumatology* (1991). Mills, W. E., *The Holy Spirit: A Bibliography* (1988). Mühlen, H., *A Charismatic Theology: Initiation in the Spirit* (1978). Idem, *Una mystica Persona: Die Kirche als das Mysterium der Identität des Heiligen Geistes in Christus und den Christen* (1967). O'Carroll, M., *Veni Creator Spiritus: A Theological Encyclopedia of the Holy Spirit* (1990). Peters, T., *God: The World's Future* (1992) 228–55. Porsch, F., *Pneuma und Wort* (1974). Rayan, S., *The Holy Spirit: Heart of the Gospel and Christian Hope* (1978). Shelton, J. B., *Mighty in Word and Deed: The Role of the Holy Spirit in Luke-Acts* (1991). Smart, N., and S. Konstantine, *Christian Systematic Theology in a World Context* (1991) 144–99. Strolz, W., ed., *Vom Geist, den wir brauchen* (1978). Taylor, J. V., *The Go-Between God: The Holy Spirit and the Christian Mission* (1973). Wijngaards, J., *The Spirit in John* (1988). World Council of Churches, *Come Holy Spirit, Renew the Whole Creation: Six Bible Studies on the Theme of the Seventh Assembly of the World Council of Churches* (1989).

❧ HUMAN RIGHTS ❧

1. Definition.   2. Theological Approach.   3. Sharpening the Issue Ecumenically.

1.   A clear definition of human rights is extremely important because on all sides these rights are abused. The growing awareness of human rights and the growing threat to them shape the image of the twentieth century. Universal validity is claimed for human rights, yet the situations in which one must fight for them differ greatly. For the inhabitants of the impoverished fringes of the earth, they mean something different from what they mean for the privileged people of the industrial countries; in countries with state socialism, they have a different sound from that in capitalist countries. The implementation of human rights is demanded throughout the entire globe, yet the different religious, cultural, and political traditions (→tradition) offer very different justifications for this. Hardly any other topic of our present age shows more clearly the interrelatedness of universalism and pluralism, an interrelatedness that determines the form of present intercultural and interreligious dialogue.

The ability to define human rights is part of the Western heritage. It has roots in Greek antiquity, which speaks of the common rights of all; human rights were as important in that tradition as they are in the Jewish-Christian tradition, which links the dignity of the human person to being made in the image of God. The demand for a particular legal formulation of human rights first emerged with the European Wars of Religion in the seventeenth century. While the English codification of human rights of this period made them dependent on citizenship and social status, the catalogue of human rights of the eighteenth century claimed universal application. These strands meet in the American Bill of Rights, which was formulated in the tradition of the Enlightenment and the French declarations of human and citizens' rights since 1789, which were said to be based exclusively on a rational philosophy. Because of this emphasis on rational philosophy, church and theology on the continent of Europe maintained a reserve toward the idea of human rights for a long time. Neither did they constitute a critical norm for the early missionary movement. Missionaries in the following period did not promote human rights per se, but evangelical, Anglican, Wesleyan, and Baptist missionaries of the period and their supporters ardently campaigned to end the slave trade and opposed the system of forced labor and indentured labor in the British Empire. A few missionaries were even involved in the independence struggles in India (C. F. Andrews, M. Sykes, etc.), Zambia (C. Morris), and South Africa (T. Huddleston and many Anglo-Catholic missionaries). Weight was first attached to human rights as such in the face of the elementary disregard for human dignity and injury to human rights during the National Socialist mass murders and the Stalinist terror and in response to the use of modern weapons of mass destruction in World War II.

The Universal Declaration of Human Rights (December 10, 1948) was a response to this situation. In it, an attempt was made to develop popular rights into general human rights. The two UN human rights conventions in 1966 are stations on this hard road. In individual national constitutions, human rights are written into the basic rights of a nation, often with different emphases and set out with different methods of implementation.

Above all, the 1966 conventions have given rise to the view that in the present-day community of nations, three differing, even conflicting, concepts of human rights are represented. The Western democracies emphasize individual civic and political rights; the countries of state socialism emphasize economic and social rights; and, especially for the nations of Asia, Africa, and Latin America, the right to self-determination by the people has priority. This observation confirms the idea that the understanding of human rights today is bound up with the conflict between industrialized countries and the Third World as much as with the ideological and power-politics conflict between East and West. Yet one should not conclude from this that the three conceptions of human rights are necessarily antagonistic to one another.

If one considers the core content of the historical catalogues of human rights as well as the contemporary ones, then one sees that freedom, equality, and participation together make up the blueprint of human rights. Human rights protect the citizens' freedom against unjust attacks, especially state violence. For this reason, freedom of belief, of conscience, and of opinion and the basic rights to justice and the protection of property are part of the classic position of those catalogues. They also proclaim, however, the equality of all people; they contain a revolutionary tendency in the face of all circumstances characterized by illegal inequality and discrimination. They also postulate real participation of all those concerned in social wealth as well as in political decisions; they thus contain the demand for the satisfaction of basic needs as the postulate of social democratization. The way that these three elements — freedom, equality, and participation — belong together in the thinking about human rights is of more fundamental importance than the distinction or contrast between individual and social rights, as well as the demand for self-determination. The task of overcoming the avoidable antagonism between these three basic conceptions of human rights is of considerable practical significance. Ecumenical Christianity could perform an important function in this area.

2. In the decades since 1945, the churches have gradually recognized that human rights are a sphere for setting the agenda for creating awareness of public responsibilities. In this regard, three questions came initially to the center of ecclesiastical and theological preoccupation with human rights. Questions were asked about (a) their theological justification, (b) their content, and (c) the responsibility of the churches to put them into effect.

a. The question of universal validity and Christian justification constitutes a basic problem of every theological concern with human rights. In Protestant theology, the insight into the historicity of all recognition of human rights is opposed to ideas of natural law. Sometimes, therefore, a theological justification of human rights has been rejected precisely because of its universal character. In contrast to this, in the Reformed tradition above all, the universality of human rights is based on "God's claim on humanity." Since the secular development of human rights, as well as its legal character, takes a back seat in such a way of arguing, it is suggested that one should ask questions on the basis of the analogy between human rights and the basic content of Christian faith, and so clear the ground for the involvement of Christians in human rights.

b. The three basic elements of human rights require theological interpretation. Because the basic catalogues of human rights appeal to the unassailable freedom and equality of all people, a general definition of "people" is required, one that cannot, then, be derived from limited, specific experience. This definition can be deduced from the Christian belief that a person is constituted by his or her relation to God. This justifies the inviolability of the human person, which leads to criticism of all forms of oppression and denial of rights. Human rights, when expressed in legal form, serve this concept of the inviolability of the human person.

c. The churches can contribute to the development of a consensus that human rights transcend religious, national, or ideological boundaries. A credible campaign by the churches on behalf of human rights presupposes, at the very least, an explanation of how these rights can be applied within the churches themselves. Within the churches' approach to human rights, a special emphasis is laid on the area of religious freedom; their responsibility, however, is not limited to this subject. Information and the creation of public awareness are equally important forms of activity for the churches to take up, as well as direct intervention on behalf of individuals or groups who cannot secure their rights themselves.

3. Ecumenical experience has led, and continues to lead, to new emphases in the theological discussion on human rights. In the process of decolonization, the question of the relationship of individual and social human rights, as well as the relationship of human rights to a people's rights of self-determination, gained urgency for the churches. The experiences of the churches in Asia, Africa, and Latin America made it necessary to question the agents and the aims of human rights in their most acute form. At the cutting edge, driven by →liberation theology, questions about three issues came to the fore: (a) about the agents of human rights, (b) about the level of their achievement, and (c) about their function in the church.

a. Regarding the question of whose rights are involved in human rights, the various liberation theologians reply, in consequence of a basic biblical consideration of rights, that human rights are to be understood as the rights of the poor.

Legitimacy can be claimed only when human rights are set out according to the perspective of the weak and oppressed. The biblical and theological observation that the rights of the poor provide a touchstone for every system of law gives this perspective a theological weight that cannot be ignored.

b. Liberation theologians' emphasis on →liberation from all situations of exploitation and oppression provides a framework for speaking about human rights that functions as a calculated corrective mechanism for the current European and North American interpretation of such rights. According to the latter, human rights are treated like property which must be defended against attack (with the help of a legal system for the protection of rights). In contrast to this, the ecumenical discussion reminds us that human rights must first and foremost be achieved through political argument and, if necessary, through political struggle. Such a struggle aims at liberation which will give the same rights to all. The tradition of human rights also contains the question of how, in the process of liberation, personal freedom can be safeguarded and the rights of minorities can be protected in newly achieved national self-determination.

c. When human rights are treated from the perspective of the poor, the prophetic task of the church gains a special emphasis. While remaining cognizant of the conflict between its pastoral and its prophetic task, the church must be ready to speak a prophetic word when a political system systematically disregards or suspends the rights of individuals or groups. This applies especially when state domination is built on the denial of the basic rights of the majority of the population.

WOLFGANG HUBER

Bibliography

Alston, P., "Conjuring Up New Human Rights: A Proposal for Quality Control," *AJIL* 78 (1984) 607ff. Asante, S. K. B., "Nation-building and Human Rights in Emerging Africa," *CILJ* (1969) 72ff. Bellah, R. N., et al., *The Good Society* (1991). Idem, *Habits of the Heart* (1985). Bonino, J. M., "Whose Human Rights?" *IRM* 66 (1977) 220–24. Brownlie, I., ed., *Basic Documents on Human Rights* (1971). Chapelle, P. de la, *La déclaration universelle des droits de l'homme et le catholicisme* (1967). *The Church and the Rights of Man,* vol. 124 of *Concilium* (1979). Corecco, E., et al., eds., "Les droits fondamentaux du chrétien dans l'église et dans la société," in *Actes du IVe Congré International du Droit Canonique* (1980, 1981). Coriden, J. A., ed., *The Case for Freedom: Human Rights in the Church* (1969). Drinan, R. F., *Cry of the Oppressed: The History and Hope of the Human Rights Revolution* (1987). Dworkin, R., *Taking Rights Seriously* (1977). Elsbernd, M., *Papal Statements on Rights: A Historical Contextual Study of Encyclical Teaching from Pius VI–Pius XI (1791–1939)* (1985). Falconer, A. D., ed., *Understanding Human Rights* (1980). Geyer, A., *Toward a Theology of Human Rights* (1978). Grulich, R., *Religions — und Glaubensfreiheit als Menschenrecht* (1980). Henkin, L., *The Rights of Man Today* (1979). Hollenbach, D., *Claims in Conflict: Retrieving and Renewing the Catholic Human Rights Tradition* (1979). Huber, W., and H. E. Tödt, *Menschenrechte: Perspektiven einer menschlichen Welt* 3 (1988). International Theological Commission, *Propositions on the Dignity and Rights of the Human Person* (1986). Lendvai, P., ed., *Religionsfreiheit und Menschenrechte: Bilanz und Aussicht* (1983). Lissner, J., and A. Sovik, *A Lutheran Reader on Human Rights* (1978). Little, D., *Human Rights and the Conflict of Cultures: Western and Islamic Perspectives on Religious Liberty* (1988). Lochmann, J. M., and J. Moltmann, *Gottes Recht und Menschenrechte Studien und Empfehlungen des Reformierten Weltbundes* (1976). Machan, T. R., "Some Recent Work in Human Rights Theory," *APQ* 17 (1980) 103ff. Meron, T., ed., *Human Rights in International Law,* vol. 1/2 (1984). Newberg, P. R., ed., *The Politics of Human Rights* (1980). O'Grady, R., *Bread and Freedom: Understanding and Acting on Human Rights* (1979). Okechukwu, S. N., *The Right to Life and the Right to Live: Ethics of International Solidarity* (1990). O'Mahony, P. A., *The Fantasy of Human Rights* (1978). Przetacznik, F., *The Catholic Concept of Genuine and Just Peace as a Basic Collective Human Right* (1991). Robertson, A. H., *Human Rights in Europe* (1977). Schrey, H. H., "Wiedergewinnung des Humanum? Menschenrechte in christlicher Sicht," *ThR* (1983) 64–83. Smith, B. H., "Churches and Human Rights in Latin America," *JIAS* 21 (1979) 89–127. Sohn, L. B., and T. Buergenthal, *International Protection of Human Rights* (1973). Swidler, L., and H. O'Brien, eds., *A Catholic Bill of Rights* (1988). Thils, G., *Droits des l'homme et perspectives chrétiennes* (1981). Tödt, H. E., "Menschenrechte — Grundrechte," *Christlicher Glaube in moderner Gesellschaft* 27 (1982) 5–57. Traer, R., *Faith in Human Rights: Support in Religious Traditions for a Global Struggle* (1991). Weingärtner, E., *Human Rights on the Ecumenical Agenda* (1983).

I

❧ INCULTURATION ❧

1. Historical Background. 2. Problems with Culture Encounter. 3. Systematic Considerations. 4. Practical Considerations. 5. Models.

1. In the early church it was taken for granted that the *cultures* which Christianity encountered were the starting point and expression of the Christian faith. The addressees of the gospel were real human beings who, stamped by definite religious and moral ideas, worshiped God in their own way and expected meaning and fulfillment from their way of life and religion. In such concrete communities the Christian message had to articulate itself intelligibly. Many elements of the traditional religious cultures could be adopted without any difficulty; others had to be reinterpreted in the light of the Christian faith; and some had to be rejected as contrary to the faith. Through this process of assimilation, transformation, and contradiction, an objectification of the Christian faith arose which is called the Christian religion. Such a process took place first in the encounter with Judaism, then with Hellenism and in the Roman Empire, and finally also in the Gallic-Germanic sphere. Although the transitions did not proceed without friction, they nevertheless did so in an organic manner. It was only when the self-image of the church gradually grew — for example, in the Constantinian era, during the further development of theology in the Scholastic period, and during the conquests by the Catholic nations Spain and Portugal in the East and West Indies — that the doctrines, forms, and structures of Christendom were consolidated. The message of Jesus developed clearer contours, but such a development took place in a more or less homogeneous cultural sphere, and as a result the encounter with other cultures became more difficult or even problematic. The arduous process of detaching the church from the dominating Western culture has been characterized by concepts such as adaptation and accommodation and, in more recent times, by neologisms such as "indigenization," "contextualization," "incarnation," and "inculturation." The different words place different accents, but all have the same purpose, namely, the integration of cultures with the Christian faith. Provided the spirit and message of the gospel laid down and further developed in the (faith) tradition of the church are maintained, each →culture ought to have the right to develop its own form and formulation of the faith.

2. The Congregation for the Propagation of the Faith's instruction of 1659 to the vicars apostolic is impressive but unfortunately an exception: "What could be more absurd than to introduce France, Spain, Italy, or any other European country into China? It is not these but rather the faith that you should bring." The →rites controversy, one of the saddest chapters of mission history, was also a question of exaggerated Europeanism and lack of understanding for Indian and Chinese thinking. Benedict XV called the increasing nationalism on the mission field and the mixture of mission and →colonialism "a plague most deadly to ... apostleship, which would kill in the preacher of the Gospel every activity for the love of souls, and would undermine his authority with the public" (*Maximum Illud*). Vatican II returned to early Christian thinking when it compared the →word of God with a seed which grows out of the good soil watered by the divine dew, absorbing moisture, transforming it, and making it part of itself so that eventually it bears much fruit (*AG* 22).

The Protestant churches, subscribing to the general degeneration of human beings by sin, and in recent times under the pressure of Barthian theology, experienced even more difficulty with the integration of gospel and culture. Whereas G. Warneck, B. Gutmann, C. Keyßer, and others grappled with the problem from the angle of praxis, the wrestling with theory is still going on. The World Council of Churches' document *Ecumenical Affirmation: Mission and Evangelism* (1982) takes no stand on this concrete issue, but, like Catholic theology, it takes the incarnation of Christ as the starting point when it says: "The self-emptying of the servant who lived among the people, sharing in their hopes and sufferings, giving his life on the cross for all humanity — this was Christ's way of proclaiming the Good News, and as disciples we are summoned to follow the same way" (no. 28; cf. no. 26).

3. It was not until this century that the theme of accommodation was *systematically* treated. According to J. Thauren, accommodation includes "all endeavors aimed at reaching out and adapting to the national spirit, living conditions, and cultural development within certain limits." H. W. Schomerus, who spoke of "religious accommodation," was severely criticized because of the danger of misunderstanding and syncretism. G. Rosenkranz used the term *Anknüpfung* and listed three possibilities: placing oneself in the situation of the other, extracting and utilizing values, and accompanying the other to a new level above the other two. T. Ohm distinguished three steps: accommodation (adapting to human beings and peoples); assimilation (taking over some elements from others); transformation (reshaping, ennobling, transfiguring, "baptizing" these elements). A far-reaching move made by the Holy See which defused the discussion about the "contextualization" of Christianity was the revocation of the unfortunate rites decrees *Ex Illa Die* (March 19, 1715) and *Ex Quo Singulari* (July 5, 1742). Pope Pius XII emphasized with great clarity the axiom often expressed by the Congregation for the Propagation of the Faith: "The Church from the beginning down to our time has always followed this wise practice: let not the Gospel on being introduced into any new land destroy or extinguish whatever its people possess that is naturally good, just or beautiful" (*Evangelii Praecones*).

Accommodation as a help for the encounter between human beings and as a means for better →communication is not questioned. A positive attitude to ancestor worship (→ancestor worship I and II), for example, is nowadays facilitated insofar as we can now distinguish between the religious and the profane. Although in concrete questions of ethical and religious accommodation a consensus cannot yet be foreseen, a theological rapprochement is made possible by trying to see the process of the encounter of gospel and culture analogically to the incarnation event. Just as the Logos took on a concrete human nature and this concrete human being was a revelation of God, so should the message be "incarnated" in every new culture. That means that it should take a shape appropriate for each people and be the revelation of the merciful love of God in a new way. From this angle it is not a falsification or watering down of the word of God but the continuation of the incarnation of the Lord in new cultures, a growing of the Mystical Body of

Christ to its fullness, so that God may be all in all. This is basically the meaning of inculturation today.

4. A. R. Crollius paraphrases inculturation as "the integration of the Christian experience of a local church into the culture of its people in such a way that this experience not only expresses itself in elements of this culture, but becomes a force that animates, orients, and causes innovation within this culture so as to create a new unity and communion, not only within the culture in question but also as an enrichment of the Church universal." The neologism "inculturation" goes back to the anthropological concept "enculturation" and gained access to missiology through the writings of P. Charles and J. Masson. Through the Thirty-second General Assembly of the Jesuits (1974) and a petition of the Jesuit superior general at the 1977 synod of bishops it found its way into the papal document *Catechesi Tradendae,* and ever since "inculturation" has been one of the most frequently used terms in Catholic missiology. Though the underlying idea is not strange to Protestant missiology, the word itself is still treated with some reserve mainly because Protestant theology more strongly emphasizes that culture, just like all created things, "is a quantity broken by the power of sin" (S. Jacob). Catholic theology does not deny the latter, but it emphasizes more that the human being created according to the image of God in spite of sin deserves "respect and love," has a noble destiny, and possesses an "element of the divine"; consequently, it tends to give more emphasis to the possibilities of "dialogue" with the human condition (see *GS* 3). Vatican II knows that "without a creator there can be no creature" but at the same time emphasizes that "by the very nature of creation, material being is endowed with its own stability, truth and excellence, its own order and laws" which should be recognized; however, because of sin, "the hierarchy of values has been disordered," and it is "intermingled" with evil and therefore requires redemption through Christ (see *GS* 36–37).

Inculturation covers the most varied spheres of Christian life: catechesis and liturgy, discipline and church law, popular piety and custom, language and literature, art and architecture, moral and dogmatic theology. It is felt most urgently in first proclamation and in the founding of new churches, that is, in the first encounter with new cultures. Vatican II's *Lumen Gentium* excluded nothing when it said: "In virtue of this catholicity each part contributes its own gifts to the other parts and to the whole Church, so that the whole and each of the parts are strengthened by the common sharing of all things and by the common effort to attain to fullness in unity" (*LG* 13).

5. In order to clarify what contextualization or inculturation of the gospel is all about, we refer to various models. S. Bevans speaks of six models: the translation, anthropological, praxis, synthetic, transcendental, and countercultural models. The translation model is not concerned about a word-for-word translation and consequently takes the different cultures seriously, at least to a certain extent. But the point of departure is the supracultural message which goes out to the cultures and "baptizes" them. The anthropological model begins with the fundamental goodness of human beings and culture and rearticulates the faith under the various cultural conditions. As U Khin Maung Din says: "The Burmese and Buddhist understanding of Man, Nature, and Ultimate Reality must also become inclusive as a vital component in the overall content of the gospel." The praxis model, strongly influenced by the method which undergirds →liberation theology, understands revelation as God's ongoing action in history. That is why it analyzes reality, often very complex, in order to arrive at Christian behavior (orthopraxis instead of orthodoxy). The synthetic model insists that no culture is absolutely unique but rather has grown in the encounter with other cultures, is developing all the time, and can be enriched in the encounter with Western-Christian culture. Since God is present in all cultures, we must be open to all of them, enter into dialogue with them, learn from them, and allow ourselves to be formed by them. To be included in this model is what might be called the "semiotic" model, a model developed above all by R. J. Schreiter. This form of the synthetic model seeks to discover Christ not only in the values, symbols, and patterns of behavior but also in the situations and events affecting peoples; above all, it seeks to formulate "local theologies" from their "texts" (key symbols); here, gospel and tradition are more a test than an epistemological source. The transcendental model takes as its point of departure the authentic individual who by attending to the transcendental imperatives (be attentive, be intelligent, be reasonable, be responsible) articulates faith as an authentic believer and an authentic cultural subject. Finally, in the countercultural model (one which Bevans is in the process of developing), culture is taken seriously but is regarded with utmost suspicion. Inculturation is accomplished as culture is unmasked as sinful and critiqued by the culturally conditioned but divinely sanctioned message of the gospel.

None of these models should have a claim to exclusivity. The precondition for all reflection must be that the Christ-event is unique, that all Christian theology thus lives from the one word of God bestowed in Jesus Christ, and that, consequently, Christian history in the individual countries can be understood only in the context of comprehensive Christian history. However, since the encounter of Christ's message and the world happens in concrete human beings and in communities of quite different historical, social, and cultural situations, those who accept the message in faith and live it in different situations must also be allowed to reflect on it in their different psychological and cultural backgrounds, that is, theologically rework and consequently also formulate it in a different way. It is quite clear that this is more than simple didactic adaptation. It is also indisputable that this is different from the mere transmission of traditional "Western theology." But whether and in which sense one can talk of "continuous new creation" (H. Rücker) or "radical innovation" in new cultures (J.-M. Éla) must be discussed in greater detail. Whoever affirms plurality in theology will affirm the image of the seed which "sprouts in different soils, in different climates in new forms and still retains the identity of its origin and nature" (J. Neuner).

KARL MÜLLER, SVD

Bibliography

Arbuckle, G., *Earthing the Gospel* (1990). Bevans, S. B., *Cultural Expressions of Our Faith: Church Teachings and Pastoral Responses* (1993). Idem, *Models of Contextual Theology* (1992). Idem, "Models of Contextual Theology," *Missiol* 13/2 (April 1985) 185–202. Bevans, S. B., and N. Thomas, "Selected Annotated Bibliography on Missiology: Contextualization/Inculturation/Indigenization," *Missiol* 19/1 (January 1991) 105–8. Burrows, W. R., "A Seventh Paradigm? Catholics and Radical Inculturation," in W. Saayman and K. Kritzinger, eds., *Mission in Bold Humility* (1996) 121–38. Chupungco, A. J., *Cultural Adaptation of the Liturgy* (1982). Idem, *Liturgical Inculturation, Sacramentals, Religiosity and Catechesis* (1992). Idem, *Liturgies of the Future* (1989). Costa, R. O., *One Faith, Many Cultures* (1988). Cote, R. G., *Revisioning Mission* (1996). Crollius, A., R., *Inculturation: Working Papers on Living Faith and Cultures,* multiple vols. (1982–). Idem, "What Is So New about Inculturation? A Concept and Its Implication," *Gregorianum* (Rome)

61 (1980) 253–73. Fleming, B. E. C., *Contextualization of Theology: An Evangelical Assessment* (1980). Francis, M. R., *Liturgy in a Multicultural Community* (1991). Fung, J. M., *Shoes-Off Barefoot We Walk: A Theology of Shoes-Off* (1992). Geertz, C., *The Interpretation of Cultures* (1973). Gensichen, H. W., "Evangelium und Kultur: Neue Variationen über ein altes Thema," *ZMiss* 4 (1978) 197–214. Gilliland, D., ed., *The Word among Us: Contextualizing Theology for Mission Today* (1989). Gnilka, C., *Chresis: Die Methode der Kirchenväter im Umgang mit der antiken Kultur* (1984). González, J. L., *Mañana: Theology from a Hispanic Perspective* (1990). Idem, *Out of Every Tribe and Nation: Christian Theology at the Ethnic Round Table* (1992). Gritti, J., *L'expression de la foi dans les cultures humaines* (1975). Haleblian, K., "The Problem of Contextualization," *Missiol* 11/2 (1983) 95–111. Jacob, S., *Das Problem der Anknüpfung für das Wort Gottes in der deutschen evangelischen Literatur der Nachkriegszeit* (1935). Joly, R., "Inculturation et vie de foi," *Spiritus* 26 (1985) 3–32. Kinsler, F. R., "Mission and Context: The Current Debate about Contextualization," *EMQ* 14 (1978). Kraft, C. H., *Christianity in Culture* (1979). Luzbetak, L. J., *The Church and Cultures* (1988). Müller, K., "Accommodation and Inculturation in the Papal Documents," *Verbum SVD* 24 (1983) 347–60. Idem, *Missionarische Anpassung als theologisches Prinzip* (1973). Neuner, J., "Inkulturation in Indien," *GuL* 52 (1979) 171–84. Poupard, P., "Evangélisation et nouvelles cultures," *NRTh* 99 (1977) 532–49. Idem, "Foi et culture dans les mutations de notre temps," *CF* 1/2 (1993) 81–97. Idem, "L'inculturation de la foi et l'evangélisation des cultures," *CF* 2/1 (1994) 1–14. Santos Hernández, A., *Adaptación misionera* (1958). Scherer, J. A., and S. B. Bevans, *New Directions in Mission and Evangelization,* vol. 1, *Basic Statements 1974–1991* (1992). Schineller, P., *A Handbook on Inculturation* (1990). Schreiter, R. J., *Constructing Local Theologies* (1985). Schreiter, R. J., ed., *Faces of Jesus in Africa* (1991). Shorter, A., *Toward a Theology of Inculturation* (1988). Stackhouse, M. L., *Apologia: Contextualization, Globalization, and Mission in Theological Education* (1988). Sugirtharajah, R. S., ed., *Asian Faces of Jesus* (1993). Sundermeier, T., *Das Kreuz als Befreiung* (1985). Thauren, J., *Die Akkommodation im katholischen Heidenapostolat* (1927). Van Nieuwenhove, J., and B. K. Goldewijk, eds., *Popular Religion, Liberation and Contextual Theology* (1991).

❧ INDIAN THEOLOGY ❧

1. Renascent Hinduism.   2. Nationalism and Social Justice.   3. Interfaith Dialogue.

1.   It is significant to note that R. Boyd's *An Introduction to Indian Christian Theology* sees the leaders of the cultural renaissance of the nineteenth century as the pioneers in reflections on Indian Christianity. It was in the process of their struggle to assimilate the cultural impact of Western Christianity and secular humanism that they raised the question of an Indian understanding of Christ and an indigenous Christianity. Indian Christian thinkers thus began to formulate an indigenous theology and its fundamentals when they analyzed the relation between Christian apologetics and the Indian Renaissance; in short, it was participation in and dialogue with the Indian Renaissance that led them to take up the theological challenge underlying it.

Rajah Ram Mohan Roy, the founder of the Brahmo Samaj, was a monotheist who fought against the monism and polytheism of traditional Hinduism in the name of a prophetic religious consciousness which would support the moral regeneration of Indian society. In 1820 he produced for his Brahmo congregation *Precepts of Jesus — the Guide to Peace and Happiness*. It consisted of the Sermon on the Mount and the parables from the Synoptic Gospels and pictured Jesus as the moral teacher and religious messenger par excellence. When J. Marshman of the Serampore missionary trio criticized Roy for not acknowledging the deity and atonement of Jesus Christ, Roy reaffirmed his views that any incarnation of God smelled of a polytheism much like that of traditional Hinduism and that forgiveness of sins required only repentance and no atonement; he also reaffirmed that he considered Jesus to be the exemplar of the highest morality and the pre-existent firstborn of all *creatures*. As the Brahmo Samaj for a time became the spiritual home of educated Hindus of Bengal and Maharashtra, the issues involved in the Roy-Marshman controversy were kept alive in the defense of the Christian faith against Brahmo theism. L. B. Day and K. M. Banerjee of Bengal and N. Goreh and P. Ramabhai of Maharashtra continued to controvert not only classical Hinduism but also Brahmoism, especially its rejection of incarnation and atonement. But K. M. Banerjee felt that it was not enough to controvert Hinduism and neo-Hinduism but that response to their challenge should lead to an indigenous Christianity expressing universal Christian truths in the language of Indian religious culture. So he wrote *Arian Witness* (1875), *Two Essays on Supplements to the Arian Witness* (1880), and *The Relation between Christianity and Hinduism* (1881) to illustrate the thesis that there is Vedic testimony to Christ. Banerjee endeavored to show "that Christianity was the fulfillment of Vedic religion. It was no longer Christianity and Hinduism contrasted, but Christianity as fulfillment of Hinduism. For him, no one could be a true Hindu without being a true Christian. It was Krishna Mohan who spoke of Indian Christians as 'Hindoo Christians,' a term which Brahmobandhav Upadhyaya popularized later" (Philip 1982, 113).

Banerjee especially mentions that the Vedic idea of *Prajapati* finds its historical fulfillment in Jesus Christ: "The meaning of *Prajapati,* an appelative variously described as a Purusha begotten in the beginning, as Viswakarma the Creator of all, singularly coincides with the meaning of the name and office of the historical reality of Jesus Christ; and no other person than Jesus of Nazareth has ever appeared in the world claiming the character and position of the self-sacrificing *Prajapati,* at the same time mortal and immortal" (Philip 1982, 116).

L. B. Day's "memorandum" to the mission authorities entitled "The Desirableness and Practicability of a National Church of Bengal" was also a positive response to the Brahmo challenge of making Christianity a source of authentic national unity and regeneration. It conceived for the first time a national church unifying all the churches, including the Roman Catholic, on the basis of the Apostles' Creed.

After Roy, the Brahmo leader K. C. Sen reacted against Roy's purely unitarian moralistic interpretation of Jesus Christ. He produced the seminal idea of God as "uni-trinity" (*sat-chit-ananda* [truth-consciousness-bliss]), Jesus Christ being the incarnation of the *chit.* He also interpreted the ten incarnations of Vishnu from fish, animal, and half-man to Rama and Krishna as the symbolic representation of God's creation of the world through an evolutionary process, the climax of which was Jesus Christ the divine Son.

After Jesus, the religious history of humanity is the dispensation of the Holy Spirit, who traverses the whole humanity, transforming it in the likeness of Jesus. Thus divinity coming down to humanity is the Son; divinity carrying up humanity to heaven is the Holy Spirit. Keshub formed the Brahmo congregation as the Church of the New Dispensation, which he claimed was the fulfillment of Hinduism; and he invited the established Christian churches in India to unite with his church and to create the One Christ-centered Universal Church of the New Dispensation.

Though the missions and churches rejected Keshub's religious syncretism, his doctrines of God as *sat-chit-ananda,* of the world as a creative evolutionary process of self-revelation of God, of Christ as divine humanity, and of the church as the dispensation of the Spirit providing a Christ-centered harmony of religions came to prominence later in Indian Christian theology.

From the ranks of the Brahmo Samaj, a Bengalee took baptism in 1881 and became a Roman Catholic monk, taking the name B. Upadhyaya. He pursued Keshub's idea of the divine trinity of *sat-chit-ananda* and wrote a Christian hymn of adoration to God who is being-intelligence-bliss, in which the second person is adored as "the Son, Uncreated, Eternal Word, Supreme, the Image of the Father whose form is Intelligence, Giver of highest Release." It has become a hymn of the Indian church in recent years. Upadhyaya wrote: "We are Hindus as far as our physical and mental constitution is concerned, but in regard to our immortal souls we are Catholics. We are Hindu-Catholics." In the periodicals *Sophia* and *Twentieth Century* he elaborated his theology first in Vedic terms but later also in the Vedantic terms of Sankara and Ramanuja. He was eager to start an order of Indian Christian *samnyasis,* but the Vatican refused permission. This convinced him that a truly Indian Christianity required an independent Indian nation. So he entered the struggle for political freedom and died in prison. Though he remained long-forgotten, Upadhyaya is recognized today as the pioneer of Indian Christian theology.

Brahmo theism and moralism declined in India with the revival of Vedantic traditions of *advaita* and *visishtadvaita* and the Vaishnava tradition of avatarism. Under the leadership of S. Vivekananda the Ramakrishna movement emphasized the vedantic philosophy of self-realization and the interior spiritual vision of unity-in-diversity as the essence of Hinduism. Vivekananda himself popularized *dvaita* (dualism), *visishtadvaita* (qualified dualism), and *advaita* (nondualism) as a ladder of spiritual journey and sought to give room in it for *karma, bhakti,* and *jnana* paths of salvation. S. Radhakrishnan and Aurobindo Ghosh had their own interpretations of the *advaitic* relation between unity and pluralism. The new exposition of nondualism distinguished it from monism and gave room for plurality and affirmed *eswara* as the cosmic view of *brahman.* It saved the world and the moral imperative of social transformation. In its new forms, the Vaishnava tradition of many avatars (incarnations) with special emphasis on Rama and Krishna elevated *bhakti* mysticism, with its personal communion with God and egalitarian approach to society, as the ultimate in religion. New interpretations of the Bhagavad Gita provided its scriptural basis.

This return of neo-Hinduism to the *advaita* and avatar traditions of Hinduism brought two challenges to Indian Christian theology. One was to define the spiritual interiority of fellowship with God through Jesus Christ in relation to the experience of *advaitic* or *bhakti* mysticism; and the other was to interpret the uniqueness of the person of Jesus Christ as redeemer of the world in the metaphysical categories of the *advaitic* or avatar traditions.

The interiority of the *advaitic* spiritual experience transcends all religious names (*nama*) and forms (*rupa*); and as *atman-brahman* identity it is unmediated self-realization. It is a cosmic spirituality of liberation from the very distinction between the one and the many in the world. Many Catholic Christian monks have been deeply attracted by this unitive vision of the Hindu *samnyasin,* the more so as Christian activism has been producing intense divisions and conflicts.

The French Catholic monks who became Indian Christian *samnyasins* (taking names like Parama Arubi Anandam and Swami Abhishiktananda) came together with a group of Christian Ashramites and theologians to seek to define and grasp the Hindu *advaitic* vision in tri-unitarian terms. Following Keshub and Upadhyaya, they pursued the triune God *sat-chit-ananda* and the spirituality of nonduality underlying it; they followed the tradition of Christian mysticism represented by Eckhart, St. John of the Cross, and the Eastern Orthodox doctrine of theosis, all of which see Christian personalism as beyond the impersonality and the unipersonality of the divine.

Satchidananda — a Christian Approach to Advaitic Experience, by Swami Abhishiktananda, first published in French in 1965, is an important reflection. It began as a Christian reflection on the challenge of R. Maharshi to the Christian church. The author says:

> As Christ himself taught, only he who is willing to risk all, including his own self (anima, psyche [Lk 9:24]), can enter the Kingdom. Without complete renunciation [and] stripping of self, loss of self, there is no possibility of following Jesus in his return to the Father, the source and Principle of all.
>
> The "quest of the self" recommended by Sri Ramana Maharshi in its own way amounts to the same thing as that call to death which abounds in the Gospel, whose acceptance is paradoxically the very means of overcoming death by undergoing it. It also very closely resembles the *todo-nada* of St. John of the Cross. (1974, 64)

In *Hindu-Christian Meeting Point in the Cave of the Heart,* Swami Abhishiktananda says that India will never take the message that humanity encounters God as creatures, children, and sinners until "it is freed from the dualistic presuppositions which too often color our conceptualization and expression of it" (1969, 127).

Swami Abhishiktananda recognizes that it is difficult for "an interiorized cosmic religion to allow that any form of historic religion as such should be true absolutely or could speak definitely about God." He asks whether the historicity of Jesus Christ, which was "dated in time (involving, e.g., the birth of Jesus under Caesar Augustus, his teaching under Tiberius, his execution under the procurator Pontius Pilate"), can be "interiorized" without losing its "temporal character." His own answer is that "stated in these terms the problem is insoluble"; he opts for a solution at the level not of theology but of *anubhava* (spiritual experience).

M. S. Rao, a convert from Hinduism to Christianity, in his pamphlet *Ananyatva: Realization of Christian Non-duality* distinguishes between monism and nonduality and shows that the Greek doctrine of *perichoresis* (coinherence), which underlies the doctrines of the Trinity and incarnation, provides a framework for incorporating the *advaitic* experience into Christian personalism. In his opinion, *mystica, theosis,* and *perichoresis,* all used by the Greek Fathers, point to a divine-human union not unlike that of the *advaita* union; unlike the *advaita* union, however, it is not ontological but pneumatological, that is, union in the Holy Spirit and not identity of nature. He also makes a distinction between Christ's oneness with God, which is hypostatic (in substance), and the disciple's oneness with God, which is mystic — mediated through Christ. Rao rejects I-it and I-Thou relations and proposes I-in-Thou and Thou-in-me relations, that is, relations of mutual interpenetration in the Spirit.

A. J. Appasamy, who was more Protestant (he later became bishop of the Church of South India), followed the *bhakti* tradition because he thought that Christian personalism, with its affirmation of creatureliness, sinfulness, and sonship/daughterhood, was never safe in the *advaitic* context. In his opinion, the *mahavakya,* or Christian, mysticism emphasizes "Abide in me and I in you" (denoting mutual indwelling) and not "I and my Father are one" (which is interpreted as a relation of identity by Hindu *advaitins*). Even in Jesus' relationship with God, according to Appasamy, there was not only unity but also dependence. The church always had mystics, even mystics whose experience obliterated distinctions between humanity and God. But in judging the orthodoxy of mystics, the test of the church was impeccability. Appasamy considered this an excellent test, one badly needed in India. He saw both the metaphysical and moral levels in the ideas of sonship and fellowship with God. It was a union of "nature" and "will." In fact, S. S. Singh, whose biography Appasamy wrote with B. H. Streeter, was his ideal of Christian mysticism.

It has been always difficult for Christian theology to interpret the One-for-all and once-for-all incarnation of God in Jesus Christ in terms of Hindu religious thought and experience. Upadhyaya never used the word "avatar" for the divine incarnation in Jesus because avatars were a lower order of divinity than *sat* and because there were many avatars who descended to the world to destroy wickedness and restore the established moral order. In *Christianity as Bhakti Marga*, Appasamy adopted the concept of avatar, but he differentiated the person of Jesus as the supreme avatar and his work as redemptive. V. Chakkarai's books *Jesus the Avatar* and *The Cross and Indian Thought* differentiate Jesus from Hindu avatars by affirming that as mediator of God to the world (the incarnation of the *chit* and *rupa* of the being of God), the *sat* is permanent and dynamic.

P. Chenchiah conceived incarnation in Jesus as "the perfected human body receiving the full divinity of God into permanent integration." From this standpoint, he rejected the Barth-Kraemer ideas of the incarnation of God in Jesus precisely because they resembled the Hindu avatar concepts.

Chenchiah followed Aurobindo's *Integral Vedanta,* which rejects the *sankara* concept of the unreality of the many, with *brahman* as the only reality, but sees *brahman* as emptying itself to manifest itself in the many of the creative process, by spiritualizing it. Chenchiah also pursued the *suddhadvaita* line of Vallabha, which gives primacy to the avatar, the absolute supreme reality of Krishna. Therefore, for Chenchiah, Jesus was God taking a body permanently in the historical process in his adventure of ever-new creation.

In his *Preface to Personality,* a discussion of "christology in relation to Radhakrishnan's philosophy," S. Singh uses the framework of Radhakrishnan's neo-*sankara* philosophy for his interpretation of Jesus. Radhakrishnan sees ultimate reality as involved in pluralism without being exhausted by it or annihilating it. "In this context individuality as laying claim to absolutism would be denied. But insofar as it aligns itself with the pattern of ultimate reality it is affirmed and preserved." This, says Singh, corresponds to the conception of individuality as revealed in Jesus Christ:

> The whole life of Jesus the Christ, and particularly the cross, bears witness to the phenomenon of the destruction of individuality as laying claim to absolutism. On the other hand, by positive righteousness he made himself so transparent to the divine that no contradiction remained between divinity and Humanity. The relation of perfect union was achieved. By making humanity transparent, by stripping it off from any possibility of its asserting itself in its own right, the humanity was not by any means absorbed in divinity, but only became completely responsive. Therefore, the

God-Man is not only a reality in history, but it is also beyond it. (Singh 1952, 109–10)

The resurrection represents a historical individuality which is spiritual. In it historical reality is "taken up into the consummation of things and is preserved in the essential structure of Reality."

We have only illustrated certain types of Indian Christian theology which have arisen in dialogue with neo-Hinduism.

2. Renascent Hinduism was a prelude to the emergence of Indian nationalism and its struggle for national independence. This struggle, under the ideological leadership of G. K. Gokhale's liberal-democratic secularism, B. G. Tilak's Hindu nationalism, M. Gandhi's nonviolence, and M. Nehru's socialism brought not only political independence but also the search for an ideology of social humanism as the foundation for nation building and a just transformation of society. Indian Christians participating in the political struggle for freedom and later in the programs of action for economic development and social justice developed their own theological anthropology (relating person, society, and state) in dialogue with the national ideologies of social humanism current in India. In that context, they also helped to clarify the meaning of Jesus Christ and the nature and form of the Christian church and its mission in a pluralistic national community. G. Thomas's *Christian Indians and Indian Nationalism 1885 to 1950: An Interpretation in Historical and Theological Perspectives* is a very illuminating survey of the theological insights that arose in this context.

In the preindependence period, the Christian Nationalism movement emerged, urging Christian participation in the political struggle for India's freedom. One may take K. T. Paul, a YMCA leader, as representative. His *Christian Nationalism and British Connection with India,* his several articles on Christian citizenship in modern India in the YMCA and NCC journals, and his speeches at the Round Table Conference give the context of his thinking. Based on them, one may say that Christian Nationalism sought, first, to define the meaning of the British-Indian connection in light of the providence of God and of Indian independence as the fulfillment of Christians' providential purpose; second, therefore, to urge members of the Indian national movement not to preserve their minority "communal" interests or buttress them with safeguards but rather to work for a common nationhood and nation-state that transcended all religious or ethnic "communalism" and was based on the universal rights of the human person and peoples; third, to define the relevance of Christ and the fellowship in Christ for developing the criteria and spiritual resources for building a casteless democratic community; and fourth, to urge that the church become liberated from control of missions and Western denominationalism, enabling it to become a united and indigenous fellowship oriented to its evangelistic and prophetic mission to the whole national community.

These theological emphases are found also in the writings of S. K. Rudra, S. K. Datta, Bishop Azariah, J. de Souza, and others. After independence this tradition was continued by the Christian Institute for the Study of Religion and Society, as shown by the book *Christian Participation in Nation-Building.* B. Hoffman's *Christian Social Thought in India 1947–'62* and G. Shiri's *Christian Social Thought in India 1962–'77* are relevant for understanding the dialogue between Indian Christianity and ideologies of nation building in postindependent India.

Here, we shall confine our survey to just two aspects of Indian Christian anthropology. The first aspect concerns the church as mission to the whole people of
India and the fellowship in Christ as the sign of true community. The Christian
Nationalist stand for "secular-national" as against "religious-communal" politics
was based on a theological conviction that the church represented not the narrow
interests of the Christian community but the genuine human and spiritual interests of all peoples of India and that, therefore, the preservation of the church as a
static minority community with communal safeguards was a denial of the nature
and mission of the church. Both S. K. Datta and K. T. Paul saw the church as "a
potent factor and bond of unity in the corporate and national life of the people."
This consciousness of the Indian Christian leadership helped propel Christians'
fight against the British plan of imposing a communal electorate and against advocates of a Hindu state and Pakistan. In advocating a secular nationalism, the
Indian Christians did not make religion a private affair unrelated to the ethics
of public life. On the contrary, it was their conviction that a secular state which
protected the citizenship rights of religious freedom for all persons was the best
framework for the church to make its contribution to the renewal of Indian life.

To make that contribution, it was the Christian Nationalist conviction that the
fellowship of the church must transcend both Western denominationalism and
Indian caste. It is significant that the Tranquebar Declaration of South Indian
church leaders, which started the church union negotiations that culminated in
the Church of South India, pointed to the church's mission to the nation as the
basic reason for church unity:

> We believe that the challenge of the present hour, and the present critical
> situation in India itself, call us to mourn our past division and turn to our
> Lord Jesus Christ to seek in Him the unity of the body expressed in one vis-
> ible church. We face together the titanic task of winning India for Christ —
> one fifth of the human race. Yet, confronted by such an overwhelming re-
> sponsibility, we find ourselves rendered weak and relatively impotent by our
> unhappy divisions, for which we were not responsible and which have been
> as it were imposed on us from without, divisions which we did not create and
> which we do not desire to perpetuate.

S. K. Datta pointed out that for the sake of the church's mission to India, the
church must overcome "the divisions of Western Christendom" as well as the danger of splitting up the church into "caste churches." In the mind of the Christian
Nationalists, the church's primary contribution to the renewal of corporate life was
and would continue to be through the ferment created by the quality of fellowship
of the Indian church.

The second aspect concerns a cross-centered anthropology. M. Gandhi's advocacy of nonviolence in the national struggle for independence coupled with his
recognition that Christ's Sermon on the Mount and Christ's death on the cross
had inspired him brought about the lively debate in India on the meaning of the
cross for political philosophy. It was this that led the Indian Christian Nationalists to give attention to the relevance of a cross-centered anthropology for politics
in general and for political struggle for freedom and justice in particular. In its
turn, it also illumined christology.

A. G. Hogg, in his Christmas sermon at the world missionary meeting at
Tambaram in 1938, spoke in terms of Gandhi's thought and referred to the

incarnation as the transcendent *satyagraha* of God against evil in humanity. More recently, I. Jesudasan's *A Gandhian Theology of Liberation* affirmed that Gandhian *satyagraha* is a manifestation of Christ's incarnation.

It was probably C. F. Andrews who first emphasized in the Indian setting the idea of "Christ the Son of Man suffering in each indignity offered to the least of his brethren, Christ the divine Head of Humanity in whom all the races of mankind are gathered into one" (1912, 174). For Andrews, Gandhi, and R. Tagore, the crucified Christ was the symbol of God's identification with oppressed humanity and of the unity of humankind; they integrated that symbol into the nationalist philosophy, politics, and art. To illustrate Tagore's poem "The Son of Man," N. Bose painted Jesus on the cross. But following that, all the painters of the Bengal school and even others painted Christ on the cross to reveal a new vision of God or a new hope for oppressed humanity.

Political thinkers also talked about this symbolism. To a Christian delegation, A. Mehta, then planning minister, said that Christians who believe in the agony of God wherever human beings suffer must share that agony and must manifest it in their action. R. Lohia, a socialist leader, has said that though he did not believe in God, the figure of Christ on the cross had fascinated him as one symbol of hope for tortured humanity.

Indian Christian theology has emphasized that the cross means not only divine forgiveness but also divine identification with the poor and the oppressed. Recently, India's younger theologians and social action groups have been emphasizing this aspect of the meaning of the cross as providing the spirituality and theology for the church's identification with the struggle of the poor and the oppressed for justice. It has also provided a common basis from which the →Ecumenical Association of Third World Theologians (EATWOT) has constructed a theology of liberation.

S. Rayan's contribution to an Indian theology of the relation between faith and history is made in relation to his exposition of the Bhagavad Gita. He notes that commentaries on the Gita have been written by many Indian philosophers and national leaders of modern India from Tilak to Radhakrishnan, from Gandhi to Bhave. This fact is evidence of the Gita's relevance to the historical decisions India is called to make in our time. This relevance lies in the historical crisis Kurushetra creates for Arjuna as the representative of humanity. In that situation the human being has to act. The real problem is that work is at once necessary for life and dangerous for salvation. The solution is in *nishkamakarma* (work without selfish desire) for the goal of *lokasamgraha* (the gathering and holding together of the world in wholeness), especially as such work is offered as sacrifice to the Person of the Lord who is present within the stream of history, the *antaryamin*.

3. Interfaith and intrafaith dialogues are inherent in the use of Hindu categories of thought for Christian theologizing as well as in the search for an anthropology adequate for India's nation building. This inevitably led Indian Christians to formulate an Indian theology of religious and ideological faiths and of dialogue with them. We cannot go into a detailed exposition of the history of this formulation, but the theological trends which have produced, for example, R. Panikkar's *Unknown Christ of Hinduism* and *The Trinity and World Religions,* P. Devanandan's *Christian Concern in Hinduism,* and the collection of essays *Preparation for Dialogue* deal with Christ and religions and may be quickly surveyed.

Briefly stated, the new Catholic theology of religion takes its start from R. de Nobili's adaptation theory, which he practiced in Tamilnadu. It sought to distinguish between culture and religion in Hinduism and to adapt Hindu culture to the Christian religion. The new thinking spurred by Vatican II sees Christ and his kingdom as transcending, transforming, and fulfilling all religions and sees the church as the universal sacrament of this fulfillment. Panikkar stands in the tradition of conciliar and postconciliar developments.

Panikkar affirms the presence and activity of the eternal Christ of God in all religions, and he holds that this presence and activity bring salvation to the religions' adherents through their own sacraments. Christ is the "only mediator," but he is "present and active" in every authentic religion as it seeks the ontological link between the absolute and the relative or searches for the mediator between God and the world in whatever name or form. The Christ of Christianity, the *eswara* of Vedantic religion, the Logos of Plotinus, and the *thathagatha* of Buddhism are parallel mediating links. Panikkar thinks that since faith transcends belief-systems, these different and apparently conflicting mediating principles may be "pointing to the same mystery." In any case, the meeting of faiths at the level of the mediating symbols makes possible real interfaith dialogue about that mystery.

In this context, Panikkar interprets the role of historical Christianity and its relation to other religions as follows. First, as already stated, historical Christianity and its sacraments, which are centered around Jesus as the Christ, reveal the universality of saving grace operating in all religions. But since it is an operation which has its urge toward fullness and especially toward fullness in Christ, Hinduism is "a kind of Christianity in potency."

Second, argues Panikkar, Western Christianity is, historically, ancient paganism, or, more precisely, the complex of Hebro-Hellenic-Graeco-Latin-Celtic-Gothic-Modern religions, all converted to Christ more or less successfully. Similarly, Indian Christianity should be Hinduism, itself converted, or Islam, Buddhism, whatever it may be. This conversion, of course, involves continuity and development as well as transformation and revolution in all religious traditions. How Christianity needs to grow or how Hinduism or modern humanism has to change, we may not yet know.

The new Protestant Indian thought on other religions in this century starts with J. N. Farquhar's *The Crown of Hinduism*. It saw Christianity as the "fulfillment" of Hinduism. The challenge to it came at the World Missionary Conference at Tambaram (Madras, India, 1938) from the Barthianism of Kraemer's *Christian Message in a Non-Christian World*. The latter interpreted all religions, including empirical Christianity, as human efforts at self-justification before God. Christianity, constantly living under this judgment, is the sole means of new life in grace.

The Indian Christian challenge to Kraemer came from the theological group behind the book *Rethinking Christianity in India* and later from D. G. Moses's *Religious Truth and the Relation between Religions*. As we saw earlier, P. Chenchiah criticized the Barthian idea of incarnation as akin to the Hindu idea of avatars, arguing that the Barthian view conceived Jesus Christ as only a tangential touching of history and not as full entry of God into history to create a new humanity. Moses argued both against Kraemer's idea of total discontinuity between Christianity and other religions and against Radhakrishnan's approach of seeing all religions as relative forms of one religion.

P. Devanandan developed Chenchiah's doctrine of the new humanity in Christ on a post-Kraemer basis. Devanandan conceded Kraemer's Barthian view that the realm of religion (and ideology) is the realm of law pointing to a divine salvation which law cannot realize, and, therefore, it is to be judged and abolished by divine grace in Christ.

Therefore, as a common response to the cross broke down the wall between the Jew and the Gentile in early Christian history, today the common Hindu and Christian and secular response to the ferment of the gospel and the new humanity in Christ, however partial, must be seen as lowering if not abolishing the walls between Christianity and other religious or ideological faiths.

Therefore, Devanandan discerned the work of Christ within the Hindu Renaissance. He saw that renaissance as stimulated by the teaching of Jesus Christ and the agape-centered anthropology which visualizes humanity as persons-in-community oriented to a spiritual fulfillment in the kingdom of Love. He also saw Christ at work where secular ideologies give up their utopianism and revise their understanding of human alienation to include not merely social but also spiritual alienation, thus becoming more realistic. And interfaith dialogue in Christ for him was dialogue on the "new anthropology," which directly or indirectly raised questions of "theology" and its reformulation in all religions and ideologies.

Panikkar and Devanandan, by posing the faith response to Christ as transcending Christianity and other religious and secular ideologies, raised the question whether a Christ-centered *koinonia* of faith could be formed within the Hindu religious community or within a secular ideological community or across all religious and ideological barriers. There is, indeed, a tradition of individual Christian believers from K. Chetty and M. Parekh to many today who have stayed within the Hindu religious community while maintaining fellowship with Christians and openly confessing Christ. Chetty was unbaptized. Parekh was baptized. K. C. Sen's Brahmo Church in the nineteenth century and S. Rao's *brahmin* group in Andhra Pradesh in the twentieth century were not the only spiritual fellowships in the Hindu fold that acknowledged Christ. There was also the effort of the poet N. V. Tilak to build "God's durbar," a Christ-centered fellowship of the baptized and unbaptized. The assumption is that baptism in India's religious communal context has acquired a communal rather than a sacramental character, like circumcision in the early period of church history. The search in Indian Christian theology is for a communal form of the eucharistic fellowship acknowledging Christ in the Indian context.

M. M. THOMAS

Bibliography

Abhishiktananda, S., *Hindu-Christian Meeting Point in the Cave of the Heart* (1969). Idem, *Satchidananda — a Christian Approach to Advaitic Experience* (1974). Amaladoss, M., *Making All Things New* (1990). Andrews, C. F., *Renaissance in India* (1912). Appasamy, A. J., *Christianity as Bhakti Marga* (1928). Idem, *My Theological Task* (1964). Idem, *What Is Moksha?* (1931). Appasamy, A. J., and B. H. Streeter, *The Sadhu* (1921). Baago, K., *Library of Indian Christian Theology: A Bibliography* (1969). Idem, *Pioneers of Indigenous Christianity* (1969). Banerjee, K. M., *The Arian Witness* (1875). Idem, *Dialogues on Hindu Philosophy* (1861). Idem, *The Relation between Christianity and Hinduism* (1881). Idem, *Two Essays on Supplements to the Arian Witness* (1880). Boyd, R. H. S., *An Introduction to Indian Christian Theology* (1975). Bürkle, H., ed., *Indische Beiträge zur Theologie der Gegenwart* (1966). Chakkarai, V., *The Cross and Indian Thought* (1932). Idem, *Jesus the Avatar* (1927). Collet, S. D., ed., *The Life and Letters of Raja Rammohan Roy* (1900). Datta, S. K., *Desire of India* (1908). Day, L. B., *An Antidote to*

Brahmoism (1867). Devanandan, P. D., *Christian Concern in Hinduism* (1961). Idem, *Preparation for Dialogue* (1964). Devanandan, P. D., and M. M. Thomas, eds., *Christian Participation in Nation-Building* (1960). Farquhar, J. N., *The Crown of Hinduism* (1913). Gensichen, H. W., "Auf dem Wege zu einer indischen Theologie," *NZSTh* 1 (1959) 326–49. Goreh, N., *Theism and Christianity* (1882). Hoffman, B., *Christian Social Thought in India 1947–1962* (1967). Jesudasan, I., *A Gandhian Theology of Liberation* (1985). Kraemer, H., *The Christian Message in a Non-Christian World* (1947). Marshman, J., *A Defence of the Deity and Atonement of Jesus Christ in Reply to Rammohan Roy of Calcutta* (1822). Missionswissenschaftliches Institut Missio e. V., *Theologie im Kontext: Informationen über theologische Beiträge aus Afrika, Asien, Ozeanien und Lateinamerika* (monthly). Philip, T. V., *Krishna Mohan Banerjee — Christian Apologist* (1982). Mookenthottam, A., *Indian Theological Tendencies* (1978). Moses, D. G., *Religious Truth and the Relation between Religions* (1950). Oosthuizen, G. C., *Theological Battleground in Asia and Africa* (1972). Idem, *Theological Discussions and Confessional Developments in the Churches of Asia and Africa* (1958). Osthatios, M., *Theologie einer Klassenlosen Gesellschaft* (1980). Panikkar, R., *The Trinity and World Religions* (1970). Idem, *The Unknown Christ of Hinduism* (1981). Paul, K. T., *British Connection with India* (1928). Idem, *Christian Nationalism* (1921). Puthiadam, J., "Überlegungen zu einer indischen Theologie," *ZMRW* 67 (1983) 206–19. Rao, M. S., *Ananyatva: Realisation of Christian Non-duality* (1964). Rayan, S., "Indian Theology and the Problem of History," in R. W. Taylor, ed., *Society and Religion* (1974) 167–93. Roy, R. R. M., *Precepts of Jesus: The Guide to Peace and Happiness, Extracted from the Books of the New Testament, Ascribed to the Four Evangelists to Which Are Added the 1st, 2nd and Final Appeal to the Christian Public* (1934). Samartha, S., "The Cross and the Rainbow: Christ in a Multireligious Culture," in R. S. Sugirtharajah, ed., *Asian Faces of Jesus* (1993). Shiri, G., *Christian Social Thought in India 1962–1977* (1982). Singh, S., *Preface to Personality* (1952). Taylor, R. W., *Jesus in Indian Paintings* (1975). Thangaraj, T., *The Crucified Guru: An Experiment in Cross-cultural Christology* (1994). Thomas, G., *Christian Indians and Indian Nationalism 1885–1950: An Interpretation in Historical and Theological Perspectives* (1979). Thomas, M. M., *The Acknowledged Christ of the Indian Renaissance* (1969). Idem, *Some Theological Dialogues* (1977). Idem, "Some Trends in Contemporary Indian Christian Theology," *RelSoc* 24 (1977) 4–18. Wagner, H., *Erstgestalten einer einheimischen Theologie in Südindien* (1963). Wietzke, J., *Theologie im modernen Indien: P. D. Devanandan* (1975).

❧ INITIATION IN DIVERSE CONTEXTS ❧

1. Terminology and History of Research. 2. Manifestations, Forms and Inner Structures of Initiation. 3. Christian Initiation: Mission, Contextual Theologies, and Questions Referred Back to Western Theology.

1. Generally, by "initiation" is understood a ritual to mark the transition into a new religious or social status. The term is derived from the Latin *initiare,* which, together with the noun *initiatio,* is found in various ancient sources on the mystery cults. One difficulty consists of limiting the term "initiation" to "rites of passage," as in A. van Gennep's concept (1909). If one tries, with van Gennep, to understand as "rites of passage" all those ceremonial patterns "which accompany a passage from one situation to another or from one cosmic or social world to another" (van Gennep 1960, 10), the similarity in meaning to the term "initiation" becomes clear. So it is not surprising that until today in the history of research no consensus about the precise meaning and mutual limits of the two concepts could be reached (see Berner 1972, 1–3).

In cultural →anthropology there is the tendency to restrict the use of the word "initiation" to such rites as introduce certain candidates into closed groups (secret societies, brotherhoods, mystery pacts), or into special functions such as that of a shaman or witch (Panoff and Perrin 1982, 148; differing from Berner 1972, 231–32). In any case, the term "initiation" is placed in the phenomenology of religion under the broader category of "rites of passage" because there is a form of initiation implicit in every "passage" into a new "status." The broad understanding of the term, underlying the meaning here, is influenced by M. Eliade's definition of initiation as a "body of rites and oral teachings whose purpose is to produce a decisive alteration in the religious and social status of the person to be initiated" and which "more or less clearly imply a ritual death followed by resurrection or new birth" (Eliade 1959, x–xii).

2. Initiation rites can be found in all cultures and therefore can be seen as a secured anthropological "universal." A. van Gennep's characterization of rites of passage is still valid for the common inner structure of all initiation rites. At the beginning there is usually a phase of preparation and separation (*séparation*), which is followed by an ambivalent transition or liminal state (*margé*). The special significance of this transitional period as a dangerous state of "betwixt and between," in which the candidates no longer belong to their former group but do not yet belong to the new community, has been described by V. W. Turner especially. Rites of incorporation (*rites d'agrégation*), rites which effect the (re)acceptance into the community, form the conclusion. In the course of these three stages, the initiates (neophytes, novices) are dramatically cut off from their former life; this is in most cases effected also by separating them spatially from their relatives (seclusion in an initiation camp, etc.). In the course of the initiation, they go through tests of courage and self-castigation and also special apotropaic acts (purification, fasting), partly communicated in a secret language. The "elders" who conduct the initiation mediate the secret and previously unknown knowledge step-by-step to the candidates (mainly a demonstration of the *sacra*), whose attainment is made visible physically by various permanent mutilations (knocking out of teeth, tattooing, circumcision). These mutilations serve from now on as marks distinguishing them from noninitiates and alien groups (Worms and Petri 1968, 270).

In research into comparative religion, distinctions between three kinds of initiation have been established: (*a*) life-cycle rites or age-group initiations, especially puberty rites, which mark the passage of an entire age group (collective ritual) from childhood to adulthood; (*b*) entry into secret societies and brotherhoods; (*c*) magic-mystical calls to shamans, for example, medicine men (see Eliade, Bleeker, Gerlitz).

a. Life-cycle rites are especially strong in the tribal context. They are based on the experience that human life, from birth to death — and beyond death — is a continuous process which is marked by definite stages or watershed moments. In an analogy with nature, whose annual cycle passes through "death" and "rebirth," human life is structured as a cycle through a series of "deaths" and "rebirths." The essential passages are birth, puberty, marriage, and death — nevertheless, one finds many more far-reaching distinctions in some tribal societies.

Birth rites are particularly strongly observed in those cultures in which a preexistent form of human personality is presumed. Thus there is, for example, among some Bantu peoples, the concept of alternating generations reproducing themselves; the birth rites are, therefore, shaped as "rites of passage" in the form of the life of the child (Thiel 1977, 292).

Puberty rites have always played a special role in the context of the →theology of mission. In the first place, puberty rites deal with "a social puberty" (passage of children into the adult community) and not with a biological state. Therefore, the age at which the initiation rites take place fluctuates between seven and eighteen. In the course of the puberty rites, the candidates are inducted into full membership of the community; this is mainly preceded by a long training for future adult life. The climax of the ceremonies, which as a rule are conducted in seclusion from the rest of the community (in an uncultivated place as opposed to the village), is the experience of "death" (with accompanying "rebirth"), mainly in connection with a *descensus ad inferos* or *regressus ad uterum*. In the Keyo initiation, the candidates must, for example, first repeatedly crawl through a long tunnel, while at the same time they are confronted with hornets' stings; later they must force their way through a tunnel in water; at the end the spectators sing, "Our sons saw the underworld and came back" (Welbourn 1968, 228). The candidates in various Australian aboriginal tribes must crawl into special holes at the places of initiation, where the symbolic expression of the concept of dying and being buried, and of a return to the mother's womb, is created (Worms and Petri 1968, 269).

Different rites are also grouped around marriage, which among most peoples is seen as the final passage into full productive being for society; these rites help one cope with the transition into this new status. Among peoples with patrilocal living arrangements, the rites for women are especially important, because for them the move into a new family means a decisive change (Thiel 1977, 294; Mbiti 1970, 167ff.).

Just as for many people birth is experienced as a passage into the present world, so death is, by analogy, not the final point in life, but a passage into another form of existence. In several traditional religions of Africa, a good (i.e., natural) death is interpreted as merely the passage from the village of the living to the village of the ancestors. It is the summit on the long-yearned-for way to becoming an ancestor (→ancestor worship I and II). In some cultures, the dead are buried in a squatting position in a cowhide, which is a clear image of the birth process and which points to their "rebirth" in the otherworldly village of the ancestors. (It must be said, however, that most Africans do not speculate overmuch about death; they accept it, but as a natural phenomenon.)

b. The rites of mystery religions and secret societies share the same structural process as puberty rites, but their secret character comes out in a special way. Because of the instruction of secrecy toward outsiders, the details, for example, of the "great mysteries" of Eleusis, are almost entirely unknown right up to the present day. The climax of the initiation feast was indeed, as a rule, the vision of the *sacra* or *numina* (Berner).

c. In contrast to the initiation rites discussed above, the direct relationship to the community is lacking in the initiation of a shaman (medicine man, healer). What is involved here is the individual vocation to a specific office or to a special function. There are some specific elements which are encountered only in the shaman's vocation. These include mainly the "initiation illness," a syndrome of fits, ecstasies, dreams, and hallucinations which marks out the men and women for the shaman's calling. Dismemberment and renewal of the body, voyages to heaven, and journeys are symbolic stages in the initiation process (see Eliade 1964).

Further subclassification or arrangement into type-forms are possible: the call to a particular position of leadership (investiture of a king) or initiation into a particular religious community. The latter plays an important role in societies of religious pluralism because by it adherence to a particular community is documented from within and without (e.g., circumcision and reciting the Fatiha in Islam). Besides that, one must also take into account profane works of initiation, which either have been kept in their secularized form in "secularized" societies (e.g., initiations into college fraternities or sororities) or take on the appearance of neosacral functions (e.g., the inauguration of a national leader). Further consideration should be given to entrance into the Boy or Girl Scouts, housewarmings, building dedications, ship or boat launchings, ceremonies on crossing the International Date Line, craft and guild examinations, academic final examinations, dissertation defenses, and so on.

3. In the Christian tradition, the same turning points in life (birth, puberty, marriage, and death) are accompanied by rites of passage. Even for those Christians who do not practice their religion or attend church regularly, children are still presented for baptism and confirmation; church weddings are still common; and church burials are often preferred. The understanding of baptism in the post-Easter community (→baptism) already contained the imagery of death and resurrection (Rom 6:4–11; Ti 3:5), along with the integration of the baptismal candidate into a new relationship to the community (the church as Body of Christ).

With the general spread of infant baptism, the practice of confirmation was slowly but steadily established, with the removal to it of some of the rites which originally belonged to baptism (anointing, laying on of hands); through confirmation, the candidates are brought into full membership of the Christian community after reflection on the baptismal event.

As "the sacrament of mission," Christian baptism stands in tension with the traditional initiation rites of different cultures (→rites controversy). For hundreds of years the dichotomy between traditional initiation and Christian initiation was stressed in Christian missionary practice. This led in most cases to dramatic initiation controversies in Asia, Africa, and Oceania because the renunciation of traditional worship of the deity and the ancestors was accompanied by a basic rejection of initiation rituals. First-generation Christians in particular forfeited integration into their native community because of this (see Popp 1969, 71–72; Turner 1979, 239). Where such conflicts became unbearable for the participants, "independent churches" (→African independent churches) arose and effected an original integration of traditional and Christian points of view and rites.

On the basis of these experiences and in the wake of the general turning toward "non-Christian" religions (→theology of religions), a new reflection took place in the second half of the twentieth century on the significance and value of traditional initiation practices in relation to Christian initiation. The discussion has chiefly taken place in Catholic circles — mainly in relation to the opening to other religions achieved at Vatican II (*NA* 2; see also *LG* 13–14; *AG* 7–10, 22; →Vatican Council II). One text, much quoted in present discussions, says: "In mission lands initiation rites are found in use among individual peoples. Elements from these, when capable of being adapted to Christian ritual, may be admitted along with those already found in Christian tradition" (*SC* 65). Recently, a more critical approach has been adopted because the council seemed to talk only about selective "adaptation" of existing customs, which in fact would lead to an artificial mixing of preexisting rites and Christian rites. In contrast to this, a full "new creation" and "organic unity" of traditional and Christian elements in liturgical rites are advocated in relation to the teaching of incarnation, whereby the →inculturation of the gospel can take place only within a real "becoming flesh" within traditional culture. New breakthroughs in Catholic liturgical practice have been registered since the introduction of the Rite of Christian Initiation of Adults in 1972 and through the creation of "neophyte communities."

On the Protestant side, the judgment of traditional initiation rites is very different. While some evangelical and fundamentalist missions in particular still propagate a Western "Christianity for export" and incline toward a denial of traditional culture as "heathen," others have made the first attempt at intercultural "new creation" in the Christian practice of initiation. Until now there have been in Protestant theology of mission notably stronger reservations against traditional initiation rites and even against the view of baptism as a sacrament of initiation.

G. Vicedom draws attention to a certain anticipation of baptism among the "heathen" that "comes very close to the [Christian] understanding of baptism"; he sees this in concrete form in pre-Christian initiation rites. Of course, he recognizes here a point of contact for Christian preaching, but these ("heathen") cults conceal "the essence" and are to be understood as arbitrary "attempts of human beings to put an end to the misery of death" (Vicedom 1960, 11–12). According to H. Bürkle, baptism has a very pronounced confessional function in mission, in the sense that it is a personal moment of decision. Otherwise, Christian baptism must be defended in terms of its "character of incorporation." The initiation rites of traditional religions emphasize, as M. Ntetem has shown, the self-integration of the initiated, incorporation into the society of the living, and incorporation into the community of the ancestors (the "living dead"). Following B. Bujo's concept of human existence as a vital participation in the source of life through participation in a community, one could join Bürkle in understanding baptism as an act of initiation into the (new) community, but also at the same time as "the integration of individuals in a no less corporative way into the new mystical unity of the Body of Christ," whereby a "discharge" of the pre-Christian religious connections from their "soteriological function" can result (see Bürkle 1979, 101–7; Bujo 1992, 18–23). Against this background, the new liturgical creations in the context of traditional initiation are justifiable — as, for example, B. Sundkler reports of the Anglican missionary W. V. Lucas — insofar as they give a living expression to the thought of the incarnation of the gospel.

In the field of contextual theologies in Africa (→African theology), one finds some starting points which relate explicitly to traditional initiation customs. "When the African meets Jesus Christ, he sees in him the Son of God, the Lord of life and death, the one who, through his life, teaching, miracles, suffering and death and his resurrection, is the highest master of initiation for the human being" (Mveng 1978, 79). In A. T. Sanon's plan for rooting the gospel in the area of African tribal initiation, Christ as the master of initiation is the basic theme. Sanon's basic consideration consists of emphasizing Christ's "act of redemption after the fashion and reality of initiation" (Sanon 1982, 111–12). Jesus' Jewishness (circumcision), his way of suffering unto the cross, and finally his resurrection are understood by Sanon as steps in an initiatory process or drama, which, in the passage from life to death, reminds Sanon of the traditional initiation process. The Easter rhythm of death, burial, resurrection, and ascent to glory is an initiation ritual: already in Paul's writings, baptism is understood as being taken into Christ's initiation. To be initiated means, therefore, "to enter into Christ's own initiation and to take part in his trials" (Sanon 1982, 125). So there is and remains the "community formed after a hard, crucifying, first initiation to Christ... on the way of initiation" — "a gaze fixed and steady on the master of initiation" (Sanon 1982, 111).

Even if Sanon's initiatory interpretation of the Christian experience of salvation is strongly oriented toward the historical →Jesus in its details, the presentation already has the tendency to interpret the whole mission of Jesus in an initiatory way in the framework of a descendant christology.

C. Nyamiti has brought out this thought even more strongly, in that he sees the initiation character of Christ's act of salvation in relation to humiliation (*kenosis*) and exaltation. The incarnation and humiliation of Christ are to be understood as separation rites, while the resurrection and exaltation signify the (re)incorporation into the eternal trinitarian community, "the Trinitarian tribe" (Nyamiti 1984, 179–80). Nyamiti attempts to present this "internal Trinitarian initiation ritual" as an archetype, the hidden background and highest realization of all initiation rites.

B. Bujo also emphasizes the preeminently theological significance of the trinitarian event: "[O]nce initiated into the inner life of God, Jesus brings this initiation to expression in creation and lives it for the benefit of humankind. It is finally and definitively endorsed by the Father and taken up into divine glory through passion, death and resurrection" (Bujo 1992, 86). Like Nyamiti and Ntetem, Bujo takes up in this connection the idea of the ancestors linked with the tribal initiation, in that he describes Christ as the "archetypal ancestor" or "original ancestor." Bujo further reflects critically on the social *Sitz im Leben* of an African theology, which is characterized by an explicit harking back to indigenous tradition. He warns against conserving antiquated native traditions to the disadvantage of the liberating and integrating functions of religion in the concrete social situation in Africa.

In Melanesia, where the extensive practice of male initiation still exists, P. F. Gesch and R. Schroeder have produced initial but pioneering work. It remains, however, for indigenous Melanesian subjects to develop a more theological understanding of these practices and to integrate them into liturgical and ecclesial practice.

Both these African and Melanesian attempts should also be understood as queries about our Western theological practices. Where the serious task of a theology in the context of cultures (→contextual theology; inculturation; intercultural theology) gives way to the postcolonial interest of preserving, as in a museum, exotic initiation traditions which have long since lost their relevance and vitality in a particular society, the Western theology of mission is compromised afresh. Even when, after a long period of rude rejection of indigenous customs, a welcome opening toward "contextuality" has taken place, it remains to be asked repeatedly who propagates the integration of traditional initiation practices and Christianity, and with what interest at heart. As long as this takes place within the framework of an indigenous theology, which in this way makes the theme of "incarnation" of the gospel in the culture a necessity, the "sending churches" have no justification for barring this practice from "mission churches" which have long since been "emancipated" from them. In no cases should the old practices of initiation of traditional religions be used again as a reservoir for a new "colonial exploitation of resources" (Kuhl 1977, 266–67). The opening can be welcomed unreservedly only where "new creations" are achieved in the local congregations, because only in this way will the need for a new "incarnation" of the gospel be taken into account. The "indigenous churches" then enter into the intercultural dialogue of the one ecumenical world as equal partners — to the mutual enrichment and questioning of the members.

The experience that only an integration of "primary" and "secondary" religious experience takes account of the wholeness of life could become real for Western Christians, especially in dialogue with the initiation tradition of African tribal societies. A deepened understanding of the present secularized situation is possible against a background of initiation practices — especially an understanding of why the four chief rites of passage in life still determine the occasional practices of nominal Christians in churches of the more secularized and developed countries of Europe, North America, and Australia. The debate with the initiation traditions of the indigenous churches of Africa, Asia, and Melanesia should force Western Christianity "to clarify the common points as well as the profile of the traditions grown in a new inter-cultural horizon" (Volp 1987, 39). The deficits in the ritual accompaniment of life-crises could also be uncovered thereby, as T. Sundermeier has shown, for example, for death and burial rites.

ANDREAS GRÜNSCHLOß

Bibliography

Berilengar, A., "L'initiation traditionelle, un processus d'intégration sociale," *Telema* 17/65 (1991) 65–70. Berner, W. D., *Initiationsriten in Mysterienreligionen, im Gnostizismus und im antiken Judentum* (1972). Bettscheider, H., "Afrikanische und christliche Initiation: Theologische Begrüdung," *Verbum SVD* 18/4 (1977) 304–18. Bischofberger, O., "Die Idee der Wiedergeburt zu neuem Leben in der christlichen Taufe und in der traditionellen afrikanischen Initiation," *NZM* 27 (1971) 241–52. Bleeker, C. J., *Initiation* (1965). Bohren, R., *Unsere Kasualpraxis — eine missionarische Gelegenheit* (1961). Bujo, B., *African Theology in Its Social Context* (1992). Bürkle, H., *Missionstheologie* (1979). Bürkle, H., ed., *Theologie und Kirche in Afrika* (1968). Cavallotto, G., "Una iniziazione a dimensione catecumenale: Quale itinerario e quale chatechesi," *CatMiss* 6/1 (1990) 13–25. Cornehl, P., "Frömmigkeit — Alltagswelt — Lebenszyklus," *WPKG* 64 (1975) 388–409. Eliade, M., *Cosmos and History: The Myth of the Eternal Return* (1959). Idem, *A History of Religious Ideas* (1978). Idem, "Initiation: An Overview," *ER* 7 (1987) 225–29. Idem, *Rites and Symbols of Initiation: The Mysteries of Birth and Rebirth* (1965). Idem, *Shamanism: Archaic Techniques of Ecstasy* (1964). Gennep, A. van, *The Rites of Passage* (1960). Gensichen, H. W., *Das Taufproblem in der Mission* (1951). Gesch, P. F., *Initiative and Initiation* (1985). Jetter, W., *Symbol und Ritual: Anthropologische Elemente im Gottesdienst* (1978). Kaebler, W., "Men's Initiation," *ER* 7 (1987) 229–34. Kigasung, W., "The Value of Bukawa Initiation," *Point* (1978) 128–39. Kuhl, J., "Neue afrikanische Initiationsriten und ihre Bedeutung: Versuche in jungen katholischen afrikanischen Kirchen," *Verbum SVD* 18/4 (1977) 265–79. Lincoln, B., "Women's Initiation," *ER* 7 (1987) 234–38. Luykx, B., "Die Seele des Afrikaners und der christliche Gottesdienst," in H. Bürkle, ed., *Theologie und Kirche in Afrika* (1968) 265–76. Mbiti, J. S., *African Religions and Philosophy* (1970). Meyerhoff, B. G., L. L. A. Camino, and E. Turner, "Rites of Passage, an Overview," *ER* 12 (1987) 380–86. Müller, K., *Mission Theology: An Introduction* (1987). Mveng, E., "Christus der Initiationsmeister," in T. Sundermeier, ed., *Zwischen Kultur und Politik* (1978). Nyamiti, C., *Christ as Our Ancestor* (1984). Panoff, M., and M. Perrin, *Taschenwörterbuch der Ethnologie, Begriffe und Definitionen zur Einführung* (1982). Popp, V., ed., *Initiation — Zeremonien der Statusänderung und des Rollenwechsels: Eine Anthologie* (1969). Power, D., and L. Maldonado, eds., *Liturgy and Human Passage*, vol. 106 of *Concilium* (1979). Prickett, J., ed., *Initiation Rites* (1978). Ratoingar, N., "Le Yondo, initiation traditionelle du peuple Day an Tchad," *Tel* 17/65 (1991) 51–62. Ratschow, C. H., *Die eine christliche Taufe* (1972). Sanon, A. T., "Jesus, Master of Initiation," in R. J. Schreiter, ed., *Faces of Jesus in Africa* (1991) 85–102. Sanon, A. T., and R. Luneau, *Enraciner l'évangile: Initiations africaines et pédagogie de la foi* (1982). Schroeder, R., *Initiation and Religion: A Case Study from the Wosera of Papua New Guinea* (1992). Sundermeier, T., "Interreligiöser Dialog und die 'Stammesreligionen,'" *NZSTh* 23 (1981) 225–37. Idem, "Die 'Stammesreligionen' als Thema der Religionsgeschichte," in T. Sundermeier, ed., *Fides Pro Mundi Vita: Missionstheologie heute* (1980) 159–67. Idem, "Todesriten als Lebenshilfe: Trauerprozess in Afrika," *WZM* 29 (1977) 129–44. Idem, "Todesriten und Lebenssymbole in den afrikanischen Religionen," in G. Stephenson, ed., *Leben und Tod in den Religionen* (1980) 250–59. Sundkler, B., *The World of Mission* (1965). Thiel, J. F., *Grundbegriffe der Religionen schriftloser Völker* (1984). Idem, "Initiationsriten als Übergangsriten Tod und Auferstehung bezeichnend," *Verbum SVD* 18/4 (1977) 291–303. Turner, V., "Betwixt and Between: The Liminal Period in Rites of Passage," in W. A. Lessa and E. Z. Vogt, eds., *Reader in Comparative Religion: An Anthropological Approach* (1979) 234–43. Uzukwu, E. E., "Traditional Initiation Rites: Anthropological and

Religious Viewpoints," *Lucerna* 7/1 (1986–87) 31–41. Vicedom, G., *Die Taufe under den Heiden* (1960). Volp, R., "Die Taufe zwischen Bekenntnisaet und Kasualhandlung," *PTh* 76 (1987) 39–55. Weckman, G., "Secret Societies," *ER* 13 (1987) 151–54. Welbourn, F. B., "Keyo Initiation," *JRA* 1 (1968) 212–32. Widengren, G., *Religionsphøanomenologie* (1969). Worms, E. A., and H. Petri, "Australische Eingeborenen-Religionen," in H. Nevermann, ed., *Die Religionen der Südsee und Australiens* (1968) 125ff.

❦ INTERCULTURAL THEOLOGY ❦

1. Roots of Intercultural Theology. 2. Concepts. 3. Guidelines to an Intercultural Theology. 4. Intercultural Dialogue.

1. Extensive experiences with people and products from different cultural traditions are characteristic for our century and have resulted in new intercultural phenomena: fashions, recipes, music, medical and psychiatric forms of therapy, and esoteric and religious experiences. But they are also leading to destructive reactions: ghettoes, xenophobia, racism, insecurity, and lack of orientation. These manifestations of the culture of life and the anticulture of death are symptoms of the "sudden and far-reaching changes" (*GS* 1–2) which also challenge theology (*GS* 4, 11). Three main developments lead to "intercultural" theology.

a. Demographic shifts. As a result of the population explosion, the population of Europe (without the former Soviet Union) is increasingly becoming a minority (1960: 14 percent; 1980: 11 percent of the world population), and the economic and political power centers are shifting from the European *mare nostrum* to the *mare nostrum* of the Pacific (China, Japan, Australia, Chile, Peru, Mexico, California). By 1981, another major change had occurred: only 47 percent of Christians still belonged to the white race. These developments are accompanied by various people's efforts to become independent in the mental, economic, social, and political spheres. On the theological level, this goes hand in hand with the demands for autonomy of the →local churches. In this tension-laden challenge of "universality-particularity," the synodal principle becomes an inevitable condition for the survival of the church.

b. Diverse "languages." This "intercultural circulation" and sociodemographic metamorphosis strengthens the consciousness that diverse — semantic and cultural — forms of expression are also justified in the Christian community of faith (see *GS* 44 and *EN* 63). What is meant are not only the verbal and nonverbal theological signs and theological interpretative models but also the different religious sensibilities of world cultures with their corresponding culture of women and culture of men. "Intercultural" theology is based on the evidence that there is no longer any common binding and normative language either throughout the world or within the church.

c. Christ and the Christians. Even the witness of →Jesus Christ is affected and qualitatively enriched by these demographic and cultural-anthropological shifts. The tension between Christianity and the cultures of the Christians of the Occident, Africa, Latin America, Asia, and Oceania makes those Christians realize that the reality of Christ is more than they — as geographically and culturally determined Christians — can theologically understand and liturgically express. The same applies to the christological creeds in the Hebrew-Greek New Testament, to the models of christologies in the Eastern Greek and Western Latin churches, to the christological and soteriological models of modern times in the West, as well as to the new understandings of Christ in the African, Latin American, and Asian contexts.

Since the end of colonialism, the community of Christ and the community of Christians no longer coincide; even less so the community of Christ and various denominations. Hence, Christian intercultural theology opens itself to a growing interreligious theology in which the relationship between Christ and the cultures (according to the various backgrounds of experience and dimensions of understanding) is interpreted according to one among a number of models — for example, those of fulfillment, judgment, salvation transcending religions and history, invitation to conversion, or solidarity in suffering.

2.   The concept "intercultural theology" does not mean first and foremost a program aiming at a universal transcultural theology. It means, rather, a method which addresses forms of expression of the eternal message of the gospel ("salvation of God for all people in Jesus Christ") that are different from those grown out of one's own intellectual, liturgical, socioethical, pastoral, mystical, and political culture; these various forms of expression are received and reflected on by the members of the particular local churches with quite different cultural backgrounds.

In order to engage in this theologal and theological process which transcends national and cultural boundaries, we have to examine more closely the three basic anthropological concepts: culture, inculturation, and acculturation.

a. Culture. Culture is defined differently according to the more or less psychological, sociological, economic, or philosophical interpretations of existence. Functionally, it can be described as a plan (model, code, paradigm, system of interpretation, store of experience, *nomos*) which enables a particular society to guarantee its material survival (food, clothing, housing, health), its security in interpersonal communication (roles, kinship and friendship networks, forms of authority, social responsibility, conflicts, celebrations), and the answer to the basic questions of human existence (e.g., how to deal with suffering and death, transcendence, the profane and the holy, worldviews, the origin and goal of the history of the individual and of humankind as a whole, responsible choice, etc.). If these behavior patterns, world models, values, and "theologies" transmitted from generation to generation are not understood relatively and in relation to the various historically developed milieus but are fixed as historically absolute and normative, then a complex of reflexes and attitudes arises which is called "ethnocentrism"; it is characterized by prejudice, racism, feelings of superiority, intolerance, a colonialist mentality, religious arrogance, theological Eurocentrism, and refusal to communicate. If these models — with their corresponding ethnocentric behavior patterns — no longer guarantee the expected security because of processes like the above-mentioned social mutations, then we are confronted with anomic reactions such as malicious aggressiveness, sadism, suicide, torture, authoritarian and judgmental punitiveness, and inquisition.

b. Enculturation. The culture handed down (with its values and antivalues) confronts the new generation as a given, evident, objective quantity. The pedagogical mechanism through which these behavior patterns and evaluations become subjective thought structures and ways of acting is called enculturation (or socialization, internalization). "Language" (including extra- and paralanguage) is the decisive instrument of enculturation for the "significant others" (e.g., parents, relatives, teachers, theologians) who are entrusted by society with the responsibility for these processes of "becoming human," according to the model of the particular culture or subculture: a human being is the sum of his/her reactions to the environment.

c. Acculturation. As suggested above, these cultural models are not static but constantly in phases of development and encounter. These voluntary, planned, or imposed initiatives and phenomena within and between cultures are described as acculturation; →evangelization, missionary expansion, intercultural and inter-religious dialogue, and postcolonial self-esteem are illustrations of socioreligious change. In theological terminology, the encounter between people stamped by different cultural and religious-theological paradigms (the totality of ways of behavior and convictions of a society) is described by the neologism →inculturation. An example of this change of paradigm, in which the many different local paradigms merge as partial elements into a new, more comprehensive paradigm, is intercultural theology.

3. The above-mentioned demographic, sociological, and christological mutations and the anthropological references to "culture" lead to an increasing divergence between the basic theological themes worked out in the First and Second Worlds and the concerns of Third World theologians. Whereas the main concern of the theology in the industrialized and postindustrial societies is how faith in God can still be justified in the secularized world, the basic question of Third World theology is where and how there can still be a place for hope in an inhuman world stamped by the anticulture of death. For an intercultural theology, basic experiences such as these result in changes of emphasis which can be broadly systematized by means of the following propositions.

a. Intercultural theology is that scientific discipline concerned with God and the offer of salvation which operates in a given culture without absolutizing it. Theologies of the Eucharist and of the breaking of the Bread differ according to whether the believing Christians live in an environment destroyed by famine — and thus without bread to break — or whether they live in a highly industrialized consumer society where they share responsibility for the wholesale waste of bread which causes famine elsewhere. It is an ortho-practical sin (a heretical structure) to receive the eucharistic body in the liturgy while in everyday life allowing the social body of the Lord to die (see 1 Cor 11:18–23; Mt 25:31–46).

b. The method of intercultural theology depends on the social context. The academic and scientific theology of the Mediterranean tradition rooted in Europe (→European theology) is, therefore, still basically valid. But from the perspective of intercultural theology, its method and academic way of working can no longer be regarded as the exclusive and normative way of doing theology. The experiences with →popular religion in the basic ecclesial communities of the Third World, but also in the "cult" groups in the West, show how the people (→"people" [*Volk*], "nation") becomes the subject of theology (which then focuses on, e.g., charismatic phenomena, local hymns and narratives, meditation and sociopolitical resistance, and healings) and how a corresponding liturgical and pastoral language and a theological method take shape.

c. The research methods and community models of Western academic theology can and must be enriched by alternative forms of doing theology. Liturgical music, the language of dance, practical methods of meditation, pedagogical methods, and political peace strategies come within the scope of intercultural theology as well as the ethical discussions about genetic engineering, the risks of information science, or the painstaking historico-critical work with biblical texts.

d. Thus, intercultural theology does not dispense with the methods of rational and analytical science developed in Western culture. It demands, however, that this critical examination be applied also to the total process of intercultural, inner-ecclesiastic, and interreligious communication in which the West is only one of the participants.

4. The horizon of intercultural theology is "the global village" (M. McLuhan) in which the message of the gospel can and must be witnessed to in different cultural registers. The Christian, intercultural dialogue manifests new dimensions of the "kindness and love of God" (Ti 3:4) and hence leads to a qualitatively more comprehensive catholicity and ecumenism, in which Christ and his gospel are liberated from their "Western captivity."

RICHARD FRIEDLI

Bibliography

Please consult the bibliographies for the articles "Contextual Theology" and "Inculturation."

J

❧ JAPANESE THEOLOGY ❧

1. The Problem of Interpreting the Bible. 2. The Theology of the Cross. 3. The Adoption of Dialectic Theology and Its Effect. 4. The Theology of "Emmanuel." 5. Interfaith Dialogue. 6. Church History. 7. Japanese Christian Liberalism. 8. Catholic Theology.

1. After the intense arguments of the 1970s, the problem of the Bible became very lively once more in the Japanese theological context. The question of the canon of scripture came to the fore. The human form of →Jesus of Nazareth was separated from the Christ of preaching, and Jesus was understood as a social and political reformer. This picture of Christ was created mainly by theologians of the No Church movement (Mu-Kyokai), which goes back to Uchimura Kanzo (1861–1930). Uchimura belonged to the Sapporo Band — which an American professor and missionary, W. S. Clark (1828–86), had founded — and started his Mu-Kyokai movement in 1901. The prefix *Mu* (nothing) does not mean destroying or ignoring the church; rather, it underscores Uchimura's opinion that Christianity is neither a church nor an institution but the living person of the Lord Jesus Christ, who creates personal relationships among believers. The Mu-Kyokai movement denies the profession of a pastor and the necessity of the sacraments. It brings criticisms of the different denominations to light. The movement itself consists of living communities of the invisible church. The center of the community is the Bible. Worship means interpreting the Bible. The leader of the service and of the assembly is a layperson who works in a secular profession. Many leaders are active as authors, writing or publishing commentaries, concordances, their own journal for Bible study, and so on. Uchimura published his journal, *Bible Studies,* from 1900 until his death. Bible study is thus the most important work for Mu-Kyokai, and important Japanese students of the Bible are members of the movement. One should mention here as disciples of Uchimura, Tsukamoto Toraji (1885–1973), Kurosaki Kokichi (1886–1970), Sekine Masao (b. 1912), Kanda Tateo (b. 1897), and Maeda Goro (1919–80). The leading Japanese theologians have come from this circle of Bible scholars who turned against the traditional understanding of Jesus Christ and the scriptures. Arai Sasagu (b. 1930) states that the archetype of the human Jesus stands in contrast to the picture of the Jesus of Christianity and that Jesus must be understood as the friend of godless and weak human beings. Tagawa Kenzo (b. 1935) interprets the human Jesus in political terms. He himself, as a representative of the New Left, was a leader of the rebellious students of the 1970s. Yagi Seiichi (b. 1932) relativizes the Bible and sees it in line with other sacred writings, just as he relativizes the image of Jesus in terms of the images of other religious leaders. With this he constructs a systematic understanding of the religious existence of all people. Watanabe Zentra (1885–1978) and Takemori Masaichi (b. 1907), among others, have dedicated themselves to the interpretation of the Bible within the church. They seek to mediate between Bible studies and preaching in the life of the church.

2. The theology of the cross in Japan was put into words by Kitamori Kazoh (b. 1916) in his main work, *The Theology of the Pain of God* (1946). The *locus classicus* for the concept of the pain of God is for him Jer 31:20, "Therefore my heart yearns for him." According to Kitamori, the pain of God is not exactly identical with the love of God. The direct love of God is nothing other than law. The pain of God is the love of God at the cross of Jesus Christ. Therefore, the pain of God is more comprehensive than the direct love of God and contrasts with God's love for sinners. For Kitamori, the following three ways of thinking are significant. First, there is God's love which is not accepted by human beings and rules as law over them. The true and living God gives up the rebel sinners to death. Second, Kitamori thinks of the wrath of God. From the love and the wrath of God, according to him, a third force comes into existence at the cross of Jesus — the pain of God. The concept of the pain of God describes the tension between the love and the wrath of God. The pain of God consists, on the one hand, of this: that God cannot forgive those who are loved. On the other hand, it consists of this: that God forgives and therefore does what God cannot do. After quoting Luther's words, "Then God is in conflict with God," Kitamori declares: "The God who must give up the sinner to death is in conflict with the God who loves the sinner. The fact that they are both the same God is the pain of God." The word *tsurasa* refers to the feelings associated with suffering pain (*itami*). The concepts are thus allied but distinguishable. In the traditional Kabuki Theater one often finds plays with examples of *tsurasa*. A good example can be found in the play *Terakoya*. There the hero, Matsuomaru, learns that the enemy want to kill the son of his feudal lord. Matsuomaru and his wife deliberately send their own son into the same school (Terakoya) where the lord's son is, in order to let their son die in his place. When Matsuomaru learns that his son has died as a substitute and that the son of his lord has escaped, he cries silently with his wife and says to her, "Be glad, wife, that our son has done his duty." *Tsurasa* really works when someone gives oneself or a beloved child up to death in order to save the life of a third person. *Tsurasa* and *itami* are given a theological quality by Kitamori and form the center of his theology of the cross.

Kitamori was baptized in the Lutheran Church and studied in a Lutheran seminary. The influence of Luther's theology on Kitamori is very great. After his studies in the Lutheran seminary, he studied further at Kyoto University. He primarily attended the lectures of Tanabe Hajime (1885–1962), who was influenced by Jodo (Shin) Buddhism and who, after the Zen Buddhist philosopher Nishida Kitaro (1870–1945), was the leading personality in the Kyoto school of philosophy. Thus Kitamori was very strongly influenced by Jodo (Shin) Buddhism. His statement that Jesus Christ heals our human wounds by his own wounds is echoed in the Buddhist proposal that illness (for humans, the result of foolish love) can be healed by illness (the mercy of the Amida-Buddha). One can also see the influence of Confucianism in the facts that Kitamori holds that the relationship between Matsumaru and his feudal lord in the play is more important than the life of his son and that pain is interpreted here as being that of the father, not of the son. When *The Theology of the Pain of God* was published shortly after World War II, it found enthusiastic readers outside the church. Kitamori became the leading theologian and spokesman of the Kyodan Church (the United of Christ in Japan), from which came important moves to understand Lutheran theology in Japan, for example, the efforts of Kuramatsu Isao (b. 1928). Kitamori has been criticized for dissociating the reality of the pain of God from the plane of social ethics; in response to this criticism, he always emphasizes the transcendent character of the pain of *God*.

3. When the Japanese church was mature enough to create its own theology, dialectical theology came to Japan. Anglo-American theology, which the missionaries had brought with them, was directed to mission and the creation of the congregation/church. It became normative for the great Christian personalities, for example, Uemaraa Masahisa (1858–1925), Ebina Danjo (1856–1937), and Takakura Tokutaro (1885–1934). The dialectic theology of the 1930s, which came from Europe, worked against this in the direction of the construction of a theological system for the Japanese. For this reason, dialectical theology in Japan means not only a theological movement but the mode of thought which generally gave Japanese theology a decisive impulse. One can say that Japanese theology began with dialectical theology and that it is still influenced by it, especially by K. Barth. Kumano Yoshitaka (1898–1981) introduced dialectical theology in his book *Compendium of Dialectical Theology* (1932) and wrote, among other things, a three-volume dogmatics in which he emphasized the importance of the existence of the church. The church is the holy place in which the eternity of God takes concrete form. The church as the Body of Christ takes on the function of mediator. It is the church, not human experience, which is the fundamental factor in the continuity of the faith (this runs against liberalism). The real church is the visible church, and the character of history is essential for the church (in opposition to Mu-Kyokai thought). Kuwada Hidenobu (1895–1975), Kan Enkichi (1895–1972), Takizawa Katsumi (1909–1984), Yamamoto Kano (b. 1909), and others have introduced Barthian theology to Japan. The peculiar feature of the way Barth was received before World War II lies in the fact that his theology was misunderstood as belonging mainly to the "groves of theological academia." In the same way, the character of God as wholly other and the emphasis on →eschatology were misunderstood, as if concrete history and human endeavor should be eliminated by this or the history of the resurrection of Jesus Christ should replace the history of the cross. Therefore, it cannot come as a surprise that Barth's theological works on the political responsibility of Christians received little notice in spite of the efforts of E. Hessel (a Confessing Church missionary in Japan and a disciple of Barth's) and were not translated at all. Also, the theological conflict between Barth and E. Brunner and F. Gogarten over natural theology, which was much discussed, was understood almost exclusively in terms of orthodoxy, and very little reflection took place on the political consequences. Attempts to understand Barth's theology in its totality were first made only after World War II. One consequence of these new concerns is the confession of guilt of the Kyodan, which was initiated by Suzuki Masahisa (1912–69). Besides Barth, other Western theologians — E. Brunner, D. Bonhoeffer, P. Tillich and R. Bultmann — were introduced into Japan, and each has found adherents.

4. Takizawa Katsumi (1909–1984) studied on the recommendation of his Zen Buddhist teacher of philosophy, K. Nishida, under K. Barth in Bonn and later developed a "theology of Emmanuel." In Nishida's thought, Takizawa found the destination of the individual person, according to which the Absolute is not to be thought of as the abstract transcendent but as that which is together with the individual. The individual is much more the place in which the Absolute expresses itself. Inseparable unity, unconfusable difference, and irreversible order between the Absolute and the individual belong to the structure of the place where the individual is. While Nishida labels this circumstance "the self-identity of that which conflicts with itself," Takizawa expresses this with Christian concepts, in which he considers the philosophy of Nishida as the anonymous truth of the Christian gospel. What Nishida means by the individual's destination is summarized by Barth in the formula "Emmanuel" ("God-with-us"). Barth's formula, according to Takizawa, describes the fact that the absolute God relates personally to all people. The basic human destination is essentially nothing other than the relationship of God to people. Takizawa's thoughts can be summarized in three points:

a. The fact of Emmanuel as the basic destination of human beings. In the total unity of God and the human, in which the unconquerable difference and the absolute irreversibility prevail at the same time, human sins and original sin are thoroughly and utterly destroyed, and the promise, as well as the order, of new life is given. The human being is, in the fact of Emmanuel, truly human. The reality of Emmanuel signifies the being together of entirely unequal things. Therefore it cannot come about from the human side but can only be given by God. The human should be aware of this and give thanks. Faith means enlightenment on the question of Emmanuel. There is no time and place where this fact does not prevail. The fact of Emmanuel is not a single historical fact, limited by conditions of time and space, which should be somehow communicated and universalized. And Emmanuel is not an idea which should be retrospectively historicized and individualized. Emmanuel itself is already a wholly concrete fact.

b. Fact and sign. The fact of Emmanuel affects all people but is different from its sign in the world. The fact seeks and creates the sign, but it is not identical with it, because both are qualitatively different. If one confuses fact and sign, either the historical sign of the eternal fact is lost, or the eternal is reduced to the level of the historical.

c. The human Jesus as the sign. The human Jesus, according to Takizawa, is not the fact itself but the sign, that is, the prototype of real humanity. The word of God becoming flesh means, then, not the creation of an absolute relationship between God and human beings but the creation of signs of the relationship. The difference between the human Jesus and the prophets lies in his being the perfect sign. The cross of Jesus Christ is the sign at the center of all signs. The forgiveness of sins happens not at the cross as a sign; rather, the crucifixion itself is the sign that death is not the end. The resurrection means the revelation of Emmanuel, according to which the fact of Emmanuel without sign (i.e., Jesus of Nazareth) really exists. Takizawa's theology relativizes the form of the human Jesus and Christianity as a religion and inquires into the possibility of alterations in the essence of the system of Christian theology.

5. Interfaith dialogue between Buddhism and Christianity entered a new phase through Takizawa, a phase in which not only mutual discussion in the sense of comparative religion takes place but a new form of theology is sought. Yaeiichi (b. 1932), a descendant of the Mu-Kyokai, is influenced by Zen Buddhism and the Bultmann school of New Testament research. In his debate with Takizawa, he attempts to present a new system of the philosophy of religion. For S. Yagi, human existence in Buddhism is identical with human existence in Christianity. According to Yagi, Christian existence is one possibility of the universal existence of humanity, and if it is called Christian, then it is because it came into being through Christian proclamation. It is important for him to understand true existence as religious existence, for he believes the latter underlies all human existence. An important, but not exclusive, support for this is the New Testament. True existence is the acceptance which comes into being in deciding what is real, not what one thinks of as "being." The ground of true being is nothingness, in the sense that being is a predicate of nothingness. If true existence is effective in people, then, according to Yagi, it is none other than the creation of pure contemplation. Pure contemplation in which one is set free from all worries dedicates itself to free and creative thought, that is, to love and to relationships with others. True existence does not proceed from human spontaneity but speaks of transcendence, which is at the same time the immanent. Therefore, true existence must be a religious existence. Religious existence, according to Yagi, conceals three moments in itself: (a) the reality of transcendence; (b) its address to existence; and (c) the subjectivity of existence, which is responsible for its decision. Yagi explains the origin of New Testament thought with the concept of religious existence and finds religious existence in its pure form in the words of Jesus: "The Sabbath was made for people, not people for the Sabbath" (Mk 2:27). Besides Yagi, Honda Masaaki (b. 1929) and other Catholic theologians think along the same lines, while Haatano Seiichi (1877–1950), Agiga Tetsutaro (1899–1977), and Muto Kazuo (b. 1913) are among the great personalities of the philosophy of religion in the traditional sense.

6. One can say that the study of Christian theology in Japan began in the field of history. R. von Koeber (1848–1914), who belonged to the history-of-religions school, taught principally the history of philosophy, but also theology, in the Imperial University of Tokyo (1893–1914). Hatano Seiichi and Ishiwara Ken (1882–1976) were well-known students of his. Hatano published studies on Paul and primitive Christianity and essays in the philosophy of religion. Ishiwara published some works on the history of Christianity and Christian theology. Both were trailblazers in the field of research into history and exercised a great influence on the rising generations of theologians in the universities. Until the present day, studies in the field of the history of theology in Japan are still dominated by the outlook of the history-of-religions school.

7. Christian liberalism in Japan was represented by Ebina Danjo and Kagawa Toyohiko. Ebina (1856–1937) became famous as a minister because of his ability as a preacher. He won many hearers. Most were students who later became leading figures in different areas of academia and state affairs. In theological terms, Ebina denies the divinity of Jesus Christ and therefore the Trinity. According to him, God is our Father, and we humans are God's children. Jesus Christ gives us the certainty that we can pray to our heavenly Father together with him. Ebina does not see worship and veneration as appropriate behavior for humans, who are animated by God's Spirit, but it is their task to prove themselves in word and deed in following Jesus. The spiritual presuppositions for Ebina's theology can be seen, on the one hand, in his national consciousness as a Japanese and, on the other, in Confucianism. In his writings the Confucian ethics are not devalued by the gospel; rather, their demands are fulfilled. Therefore, his theology is based on the goodwill of human beings and their conscience. Ebina emphasizes moral consciousness as well as the personal education of men and women. For him Jesus is the model of the ideal human being.

Kagawa Toyohiko (1888–1960) was well known as a Christian because he actually lived out and demonstrated Christian love for the poor, the downtrodden, the slum-dweller. He was extremely active as an author, a preacher, and a leader of a trade-union movement. His theology is not systematic. So, for example, he does not explain the connection between the Christian faith and the solution of social problems. Kagawa was no theoretician, but a practitioner, and equally a poet and prophet. The tendency of his theology can be described as liberal. On the one hand, he emphasizes the cross of Christ and the love of God, which is revealed in his work of reconciliation. On the other, we find in him a clearly idealistic ethic and an optimistic eschatology: Christians who have experienced the love of God love their fellow human beings, and Christians redeemed by God work for liberation among their fellow human beings. Redeeming love is lived and made real by such Christians in society. In this way, the reign of God is built in the history of our world.

Japanese Christian liberalism is less interested in theological questions than in social problems and Japanese culture. It takes the view that Christianity must first adapt to Japanese culture and society in order to change them slowly from within. Under no circumstances should it call for a kind of revolution against culture and society. Because of the lack of a firm theological foundation, a liberal proclamation can lead to assimilation of the gospel with Japanese culture and society. In that regard, dialectical theology had an easy time with liberalism and was able to vanquish it theologically without any problem. A certain weakness in theological arguments and strength in respect to social involvement in liberalism were matched on the other side by the theological strength of dialectical theology and the weakness of Japanese Barthianism in relation to social and political involvement. Japanese liberalism ended with World War II in Japan. Its interest in society was taken up and developed further by the younger Barthian students, as well as by the New Testament specialists who dedicated themselves to the study of the historical Jesus.

8. The leading tendencies in Catholic theology can be indicated in the following four points.

a. The debate between Buddhism and Christianity has been taken up by a group of Catholic theologians. In this connection, the theologians H. Dumoulin (b. 1905), H. Lassalle (b. 1898), and other non-Japanese Catholics should be mentioned, as well as Kadowaki Kakichi (b. 1926) and Onodera Isao (b. 1922). Because of his experience of Zen, Kadowaki is concerned to compare Buddhist thought with Christian thinking; that is, he compares the method of thought, not the concepts and teaching of the faiths. There is no place for a higher third position in this kind of comparison. One's own religious experience can only be deepened by personal encounter and discussion. Onodera, in contrast, creates his own theology, described by him as "topological," through the comparison of Catholic theology with Buddhist philosophy.

b. The traditional task of Catholic theologians is involvement with philosophy, especially with that of Thomas Aquinas, Bonaventure, Augustine, and so on. In this field, the most important figures, all of whom provide a strong impetus *against* the Japanese world of thought, are Matsumoto Masao (b. 1910), Takahashi Wataru (b. 1909), Imamichi Tomonobus (b. 1922), Yamadara Akira (b. 1922) and Inagaki Ryosuke (b. 1928).

c. In the field of New Testament theology, two key works that have been published in German are the following: Ibuki Yu, *Die Wahrheit im Johannes-Evangelium,* and Mioshi Michi, *Der Anfang des Reiseberichts Lk 9, v 51 — 10, v 24: Eine redaktiongeschichtliche Untersuchung.* With both these publications, Catholic New Testament research took an important step forward in an area where Protestant theologians had already made a definite advance. The question of the origin of christology is discussed with especial intensity. The general tendency becomes clear in the emphasis on the identification of the historical Jesus with the Christ of the kerygma. Takayanagi Shunichi (b. 1932) says, for example, that the contrast between the historical Jesus and the Christ of faith is incorrect. Takayanagi is a systematic theologian and has written a three-volume work, rich in doctrine, about the history of the intellectual background of the phenomenon "city."

d. Of some significance as well are a number of Japanese translations of important Western theological works.

YOSHIKI TERAZONO

Bibliography

Anderson, G. H., ed., *Asian Voices in Christian Theology* (1976). Aono, T., *Kreuz und Auferstehung bei Paulus: Ein Plädoyer für die Theologie K. Takizawas und S. Yagis* (1984). Araki, T. J., *Takakura Tokutaro (1885–1934): Sein Leben und Werk im Rahmen der japanischen Theologiegeschichte* (1990). Barksdale, J., "Yagi and Takizawa: Bultmann vs. Barth in Japan," *JMB* 24 (1970). Barth, D., *Taten in Gottes Kraft: Toyohiko Kagawa, sein Leben für Christus und Japan* (1950). Best, E. E., *Christian Faith and Cultural Crisis: The Japanese Case* (1966). Böttcher, W., *Rückenansicht: Perspektiven japanischen Christentums* (1973). Caldarola, C., *Christianity: The Japanese Way* (1979). Cho, K. T., "An Essay on Kagawa Toyohiko," *AsCS* 3A (September 1960). Idem, "The Ideological Spectrum in Asia," in E. de Vries, ed., *Man in Community* (1966). Dehn, U., "Auf der Suche nach Geschichten von Menschen: Eine Theologie der Welt in Japan," *ZMiss* 16 (1990) 67–74. Demura, A., "Calvin Studies in Japan," *NEAJT* 1 (1968). Dohi, A., "Christianity in Japan," in T. K. Thomas, ed., *Christianity in Asia: North-East Asia* (1979). Doi, M., "The Nature of Encounter between Christianity and Other Religions as Witness on the Japanese Scene." in G. A. Anderson, ed., *The Theology of Christian Mission* (1961) 168–78. Drummond, R., *The History of Christianity in Japan* (1971). Elwood, D. J., ed., *What Asian Christians Are Thinking: A Theological Source Book* (1976). Endo, S., *A Life of Jesus* (1978). Idem, "On My Literature," *JMB* 26/10 (November 1972) 597–601. Idem, *Silence* (1979). Fox Young, R., "The 'Christ' of the Japanese New Religions," *JCQ* 57 (1991) 18–28. Fritsch-Oppermann, S., "Trihaya und Trinität: Über einige Aspekte des christliche-buddhistischen Dialogs in Japan," *ZMiss* 17 (1991) 224–37. Furuya, Y., "A Critical View on the So-called Asian Theology," *TSJ* 21 (1982). Idem, "The Influence of Barth on Present Day Theological Thought in Japan," *JCQ* 30 (1964) 262–97. Germany, C. H., *Protestant Theologies in Modern Japan: A History of Dominant Currents from 1920–1960* (1965). Hamer, H. E., "Der rheinische Beitrag zur Ostasien-Mission," *MEKGR* 33 (1984) 403–84. Idem, "Zur Verfolgung des rheinischen BK-Missionars Egon Hessel," *MEKGR* 34 (1985) 159–72. Hatano, S., *Time and Eternity* (1963). Hecken, J. L. van, *The Catholic Church in Japan Since 1859* (1963). Hesselink, I. J., "Emil Brunner in Japan," *JCQ* 33/2 (spring 1967). Honda, M., "Interdialogue between Buddhism and Christianity in Japan," *TSJ* 20 (1981). Iglehart, C., *A Century of Protestant Christianity in Japan* (1959). Ikado, F., and J. R. McGovern, *A Bibliography of Christianity in Japan: Protestantism in English Sources, 1859–1959* (1966). Inagaki, R., "Scholastic Studies in Japan: A Survey," *NEAJT* 4 (March 1970). In-ha, L., "A Sojourner's Theology," *JCQ* 56 (1990) 42–46. Jennings, R. P., *Jesus, Japan and Kanzo Uchimura: A Study of the View of the Church of Kanzo Uchimura and Its Significance for Japanese Christianity* (1958). Kagawa, T., *Christ and Japan* (1934). Kakichi, K., "The Baptism of Jesus: Noh Play and Mass," *JMB* 44 (1990) 3–10. Kaori, M., "The Power of Drama." *JMB* 44 (1990) 36–41. Kitagawa, J. M., "The Asian Tradition with Special Reference to Japan," *AThR* 71 (1989) 241–60 and 72 (1990) 62–84, 175–98. Idem, *On Understanding Japanese Religion* (1987). Idem, "Some Reflections on Theology in Japan," *ATR* 43 (1961) 1–19. Kitamori, K., *Theology of the Pain of God* (1965). Koyama, K., *Mt. Fuji and Mt. Sinai: A Pilgrimage in Theology* (1985). Idem, *No Handle on the Cross: An Asian Meditation on the Crucified Mind* (1977). Kumagawa, Y., and D. L. Swain, *Christianity in Japan 1970–91* (1991). Laube, J., "Hajime Tanabe's View of 'Radical Evil,'" *SID* 1 (1991) 101–15.

Lee, K. S., *The Christian Confrontation with Shinto Nationalism* (1966). Lee, R., *Stranger in the Land: A Study of the Church in Japan* (1967). Mueller, G. A., *The Catechetical Problem in Japan 1549–1965* (1967). Nemeshegyi, P., "Theology of the Way: An Attempt of Inculturated Theology in Japan," *StMiss* 45 (1996) 153–67. Ogata, M. B., "What We Can Learn from Japan's New Religious Movements," *EMQ* 27 (1991) 362–69. Ogawa, K., *Die Aufgabe der Neueren evangelischen Theologie in Japan* (1965). Idem, "Zum Verständnis der Auferstehung Jesu Christi aus japanischer Sicht," *ZDTh* (1988) 227–40. Oguro-Opitz, B., *Analyse und Auseinandersetzung mit der Theologie des Schmerzes Gottes von K. Kitamori* (1980). Parker, F. C., "Baptist Missions in Japan 1945–1973: A Study in Relationships," *JCQ* 40/1 (1974). Phillips, J. M., *From the Rising of the Sun: Christians and Society in Contemporary Japan* (1981). Piovesana, G. K., *Recent Japanese Philosophical Thought 1862–1962: A Survey* (1963). Rosenkranz, G., ed., *Christus kommt nach Japan* (1959). Shimizu, M., *Das "Selbst" im Mahayana-Buddhismus in japanischer Sicht und die "Person" im Christentum im Licht des Neuen Testaments* (1981). Sottocornila, F., "The Tea Ceremony and the Mass: Towards Inculturation of the Liturgy in Japan," *JMB* 44 (1990) 11–27. Spae, J. J., *Buddhist-Christian Empathy* (1980). Idem, *Christian Corridors to Japan* (1965). Idem, *Christianity Encounters Japan* (1968). Idem, *Christians of Japan* (1970). Idem, *Japanese Religiosity* (1971). Sundermeier, T., "Das Kreuz in japanischer Interpretation," *EvTh* 44 (1984) 417–40. Suzuki, D. T., *Mysticism: Christian and Buddhist* (1957). Tagawa, K., "The Yagi-Takizawa Debate," *NEAJT* 2 (1969). Takizawa, K., *Das Heil im Heute: Texte einer japanischen Theologie* (1987). Idem, *Reflexionen über die universale Grundlage von Buddhismus und Christentum* (1980). Idem, "Zen Buddhism and Christianity in Contemporary Japan," *NEAJT* 4 (1970). Terazono, Y., *Die Christologie Karl Barths und Takizawas* (1976). Idem, "Über das Handeln der Menschen und das Christusverständnis in der theologischen Bemühung Takizawas," in H. Reiffen, ed., *Christen und Marxisten in unserer Gesellschaft heute* (1983). Terazono, Y., and H. Hamer, eds., *Brennpunkte in Kirche und Theologie Japans* (1986). Yagi, S., "The Dependence of Japanese Theology upon the Occident," *JCQ* 30/4 (1964). Yagi, S., and U. Luz, eds., *Gott in Japan: Anstösse zum Gespräch mit japanischen Philosophen, Theologen, Schriftstellern* (1973). Yamamori, T., *Church Growth in Japan* (1974). Yasui, T., *Christus und Buddha* (1981). Young, J. M. T., *The Two Empires in Japan: A Record of Church-State Conflict* (1958).

❧ JESUS ❧

1. The Quest for the Historical Jesus. 2. Sociological Approach. 3. Jewish and Anti-Jewish Interpretations. 4. Political Interpretations. 5. Cultural Integration. 6. Non-Christian Interpretations.

"Without being guilty of an exaggeration, one can say that the question of the historical Jesus has become one of the most important problems, if not the most important problem, of theology" (F. Gogarten). The interest in Jesus is intense not only in classical Western theology but also in Christian communities in all parts of the world. Even non-Christians, chiefly Marxists, have been confronted with Jesus of Nazareth. Ultimately, the question of Jesus is posed not only as the question of the historical Jesus, in the sense of the central European tradition of historical criticism. Cultural and contemporary social conditions have far more of an influence on the preoccupation with Jesus. In the same way, the academic approach plays a large part, as well as the particular perspective and special interests of the inquirer. Six models of interpretation can be outlined.

1. The "quest for the historical Jesus" has been a major preoccupation of theology from the beginning of the Enlightenment up to the present day. Its history is one of an increasing distinction being made between the church's dogmatic convictions about Jesus Christ (→christology) and the historically verifiable knowledge about Jesus of Nazareth. At the beginning, there was the intention to free Jesus, who was conceived as "chained to the rock of church doctrine" (A. Schweitzer). Most of the time the only Jesus to emerge was one who conformed to the spirit of those particular times. Schweitzer set up a literary monument to the "life of Jesus research" which at the same time was its obituary notice (1906). This process of research gave exegesis an increasingly narrow basis of assured insights about Jesus. Liberal theology denies that one can write a biography of Jesus (A. von Harnack: *vita Christi scribi nequit*), yet our knowledge suffices for a "character sketch" of Jesus. This possibility bids farewell to the form-criticism exegesis (especially R. Bultmann's) but means that one can reconstruct the outlines of Jesus' message, even if the authenticity of a particular single saying cannot be guaranteed.

The quest for the historical Jesus appeared to be lost for a time in the insights of the dialectical theology movement especially, as well as in the methodological "aphorisms" in relation to the sources for research into Jesus. Bultmann declared the question of the historical Jesus to have failed; this claim was based not only on Bultmann's "brazen skepticism" about the question but also on problems associated with historical criticism itself (the failure of theories about the literary sources for the oldest, most authentic source about Jesus, the insight of form criticism that the oldest oral tradition was itself already shaped by the faith of the original community). Bultmann's declaration is rooted in theological ground; faith does not depend on the historical form of the Nazarene; rather, it comes from the church's preaching of Jesus as Christ. Theology cannot, and should not, go back behind the kerygma. From a different perspective, K. Barth criticized the quest for the historical Jesus by reacting to the doctrine of the anhypostasia. A. von Harnack, against the point of view of the dialectical theology movement, had already expressed his fears that it would put a "dreamed-up Christ" in the place of the real Christ, because it had abandoned historical research. His questioning reappears in an altered form in the Bultmann school.

"The new quest" (J. M. Robinson) for the historical Jesus developed above all in the circle of students around Bultmann (E. Käsemann, G. Ebeling) and, for a time, and in appearance only, reversed the lines drawn between liberal and kerygmatic theology. Therefore, the differences within historical criticism were not so great as they had been earlier; for example, there was common ground between J. Jeremias, who wanted to establish the historical authenticity of individual sayings of Jesus as *ipsissima vox,* and Bultmann himself, who admittedly had no doubts about the tenor of Jesus' preaching, even when he did have doubts about individual sayings. In all the vehement and hectic revival of the question of the historical Jesus, Käsemann has not gone further than Bultmann when he considers it historically possible to recognize "characteristic features of Jesus' proclamation." Bultmann had no doubts about this. At any rate, there is a difference between Bultmann, Käsemann, and Jeremias in their estimation of the significance of the relevance of the historical knowledge of Jesus of Nazareth for the faith. Three positions are possible in relation to such knowledge. First, Bultmann offers a position of radical negation, according to which one cannot and must not go further theologically than the "coming of Jesus." Second, Jeremias offers an affirmative position, according to which the historical Jesus becomes the criterion of christology, for example, of the kerygma. Third, Käsemann (like Bultmann) points to the New Testament itself for support for his position. Bultmann would say that Paul and John are content with the pure "that"; Käsemann would say that if the pure "that" were sufficient, the origins of the Gospels as recollections of the life and work of the earthly Jesus remain inexplicable.

Somewhat along the lines of the "new quest" is E. Schillebeeckx's *Jesus: An Experiment in Christology*. Schillebeeckx uses sophisticated historical methods and (in the 1970s, when the book was written) the latest biblical scholarship in an attempt to paint a picture of Jesus that would to lead the believer to a "disclosure experience" of Jesus' meaning in history and especially in the contemporary world.

Despite the differences, all these positions aim at an individual image of Jesus within the contours of the history of religion and of ideas. In contrast, the most recent sociological and social-historical research into Jesus opens a new page in the history of the quest for the historical Jesus because it does not separate the earthly Jesus from his followers and seeks to understand him in the context of his contemporaries. This new interest in Jesus would be unthinkable without the impetus from Latin American →liberation theology.

2. The new question posed by social history and sociology about Jesus does not focus only on the individual person of Jesus or precise historical situations of his life. It works methodologically on "making concrete or individual examples out of the typical" (W. Conze). Two approaches can be distinguished in methodological and theological terms. On the one hand, there is the materialist reading (examples are works by F. Belo, M. Clevenot, and K. Füssel) created in the sphere of Romance linguistics and language-theory; the approach links the positions of historical materialism with textual theories of French structuralism. On the other hand, there is the exegesis which stands in the academic tradition of historical criticism and expressly connects it with social history and sociology (see works by L. Schottroff, W. Stegemann, and G. Theissen); this approach plays a significant role in North American exegesis (see J. Elliott and W. A. Meeks). The materialist reading is of course emphatically interested in the "subversive," "messianic action" of Jesus, not in the historical Jesus. The "action" (praxis) of Jesus, then, means here the action of an "actor" in a narrative, not the real behavior of the man from Nazareth. Belo considers the quest for the historical Jesus among the fundamental mistakes of the idealist school of history. In line with the historical-critical approach, G. Theissen systematically poses the Jesus question in reference to the "sociology of the Jesus movement." According to this, Jesus is the founder of a movement of "wandering charismatics" whose radical ethos (no families, no homes, no possessions) was the expression of a specific, real-life situation. This Jewish renewal movement, which grew out of the crisis of the society of those days, had, according to Theissen, drawn its recruits from the "marginalized middle class." Countering this, Schottroff and Stegemann consider that Jesus himself and his disciples belonged to the lowest class of the Judeo-Palestinian society of their time and that Jesus founded a "movement of the poor for the poor" (W. Stegemann). Exactly in the same way, Jesus' death on the cross can be explained in terms of social history by the fact of the politics of the occupying power, which brutally suppressed the (unarmed) movement of enthusiasts. As far as this goes, Jesus' death was no miscarriage of justice (as Bultmann maintains), and Jesus was no revolutionary (as M. Hengel claims), yet he still died as an anti-Roman rebel and was regarded as such by the Romans. The social-historical aspect of research into Jesus has been taken up especially by theologians from the Third World, who base their liberation christology on the historical Jesus. In the United States, J. D. Crossan has used sociological and anthropological sources for his study of Jesus, and, in a less controversial way, J. Meier also has employed the social sciences in his important work.

The psychological interpretation of Jesus has received much attention in the German-speaking world, as in the United States. Indeed, Freud was not interested in the real man from Nazareth but concentrated on the christological doctrine of sacrificial death, through which the tribe of the fathers was changed into a "community of brothers." E. Fromm linked this totemist aspect with Marxist criticism of society. According to Fromm, Jesus' summoning of the oppressed to freedom was the "Son's putsch" against the "Father God"; after Christianity became the religion of the ruling classes, it became necessary to resolve this in "the harmony of the eternal unity of being" of Father and Son. T. Brocher understands the sacrificial death of Jesus as a countermodel to the Oedipus myth: here the son is sacrificed while the father triumphs. The Oedipus myth may have uncomfortable implications, but so does Christianity: by preaching an attitude of sacrifice in the subordination of the son, it can open the way for toleration of dictators (the "fathers" who demand sacrifice). K. Niederwimmer understands Jesus in his depth-psychology interpretation as a "symbol for human existence," especially as a symbol (and justification) of "failure." J. Scharfenberg wants to weaken the criticism of the psychology of "filial sacrifice"; thus he explains the Pharisees as representatives of an obsessive-neurotic system, from which Jesus called people.

3. J. Weiss (*Die Predigt Jesu vom Reiche Gottes* [1892]) and E. Schürer (*Geschichte des Judentums im Zeitalter Jesu Christi* [1901]) attempted to understand Jesus logically from the Judaism of their day. W. Bousset opposed this in his *Predigt Jesus in ihrem Gegensatz zum Judentum* (1892). His "portrait of decadence" (E. Stegemann) influenced generations of New Testament scholars. Bultmann considered the preaching of Jesus, who was a Jew and not a Christian, as one of the prerequisites of New Testament theology. For Käsemann, Jesus was first an "evangelist" and not a "bearer of the law." He is not interested in exploring the Jewishness of the historical Jesus. He emphasizes that the historical Jesus had broken with Judaism and had even overcome it. The picture of Jesus drawn by many Christian exegetical scholars is broadly a presentation of profound and permanent conflicts of Jesus with Judaism. Not infrequently Jesus is described (favorably) as the sovereign lawbreaker (H. Braun). Many Jewish authors consider this picture of Jesus to be a Christian projection. D. Flusser makes us consider whether secret anti-Semitism is concealed behind this zeal. Under the impact of the Holocaust, even Christian theologians are beginning to classify Jesus in the Judaism of his time. J. Klausner's interpretation of Jesus remains fundamental to this (and within Judaism itself). He shows that Jesus' teaching can be explained by biblical and rabbinical Judaism. J. Pawlikowski's thought, as well as that of H. Perelmuter, is also along these lines. The majority of modern Jewish authors conjecture that Jesus himself was a Pharisee or at least was close to Pharisaism (D. Flusser, S. Ben Chorin, P. Lapide). They are broadly agreed that Jesus' relationship to the Torah did not go beyond the bounds of contemporary Judaism. M. Buber's statements about Jesus as "brother" have (in contradistinction to Klausner) had more effect in Christian than in Jewish circles. S. Ben Chorin's interpretation of Jesus stands more in this tradition.

4. Latin American theology prefers a christology which is mainly interested in the historical Jesus. On the one hand, it is interested in the "similarity of structures" (L. Boff) between the social situation at the time of Jesus and the South American contemporary situation. On the other hand, liberation theologians are interested in the relation between their own political action as discipleship and the "action" of Jesus. The experience of direct simultaneity with Jesus and being in touch with his power for liberation results often from the (common) "rereading" (*releitura*) of the Gospels with the eyes of the oppressed. The poor of Latin America discover in the Gospels their own social circumstances; in Jesus, they encounter "the God of the poor" and "God the worker," who is simple and human, who sweats in the streets, who is at the same time "comrade" and victor over death, and who is resurrected in every arm raised to defend the people. The resurrection in particular becomes a political message of resistance. The materialist reading of F. Belo, a former Portuguese priest, has had an influence on the *releitura* mainly in Brazil. One should not keep silent about the fact that this exposition of the Bible has been discussed in terms of anti-Semitism, in that it expresses social contrasts between Jesus' time and the present time as religious contrasts, through negative comparisons with Judaism.

In the "black theology" (→African theology; black theology) of black Americans and Africans, Christ is invested with a direct contemporary identity as the "black liberator." Black theologians underscore that Jesus not only came from the poor and belonged to an oppressed people (i.e., they were oppressed by the Romans) but also knew himself to be sent to the poor, the exploited, and the oppressed and declared war on poverty and oppression. Luke 4:19 becomes a key text here. It should be noted that this approach to the historical Jesus has come under some sharp criticism from certain exegetes, notably the U.S. scholar J. Meier.

In contrast, in South Korea, which in the 1920s showed the influence of central European theology in the social-revolutionary interpretation of Jesus as proletarian and socialist (S. Chan-Kun), a genuine Korean interpretation is achieved in which the understanding of Jesus as liberator (verified especially in the healing of the sick) gradually received a political content. This approach finds its most significant Korean expression in minjung theology, in which Jesus is understood as the friend of the minjung (collective term for the economically poor, socially and culturally marginalized, and politically oppressed people [see S. Nam-Dong]). The theology of S. Nam-Dong, which is far more radical than other Korean theologies (the Lord's Prayer is reserved for the poor alone), is not shared by Byung-Mu Ahn, the most significant representative of minjung theology today. Ahn sees the minjung in the Galilean *ochlos,* to whom Jesus dedicated the message of salvation. He identifies them with the powerless and propertyless mass of the people, as opposed to the ruling classes and the privileged. In harking back to Jesus, minjung theology is concerned not only with individual salvation but principally with the salvation of society. The key text for this is Lk 4:16–21. If one examines this theology in relation to the question of the historical Jesus, then one can say: "minjung is more interested in the Christ-event than in the kerygma. Jesus, as the one who became *sarx,* is a worker, uneducated and in poverty. Weak against the rich and mighty, he goes to Jerusalem and does not avoid confrontation. Therefore he is crucified by the mighty. The crucifixion is the 'self-ascendance of the flesh'" (Ahn). This event happens today as well in minjung events. In the suffering of the minjung, one experiences the suffering of Jesus; conversely, the present suffering of the minjung becomes clearer in Jesus' suffering. In this sense, the Jesus-event is more important than the kerygma. Minjung theology is precisely an attempt to understand the Christian faith in general and Jesus Christ in particular in and from the minjung's own cultural and social situation.

5. The cross and suffering of Christ are interpreted in other cultural areas (e.g., in →African theology; Japanese theology) under the influence of their own cultural history. Under the impact of national defeat, K. Kitamori outlined a theology of proud pain on the cross of Christ; the "nationalistic overtones" (T. Sundermeier) of this theology, set against the background of the Samurai tradition, were criticized in Japan itself. K. Takizawa interpreted the cross in the depths of *kenosis,* in the context of various cultural-religious traditions. In his writings, Jesus becomes the prototype of fulfilled humanity precisely in simply being human. The specific cultural and mythological traditions make an African theology possible, for example, by seeing in the birth, baptism, and death of Jesus the expression of his incorporation in humanity, his active participation as a member of society, and his complete identification with humanity (J. Mbiti). Traditional tribal thought interprets Christ as "chief" and understands him also as "the connecting link between the living and the dead" (P. Sandner). Among other things, he is Christus Victor, the victor over the natural and supernatural powers and forces, which manifest themselves in spirit possession, illness, even in strife and death (Mbiti). Conversely, the cultural strangeness of the Jesus encountered in the scriptures (e.g., in proclamation) can correspond to these integrative interpretations. So Lin Yu-Tang emphasizes, from his Chinese tradition, the ethical aspects of the Sermon on the Mount but praises also, in contrapuntal form to his own tradition, Jesus' clarity and the spontaneity of love, his acting instead of contemplation (C.-S. Song).

6. Naturally, christological statements come up against incomprehension from non-Christians in a special way. For M. Gandhi, the concept of incarnation was a stumbling block, yet what Jesus had done was important to him (→Indian theology). S. Radhakrishnan, a Hindu, separated the earthly Jesus as "guru" from the heavenly Christ, whom he located in the assembly of the gods, practically in a Gnostic-dualist way. A. Augstein has discovered Jesus, "the Son of Man," as the child of earthly parents. E. Bloch, V. Gardavsky, and M. Machoveč produced interpretations under the influence of modern Marxism. Bloch has emphasized the real messianic nature of Jesus and his future utopia and placed Jesus in a compressed relationship to Moses and the exodus. For Gardavsky, Jesus is the "model of a human decision for human beings" (W. Kern), while Machoveč emphasizes "Jesus for atheists" and understands Marxists as legitimate inheritors and secular successors of the cause of Jesus.

Wolfgang Stegemann

Bibliography

Boff, L., *Jesus Christ Liberator: A Critical Christology for Our Time* (1978). Brandt, H., ed., *Die Glut kommt von unten: Texte einer Theologie aus der eigenen Erde* (1981). Bravo, C., "Jesus of Nazareth, Christ the Liberator," in I. Ellacuría and J. Sobrino, eds., *Mysterium Liberationis: Fundamental Concepts of Liberation Theology* (1993) 420–39. Clevenot, M., *So kennen wir die Bibel nicht* (1978). Commission on Theological Concerns of the Christian Conference of Asia, ed., *Minjung Theology* (1983). Cone, J. H., *A Black Theology of Liberation* (1986). Crossan, J. D., *The Historical Jesus: The Life of a Mediterranean Jewish Peasant* (1991). Idem, *Jesus: A Revolutionary Biography* (1994). Dantine, W., *Jesus von Nazareth in der gegenwärtigen Diskussion* (1974). DeMesa, J. M., and L. L. Wostyn, *Doing Christology* (1989). Dupuis, J., *Who Do You Say I Am?* (1994). Gnilka, J., "Neue Jesusliteratur," *ThR* 67 (1971) 249–56. Johnson, E. A., *Consider Jesus: Waves of Renewal in Christology* (1990). Kasper, W., *Jesus the Christ* (1977). Keck, L., *A Future for the Historical Jesus: The Place of Jesus in Preaching and Theology* (1980). Kitamori, K., *Theology of the Pain of God* (1965). Knoebel, J., ed., *Christ in Melanesia: Exploring Theological Issues* (1977). Macquarrie, J., *Jesus Christ in Modern Thought* (1990). Meier, J. P., "The Bible as a Source for Theology," in G. Kilcourse, ed., *CTSA Proceedings* (1988) 1–14. Idem, *A Marginal Jew: Rethinking the Historical Jesus* (1991). Pawlikowski, J., *Jesus and the Theology of Israel* (1989). Robinson, J. M., *A New Quest of the Historical Jesus* (1966). Samuel, V., and C. Sugden, eds., *Sharing Jesus in the Two Thirds World* (1983). Sandner, P., "Jesus Christus im Bekenntnis afrikanischer Kirchen," *ZfM* 1 (1975) 68–77. Schillebeeckx, E., *Church: The Human Story of God* (1990). Idem, *Jesus: An Experiment in Christology* (1979). Schreiter, R. J., ed., *Faces of Jesus in Africa* (1991). Sobrino, J., *Christology at the Crossroads* (1978). Idem, *Jesus in Latin America* (1987). Sugirtharajah, R. S., ed., *Asian Faces of Jesus* (1993). Sundermeier, T., *Christus, der schwarze Befreier* (1973). Idem, "Das Kreutz in japanischer Interpretation," *EvTh* 44 (1984) 417–40. Theissen, G., *The Gospels in Context: Social and Political History in the Synoptic Tradition* (1991). Idem, *The Shadow of the Galilean: The Quest of the Historical Jesus in Narrative Form* (1987). Idem, *Sociology of Early Palestinian Christianity* (1978). Thoma, C., "Jüdische Zugänge zu Jesus Christus," *ThB* 7 (1978) 149–76. Yoder, J. H., *The Politics of Jesus* (1972).

❧ JUDAISM ❧

1. The Mission of Israel.   2. Mission to Israel?   3. Israel's Significance for the Mission of the Church.   4. Joint Witness of Jews and Christians.

1.   The Jewish understanding of mission has always been closely linked to the notion of "chosenness." This sense of the Jewish people's chosenness has provided a purpose for existence and sustained its members during the many trials and persecutions that have befallen them. Jews have never regarded this concept of chosenness as something resulting from special merit. Nor has it generally been interpreted as a sign of superiority over others. It has been described rather as the basis for a mission of outreach to the world, bringing knowledge of God's presence, God's omnipotence, and God's omniscience to all the nations of the earth. The ultimate goal of this Jewish mission was to be acknowledgment by all humankind of the universality of the one God. This sense of universal mission has prophetic roots, particularly the teachings of Jeremiah, Ezekiel, and, above all, Isaiah, who has God proclaim: "Turn to me and gain success. All the ends of the earth! For I am God, and there is none else" (Is 45:22). It is also rooted in the blessing of Abraham, "Be a blessing,... and all the families of the earth shall be blessed through you" (Gn 12:2–3).

When we turn to Talmudic literature, we see a continuation of the sense of mission found in the Hebrew scriptures. One of the most notable examples of this comes in the rabbinic reinterpretation of the career of Abraham. The Talmudic literature depicts Abraham as a missionary who engaged actively in disseminating his faith. Abraham's call is said to have been preceded by his profound frustration with the moral decadence rampant in the world. Through his call Abraham recognized, according to the Talmud, that God had summoned him to assist in saving the world. He was to serve as God's answer to the waywardness of the human community and commit his life, through teaching and example, to setting humankind on the course of righteousness. The verse, "And Abraham took Sarah his wife...and all the persons they had acquired in Haran" (Gn 12:5), was taken as referring to the converts they had made. The rabbis also suggested that the Torah was given while the Israelites sojourned in the Sinai Desert, regarded by them as a no-man's land, as a sign that it was not intended for the exclusive possession of the Jews but was intended to be offered to all who were open to live according to its precepts.

In the post-Talmudic period, leading Jewish thinkers continued the biblical/ Talmudic thrust regarding mission. Maimonides (1135–1205) regarded the duty of giving religious witness as a formal commandment incumbent upon all Jews. But he likewise acknowledged that such religious witness did not need to include bringing non-Jews into the fold of Israel in a formal way. The so-called pious who believed in the creator God and followed the divine commandments were assured of a share in the world to come. The Hasidic master Rabbi Nahman of Bratslav (1772–1810) described such a "pious" person as a "convert-in-essence," even if not in fact. He bases this view on the words of the prophet Malachi (1:11), who spoke of the name of God being honored among the nations of the world "from the rising of the sun to its going down." In more recent times, leading Jewish religious thinkers such as Rabbi A. I. Kook and F. Rosenzweig have depicted Judaism as offering a unique religious witness to the human community. But for both Kook and Rosenzweig this witness did not stand in opposition to the witness of other religious groups. Rather the various forms of religious witness exist in a fundamentally complementary relationship. All religious traditions are channels through which the human spirit may grow in enlightenment.

2. The question whether Christianity has a "mission to Israel" remains a disputed issue within the churches today. For years many Protestant denominations maintained formal "missions to the Jews." Many of those have now disappeared, especially among the more liberal denominations. Catholicism never had anything quite as formal in this regard. Two related religious communities, the Fathers of Sion and the Sisters of St. Mary of Sion, were founded by a Jewish convert to Christianity named Ratisbonne with the intent that they would bring other Jews into the Catholic Church. However, both religious communities tended in practice to confine their outreach to Jews historically to the realm of prayer. And since Vatican II both have become leaders in promoting dialogue with Jews rather than advocating conversion.

Overall, the Catholic Church has increasingly marginalized any organized effort to convert Jews. At the 1977 Venice meeting of the International Jewish-Catholic Dialogue, T. Federici of Rome, a member of the Vatican delegation, presented a paper in which he argued that "witness" ought to replace "proselytism" in terms of the Jewish-Christian relationship. In the subsequent published version of his paper, the term was changed to "undue proselytism." Federici defined "undue proselytism" as the use of "physical, moral, psychological or cultural constraints on the Jews, both individuals and communities, such as might in any way destroy or even simply reduce their personal judgment, free will and full autonomy of decision at the personal or community level" (see International Catholic-Jewish Liaison Committee 1988, 57). For Federici, Vatican II's *Dignitatis Humanae* had to condition any discussion of witness and proselytism. Subsequently the official Catholic position on mission/witness has been marked mostly by silence. Jews were not specifically mentioned, for example, in the Vatican document on mission entitled *Redemptoris Missio.*

Among the Protestant churches there has been a serious division of the house on the issue of "missionizing Jews." Generally the liberal denominations have severely qualified any obligation along these lines without formally renouncing it in recent years. One clear indication of this is found within the World Council of Churches (WCC). Its Consultation on the Church and the Jewish People began under the umbrella of the International Missionary Council, and that relation remained in effect until 1961, when the council was formally merged with the

WCC. This merger saw a shift of the work on Christian-Jewish relations to the WCC department engaged in dialogue with people of other faiths and a general shift in WCC documents from a missionary approach to the Jewish people toward espousal of a dialogical relationship between Jews and Christians. The 1948 Amsterdam assembly of the WCC had underlined the importance of including the Jewish people in the work of Christian evangelism, even though pressures or "unworthy inducements" were to be avoided in any missionary outreach to Jews. By 1967, however, the tone had changed. The WCC's Faith and Order Commission, meeting in Bristol, England, argued that mission should be replaced by service in approaching the Jewish community.

The shift from mission to dialogue with respect to the Jews is also evident within many Protestant denominations and regional church councils. The Lutheran World Federation in a 1982 document described the church's encounter with Judaism as mutually transforming, even though it may continue to include a witness to Jesus Christ on the part of Christians. The synod of the Rhineland Church in Germany in 1980 spoke of a shared Jewish-Christian witness to the divine presence in the world and specifically excluded Jews from the church's mission to the "peoples of the world." In the United States, the Texas Conference of Churches (1982) and the Presbyterian Church (1987) both stressed that dialogue, rather than mission, must now be regarded as the desired posture between Christians and Jews.

This discernible shift in the approach to the Jewish people on the part of many within mainline Christianity has brought about rejoinders from individual Christian theologians and from groups associated with evangelical Christianity. Two statements in particular stand out. The first is the "Willowbank Declaration" on "the Christian gospel and the Jewish people" adopted unanimously by the World Evangelical Fellowship at a consultation at Willowbank, Bermuda, in 1989. The document is critical of those Christians who have abandoned evangelistic efforts directed toward the Jewish community in light of the Holocaust and have moved to a posture of dialogue. It clearly affirms that "the concern to point Jewish people to faith in Jesus Christ, which the Christian church has historically felt and shown, was right" (art. 4.20). Such a concern must remain a central priority for the church, according to the "Willowbank Declaration." Two years later the Lausanne Committee on World Evangelism, meeting in Zeist, the Netherlands, called upon "the whole church to take the whole Gospel to the Jewish people everywhere." A follow-up conference of the Lausanne Consultation held in Jerusalem in 1995 warned churches that any viewpoint which presumed that Jews could be reconciled to God outside of Jesus did dishonor to Jesus. Its document reaffirmed the need for all Christians "to recognize the legitimacy and the urgency of sharing the Good News of Jesus, the Jewish Messiah, with those people from whom and for whom he first came."

D. A. Hagner, a member of the faculty at Fuller Theological Seminary in California (a leading evangelical institution), has argued that while dialogue is valuable and while Judaism can provide an important corrective to Christian thinking on some points and while Jews should not be approached in the same manner as "pagans," nonetheless faithfulness to the New Testament demands that the church continue to evangelize the Jews. Christians cannot regard Judaism as an alternate route to salvation. The Southern Baptists have made this point in a statement that has been strongly criticized by Jews and several Christian leaders.

3. Increasingly, Christian groups engaged in the encounter with Jews, as well as individual theologians in the dialogue, have begun to argue that Jews are integral to the ultimate "mission" of the church. Pope John Paul II has spoken of Jews and Christians as intimately related at the basic level of their identities. In other words, they are inseparably linked as partners in the emergence of the divine reign. The Episcopal theologian P. van Buren, author of the most comprehensive contemporary study of the theology of the Jewish-Christian relationship (3 vols.), has insisted that "Israel" in its fullest sense embraces both the church and the Jewish people. The fullness of the New Testament view of Israel cannot be attained, as he sees it, without a reunion of Jews and Christians.

Other theologians have emphasized that Israel's mission is to complement and correct the Christian perspective on salvation. Specifically, the Jewish tradition can enhance Christianity's sense of the basic goodness of all creation, of the centrality of community and covenant, of the importance of land, and of the demands of justice and the importance of future hope. At a deeper level, some theologians argue that the Jewish "no" to Jesus should be viewed as a constructive contribution to christological understanding, as a corrective to the many wrong turns that christology has taken over the years. Israel's refusal of the gospel may serve the church as a powerful curb against a worldly, triumphalistic ethos that has captured its self-understanding.

4. A common prophetic witness by Jews and Christians "in the face of nihilism and despair," as A. J. Heschel put it, is incumbent upon Jews and Christians today as an affirmation of the creator and redeemer of the world. Contemporary Christian-Jewish dialogue has deep roots in such an affirmation. Many of the European dialogue groups grew out of relationships forged in efforts of resistance toward the Nazis. And in the United States the early Christian-Jewish relationships developed from joint efforts led by the Federal Council of Churches, the Central Conference of American Rabbis, and the National Catholic Welfare Conference to improve the condition of the working class in the United States. This coalition played a central role in the passage of the important social legislation connected with the New Deal. Scholars such as R. Chopp and K. Adloff have explicitly linked the Christian-Jewish dialogue with common action on behalf of the suffering of the world. Only through such witness of service will the new dialogue be liberated from introversion. Such a "world mission" is rooted in a belief in the one God who, according to the hope of the Jews as well as Christians, will eventually triumph over the powers of evil and will be "all in all" (1 Cor 15:28).

JOHN PAWLIKOWSKI, OSM

Bibliography

Adloff, K., "Die missionarische Existenz des Apostles Paulus nach dem Zweiten Korintherbrief," *BThZ* 3 (1986) 11–27. Barth, K., *CD*, IV/3.2, IV.3.3 (1962). Barth, M., *Israel and the Church: Contribution to a Dialogue for Peace* (1969). Baumann, A. H., *Christliches Zeugnis und die Juden heute: Zur Frage der Judenmission* (1981). Beck, N. A., *Mature Christianity in the 21st Century: The Recognition and Repudiation of the Anti-Jewish Polemic in the New Testament* (1994) (contains comprehensive bibliography). Boccaccini, G., *Middle Judaism: Jewish Thought: 300 B.C.E. to 200 C.E.* (1991). Breuning, W., and H. Heinz, eds., *Damit die Erde menschlich bleibt: Gemeinsame Verantwortung von Juden und Christen für die Zukunft* (1985). Brocke, E., and J. Seim, eds., *Gottes Augapfel: Beiträge zur Erneuerung des Verhältnisses von Christen und Juden* (1986). Brooks, R., and J. J. Collins, *Hebrew Bible or Old Testament: Studying the Bible in Judaism and Christianity* (1990). Burrows, W., ed., *Redemption and Dialogue: Reading "Redemptoris Missio" and "Dialogue and Proclamation"* (1994). Charlesworth, J. H., ed., *Jesus'*

Jewishness: Exploring the Place of Jesus in Early Judaism (1991). Idem, *Jews and Christians: Exploring the Past, Present, and Future* (1990). Chrostowski, W., ed., *Dziece Jednego Boga* (1991). Conzelmann, H., *Gentiles / Jews / Christians: Polemics and Apologetics in the Greco-Roman Era* (1992). Croner, H., ed., *Stepping Stones to Further Jewish-Christian Relations: An Unabridged Collection of Christian Documents* (1977). Idem, *More Stepping Stones to Jewish-Christian Relations: An Unabridged Collection of Christian Documents 1975–1983.* (1985). Croner, H., and L. Klenicki, eds., *Issues in the Jewish-Christian Dialogue: Jewish Perspectives on Covenant, Mission, and Witness* (1979). Davies, A. T., ed., *Anti-Semitism and the Foundations of Christianity* (1979). Dunn, J. D. G., *The Partings of the Ways: Between Christianity and Judaism and Their Significance for the Character of Christianity* (1991). Eckardt, A. R., *Jews and Christians: The Contemporary Meeting* (1986). Idem, *Reclaiming the Jesus of History: Christology Today* (1992). Everett, R. A., *Christianity without Antisemitism: James Parkes and the Jewish-Christian Encounter* (1993). Falaturi, A., J. J. Petuchowski, and W. Strolz, eds., *Three Ways to the One God: The Faith Experience in Judaism, Christianity and Islam* (1987). Fisher, E. J., ed., *Interwoven Destinies: Jews and Christians through the Ages* (1993). Idem, *Visions of the Other: Jewish and Christian Theologians Assess the Dialogue* (1994). Fisher, E. J., and L. Klenicki, eds., *In Our Time: The Flowering of Jewish-Catholic Dialogue* (1990) (contains an extensive annotated bibliography). Idem, *John Paul II: On Jews and Judaism 1979–1986* (1987). Idem, *Spiritual Pilgrimage: Texts on Jews and Judaism 1979–1995–Pope John Paul II* (1995). Fisher, E. J., A. J. Rudin, and M. H. Tanenbaum, eds., *Twenty Years of Jewish-Catholic Relations* (1986). Hagner, D. A., *The Jewish Reclamation of Jesus: An Analysis and Critique of the Modern Jewish Study of Jesus* (1984). Harrington, D. J., *God's People in Christ: New Testament Perspectives on the Church and Judaism* (1980). International Catholic-Jewish Liaison Committee, *Fifteen Years of Catholic-Jewish Dialogue 1970–1985: Selected Papers* (1988). Lausanne Consultation on Jewish Evangelism, "Conference Statement: Jerusalem '95: Yeshua for Israel," *International Bulletin of Missionary Research* 19/4 (October 1995) 168–69. Lipson, J. G., *Jews for Jesus: An Anthropological Study* (1990). Lohfink, N., *The Covenant Never Revoked: Biblical Reflection on Christian-Jewish Dialogue* (1991). Maduro, O., ed., *Judaism, Christianity, and Liberation: An Agenda for Dialogue* (1991). Mussner, F., *Tractate on the Jews: The Significance of Judaism for Christian Faith* (1984). Oesterreicher, J. M., *The New Encounter between Christians and Jews* (1986). Overman, J. A., *Matthew's Gospel and Formative Judaism: The Social World of the Matthean Community* (1990). Pawlikowski, J. T., *Christ in the Light of the Christian-Jewish Dialogue* (1982). Idem, *Jesus and the Theology of Israel* (1989). Perelmuter, H. G., *Siblings: Rabbinic Judaism and Early Christianity at Their Beginnings* (1989). Rousseau, R. W., *Christianity and Judaism: The Deepening Dialogue* (1983). Ruether, R. R., *Faith and Fratricide: The Theological Roots of Anti-Semitism* (1974). Sanders, E. P., *Paul and Palestinian Judaism* (1977). Idem, *Paul, the Law, and the Jewish People* (1983). Sanders, J. T., *The Jews in Luke-Acts* (1987). Scherer, J. A., and S. B. Bevans, eds., *New Directions in Mission and Evangelization*, vol. 1, *Basic Statements, 1974–1991* (1992). Segal, A., *Paul the Convert* (1992). Shermis, M., *Jewish-Christian Relations: An Annotated Bibliography and Resource Guide* (1988). Smiga, G. M., *Pain and Polemic: Anti-Judaism in the Gospels* (1992). Thoma, C., *A Christian Theology of Judaism* (1980). Tomson, P. J., *Paul and the Jewish Law: Halakha in the Letters of the Apostle to the Gentiles* (1990). Van Buren, P., *A Christian Theology of the People Israel* (1983). Idem, *Discerning the Way: A Theology of the Jewish-Christian Reality* (1980). Volken, L., *Jesus der Jude und das Jüdische im Christentum* (1983). Von der Osten-Sacken, P., *Christian-Jewish Dialogue: Theological Foundations* (1986). Willebrands, J., *Church and Jewish People: New Considerations* (1992). Williamson, C. M., *A Guest in the House of Israel: Post-Holocaust Church Theology* (1993). World Council of Churches, *The Theology of the Churches and the Jewish People: Statements by the World Council of Churches and Its Member Churches* (1988). Young, B. H., *Jesus and His Jewish Parables: Rediscovering the Roots of Jesus' Teaching* (1989).

❧ JUSTIFICATION ❧

1. Fundamental Observations. 2. Old Testament and Early Judaism. 3. The Synoptic Gospels and the Pre-Pauline Tradition. 4. Paul. 5. Non-Pauline Epistles and John's Gospel. 6. History of the Church.

1. The "justification" of those without relationship to God is the content and goal of missionary preaching, as it is of every Christian endeavor. At issue is not one theme among many; justification is the fundamental theme of the New Testament. Nor is justification the leading idea of a particular theology (i.e., Pauline); it is rather the basic motif of the early Christian witness. Questions may naturally be asked not only about the occurrence of the word and its cognates — "justice," "being justified," "to justify" — but also about the congruence of such specific occurrences with the rest of the New Testament kerygma. This can be done in such a way that the terminology of justification becomes the point of departure from which one can recognize the inner coherence of the New Testament witness and the relevance of the justification theme for the Christian message as a whole. The Reformers, above all M. Luther, understood the doctrine of justification in this sense, as "central point and frontier of theology" (E. Wolf), a concept unjustifiably contested in later interpretations, which saw it merely as a particular expression of theology in Paul or even only as a "side crater" in Pauline theology itself (A. Schweitzer).

2. Justification is already an important theme in the Old Testament and is thus, with certain limitations, a fundamental concept in the whole Bible. "Justice" is no superior norm here, but conduct appropriate to the community (H. Cremer, G. von Rad). As a description of relationship, "justice" is especially influenced by the relationship between God and humankind in general and between God and God's people in particular. Only within this relationship, can it be established whether someone can be regarded as righteous or has experienced justification by God. God's own action is the action of righteousness, insofar as God keeps faith and grants →salvation. In contrast, the community's falling away from faithfulness is in itself judgment. Interestingly, in the majority of places where God's righteousness is spoken of, the plural is used in the sense of "acts of justice" or, more precisely, "proofs of justice." Only in Dt 33:21 is the singular used. Throughout the Old Testament, the "righteous acts of Yahweh" are spoken of, not "the righteousness of God," as in the New Testament. Apart from that, righteousness as the faithfulness of the community is a primary term, related to the former constitution of the covenant as understood here.

Righteousness and justification can first be shown in connection with eschatological expectations in the late Old Testament and early Judaism tradition. In Dn 9:24, the establishment of "eternal justice" is spoken of; and in the apocalyptic books of *4 Ezra* and *Ethiopian Enoch,* reference is made more often to the realization of God's justice establishing salvation at the end of time. The Qumran texts are especially informative as to the presumptions made in the New Testament way of speaking, because here, in the pre-Christian period, they speak of "the righteousness of God" and of the justification of the sinner prepared to turn around, where, nevertheless, conscientious fulfillment of a radicalized Torah has a decisive function. That this was an opinion held not only by the Qumran community is shown in related texts from the *Book of Jubilees* and the *Testament of the Twelve Patriarchs.*

3. A series of extra-Pauline texts in the New Testament speak of the "righteousness of God" or "justification." In the Synoptic Gospels, above all, it is worth noting the closing line of the parable of the Pharisee and the tax collector (Lk 18:14a), where the tax collector "went away to his house justified," and the Pharisee was not justified. The unconditional nature of justification, based on the unrestricted confession that one is a sinner, is crucial here. The statement that the righteousness which "stands before God" (M. Luther) cannot be earned, but only received, makes Mt 6:33 significant, as here the summons to the disciples is to seek "the reign of God" and "its righteousness." Accordingly, in Mt 5:6, those who are called blessed are those who "hunger and thirst after righteousness." James 1:20–21 should be seen in this connection also, insofar as the saving word can be received, while anger does not achieve "God's righteousness," but rather excludes it.

The fact that Paul did not develop his doctrine of justification independently is shown in several texts which are clearly recognizable as pre-Pauline. This is true of the saying in 1 Cor 6:11, in which the "washing away," the "sanctification," and the "justification" are descriptions of the baptismal event. All of these actions mean that in the name of Jesus and in the power of the Holy Spirit, the person baptized has received justification. That is noteworthy insofar as for Paul human justification is otherwise an event on which the human being is continually dependent and which therefore always happens anew. The christological confession of Rom 4:25 also proves to be pre-Pauline; here the forgiveness of sins is bound up with the death of Jesus, and justification with his resurrection. In other texts Paul speaks of justification effected by the *death* of Jesus, as is the case in Rom 3:24–26, where Jesus' death is shown as the propitiatory sacrifice for human sins — "evidence" of justice creating salvation. Paul has not taken over this text without changing it; he supplements it with two additions, as can be shown linguistically in the original text: he speaks explicitly about the faith of people and about the justifying activity of God always realizing itself anew in the present "now."

4. For Paul himself, in the Epistle to the Galatians as in Romans, the doctrine of justification he maintains is the explication of the "truth of the gospel" (Gal 2:5; etc.). The justification of human beings as salvation-event is based on God's promise and the realization of that promise through the person and work of Jesus Christ, especially through his death. The "righteousness of God" is thereby understood neither as a quality of God, nor as the measure of judgment, nor even simply as a gift of God, but more as action for righteousness, through which God grants salvation and through which the human person is made whole and called to respond. This action for righteousness is, according to Rom 1:17, visible and effective in the proclamation of the gospel. Since the "righteousness of God" describes the singular action of God in the sense of *justitia salutifera,* this means for Paul, on the one hand, that the promise and realization of this righteousness are independent of every invitation to human beings and of every act; this is why the law also can have only a secondary function in contrast to the promise, and an irrelevant one for salvation (Gal 2:1ff.). On the other hand, this means that all "works of the law" must be excluded as the products of human striving for self-realization and fame (Rom 3:27–28). Further, the realization of God's righteousness means that for human beings there can be no alternative to unconditional self-surrender and entrusting oneself to God, a "faith in hope against hope," whereby people can be assured that God does what God promises and keeps faith (Rom 4:18–22). Abraham is the prototype for this, according to Gn 15:6, his unconditional faith being "counted to him as righteousness" (Gal 3:6–23; Rom 4:3–25). The exclusiveness of God's gracious action, the link to the person and death of Jesus Christ, and the unconditional nature of human faith in the sense of surrendering oneself to God are for Paul the elements constituting his message of justification. That means for him that basically every person can receive salvation and that it is precisely those without God who will be justified by God (Rom 4:3–5). God has made the one "who knew no sin," that is, who had not fallen out of communion with God, "become sin" vicariously "for us," in order that we "might become righteous in him" (2 Cor 5:21), which means that we receive justification insofar as we live "in him," namely, "in the Body of Christ," belonging to him (see 1 Cor 12:13; 2 Cor 5:17). Justification includes being established again in communion with God and at the same time makes possible a new life (Rom 8:1–11). Through the word of the gospel, the promise of salvation, the person is declared righteous and at the same time is also justified, in the sense that he or she can live from God and before God. For this reason, everything can be given up for the sake of knowing Christ, because "the righteousness of God depends on faith," which gives one a secure hold and a future (Phil 3:7–11). The hope of the consummation of salvation is indissolubly bound up with faith (Rom 5:1–11). It is true that "the one who is justified by faith will live," because the righteousness of God becomes visible in the gospel "from faith to faith" (Rom 1:17).

Paul has demonstrated in Galatians that Christian life as a whole must be understood as the existence of the justified, and in Romans he has shown that justification is the action of God being made real and concrete in the proclamation of the gospel. Romans 9:30-10:17 is especially revealing for this, together with Rom 11:11–24 and 15:1–13. It is the proclamation of the gospel which brings salvation and life: "Everyone who calls on the name of the Lord will be saved. But how are they to call on one in whom they have not believed?" (Rom 10:13–14). So "faith comes from what is heard, and what is heard comes from the preaching of Christ" (Rom 10:17). For Paul, as for the whole of early Christianity, this is the basis for tireless missionary activity. It hinges on the confession, "Jesus Christ is Lord," and this is not the Lord of an individual or of a closed community, but the Lord of the world. Paul therefore quotes the hymn Phil 2:6–11. He is also convinced that, with the message of the gospel, the powers of this world, which enslave people, will be overcome. He sees the ambassadors of Christ as in a triumphal procession, in spite of all suffering and persecution, processing through the nations (2 Cor 2:14–17). He knows himself to be designated by the message to a priestly service (Rom 15:16). So it is not a matter of human words but of authoritative proclamation, which Christ himself has commissioned (1 Thes 2:13; Rom 10:15). Through the righteousness which creates salvation and becomes effective through the gospel, all differences will be removed. There is here no distinction between Gentile or Jew, nor superiority or submission of man and woman, of master and slave (Gal 3:28). It concerns the common praise of all (Rom 15:7–13). The enigma that Israel, apart from a "remnant," does not accept the message is still linked to missionary service (Romans 9–11). For the sake of the non-Jew, Israel must stand back for the moment, but will in the future come to the faith and be saved (Rom 11:23, 25–32). Missionary service, therefore, involves God's universal will for salvation. In more modern exegesis, it is rightly stated that the "righteousness of God" not only concerns the individual but also has a universalized dimension and that ultimately it is about God's justice being realized on earth (see E. Käsemann). Where God establishes God's justice, it means salvation for people.

5. In the non-Pauline letters of the New Testament, we have the same evidence concerning the unconditional nature of the message of salvation, of the basis of God's revelation in Christ, and of human trust and faith. This is not carried through with the same overall consistency as in Paul, but it is nowhere lacking. The Christian message is from its origin the unconditional message of salvation and call to faith. Jesus' message of the breaking in of the reign of God and its pre-Easter effects were nothing other than the expression of God's unlimited gift of salvation. Jesus therefore preached to the sinners and outcasts and accepted them into his community. The doctrine of justification can only be an interpretation of the message of the breaking in of the reign of God — of course, after Easter, taking into account the death and resurrection of Jesus. Because the justifying action of God overcomes sins and removes them, Christians took as their task the ministry of reconciliation through the death and resurrection of Christ, by which salvation and righteousness are mediated. Trust in the representative power of Jesus' death, as well as belonging to Jesus and his community of salvation, gained central significance for the post-Easter message. But just as the message of justification could be passed on without specific justification terminology, the message of Christ is also proclaimed in a plurality of forms and made explicit in its soteriological relevance. God's turning to humankind, bound up in the person of Jesus, thereby retains its fundamental importance because in his word and work the unconditional offer of salvation became visible.

Among the New Testament writings, John's Gospel deserves special consideration. John does not speak explicitly of justification but rather speaks of righteousness in connection with the promise of the Paraclete. This divine righteousness, according to Jn 16:8–11, has something to do with Jesus' ascent to the Father. His departure unleashes the power of life, the power which became visible in Jesus' becoming human and through which, now, sin, the world, and death are overcome. In the Fourth Gospel the theme of sin and the forgiveness of sin is not a primary one, but it is not lacking (Jn 1:29; 3:16). Jesus' death is not in the first place viewed as an act of sacrifice, but, in Jesus' death, his being lifted up and glorified are already happening — something which is spoken of first in connection with the resurrection. Jesus' death, therefore, is above all about the liberation of human beings from death and the subsequent bestowal of life (Jn 3:36; 5:24; 6:33). With the overcoming of death, the tie to the world, which is hostile to God and subjected to evil (1 Jn 5:19b), is removed. This means that salvation is granted through Jesus' word and through trust in his person, and new eternal life is given to people (Jn 11:25–26). Perhaps this interpretation of the justification event as unconditional and unlimited liberation from death and bondage to the world is the explanation of the Christian message which might be best understood today. At the same time it is an indication that the biblical tradition itself offers a variety of possibilities of approach and interpretation. Such variety has often been inadequately explained in both the church's theology and its missionary work.

6. In the history of the church the message of justification has often been restricted or transmitted fragmentarily. However, the great teachers of the church — Augustine, Aquinas, Luther, Barth — recognized its importance and explained its meaning in the context of their own times. One must explain why it was often so difficult to hold on to this message in its biblical form. The problems of translation into another language and into another nonbiblical mode of thought about righteousness and justification have definitely played a role, and this is why the concept of justification as a legal norm has come to the fore all too strongly. The real problem, however, lies in the doctrine of justification itself: it can only be taken up and transmitted in its true sense when the unconditional nature of the promise of salvation and the unreserved nature of human trust remain bound together with each other in actual life. The danger is either that the unconditional nature of the salvation leads to a situation of unbridled license or that the necessity of being bound to Christ and the Christian community leads to a surrender of grace's basic unconditional nature. Freedom, however, does not have to result in libertarianism. Conversely, obligations which should make clear the importance of human responsibility often end in moralism or clericalism. It not only requires an adequate theology to make the unity between justification as grace and justification as responsible action clear; it requires first and foremost a missionary proclamation — and today every proclamation is missionary — in which the freedom of the gospel is linked with human responsibility in a way which cannot be misunderstood as mere secular freedom.

FERDINAND HAHN

Bibliography

Alszeghy, Z., and M. Flick, *Fondamenti di una antropologia teologica* (1970). Bultmann, R., *Theology of the New Testament* (1951). Cremer, H., *Die Paulinische Rechtfertigungslehre* (1900). Forde, G. O., "Christian Life," in C. E. Braaten and R. W. Jensen, eds., *Christian Dogmatics,* vol. 2 (1984) 393–469. Fransen, P., *Divine Grace and Man* (1962). Idem, *The New Life of Grace* (1969). Haight, R., *The Experience and Language of Grace* (1979). Idem, "Sin and Grace," in F. Schüssler Fiorenza and J. Galvin, eds., *Systematic Theology: Roman Catholic Perspectives* (1991) 78–141. Härle, W., and E. Herms, *Rechtfertigung: Das Wirklichkeitsverständnis des christlichen Glaubens* (1980). Küng, H., *Justification: The Doctrine of Karl Barth and a Catholic Reflection* (1964). Meyer, C. R., *A Contemporary Theology of Grace* (1971). Müller, G., *Die Rechtfertigungslehre: Geschichte und Problem* (1977). Oman, J. W., *Grace and Personality* (1917). Pesch, O. H., and A. Peters, *Einführung in die Lehre von Gnade und Rechtfertigung* (1981). Rad, G. von, *Theology of the Old Testament,* vol. 1 (1962). Rahner, K., "Justification and World Development from a Catholic Viewpoint," *TI* 18 (1983) 259–73. Idem, "Justified and Sinner at the Same Time," *TI* 6 (1969) 218–30. Idem, "Law and Righteousness in the Catholic Understanding," *TI* 18 (1983) 274–87. Idem, "Questions of Controversial Theology on Justification," *TI* 4 (1966) 189–218. Rahner, K., and A. Darlap, "Justification," in *EnRel* 8 (1987) 215–19. Reumann, J., *Righteousness in the New Testament* (1982). Schillebeeckx, E., *Christ: The Experience of Jesus as Lord* (1980). Schweitzer, A., *The Mysticism of Saint Paul the Apostle* (1968). Stuhlmacher, P., *Gerechtigkeit Gottes bei Paulus* (1965). Welte, B., *Heilsverständnis* (1966).

K

❧ KOREAN THEOLOGY ❧

1. Historical Survey. 2. Types of Korean Theology. 3. Minjung Theology.

1. The term "Korean theology" is applied to the theological research produced and adopted by Koreans in Korea. Korean theology has developed its own central themes and identity through (a) the effectiveness of Korean spiritual-cultural traditions and (b) the specific political situation in Korea.

Korean society is religiously pluralist. Buddhism and Confucianism influence the spiritual climate of the country, together with the various popular religions (shamanism, Maitreya Buddhism, Dong-Hak teaching, and new syncretistic religions) which have an effect, above all, on the vitality and the worldview of the Korean minjung (impoverished people). The history of Christianity in Korea can be understood only if it is seen against this complex religious background. The central hermeneutical task of Korean theology has been, until this day, dialogue between the gospel and the living religious tradition of the country.

The first epoch of Korean Protestantism (1894–1910) was the time of the complete collapse of the Chosun Dynasty. A spiritual vacuum opened up, and Japan won increasing influence. Most members of the church were impoverished people without hope, mostly women. The "Nevius method" was employed by the missionaries, according to which missionary efforts were directed especially at the simplest people. The gospel brought them good news: knowledge of human rights and liberation. From the beginning of this period, Christians were actively involved in national history. The linking of the opposition movement of the minjung (the peasants' uprisings in the nineteenth century) to the awareness newly awakened by the gospel led to the active participation of many Christians in the Independence Movement of March 1, 1919, and in other national struggles during the Japanese colonial period. This patriotic and progressive tradition in the Korean church led finally to the nationalistically oriented movement for democratization and human rights of the 1970s.

In the Japanese colonial period (1910–1945), large parts of the church were depoliticized under the influence of U.S. missionaries' theology of mission, which was received uncritically. With antirevolutionary theology (the strict separation of church and state) and comprehensive evangelization campaigns (from 1907), the missionaries tried to prevent more severe suppression of church work by the Japanese. This fundamentalist direction led to isolation from the world, and even today a large part of Korean Protestantism is molded by it.

The "minjung tradition" of the church, however, remained effective underground. With the resumption of diplomatic relations between Korea and Japan in 1965, the national question came to life again in an acute form. The opposition which was then being formed reached back through the years to link up with the Independence Movement of March 1, 1919, and its thrust against Japanese expansionism.

At the same time, social contrasts were sharpened after the military coup of 1961. With the aim of rapid economic growth, Korea was integrated into the world capitalist system and submitted to a rigid development dictatorship. On account of the development goals, the ruling class, in cooperation with overseas powers, had to oppress the minjung politically, exploit them economically, and alienate them socially and culturally. The Christian groupings, which were working for democracy and human rights, also belonged to the newly awakened resistance movement. In the course of the conflict, the opposition Christians discovered the subject of the minjung as something new. Taking the suffering and the hopes of the minjung seriously once more in theological terms was the starting point for minjung theology.

2. We can roughly distinguish the following types of Korean theology: (*a*) theology of religion and culture, (*b*) fundamentalist theology, and (*c*) political theology.

a. The task of witnessing to the gospel in discussion, and confrontation, with the existing religions was first formulated theologically by Choe Byung-Hun (1858–1927). He made a distinction between the gospel of Jesus as the Absolute and the religions as the Relative. On the one hand, he evaluated Christianity and the church as religious and cultural phenomena, in continuity with and parallel to the other religions. On the other hand, he saw the gospel revealed in Jesus Christ as the fulfillment of all religions. In contrast to the attitude of fundamentalist theology, Choe recognized the relative value of other religions. The discussion over the evaluation of these religions was intensified later in the debate about indigenization in the aftermath of the reawakening of national consciousness after 1960. Yun Sung-Bum stipulated that it was necessary to revive indigenous traditions and to draw on Western elements of theology only as an addition. Discussion with the religions was taken up afresh: with shamanism (Yu Dong-Sik), with Confucianism (Yun Sung-Bum), and with Buddhism (Byun Son-Hwan). For the representatives of indigenization, these issues have to do with dialogue, not "conversion." "Conversion" gives an impression of theological imperialism. This criticism is the point of departure of a new theology of mission (Byun Son-Hwan).

b. Fundamentalism influences a good third of the Korean church. According to Park Hyung-Ryong, an authority on Korean fundamentalism, the task of Korean theology consists of holding firm to the pure apostolic tradition; for example, it also involves holding firm to the theology of the missionaries of the founding period as eternal riches. The principal catch-phrases of Korean fundamentalism are "verbal inspiration," "literal interpretation," "verbal inerrancy," and "religious exclusivism"; a large place is taken by a puritanically molded legalistic pietism; the principle of separation of church and state is emphasized; and the stress is all on the salvation of the individual soul. Korean fundamentalism uncompromisingly rejects dialogue with other religions. For it, the relationship to other religions is not a question of dialogue but of "victory in the fight."

c. Seeds of a political theology could already be seen in the work of Yun Ch-Ho (1864–1945), who, as a progressive scholar and politician, conceived of practical acts of love in political commitment and the preaching of the gospel in church as one and the same thing. Kim Jae-Jun (b. 1901) further developed a politically conscious theology through his study of the social message of the prophets. In sharp contrast to the fundamentalists' dualism of this world and the world to come, he advocated the participation of Christians in historical tasks in Korea. Christians have to bring the saving work of Christ to bear on all aspects of historical life.

Endeavors with a politically aware theology were further stimulated by the ecumenical movement and the *missio Dei* theology supported by it.

3. Contemporary minjung theology is quite critical of fundamentalism, and it incorporates the insights of both political theology and the theology of religion and culture. Minjung theology executes a radical turn in its hermeneutic, in that it attempts to view the Bible, history, and reality with the eyes of the minjung, that is, from below. This theology refuses to define the term "minjung" too narrowly, in order to avoid an ideological fixation. Minjung is a living subject: God acts in minjung events; Christians can encounter God and Christ concretely today only through active participation in these events. The main task of minjung theology, therefore, is to testify to the *missio Dei* in minjung events. In this sense, minjung theology is a *theologia eventorum* (Byung-Mu Ahn), which has the task of tracing out the movement and presence of God in historical events; the Bible and the present are expounded from this basic conviction. Events are in principle the first thing: they lay the foundations; theological reflection follows later. This applies to biblical studies as much as to systematic theology.

In the field of Old Testament studies, minjung theologians ask what experiences led the people in Israel to their ideas of God. It is not sufficient to reconstruct the process of the formation of the traditions in the Bible; rather, the life and the actual living conditions of the groups which lived and handed on these statements of faith must be researched (involved in this effort are Suh In-Sok, Kim Jung-Jun, and Park Jun-Soh). One can distinguish throughout between the idea of God of the Hebrew minjung and the image of God of the ruling classes. Suh Nam-Dong attempts to interpret the exodus-event as the secret focal point of the entire Hebrew Bible. The liberation attested in the exodus-event is seen as the *cantus firmus* of the Old Testament. God reveals Godself in the acts of liberation: possessing the land, the struggle against the Canaanite feudal system, and the program of an egalitarian society in the "Book of the Covenant" (Exodus 21ff.). Finally, Byung-Mu Ahn analyzes the significance of the strong mono-Yahwism in the Old Testament. This idea of God, the tradition in which Jesus stands, can elucidate the concept of the "reign of God."

In the field of New Testament studies, minjung theology endeavors to research the life of the historical Jesus, with critical acceptance of the earlier results of the life of Jesus research, especially the form-criticism and redaction-criticism analyses. The Jesus-event, not the kerygma, is envisaged as fundamental and primary (Byung-Mu Ahn). Minjung theology insists that the interaction and the relationship between Jesus and the crowd (*ochlos*) must be analyzed more closely. It is also the task of minjung theology to illuminate the process of the transmission of the Jesus-event. The event occurred among people who were oppressed by the political powers, exploited by the Jerusalem temple cult, and alienated by the ideology of a strongly legalistic piety. They did not play a supporting role in the drama of the life of Jesus. Rather they were living subjects and active co-stars, without whom Jesus' behavior would be unthinkable and beyond analysis. This living, not conceptually fixed, *ochlos* is the first bearer and transmitter of the Jesus-event. The analysis of these groups makes conclusions possible as to the original meaning of the Jesus-event. The Jesus-event has a lasting effect in the case of the minjung and their history and repeats itself. Jesus Christ is there in the suffering of the minjung and in their being killed; and in the resurrection, he is present in their rising up. In this sense, the minjung-event is a gateway, a medium of the presence of Jesus.

In the field of systematic theology, the main task is attesting to the confluence of the biblical minjung traditions and Korean minjung history (a task taken up by Suh Nam-Dong). This "synopsis" requires special methods: those of sociohistorical interpretation and pneumatological-synchronic interpretation. Sociohistorical analysis probes the question of "the substructure of revelation" (Suh Nam-Dong), that is, of the actual living conditions in which God's action takes place. Revelation takes the form of historical events. The pneumatological-synchronic interpretation of events attempts to see the Jesus-event as repeating itself and to attest the contemporary presence and further effect of this event in the history of the minjung.

Minjung theology places the main accent on the "narrative" and the "narration." The narration is counted as language of the body (Hyun Young-Hak), as the means of expression of simple people (Byung-Mu Ahn, Suh Nam-Dong), as medium of the social biography and autobiography of the minjung (Kim Yong-Bok). The way of looking at things derived from the sociology of literature is enlisted in order to understand the biblical narratives. In the New Testament, a distinction is made between the style of the kerygma and the style of the narratives (Byung-Mu Ahn). In the narratives, the main aspects of the life of the minjung are expressed (suffering, mourning, hope, longing). However, it is to be observed that minjung language is never "pure" but is mixed with the language and ideology of the ruling classes. It requires methods of ideology criticism to see through the superficial structures of folk narratives in which these narratives are assimilated together with the ruling ideology and to expose the real language and sayings of the minjung (Suh Nam-Dong).

Minjung theology also includes cultural theological elements; it criticizes "the theology of indigenization" insofar as it has not analyzed the traditions of Korean religions "from below," from the minjung perspective. A new encounter with traditional religions is consciously prepared (especially by Hyun Young-Hak and David Suhl). The sphere of the encounter will be minjung culture, not that of the powers-that-be. For example, Hyun Young-Hak has examined Korean masked dancing.

In the debate with Korea's cultural traditions, minjung theology has taken up the term *han*. *Han* means a suppressed vitality, a *pathein* whose bitter existence is locked up in the heart, because it can find no means of expression, because of repression by the ruling classes. It is central to minjung theology to understand the *han* of the minjung, in order to be able to prepare liberation from this pain and from the mechanisms of repression. In this context, Jesus appears as a priest, a shaman, who understands how to release the *han*. Effective in the midst of the minjung, Jesus breaks the vicious circle of repression and alienation and so makes possible the way to true liberation (Suh Nam-Dong).

Byung-Mu Ahn

Bibliography

Ahn, B. M., *Draussen vor dem Tor: Kirche und Minjung in Korea: Theologische Beiträge und Reflexionen* (1986). Idem, "Jesus and People (Minjung)," in R. S. Sugirtharajah, ed., *Asian Faces of Jesus* (1993) 163–72. Brown, G. T., "Why Has Christianity Grown Faster in Korea Than in China?" *Missiol* 22/1 (January 1994) 77–88. Chung, H.-E., *Das Koreanische Minjung und seine*

Bedeutung für eine ökumenische Theologie (1984). Chung, H.-K., "'Opium or the Seed for Revolution?' Shamanism: Women Centred Popular Religiosity in Korea," in L. Boff and V. Elizondo, eds., *Theologies of the Third World: Convergences and Differences,* vol. 199 of *Concilium* (1988) 97–104. Chung, L. O., and S. A. L. Park, "Peace, Unification and Women," in V. Fabella and S. A. L. Park, eds., *We Dare to Dream: Doing Theology as Asian Women* (1990) 65–82. Clark, D., *A History of the Korean Church* (1971). Commission on Theological Concerns of the Christian Conference of Asia, ed., *Minjung Theology* (1983). Kim, Y. B., *Messiah and Minjung: Collected Articles* (1986). Idem, *Minjung Theology: People as the Subjects of History* (1981). Lee, J. Y., ed., *An Emerging Theology in World Perspective: Commentary on Korean Minjung Theology* (1988). Lim, C. H., and A. Jung, *Bilder und Texte aus der Minjung Kulturbewegung in Südkorea* (1986). Moltmann, J., *Theologie des Volkes Gottes in Südkorea* (1984). Mun, H.-S., *A Korean Minjung Theology: An Old Testament Perspective* (1985). Nim, A. S., "Feminist Theology in the Korean Church," in V. Fabella and S. A. L. Park, eds., *We Dare to Dream: Doing Theology as Asian Women* (1990) 127–34. Paik, L. G., *History of Protestant Missions in Korea 1832–1910* (1929). Park, J. W., *Das Ringen um die Einheit der Kirche in Korea* (1985). Sundermeier, T., *Das Kreuz als Befreiung: Kreuzesinterpretationen in Asien und Afrika* (1985). Underwood, H. G., "Christianity in Korea," *Missiol* 22/1 (January 1994) 65–76.

L

❧ LAITY ❧

1. The Question of the Laity as a Question of the Church. 2. Spheres and Forms of Co-responsibility of Women and Men. 3. Structures of Co-responsibility. 4. Spirituality as Cultivation of the Christian Life.

The question of "laity" is ultimately one about the understanding of church. The difficulty about giving a clear theological definition of the word "laity" is that of determining the relationship of laity and clergy sociologically and structurally: the mutual delimitation easily becomes the focus of the discussion.

1. In a theological evaluation it must be remembered that in the early church the stress was laid not on the difference between clergy and laity but on the opposition of the church to the world from which it was called and set apart. The whole Christian community was deeply conscious of its responsibility for mission and the proclamation of salvation in Jesus Christ. As Christianity became the official religion of the Roman Empire, this "opposition" shifted increasingly into the church itself and led to the institutional separation of a "first class" (priests and monks) from the "second class" (the laity) (*Decretum Gratiani* 1142). Some developments nowadays are reminiscent of the situation in the early church; as a consequence of secularization and the modern emancipation and liberation movements, the church finds itself in a diasporan situation in which the ecclesiastical and social spheres no longer coincide. →Vatican II reflects this tendency: prior to any distribution of roles and distinction of laity and clergy, it emphasizes the equality of all believers based on baptism (*LG* 32). Before all charismatic differentiation and ecclesiastical organization, the image of the church as "people of God" gives decisive preference to the equal dignity of all Christians as brothers and sisters on the fundamental pneumatological level. In this respect "Christian" and "believer" are more meaningful terms for what "layperson," etymologically, can only hazily convey. Nevertheless, through this ecclesiological mooring the laity have again found a positive definition for their missionary mandate in today's world. Christians translate the mission of the church (→evangelism, evangelization) into action by asserting God's saving will to give life in full to all by a critical presence in the interpersonal and social situations and challenges (*AA* 5–8). According to Vatican II the laity do not participate "somehow or other" in the mission of the church but have — to use the words of the council — "as living members, the vocation of applying to the building up of the church and to its continual sanctification all the powers which they have received" (*LG* 33); and "everything that has been said of the People of God is addressed equally to laity, religious and clergy" (*LG* 30). This theological determination of the place of the laity can hardly be understood without the change from a hierarchically stamped image of the church to an understanding of the church as "people of God." The process of change must be seen in relationship to the question of →women in the church, a new understanding of ministry, participatory and synodal co-responsibility, and ecumenism; all of this has resulted in a stronger emphasis on the priesthood of all the faithful and, instead of the duality clergy/laity, the dialectical tension of ministry and

251

community. Also to be considered are the new models of parish and the basic communities in which women and men, together with the clergy, jointly take up social challenges; additional consideration must be given to the increasing collaboration of women and men in churches all around the world — full-time, part-time, or voluntary helpers in the social, cultural, catechetical, and pastoral fields. It must be acknowledged as well that, in many parts of the world, an increasing number of foreign missionaries come from the laity: organizations for lay missionaries are often sponsored by religious communities (e.g., the Maryknolls, the Claretians, the Jesuits), but there are also some that are completely lay-run (e.g., the Volunteer Missionary movement). As the laity take on more and more ministerial roles within the church, the distinction between "lay" and "cleric" is becoming less and less sharp and defined.

In this connection the conciliar decrees leave important questions open — when, for instance, the "layperson" is defined with reference to status in the world or secular character (*LG* 31; *AA* 2). "The salvation of humanity" and "the renewal of the whole temporal order" (*AA* 5) are, in the statements of the council, two intimately connected spheres. If, however, in the postconciliar discussion and in connection with the new "lay ministries," the "ministry of salvation" is assigned to the clergy and the "ministry of the world" to the laity, then not only is a course set for an ecclesiastical pathology — in which a clerical "inside" and a lay "outside" could be justified theologically — but a position inconsistent with the most seminal statements of Vatican II is maintained. The self-description of the church as the sacrament "of communion with God and of unity among all humanity" (*LG* 1) forbids approaches which separate clergy and laity into two different classes. The most challenging aspects of →liberation theology in particular originate in this statement of the council, for it emphasizes the liberating contents of the faith by understanding and reflecting on Christian life proceeding from the situation of the people (*el pueblo,* the minjung) and oriented toward action *with* and *for* them. There is a radical recognition that the "people" (→"people" [*Volk*], "nation") are the subjects of Christian and social activity.

It goes without saying that with the theological rethinking of the definition and role of the layperson as Christian and member of the church, a pattern is forming which is just beginning to be discernible in the consciousness of the church. The implications of such a pattern still need to be put into effect on the levels of missionary work, pastoral activity, and ecclesiastical structures.

2. Consequently, on the level of Christian action and pastoral work there are no spheres which are, in principle, closed to the laity. The whole people of God, rather, is the subject of ecclesiastical life. From this flows all Christians' basic participation in and co-responsibility for the church and its salvific mission in the world. This does not mean any kind of inner-ecclesiastical "laicism" but is a plea for a church alive in all its members, according to which the laity should not be satisfied with the role of objects who are simply ministered to; they should rather risk and undertake the duties and responsibilities of cooperating subjects of Christian and ecclesiastical activity. Various associations such as Catholic Action and other forms of the lay apostolate have acted as pioneers in this regard. They have expressed not only the right but also the obligation of the laity to participate actively in the mission of the church as manifested in church life and in commitment to the world. Of similar importance in the churches of the Reformation, apart from the associations, are the many different initiatives and services of the lay movement — not least the missionary conferences (→world missionary conferences), in which clergy and laity come together and collaborate.

The laity participates in all essential functions of the church and of life in the parishes and communities: evangelization with its aspects of awakening and deepening the faith (religious instruction; catechesis; faith and Bible sharing; adult education; theology; media and publicity work); liturgy and sacramental praxis (parish and group liturgies; sacramental catechesis with parents on the occasion of first communion, first confession, and confirmation; marriage); social and charitable work in the individual and social spheres (social services and projects; counseling; "consoling"; tackling social problems and challenges such as projects in the neighborhoods, Third World problems, the peace movement, and women's emancipation); and community building (associations; councils and boards; coordination of the different services; networking of the different areas of responsibility; training collaborators; disseminating information; and conscientization).

3. Against this background of the theological understanding and practical importance of the laity, questions arise about the structures of the institutional church and ecclesiastical ministries. The 1983 Code of Canon Law presupposes a clear distinction between the two states "clergy" and "laity." On a pragmatic level, it takes into account the changed awareness of the problem and the new personnel situation in pastoral ministry inasmuch as laypeople, more than before, are given the possibility to cooperate and to some extent take responsibility in exceptional situations (e.g., witnessing marriages). On the ecclesiastical level, the fundamental equal dignity of all Christians does not mean an amorphous mass; the common calling and mission are differentiated on the practical and functional level of church life. Vatican II places the particular charism of each Christian in the center of its teaching about the church as people of God. In this context the "fundamental-pneumatic" level of Christian life is to be distinguished from the "charismatic-functional" level of ecclesiastical activity, but both are like two poles of the same, inseparable reality. The variety of charisms is an expression and consequence of Christian vitality; and the ministries of the church are at the service of this vitality.

For this reason the church's ministries and services are not just a pure organizational necessity but are theologically destined to be "at the service" of the basic ministry of the church, that is, to make present the salvation inaugurated once and for all in Jesus Christ in the history of humanity. Flowing from its orientation to Jesus and the missionary commission and evangelizing task (a task in which Christians are not only subjects but always addressees also), the church is the reason and foundation of ministry — not the other way around. On this question hinges the problem of a workable church order in which unity and diversity go hand in hand, as well as the active co-responsibility of all Christians and the different ministries. In the future it might be necessary to look for and organize the structural relationship between laity and clergy on the basis of a pneumatic-fundamental equality and a charismatic-functional differentiation. Rather than a monocratic (monarchical) and democratic constitutional structure, a synodal church would probably best correspond to this theological approach. These synodal structures would have to be tried out in the various spheres and on different levels of the church. Their bipolarity would correspond to a double representation:

from "above" and from "below." In such a model the co-responsibility of all and the various ministries (and competencies) would be mutually connected and related.

4. Christian living must be cultivated and its motives constantly purified. Christian spirituality must be tested in the tension between the gospel and the world. There will always be a danger of dichotomy between religious commitment and social commitment, between ministry of salvation and ministry of the world, between withdrawal into ecclesiastical ghettoes (clericalism of the laity also) and sheepishly following the majority. The question of the laity as the question of the church shows clearly that Christian praxis must not be confined to the church itself but must understand itself as missionary openness to the world and "consume" itself serving humanity. But such missionary openness cannot be content with social welfare work; it will not do, as is often the case, to acknowledge the inspiration of the gospel only implicitly. Such an attitude cannot be kept up for long: Christian living explicitly needs critical and encouraging inspiration of the gospel which proclaims God's will to give life to all; this inspiration must find new ways of expressing itself in every new situation. For this reason individual Christians are dependent on the believing church community; they need to be constantly reminded of and helped to grow in Christian hope by recourse to the sources of the life of faith (liturgy, prayer, meditation, etc.) and realization of this hope and its practice in solidarity with others in the world. Although it has been exaggerated, there is a real truth to the idea that the world sets the agenda for the church. Because of this, the main preoccupation of the laity should not be the church as such but a church which cares for human beings and the world.

Leo Karrer

Bibliography

Aumann, J., *On the Front Lines: The Lay Person in the Church after Vatican II* (1990). Blakley, A. F., "Decree on the Apostolate of Lay People, *Apostolicam Actuositatem,*" in T. E. O'Connell, ed., *Vatican II and Its Documents: An American Reappraisal* (1986) 141–57. Boff, L., *Ecclesiogenesis: The Base Communities Reinvent the Church* (1986). Idem, *God's Witnesses in the Heart of the World* (1981). Burrows, W. R., *New Ministries: The Global Context* (1980). Congar, Y., *Lay People in the Church* (1957). Idem, *Ministères et communion ecclésiale* (1971). Idem, "My Pathfindings in the Theology of the Laity," *Jurist* (Washington, D.C.) 32 (1972) 169–88. Dabin, P., *Le sacerdoce royal des fidèles dans la tradition ancienne et moderne* (1950). Del Portillo, A., *Faithful and Laity in the Church* (1972). Doohan, L., *The Laity's Mission in the Local Church: Setting a New Direction* (1986). Idem, *The Lay-centered Church: Theology and Spirituality* (1984). Federation of Asian Bishops' Conferences, "The Vocation and Mission of the Laity in the Church and in the World of Asia," in G. Rosales and C. G. Arévalo, eds., *For All the Peoples of Asia* (1992) 177–98. Femiano, S. D., *The Infallibility of the Laity: The Legacy of Newman* (1967). John Paul II, Pope, *The Vocation and the Mission of the Lay Faithful in the Church and in the World (Christifideles Laici)* (1989). Karrer, L., "Laie/Klerus," in P. Eicher, ed., *Neues Handbuch theologischer Grundbegriffe,* 2:363–74. Kertelge, K., *Gemeinde und Amt im Neuen Testament* (1972). Küng, H., *The Church* (1967) 363–87. Lawler, M. G., and T. J. Shanahan, *Church: A Spirited Communion* (1995) 71–87. O'Meara, T. F., *Theology of Ministry* (1983). Osborne, K. B., *Ministry: Lay Ministry in the Roman Catholic Church, Its History and Theology* (1993). Peck, G., and J. S. Hoffman, eds., *The Laity in Ministry: The Whole People of God for the Whole World* (1984). Power, D. N., *Gifts That Differ: Lay Ministries Established and Unestablished* (1980). Rahner, K., "The Consecration of the Layman to the Care of Souls," in *TI* 3 (1967) 263–76. Idem, "Notes on the Lay Apostolate," in *TI* 2 (1963) 219–352. Idem, "The Sacramental Basis for the Role of the Layman in the Church," in *TI* 8 (1971) 51–74. Rajsp, A., *"Priester" und "Laien": Ein Neues Verständnis* (1982). Schillebeeckx, E., "The Typological Definition of the Christian Laymen according to Vatican II," in *The Mission of the Church* (1981) 90–117. Synod of Bishops, *The Vocation and Mission of the Laity in the Church and in the World Twenty Years after the Second Vatican Council* (1985). U.S. Bishops, *Called and Gifted* (1980). Idem, *Gifts Unfolding: The Lay Vocation Today with Questions for Tomorrow* (1990). Idem, *One Body, Different Gifts, Many Roles: Reflections on the American Cath-*

olic Laity (1987). Venetz, H. J., *So fing es mit der Kirche an* (1982). Whitehead, J. D., and E. E. Whitehead, *The Emerging Laity: Returning Leadership to the Community of Faith* (1986). World Council of Churches, *Laici in Ecclesia: An Ecumenical Bibliography on the Role of the Laity in the Life and Mission of the Church* (1961).

❧ LANGUAGE AND TRANSLATION ❧

1. Language in the Bible. 2. Language as a Means of Christian Proclamation. 3. Value of the Mother Tongue. 4. Christianization of a Language and Its Consequences.

Language and religion are bound up with each other in the closest possible way. The concepts, sentiments, and statements of a religion (→religion, religions) presuppose the existence of a language. Without reflecting on the origin of language, let it be said that it constitutes part of being human. One would be fully justified in inserting it into the declaration of article 1 of Luther's Greater Catechism where there are enumerated the individual gifts which God has given to every person at birth.

1. In the Bible, one finds few general statements about language. According to Genesis 11, humanity originally possessed a common language. The different languages are the result of divine judgment. Nevertheless, language gives people the opportunity to hear the call to pray and to praise God. Human language is involved in the incarnation, in that God uses it directly or indirectly for proclamation. Although it is also subjected to sin, it remains a great good in creation (→creation theology and missiology), and in the form of a mother tongue it belongs to basic human rights.

2. Language is not only an aid to understanding. It above all involves the expression of thought and feeling. It is fully developed only in the context of its native speaker. Therefore, in proclamation and mission to native speakers of another tongue, one must first undertake a profound study of their language. This applies also to preparation for counseling, teaching, and dialogue. It was, therefore, obvious to the missionaries of former times that they would learn the language of their assigned areas thoroughly. Phonetics, grammar, syntax, and prosodology needed intensive study, the success of which had to be proved in examinations. The missionaries thus did not encounter a tabula rasa but — as a rule — a well-ordered system, and this system was reflected in both linguistic structure and vocabulary. In Bantu languages there is a class of nouns into which all substantives are placed which refer to the magical world. In Zulu, trees, rivers, animals, and tools are included with friends and the kraal. Names are not empty sounds but potential powers whose effect can be positive or negative. Reserve about choosing names and about in-laws has its origin here. Awareness of language taboos is important for an ordered common life. An especially difficult area for the outsider is knowledge of a secret language, like that used in initiation ceremonies and in the context of secret societies.

The first task of the evangelizer, after acknowledging the holiness of the language that is to be learned, is to divest it of its character of power; subsequently, he or she must search for words in which the Christian message can be adequately communicated. Since such translation is not like arithmetic, there is no question of translation according to "formal correspondence." Because the Christian message is first of all revealed as something new through God's revelation in the Bible, one must search for expressions in other languages that are as close to the biblical meanings as possible, though the search for precise matches will be in vain. One can only use analogies. In many African languages, for example, the name of the most widely worshiped high god has been taken as the designation for God. Although such deities usually lack the essential attributes of the biblical God, there is usually no alternative. The name thus chosen, therefore, must be so changed by →preaching, teaching, and counseling that it corresponds to the biblical images of God. The same applies to all concepts and descriptions of the holy scriptures.

The translation of Christian concepts is also tied up with subjective considerations. As with the translation of biblical texts, the best analogies possible for the concepts must be sought out, and one must trust that the translation so rendered represents God's word. Basically, however, every language is capable of being translated adequately. The incarnational principle of Christianity is an assurance that language (as an "earthen vessel") offers sufficient scope to bear the Christian message.

Islam, on the contrary, is not an incarnational faith and, according to the orthodox view, cannot be "incarnated" in various languages. Allah speaks only Arabic, which is seen as a holy language whose religious document, the Koran, may not be translated. The free working of the →Holy Spirit, without which a Bible translator cannot work, has no place in Islam.

3. Both on theological and pedagogical grounds, one of the tasks of Christian mission has been to preserve and care for local languages. Such a task was accomplished not without opposition, for, in the colonial period, certain powers wanted the most exclusive possible use of a given European language. Following the colonial period, states which contained speakers of tribal languages tried to suppress those languages and allow only the use of the official language, for example, Amharic in Ethiopia. Indeed, many modern states that are still searching for national unity or identity see in tribal languages a hindrance to political development and want to suppress them. In the face of such attempts, the church must stand up again and again for the right to use one's mother tongue. Spiritual life is hindered without it.

When the right to use a mother tongue is secure, the church should move forward on other tasks relating to a given local language. Standardization is part of this. This is essential and demands compromises on all sides. A language without obligatory orthography and grammar has no future. Single-minded superiority must give way to a consensus. Nothing stands in the way of co-operation on a language of instruction as long as religious education in the lower classes in the mother tongue is guaranteed. If a national language, or even a European language, is introduced, it should only be used as a supplement in preaching. If in certain countries it is regarded as necessary to create a literature with the so-called basic vocabulary, the Bible could also be included in these considerations.

The church should have no hand in damaging a language. The attempts of the British and Foreign Bible Society translators, active since 1812, to make the Bible available to every people in its own language are to be applauded. A minimum literature should be created for even the smallest language unit. For larger groups, the New Testament or the full Bible with the relevant literature is necessary. A Christian literature should be begun in Creole; whether it should also be developed for pidgin languages should be decided on the merits of each case.

4. The variety of contexts in which the Bible was composed — contexts which stretch from the culture of the nomads to the high civilization of the ancient world — engendered a wide extension of vocabulary. This richness, interestingly enough, has been a benefit in mediating the spiritual and ethical values of the biblical revelation to various peoples. Thus, apart from a few necessary foreign words, the translator uses the existing word stock in a given language. Then, through added educational elements, but primarily through interpretation, new Christian ideas and terms are created, terms which were previously unknown to the language. In this way the language undergoes an extension of form and content. There is no sacred language for Christians; every language is concerned with God and receives thereby a special dignity. Some languages in which the future possesses limited meaning (as a consequence of cyclic thought) gain an orientation to the future after the concept of salvation history is connected with local secular history.

Finally, it should be pointed out that among peoples of traditional religions only orally transmitted popular poetry existed. With the translation of the Bible, the age of literature began. In those places, an initial explosion took place — a wide range of literature was created among those peoples; these literatures now develop independently.

The methods of language work in church and mission have changed at the end of the twentieth century. The period of great individual work is over. The future will be determined by joint work across denominational and national boundaries.

ERNST DAMMANN

Bibliography

Altree, W., *Why Talk? A Conversation about Language with Walter J. Ong* (1973). Bevans, S. B., *Models of Contextual Theology* (1992). Cassirer, E., *An Essay on Man: An Introduction to the Philosophy of Human Culture* (1965). Idem, *Language and Myth* (1946). Dammann, E., *Die Übersetzung der Bible in afrikanische Sprachen* (1975). Idem, and E. Rommen, *Contextualization: Meanings, Methods, and Models* (1989). Hiebert, P. G., *Anthropological Insights for Missionaries* (1985). Idem, *Cultural Anthropology* (1976). Knobloch, J., *Sprache und Religion* (1979). Kraft, C. H., *Christianity in Culture: A Study in Dynamic Biblical Theologizing* (1979). Lévi-Strauss, C., *Structural Anthropology* (1963) 31–97. Luzbetak, L. J., *The Church and Cultures* (1988). Mercado, L., *Elements of Filipino Theology* (1975). Miranda, D. M., *Buting Pinoy: Probe Essays on Value as Filipino* (1993). Idem, *Pagkamakabuhay: On the Side of Life* (1994). Müller-Schwefe, H. R., *Die Sprache und das Wort* (1961). Nida, E. A., *Message and Mission: The Communication of the Christian Faith* (1960). Ong, W. J., *Orality and Literacy: The Technologizing of the Word* (1988). Idem, *The Presence of the Word: Some Prolegomena for Culture and Religious History* (1981). Osborn, N. O., "Principles of Dynamic Equivalence" and "Examples from the Ilokano Popular Version Bible," *IlRev* 14 (1982) 4–27; 28–50. Renck, G., *Contextualization of Christianity and Christianization of Language: A Case Study from the Highlands of Papua New Guinea* (1987). Sanneh, L., *Translating the Message: The Missionary Impact on Culture* (1989). Stewart, E. C., and M. J. Bennett, *American Cultural Patterns: A Cross-cultural Perspective* (1991) 45–60. Weigräbe, P., *Gott spricht auch Ewe* (1968).

❧ LATIN AMERICAN THEOLOGY ❧

1. **Theology of the Colonial Period.**   2. **The Period of Independence.** 3. **The Theology of the Catholic Reform.**   4. **Neo-Scholastic Theology.** 5. **Hermeneutical Theology.**   6. **Theology of Development and Liberation.** 7. **Theology of Restoration and Reconciliation.**

Latin American theology is now over five hundred years old. It is a product of the Christian European tradition under the influence of the sociocultural situation of the New World. It is not easy to systematize because its historical sources are scattered all over the Latin American continent and the influence exercised by the African and local religious traditions has not yet been adequately investigated. The long experience of foreign economic, political, and cultural domination has left such a mark on the pastoral practice and theology of the church that it is far more concerned with foreign problems than with its own. Nevertheless, since the early days of the church in Latin America, we can find seeds of a specific and original Latin American theology. These seeds are being studied by CEHILA (Comisión de Estudios de Historia de la Iglesia en América Latina = Commission for the Study of Church History in Latin America), and this article is partially based on the commission's findings. What is related here can only be provisional, especially since the monographical studies are very scarce. For practical reasons we will give more extensive consideration to Brazilian sources.

1. In Latin America the conquerors planted civil and ecclesiastical institutions with their corresponding theology. The flourishing theology of sixteenth-century Spanish Scholasticism took root in the New World by means of academic institutions such as the universities in Mexico and Lima, the Jesuit colleges, the Dominican and Franciscan convents, and the seminaries. In these settings, theologians followed the strict Scholastic syllogistic method — the theological proofs were taken from the scriptures, church tradition (the Fathers of the Church, the councils), and natural reason; they wrote commentaries on the scriptures or the classics, in particular on the *Summa Theologiae* of Aquinas and his commentators (Cajetan, F. Suárez, John of St. Thomas, D. Bañez, L. de Molina, D. de Soto, and F. de Vitoria), or discussed speculative issues such as *De Auxiliis* or probabilism. This theology played into the hands of the conquerors because it emphasized the obligatory nature of evangelization to the detriment of the freedom of the Indians (see M. da Nóbrega) and the identification of the reign of God and divine providence with the presence of the Spanish and Portuguese conquerors in America. In the Portuguese-speaking world it was held as a basic principle that the reign of God realized itself through Portugal. "All kings are from God. The other kings too are from God but installed by human beings; the king of Portugal is from God and installed by God. Hence he belongs to God in a very real sense" (A. Vieira). Through the influence of messianic movements of the time, a holy and salvific character was ascribed to the history of Portugal and a real missionary task to the king so that the "holy war" against the Indians was regarded as justified for the foreign invaders. "In the other territories some are servants of the gospel and others not; but in the countries conquered by Portugal all are servants of the gospel" (A. Vieira). Slavery was justified as liberation and redemption for the blacks because, it was claimed, they crossed over from the slavery of the soul in Africa to liberation in the promised land (baptism in Brazil). This is a theology that confirms the politico-religious colonial system and conceives God as a God of the order established by the conquerors. Whoever opposes such an order sins, rejects salvation, and deserves to be punished by God.

When a continent is conquered by force and exposed to severe oppression, a penitential theology can emerge or take root which is the reverse of the theology of the conquering Christendom, manifesting various dimensions. The religious orders especially, influenced by the medieval tradition of *contemptus mundi* of the Augustinian and Platonic type, developed the ascetic and spiritual dimension. On the one hand, this theology made the poor give up hope and accept the evils of this life in the expectation of another; on the other hand, it made the rich demonstrate their spirit of sacrifice by performing acts of charity and giving alms. The theological and spiritual dimension reveals itself in the identification with the suffering of Christ, an identification helped by a devotion to Christ's passion that was nourished by the preaching of the missionaries. In Peru and other countries, the preaching on the seven words of Jesus on the cross assumed enormous proportions, and, even today, in many places in Latin America, Good Friday is one of the most popular liturgical feasts. The social dimension presented the situation of suffering and slavery of the Indians and blacks as the consequence of sin and the occasion for them to be converted. These people were seen in a very negative light, as people under the influence of the passions and of sin. Their suffering was part of the salvific plan of God for their redemption. One the one hand, such a theology had a conserving function and denied the legitimacy of any attempt at rebellion and liberation. On the other hand, it possessed a certain liberating function in the sense that it pointed to the suffering →Jesus as the one who is close to the oppressed in their suffering and also gives them strength to resist and courage to continue their struggle for survival; this was the basis for more critical forms of resistance by organization and →liberation. Hence the devotion to the Lord of Miracles (Lima, Peru) and to Our Lady of Guadalupe (Mexico) possessed this prophetic dimension by emphasizing the solidarity of the Lord and the Virgin with the Indians and the oppressed.

This theology also contains prophetic and critical beginnings of a theology of the underside of history. The same theology of grace which conceded the legitimacy of forcible evangelization was also interpreted as a defense of the freedom of the Indians and blacks. M. da Nóbrega, in a work entitled *Casos de consciência* (cases of conscience), treated the question of the freedom of the Indians with regard to the sacraments and worked out an official report which is regarded as one of the oldest legal and moral documents in Brazil. According to this document, the Indians are free by nature, and neither by guilt nor crime can they lose this freedom. There are no peoples who are *jure perpetuo* born for slavery — as European theologians, for example, J. Major of Paris (1469–1550), held. Such theologians defended the conquest and domination of the Indians because they live *bestialiter* and are slaves *natura*. B. de Las Casas (1474–1566), who was converted by a sermon preached by A. de Montesinos, was the first to systematize this prophetic theology. Las Casas attacked the Spaniards for their cruelties to the Indians and compared the former's chances of salvation with those of the Moors and Turks. He defended both a political and a theological thesis. This was the political thesis: America is the richest and most beautiful part of the world. Its inhabitants are human beings endowed with intelligence, boldness, and beauty. Hence the campaigns of the Spaniards against them were never justified; indeed, they were diabolical. The theological thesis is concerned with the Spaniards' image of God. Their God is gold and greed. In contrast, the image of the violated, flagellated, and crucified Christ appears among the Indians. Las Casas asserts enthusiastically that Christ is the head of the unbelievers *in actu* because he deflects them from numerous evils, inspires them with good desires, prepares them to understand and accept the teachings of the faith, enlightens them, and changes and guides their hearts, so that they understand and want today what they neither understood nor wanted yesterday, thus transforming bad tendencies into good ones. He appeals to the Thomistic teaching of divine rule and the guidance of grace. But in order to avoid misunderstandings he backtracks, calls Christ the head of the unbelievers *in potentia* only since they lack the true knowledge of Christ which is given through faith, love, and obedience. Only at the end of the world will the good belong to Christ *in actu et perfecte*. Even though he recognizes papal jurisdiction over the unbelievers, he does not agree with forced conversions. It suffices, he claims, to consider divine providence, which moves, arranges, and brings all things to completion gently and without force. God created human beings as free creatures: therefore, they cannot be forced to believe. Only when the Spaniards promote the temporal and eternal happiness of the peoples of the New World will they be able to free themselves from their sins and vices. This theology presupposes a God who is clearly on the side of the oppressed people (→"people" [*Volk*], "nation") who experience God in such nearness that God is called "*Diosito*" (literally, "little God"), as opposed to the oppressing image of the official omnipotent God of the oppressing power.

In Peru, the Jesuit J. de Acosta (1540–1600) theologically treated mission among the Indians in such a way that his work can be regarded, in one sense, as a justification of colonial conquest and degradation of the Indians. For it contains definite negative statements about the Indians and condones the military escort of missionaries to guarantee their lives in their dangerous pilgrimage seeking to end "the tyranny of the devil." In another sense, however, when we carefully scrutinize his work, we discover that the author really defends the Indians and criticizes the missionary ventures of the conquerors. The basic consideration for him is not the *plantatio ecclesiae,* and still less the *plantatio regni hispanici,* but the propagation of the gospel for the salvation of the Indians. The question of the establishment of the church is only a consequence of this. He defends the universality of salvation with biblical arguments such as the prophecy of the conversion of the Ethiopians and distant peoples (Isaiah 43), the parable of the wedding feast (Mt 22:1–14), and the dreams of Peter and Cornelius (Acts 10:1–43). The texts are applied to the Indians of the New World. Even the wildness of the Indians is transformed into a positive argument; God does not want our talents but our recognition and adoration. Their ignorance and weakness do not exclude them from participation in the sacraments of baptism, →Eucharist (Lord's Supper), and marriage. Following Augustine, de Acosta adopts an evangelizing pedagogy according to which the idolatrous images on the altar should not be destroyed until the Indians first tear them out of their hearts. And the heathen ceremonies should not be abolished until they are replaced by Christian ceremonies. In the same prophetic vein, the Capuchin F. de Jaca (b. 1645) defends the liberty of the blacks in their original state and with even more justification after their baptism. He provides biblical proof that slavery is wrong. He defends "the liberty of the baptismal font" which the baptized acquire when their names are written in the "Book of the Free" and the ransom is paid by the parents, the master, or, more often, the god-parents. Another Capuchin, E. de Moirans (1644–89), pursues the same theological path of defending the liberty of the slaves and opposes the traditional theses of the permissibility of slavery by purchase or because of crime. He advances arguments from holy scripture, civil law, and the statements of Pope Innocent XI in order to prove that slavery is against natural law, divine law, and international law — and consequently morally wrong. He obliges the slaveholder under threat of eternal damnation not only to free the slaves but also to pay them compensation for damages incurred and wages for the work performed. The same A. Vieira who, in accordance with the mentality of his time, theologically defended the colonial system also exhibits prophetic elements of denunciation: "In the state of Maranhão, Lord, there is no other gold or silver except the blood and sweat of the Indians.... From the beginning of the world, including the times of Nero and Diocletian, nothing has caused so much injustice, cruelty, and tyranny as the greed and godlessness of the so-called conquerors of the Maranhão." Before him, two Jesuit professors, G. Leite and M. Garcia, challenged the regime of slavery. They affirmed that "no slave of Africa or Brazil is being held legally" and that, unless there was a change, the way of the Portuguese in Brazil would lead to the damnation of their souls; for they are "murderers and thieves of liberty, of lands, and other people's sweat."

2. The period of independence was a time of sweeping changes. The Christendom of the New World was in crisis. The Jesuits, who played a very important part in the missionary and cultural process of America, were expelled. Independence movements broke out all over the continent. In this connection the importance of the clergy was considerable. A theology emerged at this time which no longer justified the colonial system but rather justified the struggle for freedom. It severed the links with the academic centers, taking hold of the pulpits, periodical literature, the revolutionary daily papers, and the assemblies working out the constitutions. The second phase of Scholasticism gave way to the ideas of the Enlightenment, of the apocalyptic encyclopedists. Even Thomistic and Suárezian principles were appealed to in order to justify the emancipatory process. In Mexico, J. M. Morelos y Pavón (1765–1815) developed the beginnings of an emancipatory theology while involved in revolutionary and military activity; this ended with his death before a firing squad. Morelos y Pavón demonstrates the parallels between the situation of the Jewish and Mexican peoples. Both are oppressed and cry to God for liberation. He compares Spain to Babylon with its cult of Baal that has to be destroyed. God hears the appeal of Anáhuac, entrusts him with the task of independence, provides him with freedom fighters, and leads their army. Our Lady of Guadalupe fights with God on the side of the people. In a miraculous way she liberates the Mexicans and punishes the Spaniards. Humanity is free by creation and grace. Hence the fight for independence is just and harmonizes with God's plan. Opposing it is a sin. The participants in the uprising glorify God.

Another Mexican, S. T. de Mier (1763–1827), denied the legitimacy of the conquest and of the local church of New Spain. For this he used two fundamental religious symbols of →popular religion: Our Lady of Guadalupe and the presence of Saint Thomas the Apostle in America. According to Mier, the Guadalupe image was brought by Saint Thomas himself and, having been venerated for some time and then neglected by the Indians, went missing until after the Spanish conquest when it was found again. This legend provides a theological foundation for the equality of the Mexican and Spanish churches since both have the same apostolic origin, and the folk religiosity of the Indians can be interpreted as a Christian survival and not a work of Satan. In Brazil, J. Caneca (1774–1825) defended the sovereignty of the nation because power is derived from the people. The basic institution of society comes from God but not its definite form, which is for the people to establish or change. Recognizing this power means glorifying God. This political theology defends the participation of the clergy in the temporal sphere because society as such is created by God, who is the author of the laws of nature and human reason. The bishop of Cartagena, J. Fernández de Sotomayor, tried to enlighten the citizens about their rights and duties. He pointed out the error and shame of a "religion of love" at the service of a barbaric conquest. Some priests had consolidated tyranny through the misuse and desecration of the sermon. So he rejects the legitimacy of the conquest, including the papal power to distribute parts of the world, and defends resistance and revolution as the fulfillment of the priestly office. The war of independence is holy and just; subjugation is worse than original sin because there is no kind of baptism for it. The Spaniards who persecute the Indians are like Nero with roles reversed: Christians persecute those who want to be converted. The victories over the Spaniards are compared with biblical episodes — with Judith and the Maccabees — and are viewed as works of the God of the oppressed who breaks the shackles of the Mexicans and restores to them their basic →human rights, that is, choosing and establishing their own governments. This political theology condemns forced evangelization and justifies the independence movement as an expression of love of the Catholic religion. The political emancipatory theology in Chile emphasizes the sin of tyranny, oppression, and fratricide (Gn 4:8–12; Wis 6:3–4; Sir 49:4; Mt 27:37) and the biblical dimension of emancipation, proceeding from passages in Exodus, Kings, Chronicles, and Maccabees. Appealing to the Acts of the Apostles (5:29) and the attitude of some Fathers (John Chrysostom, Gregory of Nazianzus, Ambrose, Basil), this theology defends the possibility of Christian disobedience toward the temporal power. The defense of the sovereignty of the people is supported by theological tradition (Thomas Aquinas and sixteenth-century Spanish Thomism). The antimonarchist tradition of the Old Testament (Jgs 8:23; 1 Sm 8:10–22) and texts of the New Testament (Mt 22:21; Jn 6:15; 18:36) furnish arguments criticizing the institution of the kingdom and supporting the revolution as a liberating and salvific event. There is also an attempt to justify with biblical texts the republican principle of equality (Mt 23:8–9, J. Donoso) in contrast to the authoritarianism of the monarchy (Lk 22:24–27, C. Henríquez, P. Arce). Independence is interpreted as the emergence of the free, fraternal, serving spirit of the gospel as opposed to the authoritarian and violent domination of the Spanish empire. A theology of history is developed in which the three stages of salvation history — the creation in innocence, sin, and redemption — are applied to the situation of America: the Indians before Columbus, the colonial era, and emancipated America. The influence of the Enlightenment is translated into episcopal theories, a high esteem for the early church and the patristic period, and democratic openness (J. M. Bazaguchiascúa [1786–1840]). This theology uses the same theological methods as colonial Christianity: it chooses texts supporting its political thesis, though the texts chosen are from an entirely different perspective. It thus remains a prisoner of a casuistic hermeneutic.

The turbulent years toward the end of the eighteenth century produced a climate favorable for the emergence of a messianic theology. This theology systematized the ever-present utopian yearnings within history which surface with greater intensity in times of crisis. M. Lacunza (1731–1801), a Chilean Jesuit, presents a utopian project of a reign of justice on earth within an evolutionary and dialectical view of history. He leaves behind a cosmic view of the heavenly myths and proposes the perpetual indivisibility of a renewable matter and the future of humankind. The time of happiness will dawn among the poor, the simple, and the innocent. Lacunza supports a millennium within history which will lead in the final phase to a perfect society without domination and with ownership in common. Even though his idea of a heavenly city, founded in heaven and brought to earth, might seem integralist and fundamentalist, he nevertheless radically criticizes power — the political and ecclesiastical system of the Christian West, Rome, the church hierarchy — but without giving offense to the authorities. From a universalistic and liberating perspective he understands the action of Jesus Christ as a new exodus through which the oppressing and sacralized structures are destroyed and the peoples reconciled into a single people. This happens through the instrumentality of the Christian church and will precede the reign of God in the parousia. He understands the kingdom of Christ as the continuation of human history in blessed peace and justice, because he believes in a yet incomplete process of the transformation of the human being and all his or her relationships with nature and others. The universe will not be destroyed but renewed. The glory of humanity will be not only the vision of God but also the vision and enjoyment of the whole of nature. In this way he enhances the status of matter, the evolutionary and dialectical view of history, the hope for God's reign for the oppressed, and faith in the new humanity, liberated and rulers of the universe.

3. The theology of the Catholic reform reflects the influence of the theology of the Council of Trent on Latin America. In Brazil this phenomenon — the Romanization of Catholicism — constituted a common undertaking of a group of bishops, professors, and seminary prefects. An ecclesiology is worked out in which the church is presented as a perfect, hierarchical society, necessary for salvation. It is an apologetic, clerical, and doctrinaire theology. It compiles the teachings of the magisterium without any kind of creativity; it repeats the manuals and catechisms of Europe, in particular those of Rome and France; it rejects the main opposing tendencies of the time: Jansenism, Gallicanism, regalism, and liberalism; it emphasizes the spiritual mission of the church and its autonomy and freedom from the state for the fulfillment of its mission; and it strengthens the power of the bishops in union with the pope, the supreme authority. The defense of the perfect twofold society — church and state — does not involve absolute independence but rather cooperation. The church maintains social order; the state protects and recognizes religion (→religion, religions), especially when there is virtually only one religion within a state. The nation cannot distance itself from the public religious cult (as stated by Archbishop Mosquera of Colombia). This dichotomy extends to the various spheres of life so that there is a distinction between human and secular activities, on the one hand, and spiritual and supernatural ones, on the other. Only the latter can merit eternal life and are salvific. Earth is no more than a place of exile and trial where the real problem is sin. Confession is available as an antidote to this. The spiritual and religious exercises constitute the barometer of Christian life, the sacramental actions being overvalued to the detriment of the traditional devotions of popular piety: processions, veneration of the saints, and feasts. A defeatist and pessimistic view of the world in which the church is attacked by so many enemies — this coincides with the turbulent pontificate of Pius IX — emphasizes restitution and expiation, especially to the Sacred Heart of Jesus and the eucharistic Christ, the prisoner of the tabernacle. The church appears as the symbol of spiritual power, of the hierarchy, of antiliberalism, led by a spirit of restoration and ultramontanism. But this conservative and restorationist theology did not prevent the continuation of the liberal theology of the previous period.

This continuation of liberal theology confirmed the distinction of spheres of activity: the internal sphere for religion, the sociopolitical for the →state, with distinct and separate goals. It argued that the state perverts religion by using it as an instrument. According to C. Martínez Silva of Colombia, liberalism in his country was neither a sin nor an enemy of the faith, as the conservatives wrongly maintained. For there were two liberalisms, the acceptable kind held by the majority of Colombian liberals and the other doctrinaire kind which was incompatible with the church and was condemned by Pius IX as the sum of all heresies (see P. B. Vélez of Colombia). Genuine atheism, the liberals argued, does not consist in the liberty of conscience and faith but in the mutilation of God's gifts of freedom and intelligence. In the case of the abuse of religion, the state can take action (S. Pérez). In Brazil, the liberal theses were defended by J. C. de Morais Carneiro (1850–1916), known under his religious name, Fr. Júlio María. In his first, liberal phase he tried to show how the church adapts to progress and modern civilization without losing its divine constitution. There is a liberalism that uplifts human reason and liberty just as religion does. There is another that degrades God and leads to tyranny and revolt. The church must support the democratic order, must leave the sacristy, must go where people are — with their real problems. In his second phase he began to make the poor, the lowly, and the proletariat (the fruits of the capitalist system) the preferred addressees of the church according to the example of →Jesus, who called the lowly to himself. The tyranny of capital must subject itself to the laws of equality, to the duty of justice and charity. The Christian faith must penetrate the workshops, stamp them with the Christian spirit, proclaim the dignity of the worker in the City of God. Jesus founded the church for the people and not for the upper classes, the aristocrats, the bourgeois, or the dynasties. Hence it is necessary to invite democracy "to the social feast of the gospel. Just as everywhere in the world, in Brazil there are only two forces today: the church and the people." On the one hand, liberal theology as such means progress compared with the dominating conservative tendency; on the other hand, it robs the people of their creative function in religion. Fr. Júlio María attempts to partially correct this deficiency.

4. The impulse given to Scholasticism through the interventions of the magisterium (especially Leo XIII, *Aeterni Patris* [1879]) and the European centers (Rome and Louvain) had its effect on the theology of Latin America. J. Mors, a Brazilian, published six volumes with the main theological tracts. Academic centers and seminaries adopted the school manuals, in particular those of the Gregorian University in Rome. For an emerging, intellectually more demanding laity, M. T.-L. Penido, an enlightened and anticonservative neo-Thomist, connected the intellectual and conceptual perspective of Thomism in an inductive method with an openness for the modern world and the wish for social reform. He was influenced by the intuitive method of H. Bergson and M. Blondel, especially in his study of the "religious phenomenon" in the dimension of experience. The central idea of Penido's neo-Thomism in the Cajetan tradition is the concept of analogy, searching for a middle way between the dry and abstract theology of the manuals and the immanentism of a W. James or the intuitionism of Bergson. He overcomes the intellectualistic conception of the faith through the richness of the writings of J. H. Newman and of Saint John of the Cross and explores the experiential method of knowing God. The path of this neo-Thomist ended in studies on mysticism. For him mysticism is something that does not destroy analogical knowledge but transcends and confirms it. It unmasks symbolism by maintaining the possibility of a real knowledge of God and uncovers the deficiency of anthropomorphic thinking through its recourse to negations. Penido thus offered the first *summa* of a complete theology in the mother tongue to the intellectual laity of his country. The central theme is mystery — the mystery of the church, the mystery of the sacraments, the mystery of Christ.

Another neo-Thomist, the Jesuit L. Franca (1893–1948), became known in Brazil mainly because of two theological works: *The Crisis of the Modern World* and *On the Psychology of Faith*. In the first of these he analyzes the seriousness of the present crisis and how it arose and developed, in order to emphasize the eternal cultural values of the Christian faith. Men and women, destined for the absolute, suffer from the crisis of "the terrifying defenselessness of a rational existence which has lost its orientation toward a goal." They will only find themselves again "in the orientation toward [a] transcendental goal." In the second work, Franca analyzes the act of faith as "the psychological interaction of [various] abilities which . . . come into play, the cooperation of intelligence and will which prepare and justify it [i.e., faith]," and he lists the intellectual and moral impediments of the act of faith. He backs up his remarks with numerous examples from the experience of nonbelievers, believers, and converts. In a period of a very conservative ecclesial theology and praxis in the whole of Latin America, Franca's neo-Thomism was in the direction of openness, albeit cautious and not very concerned about social issues.

5. As soon as neo-Thomism was taken up by Catholic Action and the liturgical and social movements, it ended by implosion. On a political level, Latin America experienced the spontaneous development of capitalism; on a church level, the opening was created by Pope John XXIII and Vatican II. Theology tried to give answers to the questions of a more demanding laity and the growing number of ecclesiastical movements. The liturgical movement went beyond neo-Thomistic theology by bringing into the center of its thinking the fundamental theological experience of the eucharistic mystery as the mystery of Christ and the church. The liturgy expresses itself together with Christ the Victor, present in his body the church. Redemption becomes present in and through the liturgy, the center of which is the Eucharist. The cosmos participates in this victory of Christ and already anticipates God's eschatological reign. This theology is a reaction to an individualistic, subjectivistic, and sentimental religiosity (e.g., that of M. Michler, OSB, of Rio). The practical way to overcome this religiosity is participation in the Eucharist, the sacrifice of the whole church, the *sacramentum unitatis;* another way to overcome that religiosity is to employ religious instruction with a social emphasis (T. Keller). Biblical theology is confronted with the development of modern exegesis and demythologization.

To sum up, in the period just before and after Vatican II, theology in Latin America followed the main direction of modern liberal European theology and had still to find an adequate response to the situation of the Latin American continent. The liberal model had failed because it is elitist, far from the poor, and has no interest in the social aspects of reality. Under the influence of M. Heidegger, personalism, the phenomenon of secularization, and P. Teilhard de Chardin, an existential hermeneutic was developed (by L. Boff and members of the Franciscan Theological Institute, Petrópolis, Brazil). Ecclesiology renewed itself, abandoned R. Bellarmine's model, and adopted the ideas of the mystical body (A. Lorscheider) and the sacramental dimension (B. Kloppenburg, L. Boff). The theology of Catholic Action, under the influence of thinkers like J. Maritain and E. Mounier, produced socially aware and committed activists who wanted to evangelize a world of contradictions, conflicts, and injustice and who were concerned about the problem of the relationship of church and world, evangelization and secular action, Christian commitment and political activity. This opened the way for the dialectical theology of development and subsequently that of liberation, a way which first proceeded through the theology of earthly realities (C. Koser). In Uruguay, J. L. Segundo worked out various central themes of theology (God, grace, church, sacraments, sin) in a perspective open for modern laity who belong to the most critical class of the continent. But we are still in a theological phase which is very distant from the real questions of a poor continent groaning under the weight of gross injustice.

6. In the next phase, Latin American theology began to explore new pathways, abandoning the hermeneutic phase of subjectivity and pure historicity for a more praxis-oriented hermeneutic. It could not escape the social fact of the underdevelopment of the continent. In view of a development serving the promotion of all, the theology of →development began with the perception of the alienation of the Latin American process of history and the necessity of breaking with the current colonial structures. It distanced itself from the dominant view of progress because it noticed the inhuman character of the domination of the countries of the periphery and the impossibility of their determining their own history. Increasing importance was attached to the culture of the people, conscientization, and human promotion, so that the masses could become a people, the real subjects of history. The mystery of the incarnation became the paradigm of commitment to promotion of individuals and peoples on the basis of a dynamic understanding of humanity — as persons, free creatures, and subjects of history. At the same time an attempt was made to overcome the liberal and Marxist view, moralism, and reformism, going directly to the root of the evil, the situation of injustice caused by the colonial structure (C. Mendes de Almeida). This presupposed the transition from a Greek, rather static worldview to a "historical consciousness" (H. C. Lima Vaz). The situation of underdevelopment and exploitation on the Latin American continent impeded a real unity of consciousness on a national and international level. The monotheism of creation and the mystery of the incarnation offered theological parameters for questioning the situation of capitalistic domination as well as Marxist doctrine, the anthropology of which is reductionist. Revelation presents a person who is created free, open to God and his or her brothers and sisters, and called to transform the world through activity. God is revealed through the word and the mystery of the incarnation in human history, so that the Absolute, the origin of history, makes itself the center, fact, and norm of history. This Absolute establishes humanity definitely in the category of consciousness and gives a transcendent meaning to human history. Real development takes place only where room is made for the communion of consciousness and its expansion; for the social existence of humanity is based on this communion. In a later phase, there was an attempt to go beyond this, with *Gaudium et Spes* and *Populorum Progressio* as guidelines, using the inductive method and searching for the special nature of the Third World problems. In order to suggest that the progression from underdevelopment to development is by no means smooth, it was argued that the concept of development is wider than the meaning of "continual progress." Consequently, theological thinking too had to outgrow the progressivist doctrine of the Enlightenment in favor of a theology embedded in the concrete processes of historical transformation. This implied certain options: in the first place, criticism of the presence of Christians in a profoundly anti-Christian status quo; it implied further that Christians abandon their tactical collaboration with the system and that they develop an eschatological faith which would serve as an exorcism and criticism of ideological inflexibility. It implied as well a radical willingness to inculturate ideologically; the emergence of church wherever people create conditions for fraternal unity; a thoroughly open anthropology; a Johannine view of the world (with which we can establish no alliance because of its hatreds); an understanding of domination as a hindrance for a possible church as sacrament, so that development appears as a precondition for a church-in-the-world; and, finally, an ethic of development which includes the judgment of the present (H. Assmann). In this theology of development we see the first traces of the →theology of liberation.

7. As a reaction to neoliberal and liberation theologies, conservative theologies in the exaggerated form of integralism or in the moderate form of "restoration" or "reconciliation" theology have also emerged in Latin America. The integralist theology has an ecclesiastical and a political dimension. Ecclesiastically, it reinforces Bellarmine's model of the church as a perfect and visible society, rejects the liturgical reforms, insists on biblical fundamentalism, and supports those traditional groups that have a Tridentine way of looking at things. It maintains Scholasticism in its most rigidly dogmatic form and rejects every principle of interpretation relating to situation, history, subjectivity, or a dialectical view of reality. Thus this theology retains the classical category of substance, according to which the intelligence is anchored only in the unchangeable essence of things, in the eternal truths — regardless of accidental changes or different formulations. Politically, this theology reinforces the conservative positions of the landed oligarchy in some countries and the bourgeois liberals in industrialized nations who oppose changes of a popular nature; at the same time it accepts the modernizing changes that are cultivated by these people in positions of power. After liberation theology had become established in the church of Latin America, "reconciliation theology" developed with the intention of replacing it. It presents itself as the corrective to liberation theology and, while maintaining the language of liberation, nevertheless claims to rectify the contents of liberation theology, which it regards as misleading and erroneous. It continues to speak about the fundamental option for the poor, for justice, and for the structural transformation of society, but, preferring a policy of reconciliation, it distances itself from any view of society involving struggle. Reconciliation theology rejects political mediation and concentrates on the individual conversion of hearts. Reconciliation offers the hermeneutical key for realigning the social projects with God's plan. Hence every ideology involving struggle is seen in its theological negativity, as a dynamic of death; reconciliation, in contrast, bears within itself the dynamic of life. Conflict will dissolve into the logic of reconciliation by consensus, the dynamic dialogue of complementarity and responsible cooperation through brotherly and creative encounter. This theology opposes any pastoral ministry along the lines of conscientization and organization of the people. It forgets the enormous inequality of the opposing parties and the long historical tradition of domination which makes dialogue impossible unless the weaker party, the people, can first conscientize and organize itself. It is a theological discourse that amounts to disarming the weaker and strengthening the stronger. In this sense the theology of reconciliation plays into the hands of conservative forces, rendering the people powerless.

Latin American theology has its own history. Until the emergence of liberation theology it was for the most part a pure adaptation of the European theologies (→European theology) to Latin America without originality or any special characteristics peculiar to itself. In the course of the centuries, however, it did manage to develop a theology in embryonic form which took the real needs and conditions of the colonized, enslaved, and dominated people as its starting point. After Vatican II it asserted itself in the form of liberation theology, which at present is questioned by the integralist and conservative theology of reconciliation. Nevertheless, it remains a very inspiring theology, legitimizing a liberating pastoral praxis dedicated to the poor.

J. B. Libânio

Bibliography

Acosta, J. de, *De Procuranda Indorum Salute* (1588). Almeida, C. M. de, *Nacionalismo e Desenvolvimento* (1963). André-Vincent, P. I., "L'inituition fondamentale de Las Casas et la doctrine de Saint Thomas," *NRTh* 96 (1974) 994–1052. Assmann, H., "Tarefas e limitações de uma teologia do desenvolvimento," *Vozes* 62 (1968) 13–21. Azzi, R., *Catolicismo popular no Brasil: Aspectos históricos* (1978). Bie, J. de, *God in de sermoenen van Vieira* (1970). Boff, L., *Ecclesiogenesis: The Base Communities Reinvent the Church* (1986). Idem, *Jesus Christ Liberator: A Critical Christology for Our Time* (1978). Idem, *O evangelho do Christo cósmico: A realidade de um mito, o mito de uma realidade* (1971). Bruneau, M., et al., eds., *The Catholic Church and Religions in Latin America* (1984). Cleary, E. L., *Crisis and Change: The Church in Latin America Today* (1985). Cleary, E. L., and H. Stewart-Gambino, eds., *Conflict and Competition: The Latin American Church in a Changing Environment* (1992). Comblin, J., *História da teologia católica* (1969). Idem, *Os sinais dos tempos e a evangelização* (1968). Costa, J. B. P., *Ação Católica* (1937). Dale, R., *A Ação Católica Brasileira* (1985). Dussel, E., ed., *The Church in Latin America 1492–1992* (1992). Eagleson, J., and P. Scharper, eds., *Puebla and Beyond* (1979). Ellacuría, I., and J. Sobrino, *Mysterium Liberationis: Fundamental Concepts of Liberation Theology* (1993). Franca, L., *A crise do mundo moderno* (1955). Idem, *A psicologia da fé* (1952). Goodpasture, H. M., *Cross and Sword: An Eyewitness History of Christianity in Latin America* (1989). Gutiérrez, G., *Las Casas: In Search of the Poor of Jesus Christ* (1993). Idem, *A Theology of Liberation*, rev. ed. (1988). Hennelly, A. T., *Santo Domingo and Beyond* (1993). Hoornaert, E., *Formação do Catolicismo Brasileira 1550–1800* (1974). Lacunza y Díaz, M., *La venida del mesias in gloria y majestad* (1813). Leite, S., *História da Companhia de Jesus no Brasil*, 10 vols. (1938). Lopetegui, L., *El Padre José Acosta y las misiones* (1942). Moura, O., "Direçóes do pensamento católico no Brasil do séc. XX," in A. Crippa, ed., *As idéias filosóficas no Brasil séc, XX*, pt. 1 (1978) 130–205. Nóbrega, M. da, *Diálogo sobre a conversão do gentio* (1954). Penido, M. T.-L., *O mistério de Cristo* (1969). Richard, P., ed., *Materiales para una historia de la teología en América Latina* (1981). Segna, E. V., *Análise crítica do Catolicismo do Brasil e perspectivas para uma pastoral de libertação* (1977). Segundo, J. L., *A Theology for the Artisans of a New Humanity*, 5 vols. (1973–74). Silva, J. A. da, *O movimento litúrgico no Brasil: Estudo histórico* (1983). Silveira, G. M. de, *Conhecimento de Deus e experiencia religiosa segundo M. T. L. Penido* (1973). Third Latin American Congress on Evangelism, "The Whole Gospel from Latin America to All Peoples," in J. A. Scherer and S. B. Bevans, eds., *New Directions in Mission and Evangelization*, vol. 2, *Theological Foundations* (1994) 191–98. Torres, J. C. de Oliveira, *História das Idéias Religiosas no Brasil* (1968). Vaz, H. C., *Ontologia e História* (1968). Vieira, A., *História do Futuro* (1718). Idem, *Sermóes*, 15 vols. (1907–9).

❧ LIBERATION ❧

1. The Concept. 2. Liberation in the Old Testament. 3. Liberation in the New Testament. 4. From the Fathers to Modern Times. 5. Political Theology. 6. J. Moltmann's Model. 7. Liberation Theology in Latin America. 8. Critical Evaluation of the Various Models. 9. Reaction of the Sacred Congregation for the Doctrine of the Faith.

1. It is only in modern times and especially in the →liberation theology of the twentieth century that liberation has become a theological concept in Christian theology. The traditional concept used was redemption. The questions to be answered are as follows: What has the Christ-event accomplished? Is the term "liberation" (with its connotations) today a more adequate expression for this event than "redemption"? What does liberation add to the concept of redemption? Is the term "redemption" superfluous today?

2. Liberation plays a pivotal part in the soteriology of the Old Testament. It appears especially in the exodus tradition, in the time after the exile, in Deutero-Isaiah, and also in prayer texts, for example, in the Psalms.

In the Old Testament, liberation means deliverance from an evil situation by the aid of Yahweh and not by human means. Salvation as a result of the liberating act is a salvation in this world (though it is true that the Old Testament also expresses hope in the hereafter). Some texts (Deutero-Isaiah) that come to us from the time after the exile perhaps hint at a change of the social structures. But N. Lohfink points out that these texts should be interpreted with care. He feels that some liberation theologians use the Old Testament rather superficially.

3. "Freedom" and "liberation" are not the most common terms used in the New Testament to explain the liberating action of Jesus. The concepts more frequently used are redemption, salvation, deliverance, and forgiveness. The term "freedom" has no direct political connotation. Paul uses it in an individual-existential sense.

The New Testament concepts of liberation and freedom become clearer when we examine the liberating action of Jesus and his message of the reign of God. Jesus freed humanity from the slavery of sin, but this had consequences as well for social conditions.

4. From patristic times onward the subject of liberation is treated predominantly within the context of redemption. The Fathers had different ways of looking at redemption, but in general they saw it as worked out through a process involving new knowledge, teaching, guidance, and the example of Christ.

These ideas have to be understood against the background of the Platonic notion of *paideia:* by a process of maturation through shadowy images the human person arrives at true reality. By imitating this reality (*mimesis*), that person reaches true being. This imitation of the true reality of God permits a person to share in God's life (*methexis*). Knowledge of and commitment to Christ enable men and women to achieve *mimesis* and *methexis* and thus to participate in the life of God and "become real."

The sociocultural background of the Latin Western church differs from that of the world that generated these Platonic notions. The Latin Western church thus had a different conception of liberation. It emphasized practical lifestyle and the legal structure of the community. Concepts like responsibility, guilt, and reward were central. The Latin idea of redemption, therefore, was concerned with the mending of the break between God and humanity. Such concern with the restoration of the legal *ordo* destroyed by humankind's sin found its full expression in the satisfaction theory proposed by Anselm of Canterbury.

All these different views on redemption revolve around the question of how men and women can regain their freedom: either through participation in the life of God or by the restoration of the legal order, allowing humanity to regain dignity and freedom.

In modern times the question of subjectivity has become very important. The subject seeks to emancipate itself from all restrictions, fulfill itself, and decide its own fate. Into this process of humanity finding itself, God is introduced as merely one factor in the history of the freedom of the subject. This is what modern theology takes as a starting point when it investigates the conditions for human freedom in the world and society.

5. Political theology deals with human beings as subjects before God in the concrete historical situation. If humanity becomes the subject of its history, it gains freedom. But modern emancipation ought not to be uncritically linked with Christian redemption. The history of redemption is not to be regarded simply as something which surpasses the history of emancipation. Redemption means not only liberation from political and social oppression but above all liberation from guilt and death. Redemption also includes those who fail and those who have died.

The Enlightenment produced the "bourgeois subject." This is the autonomous, reasonable, mature individual. He or she has freed himself or herself from the spiritual and religious traditions of the surrounding milieu. By fighting against such traditions — whether feudalism or absolutism — men and women win their freedom. The whole of social life is regulated by the principle of exchange. Thus men and women reject everything that does not have exchange-value. The laws of calculating reason, the marketplace, and profit are crucial. All other values belong to the private sphere. Religion becomes one service among others. The loss of tradition shows itself most clearly in the relationship to the dead. They do not fit into the exchange society, so any meaningful relationship with them is lost. The relationship to the dead becomes a private matter. What liberation means for them cannot be explained. The loss of tradition also leads to the devaluation of traditional attitudes which have no exchange-value, for example, friendliness, gratitude, and loyalty.

Thus in the Enlightenment the property-owning bourgeois person became the representative of reason. The aim was not liberation, however, but domination: domination over nature, domination in the interest of the market.

Political theology points out that this modern process of emancipation, autonomy, and freedom cannot simply be identified with Christianity. Otherwise Christianity would be a canonization of factual development. The bourgeois concept of freedom supplants the genuine Christian concept of freedom, which is critical of society.

The modern concepts "subject," "existence," and "person," with their tendency to emphasize privatization, should not be adapted uncritically. The solidarity of all subjects has to be emphasized.

Relationship to God helps constitute the subject and create its identity. In the Bible, religion is no secondary phenomenon but participates in the building up of the subject. An example of this is the way in which Israel becomes a subject in the exodus. The relationship to God does not result in the enslavement of the people but, in the face of danger, enables them to become subjects. The struggle for God and the struggle to become a free subject proceed in the same direction. The subject concerned is never the individual alone but always the person in experience with others. So the form in which the subject exists before God is "universal solidarity."

In this context remembrance and narration form categories of liberation. The destruction of remembrance prevents identity, prevents the human being from becoming and remaining subject. The deportation of slaves, for example, led to the destruction of remembrance and so consolidated their subjugation. For the sake of the subject, Christian practice must always judge the prevailing conditions with a critical eye.

6. J. Moltmann takes the theology of the cross as the starting point of his concept of liberation. The historical way of Jesus to the cross shows the concrete way to the liberation of humanity and motivates human activity toward liberation. Moltmann emphasizes the following aspects of the way of the cross:

- Jesus is condemned as a lawbreaker and blasphemer because he sets his God of promise and hope against the God of the law. Where the cross is confirmed through the raising from the dead, it becomes a protest against the prevailing conditions and a sign of hope for God's new world.

- A political punishment is imposed on Jesus. He dies as a rebel against the political powers of his time, which he opposed with his message of the exclusive lordship of God. His being raised from the dead, therefore, becomes a protest against every form of religious justification of political power.

- Jesus dies utterly deserted by God. His being raised from the dead shows that God was present in the suffering of Jesus. God is woven into the passion of humanity. In this way God gives broken humanity hope for a new and final future.

With this theology of the cross as a basis, Moltmann develops a "political hermeneutic of liberation." What does the presence of the crucified God mean for human society? The object here is not only an abstract definition of the relationship between faith and political action but the concrete religious problems of politics, that is, the vicious circles in economic and social life which obstruct true humanity and even make it impossible. The situation of the crucified God makes us aware of human situations of bondage and shows how they can be overcome. This is a question not of a reduction of the theology of the cross to a political theology but of its "interpretation as political discipleship." The political hermeneutic wants to clarify the socioeconomic conditions of the theological institutions and languages so that their liberating content can assert itself in inhuman situations.

Christian freedom and liberation must not remain abstract and on the level of principles, for this would expose concrete freedom to the danger of being reduced to the realm of the merely possible and arbitrary. Rather, people should be given the opportunity to experience the liberating presence of God in the vicious circles of human misery.

One may ask what Moltmann means by liberation. A political hermeneutic for him is a hermeneutic of life in the history of the passion of God. For this reason it includes both praxis and change of praxis. Liberation must always be practiced in specific "vicious circles" which prevent people from being really human. There are hopeless systems in the economic, social, and political spheres which lead to death. In any specific situation there are always several vicious circles which interact. And so Moltmann does not speak of liberation but of liberations (in the plural). Liberation must be simultaneously promoted in several spheres because the different vicious circles are interdependent.

In regard to the economic sphere, Moltmann speaks of the vicious circle of poverty. It consists of problems like hunger and sickness that are caused by exploitation and class rule. These conditions obtain within nations and between nations. The vicious circle of violence is connected with that of poverty. Here some of the key notions are dictatorship, suppression of →human rights and self-determination, and the arms race. The vicious circle of poverty and violence is bound up with that of racial and cultural alienation. People are robbed of their identity and manipulated. Today in this context there is the additional vicious circle of the industrial destruction of nature.

All these interrelated vicious circles lead to a sense of futility and being forsaken by God; they lead to inhumanity and death. Liberating action must assert itself in these vicious circles. In the economic sphere, liberation means social justice, providing material necessities, and workers' participation in industrial decisions. In the political sphere, it means democracy, that is, participation in and control of power. In the cultural dimension of life, liberation means the discovery of one's own identity and recognition of the rights of others. In ecological terms, liberation means peace with nature. As an answer to the sense of futility, liberation means the belief that life as a whole is meaningful. It means the conviction that God is with us as the essential meaning of life. This faith gives people the courage to live; it gives hope.

Since the vicious circles are interrelated, there can be peace (→peace and mission) among human beings and between humanity and nature only when men and women believe that life as a whole has meaning. Conversely, meaning can only be experienced where efforts are made to liberate people from all these evils. In short, as long as liberation is understood as an abstract concept only, it does not become real. For the theological concept of liberation this means that the liberation brought about by God becomes a reality only when it is realized in the afflictions of humanity. In other words, eschatology is only realized in the specific historical situation.

7. The Latin American theology of liberation (→Latin American theology) emerged out of the disenchantment with the development programs of the 1960s.

The radical rethinking of many Christians regarding the real conditions in Latin America and the possibilities for change is identified with names like H. Camara and N. Paz. At the beginning of the 1960s, a vague hope prevailed that the mass poverty of Latin America could be solved by technological solutions and development projects (→development). Because of the total lack of success of those attempts, many Latin Americans became convinced that such schemes only consolidated the traditional social structure without coming to grips with the causes of underdevelopment. The failure of these development programs convinced many Christians at the grass roots of the necessity of a break with the prevailing system. At the same time the results of Vatican II (→Vatican Council II) and the encyclical *Populorum Progressio* made many Christians wake up. CELAM (Consejo Episcopal Latinoamericano = Episcopal Conference of Latin America) took up the suggestions of Vatican II. Many theologians, taking their cue from the bishops, at various meetings contrasted the conciliar statements with the cruel reality of their continent.

Liberation theology takes the concrete situation in Latin America as its starting point. It does not do this, however, in a theoretical way but rather analyzes the concrete *experiences* of Christians in the liberating process. They articulate their problems, faith experiences, and insights in light of the reality of Christianity. This reflection takes place not only on a purely academic level but where the pulse of history beats — that is, in the liberating process. The starting point for this theology is the praxis of liberation, that is, concrete commitment to the oppressed, both individuals and entire peoples. It starts with the specific and practical option for the poor and oppressed. The whole of reality is judged and the →word of God understood from this angle.

Theology, therefore, is not the basis and pastoral practice the consequence. Theology is a reflection on the activity of the church; the presence of the Spirit has to be discovered in it. Theology should not only be concerned with the life of the church, however; it needs to draw inspiration from the problems of the world and history. Only in this way can theology really express God's word in a new way for its own time. In this way it is not static and sterile, as if it were based on "eternal" truths.

Liberation is the core concept of this theology. What does it mean and what is its relation to the theological concept of redemption? Human history is understood as a *process of liberation* of humanity. Through this process a new society with a new humanity gradually develops. It is a question of a permanent "cultural revolution" at the end of which there will be a world "where every person, no matter what race, religion or nationality, can live a fully human life, freed from servitude imposed by others or by natural forces over which humanity has not sufficient control" (*PP* 47).

Three levels of meaning are to be distinguished in the concept of liberation:

- Liberation refers to the aspirations of oppressed social classes and peoples. Their oppression is the result of conflicts which cannot be solved by a process of development. This is possible only through radical liberation.

- On a deeper level, liberation means a process in which humanity takes its fate into its own hands. It is a dynamic process in which men and women gradually develop all their dimensions to find themselves in the end new persons in a qualitatively different society.

- Finally, the process of liberation has a theological aspect. The Bible describes Christ as savior and liberator. He frees humanity from sin, the ultimate cause of any rupture of friendship, of injustice, and of oppression. Christ truly liberates — that is, he makes possible a life of community with him which is the foundation of true community.

These three processes do not run parallel but are mutually inclusive and find their full realization in redemption.

We arrive at the same result if we consider the concept of redemption. Liberation theology recognizes a change in the concept of redemption. The traditional perspective understood redemption as forgiveness of sins in the present life and consequently supernatural salvation. The new concept of redemption holds that the person who opens up to the other is in a state of salvation even when he or she is not fully aware of these things. By acknowledging the presence of grace in all people, this view grants a Christian value to all human behavior. Seen from this angle, redemption has an aspect not observed before. Salvation is no longer understood as something "otherworldly." It is already concretely active in history.

In this connection the concept of sin is also of special importance. Sin is not seen as an individual, personal, private, and internal reality which needs merely a "spiritual" deliverance without touching the order in which we live; it is rather a social and historical reality. It becomes tangible in oppressive structures, in the exploitation of people by people, in the domination and enslavement of peoples, races, and social classes. Sin, therefore, demands a radical liberation which includes political liberation. →Salvation is a historical reality. Redemption as communion of human beings with God and with one another gives direction to history, changes it, and leads it to its fulfillment.

These statements about liberation belong to the greater context of the relationship between progress within the temporal sphere and the →reign of God.

The liberation of humanity and the growth of the reign of God are both oriented to the perfect community of human beings with God and with one another. Both have the same goal. Their ways, however, do not run parallel or converge. The growth of the reign of God is a process which is realized in historical liberation insofar as this results in a fuller realization of humanity and creates the conditions for a new society. But the reign of God is more than liberation. It takes shape in the historical attempts at liberation but at the same time points to their limitations and ambiguities and so cannot be identified with historical liberations. The reign of God is a gift of God which will only be fully achieved at the end of history.

8. We have examined three models of liberation above. (*a*) J. B. Metz is critical of the rash identification of liberation and modern emancipation. Religious liberation must always be critical of the prevailing conditions in church and society. Liberation means that all persons — in the past, present, and future — are subjects before God. (*b*) J. Moltmann bases his concept of liberation on the theology of the cross. Because God is present in the suffering of humankind, God is the guarantor of final liberation. (*c*) Liberation theology starts from concrete praxis and from there arrives at its concept of liberation. All three models emphasize that one cannot proceed from an abstract concept of liberation but must take concrete history into consideration in order to learn what liberation is. They differ in their specific approaches.

Metz is against bringing humanity's history of suffering into the trinitarian history of God. According to him, a conceptual and logical mediation between salvation as a historical reality, on the one hand, and the human history of suffering, on the other, is out of the question. He attempts to solve the problem with the categories "remembrance" and "narration." In Moltmann's view, the way to liberation proceeds by way of the theology of the cross, which is itself anchored in the teaching of the Trinity. Finally, liberation theology must analyze in greater depth its relation to the social sciences, which it uses to carry out its situational analysis. In addition, the relationship between human well-being and the reign of God needs more profound reflection.

9. On March 22, 1986, the Sacred Congregation for the Doctrine of the Faith declared its position on "liberation" in an instruction entitled "Christian Freedom and Liberation." The theme is situated in the context of the history of freedom since the beginning of modern times and gives a description of the situation of freedom in the world. Progress in the realization of freedom is described, but the ambiguities of modern liberation processes are also pointed out.

The dangers for freedom can only be averted by the truth and love brought by Christ. Thus the Christian concept of freedom is emphasized. Human freedom is based on the notion that the human being is created as a free person called to enter into community with God. Freedom is the freedom of a created being. As creature, the human being is the image of God. This image of God in humanity is the foundation of freedom and dignity of the human person. This concept of freedom determines the concept of earthly liberation, which refers to the totality of the processes which aim at creating the conditions which are necessary for the realization of true human freedom.

Sin is the source of all oppression and alienation. It also creates unjust structures. Thus Christian liberation means that God has freed humanity from sin through Jesus Christ and so enabled it to live again in true freedom. The goal of liberation is the final encounter with Christ. This hope does not lessen commitment for progress in earthly matters but, on the contrary, gives it meaning and strength.

The liberating mission of the church aims at the comprehensive salvation of humanity and the world. The power of the gospel penetrates into human history; it purifies and vivifies it. At this point the instruction emphasizes in a special way the love which makes an option for the poor. It also emphasizes that structural changes in society are absolutely necessary.

The instruction treats the theme "liberation and freedom" comprehensively. The social, political, and cultural dimensions of freedom are emphasized. It also points out the importance of changing structures. Its positive evaluation of the preferential option for the poor should not be ignored. By way of criticism, it has to be said that the instruction uses an ahistorical concept of freedom; commitment to liberation is framed as an ethical claim, not as a theological dimension.

HERIBERT BETTSCHEIDER, SVD

Bibliography

Alfaro, J., *Esperanza Cristiana y liberación del hombre* (1972). Bauer, J., *Freiheit und Emanzipation: Ein philosophisch-theologischer Traktat* (1974). Bettscheider, H., ed., *Theologie und Befreiung* (1974). Boff, C., *Theology and Praxis: Epistemological Foundations* (1987). Boff, L., *Church: Charism and Power* (1985). Idem, *Ecclesiogenesis: The Base Communities Reinvent the Church* (1986). Idem, *Faith on the Edge: Religion and Marginalized Existence* (1989). Bonino, J. M., *Doing Theology in a Revolutionary Situation* (1975). Comblin, J., "La thème de la libération dans la pensée chrétienne latino-américaine," *RN* 55 (1972) 560–74. Congregation for the Doctrine of the Faith, *Instruction on Christian Freedom and Liberation* (1986). Fiorenza, F. Schüssler, "Redemption," in *New Dictionary of Theology* (1987) 836–57. Fischer, G. D., "Befreiung: Zentralbegriff einer neuorientierten lateinamerikanischen Theologie," *ThGl* 63 (1973) 1–23. Gatti, J., "Liberación," in L. Pacomio, et al., eds., *Diccionario teológico interdisciplinar*, 3 (1982) 310–18. Greshake, G., *Geschenkte Freiheit: Einführung in die Gnadenlehre* (1977). Gutiérrez, G., *A Theology of Liberation*, rev. ed. (1988). Kessler, H., *Erlösung als Befreiung* (1972). Metz, J. B., *Faith in History and Society* (1980). Moltmann, J., *The Crucified God* (1974). Paul VI, Pope, *Evangelii Nuntiandi* (1975). Rahner, K., "The Christian Understanding of Redemption," in *TI* 21 (1988) 239–54. Scheffczyk, L., ed., *Erlösung und Emanzipation* (1973). Schillebeeckx, E., *Christ: The Experience of Jesus as Lord* (1981).

✎ LIBERATION THEOLOGY ✎

1. The Sociopolitical Context of Liberation Theology. 2. The Ecclesial Context. 3. Some False Definitions. 4. The Fundamental Option for the Poor. 5. The New Hermeneutical Process. 6. The Praxis-Related Dimension. 7. The Various Trends in Latin America. 8. Africa. 9. Asia. 10. Feminist Theology and Other Forms of Liberation Theology.

In countries of the Third World and especially in Latin America, liberation theology constitutes a sociopolitical reality which not only has captured the interest of the media but has already made an impact in the political sphere. Repressive capitalistic regimes persecute its supporters and ban its publications. Regimes which are more oriented toward the masses show an interest in this theology in the hope of obtaining the support of religious groups for projects they consider liberating for the people. But liberation theology is above all an *ecclesial reality*. Local churches which are more committed to the option for the poor look to it for theoretical support and justification. A unique fact about this theology, which has emerged from countries on the ecclesial periphery, is that it has found an echo in European theology and among the highest authorities of the church.

1. Liberation theology originated in Latin America (→Latin American theology), became rooted there, and has spread to other countries of the Third World, where it has developed features proper to those contexts. Three social factors have been decisive for this development: the situation of domination and oppression, the emergence of a consciousness of liberation, and the lack of political channels to collect and develop such a consciousness. The situation of oppression has a long history. The current form is rooted primarily in the structure of First World colonialism and the slavery connected with it — a structure that was operative in Latin America from the beginning of the Spanish-Portuguese colonization. The wars of independence and the political situation resulting from them were not capable of breaking with this structure. Then followed English and American imperialism, and finally neocapitalism with its modern and refined forms of exploitation. The Latin American bishops meeting at Puebla, Mexico, drew a realistic picture of this situation. In this situation of oppression there emerges a strong *consciousness of liberation* which expresses itself in manifold activities. The 1950s witnessed the mobilization of people for nationalistic goals directed against exploitation by foreign powers. Although these movements were neutralized, either by the machinations of charismatic political figures or through the intervention of repressive military forces, they nevertheless created a climate of liberation. This gained momentum in different countries by means of an extensive campaign to bring about basic reforms in the rural sector, in public administration, in universities, in the voting system, and so on. Hand in hand with student movements in other parts of the world (United States, France, etc.), the students of Latin America organized themselves into liberation corps, some of them even in clandestine revolutionary groups. The trade unions in the rural and urban areas multiplied and became a significant presence, with their programmatic demands, particularly in Bolivia and Brazil. In the field of education, P. Freire's pedagogy enabled many people in state schools and church groups to become politically conscientized. Latin American specialists in political science began to criticize the ideology of →development which was then in vogue in their countries and pointed out that the countries of Latin America were not simply underdeveloped, in comparison to the highly developed countries, were not simply in a preliminary stage of development, and were not just about to enter a new phase of development — rather, they were "basically and constitutively dependent." The concept of "dependence" emerged as the "key element for interpreting the Latin American reality." Consequently, the political and economic option was not directed to development but rather to liberation from internal and external forms of dependence. The liberation movement was also nourished by cultural phenomena. Protest songs and films critically reflected national situations. Plays aiming at political conscientization were performed by student groups, not only on conventional stages but before the gates of factories and on the public squares. In this way the people could become aware of the situation of domination in which they lived and were able to search for political methods of liberation. Eventually in various countries numerous popular movements arose in the cities and rural areas. All these were characterized by a liberating perspective nourished by groups of intellectuals from the universities and professions. But at this juncture the political structures of the Latin American countries did not possess sufficient democratic maturity to be able to channel such energies. In most cases military coups forced these liberation movements underground. Chile succeeded in making more advances than other countries on the political level and in institutionalizing the emancipation movement. But a violent military coup brought this to a tragic end.

2.   Unlike the political authorities, the Catholic Church has often proved mature enough to integrate and channel the liberation movements. A climate of openness was already emerging during the pontificate of Pope John XXIII, especially through his encyclicals *Mater et Magistra* and *Pacem in Terris,* and such openness was consolidated by Vatican II (→Vatican Council II), especially in *Gaudium et Spes.* Militant members of Catholic Action not only had a positive influence on the clergy; aware of the yearning of the people for liberation, they were also able to tackle the theme of liberation on a theological level by using an emerging theological method that was based on a liberative praxis. This may be regarded as the beginnings of liberation theology. The movement would not have been able to spread within the church had there not been a forward-looking and open-minded group among the bishops who were able to understand the signs of the times, examine them theologically and pastorally, and, following the theological method of *Gaudium et Spes,* convert them into the resolutions of Medellín (1968). This liberating presence of the church was also felt in the sphere of basic education and in the basic ecclesial communities. Here it was possible to realize in everyday life the difficult combination of faith and life, word of God and social commitment, so that theological reflection could be integrated with praxis. This was to become the distinctive mark of liberation theology.

3.   Having given a short description of the social and ecclesial context behind the emergence of liberation theology, we would now like to point out a number of false definitions. Liberation theology is not a theology of violence or revolution. These latter veil themselves in substitute theories or narrow theology down to a strategic cover for revolutionary activities or conceptually abstract discussions. Liberation theology is not concerned with a theoretical confrontation with Marxism or a theology of class warfare; nor can it be reduced to ideology, sociology, or politics, renouncing the primacy of faith. It also cannot be regarded as a part of ecclesiastical social teaching, social ethics, or morals, thus ignoring its theological specificity. It cannot be defined as a theology that places no value on theory or is interested exclusively in the efficiency of the action resulting from it and promoted by it. Liberation theology is not the imitation or the outgrowth of certain European theologies — political theology, theology of hope, theology of revolution — nowadays in obvious decline. That would mean that the centuries-old dependence on →European theology is perpetuated and just reproduced in a clumsy and diminished manner in the Third World.

4. Liberation theology is basically concerned with the poor, not as individuals but as the multitudes in the Third World for whom the church has made an option. But this option presupposes a spiritual experience of encountering God precisely in these poor. That experience is, so to speak, the constant driving force of all theological endeavors of liberation theology. Liberation theology is the theology of a church which commits itself to a liberating pastoral ministry on the periphery of the world. It is the second step of a previous concrete commitment to engage in the noble struggle to liberate the poor.

5. Liberation theology breaks with traditional and conservative theology by its hermeneutical starting position. It cannot be classified according to the model of Scholastic theology, which concentrated on defining, explaining, interpreting, and systematizing Catholic dogmatic teaching and magisterial pronouncement. It undertakes the task of interpreting revelation within the living →tradition of the church, beginning with the present historical moment. In this it agrees with the neoliberal theology which asserted itself in the years of Vatican II, but it differs from it by introducing a new hermeneutical principle, that is, a way of reading the word of God from the situation of the poor. The historical situation of Latin America is no longer seen simply as a belated development of the European situation, the latter no longer being regarded as universal. In a very important *pretheological* step, an attempt is made to get acquainted with the real social situation of domination and of the liberation movements of the Third World, not through simple common sense but with the help of theoretical instruments of a dialectical nature. Such mediations of social analysis must be chosen with a view to the fundamental option which liberation theology makes for the liberation of the poor. Marxist analysis, just like any other instrument of analysis of reality, must subject itself to the same criteria of the spiritual option for the poor; no claim to absoluteness by science and no imposed dogmatism can be accepted. No instrument can enjoy such scientific validity that it cannot be questioned from the standpoint of science and ethics. Nor can it impose itself as fixed truth, since every human science is subject to historical limitation and bias. Nor can this scientific mediation be of such a kind that it bears within itself elements which are absolutely irreconcilable with the image of humanity, society, world, and transcendence that we find in revelation. In a word, faith exercises a negative choice in relation to the instrument of social analysis, so that it eliminates those elements which are irreconcilable with its basic option for the poor and with the revelation from which it nourishes itself. The social scientists, on their part, judge social analysis according to its degree of objectivity and scientific exactness. But the specifically theological factor consists in reflecting, in the light of the revelation, on the questions raised up by the liberating praxis. The problems brought to light through the social analysis of the situation are reinterpreted in light of the Christian scriptures and within the tradition of the church, and at the same time these theological sources are also reinterpreted in the light of the encounter with the newness of the situation and its perception in social analysis. Once again the theologian must avoid the dangers of both determinism (i.e., the interpretation of the revealed truths as if they were determined and produced by the sociopolitical situation) and dogmatism (i.e., a simple application of one type of interpretation or truth — ahistorical, abstract, unchangeable — to all situations). Here it is a question of a dialectical relationship between the concrete situation and the word of God, between the sociohistorical locus and revelation. The theological factor is the fruit of a hermeneutical triangle — the text, the context, and the pre-text. Within a pre-text (a situation of domination and the search for liberation understood through the mediation of social analysis), in an ecclesial context (church of the Third World committed to a process of liberation), an attempt is made to penetrate the meaning of the revealed text (What does God say to us about, for, and in this situation?). Consequently, liberation theology tries to answer the basic question of all theology — Who is God? — in a Third World situation. It asks: What does God say to us about salvation? How does the church understand the God revealed in the Old Testament and especially in the person of Jesus Christ in this context? How should one live as a Christian in a situation of injustice and oppression and at the same time in a process of liberation?

6. This last question leads us to the practical aspect of liberation theology. Liberation theology wants to be a theology intimately connected with praxis — that is, a critical reflection on the theological praxis itself, on the pastoral praxis of Christian communities, and on the sociopolitical praxis of Christians and people in general. Liberation theology is, first, a *theology of praxis*, for it takes the material of its reflection from the inner-theological, inner-ecclesiastical, and/or sociopolitical praxis. Praxis provides its raw material. It is, second, a *theology for praxis*, for the theological product aims at elucidating the theological, inner-ecclesiastical, and/or sociopolitical praxis. It is, third, a *theology in praxis*, for theologians must be connected in some way with the praxis about which and for which they reflect. This presupposes a genuine and concrete option for commitment to the liberating praxis of the poor. Finally, it is a *theology through praxis*, for the theology worked out must be prepared to be criticized by praxis in turn. Praxis, therefore, as a true criterion — although not the only one — will judge theology by asking whether the theological task was accomplished well or not in the sense of promoting the process of liberation and the faith within it. The criterion is *orthopraxis* — a notion which does not oppose orthodoxy but goes hand in hand with it, even though it does not regard it as the one and only criterion.

7. One trend linked with the very origins of liberation theology endeavors — working from the perspective of the liberation of the people (→"people" [*Volk*], "nation") — to liberate theological concepts themselves from their alienating and crippling elements. A second trend tries to find a dialectical connection with the culture of the people. It understands the people more in their historical and cultural dimension and less under the aspect of class; consequently, it understands the people as the subjects of *one* history and *one* →culture. It wants to express in theological categories the folk wisdom which is de facto Christian, has accompanied the people in their centuries-old struggle, and still gives them strength to resist, organize, and endure. Typical of this liberation theology is also a concern for popular religiosity, which is particularly reflected in the basic ecclesial communities. Here it tries to find a better connection between the word of God and life, the gospel and struggle, and faith and social reality in the life of the community. A third trend emphasizes in its reflection the historico-political and pastoral praxis of the more conscientized and politically oriented Christian groups, avoiding every sort of avant-gardism and elitism. The preferred places for discussing these questions are the popular movements or/and the basic ecclesial communities, which are connected with and operate within such movements. Compared to a former trend which preferentially began with the faith of the people and ended in the commitment nourished by such a faith, this way of proceeding begins with the people's struggle for existence and discovers in such a struggle a source of interpretation and understanding of the faith. In an early phase of liberation theology there were authors who preferred to start from the praxis of Christian groups whose political orientation even included the commitment to revolutionary action (not necessarily violent) and who wanted to reflect on its implications for faith. This phase corresponded to a particular stage of Latin American history which is less relevant today. In spite of what the opponents of liberation theology obstinately maintain, such a tendency is diminishing. A fourth trend sees in the liberation of the poor one of the signs of the times and tries to give it a spiritual dimension. Christians must understand and bear witness to the liberating dimension of faith in Jesus Christ. This trend sees the fact of domination as an appeal for commitment to liberation and consequently for the necessity of changes to which the Latin American people have a right. The Christian faith has something to contribute here by revealing the specifically Christian content of the liberating praxis and the specific mission of the church in the dimension of integral liberation. This theological discourse does not use the mediation of social analysis; it uses only ethics and anthropology. A fifth trend is called *teologia pé-nochão* (a "feet-on-the-ground theology"), which is worked out by theologians who are close to the people and who use the language of the people or by basic communities themselves; it is expressed on mimeographed sheets or in small pamphlets, in the form of reflections on day-to-day living and the small struggles for survival, and in the form of stations of the cross, novenas, and liturgical celebrations. Here its liberating vision of the faith reveals itself. *Teologia da énxada* (literally, "theology of the hoe") describes a theological praxis connected with the religious experience of the people for the training of future pastoral helpers and priests in rural areas. As regards subject matter, liberation theology has developed particularly in the field of christology, ecclesiology, spirituality, and theological method. An extensive series has been initiated, entitled Theology and Liberation, which treats the principal themes of systematic theology from a liberation perspective. A new exegetical method also merits attention. Further, a growing number of Protestants are contributing to the development and refinement of liberation theology.

8. African liberation theology (→African theology; black theology) originated on a continent which for a long time had suffered from domination in the forms of imperialism, →colonialism, multinational corporations, foreign capital, the activities of a national bourgeoisie, and racism. At the same time, countless liberation movements have arisen which either were able to form their own new governments or are still struggling against external and internal systems of oppression and exploitation. This theology presents itself in two different forms. One is stamped by a nativistic, cultural, and ethnographical character; the other is marked by an anthropological and sociopolitical character. Both seek to reconstruct the true image of the black people which has been greatly distorted by Europeans and white Americans.

The more culturally based theology proceeds from the observation that "the church in Africa is a church without theology and a church without theological concern" (J. Mbiti). Theology must be freed from the shackles of a white, European cultural subjugation, and the religious and cultural African heritage must be rediscovered. The intention of this kind of African liberation theology is to interpret Christ in a conceptuality relevant and essential for the African, so that the African does not have to be made "tribeless" in order to be Christian. African liberation theology chooses typical themes of African culture and compares them with similar Christian themes (e.g., communal solidarity is compared with the Mystical Body, ancestor worship with the veneration of the saints) in order to enrich both of them, not wanting to confine itself to a one-sided critique of the Christian view of the African religion or to some individual problems (C. Nyamiti). This theology presupposes that the "hermeneutical chasm" between the two religious worlds could be narrowed either by a better acquaintance with the worldview, categories, and thought systems of mythical, poetical philosophy, the "corpus" of African concepts, or through a reinterpretation of theology against the African cultural background. In a word, theology must "clothe itself in the language, style, disposition, character, and culture of the African people" (E. Fashole-Luke).

The other trend of African theology questions such a culturally based theology, pointing out the risk of turning the religious past into a myth. There is a danger of forgetting the actual, present situation of oppression and of romanticizing the ethnic past to the detriment of the analysis of present injustice (M. Buthelezi). The racial structure of violence in the system of apartheid of South Africa brought out the problem of sociopolitical liberation most clearly. The injustice of such a system implicates the white mother churches in the oppression and exploitation resulting from the investments of the First World in that country. The more rigid such a system becomes, the more intensely a black consciousness develops. It tries to relate the understanding of the gospel with the evils of racism and apartheid (S. Biko, D. Tutu, A. Boesak). It reinterprets in a liberating manner God and Jesus Christ, who now stand on the side of those racially oppressed. It tries to answer questions like: What does it mean to believe in Jesus Christ when one is black and lives in a world controlled by white racists? And what does it mean when these racists call themselves Christians? Such a theology proclaims the end of the "innocence" of whites and points out that white people will only be free when blacks are free also. Deviating in a certain measure from the former approach, this theology does not so much take African themes into consideration as it does Africans themselves and the material and spiritual condition that will enable them to become full persons, to participate fully in life and freedom. Liberation is not a part of the gospel; it is the whole of it. The situation of suffering, of oppression of blacks, and the integral liberation brought by Christ are taken seriously, in contrast to racial ideology, which has manipulated the gospel. Some prefer to emphasize the originality of African liberation theology, whereas others maintain that all theologies of liberation — of Latin America, the United States, Africa, Asia — must join forces, since they possess the same common horizon of liberation (see A. Boesak).

9. Asia has three prominent features: it is an enormous continent still harshly oppressed and exploited by the capital of the First World; it is home to a number of religions (e.g., Hinduism, Buddhism, Confucianism [→religion, religions]); and Christianity constitutes only a small minority (except in the Philippines) and is regarded as the product of Western colonialism. Asian liberation theology has to respond to these three challenges and increasingly direct its dimension of liberation to oppression, to dialogue with the great religions, and to revealing the universal character of Christianity beyond the colonial West.

The Philippines (→Filipino theology) has been acquainted with invasions, domination, and oppression from the time of the Spaniards in the sixteenth century up to the Marcos dictatorship in the late twentieth century. Filipino liberation theology undertakes a liberating interpretation of the mission of Jesus Christ based on a concrete analysis of the oppressed situation of the people, without shying away from a confrontation with Marxism, and commits the church to the struggle against injustice (see E. de la Torre, F. Claver). Such a liberation theology will only be really Filipino when it is elaborated without the categories of Western theology, when it answers questions like: What is the meaning of the present Philippine situation in the history of salvation? What does salvation mean for the Filipinos? Consequently, it must relate the interpretation of the present historical situation — making use of the experience and mediations of social analysis — to the history of salvation and redemption for today, in accordance with the holistic development and transformation of the social order. In principle, liberation theology must be worked out by the Christians of the basic communities, proceeding from their daily experiences with →prayer, creative →liturgy, dramas, songs, stories, and poetry (see C. Abesamis).

Liberation theology in India (→Indian theology) is challenged by the question, How can the presence of God and the activity of Christ be recognized in the phenomena of the great religions and in the process of liberation and development of the country? These are the signs of the times which must be theologically interpreted. The theology of the *semina verbi* (*AG* 15), which recognizes the effective and active presence of the cosmic Christ even before the actual founding of the church and outside it, permits a positive relationship between Christian theology and the great religions. These religions are mediators of salvation and expressions of God's revelation. Taking this double observation as a starting point, the liberation theology of India attempts to work out the theme of evangelization in such a way that it amounts to neither exclusiveness of nor domination by Christianity but rather a fruitful dialogue. In India, liberation means dialogue between the religions (see D. S. Amalorpavadass). The European dress of Catholicism must be laid aside as soon as possible and replaced by Hindu forms to make it acceptable to the Indian people (B. Upadhyaya). Indian philosophy constitutes a propaedeutic stage for the Catholic faith. Consequently, the Christian faith can be interpreted according to the categories of the religious and philosophical traditions of India (A. J. Appasamy). Such a task must not be limited to the interiority of the religious experience but must advance so far that it shows the gospel in its concern for the freedom struggles and its role in them. The mission of salvation and the task of humanization are integrally linked to each other — even if not identical (M. M. Thomas).

The main concern of T. Balasuriya from Sri Lanka is the relationship between a Eucharist oriented to action and its social dimension, which aims at a new world order. A. Pieris seeks to combine both liberation themes and the concerns of interreligious dialogue in his thought.

Theology in South Korea (→Korean theology) deepens the reflection on the presence of God in the midst of human suffering; it explains that God hears the misery of God's people as in the days of old (Kim Chung-Choon).

10. Particularly in the United States and in Europe, but increasingly in all other parts of the world (see V. Fabella and S. A. L. Park, A. M. Isasi-Díaz, and M. P. Aquino), feminist theology has taken on the characteristics of a liberation theology. Feminist theological analysis proceeds from the double perspective of a hermeneutics of suspicion (thought forms, society, and religion are dominated by males and are structured systematically to exclude women) and the "critical feminist principle" ("Whatever denies, diminishes or distorts the full humanity of women is . . . not redemptive" [R. R. Ruether]) and offers fresh and challenging perspectives on God, Christian anthropology, Jesus, church, and ethics. Feminist theology has developed into one of the most important and vital areas of theological research in our day and will have tremendous implications as Latin Americans, Africans, and Asians continue to theologize out of and for their own contexts.

On the increase as well are other movements in theology that contribute to and draw on the various liberation theologies. In the United States, there has emerged a distinctive form of black liberation theology and its counterpart of womanist theology. This has been both an inspiration to and an influence on the antiapartheid struggles in South Africa. Less widespread, but also important, are liberation concerns within Native American theology; and of increasing impact are liberation theologies articulated by gays and lesbians, people who are physically disabled, and advocates of the integrity of creation. While these liberation theologies have originated mostly within First World contexts, they are likely to influence theologies in the Third World as well.

All liberation theologies have one and the same basic concern. Proceeding from a situation of concrete oppression, an attempt is made to discover the liberating force of God's revelation, which is reinterpreted as a prophetic denunciation of injustice and an appeal to action.

J. B. LIBÂNIO

Bibliography

Abraham, K. C., *Third World Theologies: Commonalities and Divergences* (1990). Alves, R., *A Theology of Human Hope* (1969). Appiah-Kubi, K., and S. Torres, eds., *African Theology en Route* (1979). Aquino, M. P., *Our Cry for Life* (1994). Assmann, H., *Opresión-liberación: Desafío a los cristianos* (1971). Idem, *Teología desde la praxis de la liberación* (1973). Balasuriya, T., *The Eucharist and Human Liberation* (1979). Berryman, P., *Liberation Theology* (1987). Boesak, A., *Farewell to Innocence: A Socio-ethical Study on Black Theology and Power* (1977). Boff, C., *Feet-on-the-Ground Theology: A Brazilian Journey* (1987). Idem, *Theology and Praxis: Epistemological Foundations* (1987). Boff, L., *Church: Charism and Power* (1985). Idem, *Jesus Christ Liberator: A Critical Theology for Our Time* (1978). Boff, L., and V. Elizondo, eds., *Theologies of the Third World: Convergences and Differences* (1988). Brown, R. M., *Unexpected News: Reading the Bible with Third World Eyes* (1984). Cadorette, C., et al., eds., *Liberation Theology: An Introductory Reader* (1992). Chopp, R. S., *The Praxis of Suffering: An Interpretation of Liberation and Political Theologies* (1986). Comblin, J., *Antropologia crista* (1985). Idem, *Teología de libertação: Teologia noconservadora e teologia liberal* (1985). Cone, J. H., *A Black Theology of Liberation* (1986). Congregation for the Doctrine of the Faith, *Instruction on Christian Freedom and Liberation* (1986). Dussel, E., ed., *The Church in Latin America 1492–1992* (1992). Eagleson, J., and P. Scharper, eds., *Puebla and Beyond* (1979). Ellacuría, I., and J. Sobrino, eds., *Mysterium Liberationis: Fundamental Concepts of Liberation Theology* (1993). Ellis, M., and O. Maduro, eds., *Expanding the*

View: Gustavo Gutiérrez and the Future of Liberation Theology (1990). England, J. C., ed., *Living Theology in Asia* (1982). Fabella, V., and S. A. L. Park, *We Dare to Dream: Doing Theology as Asian Women* (1990). Ferm, D. W., *Third World Theologies: An Introductory Survey* (1986). Garcia Rubio, A., *Teologia da libertação: Politica ou profetismo* (1977). Gutiérrez, G., *Las Casas: In Search of the Poor of Jesus Christ* (1994). Idem, *On Job: God-Talk and the Suffering of the Innocent* (1987). Idem, *The Power of the Poor in History* (1983). Idem, *A Theology of Liberation,* rev. ed. (1988). Idem, *We Drink from Our Own Wells* (1984). Haight, R., *An Alternate Vision: An Interpretation of Liberation Theology* (1985). Hennelly, A. T., ed., *Liberation Theology: A Documentary History* (1990). Idem, *Santo Domingo and Beyond* (1993). Isasi-Díaz, A. M., *En la Lucha/In the Struggle: Elaborating a Mujerista Theology* (1993). LaCugna, C. M., ed., *Freeing Theology: The Essentials of Theology in Feminist Perspective* (1993). Libânio, J. B., *Evangelização e libertação* (1976). Libânio, J. B., and M. C. Bingemer, *Escatologia crista* (1985). Magaña, A. Q., *Eclesiología en la teología de la liberación* (1983). Mondin, B., *La teologia della liberazione* (1977). Muñoz, R., *The God of Christians* (1990). Nieuwenhove, J. van, and B. K. Goldewijk, eds., *Popular Religion, Liberation, and Contextual Theology* (1991). Paul VI, Pope, *Evangelii Nuntiandi* (1975). Pernia, A. M., *God's Kingdom and Human Liberation: A Study of G. Gutiérrez, L. Boff, and J. L. Segundo* (1990). Pieris, A., *An Asian Theology of Liberation* (1988). Pironio, E., *La iglesia que nace entre nosotros* (1970). Scannone, J. C., "Teología de la liberación," in C. Floristán and J. J. Tamayo, eds., *Conceptos fundamentales de Pastoral* (1983) 562–79. Idem, *Teología de la liberación y praxis popular* (1976). Segundo, J. L., *The Liberation of Theology* (1976). Sobrino, J., *Christology at the Crossroads: A Latin American Approach* (1978). Taborda, F., *Cristianismo y ideología* (1984). Thistlethwaite, S. B., and M. P. Engel, eds., *Lift Every Voice: Constructing Christian Theologies from the Underside* (1990). Torres, S., and V. Fabella, eds., *The Emergent Gospel: Theology from the Underside of History* (1978).

❧ LITURGY ❧

1. What Is Liturgy? 2. A History of the Use of the Term. 3. Liturgy and Vatican II. 4. Liturgy and Culture. 5. The Future of the Liturgy.

1. "Liturgy" is a word currently used in the Orthodox, Roman Catholic, Anglo-Catholic, and some Protestant traditions to describe the official, public worship of the church. In Roman Catholicism "liturgy" generally refers to the celebration of the seven sacraments, the canonical hours, and other rites of an authorized and public nature approved by the Holy See — such as the various celebrations that accompany the catechumenal process (the RCIA) or occasional rites such as eucharistic exposition and benediction. Eastern rite churches, especially those belonging to the Byzantine family, use the term "liturgy" only in reference to the Eucharist, which is called the "divine liturgy."

2. The word "liturgy" is derived from the classical Greek *leitourgía* — a term which has evolved over centuries of use. It is a compound expression composed of *leit* (from *leós/laós* = people), standing for the generic "public" — that which belongs to the people — and *érgon* (from *ergázomai* = to act, to work). In classical usage this term signified "a work performed for the people" but also emphasized the public nature of the activity. It was used to describe a "public works project" such as the construction of an aqueduct or the subsidizing of athletic competitions by a wealthy individual or family on behalf of their *polis* or city-state. Later, during the Hellenistic period, those who translated the Hebrew scriptures into Greek used *leitourgía* as a technical term to translate the Hebrew verbs *'abhad* and *sheret,* which were used to describe the service rendered by the priests and levites in the Jerusalem temple.

In the New Testament, *leitourgía* is used in three different ways. First, it is used to describe a good work done on behalf of another. For example, Paul uses the term to designate the collection taken up by the churches for the Jewish

Christians in Jerusalem (Rom 15:27; 2 Cor 9:12). Second, *leitourgía* is used in the traditional way to designate the levitical ritual of the Old Testament — Zechariah fulfilling his priestly service (*leitourgía*) in the temple. In much the same way, it is used metaphorically in the Letter to the Hebrews (chaps. 7–10) to link the suffering and death of Jesus Christ to the action of the high priest performing the ritual on the Day of Atonement in the Jerusalem temple. Finally, *leitourgía* is used to describe the "spiritual worship" of Christians: a "worship" that is conceived of in very noncultic ways. For example, Paul describes himself as a "minister" (*leitourgòn*) of Christ, carrying out his "priestly liturgical action" of proclaiming the gospel, so that the Gentiles might become an offering pleasing to God (Rom 15:16).

These examples point to the spiritualization of the term in the New Testament. No longer is *leitourgía* narrowly applied to the ministry of priests and levites performing the prescribed ritual in the Jerusalem temple. Now, because Jesus Christ has reconciled the world to God through his cross and resurrection, the former means of gaining access to God (sacrifice, priesthood, temple) have been subsumed in the person of Christ, who is at the same time temple, priest, and the sacrifice. Christians are "a chosen race, a royal priesthood, a holy nation, God's own people," whose ministry now is to "proclaim the mighty acts of him who called [them] out of darkness into his marvelous light" (1 Pt 2:9). The gulf between God and humanity has been reconciled. Now, not only the levitical priests can stand in God's presence in the temple, but all who believe in Christ are capable of emulating this "noncultic" priesthood and stand in God's presence by virtue of Christ's suffering and death. Their *leitourgía,* in imitation of Christ's, is a life poured out in the service of God and humanity. In this sense, Paul exhorts the Romans: "I appeal to you therefore, brothers and sisters, by the mercies of God, to present your bodies as a living sacrifice, holy and acceptable to God, which is your spiritual worship" (Rom 12:1).

After the New Testament period a gradual semantic shift took place in regard to *leitourgía* among Greek-speaking Christians. In early patristic writing, *leitourgía* not only indicated the ministry of church officials but also began to be applied to any act of divine worship. Later, its focus narrowed even further, and *leitourgía* was applied only to eucharistic worship.

In the Western church, *leitourgía* (or *liturgia,* in its Latin form) fell out of use for many centuries. Others terms such as "divine office" or "sacred rites" were used instead. With the revival of interest in Greek during the Renaissance and the birth of more critical historical studies informed by primary sources, "liturgy" became a term of preference for many scholars in the West in speaking about the official prayer of the church. The "first liturgical movement," led by P. Guéranger during the nineteenth century, also did much to popularize the word, as did the first modern liturgical pioneer, L. Beauduin at the beginning of the twentieth century. The term gradually gained official acceptance in Roman Catholic circles during the nineteenth century and became a usual way to refer to the worship beginning with the encyclicals of Pius X (*Tra le Sollicitudini,* 1903) and especially Pius XII's encyclical *Mediator Dei* (1948). It is in this sense that the word reentered the Western Christian lexicon and became the usual term used to describe worship in the documents of Vatican II and in the revised code of (Roman Catholic) canon law (1983).

3. One of the most influential liturgical documents of the twentieth century is *Sacrosanctum Concilium* (*SC*), the first document of Vatican II (1963). This statement has served as the foundation for the subsequent liturgical reform in the Roman Catholic Church — a reform that has also influenced the revision of the worship books of other Christian churches in Europe, the United States, and the developing world. This document does not so much define liturgy as describe it. Far from considering the worship of the church as a rigid set of rubrics performed by clerical specialists (the bane of Roman Catholic worship prior to Vatican II), the council clearly describes the liturgy as a "work of the people" — "the outstanding means whereby the faithful may express in their lives and manifest to others the mystery of Christ and the real nature of the true church" (*SC* 2). For this reason the liturgy is "the summit toward which the activity of the church is directed; at the same time it is the fount from which all the church's power flows" (*SC* 10).

The council further acknowledges, however, that "the liturgy does not exhaust the entire activity of the church" (*SC* 9), for the believers also engage in acts of "liturgy" as the term was originally used in the New Testament. Evangelization, catechesis, social action, and other ways of proclaiming the gospel are also forms of worship. Nor is liturgy the only time that Christians pray, for there exist in many of the churches widespread practices known as "popular religion" which, while not often officially approved (or controlled) by church authorities, are often an authentic expression of the faith of the people.

Still, basic to the identity of liturgy — as opposed to other laudable but un-official celebrations such as a communal recitation of the rosary — is that it is "the epiphany of Christ and the church." A celebration of the liturgy, whether it be a celebration of the sacraments or of the Liturgy of the Hours, is essentially trinitarian in nature and draws its basic purpose and identity from the paschal mystery of Jesus Christ. It is because of the paschal mystery of Christ that the community has come together to worship God "in spirit and in truth" (Jn 4:24). We gather to remember the mighty acts that God has performed for humanity from the beginning of time — especially in Jesus Christ — and to invoke the Holy Spirit that vivifies, enlightens, and unifies the Body of Christ. Every sacramental celebration, then, revolves around *anámnesis* (remembering, making memorial) and *epíclesis* (invoking the Holy Spirit). These two fundamental aspects of liturgy were recognized ecumenically in the so-called Lima Document (official title = *Baptism, Eucharist, and Ministry* [1982]) of the World Council of Churches in its discussion of the meaning of the Eucharist.

4. From the outset of the conciliar discussions at Vatican II, it became obvious that *aggiornamento* (updating) would be impossible without attending to the complex reality of human culture, since one of the primary goals of the reform was the people's "full, conscious and active participation" in liturgical celebrations (*SC* 14). The concern to reform the liturgy in such a way as to make it accessible to people of very different cultural backgrounds is expressed in both the first and the last document of the council, *Sacrosanctum Concilium* (1963) and *Gaudium et Spes* (*GS*; 1965).

The most dramatic change authorized by *Sacrosanctum Concilium* was the use of the local language in worship (*SC* 36). After the church had for centuries championed the Tridentine rite of Mass as an immutable monument to orthodoxy, the council's assertion that "the liturgy is made up of immutable elements divinely instituted, and of elements subject to change ... that not only may but ought to be changed with the passage of time" (*SC* 21) was a revolutionary statement indeed.

Sacrosanctum Concilium 37–40 marks a dramatic return to the principle of liturgical diversity in unity that had characterized the earliest history of the church, when the various liturgical families as different as the Byzantine, Mozarabic, and Eastern Syrian developed very distinct liturgical practices largely influenced by language and culture. The acknowledgment that the "church has no wish to impose a rigid uniformity in matters that do not affect the faith or good of the whole community" (*SC* 37) and that "provisions should be made, even in the revision of liturgical books, for legitimate variations and adaptations to different groups, regions, and peoples, especially in mission lands" (*SC* 38), opened the door to legitimate liturgical pluriformity in a Roman rite of the Catholic Church that had been "rigidly uniform" in matters liturgical with very few exceptions since the Council of Trent in the sixteenth century. *Sacrosanctum Concilium* 40 is the most important article in the document on inculturation. It makes provision for even more radical adaptations (the term "inculturation" was then not generally in use) in concert with national bishops conferences, especially in mission lands.

The implementation of the liturgical reform since the promulgation of the various liturgical books beginning in the late 1960s has been guided by a return to a simplified, and more traditional, order of worship that was to serve as the starting point for cultural adaptation. The liturgy presented in the official books (*editio typica*) is largely modeled on the style of worship practiced during the classical period of the Roman rite — the fifth through seventh centuries, the last period during which people actively participated in the liturgical celebration. This ethos, reflective of the sobriety and practicality of ancient Roman culture, is described in *SC* 34: "The rites should be marked by a noble simplicity; they should be short, clear and unencumbered by useless repetitions; they should be within the people's powers of comprehension and as a rule not require much explanation." It should be noted that simplicity and lack of repetition are not universally held cultural values, especially in relation to ritual. Rather, it is these "simple" and "unencumbered" rites that are proposed by Rome as the basis for further adaptation and inculturation by the local conferences of bishops.

5. For the past thirty years there has been a growing awareness, in both Catholicism and Protestantism, of the profoundly Eurocentric bias of the various forms of liturgy brought by European and American missionaries to non-Western cultures. Both Catholics and Protestants have embarked on revisions of their worship books and have attempted, where deemed possible, to make their proclamation of Christ and the paschal mystery more effective through forms of contextualization. The inclusion in Christian worship of dance, other ritual gestures, music, and the plastic arts — some of which draw from non-Christian traditions — has opened the door to even more radical changes in Christian worship in non-Western countries.

In Europe and North America, the culture has challenged the ability of the liturgy to speak to modern believers. Negative influences such as secularization and the rampant consumerism that fragments society have undermined the ability of liturgical symbols to proclaim the "countercultural" message of the gospel. Other movements, such as feminism, have legitimately called into question a traditional church order that limits leadership roles both within the Christian assembly and outside of it to one-half of the human race.

Much still remains to be done, however. In Roman Catholicism, after some very promising initial experiments in India, the Philippines, and parts of Africa, much of the energy to inculturate the liturgy seems to have dissipated in the atmosphere of centralization that marked the 1980s. Latin America and other traditionally Catholic areas of the world have still to embrace the call of the bishops at Puebla (1979) "that the liturgy and the common people's piety cross-fertilize each other, giving lucid and prudent direction to the impulses of prayer and charismatic vitality that are evident today in our countries" (Puebla 3.4e).

While the approval of the Roman Rite for the Dioceses of Zaire (Democratic Republic of Congo) by the Roman Congregation of Divine Worship represents a real milestone in the inculturation of the liturgy, the same process needs to be encouraged in other parts of the world where the liturgy of the church seems to be becoming increasingly unintelligible to the people. At stake is the ability of Christ's people to see themselves — their own lives — being celebrated in the liturgical expression of the suffering, death, and resurrection of Jesus Christ. In the words of the pastoral letter of the African-American Catholic Bishops, "What We Have Seen and Heard" (1984), "All people should be able to recognize themselves when Christ is presented [in the liturgy], and should be able to experience their own fulfillment when these mysteries are celebrated."

MARK R. FRANCIS, CSV

Bibliography

Amalorpavadass, D. S., *Toward Indigenization in the Liturgy* (1974). Aranda, A., *Manantial y cumbre: iniciación litúrgica* (1992). Berger, T., "The Women's Movement as a Liturgical Movement: A Form of Inculturation," *StLit* 20 (1990) 55–64. Casel, O., "Leitourgia — Munus," in *OrChr* (1932) 289–302. Chupungco, A., *Cultural Adaptation of the Liturgy* (1984). Collins, M., "Liturgy," *NDT* (1987) 591–601. Francis, M., "Adaptation, Liturgical," *NDSW* (1990) 14–25. Lyonnet, S., "La nature du culte dans le NT," in *La liturgie après Vatican II (Unam sanctam, 66)* (1967) 357–84. Madden, L., "Liturgy," *NDSW* (1990) 740–42. Marsili, S., "La liturgia, momento storico della salvezza," in *Anàmnesis,* vol. 1, *La liturgia, momento nella storia della salvezza* (1974) 33–158. National Conference of Catholic Bishops (USA), *Plenty Good Room: The Spirit and Truth of African American Catholic Worship* (1990). Neunheuser, B., "Liturgie und Mission: Entfaltung im Dialog," *ED* 32 (1978) 365–84. Senn, F. C., *Christian Worship and Its Cultural Setting* (1993 [1983]). White, J., *Introduction to Christian Worship* (1980).

∿ LOCAL CHURCH ∿

1. Ecumenical Relevance of the Local Church. 2. Different Models of the Local Church in Third World Theology. 3. Interrelation of the Models.

1. The question of the relationship between the universal church and the local churches is very relevant today. This can be seen in the Catholic Church, for instance, when the question arises concerning what authorization can be given in matters such as church structure, ministries, theology, and liturgy. But other churches struggle with similar difficulties: for instance, when churches from different traditions want to form a united church or when churches in the Third World, founded by missionaries of Western origin, want to go their own way. Consequently, autonomy is a frequently discussed concern today throughout the Christian world. Certainly there are general principles which have been accepted by councils, episcopal synods, or other leading authorities of the great churches; but that does not mean that the concrete implementation proceeds without tension. Vatican II (→Vatican Council II) laid down that the local church is not to be understood as the smallest administrative unit: "This Church of Christ is really present in all legitimately organized local groups of the faithful, which, insofar as they are united to their pastors, are also quite appropriately called churches in the New Testament" (*LG* 26). The community of all local churches constitutes the catholicity of the universal church. The apostolic letter *Evangelii Nuntiandi* (*EN*) says: "Nevertheless this universal Church is in practice incarnate in the individual churches made up of such and such an actual part of mankind, speaking such and such a language, heirs of a cultural patrimony, of a vision of the world, of an historical past, of a particular human substratum. Receptivity to the wealth of the individual church corresponds to a special sensitivity of modern man" (*EN* 62). In the history of the churches of the Reformation there have always been leaders like R. Anderson, H. Venn, and R. Allen who defended the right of the churches in the Third World to be independent, and these leaders still exercise a great influence on the general assemblies of the churches of the Reformation. The history and ecclesiology of the great Orthodox churches clearly support the principle of autonomy, but those churches find it hard to come to an understanding about the principle of universality. Pluralism and unity, local church and universal church — these are themes that concern all churches (cf. A. Camps, R. Bassham, W. R. Shenk, J. S. Stamoolis, and W. Bühlmann).

2. Third World theologians are particularly preoccupied with the question of the local church. These theologians look upon the relationship of Third World churches to the Western churches as a "captivity" or "foreign domination" (G. Cook, S. Torres, T. Balasuriya, E. Boulaga, Tu Shihua). Five different models of the local church can be distinguished in their writings (see M. Pongudom).

2.1. The first model is the house church. This church is regarded as a community of love in which poor and rich live together fraternally and share everything. The house church enables the church to fulfill its mission within a particular situation. In such a dynamic and life-giving church, religion is regarded as just as necessary for the whole of human life as a home, just as simple as a home, and as intimate in its human relationships as a household. The church is equated with a family community. During the first centuries of Christianity, this was the most important form of church life. But later too it was never entirely lost — for instance, in the old religious orders and in times of crisis, when the church became again a refuge for the suffering. Practical examples of this kind of church are base communities, independent churches, and household communities.

2.2. The second model is the institutional church. This model developed early in the history of the church, but it was more concerned in the beginning with theological stability than with the power of church leaders. This latter aspect became particularly visible toward the end of the Middle Ages and during the Counter-Reformation as a defense against opponents. The church was regarded as a perfect society which differed from all other societies. Structures of doctrine, sacraments, and ecclesiastical leadership were said to be drawn from divine revelation. Consequently, changes in the structures were almost impossible. This is true not only of the Catholic Church but also of those churches of the Reformation that have maintained a pyramidal model. An institutional church lives in the conviction that →salvation is present only in the church, and consequently this church become triumphalistic. This model of the local church shows up in the writings of Third World theologians when they point to the mainline triumphalistic churches of the West as well as to those churches' activities throughout the Third World.

2.3. The third model is the incarnated and suffering community. This community lives out its discipleship by following →Jesus of Nazareth, the incarnated and suffering Lord. The Lord became a simple human being, lived with outcasts, and died on the cross. This church never minimalizes the importance of human cultures (→culture) and history. On the contrary, it tries to incarnate the good news within them. This community incarnates itself especially in the history of suffering humanity and wants to be a suffering servant of society. One thinks here of the early church, the religious communities, and certain movements that criticize the wealth of the big churches (e.g., according to the ideals of D. Bonhoeffer, H. Cox, and J. A. T. Robinson), but also of the local churches in Africa and Asia that endeavor to promote the →inculturation and contextualization of the whole Christian life (→contextual theology).

2.4. The fourth model is the church as a sacramental and eschatological community. The grace of God brings sinners together to form a church. The grace of God is an invisible power which becomes visible in the sign of the sacraments. The church is the visible manifestation of the grace of God and salvation, and it exercises this function especially by means of the sacraments of baptism and Eucharist (→Eucharist [Lord's Supper]). At the same time the church is an eschatological community. It is the beginning of the reign of God in the world. But it is nothing final. The church is a foretaste of the coming reign of God, inaugurated →eschatology, or a church on pilgrimage. We do not necessarily have to distinguish between the sacramental church, strongly concentrated on its own members, and the eschatological church, oriented to the future. This model was worked out by Vatican II and has given a new dynamism to the Catholic Church. It has likewise made dialogue, learning from other religions (→religion, religions), and inculturation possible. The resulting dynamism has found concrete expression in other church models.

2.5. The fifth model is the church as a prophetic and liberating movement of the people (→"people" [*Volk*], "nation"). The church as a popular movement goes back far into the past: Moses was a prophet and liberator of his people. Later, when the people of God were oppressed in their own land, others were called as prophets and liberators. They prophesied against the prevailing sociopolitical and economic structures and challenged kings and powers. Jesus of Nazareth, the founder of the Christian movement, was a prophet and liberator and even a revolutionary in the eyes of the Jewish authorities. Many people in the past and the present have regarded him as such. But their motives are and have been diverse. There are those who regard Jesus as a destructive enemy of the present order and those who regard him as a creative prophet and liberator, or revolutionary, opposed to the corrupt present-day order. The church has also been and still is interpreted in this way. In the history of the church there have always been movements which devoted themselves to the liberation of the poor, women, slaves, and the oppressed or to the struggle against corruption and the tyranny of the state. As Christian churches spread into the non-Christian world they often exercised a liberating function, since the good news worked in a liberating way. But soon these churches came to be stamped by the prevailing systems, by imported structures and church order. Furthermore, churches were unable to have a prophetic and liberating effect within those societies subject to rapid social change and technological developments. As popular movements of God, the churches should listen to the voices of the oppressed and exploited. The churches should not be static institutions. Today this view is held especially in Asia and Latin America, even though the theologians of liberation on those continents underline different aspects of this message (→liberation theology).

3. It should be obvious that during the long history of the churches up to the present, these five models have played and are playing an important role. This must be regarded as the church's strength. But this analysis must be properly understood: the individual models cannot exist as such. Elements of the five models will always be found in the local churches, fluctuating according to the concrete situation of the local church. The church as institution cannot simply be disregarded. Individual local churches such as those in China, Latin America, Asia, Africa, and Oceania set different agendas. In this way new church forms arise which harmoniously blend the characteristics of different models. For example, in most of the local churches of Asia the models of incarnation and →liberation are harmonized (→religion, religions); in Africa the characteristics of both the house church and the inculturated community prevail (e.g., in the African independent churches); and in Latin America house church and prophetic/liberating community go hand in hand (e.g., in the base communities). This gives new impulses to Western local churches and shows them how to become contextual local churches.

ARNULF CAMPS, OFM

Bibliography

Amirtham, S., and J. S. Pobee, *Theology by the People: Reflections on Doing Theology in Community* (1986). Banks, R. J., *Paul's Idea of Community: The Early House Churches in Their Historical Setting* (1980). Boff, L., *Ecclesiogenesis: The Base Communities Reinvent the Church* (1986). Cook, G., *The Expectation of the Poor: Latin American Base Ecclesial Communities in Protestant Perspective* (1985). Hesselgrave, D. J., and E. Rommen, *Contextualization* (1989). Idem, *Planting Churches Cross-culturally: A Guide for Home and Foreign Missions* (1980). Hoefer, H., "Local Village Theology in India," *Catalyst* 2/2 (1981) 121–30. Kalilombe, P., "Doing Theology at the Grassroots: A Challenge for Professional Theologians," *AfER* 27/4 (1985) 225–37. Mercado, L. N., "Notes on Christ and Local Community in Philippine Context," *Verbum SVD* 21 (1980) 303–4. Mundadan, A. M., *Indian Christians: Search for Identity and Struggle for Autonomy* (1984). Pongudom, M., "Models of the Church in Church History," in *Tradition and Innovation: A Search for a Relevant Ecclesiology in Asia* (1983). Schreiter, R. J., *Constructing Local Theologies* (1985). Idem, "Teaching Theology from an Intercultural Perspective," *Theological Education* 26/1 (1989) 13–34. Shenk, W. R., *Searching for an Indian Ecclesiology* (1984). Shihua, A. T., "To Have an Independent, Self-ruled and Self-managed Church Is Our Sacred Right," in *New Beginning: An International Dialogue with the Chinese Church* (1983) 99–103. Shorter, A., *Toward a Theology of Inculturation* (1992) 251–70. Stamoolis, J. J., *The Challenge of Basic Christian Communities* (1981). Van Engen, C., "The Impact of Modern Ecclesiology on the Local Church," in *New Directions in Mission and Evangelization* (1994).

❧ MARTYRDOM ❧

1. Biblical Background. 2. History. 3. Theological and Missionary Aspects. 4. The Cult of Martyrs. 5. Summary.

1. Already in the New Testament we can see the beginnings of an understanding of martyrdom (*martyrion*) as the supreme and triumphant test endured for the name of Jesus Christ. The Book of Revelation mentions "the souls of all the people who had been killed on account of the word of God, for witnessing [*martyria* = *testimonium*] to it" (Rv 6:9). The martyr is the witness of the sufferings of Jesus Christ, who was himself "the faithful, the true witness [martyr]" (Rv 1:5; 3:14) who sealed his "witness for the truth" (1 Tm 6:13) by his blood on the cross, by his death (Col 1:20–21). For Paul, the content of the kerygma is the one who humbled himself "even to accepting death, death on a cross" (Phil 2:8). The core of the apostolic preaching, of the proclamation of the gospel, is "Jesus Christ and him crucified" (1 Col 2:2). "Here we are preaching a crucified Christ" (1 Col 1:23). For Paul, in fact, talking about the cross is both the foolishness and the glory of his preaching (1 Col 1:17–25; Gal 6:11–14). The Acts of the Apostles reports the martyrdom of the deacon Stephen (7:54–60), the first martyr of the church, who prayed for those who stoned him. In the case of Stephen in particular, the relation between "cross" and "crown" (*stavros* and *stéphanos*) is essential.

2. Since the second century the church has regarded martyrdom — that is, the execution of Christians condemned to death by the authorities because of their faith (*Shepherd of Hermas,* parable 9.28) — as the supreme form of witnessing to the Christian hope. Such martyrdom occurred especially during the bloody persecutions endured by the church for several centuries. During this time of "crisis," the martyr's cross became the unshakable rock, "like the anvil under the hammer," not only for the church but also for the world. It was due to the martyr's sacrifice that the church existed, grew, and expanded. And, paradoxically, it was through the holy stream of their blood that the fire of persecution was extinguished (Eusebius of Caesarea, *Martyrs of Palestine* 7.11). There is a rich postapostolic and patristic literature on martyrdom, in particular the *Acts of the Martyrs* and the *Passiones,* that is, the official records of the interrogations and authentic reports of eyewitnesses. Those who were present at the executions not only handed down the words of the martyrs but also introduced a liturgical cult at the site of their graves along with the veneration of their relics.

Saint Ignatius, bishop of Antioch (d. 107), also called Theophorus, longed with perseverance for the moment of martyrdom which is the imitation par excellence of the passion of Christ. "Permit me to be an imitator of the Passion of my God" (*Epistle to the Romans* 6.3). "You cannot do me a greater favor than to let me be offered as a libation to God as long as the altar is ready" (ibid. 2.2). "I am the wheat of God, and I must be ground by the teeth of wild beasts to become the pure bread of Christ" (ibid. 4.1–2). "It is now I am beginning to be a disciple of Christ" (ibid. 5.3).

The report of the martyrdom of Saint Polycarp, bishop of Smyrna (d. ca. 156), mentions "a martyrdom in conformity with the gospel" (*Martyrdom of Polycarp* 1.1). Venerated as a saint already before his death, Polycarp is called "a pleasing holocaust prepared for God," and before the stake his witness takes the form of a prayer: "Lord, almighty God, Father of your beloved and blessed Son Jesus Christ, . . . I praise Thee that Thou hast granted me this day and this hour to partake in the chalice of Christ in the company of the martyrs for the resurrection of the soul into eternal life and of the body into the incorruptibility of the Holy Spirit" (14.1–2).

The *Epistle to Diognetus* describes Christians as a new community in the world and underlines their unique role of proclaiming the coming of the Lord through their resistance and suffering: "They love all and are persecuted by all. They are misjudged, condemned, killed, and thus they win life" (5.11–12). Christians are, so to speak, taken into custody by the world; nevertheless, it is they who maintain the world (6.7). "When persecuted the Christians multiply day by day. So noble is the position assigned to them by God that they are not allowed to desert it" (6.9–10). In this period of ecumenical consolidation of the church, martyrdom symbolized the confessing and courageous church: "Can't you see that the more they are martyred the more they increase? Such exploits cannot be the work of man: they are effects of the power of God; they are the manifest proof of His coming" (7.8–9).

Origen (d. ca. 253), son of a martyr, was himself imprisoned and tortured in the persecution under Decius. During the persecution under the emperor Maximinus in 235, he wrote an "exhortation to martyrdom" in which he eulogizes the "passion of martyrdom" (see Eusebius of Caesarea, *Ecclesiastical History* 6.2.2–6; 3.3–4). He ardently desired martyrdom: "I need that baptism of which the Lord said: 'There is a baptism I must still receive'" (*Fifth Homily on Isaiah* 2).

Thanks to Eusebius of Caesarea's *Ecclesiastical History,* we have a list, however incomplete, of martyrs (he mentions a "collection of martyrs") as well as an elaborate explanation of the role of the martyrs' witness in the mission and expansion of the church. Among other things, he emphasizes how cruel the emperors were toward the Christians (5.2.6–8). For Tertullian too "the blood of martyrs is the seed of Christians" in hostile circumstances (cf. *Apologeticum* 50.13). Later the churches of the East and West compiled martyrologies or synaxaries — that is, lives of the saints and martyrs.

3. In theological and missionary consideration of martyrdom it is necessary to exclude speculations that have nothing in common with the biblical and historical meaning of the term. The following points are important:

- When proclaiming the gospel the church is always going to encounter rejection, persecution, and death. Because of sufferings and tribulations, the good news itself is concealed and distorted (Jn 16:33). The encounter between the revelation of God and human history is stamped by the sign of the cross, and the transmission of the good news is a process which involves both acceptance and rejection. In this confrontation in the name of Christ, Christians have their defender: the Paraclete, the Holy Spirit (Jn 14:16, 26). Nevertheless, Christians, although they pray unceasingly "that the world may pass away and grace appear," ought not to provoke the hostility of the world. In fact, the church has always opposed all fanatical incitement to martyrdom (e.g., the tendency of the Montanists). In the name of the Lord God Almighty (*pantocrator*), Christians have repudiated idolatry, bloody sacrifices, and the cult of the emperor. To the question, "What is wrong with saying: Caesar is Lord [*Kyrios*], to sacrifice and so on, and thus save one's life?" (*Martyrdom of Polycarp* 8.2), they have answered with steadfast repudiation. It was only in these unavoidable "confessional" situations that Christians took the risk of being "removed" from this world (Lk 9:51) by delivering their earthly life into the hands of human beings (Lk 9:44).

• From the beginning the church, when in impossible situations, has recognized the validity of the baptism of blood, the "seal of martyrdom," the baptism of fire (Eusebius, *Ecclesiastical History* 6.4.33): "May the wholly pure faith of your servant Rogatian be credited to him as baptism. And if we die by the sword tomorrow at the orders of the governor, may the blood he sheds become for him the sacrament of his anointing" (Hamman 1952, 100). It must be pointed out, however, that the church always tried to practice its ministry legally through the edification of the Body of Christ by the proclamation of the gospel, the celebration of the sacraments, mission, and the solidarity of Christians.

  As the freedom of the Orthodox churches was restricted during the Ottoman rule, the resistance of the monks was understood as a substitute for the witness of martyrdom: "The phenomenon of monasticism takes up again in the Church the witness of the martyrs of the early centuries. By the principle of nonattachment and availability for God and one's fellow human beings, the monk or nun bears witness to the eschaton inside the Church, and thus exercises a truly prophetic ministry, in showing forth the gospel's way of the Kingdom. It is the radical faithfulness of the martyrs which assures that the gates of hell shall not prevail against the Church" ("Place of the Monastic Life" 1979, 449).

• Furthermore, there is a conception that human nature, the flesh, is destined to be offered as a sacrifice, which leads to a eucharistic interpretation of martyrdom. The Christian martyr "nailed body and soul to the cross of Jesus Christ" (Ignatius, *Epistle to the Smyrnians* 1.1) is the priest who participates in the sacrifice of the eternal and celestial high priest (Heb 6:20, 7:3). The martyr's body was in the middle of the fire "not like flesh that is burnt but like bread that is baked" (*Martyrdom of Polycarp* 15.1). This is why the deed of the martyr has not only exemplary, so to speak ethical, value but also a symbolic meaning involving eucharistic intercession. Saint Cyril of Jerusalem mentions the martyrs among those who are commemorated after the anaphora: "We remember those who have passed away, first of all the patriarchs, prophets, apostles, and martyrs, that God may graciously accept our supplications through their prayers and intercessions" (*Mystagogical Catechesis* 5.9).

Eusebius of Caesarea distinguishes between the martyrs "some of whom die by decapitation, others being thrown to wild beasts, and others who die in prison," and the confessors, "who survive the tortures" (*Ecclesiastical History* 5.4.3).

The martyr is always in a state of prayer and intercession for all, for the whole world. And because it is Christ who suffers in the martyrs and with them, they try not only to save themselves but to save all people and all churches. It is precisely prayer — the petition that their executioners be forgiven — that gives them the strength to follow Jesus to the end.

4. *The Martyrdom of Polycarp* reports that the Christians tried to remove the dead body of their bishop, now crowned with the wreath of immortality, in order to venerate his holy body. Later they collected the bones from the burnt remains and deposited them in a place of worship (17.1). As a matter of fact, the eucharistic liturgy was celebrated over the grave of the martyr (13.3). Saint John Chrysostom mentions that Christians gathered at the graves of martyrs and practiced the veneration of their relics as a "pledge of intercession and consolation"; the relics were spiritual sources of blessing and healing left by these "spiritual doctors," "those crowned by Christ" (*Baptismal Instructions* 7.1–10; 8.16).

According to a very old tradition, no new church was to be consecrated without putting relics of martyrs or other saints into the foundations of the sanctuary, "underneath the altar" (Rv 6:9). But there is a fundamental difference between the adoration of the Son of God and the veneration of the saints: "We adore Christ because he is the Son of God; the martyrs, on the other hand, we love as disciples and imitators of the Lord. And this is right because of their incomparable devotion to their king and master; may we too be their companions and co-disciples" (see Eusebius of Caesarea, *Ecclesiastical History* 4.15.41–42).

5. In conclusion, it must be asserted that as long as the church preaches the gospel as the power but also the scandal of the cross (1 Cor 1:18–25; 2:1–2; Gal 6:14), rejection, whether open or covert, by the state or an idolatrous society, will remain a historical fact. Because of the scandal of the cross it is not easy for the world to enter into the mystery of Jesus Christ. The church needs courageous confessors, martyrs, saints, and the communion of saints, for it is due to their fidelity to the end that the gates of hell do not prevail against the church. But does the church have the courage and the right to propose martyrdom as a spiritual emphasis for today's Christians? Can life in Christ still be visualized as sacrifice? Can the faithful be induced to choose the path of confrontation and hostility to the extreme limits of their endurance? The conscience of the church says that we must not absolutize prophetic actions and attitudes, for we must take into account the fundamental ambiguity of human nature and its resistance to the coming of the reign of God.

JON BRIA

Bibliography

Attwater, D., *Martyrs from St. Stephen to John Tung* (1957). Bisbee, G. A., *Pre-Decian Acts of Martyrs and Commentarii* (1988). Chenu, B., *The Book of Christian Martyrs* (1990). Crews, R. D., "Martyrdom," in *DEM* (1991) 658–61. Delehaye, H., *Les origines du culte des martyrs* (1933). Eusebius of Caesarea, *Ecclesiastical History* 1–10. Giuseppe, R., *The Age of Martyrs: Christianity from Diocletian to Constantine* (1959). Hamman, A., *Prières des premiers chrétiens* (1952). Lash, N., "What Might Martyrdom Mean?" *ExAud* 1 (1985) 14–24. Marlone, E. E., *The Monk and the Martyr: The Monk as the Successor of the Martyr* (1950). "The Place of the Monastic Life within the Witness of the Church Today," *IRM* 68 (1979). Pobee, J. S., *The Theme of Persecution and Martyrdom in the Letters of St. Paul* (1985). Rahner, K., *Zur Theologie des Todes mit einem Exkurs über das Martyrium* (1958). Sherman, J. E., *The Nature of Martyrdom: A Dogmatic and Moral Analysis according to the Teaching of St. Thomas Aquinas* (1942). Thoonen, J. P., *Black Martyrs* (1941). Till, W. C., *Koptische heiligen- und martyrerlegenden: Texte, Übersetzungen und Indices* (1935). Triebel, J., "Leiden als Thema der Missionstheologie," *JMiss* 20 (1988) 1–20. Von Campenhausen, H., "Das Martyrium in der Mission," in *Kirchengeschichte als Missionsgeschichte*, vol. 1, *Die Alte Kirche* (1974) 71–85.

❧ MINISTRY, OFFICE OF ❧

1. Fundamental Considerations. 2. Ministry in the Young Churches.

Due to impulses from Vatican II and from the various initiatives in dialogue between Christian churches, there has been much development in the theology of the office of ministry in recent decades. Until approximately twenty years ago, the positions of the Catholic and Orthodox churches, on the one hand, and of the Reformation churches, on the other, were regarded as fundamentally different and irreconcilable. Since that time it has emerged that a consensus about fundamental considerations is possible after all.

1. This fundamental consensus concerns the following points: that, sent by Jesus Christ and enabled by the Holy Spirit, the whole church has the task in the world of being an effective sign of the →salvation purchased by Christ; that each Christian has a special charism to cooperate in this task; and that through his Spirit, Christ also gives to his community various ministries for the building up of his body.

The special ministerial office in the church stands in the succession of the apostles. It is not merely a practical arrangement of the community or the delegation of the community's own authority, but an office instituted by Christ. Consequently, the office-bearer not only is in the community but also stands over against the community, equipped with authority in the name of Christ. But this authority is to be understood only in relation to Christ. Jesus Christ is the real agent who commissions the office-bearer. Thus the office-bearer is the personal sign of the Lord working now in his community.

Consequently, when the Catholic tradition describes the office-bearers as priests, this can mean only that in the Holy Spirit they participate in and make present the one priesthood of Jesus Christ. The Reformation tradition prefers to avoid the title priest in order not to endanger the understanding of the uniqueness of Christ's priesthood.

The spiritual office of ministry defined in this sense is necessary for the church (*iure divino*); but in its concrete form it must always be open for ever-new forms according to the historical situation.

Concerning the function of the ordained office-bearer, the 1981 declaration of the Roman Catholic–Lutheran Joint Commission states: "Our churches are thus able today to declare in common that the essential and specific function of the ordained minister is to assemble and build up the Christian community by proclaiming the word of God, celebrating the sacraments and presiding over the liturgical, missionary and diaconal life of the community."

The ministry is conferred by ordination, which is administered by laying on of hands and prayer. Through ordination the ordained becomes a member of the company of office-bearers and the gift of the Holy Spirit is promised and granted for the exercise of his or her mission. Whether the ordination so understood is called a sacrament or not is a question of the different understandings of sacrament.

Ordination can be conferred only once and is a commitment for life. This is also the basic meaning of the Catholic teaching on the so-called indelible character, by which it is taught that the office-bearer is engaged for life and God abides by God's own promise and works through this chosen person even when the latter existentially fails to measure up to his or her commission.

It is generally accepted that the division into the three-tiered ministry of bishop, presbyter, and deacon developed through a long process in the course of the first centuries before it became a generally accepted structure. Even if all churches did not retain this structure, it is recognized that the churches need these different aspects of the ministerial office in some form or other.

The papal ministry is still a difficult question. It is significant, however, that in the Catholic Church the college of bishops has achieved new recognition and status and that in other churches there is a growing awareness of the need for an office of unity.

Of course in all churches there are also opinions which deviate quite considerably from the consensus described above, and it is still an open question to what extent the consensus worked out by the official commissions will actually be accepted by the churches. Furthermore, the question of women's ordination has become a new matter of dispute about which various churches hold opposing opinions.

2. For those churches that have grown out of the missionary movement, this theological consensus offers guidelines for the necessary task of organizing the ecclesiastical offices of ministry according to social and cultural circumstances. In any case, care should be taken in the churches' praxis to give attention to the theological foundation since it offers an opportunity for practical rapprochement where the various churches are confronted with similar problems, as in the Third World.

The Catholic Church, with its firmly established office precisely determined by canon law, has always suffered from a shortage of priests in those parts of the world. Consequently, from the very beginning, for practical rather than theological reasons, laypeople (→laity) have played a great part in the life of the communities. These laypeople have usually been called catechists. In the beginning they often had little formal education, but being fired by great apostolic zeal they contributed inestimable services to the missionary cause. In accordance with preconciliar ecclesiology they were understood simply as helpers of the priest. Because of changed political and educational situations in these countries and the emphasis on the independent role of the laity in the ecclesiology of Vatican II, a search for a new understanding of the catechist's call began in the 1960s. In many countries academies for the formation of qualified catechists were established according to the recommendations of the council in *AG* 17.

Vatican II also brought about a new recognition of the Christian community in general, at the grassroots level. In the younger churches — especially with their immense parishes and scattered people — base ecclesial communities were established in which Christians could practice their faith together. In these communities a whole range of ministries has been developing in full accordance with the aforementioned theological consensus and its emphasis on the Spirit's bestowal on the church of a wealth of ministries according to the needs that arise. These ministries include, among other activities, leadership of small groups, animation of Bible study, responsibility for liturgy and worship, and responsibility for mutual help in solidarity with the poor. The element of solidarity with the poor, which must characterize this ministry by the church, is strongly emphasized by the →World Council of Churches.

The Catholic Church is recognizing more and more that the shortage of priests is not a temporary problem; it is a structural problem arising from the present "priest model," which has been increasingly found to be inadequate. Most younger churches contain small communities of Christians widely scattered, with poor road or rail communications. Thus, for example, the approximately four million Catholics of Indonesia live in about ten thousand ecclesiastical units. At present there are about one thousand priests in the pastoral ministry in Indonesia, but ten thousand would be needed to give each community a resident pastor. This is not possible, however, given a full-time, academically educated, celibate priesthood. Besides, such a person is overqualified for a small community. Thus everywhere we see emerging, even if in different forms, the ministry of community leader.

In general, two theories are put forward for the legitimization and further development of this ministry. One theory assumes that priestly ordination bestows the authority to preside over the →Eucharist (Lord's Supper) and administer absolution, all other duties being regarded as lay ministries. According to this view, the role of community leader is the crowning point of the lay ministries. The other theory sees ordination as the conferring of authority for the ministry of leadership in the name of Christ, with presiding at the eucharistic celebration as its climax. This theory entails the conclusion that those who are installed as de facto leaders of the community should also receive the necessary authority and spiritual help by means of ordination. In the light of the aforementioned theological consensus, the latter opinion is to be preferred. According to this view, in addition to the traditional priests there should in the future be other ministers, without academic theological training (→theological education), married, and with secular professions apart from their activities as pastors of small communities. These ministers would work under the guidance of the more highly trained priests. The problem of two classes of priests would not be serious since two very different things are not easily compared.

Various bodies have already called for this new form of ordained pastorate, but it was rejected by a small margin of the 1971 synod of bishops. Nevertheless, the last word about this matter has probably not been spoken.

The council's idea, in *AG* 16, for the commissioning of deacons has up to now found little response in the younger churches. That is understandable since in this way the problem of communities without access to the Eucharist is not solved. Further, in this scheme, the deacons would be "stop-gap" pastors and would not be able to develop their own professional image.

The Reformation churches have less rigid regulations and consequently find it easier to establish new ministries. In some ways they could serve as a stimulus for the Catholic Church, and Catholics could learn from their experience, as is already happening in very concrete ways, for example, in South Africa (see O. Hirmer). The Protestants should put still more emphasis on qualifications and better training at the various stages of the ecclesiastical ministry; here they can profit from the experience of the Catholic Church.

The restructuring of ecclesiastical ministries in the younger churches is a very important factor in the effort to make the churches at home in their own culture (→inculturation) and free them from too much dependence on foreign resources. That the churches must stand on their own feet as regards personnel and finances is also of vital importance. Only in this way can the younger churches be assured of healthy growth.

GEORG KIRCHBERGER, SVD

Bibliography

Achutegui de, P. S., *Asian Colloquium on Ministries in the Church, February 27–March 5, 1977* (1977). Amalorpavadass, D. S., *Ministries in the Church in India* (1976). Anderson, R. S., *Theological Foundations for Ministry* (1976). Antoniaszzi, A., *Arbeitsgemeinschaft ökumenischer Universitätsinstitut: Reform und Anerkennung kirchlicher Ämter* (1973). Burrows, W., *New Ministries: The Global Context* (1980). Cook, B., *Ministry to Word and Sacrament: History and Theology* (1976). Cordes, P. J., *Sendung zum Dienst: Exegetisch-historische und systematische Studien zum Konzilsdekret vom Dienst und Leben der Priester* (1972). *Eucharist and Ministry: Lutherans and Catholics in Dialogue IV* (1970). Groupe des Dombes, *Le ministère de communion dans l'Eglise universelle* (1986). Haendler, G., *Luther on Ministerial Office and Congregational Function* (1981). Hickey, R., *Africa: The Case for an Auxiliary Priesthood* (1980). Hirmer, O., *Die Funktion des Laien in der katholischen Gemeinde* (1973). Hultgren, A., "Forms of Ministry in the New Testament," *Dlg* 18/3 (1979) 201–12. Jenson, R. W., "Ministries Lay and Ordained," *Partners* 3/5 (1981) 12–13. Marins, J., and T. M. Trevisan, *Comunidades eclesiales de base* (1975). Meyer, H., and L. Vischer, *Growth in Agreement: Reports and Agreed Statements of Ecumenical Conversations on a World Level* (1984). Monsengwo, P. L., "Die Gemeindeleiter: Ein Experiment der Evangelisation in Zaire," in *Evangelisation in der Dritten Welt* (1981). Idem, "Neue Formen des amtes in christlichen Gemeinschaften," *PMVB* 50 (1974). Idem, "Römische Bischofssynode: Dokument über das priesterliche Dienstamt," *HerKor* 25 (1971) 584–91. Idem, *Sacra Congregatio pro Gentium Evangelizatione, Catéchistes in Afrique, en Asie et en Océanie, Etude Synthétique, Commission pour la Catéchèse et les Catéchistes* (1972). Parvey, C. R., *Ordination of Women in Ecumenical Perspective* (1980). Power, D. N., *Gifts That Differ: Lay Ministries Established and Unestablished* (1980). Schillebeeckx, E., *The Church with a Human Face: A New and Expanded Theology Ministry* (1987). Schütte, H., *Amt, Ordination und Sukzession im Verständnis evangelischer und katholischer Exegeten und Dogmatiker der Gegenwart sowie in Dokumenten ökumenischer Gespräche* (1974). Thurian, M., *Churches Respond to Baptism, Eucharist, and Ministry* (1986). Vischer, G. H., *Apostolischer Dienst: Fünfzig Jahre Diskussion über das kirchliche Amt in Glauben und Kirchenverfassung* (1982). Wainwright, G., "Reconciliation in Ministry," in *Ecumenical Perspectives of BEM* (1983). World Council of Churches, *Baptism, Eucharist, and Ministry* (1982).

❧ MISSIOLOGY ❧

1. Historical Background. 2. Structure.

1. The Protestant and Catholic "awakening to world mission" since the end of the eighteenth century constitutes the historical background of the beginnings of missiology, founded as a branch of theology in the Protestant church in the nineteenth century and in the Catholic Church in the first half of the twentieth century. J. F. Flatt, J. T. Danz, C. Beckenridge, and K. Graul prepared the ground for Protestant missiology. F. Schleiermacher also gave a place to mission in his practical theology. This approach to the subject of mission was at first supplemented by the inclusion of the missionary dimension in treatments of church history. The way to an independent approach to the discipline and to a comprehensive critical elucidation of the subject was paved by A. Duff in Edinburgh (1867) and most importantly by G. Warneck in Halle (1897). Warneck worked out a comprehensive foundation for missiology on the basis of biblical orthodoxy, revivalist piety, and a romantic view of the world reminiscent of Herder and Schleiermacher. His outline of a Protestant mission theory in his *Evangelische Missionslehre* also had an effect on the founder of Catholic missiology, the church historian J. Schmidlin, who, at the suggestion of the Prussian ministry for education, began to lecture on missiological topics at the Catholic Faculty of Theology in Münster in 1910.

It must be pointed out, however, that Catholic missiology had forerunners — for instance, J. B. Hirscher in the nineteenth century — who like Schleiermacher made mission a part of practical theology. Furthermore, there were numerous individual contributions pertaining to missiology or mission praxis in both the Protestant and Catholic spheres before the establishment of an independent theological discipline, not least because of the missionary experience with non-Christians which, over centuries, took mission into consideration. "Mission" included here linguistics, comparative religion, and anthropology. Reflecting the first missiological outline by Warneck, Schmidlin endeavored to give a scientific and theological framework to Catholic missiology. His organizational goal was to establish an institute and promote interdisciplinary cooperation with other missiologically relevant faculties (e.g., comparative religion). Even if this organizational perspective could be realized in Catholic missiology only in a limited way, after the first beginnings in Münster, there was a rapid development of missiology in Catholic faculties in Germany, the Netherlands, Switzerland, Rome, and beyond. Protestant missiology experienced a boom after World War II and since the 1950s has created chairs in numerous theological faculties in Germany as well as in Scandinavia, the Netherlands, and especially the United States. In contrast, in spite of the importance of German missiology — in particular the Münster School, which together with Louvain had a significant influence on Vatican II (→Vatican Council II) — it has not been possible to increase the Catholic missiological presence at the university level in the country regarded as the cradle of Catholic missiology.

It must be generally observed that missiological themes and questions in both the Protestant and Catholic spheres have detached themselves from missiology and are investigated in other theological branches but without in this way leading to a missionary theology determined by the subject "mission" in the traditional sense. Despite the fact that impulses for a reorientation of missiology are coming precisely from theological concepts and initiatives from outside missiology, these impulses are hardly able to do justice to the complexity and range of the area covered by missiology because they take the methodological differentiation too little into account. There are a great number of problems and questions that have an effect on missiology and give its research and teaching a special orientation (→theology of mission): ecumenism; the postconciliar fostering of responsibility in the local church; development and the sociopolitical, economic, and ecclesiastical problems in the Third World; the dramatic decline of European ecclesiastical and theological traditions; and the recognition of responsibility for the emergence of contextual theologies (→contextual theology). The experience with contextual theology in particular has raised numerous new issues which demand further development, such as: the experience of "unity and diversity" as a new dimension for both Protestants and Catholics; the dimension of catholicity beyond a confessionally determined one; the opening up of Christian churches and theologies to the concrete sociocultural context with its specific challenges and transcontextual ramifications; the rather unexpected reconstitution and revitalization of non-Christian religions in spite of simultaneously expanding secularizing tendencies in technocratically oriented societies; the realization of a common commitment to peace among churches and religions in spite of their historical burden of guilt for wars of religion, oppression and extermination of people, and their hesitant commitment to the removal of causes of conflicts; and the question of the ecclesiastical, that is, the Christian or religious contributions to the change of existing social structures, constraints, and forms of domination. These and other areas of interest and inquiry influence and mold missiology as a discipline and give to its methodology and teaching a special orientation.

The plurality of missiology at present; the critical analysis of its own history (still hardly begun and by no means brought to a logical conclusion) and of its role within community, theology, local churches, and the "world church" (the *oikoumene* [→ecumenism]); and especially the question of how the philosophy of science clarifies the self-understanding of missiology in connection with, among other things, the definition of the specific object of missiology and its methodology — all these various aspects show that in this phase of change and reorientation missiology needs critically to take stock of its achievements and develop them further. This presupposes that missiology will increasingly become inserted into the concrete realities of local churches and the various contextual ways of living the faith and doing theological reflection. The development of the churches and theologies in the Third World, the increasing differentiation between being a Christian and being a church member, the experience of a common faith despite the diversity of Christian traditions, the movement toward the foundation of religious truth outside Christianity through dialogue, the participation in the riches of other cultures and religions by jointly experiencing and organizing events beyond the traditional rites and rituals — all these issues present missiology with a variety of tasks for which this branch of theology does not seem to be prepared. Those theological ways of thinking that up to now dominated missiology and the theological categories are changing. In addition the concept of mission itself has become less clear. This necessarily has an effect on the definition of the object of missiology, its goals, and the organizational structure of its work.

2. The combination of missiology and comparative religion in the Protestant sphere and within the framework of Christian ecumenism offers the possibility of theological reflection on mission with reference to its religious history and sociocultural contexts along with a critical analysis of mission praxis. From case to case, the main stress of mission research is differently placed and as a rule points to some specific experience on the part of the missiologist outside of his or her own European or North American church. In addition the main streams of Reformation theology are reflected in the missiologies as well as the evaluations of non-Christian religions, cultures, and social structures. Within ecumenical circles and in the life of particular churches, missiology not only affects the way mission is understood and practiced but conversely also receives from within the *oikoumene* stimuli for the deepening and modification of theological models and for the development of practical mission orientations. Increasingly this leads to a dialogical opening and cooperation between Protestant, Catholic, and Orthodox representatives of missiology and mission.

At the same time, within the Protestant church there arises the special ecumenical problem of evangelical mission practices and evangelical missionary training together with the different comprehension of missiology among the Orthodox. Just as in Catholic missiology — confirmed in its work by Vatican II and challenged anew by theology as a whole — Protestant missiology is dedicating itself anew to the basic questions of missiology: definition, foundation, goal, and realization of mission. Furthermore, since Warneck and Schmidlin, the specific mission themes treated by missiology correspond to the branches of theology — mission exegesis, mission history, global ethics, and so on. To complement these categories in the sphere of practical missiology, mission methodology (pastoral theology) must be added, especially in reference to the training of missionaries and the description of present-day mission and missionary statistics.

What has proved particularly fruitful for missiology is the cooperation with other (including nontheological) disciplines such as comparative religion, cultural anthropology, linguistics, and sociology. This can lead to shifts in emphasis. On the one hand, today missiological communications research receives special attention. On the other hand, peace and conflict research and special branches of comparative religion are also being considered. The influence of so-called political theology or socially oriented Third World theologies promotes the inclusion of sociological and sociocritical approaches. In this way a broad field of differentiation and cooperation with other scientific disciplines is opened to missiology. Nevertheless, some cultural manifestations have not yet been widely considered as objects of missiology: for example, the broad field of →art. But in spite of all the very relevant individual and special studies, it becomes obvious that a comprehensive concept of missiology is lacking. In general a contextual orientation, which leads beyond the question of inculturation, dominates the discussion. The European tradition and the dominance of the religious history of Europe are viewed in new ways and critically evaluated. Intercultural and interreligious approaches have contributed to a spirit of dialogue in churches and theologies by placing such matters as mission, creeds, theologies, historical manifestations of church, the linkage of mission with European colonialism, and the relationships and mutual influence of religions within a comprehensive framework of historical and factual-theological contexts. Such studies in particular provide an insight into the historical dimension of Christian life and show that in the evangelization process Christianity needs the enriching concrete encounter with that which is different and not merely contact with different systems of salvation.

For the further development of missiology it will be crucial to determine whether it can legitimize itself as an independent, officially recognized branch of theology. Impulses for redefining missiology, for instance, in the direction of a "comparative theology" (A. Exeler; T. Kramm), need further critical investigation. Of greater theological consequence is the problem raised by theologians like L. Rütti who detach mission from its ecclesiocentrism and refer faith to its responsibility for the world. The problem with these two new approaches is that they not only reduce the complexity of missiology and the theology of mission but overlook whole areas of human and religious existence. On the one hand, Rütti's conception in particular seems to allow no avenue for a proper evaluation of the religions. On the other hand, any social reference in regard to the Christian faith points out that mission's service of witness to salvation is tied to social structures that must be burst open by the dynamism of the gospel in solidarity with the poor and the socially and religiously marginalized. This solidarity is manifested in living, suffering, working, and hoping with others. In this sense, the contextual theologies of the Third World remind us of the theological dimensions of missiology which enable the church and theology to recognize how they are conditioned by and linked to their respective contexts; to recognize how they can transcend them; and — in regard to the Christian faith, to theology, to the reality of church, and to practicing human solidarity as a response to God's own solidarity with humanity — to recognize themselves as the foundation and goal of mission.

In this sense, and within the framework of contextuality, the question of transcontextuality and intercontextuality must be addressed. But these questions must be linked up with the more comprehensive interreligious and intercultural processes not only of mission in the strict sense but of Christian identity in general.

HANS-JÜRGEN FINDEIS

Bibliography

Allen, R., *Missionary Principles* (1964). Anderson, G. H., and T. Stransky, eds., *Mission Trends* 4 vols. (1994–). Bevans, S., *Models of Contextual Theology* (1992). Bosch, D. J., "The Structure of Mission: An Exposition of Matth. 28:16–20," in *Exploring Church Growth* (1983) 218–48. Idem, *Transforming Mission: Paradigm Shifts in Theology of Mission* (1991). Buchwalter-King, G., and R. J. Schreiter, "Fundamental Issues in Globalization," *TEd* 9, supplement 1 (1990). Idem, "Globalization: Tracing the Journey, Charting the Course," *TEd* 30, supplement 1 (1993). Idem, "Globalization and the Classical Theological Disciplines," *TEd* 29/2 (1993). Exeler, A., "Wege einer vergleichenden Pastoral," in L. Bertsch, ed., *Evangelisation in der Dritten Welt* (1981) 92–121. Gensichen, H. W., *Glaube für die Welt* (1971). Glasser, A. F., and D. McGavran, *Contemporary Theologies of Mission* (1983). Hesselgrave, D. J., *Contextualization: Meanings, Methods, and Models* (1989). Kiss, C., *Mission-in-Reverse: A Contemporary Approach to Mission* (1987). Kroeger, J. H., *Mission Today: Contemporary Themes in Missiology* (1991). Kramm, T., *Analyse und Bewährung theologischer Modelle zur Begrundung der Mission* (1979). Kunkel, F., *Theological Perspectives of Mission Education* (1985). Müller, K., *Mission Theology: An Introduction* (1987). Muzorewa, G. H., *An African Theology of Mission* (1990). Neely, A. P., *Christian Mission: A Case Study Approach* (1995). Neill, S., *CDCW* (1975). Newbigin, L., *The Open Secret: Sketches for a Missionary Theology* (1994). Niles, D. T., *Upon the Earth: The Mission of God and the Missionary Enterprise of the Churches* (1962). Phillips, J. M., and R. T. Coote, *Toward the 21st Century in Christian Mission* (1993). Schmidlin, J., *Katholische Missionslehre im Grundriß* (1919). Scott, W., *Karl Barth's Theology of Mission* (1978). Scherer, J. A., *Gospel, Church and Kingdom: Comparative Studies in World Mission Theology* (1987). Idem, "Missiology as a Discipline and What It Includes," *Missiol* 14 (1987) 507–22. Scherer, J. A., and S. Bevans, *New Directions in Mission and Evangelization*, vols. 1 and 2 (1992, 1994). Shorter, A., *Toward a Theology of Inculturation* (1989). Sundermeier, T., "Konvivenz als Grundstruktur ökumenischer Existenz heute," *ÖEH1* (1986) 49–100. Tippett, A. R., *Introduction to Missiology* (1987). Verkuyl, J., *Contemporary Missiology: An Introduction* (1978). F. Verstraelen, et al., *Missiology: An Ecumenical Introduction: Texts and Contexts of Global Christianity* (1995). Waits, J. W., W. Lesher, and R. J. Schreiter, "Globalization and the Practical Theological Disciplines," *TEd* 30/1 (1993). Warneck, G., *Evangelische Missionslehre*, 5 vols. (1892–1903). Wiedenmann, L., *Herausgefordert durch die Armen* (1983).

❧ MISSION IN NON-CHRISTIAN RELIGIONS ❧

1. Various Basic Patterns. 2. Individual Religions.

1. With regard to mission by non-Christian religions, that is, to their expansion and propaganda, various patterns of behavior are found in the history of religions.

1.1. There are a considerable number of religions which have no expansionist intentions and thus cannot be regarded as missionary by nature. Examples of these religions are found mainly in those ethnically homogeneous cultures that regard membership of the group as the decisive characteristic of their identity. Accordingly, the individual is seen mostly as a member of the community. In Africa, for instance, religion is not meant for the individual but first and foremost for the community to which the individual belongs. Mission to the individual is not really possible. Where it does happen, however, conversion is an act against the community and its values and is evaluated or punished accordingly. It goes without saying that such a tribal society never does anything on its own initiative to transfer its culture and religious code of behavior to other groups or tribes.

The same is true of the official culture/religion of Japan, Shintoism, with the exception of a few particular Shinto sects. Any expansion — even if it is desired by foreigners outside of Japan willing to be converted — is not intended. The erection of Shinto shrines outside of Japan does not correspond to the self-image of this religion, which is linked to Japan as a country. Consequently, Shinto shrines are to be erected only where the Japanese emperor (*Tenno*) reigns. This explains the existence of Shinto shrines in the territories outside Japan occupied by the Japanese (e.g., Korea) in connection with the military and political expansion at the end of the nineteenth and in the first half of the twentieth centuries.

In approximately the same way, classical Hinduism also spread through the influence of Hindu rulers by means of political and military expansion. Furthermore, there was a certain cultural and religious Hinduization in countries east of India and in Indonesia as a result of cultural superiority and, now and then, also in connection with Buddhist mission. To the extent that the meager documentation from the early period of the religious history of Southeast Asia and Indonesia permits conclusions about the expansion of Hinduism, it seems that there were no expansionist intentions nor a conscious campaign for Hinduization. Even in India such an attempt cannot be detected until the nineteenth century — apart from the zealous preaching of individual gurus who won over some followers. Things began to change, however, at the end of the nineteenth century.

1.2. External circumstances initiate missionary activities. Hinduism at the end of the nineteenth century is a good example of this principle. Having participated in the World Parliament of Religions in Chicago in 1893, Vivekananda founded the Vedanta movement and the Ramakrishna Mission, the first organizations for the spread of Hinduism in the West. It was in the English-speaking world (Great Britain, the United States) that Indian religions — for example, the Ramakrishna Mission — began to speak of mission for the first time. The Zen master Shaku Soyen from Kamakura in Japan also came to Chicago and later sent his disciple D. T. Suzuki to the United States to promote the publication of Buddhist scriptures. Representatives of Jainism were also in Chicago and soon afterward established the Mahavira Brotherhood in London. These constituted the first attempts by Eastern religions to carry on mission in the West. Since the 1960s this movement has become very strong.

Historically speaking, Judaism and Confucianism too are among the ethnic-regional religions that, at least at certain periods, advocated the reception of converts and an expansion of their influence.

1.3. Apart from Christianity, three religions in particular have made a universal claim to religious truth: Buddhism, Manichaeism, and Islam. Taking a closer look at the religious propaganda and expansionist aims of these religions one can detect two different conceptions: Buddhism and Manichaeism address their saving message to individuals; Islam has the whole community in mind.

Whereas Manichaeism from the very beginning systematically carried on missionary work and Mani himself advocated a high degree of acculturation as a program for →inculturation, the world mission of Buddhism seems to have begun only in the third century B.C.E. through Emperor Asoka. The goal of Buddhist preaching was to help those searching for truth and lead them along the Buddhist path of selflessness. There was no intention of thoroughly penetrating all spheres of social life with Buddhist thinking. Consequently, for the laity, Buddhist ethics was confined to some basic principles but otherwise tolerated other values and moral concepts of a non-Buddhist origin.

Islam makes an unequivocal universal claim (see Koran 9:33). Its goal is a community (*umma*) that appeals for what is good, lays down what is right, and forbids what is reprehensible — and all this through faith in God (see Koran 3:104, 110). Consequently, the invitation (*da'wah*) to faith (usually translated as "mission") has a twofold task: internally, the maintenance of Islamic order (*sharia*); externally, the expansion of the "house of Islam."

1.4. Following the example of Christian mission, new .sects within Buddhism and Islam, as well as many of the so-called new religions (e.g., Bahai, Unification Church), intensively pursue missionary activity in their countries of origin, many of them also worldwide, quite often with considerable success.

2. For a long time "mission" was considered an exclusively Christian term, its use being restricted to activities propagating the Christian faith. Even in the phenomenology of religions (at least in Europe), "mission" was often reserved for Christianity alone. Consequently, there are few systematic, cross-cultural, and comparative studies of missions and missionary activities that have yet been produced. But the encounter of religions in our time calls for a correction in this respect. Not only world religions but also local, tribal, and so-called primitive religions are beginning to spread their faith.

Considering this new situation, G. van der Leeuw asserts that "the dynamic of religions, further, is displayed in mission. This may in the first place be completely unconscious, and merely a reciprocal influence of religions which is the outcome of local proximity, cultural interchange, *etc.* It is called mission, however, because it is a result of speaking forth, of utterance and testimony, and is accompanied by all sorts of transpositions in the life of both the influencing and the influenced religion.... But as soon as missionary expansion is understood to be the essential activity of the community, it receives a quite different character. Its influence then becomes a fully conscious propaganda of doctrine and worship, and generally of the specific characteristics of a religion" (van der Leeuw 1963, 611–12).

Turning to concrete examples of non-Christian missionary activities we shall restrict ourselves to some outstanding world religions competing today with Christianity and changing the religious situation of the Western world: Buddhism, Islam, and Indian religiosity.

2.1. *Buddhist mission.* Apart from the fact that the Buddha himself sent out disciples, three features facilitated the spread of Buddhism: (*a*) The members of the Buddhist community rejected the Indian caste system and so were free to contact people indiscriminately. (*b*) Mahayana Buddhism in particular was inclined to adopt non-Buddhist deities, customs, and convictions and to reinterpret them in the light of Buddhist doctrine. (*c*) Unlike the Brahmanist tradition, Buddhist scriptural traditions were not attached to any sacred language and hence admitted translations and transformations into other languages such as Chinese and Japanese.

The way of the Buddha was mainly spread by wandering monks, pilgrims, and students who visited the famous monasteries in India, Tibet, and China; who practiced and studied under the guidance of a master; and who returned home with Buddhist texts. In certain periods of history Buddhism was even propagated under the patronage of emperors and kings (e.g., Asoka in India in the third century B.C.E.; the kings of the Kushan Empire in the first and second centuries C.E.; in medieval China, Korea, and Japan). The missionaries mainly used land or sea trade routes.

China became the second main center for the propagation of Buddhism outside India. According to historical records, Buddha's teaching was introduced to China for the first time between 65 and 67 c.e. After this introduction, the history of Chinese Buddhism is the history of the Chinese Buddhist mission as well. It includes the spread of Buddhism to Korea and Japan and is concerned with the development of the various forms of canonical scriptures in China and Japan and of Buddhist schools or sects as well.

Leaving aside the historical details, which would also have to deal with the spread of Buddhism to Tibet and in Southeast Asia, it is worth mentioning that the features of modern Buddhist mission can be studied especially in Sri Lanka, Vietnam, Thailand, Korea, and Japan — countries where in recent times the various occidental influences of Christianity, Western civilization, science, and technology have been strongly felt. The present encounter with the West led to (a) the development of modern apologetics (e.g., K. N. Jayatilleke [1920–70]); (b) churchlike organizational structures (see, besides the local structures, the various forms of international confederations, social activities in the field of education, health care, etc.); (c) new Buddhist-inspired religious groups (e.g., in Japan, Rissho Koseikai, Sokagakkai, etc.); and (d) the building up of Buddhist centers in Europe and the United States and the propagation of practices and doctrine among Westerners.

2.2. *Islamic mission.* The duty of spreading Islam is mentioned in many passages of the Koran (see 3:19, 99–100; 16:125–26; 22:66–67; 36:69–70; 38:87–88; 42:14; etc.). The basic Arabic term is *da'wah,* which means to invite, to call, to summon. It is used in the sense of inviting people to embrace Islam as the true religion, calling upon God in prayer. For centuries it implied political orientations and the spread of Islamic statehood. Today it mainly "refers to Islamic missionary activities, which are increasingly characterized by long-range planning, skillful exploitation of the media, establishment of study centers and mosques, and earnest, urgent preaching and efforts at persuasion. *Da'wah* as mission should never be spread by force (cf. 2:256)" (*ER* 4:245). Undoubtedly, *da'wah* is strongly emphasized in the Islamic revival of the late twentieth century.

Nevertheless, Islamic mission cannot be discussed without reference to the understanding of *jihad* (see *jahada:* to endeavor, to strive, to struggle). Although *jihad* also refers to the struggle against one's own evil inclinations, it usually points to the spread of Islam. This can be peaceful (*jihad* of the tongue or the pen) or forceful (*jihad* of the sword). Consequently, it is not simply the "holy war," although in about two-thirds of the instances where the verb *jahada* occurs in the Koran, it refers to warfare. The close connection of religious and political interests in Islam led to the simple conclusion that in history Islam was mainly propagated by force. Yet a critical examination of the Islamic mission has to take into account the various reinterpretations of *jihad* in modern times (see *ER* 8:83–91).

2.3. *Indian religiosity and its mission in the West.* As mentioned before, the occidental term "mission" was applied for the first time in a non-Christian religion by the Ramakrishna Mission, founded in 1897 by Svami Vivekananda (1863–1902), the most fervent disciple of Sri Ramakrishna (1834–86). In the case of this neo-Hinduist movement, the quest for mission implied the transformation of Hinduism from an ethnic religion to a world religion; it changed from a caste-bound religion to a religion of free choice and possible conversion. The second presupposition for a mission-oriented religion, namely, that it has to offer a message of universal salvation and liberation, can be proved by the history of Hindu religion and religiosity and its development during the various periods. Important factors are the following: the appearance of Buddhism and the reaction of Brahmanism, which led to the disappearance of Buddhism in India; the encounter with foreign religions like Islam and Christianity; the competition of India's "great" and "little" (or popular) traditions; the constantly occurring call for a universal religion inside of India; and the development of neo-Hinduism in the period of colonialism and independence. The various experiences of interaction with other religions, between religion and sociopolitical events, and between cult and meditative or speculative insights prepared India in a special manner for coping with the problems of modern times. Among these are the encounter with religions outside of India and the challenges of Western scholarship, technology, and political ideas. Moreover, the rejection and criticism of Christianity in many places in the West suggested Asian religions as possible alternative ways of salvation.

The special character and pluriformity of Hindu religiosity as well as the development of modern syncretism in Asian religious life gave rise to a variety of religious groups and ways in the West through which Hinduism in particular and Asian religiosity in general exercise their influence. The patterns of propagating the Asian religions differ widely. Not all religions call for conversion. In many cases a double membership in different religions is allowed. Besides, the aims of the religious groups are not completely identical. However, a number of common features are emphasized, including: the integral understanding of salvation comprising physical health (healing) and psychological insight (consciousness of mind, enlightenment); the unity of nature and humankind; the divine as identity of the cosmos and humanity; and wisdom and love. Westerners often feel a strong fascination regarding the spiritual leaders and guides of the Asian religions. The small religious communities give the feeling of safety and make them a place of security. Moreover, the indirect missionary methods contrast with the missionary activities and methods applied in modern church history. The main attraction of Asian groups is precisely the fact that they stand in opposition to the Christian churches in the Western Hemisphere and often reveal the shortcomings of the churches.

PETER ANTES AND HANS WALDENFELS, SJ

Bibliography

Ahmad, K., and D. Kerr, *Christian Mission and Islamic Da'wah* (1982). Barker, E., *Of Gods and Men: New Religious Movements in the West* (1981). Bulliet, R., *Conversion to Islam in the Medieval Period* (1979). Ch'en, K., *The Chinese Transformation of Buddhism* (1973). Corless, R. J., *The Vision of Buddhism: The Space under the Tree* (1989). Decret, F., *Mani et la tradition manichéenne* (1974). Hummel, R., *Indische Mission und neue Frömmigkeit im Westen* (1980). Hutten, K., and S. Kortzfleisch, *Asien missioniert im Abendland* (1962). Jomier, J., "Mission dans l'Islam," in *DictR* (1984). Meinhold, P., *Die Religionen der Gegenwart* (1978). Nasr, S. H., *Islamic Spirituality*, 2 vols. (1987). Needleman, J., and G. Baker, *Understanding the New Religions* (1978). Oxtoby, W. G., *The Meaning of Other Faiths* (1983). Van der Leeuw, G., *Religion in Essence and Manifestation: A Study in Phenomenology* (1963). Zürcher, E., *Buddhism: Its Origin and Spread in Words, Maps, and Pictures* (1962). Idem, *The Buddhist Conquest of China*, 2 vols. (1972). Idem, "Buddhist Missions," in *EncRel* (1987).

❧ MISSION LAW ❧

1. Concept. 2. Sources of Law. 3. Agents of Mission. 4. Missionary Personnel. 5. Missionary Work. 6. Mission and Law.

1. The term "mission law" refers to all legal norms concerned with the propagation of the Christian faith among non-Christian peoples. In the postcolonial era these norms are confined in the civil sphere to regulations about religious freedom and the unhampered proclamation of a religious message. Within the church, mission law means all norms of general canon law connected with the propagation of the faith. Especially important are the particular guidelines through which the church can adapt itself to the realities of individual cultures.

2. The results of the development of law in the Catholic Church after Vatican II can be found in the Code of Canon Law (CIC) 1983, in particular in cans. 781–82, and also in cans. 371, 420, 450.1+2, 502.4, and 1018, which deal with apostolic vicars and prefects.

The further development of mission law is primarily the task of the Congregation for the Evangelization of Peoples (formerly, the Congregation for the Propagation of the Faith [founded 1622]). The faculties formerly granted to the heads of the local churches in the missions are no longer granted after the transition in canon law from the principle of delegation to the principle of reservation. For the further development of particular laws, those responsible, apart from the local ordinaries (bishops, vicars, and prefects apostolic [cans. 375–76]), are the plenary councils (can. 439), provincial councils (can. 440), and episcopal conferences (cans. 447–59). These latter are becoming increasingly important. In addition, there are the mission statutes of the individual missionary institutes and contracts between the bishops of mission dioceses and missionary institutes (can. 790.1 n. 2).

Within the Protestant missions the establishment of law and legal order is determined on a regional basis. Legal norms are found in the mission-church statutes in which the missionary societies give the mission congregations a fixed church order. Some of these codes take a particular confession as their basis and then add church legislation. Others begin with church order and later integrate the confessional dimension (*AMZ* 9 [1882] 27–43).

Church discipline is of crucial importance for the development of congregations and the advancement of younger churches. It regulates the external life of the community and is also necessary for the gradual transition from a non-Christian religion to Christianity and for the formation and sensitizing of consciences. Rules are established concerning daily living (e.g., polygamy) and participation in Holy Communion and in the life of the congregation, which makes these codes a part of the development of church law.

3. Whereas according to can. 1350.2 of the CIC of 1917 the responsibility for mission work lay exclusively with the Apostolic See, the CIC of 1983 adopted the basic principle of Vatican II that "the whole church is missionary by its very nature" (*AG* 2, 35; see can. 781). The whole people of God is asked to make a contribution to mission work (can. 781). This maintains the importance of the church as the "primary sacrament" for missionary work. For carrying out this missionary task, the overall direction and coordination of all initiatives and activities are entrusted to the pope and the college of bishops (can. 782.1). The fact that the college of bishops is mentioned shows the new attitude of Vatican II (*LG* 23, 25; *ChD* 3; can. 756.1). This responsibility lies, as it did before, with the Congregation for the Evangelization of Peoples (can. 360; *AAS* 59 [1967] 915–18). The missionary institutes, the mission aid societies, and all missionaries, including the religious in their missionary activities, are subject to this congregation. It organizes collections for mission work and fosters initiatives of a missionary nature. In mission territories it exercises authority which is elsewhere reserved to other congregations. Excepted are questions of faith, prescriptions about rites, marriage nullity processes, processes concerning ordinations, and matters concerning universities and studies. The college of bishops in this congregation acts on behalf of the whole church by means of representatives. These representatives are nominated after consultation with the episcopal conferences and can cast votes (*AG* 29). The episcopate as a whole also exerts an influence through the synod of bishops, which, according to can. 342, assists the pope in the administration of the universal church. In the particular churches (can. 368) the individual bishops, as sponsors of the universal church and all churches, have special responsibility for mission work, especially for "arousing, fostering and sustaining missionary initiatives" in their territories (can. 782.2). In this way their responsibility beyond the bounds of their dioceses is expressly emphasized. All diocesan bishops are obliged to care for the promotion of missionary vocations and to appoint a mission consultant who promotes missionary undertakings in the diocese, especially the pontifical mission aid societies. There is to be an annual day for the missions in the diocese, and an appropriate contribution for the missions is to be sent annually to the Apostolic See (can. 791). In addition, the episcopal conferences have the responsibility of establishing and promoting institutions in which students and workers from mission countries will be warmly received and given pastoral care (can. 792). A special passage deals with diocesan bishops in mission territories. A hierarchy with diocesan bishops who govern their territories in their own names is not yet everywhere established, but there are today only a relatively small number of apostolic vicars and prefects in these areas who are subject to the Congregation for the Evangelization of Peoples and who administer their territories in the name of the pope. It is the duty of the ordinaries to lead, promote, and coordinate missionary undertakings in their territories. After the transition from the *ius commissionis* to the *ius mandati* in 1969, missionary activity in the dioceses (but not in the vicariates and prefectures) is entrusted no longer to the missionary institutes but to the bishops (see the instruction *Relationes in Territoriis Missionum,* February 24, 1969 [in *AAS* 61 (1969) 281–89]). The bishops are obliged to draw up a contract with the superiors of missionary institutes working in their dioceses. This contract is confirmed by a mandate of the Apostolic See. All missionaries, including the religious and their helpers, are bound by the provisions of the diocesan bishop. In the vicariates and prefectures the *ius commissionis* remains in effect (see the instruction *Quum huic,* December 8, 1929 [in *AAS* 22 (1930) 111–15]). Here the institutes are still the agents of mission.

Just as the mutual relationship of mission and unity urges the "younger churches" within the Protestant churches to form unions, it provides a stimulus for the sending churches also to integrate church and mission. Two factors come into play at this point. The younger churches want to be independent as members of the one church of Christ and realize their missionary responsibility side by side with their mother organizations. On a theological level this movement was inspired by the idea of *missio Dei,* the church's new consciousness as a participant in the mission of God (promoted at the missionary conferences at Tambaram in 1938 and Willingen in 1952). The World Missionary Conference in Accra, Ghana (1957/58), discussed at length the question of integrating the World Missionary Conference (→world missionary conferences) into the World Council of Churches, that is, the relation between mission and church. The integration took place in New Delhi in 1961.

The first realization of this movement on a national level took place in Holland in 1950. The Netherlands Reformed Church, conscious of its apostolic duty, took responsibility for the work of the missionary societies within its sphere. In the Federal Republic of Germany, the Arbeitsgemeinschaft für Weltmission (Protestant Liaison Board for World Mission), founded in 1964, contributed to the gradual integration of the Evangelical Church in Germany and the German Evangelical Missionary Conference. In northern Germany, the North Elbian Center for World Mission and Church Service was founded in 1971 as a partner to the North Elbian churches. In southwest Germany, the Protestant Missionary Society of Southwest Germany was constituted as "a union of Protestant churches and missions." By means of regional church legislation in Bavaria, the Missionary Society of the Evangelical-Lutheran Church in Bavaria was founded.

The setting up of agencies for promoting missions in the old German "Landeskirchen" (territorial churches) was not easy, in either a constitutive or a confederative form, and therefore took a long time. But it was also a question of living and visibly realizing "the variety of structures and goals...in the unity given to us in Christ" (statement from the Bangkok conference).

4. Concerning missionaries sent by the appropriate ecclesiastical authority (which does not necessarily have to be the highest authority), the CIC of 1983 states that both indigenous and nonindigenous missionaries can be chosen. These missionaries can be secular clergy, religious, or lay members of the church (can. 784). Hence all religious sisters and brothers and also laypeople from secular disciplines are recognized as missionaries and not just as helpers. No distinction is made between missionaries working contractually for a limited period of time and missionaries for life. There is a special mention of catechists, who, after being given an appropriate formation, are to be encouraged to do mission work (can. 785).

5. The CIC of 1983 lays down the planting of the church among the peoples and the founding of new churches as the goal of missionary activity (can. 786). This should be carried on by the testimony of word and life. While cultural distinctiveness is to be respected (→inculturation), special emphasis should be placed on dialogue (can. 787.1). The decision to accept the faith must be free (can. 787.2). The code mentions as steps of initiation: the preliminary catechumenate; the catechumenate proper with introduction into the mysteries of salvation; the practical Christian life; liturgy; works of charity; and the apostolate. The episcopal conference should establish norms for the catechumenate (can. 788). A more intensive pastoral care of the newly baptized is demanded (can. 789).

6. Within the discussion about mission and law, the position of mission within the framework of general international law is important. In modern treaties and constitutions the right to carry on (Christian) missionary work and the free exercise of religion are always laid down. But how this is understood in practice depends on the attitude of the various states and their commitment to natural law. This also means that the Catholic and Protestant missions have differing attitudes and aims regarding their legal status in treaties and constitutions. In reality the regulations and legal details are more or less the same since the question revolves around Christianity in a general sense. The main goals to be achieved are freedom of religion and confession, freedom of public worship and cultural activities, and freedom to carry on Christian service. These demands were formulated at the World Missionary Conference at Tambaram (1938). Even if the demands of freedom of mission and church are met in principle, the church has to proclaim the demands and claims of God without, however, identifying God's claims with its own.

PAUL ZEPP, SVD

Bibliography

Beversluis, L., *A Source Book for Earth's Community of Religions* (1995) 124–223. Bonino, J. M., "Whose Human Rights?" *IRM* 66 (1977) 220–24. Corecco, E., *Die Grundrechte des Christen in Kirche und Gesellschaft* (1980). Idem, *Die Menschenrechte im ökumenischen Gespräch: Beiträge der Kammer der EKD für öffentliche Verantwortung* (1979). Dworkin, R., *Bürgerrechte ernstgenommen* (1984). Falconer, A. D., *Understanding Human Rights* (1980). Frenz, H., *Stimme der Verstummten: Vom Einsatz für die Menschenrechte* (1983). Furger, R., and C. Strobel-Nepple, *Menschenrechte und katholische Soziallehre* (1984). Geyer, A., *Toward a Theology of Human Rights* (1978). Gort, J. D., "The Ecumenical Reception of Human Rights," in *MissS* 11/1 (1994) 76–107. Grulich, R., *Religions- und Glaubensfreiheit als Menschenrecht* (1980). Henkin, L., *The Rights of Man Today* (1979). Hollenbach, D., *Claims in Conflict: Retrieving and Renewing the Catholic Human Rights Tradition* (1979). Honecker, M., *Das Recht des Menschen: Einführung in die evangelische Sozialethik* (1978). Huber, W., and H. E. Tödt, *Menschenrechte: Perspektiven einer Menschlichen Welt* (1978). Lendvai, P., *Religionsfreiheit und Menschenrechte: Bilanz und Aussicht* (1983). Lissner, J., and A. Sovik, *A Lutheran Reader on Human Rights* (1978). Lochmann, J. M., and J. Moltmann, *Gottes Recht und Menschenrecht: Studien und Empfehlungen des Reformierten Weltbundes* (1976). Lorenz, E., *How Christian Are Human Rights?* (1981). Moltmann, J., "A Christian Declaration on Human Rights," in *Reformed World* 34 (1976) 58–72. O'Mahony, P. A., *The Fantasy of Human Rights* (1978). Schnur, R., *Zur Geschichte der Erklärung der Menschenrechte* (1964). Schrey, H. H., "Wiedergewinnung des Humanum? Menschenrechte in christlicher Sicht," *ThR* 48 (1983) 64–83.

❧ MISSION PATRONS ❦

1. Francis Xavier. 2. Thérèse of Lisieux.

In 1927 two saints, the French Carmelite Thérèse of Lisieux and the Basque Jesuit Francis Xavier, were together affirmed as "patrons of all missions." Within vastly differing life-situations, each of these saints practiced heroic and lifelong self-giving on behalf of the missions. Now wholly embraced within the communion of saints, they continue this dedicated participation in their new role as intercessors.

1. The young Francis Xavier (1506–52), born of noble blood, was a student preparing for a career of wealth and status as a diocesan priest when he met Ignatius of Loyola. It took several years for the future founder of the Society of Jesus to win him over to the vision of a life of gospel poverty and mission, but once Francis made his decision he became Ignatius's most trusted friend and collaborator among the first group of companions. When the nascent society was asked by the pope to provide two men for mission in the Indies, it was with the greatest sorrow that Ignatius allowed Xavier to substitute for another who had become ill.

Departing in 1540, Xavier would never see the shores of Europe again. On his several subsequent sea and land journeys in service of his mission, he endured bad food and water, lengthy delays, pirate threats, the vagaries of unreliable captains, near disasters during storms, and other grueling hardships. This first trip, with a destination of Goa in India, took over two years.

Upon arrival in India, Xavier quickly set about the work of evangelization. After only a few months in Goa, he was asked to work among the Parava people on the Indian coast opposite Sri Lanka. Xavier devoted himself wholeheartedly to teaching and caring for these low-caste fishermen, who were subject to much mistreatment by fellow Indians and Europeans alike. Even after he had moved on to other missions in Malaysia, Indonesia, and Japan, Xavier had a special care for the Parava people and attempted — with little success — to protect them from the cruelty so frequently visited upon them.

Although he apparently was never able to become proficient in the languages of the peoples he served, from the first Xavier made a policy of seeking to reach them in their own language rather than (like earlier missionaries) requiring converts to learn Western language and culture. He would typically begin his evangelization by finding collaborators who would assist in translating the creed and basic prayers into the local language and then teaching these in sung form. Later on he would sometimes have a local Christian preach while he stood by praying for the success of the effort. Despite his linguistic difficulties, Xavier was evidently a very charismatic communicator; in each of the locales where he worked, a strong indigenous Christian community became well established.

Xavier was indefatigable in his zeal to expand and enhance the effectiveness of his mission. In Japan, lack of success in his initial efforts led him to the innovative insight that communication required taking on not only the language of the local people but their dress and comportment as well. After this breakthrough was approved by the authorities, he was able to convert several Japanese who, without ever learning a European language, carried out significant campaigns of gospel preaching. Meanwhile, discovering that the Asian people regarded China as the cultural capital of the world, Xavier became convinced that the full success of his mission of evangelizing the Orient required him to shift the focus of his attention there. It was not to be, however. After only twelve years on mission, but already a legend in both Europe and Asia, the forty-six-year-old Jesuit died of a fever while on the way to China.

2. Thérèse Martin (1873–97) joined the order of Discalced Carmelites in Lisieux, France, at the age of fifteen. Carmelites, beginning with the first disillusioned crusaders who became hermits on Mount Carmel in twelfth-century Palestine, have always had a strong awareness of participation through prayer in the worldwide development of the church. The sixteenth-century Discalced reform of the Carmelite order took root during the same period of missionary expansion in which Francis Xavier participated. Discalced Carmelite communities, especially the enclosed monasteries of women, traditionally take very seriously the responsibility to offer prayer and sacrifice for the intentions of those on mission. The future saint Thérèse exemplified this tradition in a superlative way throughout her brief life.

Even as a child Thérèse was imbued with a spirituality that taught her to offer up her small sufferings and problems as prayers on behalf of those in extreme need. In her early years in Carmel, she developed this more fully into her "little way" — a spirituality of complete hiddenness and ordinariness in which one offers each moment very simply to God. Her famous title, "The Little Flower," derives from her image of herself as only one among millions of little flowers on the hillside, each giving its all in joy and praise to God. Her success in living this spirituality is indicated by the fact that during her lifetime many of her sisters in community regarded her as a very ordinary Carmelite; only a few recognized the extraordinary virtue that was developing in their midst.

Thérèse's writings and conversations included frequent specific references to missionaries and the missions. Indeed, Thérèse greatly desired to be a missionary herself by participating in a foundation her community was about to make in Hanoi, but her failing health prevented her from making the journey. Rather than weakening her commitment to the missions, this seemed to strengthen it. She took on special responsibility for two "spiritual brothers," Rev. Maurice Bellière (missionary to Africa) and Rev. Adolphe Roulland (missionary to China), promising to pray and sacrifice daily for their work. She also developed a great devotion to a young missionary martyr, Théophane Vénard, who had been beheaded in Hanoi in 1861. His picture and his memory were constantly with her during the last six months of her life, as she endured a slow and horribly painful death from the effects of tuberculosis.

Thérèse's understanding of her role in mission work revolved primarily around her sense of sharing in Christ's redemptive suffering. Some of the concrete ways in which she required herself to participate in that suffering may come across as artificial or even morbid today, but the core doctrine is sound. Even as she spoke a great deal about suffering, she was very clear that what really matters is love. The offering of sufferings is not for its own sake but rather is a gift of love that is willing to endure anything for and with the beloved. Thérèse's passionate love led her to long intensely to do all things for God; she spoke explicitly of wanting to be priest, apostle, doctor of the church, martyr, warrior, missionary, and prophet. She concluded, however: "My vocation, at last I have found it.... MY VOCATION IS LOVE!...[I]n the heart of the Church, my Mother, I shall be Love. Thus I shall be everything, and thus my dream will be realized."

In one of her striking images, Thérèse compared herself to a barely glimmering candlewick which, although placed in a dark corner of the sacristy, can be used to light thousands of candles, filling the whole church with light. Thus we see how this young contemplative sister was gifted with an extraordinary degree of conviction that even the smallest action done in the love of God can bear fruit for the entire people of God. Her example of consistently seeking to live her simple hidden life in a way that would benefit those most in need — especially missionaries and those in mission lands — offers a model of participation in the missions for others who may never have the opportunity to leave their own lands or cultures.

The very different lives of these two saints, now placed side by side as patrons of the missions, offer a potent image of diversity of vocation in the family of God. The commonality in their vocations, however, is equally significant: both placed their lives entirely in the hands of God, endured profound sufferings with love and faith in conscious imitation of Christ, heroically gave of themselves for the good of others, and gave public witness to the centrality of prayer in the life of a Christian disciple. These qualities exemplify the spirit of Christian mission, in whatever time or place it may be lived. The lives and persons of these two canonized saints, along with those of all of like spirit, remain permanently in our midst as a living witness to Christ's mission of transforming love.

MARY FROHLICH

Bibliography

Francis Xavier
Brodrick, J., *St. Francis Xavier* (1952). Recondo, J. M., *San Franciso Javier: Vida y Obra* (1988). Ross, A. C., *A Vision Betrayed: The Jesuits in Japan and China, 1542–1742* (1994). Schurhammer, G., *Francis Xavier: His Life and Times*, 4 vols., (1973–1982). Idem, *Saint Francis Xavier, the Apostle of India and Japan* (1928). Xavier, Francis, *The Letters and Instructions of Francis Xavier*, trans. M. J. Costello, (1992). Idem, *Monumenta Xaveriana* (1899–1912).

Thérèse of Lisieux
Balthasar, H. U. von, *Thérèse of Lisieux: The Story of a Mission* (1954). Combes, A., *Saint Thérèse and Her Mission: The Basic Principles of Thérèsian Spirituality* (1955). Furlong, M., *Thérèse of Lisieux* (1987). Gaucher, G., *The Passion of Thérèse of Lisieux* (1989). Idem, *The Story of a Life: St. Thérèse of Lisieux* (1982). Sullivan, J., ed., *Carmelite Studies*, vol. 5, *Experiencing Saint Thérèse Today* (1990). Thérèse of Lisieux, *General Correspondence: Saint Thérèse of Lisieux*, 2 vols., trans. J. Clarke (1982). Idem, *Story of a Soul: The Autobiography of St. Thérèse of Lisieux*, trans. J. Clarke (1975). Idem, *St. Thérèse of Lisieux: Her Last Conversations*, trans. J. Clarke (1977).

∞ MISSION STATISTICS ∞

1. Concept and Purpose. 2. The Universality of Christianity. 3. The Vitality of Christianity. 4. The Growth of Christianity. 5. The Main Categories.

1. Mission statistics can be defined as the systematically collected numerical presentation of the development of mission. In the past it was a subdivision of mission history. D. B. Barrett divides mission history into five periods: the Apostolic (or Pneumatic) Era (30–500 C.E.), the Ecclesiastical Era (500–1750), the Church Growth Era (1750–1900), the Global Mission Era (1900–1990), and the Global Discipling Era (1990–). It is obviously difficult to get exact figures from the past centuries of mission history, but general estimates are possible. For the future, only probable data can be given. From the present situation we can observe certain trends: for example, the accessibility of the Christian faith to all peoples. According to Barrett, the five periods correspond to five commands contained in the missionary mandate of Jesus Christ: Go! Baptize! Convert! Evangelize! Disciple! Mission statistics ought not to be regarded as a triumphalistic presentation of Christianity; rather the aim is to remind Christians of Christ's command concerning "the great divine work of universal mission" in which they should take an active part. Hand in hand with mission geography, mission statistics provide a concrete and expressive description of the expansion of Christianity. They are "probably the quickest, most scientific and most objective way of presenting large amounts of highly condensed and accurate information, and of describing large groupings of peoples and their activities at particular points in time" (D. B. Barrett). They can serve as a valuable corrective to both an exaggerated optimism and a depressing pessimism since they furnish statistical data with objective accuracy. Consequently, they offer a solid foundation for missionary planning, in which positive and negative factors have to be taken into consideration. In the highly regarded *World Christian Encyclopedia* (*WCE*), Barrett bases the growth curve of Christianity on the statistical data of the years 1900, 1970, 1978, 1980, 1985, and

2000 in order to arrive at the best possible estimates. He uses a relatively simple method in which he calculates the natural process of growth and the increase in the number of Christians by conversion. He relates both factors to a given group and thus arrives at the growth in percentages. Considering the small growth rates, the difference between this simple method used by Barrett and the complicated representation of the growth curve by demographers is of very little importance.

2. Mission statistics illustrate the universality of Christianity. We see from the *WCE* that there are only a few countries where there is no Christian church; in others, Christians are a minority; and in still others Christianity is deeply rooted and sometimes embraces (at least nominally) the whole population. Islam, in contrast, is particularly widespread in Indonesia, the Middle East, and North Africa. Whereas the Bible is translated into fifteen hundred languages, that is, 96 percent of the languages of the world, the Koran is available only in a very few translations, and these are not officially recognized. Buddhism embraces many countries of Southeast and East Asia; Hinduism is primarily a religion of India, Taoism of China, and Shintoism of Japan. Compared with the other great world religions, Christianity is a universal religion which has taken root in most countries. Nevertheless, mission statistics draw our attention to the new attitudes of Christianity toward the other religions. Whereas it was taken for granted in the nineteenth century that the non-Christian religions would eventually — under the influence of Western science and the spread of Christianity — lose their attraction and completely disappear, such an opinion is doubted today. These religions have become the object of academic study, and with increasing dialogue a new attitude toward these religions has been fostered.

3. Mission statistics also show the vitality of Christianity, which is growing in spite of obstacles, animosities, and persecutions. In 1980, twenty-five countries were completely and twenty-four others partly closed to Christian missionaries. The figure for Christian ministers was estimated at 3.2 billion, of whom 249,000 were foreign missionaries; 35,000 came from Communist countries. Barrett estimated the number of evangelized people in the world in 1980 to be 2.994 billion. Of these 1.433 billion were Christians and 1.561 billion non-Christians (who know Christianity and the gospel but are not officially Christians). The number of unevangelized was 1.381 billion. Of great importance for the development of Christianity is the shift of the majority of Christians from the North to the South, that is, to those who live in the Third World. The number of Christians who live in the Third World is presently estimated to be 60 percent of the total.

4. Mission statistics, especially those in the *WCE,* have refuted and corrected the myths about the decrease of Christianity and growth of Islam. The claim about the drop in the proportion of Christians was based on the supposition that their numbers were remaining static, whereas the non-Christian world was growing rapidly because of the population explosion. But mission statistics show that many Christian countries have recorded a large population increase. From the *WCE* we also see that since 1900 the decrease of the proportion of Christians is very small. In Africa, for example, the numbers have greatly increased. The claims about the strong growth of Islam in Africa were based on the assumption that five times as many people convert to Islam as to Christianity. Indeed, in Africa, Islam is rapidly increasing only in the countries of the former French colonies, not in the

English-speaking world. In twenty-nine African countries Islam forms a noticeable minority. It would seem that African peoples are less inclined now than at the beginning of the century to think that Islam meets their religious and cultural needs. At present Christians in Africa are rapidly increasing. In and to the south of Zaire (Democratic Republic of Congo), Islam is hardly known. It is estimated that the number of Christians south of the Sahara in the year 2000 will be around 300 million in a population of 360 million. That would add up to more Christians than the estimates today for north and west Europe and for North America.

5. Mission statistics describe four main categories: (*a*) missionary personnel (missionaries, priests, ordained preachers, catechists, sisters, brothers, lay helpers, teachers, nurses, development assistants); (*b*) missionary institutions (stations, churches, schools, charitable institutions, hospitals, and orphanages); (*c*) missionary activity, consisting of various forms of proclamation, administration of the sacraments, and the celebration of divine services; and (*d*) numbers of local Christians. In more recent times, local missionary personnel increasingly perform the above-mentioned tasks. Finally, mission statistics provide important information about the sending churches.

WILLI HENKEL, OMI

Bibliography

Barrett, D. B., "Annual Statistical Table on Global Mission," *IBMR* 14 (1990) 26–27 (annually since 1990). Idem, "Five Statistical Eras of Global Mission," *Missiol* 12 (1984) 21–37. Idem, *World Christian Encyclopedia* (1982). Idem, *World Evangelization Database* (1992). Barrett, D., and T. Johnson, *Our Globe and How to Reach It* (1990). Brierley, P., *World Churches Handbook* (1997) Bush, L., *AD 2000 and Beyond Handbook* (1992). Grundemann, R., *Klein Missionsgeographie und-statistik* (1901). Johnstone, P., *Operation World* (1993). MARC, *North American Protestant Ministries Overseas* (1980). *Missiones Catholicae,* 1886, then yearly until 1892, 1895, 1896, 1901, 1907, 1922, 1930, 1950. Myers, B. L., *The Changing Shape of World Mission* (1993). *Notizie statistiche delle missioni di tutto il mondo dipendenti dalla S. C. de Propaganda Fide* (1844). Pate, L., *From Every People* (1989). Schmidlin, J., *Einführung in die Missionswissenschaft* (1925) 100–101. Siewert, J., *Mission Handbook USA/Canada: Protestant Ministries Overseas* (1993). Wilson, S., and J. Siewert, *Mission Handbook: North American Protestant Ministries Overseas* (1986). *World Churches Handbook* (1996).

❧ MISSIONARY METHODS ❧

1. Missionary Methods in General. 2. The Theological Context. 3. Reductions and Christian Colonies. 4. Missionary Methods in the More Recent Missiological Discussion.

1. Missionary methods and missionary praxis are to a great extent determined and theologically sustained by the theological foundation of mission (→theology of mission) and evangelization. Thus the term "missionary methods" refers to the procedure through which the reign of God is established on earth, the church is planted in the people (→"people" [*Volk*], "nation"), and the gospel is proclaimed among those who have not yet heard it. These goals are reached by different stages: the preparation and training of missionaries, making contact with groups or peoples, the conversion of individuals or groups, and the founding and consolidating of a Christian community.

Perhaps here we can refer to *Catechesi Tradendae* 1, which describes catechesis as "the whole of the efforts within the church to make disciples, to help people to believe that Jesus is the Son of God," a description which includes both mission and the fostering of growth in the faith.

In more recent missiological discussions, missionary methods and methodology do not have the importance they had in the earliest days of →missiology. Complaints have been made repeatedly that these areas are not adequately grounded (T. Ohm). But even in that early phase it was already being pointed out that missionary methods and their study and especially missionary methodology were weak points in this new theological discipline. According to C. Grundmann, the "model method" of mission was by no means as well established as other questions within missiology. The necessary preliminary research in the form of evaluation and assessment of special mission history was still lacking.

At the World Missionary Conference in Edinburgh (1910) (→world missionary conferences) the question of missionary method was very important. The problem was to get the worldwide missionary activity established within the churches. The participants wanted to do justice to the scope of the task, the need of the hour, by means of a plan. They believed that for this plan they had to design a method, a strategy, a tactical approach. But it was also emphasized that each country and people needed, even had the right to, its own missionary method. Nevertheless, in the actual implementation of mission there are activities common to all situations: proclaiming the gospel, founding and organizing communities, disseminating the Bible. Other missionary activities are variable: the founding of schools and medical missions, the production and distribution of Christian literature, the advancement of individual groups, and the founding of associations.

Down through history (→history of mission) we can discern varied missionary methods which were conditioned by the missionaries themselves, their nationality and particular religious order, or their church affiliation. At the same time the different cultures (→culture) and social structures, economic systems, and particular histories of individual peoples have an effect. The theological classification of the peoples to whom the mission comes with its message and the evaluation of their tradition and religion (→religion, religions) also result in the emergence and choice of different missionary methods.

But the decisive factor in missionary methodology is the distribution and planned assignment of missionary personnel (see J. Mott, J. Schmidlin). The central questions about missionary method are: In a given territory, is extensive or intensive missionary activity to be used? Should it act sporadically or concentrically? In theoretical reflections on this problem, one sometimes finds emphasis on one of these poles to the exclusion of the other. But when concrete examples are examined, one observes that these different approaches are used at different stages within the history of individual mission territories. The missionaries first employ a more extensive working method and then, for the securing and deepening of the evangelization, they change over to more intensive methods. After a more sporadic evangelization, they concentrate on the central parishes and main stations and try to consolidate the Christian message. This is more or less what happens in each individual mission as well as in the whole history of mission.

2. For missionary work and the development of a missionary method it is important that missiology reach out to other academic disciplines: →anthropology, comparative religion, sociology (with emphasis on its forms and methods), and history (especially as it relates to historical processes and →development). Missiology must accompany the concrete realization of mission critically and theologically, not forgetting to be self-critical, so that the praxis is reflected and justified, the identity of the task maintained, and the world reference of the message realized. At the same time this scientific and theological reflection must always ask whether the radius of action "is broad enough to reach even a culturally, socially, and religiously 'remote' addressee in his own reality and stimulate an authentic new response" (H. W. Gensichen). The question must also be asked whether the contact with a particular people is not causing changes which result in a loss of identity in the cultural and social sphere.

The possibilities of the new media for the transmission of the gospel message have to be examined. In addition, the fundamental principles of communication research must be taken into account (→communication).

3. In the course of mission history certain missionary methods have led to fierce controversies (accommodation, →rites controversy, adaptations in the social sphere). Methods have been developed which affect not only particular areas of social and cultural life but almost all facets of life (→inculturation).

In the Spanish and Portuguese colonies, reductions have a long history. These reductions were villages in which indigenous people either voluntarily or under compulsion were "reduced" to abandoning their nomadic or seminomadic life to live as "law-abiding" people (*ad ecclesiam et vitam civilem reducti*). Catechumens and new Christians under the leadership of missionaries lived in these settlements, which were to a great degree independent and self-governing. There were religious, political, and social reasons for their founding. The goals were the education of the people, the consolidation of Christianity, and the social uplift of the population. Gathering the people in this way was intended to protect them from the conquerors, bring about social reforms hand in hand with evangelization, and establish a true Christianity — to create the "new man" in Latin America (→Latin American theology). Despite all their drawbacks the reductions were a form of Christian resistance against the colonial powers, an anticolonial utopia. They constituted a missionary method with great advantages but also with enormous weaknesses, one of the latter being that they ultimately led to the ritualization of life rather than a missionary Christianity. The reductions were a concern not only of the religious orders, especially the Jesuits, but also of the clergy and bishops, who increasingly showed solidarity with the interests of the indigenous people and the Jesuits. They denounced the social injustice which made it impossible for the people "to find true liberation in Christianity."

After 1850 the idea behind the reductions was taken up by Catholics and Protestants in many countries around the world in a form known as Christian colonies. These were artificial settlements set up by missionaries as a result of pastoral strategy or socioeconomic considerations. Although the basic idea was the same in all these Christian enclaves, they were of course stamped by their different historical, cultural, social, and geographical contexts. Some of these villages were established with the intention of creating a Christian community and a favorable climate which would be the preliminary steps toward an indigenous church and the preparation for a local clergy. Here the establishment of new social and economic institutions was of great importance, and the existing social order and natural groupings had to be destroyed in favor of the new, artificially created settlements. Other Christian colonies were established for other social and religious reasons (e.g., the mission to Muslims, natural catastrophes, helping orphans). In most cases, the settlements failed to achieve their long-term goals, often because of a lack of apostolic and missionary dynamism. The villages constituted isolated enclaves within a people and so were incapable of working like "leaven." Because of the great importance of social and economic conditions in these villages, the primacy of religious, missionary activity could easily be lost sight of. Even if the Christian colonies at the time of their establishment were a necessary requirement of adaptation to the economic, social, and cultural preconditions of the mission countries, today they are generally rejected as a missionary method. Where necessary, though, some settlements are still functioning.

4. In the more recent missiological debate, the methodological approaches and concerns of R. Allen (1868–1947) and R. Anderson (1796–1880) have had considerable influence. They are imbedded in the theological discussion about the independence of the younger churches and the "three-self" formula. The basis of Anderson's mission theology was the unshakable conviction of the necessity of evangelizing the world in his time and the firm resolve to do it. Anderson referred to the missionary method of Saint Paul, with his surprisingly rapid founding of local churches supplied with all ecclesiastical authority and responsible for the continuation of the mission. The goal of mission is, therefore, according to Anderson, world evangelization through self-propagating and independent local churches. Only means and methods which aim at this can be recognized. Oral preaching is of primary importance and goes hand in hand with the direct organization of the local church. The linkage of preaching and church organization is not a question so much of dogma as of mission strategy. In addition to the main task of creating churches by means of preaching and organization there are the secondary means of education and printed literature. The importance of these for →conversion is small. The main purpose is the consolidation and advancement of the mission church and the formation of the next generation.

R. Allen designed his own missionary method, spelled out in *Missionary Methods: St. Paul's or Ours?* (1912), in which he presents his view of the Pauline missionary method and draws conclusions for missionary activity, although in his time the importance of the Pauline method for modern mission had already become controversial. The decisive characteristic of the missionary method of Paul (→Paul the apostle as missionary), in contrast to modern methods, is that he transferred church authority immediately to the young churches as a means of self-maintenance and self-propagation. Hence this transfer is not the terminus of a development process but the beginning. He preached in central places from which the proclamation then spread. Faith in the leading power of the Spirit enabled Paul to confer great independence on the young communities. Basically every organization must be set up in such a way that it is acceptable to the community.

The missionary method of the North American Presbyterian J. L. Nevius (1829–93), the so-called Nevius Method, played an important part in the church of Korea and in mission in general. Nevius was a missionary in China who in 1890 was invited by missionaries in Korea to come over and advise them. There he formulated his method, the basic principles of which he had worked out before and which involved "planting and development of missionary churches." The Nevius Method is not suitable as a working method in an organized community; it is intended for the initial stages of a mission. This method was widespread and popular in China, but for the Korean church in particular it was of enormous importance, and the rapid growth of the church in Korea is attributed to the Nevius Method. According to this missionary method, the Bible stands in the center of evangelization. The missionaries are always itinerant preachers. Each Christian, including the newly converted, instructs another in the Bible and is in turn instructed. And every member of the community is responsible for passing on the gospel. Every group does missionary work under the guidance of an unpaid leader who will be the future pastor. The communities are self-governing and themselves responsible for building up the church, including their places of worship. When the community is fully organized, it also pays its own pastor. The planned and systematic Bible study makes every member of the community a leader or helper in the Bible circle. Life is characterized by a strict biblical discipline. The program called "Church Growth" (→Church Growth movement) could be classified as a missionary method. The focal point is the missionary "strategy," a word and concept dear to the heart of D. A. McGavran. Case studies are gathered and evaluated, then statements about the possibility of and the conditions for rapid church growth are made. According to this school, the present hour demands church growth — this is the challenge to mission today. There is at present a great readiness to accept the gospel in many places, and the growth of the church takes place in unimaginable dimensions. It is necessary to seize this opportunity by drawing up the priorities of missionary activity according to the guidelines of church growth. The methods used for church growth must be adapted to each particular situation, but of course there are general principles that always apply. All obstacles to church growth must be eliminated (e.g., →polygamy). The communities should be set up within sociologically homogeneous groups or units and should not usually cross their boundaries (like castes in India). It takes time for a comprehensive Christian fellowship to grow. Another principle is that one should primarily evangelize those groups that are especially receptive and cultivate less intensely those fields that show little promise.

The basic theological decisions that stand behind this mission strategy are uncritical. Moreover, a biblicist and literal use of the Bible text can be observed. Dogmatic decisions are made which may not be sustained by the broad range of Christian theology. This program draws attention to an important aspect of mission, but the question about the nature of the church is not answered. It can easily become an end in itself and overlook the theological foundation of evangelization in the *missio Dei*. The theological reference to the dynamic of the →Holy Spirit should not blind us to the fact that this method can easily divert attention away from the heart of the gospel message.

Josef Schmitz, SVD, and Horst Rzepkowski, SVD

Bibliography

Allen, R., *Missionary Methods: St. Paul's or Ours?* (1912). Ashby, P. H., *Christian Missions and Their Approach to Contemporary Primitive Cultures* (1951). Auf der Maur, J., "Die Missionsmethode im Frühmittelalter," *EMM* 108 (1964) 124–35. Barrett, D. B., and J. W. Reapsome, *Seven Hundred Plans to Evangelize the World: The Rise of a Global Evangelization Movement* (1988). Beaver, R. P., "Rufus Anderson: To Evangelize, Not Civilize," in *Mission Legacies* (1994). Beckmann, J., *Die katholische Missionsmethode in China in neuester Zeit (1842–1912): Geschichtliche Untersuchung über Arbeitsweisen, ihre Hindernisse und Erfolge* (1931). Bevans, S. B., *Models of Contextual Theology* (1992). Beyerhaus, P., *Die Selbständigkeit der jungen Kirchen als missionarisches Problem* (1959). Boff, C., *Ecclesiogenesis: The Base Communities Reinvent the Church* (1986). Idem, *Feet-on-the-Ground Theology: A Brazilian Journey* (1987). Bonino, J. M., *Doing The-*

ology in a Revolutionary Situation (1975). Borges, P., *Metodos misionales en las cristianizacion de America siglo XVI* (1960). Clark, C. A., *The Korean Church and the Nevius Methods* (1928). Cone, J. H., *Black Theology and Black Power* (1969). Davis, J. M., *New Buildings on Old Foundations: A Handbook on Stabilizing the Younger Churches in Their Environment* (1945). Dayton, E. R., and D. A. Fraser, *Planning Strategies for World Evangelization* (1981). Fabella, V., and M. A. Oduyoye, eds., *With Passion and Compassion: Third World Women Doing Theology* (1988). Forman, C. W., "A History of Foreign Mission Theory in America," in *American Missions in Bicentennial Perspective* (1977). González, J. L., *Mañana: Christian Theology from a Hispanic Perspective* (1990). Haas, O., *Paulus der Missionar* (1971) 82–87. Held, H., *Christendörfer: Untersuchung einer Missionsmethode* (1964). Hennelly, A. T., "Theological Method: The Southern Exposure," *TS* 38/4 (1977) 718–25. Hertlein, S., *Wege christlicher Verkündigung: Eine pastoralgeschichtliche Untersuchung aus dem Bereich der katholischen Kirche Tanzanias*, 2 vols. (1976, 1983). Hoornaert, E., *The Memory of the Christian People* (1989). Latourette, K. S., *A History of the Expansion of Christianity*, 7 vols. (1937–45). Loewen, J. A., *Culture and Human Values: Christian Intervention in Anthropological Perspective* (1975). McGavran, D. A., *The Bridges of God: A Study in the Strategy of Missions* (1955). Idem, *Church Growth and Christian Mission* (1965). Idem, *Understanding Church Growth* (1980). Neely, A., *Christian Mission: A Case Study Approach* (1995). Neill, S. C., "Strategy for Missions," in *CDCW* (1970). Ohm, T., *Das Katechumenat in den katholischen Missionen* (1959). Polzen, C., *Rules and Precepts of the Jesuit Missions of Northwestern New Spain* (1976). Ritzson, J. H., *Christian Literature in the Mission Field* (1915). Robert, D. L., "From Missions to Mission to beyond Missions: The Historiography of American Protestant Foreign Missions since World War II," *IBMR* 18/4 (1994) 146–62. Sanneh, L., *Translating the Message: The Missionary Impact on Culture* (1989). Scherer, J. A., *Missionary, Go Home! A Reappraisal of the Christian World Mission* (1964). Schreiter, R. J., *Constructing Local Theologies* (1985). Segundo, J. L., *The Liberation of Theology* (1976). Shenk, W. R., *Exploring Church Growth* (1983). Idem, "Henry Ven: Champion of Indigenous Church Principles," in *Mission Legacies* (1994). Sobrino, J., *Liberación y cautiverio: Debates en torno al metodo de la teología en América Latina* (1975). Stackhouse, M., *Apologia: Contextualization, Globalization, and Mission in Theological Education* (1988). Stott, J. R. W., *Down to Earth: Studies in Christianity and Culture* (1980). Stromberg, J., *Mission and Evangelism — an Ecumenical Affirmation* (1983). Tamez, E., *Through Her Eyes: Women's Theology from Latin America* (1989). Thistlethwaite, S. B., and M. P. Engel, eds., *Lift Every Voice: Constructing Theologies from the Underside* (1990). Tucker, R. A., "Female Mission Strategists: A Historical and Contemporary Perspective," *Missiol* 15/1 (1987) 73–89. Van Engen, C. E., "A Broadening Vision: Forty Years of Evangelical Theology of Mission," in J. A. Carpenter and W. R. Shenk, eds., *Earthen Vessels: American Evangelical Missions, 1880–1980* (1990). Waliggo, J. M., "Making a Church That Is Truly African," in *Inculturation: Its Meaning and Urgency* (1986). Winter, R., *Reaching the Unreached: The Old-New Challenge* (1984).

❧ MISSIONARY SOCIETIES ❧

1. History of Catholic and Protestant Missionary Societies. 2. German Protestant Missionary Societies. 3. Orthodox Mission. 4. Cooperation.

1. A historical consideration of Catholic missions reveals that to a great extent they were carried on by monks, religious orders, and congregations. Thus in the Middle Ages it was the religious who were the missionaries: Benedictines, the Celtic missionaries, Cistercians, Premonstratensians, Trinitarians, and eventually the Dominicans, Franciscans, Carmelites, and Augustinians. Then followed other orders, for instance, the Jesuits and many recent congregations such as the Picpus Fathers, Oblates of Mary Immaculate, Marists, Pallottines, Holy Ghost Fathers, Salesians, Scheut Fathers, White Fathers, Divine Word Missionaries, Sacred Heart Missionaries, and Holy Family Missionaries. Following the model of the Société des Missions Étrangères (Paris Foreign Missionaries), various missionary societies of secular priests were founded: the Milan Foreign Missions Seminary, the African Missionaries (Lyons), the Mill Hill Fathers, the Maryknoll Fathers. In addition, there have been a large number of women's missionary orders over the course of history, especially since the last century, although it is only recently that they have been recognized within missiological discussions.

By their spirituality, organization, tradition, and experience the orders seemed to be predestined for missionary work. That is why Thomas à Jesu (1564–1627) — a Spanish Carmelite who promoted the establishment of the Roman Congregation for the Propagation of the Faith — was of the opinion that orders and congregations were the most suitable instruments of mission, and that is also why, as mentioned above, the history of Catholic missions is to a great extent the history of religious orders. The fact of their historical contribution was underlined by Vatican II: "Religious institutes of the contemplative and active life have up to this time played, and still play, the greatest part in the evangelization of the world" (*AG* 40; see *EN* 69). With the increase of missionary awareness in the Protestant world, a similar phenomenon developed: more and more missionary societies came to carry on missionary work, even if their origin, relationship to the church, and motivation were quite varied. Although the origins of the missionary societies have not yet been investigated and worked out in detail, it would seem that initially they were near to the monastic ideal. Their ancestral line includes the remains of monasticism, the "religious societies" in England, and the revival movement of the Moravians, who from the beginning were very active in mission. Mission was seen as a direct expression of the dynamism of the community, which needed a specific organ for this purpose.

This dynamism for mission took shape in the new missionary societies. The development was promoted and hastened by the tendency in the nineteenth century to form associations. Due to the initiative of W. Carey (1761–1834), the Baptist Missionary Society was founded in 1793. With the founding of this society, mission became the responsibility of well-organized and structured groups. In 1795, the London Missionary Society was founded, followed in 1796 by two Scottish missionary societies and in 1797 by the Netherlands Missionary Society. In 1799, the Church Missionary Society was founded by Anglicans who had withdrawn from the London Missionary Society, which had been at first nonconfessional but later took on a Congregationalist form. In the German-speaking world, the Deutsche Christentumsgesellschaft (German Christianity Fellowship, founded 1780) acted as a hub and catalyst for mission activity. There were some forerunners: the Danish-Halle Mission (1705), closely linked to the colonial idea, and the Moravian Mission (1732), which was constituted fully as a free church organization. Other individual initiatives, such as that of J. von Welz, also played an important role.

Other societies that organized early in the nineteenth century included the British and Foreign Bible Society (1804), the London Society for Promoting Christianity among the Jews (1809), the American Board of Commissioners for Foreign Missions (1810), the Edinburgh Medical Missionary Society (1814), the American Baptist Missionary Board (1814), the Basel Mission (1815), the American Bible Society (1816), and the Berlin Society (1824).

Because many European Protestant churches were unable or unwilling to initiate, administer, or support foreign mission, voluntary mission societies came into being throughout Europe in the nineteenth century. The "great century" of Catholic and Protestant missions is often associated with the nineteenth century. European churches played the dominant role during this time in regard to mission and church expansion. The formation and structure of these early independent mission societies, and their formal and informal relationships with the established churches as the nineteenth century progressed, had a great impact on the early development of mission societies in the United States before World War I.

Whereas nineteenth-century mission was dominated by European mission societies, American Protestant missions became a strong force in the twentieth century. The United States was considered a mission field by the European missions until the middle of the nineteenth century for Protestants and until 1907 for Catholics. But with the religious revivals, energy, and optimism associated with mid–nineteenth-century America, the now "Christian America" moved from being a mission field to becoming the major source of missionary activity. The missionary societies in the United States had become by 1914 quite organically linked with the official structures of their respective churches, and a more directed connection between mission societies and the churches' own comprehension of mission became more apparent. Today, the largest total number of missionaries being sent out by any nation comes from U.S.-based mission societies. Missionary sending by European nations has shown a downward trend since 1975.

Although this general trend in North American and European mission will probably continue well after the year 2000, one of the newest and most significant developments is the increase in missionaries sent out by "non-Western" nations. The average growth rate of Third World Protestant missionaries during the 1980s was 13 percent. Over thirty-six thousand Protestant missionaries were sent out from the Third World nations in 1988. Those nations with the greatest number of missionaries are India, Nigeria, Zaire (Democratic Republic of Congo), Myanmar, Kenya, Brazil, the Philippines, Ghana, Zimbabwe, and Korea.

Since the late 1960s, Catholic religious orders in western Europe and North America have seen a dramatic reduction of male and female vocations. Lay missionary societies, such as the Volunteer Missionary Movement (VMM), founded in 1985 by E. Gateley, have begun to fill this vacuum. In contrast, in Africa, Asia, and Latin America, there has been a steady increase of new members in the religious orders who are willing to accept the call to missionary work. This trend has resulted in both a renewal of older religious orders and the formation of new indigenous ones.

2. The development of the German missionary societies can be divided into three main stages (see J. Richter and J. Hermelink).

2.1. The great German missionary societies arose with the express intention of avoiding confessional differences so as not to transfer them from Europe to their new communities, although later the confessional characteristics made themselves felt anyway overseas. Among these societies were the Basel Mission (1815), the Berlin Missionary Society (1800), the Rhenish Missionary Society (1828), the North German Missionary Society (1836), and the Gossner Mission Society (1836).

2.2. Reflection on the church and its confessional structure led to a second wave of missionary societies. They often arose by simply splitting off from existing mission societies. Thus in 1836 the Dresden Mission Association broke away from the Basel Mission, regarding itself as a mission of the Lutheran Church. In 1848 it transferred to Leipzig, becoming known as the Leipzig Lutheran Missionary Society and, as such, as the continuation of the Danish-Halle Mission. The Hermannsburg Mission was founded by L. Harms in 1849. Because of confessional differences, the present Mission Society of Evangelical Lutheran Free Churches branched off from the Hermannsburg Mission in 1892. The Neuendettelsau Missionary Society also understood itself as expressly "in the spirit of the Lutheran Church."

2.3. Neopietism, especially under Anglo-Saxon influence, provided further impulses for the creation of mission societies. Inspired by J. H. Taylor and the China Inland Mission (1865) — one of the largest missionary societies at that time — there arose the missionary societies of Barmen (1889), Liebenzell (1892), Neukirchen (1878), and a large number of similar foundations. In addition there were missionary societies founded for special tasks, for example, the preparation of women for charitable work.

3. In the Orthodox churches from the seventeenth through the twentieth centuries, missionary activity was confined almost exclusively to Russian initiatives. The "great captivity" of the ancient churches of the Middle East under the Islamic rule of the Ottoman Empire made most mission efforts difficult if not impossible. In Russia, the tradition of mission expansion by "colonist monks" was stifled from 1682 to 1796 by strict imperial controls. The basis then of most new missionary work, while difficult to compare with Catholic and Protestant trends, was found primarily within the monastic communities. From 1828 until the Russian Revolution in 1917, various Orthodox mission ventures were undertaken not only to reverse the trends of apostasy to Islam among the eastern Russians but to plant new churches and construct and maintain numerous charitable and educational institutions. The Russian Revolution brought a sudden close to the missionaries' work.

Today a number of societies in the Orthodox Church have accepted the mandate of mission work in foreign places such as Uganda, Tanzania, Kenya, and Sudan. One of these societies is Syndesmos ("uniting bond"), which was founded in 1953 at the initiative of Orthodox involved in the WCC youth department. Participation in the ecumenical movement along with the care of Orthodox living in countries without traditional Orthodox presence are high priorities for the society, which is a federation of youth movements and theological schools within local Eastern Orthodox churches. In 1989 it had forty-nine member movements in twenty-three countries in Europe, the Middle East, Asia, Africa, North America, and Latin America.

4. Because of the great variety of missionary societies and schools of piety and different kinds of relationships between mission societies, religious orders, mission councils, and churches, cooperation and integration have become very urgent issues in regard to missions. The integration of the International Missionary Council into the WCC at New Delhi (1961) is one basic answer to the question of the place of mission within the churches and the position of the missionary societies. But this integration has led to consequences on the grassroots level which have not been easy to resolve. Due to major changes after Vatican II, cooperation has developed on many levels between Rome's SEDOS (Servizio de Documentazione e Studi), the WCC's CWME (Commission on World Mission and Evangelism), and several evangelical and Orthodox mission agencies.

RICHARD H. BLIESE AND HORST RZEPKOWSKI, SVD

Bibliography

Adam, A., "Das Mönchtum der Alten Kirche," in *Kirchengeschichte als Missionsgeschichte,* vol. 1, *Die Alte Kirche* (1974) 86–93. Auf der Maur, I., "Das alte Mönchtum und die Glaubensverkünd-igung," *NZM* 19 (1962) 275–88. Idem, "Motive der Glaubensverkündigung im frühen Mönchtum," *NZM* 18 (1962) 275–88. Idem, "Werden, Stand und Zukunft des afrikanischen Mönchtums," *NZM* 23 (1963) 110–15. Barrett, D., *World Christian Encyclopedia* (1982). Beach, H. P., and C. H. Fahs, *World Atlas of Christian Missions* (1911). Beaver, R. P., *American Protestant Women in World Mission* (1980). Bosch, D. J., "Historical Paradigms of Mission," in *Transforming Mission* (1991) 181–348. Camps, A., "The Catholic Missionary Movement from 1492 to 1789," in *Missiology: An Ecumenical Introduction* (1995) 213–21. Idem, "The Catholic Missionary Movement from 1789 to 1962," in *Missiology: An Ecumenical Introduction* (1995) 229–36. Dayton, E. R., *Mission Handbook: North American Protestant Ministries Overseas* (1976). Foster, J., *They Converted Our Ancestors: A Study of the Early Church in Britain* (1965). Frank, S., "Das beschauliche Kloster im Missionsland," *ZMRW* 46 (1962) 92–102. Geldbach, E., "Der Einfluß Englands und Amerikas auf die deutsche Erweckungsbewegung," *ZRGG* 28 (1976) 11–122. Goddard, B. L., "Agencies," in *The Encyclopedia of the Modern Christian Missions* (1967). Gundert, H., *Die evangelische Mission: Ihre Länder, Völker und Arbeiten* (1903). Henkel, W., "Gestaltnahme von Bekehrungsvorstellun-gen bei Ordensgründungen im 19. Jahrhundert," in *Mission: Präsenz-Verkündigung-Bekehrung?* (1974) 102–14. Jongeneel, J. A. B., "The Protestant Missionary Movement up to 1789," in *Missiology: An Ecumenical Perspective* (1995) 222–28. Kasbauer, S., *Die Teilname der Frauenwelt am Missionswerk* (1928). "Mission Boards and Societies," in *The Concise Dictionary of Christian World Mission* (1971) 389–405. Nemer, L., *Anglican and Roman Catholic Attitudes on Missions* (1981). Religious Tract Society, *Handbook of Foreign Missions* (1888). Rosenkranz, G., *Die christliche Mission: Geschichte und Theologie* (1977). Stoffel, O., *Die katholischen Missions-gesellschaften: Historische Entwicklung und konziliare Erneuerung in kanonischer Sicht* (1984). Stransky, R., "Missionary Societies," in *The Dictionary of the Ecumenical Movement* (1991) 696–99. Sundermeier, T., *Mission, Bekenntnis und Kirche* (1962). Tracy, J., *History of the American Board of Commissioners for Foreign Missions* (1842). Van den Berg, J., *Constrained by Jesus' Love: An Inquiry into the Motives of Missionary Awakening in Great Britain in the Period between 1698 and 1815* (1956). Väth, A., *Die Frauenorden in den Missionen* (1920). Verstraelen-Gilhuis, G. M., "The History of the Missionary Movement from the Perspective of the Third World," in *Missiology: An Ecumenical Perspective* (1995) 253–62. Wasserzug-Traeder, G., *Deutsche Evangelische Frauen-missionsarbeit* (1927). Weber, O., "Kirchenmission? Eine Mission in gegliederter Vielfalt," *EMZ* 17 (1960). Webster, D., *Missionary Societies — One or Many?* (1960). Wind, A., "The Protestant Mis-sionary Movement from 1789–1963," in *Missiology: An Ecumenical Introduction* (1995) 237–52. Yannoulatos, A., "Monks and Mission in the Eastern Church during the Fourth Century," *IRM* 58 (1969) 208–26.

N

❧ NEW RELIGIOUS MOVEMENTS ❧

1. The White Race as a Stumbling Block.   2. The White Religion as a Stumbling Block.

More than twenty years ago H. W. Turner introduced the expression "new religious movements" as a technical term in the study of religion. It conveys more meaning than other expressions. On the one hand, it contains no overt or covert value judgments as is the case, for example, with "neoheathen," "syncretistic," or "sectarian." On the other hand, it is more comprehensive than names that are limited to only one aspect, such as "nativity movements," "revitalization movements," or "crisis cults."

The term "new religious movements" should not, however, be defined too loosely. "New" refers to the history of religion from 1800 to the present day. Many religious movements came into existence in the period between the two world wars. "Religious" in the context of this article means having a connection with the Christian mission. "Movement" refers to the infant stages of a religion. It starts with a founder figure and a body of disciples and advances toward adulthood as an organized community with set rules and rituals, dogmas, and a hierarchy of offices. In a movement much remains in flux. It is the time of new departures, of freedom and creativity.

If it had not been for the Christian mission, thousands of new religious movements would not have arisen or would have been totally different in their initial formation. Millions of Christians with black, brown, yellow, and red skins turned their backs on white Christians. The reasons are twofold. A primary motive for the birth of some new Christian movements concerns race; many protested against racist humiliation. A second motive concerns religion; many protested against a patronizing attitude and contempt shown toward their own culture. Until the end of the colonial period, external pressure triggered these movements (→colonialism). Since that period they have been created by the desire for inward liberation (→liberation theology), independent spirituality, and respect for traditional culture and "pagan" antecedents (→contextual theology).

1.   Whites, whose technical equipment made resistance impossible, came in masses. White colonists overseas did not lose their arrogance even when, for example, black Africans were shown to be more clever or skillful. White missionaries often ruled their congregations paternalistically and with a heavy hand.

1.1.   The Lutheran Bapedi Church originated in 1892 in the Transvaal in South Africa. Thirty-nine elders under the leadership of the first Pedi pastor, M. Sebuschane, withdrew from the Berlin Mission. They wanted to remain loyal to "our dear Dr. Martin Luther" and did not seek any change in the liturgy and church constitution that they had adopted, but they no longer wanted to obey the missionaries. The Germans did not trust the South Africans with any independence. They did not treat them as partners or as Christian sisters and brothers but only gave orders. After reluctantly ordaining Sebuschane, the Germans let inexperienced whites order about this highly esteemed black leader, whom the community revered as "Father." The Africans no longer wanted to be treated as children or to be "carried on the back until we have gray hair," as they put it (→African independent churches).

The Iglesia Filipina Independiente was founded by Roman Catholics. In 1896 the Catholic Filipinos rose against the Catholic Spanish. G. Aglipay, a priest, became chaplain to the rebel army. Some of the Spanish priests and bishops fled with the retreating Spanish army; some were taken prisoner. Aglipay demanded Filipino bishops for the Filipino clergy. When the central administration of the church still insisted on Spaniards, Aglipay and his followers renounced their connection with Rome. In 1902 the new church was officially recognized in Manila by the new colonial power, the United States. For a long time it had been suspected that seminary education for the local clergy had been deliberately kept at a very low level and that Filipino ordinations were deliberately limited to a few. A victim of this kind of discrimination was A. de la Cruz. As a Filipino he was not allowed to join a religious order or become a priest. He therefore founded the Confradia de San José, which was joined by thousands in the provinces of Quezon, Laguna, and Batangas. The church, however, continued to refuse to recognize him, and he was executed by the Spanish in 1841.

These specific examples show typical characteristics and racist patterns of behavior. The reason for many protests was racism. White church superiors were the problem. In the initial stages of protest, the protesters only wanted to get rid of these superiors. They wanted to keep the other facets of the church — the doctrine, ritual, forms of organization, and so on. Later on, new reasons for protest produced new forms of church. Hundreds if not thousands of Christian movements came into existence because of these first injustices. In Europe there was much talk of African "Ethiopianism," which was feared as something highly dangerous.

1.2. The national hero of all Filipinos is J. Rizal. Being called "Indio" by the Spanish offended him from his childhood days. From that point on he tried to discover what right whites had to hold such a low opinion of nonwhites. Rizal was an eye-specialist. He traveled around the world, and once, while the guest of a pastor in Odenwald, he compared German village life with that of villages at home. In Berlin he published a revealing book about this which was immediately banned at home. In Manila he founded a political league. He was banned, arrested, and condemned, and in 1896, as the uprising broke out, he was executed.

The Iglesia Watawat ng Lahi links faith in Christ with faith in Rizal. Both were Asiatics; both healed people; both loved the little people above all; both hated the darkness — that of the Pharisees and that of the Spanish. Both were persecuted by the unholy alliance of throne and altar; both stood before biased judges who charged them with provoking unrest; both were executed by their enemies; both gave their lives to bring justice, freedom, and peace; both forgave their murderers; the deaths of both meant the beginning of the end of great colonial empires. At the end, according to this church, Christ will transfer all power to Rizal, who will come again to judge the people and lead the faithful to a new Jerusalem.

Since the end of World War I, the message of the "Elder Brethren," a carefully kept secret from the whites, circulated in northern and southern Rhodesia (Zambia and Zimbabwe), in the Congo (Zaire — Democratic Republic of Congo), and also in Angola and Mozambique. The Elder Brethren are the Africans who were taken into slavery, the Ba-America. They have made America mighty because they invented everything: airplanes, cars, radios, and so on. The black race must therefore be superior to the white race. The Africans must have been misled about this by the whites. When the first airplane was seen in the sky, many believed that the Elder Brethren had come from America to see for themselves whether what the whites say about the blacks was true, namely, that they are not really human beings, but apes with tails. The Ba-America became a collective messiah in the Central African Watch Tower movement, Kitawala, whose goal is to end the domination of the whites in Africa and inaugurate a kingdom of peace for Africans alone.

These examples show what the religious response to the racist attitude of whites in general, not only of missionaries, can be. The daily message to natives from white superiors in government, from businesspeople, or on the plantations was that they were inferior. Those who went to school learned everything about the white nations and next to nothing about their own history. When they realized that they could change neither whites nor white opinion of nonwhites, they had to choose between resignation and faith in the eventual vindication of their race.

1.3. There were colonies in which Europeans experienced significant health risks. Villagers consequently rarely saw a white man. There were other colonies in which land-hungry Europeans pushed the natives from their land. In countries such as these, racism, and the religious protest against it, took on a merciless appearance.

At the end of 1890, white soldiers attacked a group of Indians at Wounded Knee in South Dakota and massacred men, women, and children. The dead were Sioux followers of a new religious movement which the whites called "Ghost Dance." One year earlier the Oglala Sioux had heard that the Messiah had appeared and that he would help the Indians and not the whites. That made the Indians happy. They sent out emissaries who found the prophet Wovoka, a Paiute, and returned home with his message. In October 1890, Short Bull, one of those sent, explained to his fellow tribespeople from Pine Ridge that they must gather together and dance (dancing is an Indian way of praying and worshiping). Then the earth would tremble and the dead return. After that, God would make a great whirlwind which would destroy almost all whites. Only four to five thousand whites would remain alive on the whole earth.

Blacks have also been victims of white ruthlessness in America. Their forefathers were needed as slaves. Their masters would not share anything freely with slaves, not even their faith. Far ahead of the "major" denominations, certain nonconformist groups went to the slaves in Jamaica: missionaries came from the Moravians, Methodists, and Baptists. Black preachers were especially successful. After slavery was abolished by law, the emancipated slaves liberated themselves from the forms of piety of their former owners in the great revival of 1860. At that time Pukumina, an African popular religion, came into being and opposed Christian missionaries. Blacks still yearned for their roots, for Africa, the land of the Moors, as it is called in Luther's Bible, or Ethiopia, as in the English Bible. Haile Selassie (formerly known as Ras Tafari Makonnen) was crowned emperor of Ethiopia in 1930. The newspapers of the day reported much about the "King of Kings," the "Victorious Lion of the Tribe of Judah." Soon Jamaicans were hailing him as the messiah of the blacks. They longed for the day when Ras Tafari would take them home to Africa. The emperor was overthrown and executed in 1975, but since then many in Jamaica have claimed to feel his spiritual presence even more strongly. Now he is with them in everything they do.

2.   Intentionally or unintentionally, white missionaries set out to fashion the whole world in their image. Many nonwhite Christians in the mission churches opposed this kind of ministry. They wanted their piety to be meaningful, that is, to be expressed meaningfully in their own way. Unlike most whites, who thought of salvation in terms of the world to come, the nonwhites expected judgment and salvation to come in this life, a view the whites dismissed as ignorance or superstition.

2.1.   "The best thing about Ringatuu is that it is a New Zealand religion. Every country has its own religions, its own faiths. Ringatuu and Ratana [another Maori church] are the two most important religions which have grown up here in our own land. They belong here." This was the argument of Paora Teramea, who was president of Ringatuu in 1938. Te Kooti, a prophet and guerrilla leader, founded it. He gave Christianity a Maori meaning. For example, Bible translators had translated "daily bread" as *taro*, a substance that had to be imported first from the tropics. Te Kooti left this absurd request out of the Lord's Prayer. The Maoris once ate both hated enemies and despised slaves, a practice that came to be reflected in the Eucharist. A few dignitaries of the Ringatuu participated in the Lord's Supper (→Eucharist [Lord's Supper]) once a year, on behalf of all. Sacred things are taboo for the Maori. Holy scriptures are passed on by word of mouth. There are no holy books. God's word has power, which is why Ringatuu priests can heal people. Services are conducted not in daylight but at night, not on Sunday but once a month on a special remembrance day, not in a church but in the holy place of a clan, the Marae. On the following morning, the faithful dissolve the taboo with a common meal which leads them back into everyday life.

The adherents of many new religious movements have answered one basic question in the negative. It is the question whether one can have the actual substance of Christianity only in its European form. This form appears alien to non-Europeans, often inconceivable, sometimes even preposterous. Must they first try to learn to feel and think as whites? They want to be Christians in these new religious movements in their own way. The next example demonstrates the problems which arise from this.

Peyote mainly produces visions of personal significance. This is why the Indians in Mexico used the cactus for religious purposes. The Spanish prohibited its use as a heathen practice. Only the Huichol and a few others who were able to evade the missionaries still use peyote today as a sacrament. Prairie Indians also consider the cactus to be holy. When the government in Washington wanted to ban peyote in 1918, the anthropologist J. Mooney advised six tribes to found the Native American Church. Their rituals, mainly for the healing of the sick, take place by night in a traditional teepee and are composed of prayers, songs, the peyote-sacrament, and the contemplation of faces, since the power of peyote bestows extraordinary knowledge of things not of this world. "The white man talks about Jesus," as a Comanche once expressed it, "but we talk to Jesus."

2.2.   What has appeared logical to whites in the nineteenth and twentieth centuries can appear absurd to others, since different cultures develop different thought patterns. Since the Enlightenment, whites, including missionaries, have been taught that the power of magic could not be proved scientifically and, therefore, that it does not exist. Anybody who practices it is a fraud; anybody who fears it suffers from a mania. Elsewhere, for example in Africa, witchcraft is regarded as logical, because people do not give up at the point where scientists who talk of "coincidence" do. Why did this roof fall on this man? Because the roof supports were rotten. Africans know that too. But why did that particular person sit under that particular roof at that particular moment when, for completely natural reasons, it collapsed? Many Africans see in this type of scene the possibility of the efficacy of witchcraft. In witchcraft they recognize the expression of human hatefulness. Africans cast spells out of envy, jealousy, and revenge. They need means of defense, and their traditional religions offer them protection against evil. Whites, colonial administrators as much as missionaries, dismantled this system of protection. They did not offer anything new in its place. Instead they surrendered the defenseless people to the hatred of their neighbors.

In 1918 soldiers demobilized from World War I brought back to the colonies a devastating influenza which claimed an extraordinary number of victims. The authorities banned public meetings and closed markets, schools, and churches. But it is precisely at times of the greatest emergency that African logic demands intensive prayer on the part of many people. At that time Nigerians who were praying met secretly in the bush. These "Aladura" later stayed together and also avoided the white missionaries, the "careless shepherds who let the wolves into the flocks of sheep," who did not know how to protect their congregations from witches and sorcerers. Mission churches were feared as "houses of the dead" in which death, not life, ruled.

Complacent whites had let the sin of witchcraft proliferate. Africans made desperate attempts from time to time to control it again. From 1955 onwards black Christians in the Bemba areas of present-day Zambia went over from the white missionaries to A. Lenshina, a black prophetess, because she promised "to make the land pure." She would then remove the oppressive burden of bewitchment and countermagic. Sinners acknowledged their fear and hatefulness in public. Absolved of their guilt, they were protected by the "baptism" of this woman sent from God. Shortly before the birth of the state of Zambia, Lenshina came into conflict with black politicians. Her movement came to an early end in violence. She herself was isolated and died as a prisoner. The way of salvation that she offered will not be forgotten for a long time.

2.3. The mass media have introduced to the world the spirit healers of the Philippines. Reports of bloody operations performed without a knife first put reporters on the trail of this intriguing story. The Union Espiritista de Filipinas is a movement with a long tradition. It was founded in 1905 by J. Ortega, a lawyer and a disciple of A. Kardec. Today its leaders emphasize the "scientific" basis of spiritualism, which is not a religious denomination and does not have its own dogma or rituals. In Kardec, the word of Jesus is believed to be fulfilled and the Holy Spirit, the promised comforter, to be visibly at work. Other helpful spirits are subordinate to him: St. Sebastian, St. Timothy, St. Thomas Aquinas, the Holy Virgin, even Jesus himself. In addition, Confucius, as well as famous doctors from different cultures and periods of history, is considered to be active. The spirits work through human mediums, who are gifted in various ways: a *medio curandero* heals the sick; a *medio vidente* sees and hears spirits and can speak to them; a *medio escribiente* takes down dictation; a *medio parlante* is a mouthpiece. The assembled congregation provides a framework for such acts. The congregations asks God and the Holy

Spirit for assistance and says the Lord's Prayer and the rosary. Patients should not believe in the medium; they must rather believe in the teachings of the Bible.

The spiritualist movement began in about 1850 in the United States when modern medicine — in which theologians were no longer involved — was moving toward unprecedented successes. Today it is said that there are fifty million spiritualists, with a particularly large number in South America, mainly in Brazil. About fifty years later the Pentecostal movement started, also in the United States, with its baptism in the Spirit, speaking in tongues, and healing. Believers also encounter spirits, angels, Christ, and God. From the very beginning African logic has played a role in the piety of Pentecostals. The Pentecostal movement has reached Africa and expanded very rapidly there.

It is there that one finds "authentic Pentecostals" such as the "Chosen One of God," J. Ikechiuku, an Ibo, who founded St. Joseph's Chosen Church of God. He teaches baptism in the Spirit, considering all those who are baptized only with water to be merely nominal Christians. He knows the working of the Holy Spirit to be speaking in tongues, shaking, crying "Hallelujah," prophesying. After that, he says, a person cannot remember individual details, because he or she is filled with unspeakable joy. But above all, he proclaims that the Holy Spirit gives power. Prayer-power is also possessed by "inauthentic" Pentecostals, the numerous African prophets. God effects salvation through them in the here and now and grants recovery from illness, success in examinations, acquittal by a court, or long-awaited offspring to a family. Christian prophets are also known to Africans as "spiritual filling stations." Even the empty "mission Christians" come openly or in secret to let themselves be filled up again and again. Members of the Kenyan Church of the Spirit (Dini ya Roho) explain that the missionaries taught them to worship Christ. His influence, however, became weak. So they prayed, and it was revealed to them that they should worship the Holy Spirit. His power is strong. "We believe in God and in His Son, Christ, but we worship the Spirit!"

HANS-JÜRGEN GRESCHAT

Bibliography

Anderson, E., *Messianic Popular Movement in the Lower Congo* (1958). Anderson, G. H., *Studies in Philippine Church History* (1969). Artificio, M. V., *Union Espiritista Cristiana de Filipinas* (1974). Axenfeld, K., *Der Äthiopismus in Südafrika* (1906). Baeta, C. G., *Prophetism in Ghana: A Study of Some "Spiritual" Churches* (1962). Barrett, L., *The Rastafarians* (1977). Benz, E., *Messianische Kirchen, Sekten und Bewegungen im heutigen Afrika* (1965). Burridge, K., *New Heaven, New Earth* (1969). Chesi, G., *Geistheiler auf den Philippinen* (n.d.). Clark, P., *"Hauhau"* (1975). Coleman, J. A., and G. Baum, *New Religious Movements* (1983). Foronda, M. A., *Cults Honoring Rizal* (1961). Gerber, P., *Die Peyote-Religion* (1980). Greenwood, W., *The Upraised Hand* (1942). Greschat, H.-J., *Kitawala* (1967). Idem, *Mana and Tapu* (1980). Idem, *Westafrikanische Propheten* (1974). Henderson, J. M., *Ratana* (1963). Hoekema, A. A., *The Four Major Cults: Christian Science, Jehovah's Witnesses, Mormonism, Seventh-Day Adventism* (1986). Kamphausen, E., *Anfänge der Kirchlichen Unabhängigkeitsbewegungen in Südafrika* (1976). Marriott, A., and C. K. Rachlin, *Peyote* (1971). Melton, J. G., *The Encyclopedic Handbook of Cults in America* (1986). Michels, P., *Rastafari* (1979). Mooney, J., *The Ghost Dance Religion* (1965). Nicholas, T., *Rastafari* (1979). Owens, J., *Dread: The Rastafarians of Jamaica* (1976). Peel, J. D. Y., *Aladura* (1968). Schlegel, S. A., *Espiritista Science* (1965). Seeson, I., *Bibliography of Cargo Cults* (1952). Sundkler, B. G. M., *Bantu Prophets in South Africa* (1961). Trompf, G., *Prophets in Melanesia* (1977). Turner, H. W., *Bibliography of the New Religious Movements in Primal Societies*, vol. 1, *Black Africa* (1977); vol. 2, *North America* (1978). Idem, *The Church of the Lord (Aladura)*, 2 vols. (1967). Idem, *Religious Innovation in Africa* (1979). Wilms, A., *Rastafari* (1982). Worley, P., *The Trumpet Shall Sound* (1957).

❧ NORTH AMERICAN MISSION THEOLOGY ❦

1. History.   2. Contributions to Missiology.   3. Regional Contributions. 4. Assessment.

1. Although missionaries began going out from North America already at the beginning of the nineteenth century, theological contributions to missiology were slow to develop. This is partially accounted for by the pragmatic bent of peoples from North America, but perhaps also because mission was not centralized and issues of colonial management did not arise. Likewise, many of those who occupied chairs of missiology in seminaries and divinity schools were typically church historians by training and so focused their attention more on history than contemporary theological reflection. These historians to be sure contributed significantly to historical understanding (one thinks especially of K. S. Latourette and R. P. Beaver in this regard).

Well into the contemporary period, multiauthor collections of essays or collaborations with missiologists elsewhere in the English-speaking world marked North American missiological production (e.g., the five volumes of essays entitled *Mission Trends* edited by G. Anderson and T. Stransky). For the most part, book-length works addressing theological issues in mission only began appearing in North America toward the end of the 1970s. This tradition continues in the series New Directions in Mission and Evangelization, edited by J. A. Scherer and S. Bevans.

2. North American contributions to mission theology can be divided into four categories: general missiological works, inculturation, dialogue and the theology of religions, and missionary spirituality. An important and influential work was *Communicating Christ Cross-culturally,* by the evangelical Protestant D. Hesselgrave. O. Costas's work was also significant. From a more conciliar point of view, J. A. Scherer's *Gospel, Church and Kingdom* provided a comprehensive theology of mission. C. Stuhlmueller and D. Senior authored a comprehensive work on the biblical foundations of mission. In addition, there are works that address more specific issues, such as Canadian J. Bonk's *Missions and Money.* The Church Growth movement has also produced some works to develop a supporting theology and critiques of the movement.

A number of important works have contributed to the literature on inculturation. An early work was L. Luzbetak's *The Church and Cultures* (1963; new and revised edition, 1988). S. Bevans, C. Kraft, A. Peelman, and R. J. Schreiter have all published books on the subject that have gained attention worldwide.

One could say that, with the exception of India, the United States has been leading the way in literature on interreligious dialogue, especially as it relates to the theology of religions. P. Knitter's work has been in the forefront here, but J. DiNoia and S. Mark Heim should also be mentioned. W. R. Burrows has edited an important collection on the Vatican document *Dialogue and Proclamation.* Further, a new generation of scholars, combining expertise in Christian theology and other religious traditions, is developing the area of comparative theology. The work of F. X. Clooney has been pathbreaking here.

Missionary spirituality has also received attention, in an early work by M. Reilly, and more recently by A. Gittins.

3. A number of North Americans have written works that have focused on specific regions or have contributed to regional theologies. African-American theologian J. Cone has produced a series of works and has educated a generation of theologians whose work has been influential in the development of black theology in South Africa. Their work has also been significant in helping to explicate the full impact of racism. R. R. Ruether's wide-ranging work has left its mark on feminist theologies worldwide. More recently, African-American (womanist) and Hispanic or Latina (mujerista) feminist theologians have also contributed to the global development of feminist theologies. Within North America, A. Peelman's work on the First Nations in Canada has been an important contribution in Native American studies. D. Hall's trilogy on faith in North America has become a kind of benchmark for contextual efforts. A similar project is the Gospel and Our Culture Network, inspired by the work of L. Newbigin, which has thus far produced one collection of essays. Besides the work of African-American theologians already mentioned, there is a burgeoning literature coming from Hispanic or Latino theologians that has addressed especially hybridity (or mestizaje) and issues of popular religion.

4. Inasmuch as North American contributions to mission theology have been relatively recent, it is difficult to assess their long-term effect. The contributions have been most notable in the areas of inculturation and the theology of religions. In the former area, the widespread concern for inclusion of the social sciences in missiological perspective is most evident. In the latter area, both the religious pluralism in which the United States and Canada live and interest in the philosophical issues of multiculturalism have stimulated interest. The new area of comparative theology promises significant insights into how religious traditions might interact. The fact of the increasing number of students from countries outside North America now studying in theological centers in the United States and in Canada will no doubt inspire more missiological thinking in the future.

Robert J. Schreiter, CPPS

Bibliography

Anderson, G., and T. Stransky, eds., *Mission Trends,* 5 vols. (1974–81). Aquino, P., *Our Cry for Life* (1993). Beaver, R. P., *All Loves Excelling: American Protestant Women in World Mission* (1968). Bevans, S., *Models of Contextual Theology* (1992). Bonk, J., *Missions and Money* (1991). Burrows, W., ed., *Redemption and Dialogue* (1993). Clooney, F., *Theology after Vedanta* (1993). Cone, J., *Black Theology and Black Power* (1969). Idem, *A Black Theology of Liberation* (1970). Costas, O., *Christ outside the Gate* (1982). Deck, A. F., *The Second Wave: Hispanic Ministry and the Evangelization of Cultures* (1989). DiNoia, J., *The Diversity of Religions* (1992). Gittins, A., *Bread for the Journey* (1993). Hall, D., *Confessing the Faith* (1996). Idem, *Professing the Faith* (1993). Idem, *Thinking the Faith* (1989). Heim, S. M., *Salvations* (1995). Hesselgrave, D., *Communicating Christ Cross-culturally* (1978). Hunsberger, G., and C. Van Gelder, eds., *The Church between Gospel and Culture* (1996). Knitter, P., *Jesus and the Other Names* (1996). Idem, *No Other Name?* (1985). Kraft, C., *Christianity in Culture* (1979). Latourette, K. S., *A History of the Expansion of Christianity* (1937–45). Luzbetak, L., *The Church and Cultures* (1988 [1963]). Peelman, A., *Christ Is a Native American* (1995). Idem, *L'Inculturation* (1991). Peters, G., *A Theology of Church Growth* (1981). Reilly, M., *Spirituality for Mission* (1976). Ruether, R., *Sexism and God-Talk* (1983). Scherer, J., *Gospel, Church and Kingdom* (1987). Scherer, J., and S. B. Bevans, *New Directions in Mission and Evangelization* (1992–). Schreiter, R. J., *Constructing Local Theologies* (1985). Schroeder, R., "A Snapshot of Missiology in North America," *VerbumSVD* 4/37 (1996) 401–12. Shenk, W., ed., *Exploring Church Growth* (1983). Stuhlmueller, C., and D. Senior, *Biblical Foundations of Mission* (1983). Williams, D., *Sisters in the Wilderness: The Challenge of Womanist God-Talk* (1993).

❧ ORTHODOX MISSION ❧

1. Past and Present. 2. Theological Basis. 3. Meaning of Mission. 4. Importance of Mission. 5. Motive of Mission. 6. Goal of Mission. 7. Activities of Mission.

1. The Orthodox Church has always exercised mission mainly through its national churches within the framework of the historical realities of their respective countries. Today a modest contribution to missionary work is being made by the Orthodox Church — mainly by Greek-speaking Orthodoxes — in some African countries (Uganda, Kenya, Tanzania, Zaire [Democratic Republic of Congo], Ghana, Cameroon, Nigeria) and in Asia (Korea, Japan, India).

Early Orthodox works on mission were produced mainly in Russian. Beginning in the nineteenth century, however, Greeks began to contribute in a modest way, and, since the middle of the twentieth century, there has been a significant increase in works by Greeks in connection with their assumption of mission work. This literature is mainly historical in nature and only to a small extent theoretical. The few theoretical works are fragmentary; though there has been an increase in this literature especially in the past decades, nevertheless no complete theory of Orthodox mission has yet been compiled.

The theological faculty of the University of Athens recognized missiology as a theological subject in 1970, and in 1978 a corresponding academic chair was established.

2. The will and energy of God for the realization of the divine economy manifest themselves simultaneously in pluriformity and uniformity. This unity is based not only in the common starting position and ultimate goal of the acts of the divine economy but also in the close relationship of these acts to one another as mutual functions and as manifestations of divine qualities and results. At the same time, each of these acts maintains its own way of functioning, uniform in essence but nevertheless multiform, each act expressing itself analogically to the part that it has to fulfill.

Mission is the result of the cooperation by which the divine and the created, each according to its own measure, awaken the fallen creation to participate in →salvation and fulfillment. This function is expressed "at various times and in various different ways" (Heb 1:1) according to the different stages on the way to salvation. In light of the incarnation, mission as life-giving witness to all humanity works toward the beginning of a new age, particularly with regard to the saving call to those outside the church.

3. In endless love the triune God forged a plan to save fallen humanity within history as well as to make humankind divine through grace and immortalize nature in the eschaton, when God will be "all in all" (1 Cor 15:28).

God brings about the fulfillment of this goal both through continual care and through divine grace, in which humanity is a participant. At the same time God undertakes specific initiatives in which God uses the angelic powers positively and those of the evil spirits negatively, and in which God works hand in hand with humankind in conjunction with both animate and inanimate nature.

In the course of history these acts reach a climax in the decisive moment of the incarnation of the Logos and the founding of the church which he brought about. From this point on, the participation of the individual in the saving work of God is no longer incidental but rather is cooperative — as in the Old Testament, where the totality of the Israelites as "people of God" played a decisive role for the individual person.

Within the new people of God both the church as a whole and each of its members contribute organically to the work of salvation — not independently but in relationship to each other. By "church" we mean here the whole church, including the church triumphant, insofar as it is participating in the work of salvation. Its contribution consists especially of intercession but also of the example of individual Christians and of the manifold supernatural works which have an effect on non-Christians.

The kind of human cooperation in the work of salvation in the old and new people of God depends to some degree on the partial and complete revelation of God in God's mutual relationship as "unity in Trinity and Trinity in unity" in the Old Testament and New Testament. This new way of human participation in the plan of the divine economy constitutes mission. From this angle, mission is a part of the salvation willed by God, namely, the part realized by the church and its members in history. That mission makes an essential contribution to the work of salvation ushered in by the incarnation does not mean that it works in an exclusive way. This non-exclusiveness of the work of mission is true with regard to initiatives, possibilities, and results. Mission possesses no exclusivity with regard to initiative, for God is witnessed to by all of creation, also by people who do not formally belong to the "saved." Mission initiative includes rousing the consciences of individuals, who then serve as self-appointed preachers (Mk 1:45, 7:36; Jn 4:39, 9:17–27; Acts 10:24–25) or as wonder-workers (Mk 9:39; Lk 9:50) or operate indirectly (Acts 5:34) or passively (1 Cor 7:12). As far as possibilities are concerned, the mission has no exclusive character either, for God not only prepares people for their work but also leads and accompanies them by means of grace. As far as results are concerned, the role of mission in the work of salvation consists of preparing the ground. The motive of salvation belongs to God alone both now and at the last judgment (Rom 2:14; 1 Cor 5:13; Rv 20:12; see also Rom 9:16; 1 Cor 3:6; 2 Cor 3:5; Phil 2:13; Mt 3:9; 12:41–42).

4. The fact that mission contributes decisively to the salvific work of the triune God in history is sufficient to demonstrate its importance. If it is simultaneously seen in the general sense mentioned above and also with regard to the eschatological dimension as salvation and deification of the individual and the preparation of the totality of individuals as church for the final encounter with the ever-present, coming Lord, then its meaning is crucial. This great importance was attached to mission already in the earliest days in the life of the church when it was recognized that the Holy Spirit had entrusted the apostles with the highest dignity of spiritual ministry (1 Cor 12:28; Eph 4:11; Acts 6:2; 1 Cor 1:17). That this opinion was generally held by the church can be proved from the whole of tradition, for example, in the writings of Origen, John Chrysostom, Pseudo-Oikoumenios, and Euthymius Zigabenus.

5. If God included mission in the plan of salvation — which from eternity (before the creation of the angels) was conceived as an expression of the fullness of God's love reaching its climax in the incarnation (Jn 3:16; 1 Jn 4:9) — then mission can have no other motive than love. When we speak of love here we are referring not to individual events of mission but to its inner dynamism.

Consequently, all other motives, such as the accomplishment of a commission (Mt 2:19), an inner necessity (1 Cor 9:11), or the glory of God (2 Cor 4:15; 1 Pt 4:11), must be based on a misinterpretation because they are only a partial interpretation of the whole. In other words, behind the different formulations of the fragmented concepts there is no attempt to find the common context of meaning and its derivation from a common general source.

If love then constitutes the motive of mission, it is also the criterion of all its works. Any work that does not correspond to the model of the incarnation (kenosis and acceptance) — the only proper form of love in practice — does not serve the goal of mission and is instead the expression of a doubtful form of mission. There have always been such forms of mission in the church. The conditioning circumstances have been various, ranging from what was evil (Acts 8:9–24) and forbidden (2 Cor 11:13–26; Gal 2:4) to the later emerging mixture of mission and politics to that which was less reprehensible (Phil 1:15). In many of these cases — no matter what the share of responsibility of the representatives of mission who arbitrarily falsified the real missionary objective — the work was nonetheless a success (Phil 1:18). This shows the priority which God has in mission.

6. Mission is an eschatological event not only because of its importance for the new era ushered in by Christ but also in the sense of its decisive contribution to the advent of the eschaton (Mt 24:14). Accordingly, mission naturally reaches its goal within history.

Within this period it is the goal of mission to appeal to people to become members of the body of the church, which is the ark of salvation, the eternal extension of the Body of Christ. In accordance with this plan, mission turns to people who are outside the church. Missionizing those who are already members of the church is not allowed (Rom 15:20), especially when the preachers of this mission proclaim different dogmas (Gal 1:6–7). An exception to this rule would be the case of a church whose teaching is so far from the truth that its members are soteriologically in the same position as people outside the church, or are even in a worse situation than these. The spiritual building up of the church by missionaries of the same faith is quite a different matter (Acts 18:25; 1 Cor 3:6; 16:12), as is the reevangelization of members of the church who have somehow lost their connection with the community.

If the goal of mission is to appeal to people to become members of the body of the church, this plan is fulfilled even if the desired result is not realized — that is, if they do not enter the church — since this decision, because of human liberty, is not within the responsibility of mission. Therefore, the mere appeal to the peoples to be converted — on condition that baptism is not refused — can fully fulfill the plan of mission (Mt 24:14, in conjunction with Lk 18:8).

7. The church as a whole, as liturgical community and administrator of grace, has the responsibility of exercising mission. Each of its members has a similar responsibility, especially those who are particularly gifted for and invited to perform the task of mission. The essential condition for exercising mission on the part of the missionary is love. This love is expressed in practice according to the model of the incarnation — that is, through kenosis and acceptance — which also determines the theological principles of missionary work.

Taking kenosis as a model, agents of mission should, on the one hand, divest themselves of worldly connections and earthly notions so that they preach only Christ. On the other hand, the mission as such must adapt itself to the relevant life-situations. According to the model of acceptance, mission must take the whole person into account, not as an abstract concept but as a living reality with his or her spiritual, physical, and environmental problems and needs. Mission is also obliged to respect the values of the peoples. In this way mission inserts itself into its milieu and transforms that milieu into the body of the church.

Missionary work consists of sending and preaching (Rom 10:14–15). Sending can be understood spatially, in the sense of departure and transference to another place, and symbolically, in the sense of care for one's neighbor and the use of various modern means of communication. Preaching is to be understood both as word and deed and as dialogue and cooperation.

The contents of the preaching are twofold. One part concerns the receiver to whom it is directed, the other the message which it contains. The contents of the first part are: (a) the human being in relation to his or her milieu, personality, and the meaning of his or her life; (b) the affirmation of each person's dignity both as an individual and as a member of a community; and (c) the fact that no one can reach the goal of his or her existence either intentionally or actually, in either the secular or the religious sphere.

The contents of the second part are: (a) the message of salvation in Christ as victory over evil and death and as involving the present and future; (b) the teaching of the necessity of repentance for salvation, in other words, the necessity of faith and entrance into the church; and (c) the importance of the consequences of accepting or rejecting preaching — consequences for the present and the future life beyond the grave.

The substance of the missionary preaching is no ordinary human word but the "word of life for life," a substantial word that involves the participation and continuation of the incarnate →word of God. For this reason preaching is an act of the highest responsibility for both preacher and listener.

If the word of proclamation is a living word that comes from the whole person and relates to the whole person, then it extends to the human being as a psycho-somatic unity but also to his or her relationships to other people and to material nature. Accordingly, the acceptance of the preaching has positive consequences not only for the individual but for his or her whole environment.

It is from this unifying perspective, whose fulfillment is to be expected in the posthistorical life of humanity, that each social work of mission gets its meaning and justification. Wherever mission work is pursued independently, or without the word of life, it preaches the division of the world. In this case mission would continually betray the one who gave it its mandate, burden its agents with meaningless responsibilities, and ultimately remain fruitless.

ELIAS VOULGARAKIS

Bibliography

Alivisator, H. S., "Die Frage der außeren und inneren Mission der orthodoxen Kirche," in *Procès Verbaux de premier Congrès de Théologie Orthodoxe à Athènes* (1936). Bria, J., *Go Forth in*

Peace: Orthodox Perspectives on Mission (1986). Calian, C. S., "The Scope and Vitality of the Orthodox Missionary Activity," *OBMRL* 5/6 (1964). Lemopoulos, G., *The Holy Spirit and Mission* (1990) 89–100. Nissiotis, N., "Die ekklesiologische Grundlage der Mission," in *Die Theologie der Ost-Kirche im ökumenischen Dialog* (1968) 186–216. Idem, *Die Theologie der Ostkirche in ökumenischen Dialog* (1968). Oleksa, M., *Orthodox Alaska: A Theology of Mission* (1986). Panagoupolos, I., *Ekklesiologia kai kierapostole* (1972). Papapetrou, K., "Kirche und Mission: Zum Missionsverständnis der orthodox-katholischen Kirche," *Kyrios* (Berlin) (1966) 105–16. Patronos, G., *Biblikes proipotheseis tes hierapostoles* (1983). Philippides, L., *Hagiographike themeliosis tes christianikes hierapostoles* (1956). Scherer, J., and S. Bevans, *New Directions in Mission and Evangelization* (1992) 203–50. Schmemann, A., *Church, World, Mission: Reflections on Orthodoxy in the West* (1979). Idem, "The Missionary Imperative in the Orthodox Tradition," in *The Theology of the Christian Mission* (1961) 250–57. Stamoolis, J. J., *Eastern Orthodox Mission Theology Today* (1986). Idem, *An Examination of Contemporary Eastern Orthodox Missiology* (1980). Veronis, A., "Orthodox Concepts of Evangelism and Mission," *GOTR* 27 (1982) 44–57. Voulgarakis, E., *He hierapostole kata ta hellenika keimena apo tu 1821 mechri tu 1917* (1971). Idem, "Mission and Unity: From the Theological Point of View," in *Poreuthentes* 24 (1965) 4–7; 26 (1965) 31–32; 27/28 (1965) 45–47. Yannoulatos, A., "The Purpose as Motive of Mission," *IRM* 54 (1965) 281–97. Idem, "Thy Will Be Done," in *The San Antonio Report* (1990). World Council of Churches, *Mission from Three Perspectives* (1989).

P

❧ PARTNERSHIP IN MISSION ❧

1. Development. 2. The Understanding of Partnership. 3. Models.

The term "partnership" has undergone a change of meaning in its ecumenical use, so that it now has little in common with the original commercial understanding of the term.

1. It is no coincidence that the term "partnership" is now to be found in the ecclesiastical missionary vocabulary. Developments in church history — for example, the coming into existence of independent churches in the "mission fields" of European and American missionary societies — have resulted in changes in attitudes toward mission. Even before World War II it was becoming clear that the paternalistic epoch in which the Western missionaries bore the responsibility for church developments in "their" mission fields was coming to an end. This process was then speeded up by the war.

The turning point in the development of relations between the Western missions and the mission churches — between the "sending" and the "growing" churches, as people liked to distinguish them in the 1920s — was the World Mission Conference organized by the International Missionary Council at Whitby, Toronto, in 1947 (→world missionary conferences). This was the first world mission conference at which the representatives of world Christianity faced each other as partners. They discovered each other through the impression created by the reports on the stamina and suffering of a large number of the younger churches during the war, and they reacted to each other with the firm determination that in the future the fulfillment of the Great Commission should be a common task of the "older" and "younger" churches (terminology that was maintained for lack of a better alternative). So the formula "partnership in obedience" was introduced with regard to the missionary command of Christ, becoming a signpost for the definition of relations between churches. This formula had such a liberating effect on the participants at the Whitby conference that it triggered discussions during the following decades on the question of what constitutes a true, trustworthy, mature partnership — discussions which showed how difficult is the path from awareness to action.

2. What does partnership mean? How does it work in actions that are jointly conducted and intended to serve the purpose of the fulfillment of the Great Commission?

Partnership, of course, always includes joint action. In this respect it is distinguished from the terms "brotherhood" or "sisterhood," which, when referring to communion based on Jesus Christ, emphasize more strongly the common confession of faith. That said, one should not ignore the fact the joint fulfillment of the missionary commission indeed rests on the foundation of faith, a conception that has been articulated by the →World Council of Churches (WCC). Further, it should not be overlooked that the term "partnership" was sometimes felt to be inadequate to describe the relationships, as measured by scripture, of cooperation by churches and missions in the "six continents." For example, P. Potter replaces "partnership" with "companionship" because "the term 'partner,' which implies, in the original sense of the word, a division of property, no longer suffices, and instead of this, one should rather talk of 'companionship': that is, the one who eats bread with me."

Partnership should be the basis of joint missionary action. That means that partnership is not an end in itself but is engaged in for the sake of mission. Partnership should be understood as "an instrument for the fulfillment of the common task." But how should a fruitful partnership be brought about when the partners are unequal? Many factors can contribute to this inequality: difference in origins, differing outlooks on life and the world, different standards of living and lifestyles, the gulf between the rich and the poor, and so on. The impossible becomes possible if the inequality is first accepted, if the partner is respected, if the present dependence is recognized. Thus it is not the others who need our help, but we who need them; the byword becomes "interdependence."

One reproach brought by the African and Asiatic churches runs as follows: up until now, the Western churches have led us and decided what was good for us. We were stamped with your pattern and example. It was your lifestyle that was the example for us; you brought us the message in European clothing. We were not your partners, but you were the parents and we were the children; you were the teachers, we the pupils.

The way out of this debilitating relationship is partnership. Where partnership is made the norm for living and working together, each partner must have a higher regard for the other than for herself or himself (Phil 2:3), "in honor preferring the other" (Rom 12:10). With the affirmation of partnership, the burden of inequality can be overcome. The partners face each other with their weaknesses and their gifts; they are at the same time giver and receiver. The practical consequences of partnership are that, after the one-way traffic in the past, knowledge and experience begin to flow both ways. The knowledge increases that we are indeed "yoke-fellows" (*dongan saauga* — a Batak term for two oxen who draw a cart together under the same yoke) and that we are partners in mission, partners who are called to joint action in mission to fulfill the task of world mission to which we are commissioned.

Put briefly: partnership means that, despite all inequalities, the partners are accepted as such; each is accorded full equality; and the freedom of decision of each is respected. Only with this attitude toward each other can partners take risks to fulfill the Great Commission.

To describe partnership theoretically is not the most difficult task. The problem arises when one tries to carry out the joint task for which one is responsible. There must be clear agreement, for example, about the description of the task in accordance with the present-day understanding of mission. The difficulties do not lie in an inability to name a wealth of tasks (e.g., projects which need cooperation in finance and personnel and which help promote development, exchange of personnel, mutual visitation work, scholarships, and literature programs), but more in the delineation of what mission means today. If we define mission as the crossing of boundaries between faith and unbelief, then an immeasurably large field of work is staked out in which witness to Jesus Christ in preaching and service is to be organized. It covers the whole world. But does it need a partnership coalition at all, if each is called to fulfill the Great Commission in his or her own locality? Is not every church called to missionary preaching and missionary service where it is? It is especially this calling which forces us to look for a partner. In this way, each bears the other's burden and becomes a "helpmate in the joy" of the partner. So partnership in practice helps the partners to recognize that one can learn from the other only in joint action. Partnership in mission is the visible sign that each listens to the other and will act together with the other.

It still remains to add that discussions about partnership in the last decades have influenced and advanced efforts toward the integration of church and mission. One part of the partnership discussion was related to the "moratorium" discussed mainly at the World Mission Conference at Bangkok (→world missionary conferences) in 1983 and then in the following years. The idea behind the moratorium was that a break in partnership for a given period would promote self-discovery and self-awareness. In 1982, in a document entitled "Mission and Evangelization," the WCC had made the following pronouncement about the notion of a moratorium: "Moratorium does not mean the end of the missionary vocation, nor of the duty to provide resources for missionary work, but it does mean freedom to reconsider present commitments and to see whether a continuation of what we have been doing for so long is the right style of mission in our day. Moratorium has to be understood inside a concern for world mission."

3.   Finally, a few examples of partnership relationships should be given.

3.1.   The Communauté Évangélique D'action Apostolique (Evangelical Community for Apostolic Action) is a union of churches that originated from the Paris Mission, with its supporting churches in France and francophone Switzerland. The community was first brought into existence under the title "Common Missionary Action of the French-speaking Churches." The first joint undertaking was missionary work with the Methodist Church of Dahomey in the area of Fon. In 1972 the Paris Mission dissolved itself, and the Communauté was created. The management committee consists of nine delegates from Europe and overseas.

3.2.   The Europäische Arbeitsgemeinschaft für ökumenische Beziehungen mit Indonesien (European Working Group for Ecumenical Relations with Indonesia) sprang in 1974 from the Kontinentale Kommission für Kirche und Mission in Indonesien (Continental Commission for Church and Mission in Indonesia), itself founded in 1962. It is a panel which works together in partnership with the community of churches in Indonesia (the PGI). The group has identified for itself as a special task to intensify a two-way flow of information and experience "to give a helping hand to the PGI in its tasks." The bilateral relationships of individual European churches and missions with their Indonesian partners are not affected by these multilateral links.

3.3.   Two other examples are the Lutheran Coordination Services (LCS) and the Evangelical Lutheran Church in Tanzania (ELCT). After the ELCT was founded in 1963, efforts were begun to bring together in one forum the various existing connections among European and American Lutheran missions that had settled in Tanzania after World War II. These efforts resulted in the creation of the LCS in 1973. The LCS constitution of 1974 says, "The LCS should act as forum for consultation and discussion. Its members will keep in sight all aspects of their relationships to the ELCT and its synods and dioceses." An agreement similar to a contract between partners has been drawn up between the LCS and ELCT. It says that the LCS is an instrument of coordination for both partners and that they wish to share the responsibility for the proclamation of the Christian message and the direction of Christian service.

3.4. Finally, reference should be made to the many and various efforts to initiate partnership relations between congregations and church circles in Europe and corresponding bodies in Africa and Asia, a sign of a healthy concern to allow real partnership to develop. The danger certainly exists that these grassroots relationships may tend toward becoming merely idealistic friendships, but this danger can be avoided when the original aim is maintained: "The aim of partnership is the sharing together in the witness and service of the church, so that all people may be saved and come to the knowledge of the truth, and may praise God and give thanks. Christians from different cultures learn in partnership to understand each other and grow together in shared praise of their Lord (1 Tm 2:4; 2 Cor 9:12; Psalms 96; 45; 147)."

3.5. In seeking to provide a basis for the demand for partnership-type cooperation, Vatican II looked to the collegial nature of the church. Because a "collegial union is apparent in the mutual relations of the individual bishops with particular churches and with the universal church," and because "the one and only Catholic Church" exists through these individual churches (*LG* 23), partnership and the responsibility of the churches for each other are demanded in theological terms. The bishops as heads and shepherds of the member churches, insofar as they are at the same time members of the college of bishops and rightful successors of the apostles, are held to care for the whole Church "by reason of Christ's command and prescription" (*LG* 24). Thus partnership becomes responsibility for one another in the widest sense. The difference between giving and receiving, old and young, and rich and poor among the churches is basically removed, and all parts share their riches. All have equal rights and equal duties in the ecumenical councils, in the bishops' synods, in the hierarchy of the church, and in responsibility for the whole church. Particular partnerships between groups and congregations, between dioceses and countries, between missionary societies and missionary bishops, and so on, are meaningful when they serve the whole.

3.6. Vatican II's clear emphasis on the office of bishop also had consequences for the relationships of →missionary societies to the bishops of the younger churches. The *Ius Commissionis* was replaced by the *Mandatum*, that is, the bishop who relies on the help of missionary societies invites them to work with him and regulates the relationship by a contract. Within the individual orders there are still pluriform structural relationships, but the principle of full equality of all the individual members and the responsibility for each other of individual provinces within the order is generally valid. To the extent to which the members of the younger churches also share in the missionary task of their religious communities and are themselves represented in the central leadership, the frontiers and differences disappear, and communities are created that serve the one common missionary commission, overriding differences and origins.

GUSTAV MENZEL AND KARL MÜLLER, SVD

Bibliography

Freytag, W., *Der große Auftrag: Weltkrise und Weltmission im Spiegel der Whitby-Konferenz des Internationalen Missionsrates* (1948). Freytag, W., and H. J. Margull, eds., *Keine Einbahnstraße: Von der Westmission zur Weltmission* (1973). Jansen Schoonhoven, E., *Wederkerige assistentie van kerken in missionair perspectief* (1977) 48–49. Lindquist, I., *Partners in Mission* (1982). Merker, H., *Partnerschaft statt Patenschaft: Chancen und Grenzen von Partnerschaftsprogrammen und Direktkontakten — Dritte Welt Information* (1986) 718. Müller-Krüger, T., *In Sechs Kontinenten: Dokumente der Weltmissionskonferenz* (1963) 64. Nababan, S. A. E., *Ökumenische Partnerschaft: Ein Arbeitspapier des Amtes für Mission und Ökumene der Evangelischen Kirche in Hessen und Nassau* (1985). Idem, "Zusammenwachsen zu mündiger Partnerschaft," *ZM* 9 (1983) 69–71. Rakotoarimanana, V., "CEVAA — a Response to the Gospel's Demands," *IRM* 62 (1973) 407–14. Ranson, C. W., *Renewal and Advance: Christian Witness in a Revolutionary World: The Whitby Meeting of the IMC, July 1947* (1948). Rosenkranz, G., *Die christliche Mission* (1977). Schekatz, H., "Learning the Meaning of Partnership," *IRM* 62 (1973) 415–24.

❧ PAUL THE APOSTLE AS MISSIONARY ❧

1. Paul's Vocation as "Apostle to the Gentiles." 2. Missionary Journeys. 3. Understanding of Mission and Missionary Praxis. 4. Teaching on Justification by Faith.

1. Around the beginning of the first century C.E. Paul was born in Tarsus, the capital of the Roman province of Cilicia in Asia Minor. As the offspring of a diasporan Jew, he was a product of both the Jewish and the Greco-Roman worlds. Both had a powerful influence on him, even though the Jewish law school of the Jerusalem rabbinate (Gamaliel [Acts 22:3]) made a particularly deep impression on him in his youth (see Phil 3:5; Gal 1:14).

Paul's encounter with the risen Lord near Damascus (ca. 33 C.E.) was the turning point in his life. "Saul," the church's persecutor (Acts 9:1; Gal 1:13), became Paul, the apostle of Jesus Christ and a committed preacher of the gospel. In Gal 1:15–16, he gives some biographical details about the call which changed his life: "Then God, who had specially chosen me while I was still in my mother's womb, called me through his grace and chose to reveal his Son to me, so that I might preach the good news about him to the pagans." With obvious allusion to the vocational theme of the Old Testament prophets (Jer 1:4–5), Paul attributes his vocation to God's call. Most probably he also deliberately refers to the role of the Suffering Servant (but without Isaiah 53): "It is not enough for you to be my servant, to restore the tribes of Jacob and bring back the survivors of Israel; I will make you the light of the nations so that my salvation may reach to the ends of the earth" (Is 49:6). (This text is quite properly applied in Acts 13:47 to the mission of Paul and Barnabas.) In his calling, Paul sees the operation of the saving will of God, which remains directed beyond Israel to the peoples of the world. Consequently, the grace of God as his vocational grace (1 Cor 15:10) also embraces the activity of the apostle through which the salvation of God is proclaimed and transmitted to all humanity.

Paul's main concern in Gal 1:15–16 is the revelation granted to him by God (which, in the context of this passage, also explains his reserve toward human authorities). God has manifested Godself so decisively to the "zealot" Paul that he recognizes the Son of God in Jesus. The wording in verse 16 ("to reveal his Son to me") leaves no doubt that this recognition is a grace, that is, that it transcends the rational possibilities of the logical thought processes of a scribe. The recognition of Jesus as the Son of God becomes the theme of Paul's proclamation. There is a causal relationship between revelation and mission which convinces him of his obligation to preach the gospel: "Not that I do boast of preaching the gospel, since it is a duty [*ananke*] which has been laid on me" (1 Cor 9:16).

2. As an apostle called by God, Paul was above all a missionary preacher of the gospel, even though consolidating the communities in the faith was also a part of his apostolic mission. His letters in particular are a testimonial to this.

The Acts of the Apostles gives us a fairly comprehensive account of Paul's missionary activity. Here we get a picture of his three missionary journeys, each of which begins in Antioch in Syria. The first journey takes Paul, together with Barnabas, to Cyprus and then farther to South Asia Minor to the provinces of Pisidia and Lycaonia. The second and third missionary journeys are quite different from the first. Acts 15:1–35 reports the problems arising from Paul's Gentile mission in the Antioch community, which did not practice circumcision, and the solution to these problems at the Council of Jerusalem. Luke has correctly assessed the importance of this assembly of the early Christian leaders which was so decisive for the future of the missionary movement of the early church, and he makes it the foundation of Paul's two great missionary journeys (Acts 15:36–18:22; 18:23–21:17). The second journey takes Paul first (probably overland) to Asia Minor by way of Derbe and Lystra and "through Phrygia and the Galatian country" as far as Troas. From there, at the special prompting of the "Spirit of Jesus" and because of a vision of a Macedonian, he continues to Greece. Here he engages in varied but very fruitful activity. He manages to found communities at all the important places: Philippi, Thessalonica, Beroea, Athens (with rather less success), and especially at Corinth, where he stays for a year and a half. He returns by the sea-route from Cenchreae via Ephesus (where he stays only long enough to announce a later missionary visit) and proceeds to Caesarea and Antioch. Luke adds the third journey immediately after a short stay in Antioch: Paul wanders through Galatia and Phrygia and reaches Ephesus, where he stays two and a half years and, in the form of regular instruction ("daily...in the lecture room of Tyrannus" [19:9]), establishes a mission center for the province of Asia. With enigmatic brevity, Acts 20:1–3 then reports about his journey to Macedonia and Greece (probably Corinth), where he remains three months. After this he returns via Macedonia, Troas, and Milet to Caesarea, his journey ending with his arrest in Jerusalem.

Luke's account of Paul's missionary activity follows a definite plan by which the word of God should proceed into the whole *oikoumene* through the mission work of Paul, the great apostle to the Gentiles (see Acts 20:24). No matter how much this plan determines the structure of Acts, so that even the individual accounts are part of the general scheme, there is no reason to doubt that Luke is essentially faithful to history. As a matter of fact, the reliability of Luke for the account of early Christian history is greater than is often conceded, considering the theological aim of the two books he wrote. He has recourse to traditions and sources which in many cases can lay claim to authenticity even for details. The sequence of the three missionary journeys and the details of Paul's stay in specific places still provide a useful framework of events even for historical-critical inquiry into the "true" picture of his missionary activity. The information contained in the Pauline letters can often be easily related to this framework. The reliability of the account is also supported by a synchronic coordination of individual dates from secular history. Reference can here be made in particular to the importance of an inscription found in Delphi which enables us to calculate the exact time the proconsul Gallio mentioned in Acts 18:12–17 stayed in Corinth. These details afford an approximate dating of the journeys and sojourns of Paul. According to this, then, we have the years 49 to 58 for the principal time of his missionary activity — that is, according to the account of the Acts of the Apostles, for the second and third missionary journeys. During this time the authentic Pauline letters were written: 1 Thessalonians (about 50 C.E.), Philemon, Philippians, 1 and 2 Corinthians, Galatians (about 55–57), and Romans (written in the winter of 57/58 from Corinth [see Acts 20:2–3]). The missionary work of Paul on his travels through the *oikoumene* was one of the main factors contributing to the historical success of the Christian faith. Because of his unparalleled efforts for the proclamation of the gospel among the Gentiles, he became the very epitome of the Christian missionary.

3. Paul was not the first missionary of early Christianity; he came into contact with Christianity when it was already a missionary movement. He began to play an active part at Antioch (Acts 13:1–3) and made use of the initial missionary experience. After the Council of Jerusalem, he pursued his missionary activity in greater independence from Antioch. In the sphere of Hellenistic Judeo-Christianity, Paul together with Barnabas had already recognized and carried out the Gentile mission as a theological possibility and necessity, that is, as the gathering of the eschatological people of God for the *Kyrios* reaching out beyond Israel to the Gentile world. He later gave a more radical expression to this very universal determination of the people of God. It is from this perspective that Paul's use of the word *ethne* (Gentile) must be understood. In Paul's day, calling the non-Jews or non-Christians "Gentiles" or "heathens" was not derogatory, as is occasionally suspected in modern usage, even in missiology. Paul does not confine himself to the Gentiles in contact with the synagogues (even though the proselytes perform the function of bridges for his mission) but turns to the focal points of the heathen world, to the cities and regional centers, and tries to found there Christian communities as new centers of the universal people of God. His goal is more ambitious than that of the missionary community at Antioch: he wants to go beyond Asia Minor and Greece to Rome and, if possible, as far as Spain. In this regard he says in Rom 15:23–24: "For many years I have been longing to pay you a visit. Now ..., having no more work to do here, I hope to see you on my way to Spain." The intention of going to Rome and Spain in the future, which he links here with his past missionary activity in the eastern Mediterranean ("from Jerusalem to Illyricum" [15:19]), is not motivated by the bustling restlessness of a zealot but springs from the very core of his gospel. Paul has the whole *oikoumene* in view because he feels himself called as the envoy of Jesus Christ to proclaim him as the *Kyrios* of the world and to assert his claim made in the gospel. In the apostle's gospel, God reaches out beyond Israel and even now makes God's saving power effective among the peoples called to eschatological salvation in the sign of God's crucified and risen Son. Hence the course of the gospel through the world becomes God's "triumphal march" in which he takes his apostle along as a prisoner that he might be like a "sweet smell" of Christ through his service "for those who are being saved" (2 Cor 2:14–15). The gospel is a message for the world beyond Israel, and Paul as its specially called preacher is totally preoccupied with this eschatological work of proclaiming salvation in Jesus Christ throughout the *oikoumene* — "world mission" in the best sense of the word. It is this vision of mission to which Paul has given an unmistakable theological foundation. For this he could appeal to the Old Testament motif of the eschatological pilgrimage of the nations to Zion (Is 2:1–5; Mi 4:1–3; see Is 51:4) and to the openness of the original Jewish-Christian community caused by the movement of the Spirit. It is remarkable that Paul does not relegate the gathering of the peoples at Zion to some remote final stage of history but prepares for it already in the present through the universal proclamation of the gospel and sees it proleptically realized in God's *ecclesia* composed of Jews and heathen. For good reason Paul includes the collection for the "saints in Jerusalem" as a reference to the anticipatory gathering of all peoples at Zion. The journey to Jerusalem (Rom 15:25–27; see Acts 20–21) consequently becomes "nothing less than a sign of the Gentiles' eschatological thank-offering and the nations' pilgrimage to Zion. But it is in fact only a sign" (Hahn). In particular Paul sees in it the repayment of the pagan's debt to the early Jewish-Christian community because pagans too now have a share in the spiritual possessions of that community. The priority of the Jews and Israel in salvation history that pervades the Epistle to the Romans from 1:16 onward is linked in Paul's mind with the preferential position of the early Jerusalem community, even though the promise given to Israel will be finally realized in the eschatological saving of the "rest of Israel" (11:25–26).

It becomes obvious that the theological conception of the mission to the Gentiles developed by Paul is encompassed in the perspective of salvation history through the promise made to Israel and its eschatological realization, merging the people of the promise with the peoples of the world, but also even now making possible a universal community of salvation based on faith in Jesus. That is why the constitutive sign of that mission is its openness to the peoples of the world in need of salvation and to Israel, whose path to salvation, despite being cut off temporarily, is not without hope but remains enveloped by God's promise of grace.

The founding of communities was also a part of Paul's missionary praxis. According to Paul, these communities understood themselves not merely as associations of like-minded individuals or only as helpful bases for further missionary activity (which they certainly were: see Phil 1:5; 4:10–19; Rom 15:24) but as outposts of the "new creation" already in force. "And for anyone who is in Christ, there is a new creation; the old creation has gone, and now the new one is here" (2 Cor 5:17). Paul's missionary work is eschatologically motivated and oriented. He shares the early Christian expectation of an impending parousia of Christ, and for this reason mission is "urgent" (D. Zeller). Nevertheless, there is some time left before the end to "prepare the communities for the encounter with Christ when he comes again" (Zeller). So this expectation of the parousia did not motivate the apparent hurry and restlessness of Paul the missionary — for instance, with the idea that "the measure of expansion is decisive for the dawn of salvation" (W. Wiefel) — but rather the motivation was the orientation of the communities to the coming Christ and their practice of the basic Christian attitude of hope for the fullness of the salvation begun in the gospel and already realized in germ. The rather brief time, as Paul understood the present (1 Cor 7:29; see Rom 13:11; Phil 4:5), demands concentration on the essentials. In spite of the end of time and its demands Paul does not overlook the importance of "church" in the present.

The new eschatological dimension which the believers have gained in baptism draws them together into the "Body of Christ" (1 Cor 12:27), that they might live a "new life" (Rom 6:4) inspired by the "love of Christ" (2 Cor 5:14).

Paul feels a continued responsibility as "father" toward the new communities he had founded (see 1 Cor 4:14). "That is why I beg you to copy me." The teaching and example of the apostle became the model for the communities. But this did not mean that they were dependent or treated as immature. On the contrary,

Paul believes that by the grace of the Spirit working in them they are able to regulate their own affairs, especially their community life. Realistically speaking, one could say that Paul, at least partially, overestimated his people in this respect. If they managed to survive beyond the initial stages it was because early in the postapostolic time they gave a stronger profile to community ministries. Here we refer especially to Eph 4:7–16 as well as to the ministry of presbyter in the pastoral letters (Acts 14:23; 20:17–35). Nevertheless, the principle of the working of the Spirit to which Paul appealed for theological (and not so much for canonical) reasons remained basic and characteristic also for the church of later times.

4. Jesus Christ, the crucified and risen Lord, stands in the center of the Pauline proclamation. Where Paul, as for instance in 1 Cor 2:2, gives special emphasis to the reality of the crucified Lord for some reason, the raising of the crucified one as proclaimed in the early Christian confession of faith (1 Cor 15:3–5) is the natural and necessary precondition for speaking with theological propriety about the cross. In this way the cross of Jesus Christ becomes for Paul the epitome of the salvation bestowed by God, which all human beings as sinners achieve only by the "obedience of faith" (Rom 1:5); and this applies to both Jews and heathens (1:16–17).

It is precisely this fundamental significance of the death on the cross or death and resurrection of Christ as locus and means of God's gift of salvation that Paul reflects on most profoundly in his teaching on justification. The special quality of this "teaching" as a theologically reflected proclamation should be observed. The terminology and concept of justification that Paul inherited from the Old Testament and the Jewish tradition already applied soteriologically, thus enabling him to present the salvation event in the model of a covenant relationship between God and God's people. This context can be easily recognized from passages like 2 Cor 5:21, Rom 3:25–26, and 5:1, which mention God's "justice," that is, the action of God justifying sinners. But Paul develops this idea in two directions: certainly the grace of God which forgives sin is mediated in and through the expiation of Jesus Christ, but this expiation of Christ works *through faith* so that whoever accepts the expiation of Christ experiences the justice of God as an event that creates anew. Faith which accepts Jesus Christ as the foundation for the saving action of God no longer needs the "works of the law." Since the works of the law were presented to the Gentile Christians by Paul's Jewish-Christian opponents in the Galatian communities as an (additional) condition for salvation, Paul comes to the antithetic formulation of his proclamation: "What makes a person righteous is not obedience to the law, but faith in Jesus Christ" (Gal 2:16; Rom 3:28). Thus the faith of the believer is imputed to him or her as justice — through grace and not through merit, just as God acted toward the believer Abraham (Gn 15:6 in Rom 4:3; Gal 4:6). Consequently, if salvation is the unmerited and unmeritable act of God toward sinners who make an act of faith, then the Christ-event in which the action of God has its historical basis and locus offers the possibility of salvation for *all*. The "precondition" for obtaining salvation is thus the sinfulness of Jews and Gentiles. All are equal in this, so that all may be saved in grace. The universality of salvation that Paul championed in his missionary program, sometimes against certain objections and opposition, had its ultimate base in the biblical view of God (Rom 3:29–30) and found its theological anchor in his teaching on justification.

KARL KERTELGE

Bibliography

Adloff, K., "Die missionarische Existenz des Apostels Paulus nach dem Zweiten Korintherbrief," *BThZ* 3 (1986) 11–27. Allen, R., *Missionary Methods: St. Paul's or Ours?* (1912). Bornkamm, G., *Paul* (1995). Bosch, D., *The Transforming Mission* (1991) 123–80. Bussmann, C., *Themen der Paulinischen Missionspredigt auf dem Hintergrund der Spätjudisch-hellenistischen Missionsliteratur* (1971). Dahl, N. A., *Studies in Paul: Theology for the Early Christian Mission* (1977). Dunn, J. D. G., *Unity and Diversity in the New Testament* (1977). Gilliland, D. S., *Pauline Theology and Mission Practice* (1983). Hahn, F., *Mission in the New Testament* (1965). Idem, "Das Verständnis der Mission im Neuen Testament," *WMANT* 13 (1965). Hultgren, A. J., *Paul's Gospel and Mission: The Outlook from His Letter to the Romans* (1985). Keck, L., *Paul and His Letters* (1979). Legrand, L., *Unity and Plurality: Mission in the Bible* (1990). Lovat, R. I., *Paul and the Universal Mission of the Church* (1987). Meier, J. P., *The Mission of Christ and His Church: Studies on Christology and Ecclesiology* (1990). Ollrog, W. H., "Paulus und seine Mitarbeiter: Untersuchungen zu Theorie und Praxis der Paulinischen Mission," *WMANT* 50 (1979). Senior, D., and C. Stuhlmueller, *The Biblical Foundations for Mission* (1983) 141–312. Smyth, B. T., *Paul: Mystic and Missionary* (1980). Spindler, M. R., and P. Middelkoop, *Bible and Mission: A Partially Annotated Bibliography 1960–1980* (1981). Stendahl, K., *Paul among Jews and Gentiles* (1976). Wiefel, W., "Die missionarische Eigenart des Paulus and das Problem des frühchristlichen Synkretismus," in *KZRT* 17 (1975) 218–31. Zeller, D., "Theologie der Mission bei Paulus," in *Mission im Neuen Testament* (1982).

❧ PEACE AND MISSION ❧

1. Peace and Development. 2. Encounter with Other Religions. 3. Peace as the Peace of God.

In the →theology of mission, the theme of peace is as rarely treated as is "mission" in peace studies. There are good and not so good reasons for this oversight. Many people no doubt believe that the time is past when a missionary might try to negotiate a peace treaty, as C. F. Schwartz did in the war between the British East India Company in India and the Sultan Hyder Ali in 1780. Others often think, rightly or wrongly, that the peace of heart and soul, which the Christian faith promises, does not measure up against the threat to humanity from nuclear war. Furthermore, it cannot be expected that the theology of mission will work in the problematic field of peace ethics, which is as wide-ranging as it is controversial. The question therefore remains whether and how — apart from individual events in mission history and a general sympathy toward peace — an up-to-date theology of mission can take up the "peace angle" (R. Friedli) in its area of concern and draw consequences from it.

1. The first guiding principle is the relationship between peace and →development, as it is generally accepted today in ecumenical circles. C. F. Schwartz, a Lutheran missionary in India, noted this relationship in his own way as he emphasized and interpreted his peace mission as a countermove against the politics of exploitation of the colonial power (see W. Germann 1870, 306ff.). The general assembly of the Lutheran World Federation in Dar-es-Salaam in 1977 adopted the same attitude for today: "Advocacy of justice is an essential, integral part of the mission of the Church" since "justice under the law of God is a witness to the universal authority of God's law over the whole of His creation." Without this justice, there is no peace. As far back as the Old Testament, peace is understood not only as the absence of war and violence but as a condition in which "steadfast love and faithfulness will meet; righteousness and peace will kiss each other" (Ps 85:10), and in which the total well-being of humanity will thus come to its fulfillment in community under God. That the whole service of Christians is directed toward people who are made in the image of God and that God provides for their every need are the logical consequences of a conception in which "development is the new name for peace."

2. A second area in which the question of peace as a missionary problem arises is the meeting of religions. Although Christianity came into the ancient world as a religion of radical love and peace, in its later development the Christian "gospel of peace" was only too often refuted by what in fact took place: holy war, direct or indirect missionary war, "the just war," modern "bellicosity," but also compromises with the mechanisms of social conflict (e.g., caste). These are all realities in the history of Christianity which cannot be blotted out by the existence of the historical peace churches or modern peace movements and which place a heavy strain on the missionary credibility of the Christian message. The picture is admittedly no less ambivalent in other religions. None of them presents itself as an outright power for peace. None of them has hitherto managed to create a new being or a new society that could overcome the forces of violence. None of them can be absolved from co-responsibility for the minimal form of peace which alone can ensure survival today. Each must start on its own to direct its thoughts toward peace in order to prepare for the change in awareness without which there is no peace. By trying to make up for historical shortcomings and by learning to renounce every religious legitimation of war and violence, Christianity can, in solidarity with other faiths, help to introduce the conversion to peace without which life with justice for all remains an illusion. Here the World Conference of Religions for Peace has a significant role to play in the recovery of the consciousness of the world mission of the Christian faith.

3. The real focal point that brings Christian mission and the peace mandate together will not be reached until the will to have peace is reconnected to the faith, that is, to the peace of God which is higher than the calculations of reason and in the light of which all those things that undermine action for peace are exposed: that is, the reality of sin, which keeps its influence even in the world of religion, and the inadequacy of all human "peacemaking" in this world. Also, we cannot expect religions to be capable of solving the problems of war and peace with, so to speak, ideological miracle-working weapons, in the sense of an absolute peace ethic. The effectiveness of such an ethic is threatened right at the outset by the doctrinal differences of the main religions. We can hardly expect Hindus, Muslims, and atheists to base their efforts for world peace on the Christian position, any more than Christian action for peace can deny its basis in faith in God's justification for sinners. How then can the difficulty be overcome, so that the path of the peacemaker does not become in effect a *via triumphalis* but is seen instead as a way of abnegation and suffering? How then can one overcome the permanent contradiction between, on the one hand, the consistent denial of power and, on the other, the need to oppose violent oppression and denial of rights with a counterforce? No theory of "just war" is a match for this ambivalence, any more than is a theory of a "just peace." What Augustine of Hippo knew long ago has to be rethought in terms of the relationship of Christian mission and Christian action for peace: only *sub aeternitatis,* which goes beyond the reality of all actions for peace, can we hope for an end to the "absurdity of war" and for lasting peace with justice.

HANS-WERNER GENSICHEN

Bibliography

Beinton, R. H., *Christian Attitudes toward War and Peace: A Historical Survey and Critical Re-evaluation* (1960). Brown, R. M., *Making Peace in the Global Village* (1981). Cahill, L. S., *Love Your Enemies: Discipleship, Pacifism, and Just War Theory* (1994). Driedger, L., and D. B. Kray-bill, *Mennonite Peacemaking: From Quietism to Activism* (1993). Duchrow, U., and G. Liedke, *Shalom: Biblical Perspectives on Creation, Justice and Peace* (1987). Fenton, T. P., *Third World Struggle for Peace with Justice: A Directory of Resources* (1990). Ferguson, J., *War and Peace in the World's Religions* (1978). Friedli, R., *Frieden Wagen* (1976). Friesen, D. K., *Christian Peace-making and International Conflict* (1986). Gensichen, H. W., *Weltreligionen und Weltfriede* (1985). Germann, W., *Missionar C. F. Schwartz* (1870). Küng, H., *Global Responsibility: In Search of a New World Ethic* (1991). Lasserre, J., *War and Gospel* (1962). Laszlo, E., and J. Y. Yoo, *The World Encyclopedia of Peace* (1986). Lauderville, D., A. J. Tambasco, and P. J. Wadell, "Peace," *CPDBT* 709–14. Lorentz, E., *Kirchen für den Frieden* (1983). Macquarrie, J., *The Concept of Peace* (1990). Musto, R. G., *Catholic Peacemakers: A Documentary History* (1993). Idem, *The Peace Tradition in the Catholic Church: An Annotated Bibliography* (1987). Parliament of the World's Religions, *A Global Ethic: The Declaration of the Parliament of the World's Religions* (1993). United States Catholic Conference, *Peacemaking: Moral and Policy Challenges for a New World* (1994). Yoder, P. B., and W. M. Swartley, *The Meaning of Peace: Biblical Studies* (1992). Weigel, G., *Tranquillitas Ordinis: The Present Failure and Future Promise of American Catholic Thought on War and Peace* (1987).

❧ "PEOPLE" (VOLK), "NATION" ❧

1. The Historical and Colloquial Meaning.   2. Meaning in the Bible. 3. Missiological and Ecumenical Meaning.

1.   The meaning of the term "people" (*Volk, pueblo, peuple, populo*) has been al-tered in the course of history in correspondence to the social and political interests of those in power at any particular time. In the German language in particular we have to deal with an ambiguous historical category which is always an expres-sion of the contemporary understanding of the sociopolitical situation, going far beyond its descriptive quality. The most important cultural sources of the modern term "people" (and this applies equally to the history of theology) lie in the ideas of the romantic movement: people as an "organic" element of "nature" and also as those who advance history; Herder's concept of the individuality of the people, shown in its language and history, leading to his postulate of a specific "soul of the people"; and, finally, the wars of liberation as "national experiences." Its philosoph-ical roots are to be found in idealism (convergence of the German and Prussian "national spirit" and "world spirit," respectively, through Hegel), and its political roots are found in the emancipation program of the French Revolution (question-ing of the principles of absolutism and the corporative state; the introduction of the sovereignty of the people and the democratic republic). The experiences of the twentieth century make the suitability of the term "people" appear questionable for a description of the historical process. The breakdown of the European nation-alisms (which were defined to a greater or lesser extent on biological or "popular" bases) in World War I led to the foundation of the League of Nations, as interna-tionalism became the leading idea in Christianity and socialism. The usurpation by fascism of the traditional term "the people" (*das Volk*) during the Nazi era not only compromised the meaning of the term but led to the division of Germany into two states. Telecommunications, the threat of atomic war, and the tendency toward removing differences in an international mass civilization make the use of the term increasingly unnecessary. In its place the term "society" (*Gesellschaft*), which carries no historical burden and which can introduce important distinctions, has won general acceptance. In colloquial speech, the experience that "people" has a historical and therefore changeable quantity (and also a cultural one) has resulted — at least in Europe — in the concept's applying less to a racial, ethnic, or even culturally homogenous group and describing more a united entity bound together by common history, language (possibly a lingua franca), and nationality. The term partly overlaps the terms "state," "nation," and "population." The status that the term "people" enjoyed in the nineteenth century seems to have been taken over in the twentieth century by the term "humanity."

2. In the Bible, "people" appears with different meanings and concepts. Two threads can be distinguished in the Old Testament. First, the Hebrew *goy* (mentioned 555 times, usually in the plural, *goyim*) indicates first of all a claim to territorial, linguistic, ethical, or even possibly state unity (Genesis 10). In this sense it is also occasionally applied to Israel (e.g., Gn 12:2). Normally, however, particularly in the plural (*goyim*), it refers to the mass of peoples as opposed to Israel. In the religious sense particularly, *goyim* stands for the heathen (Ps 2:1), in contrast to the one and exclusive people of God or the people of the possession (Gn 19:5). Second, in the phase of the forming of the state, the Hebrew *'am* — originally a term indicating close blood relationship — is used 1800 times to describe Israel as the people of God and of the covenant (Dt 7:6). In this usage it is not the people as such that is the determining factor but the choice and grace of God, as in the New Testament conception of the people of God. A more secular comprehensive term is *'am ha'ares* (people of the land [see Gn 23:7; Jer 1:18; Ezr 3:3; and Neh 10:31]). In the rabbinic literature the term indicates, however, the lowest stratum who do not know the law, so that *'am ha'ares* approaches in meaning the New Testament *ochlos*. This partly negative characterization of the peoples is not maintained in all scriptures (cf. Genesis 11 with Dt 32:8). In the prophetic crisis the peoples were recognized as tools of God's wrath or love toward Israel (Hos 8:10; Am 9:9; Is 45:1ff.). The prophetic proclamation in particular presents a modification of the relationship between the peoples and the people of God that rejects "the people" as an ethnological category and widens the concept of the people of God in the sense of universalizing and eschatologizing the pledge of salvation to Israel (the remnant of Israel) with the inclusion of the believers from the peoples (Is 25:6; Mi 4:1; Zec 8:20).

The LXX normally translates *goy* with the Greek *ethnos* (and *goyim* with *ethne;* approximately 1000 places) and *'am* with the Greek *laos* (about 2000 times). These concepts are also found with characteristic variations in the New Testament. By *ethne* (peoples [162 references in the New Testament]) is meant the "heathen," particularly in contrast to the Jews or Christians (Mt 6:32; Lk 21:24; Gal 2:15). The salvation history distinction between Israel and the peoples is not removed but bridged by the Christ-event (Acts 10:35; Eph 2:1ff.). Paul stands for the continuing preeminence of Israel as the original people of God and at the same time finds a theological foundation for the call, set free from the law, to the peoples as well (Romans 9–11). The people of God is enlarged around the church assembled out of the peoples. It does not take the place of Israel but is additional to it. With this, however, the ethnic barrier falls away. Humanity as a whole is the target of God's saving will, and through Jesus Christ humankind has already been chosen in advance to constitute the people of God (K. Rahner). *Laos*, originally "men" in the military sense (141 references), indicates, on the one hand, in continuity with the Old Testament, Israel (expressly in Acts 4:10). On the other hand, Old Testament honorary titles such as "people of God" (*laos tou theou*) and "people of the possession" (*laos periousios*) were carried over to the Christian church (Acts 15:14; 2 Cor 6:16; Ti 2:14; 1 Pt 2:9). The church thus sees itself as the (new) eschatological people of God conveying the Old Testament promises (*typos*) to a reunited humanity (Acts 2), constituted by the criteria of faith, not the criteria of individual origins (1 Cor 12:13; Col 3:11). Finally, the term *ochlos* is frequently found in association with *laos,* meaning crowd, people, humbler people (1174 references, especially in the Gospels and in Acts). It describes the group of people who are despised (and feared) by the ruling circles as uneducated or lacking in means; these are those to whom Jesus devoted himself (Mt 2:25). The company of disciples are also on occasion called *ochlos* (Lk 6:17; Acts 1:15), so that the term "people" receives a sociological shade of meaning that is worth thinking about in ecclesiological terms. The special announcement of the →reign of God to the poor, to those who are not integrated into society, and to the underprivileged points out that the people of God is not to be identified with the inevitably exclusive interests of church institutions.

3. Mission has always had to deal with "peoples" and thus also with the problem of the relation between the Christian message and already existing religions and cultures (→rites controversy). However, in reaction to the religious individualism of pietism and its practice of individual conversion and under the influence of the nineteenth century's way of looking at the people (see par. **1,** above), the people came to be regarded as the group targeted in Christian missionary work. The German Protestant missionary movement in particular worked toward so-called grassroots churches of the people or the building up of the church on the most intact ethnocultural basis possible. The path of preferring collective Christianization of a people, which G. Warneck adopted in his "doctrine of mission," even if in a diluted form, was continued in practical and theoretical terms, especially in the work of C. Keysser and B. Gutmann (the people as an organism, and so-called linkages "rooted in the soil," respectively). At the World Missionary Conference held at Tambaram in 1938 (→world missionary conferences) the German delegation (including W. Freytag, S. Knak, and M. Schlunk) distanced themselves from the ecclesiocentric and internationalistic groundswell of the conference by a special resolution. "The differences between peoples with their different forms of government, the differences between races with their different natural gifts" were described as God-given and of permanent validity. The fact that Schlunk to some extent looked after the foreign political interests of "national socialism" at Tambaram necessitated this formulation. The fact that Schlunk took seriously the foreign interests of national socialism in Tambaram still demands an explanation. However, theologically what was clear (and what is generally clear concerning the evangelization of whole peoples) was that the elevation of the folk-concept (*Volksgedankens*) of "the people" was not biblically grounded and had a tendency toward natural theology (→theology of mission). Behind the necessary efforts at indigenization and →inculturation of the gospel there stood the interest in conserving or creating rationalized residues as well as the undervaluing of the eschatological reservation under which a people as well as the church stand. As long ago as 1895, F. M. Zahn had pointed out that the thesis of Christianizing peoples misuses the concept of *ethne* exegetically and that theologically it serves as self-vindication.

The aim of mission should not be the "Christianized community of the people" but the Christian church which exists ecumenically in a multitude of forms — and ultimately, the aim should not even be this, but only "the kingdom of God and his righteousness." J. C. Hoekendijk's work (→missionary methods) is still of fundamental importance not only for determining the relation between people and church in German missiology but also in new versions of thinking about peoples, such as the "people approach" of the (Evangelical) World Evangelization Consultation at Pattaya, Thailand (1980).

At Vatican II (1962–65) the retrieval of the rich biblical and theological understanding of the image "people of God" provided the foundation for several significant ecclesiological and missiological changes in Roman Catholic theology and pastoral practice. The fact that chapter 2 of *Lumen Gentium,* entitled "The People of God," was placed before the chapters on particular functions in the church (hierarchy and laity) pointed to the reality that, in the church, a Christian is first and foremost a member of the people of God. In a hitherto hierarchically dominated church, this gave room for major developments in the theology of the laity. Also, in paragraphs 14, 15, and 16, *Lumen Gentium* speaks of the various ways by which Christians belong to (pars. 14 and 15) and non-Christians "are related to" (par. 16) the people of God. These statements have had strong implications for ecumenism, the proclamation of the gospel *ad gentes,* and the development of interreligious dialogue as an integral part of missionary activity.

In the development of ecumenism two factors have significantly altered the way of looking at the people, sociologically as well as theologically. The first was made up of the developments within the church in Latin America associated with →Vatican Council II (especially the Latin American Bishops' Conference at Medellín in 1968 [→Latin American theology]). This led to the second factor: the widespread emergence of →contextual theology across the Third World. A common starting point for these new understandings is the reality of oppressed and suffering people. This perception led to a new "not domesticated" reading (*releitura*) of the Bible and to the discovery of the incarnation of Christ in the "cellar of humanity" (C. Mesters). The Christ who is recognized by the poor and by those who live on the "underside of history" (→liberation theology) caused the churches to side with the suffering people. In a sociological sense, "the people" here consists principally of the broad mass of the deprived, who are by no means religiously, culturally, or ethnically homogeneous. In theological terms, it refers to the preferred recipients of the care and promise of God. This alteration in the social position of theology has far-reaching consequences for christology and ecclesiology. It is expressed in the slogan "the God of the poor," which stood at the heart of the World Mission Conference at Melbourne (1980) (→world missionary conferences). In →Korean theology, which comes from a land that for centuries has been characterized by foreign rule and oppression, the support of God for the suffering people (*minjung:* common people, mob) is grounded in the unconditional acceptance of the New Testament *ochlos* by Jesus (Byung-Mu Ahn). The Korean *ochlos* is here the eschatological people of God (*laos*) which is at the same time set free. It is destined to become the subject of its own history and thus to "rise again." In view of the messianic dimension, which altogether befits the people and the historic liberation project, the question once again arises from the European point of view whether there is an excessive theological and political use of the popular term "the people." However, because the starting point of liberation theology is the attempt of the threatened *people* of God to place a "spoke in the wheel" (D. Bonhoeffer), that theology's notion of the people certainly needs more from the ecumenical community than critique.

WERNER USTORF

Bibliography

Ahn, B. M., *Draußen vor dem Tor: Kirche und Minjung in Korea* (1986). Amirtham, S., and J. Pobee, *Theology by the People* (1986). Bausinger, H., B. Gustafsson, and H. W. Gensichen, "Volk und Volkstum," *RGG* 3/6:1434–40. Bertram, G., and K. L. Schmidt, "Ethnos," *ThWNT* 2:362–70. Bietenhard, H., "Volk," *TBLNT* 2/2 (1971) 1317–30. Bock, K. Y., *Minjung Theology: People as the Subjects of History* (1981). Idem, *Towards the Sovereignty of the People* (1983). Castillo-Cardenas, G., *Liberation Theology from Below* (1987). Exeler, A., and M. Metee, *Theologie des Volkes* (1978). Fraser, I. M., *Reinventing Theology as the People's Work* (1985). Hanson, H. D., *The People Called: The Growth of Community in the Bible* (1986). Hoekendijk, J. C., *The Church Inside Out* (1967). Idem, *Kirche und Volk in der deutschen Missionswissenschaft* (1967). Hopkins, D. N., *Shoes That Fit Our Feet: Sources for a Constructive Black Theology* (1993). Mathew, G., *Struggling with People Is Living with Christ* (1981). Mesters, C., *Die Botschaft des leidenden Volkes* (1982). Idem, *Sechs Tage in den Kellern der Menschheit* (1982). Moltmann, J., *Minjung: Theologie des Volkes Gottes in Südkorea* (1984). Moon, C., and L. V. Oración, "People," in *DEM* (1991). Paris, P., *The Spirituality of African Peoples: The Search for a Common Moral Discourse* (1995). Piepke, J. G., *Die Kirche auf dem Weg zum Menschen: Die Volk-Gottes-Theologie in der Kirche Brasiliens* (1985). Rahner, K., "People of God," *SM* 4 (1969) 400–402. Schlunk, M., *Das Wunder der Kirche unter den Völkern der Erde* (1939). Warneck, G., *Evangelische Missionslehre* 5 (1892–1903). Zahn, F. M., "Die evangelische Heidenpredigt," *AMZ* 22 (1895) 26–37. Idem, "Nationalität und Internationalität in der Mission," *AMZ* 23 (1896) 49–67.

❧ POLYGAMY ❧

1. Traditional Polygamy in Africa.   2. The Task of Christian Proclamation and Pastoral-Ethical Assessment of Polygamy in Africa.

Although the term "polygamy" embraces both polyandry (a marriage between one woman and several men) and polygyny (a marriage between one man and several women), it conventionally refers to the latter. Likewise, "polygamy" in this article means simultaneous polygyny.

There is no doubt that polygyny plays a role in the Old Testament. The patriarchs (Abraham and Jacob, among others) had more than one wife, and there are references to the royal harem. A clear example is King Solomon, who had seven hundred wives and three hundred concubines (see 1 Kgs 11:3). It is certain that the peoples living in the neighborhood of Israel also practiced polygamy.

Recent mission history knows polygamous marriage not only in Africa but also in other parts of the world, for instance, in New Guinea. But the best-known case is that of Africa, with which the following article will deal.

1.   Polygamy is not and never was a compulsory institution. Apart from the custom of levirate marriage (the compulsory marriage to a widow by her husband's brother), which could "force" someone to practice polygamy, in some African societies men are free to enter into wedlock with one or several women. In marriage — whether monogamous or polygamous — the following obligations must be assumed: (*a*) each monogamous or polygamous husband is obliged to support his wife or wives materially and economically; (*b*) in addition, the personality of the polygamous husband has to be such that he can maintain harmony and peace among his wives; (*c*) the husband, in particular the polygamous husband, is obliged to support his children materially and economically and bring them up according to the proven principles of the ancestral traditions.

At this point it is very important to take a look at the reasons for and functions of polygamy in Africa.

1.1. *Background.* Polygamy is not determined by sexual desire, as is often claimed; the reasons for it go much deeper. They can be summed up under three headings:

- *Childlessness.* In Sub-Saharan African marriages, infertility is a misfortune that can scarcely be tolerated. Children are a blessing from God. Besides, descendants are needed for the continuance of the clan; ancestors and descendants are mutually dependent. The dead and the living live in a kind of mystical communion. In this context a large number of children is desirable. Consequently, infertility of a first wife can lead to the practice of polygamy. It is important, however, that the first wife give permission for the practice.

- *Lack of male issue.* In tribes with a patriarchal structure the heir is always a boy. A girl can never continue the genealogy of her father. The father lives on only in the son. If there is no male issue, the husband can — with the permission of his (first) wife — take a second, third, and so on, wife in addition to the first.

- *Socioeconomic motives.* Sub-Saharan African society is mostly agricultural, lacking ultramodern technology. Understandably, in this situation, having a large number of children can be very beneficial. It is equally clear that this goal can be realized best of all within the framework of polygamy.

1.2. *The social function of polygamy.* Despite its shortcomings and limitations, polygamy has contributed to the welfare of many Africans. The following are some of its benefits:

- *The stability of marriage.* Traditional polygamy in Africa excluded divorce or made it rare. For instance, the infertility of the woman was no reason for divorce. Today more and more divorces are recorded because the churches forbid polygamy. Furthermore, in a society in which breast-feeding lasts two to three years, polygamy was seen as a great help for the husband against adultery. Today, with the introduction of monogamy, concubinage or adultery is more widespread than before and the stability of marriage is in jeopardy more than ever.

- *The enhanced status of the woman.* As a rule, the African woman fully realizes her ideal only when she is married and particularly when she has given birth. In society, the married woman — including one in a polygamous marriage — enjoys great prestige. Polygamy can even be a certain help for a barren first wife. In many tribes she is called the mother of the other wives and children, and thus, in a sense, she is not barren. Furthermore, polygamy helped protect the African woman from prostitution. It meant that more women had husbands and lived in normal marriages in which they were fully provided for. Quite often the ideal of monogamy has forced women into prostitution in African society.

- *The alliance with various families and kinship groups.* One of the most important functions of polygamy is the extension of solidarity to other families and kinship groups. Each marriage adds new members from other kinship groups to the family of the husband and so contributes to a new social relationship in which solidarity is promoted in all spheres of life.

2. An adequate judgment about polygamy in Africa cannot be made without a review of the way Christianity has dealt with traditional polygamy.

2.1. *The practice until now.* The missionary church has fought polygamy tooth and nail because it considered monogamy to be the only valid form of marriage. The polygamous man was allowed to receive baptism only if he dismissed all his wives except one, and this is still true today. The 1983 Code of Canon Law of the Roman Catholic Church insists on this practice. The only obligation it puts on the local authorities is to see to the just division of property among the dismissed wives. It is important to note that the wife to be kept does not necessarily have to be the first one. The codex here allows divorce precisely where traditional African society forbids it (can. 1148, pars. 1–3).

According to the theology on which this praxis is based, polygamy is contrary to God's plan and the equal personal dignity of man and woman. Accordingly, a polygamous marriage does not represent real love, real partnership, or real community (John Paul II has made this point). It must rather be equated with "free love" (*GS* 47). But this view has little connection with traditional African polygamy, which degrades neither man nor woman to a mere object. The polygamist not only is conscious of his responsibility for the material well-being of the woman but provides comprehensive security as well.

It would be helpful to approach the matter from the background of the Old Testament, where monogamy is the result of a long development. We may suppose that economic development, intercultural exchange, and not least the deepening of mutual love between Yahweh and the chosen people led to the transition from polygamy to monogamy.

Even if love as understood in the New Testament must eventually lead to monogamous marriage, there is no passage of which one can say with full certainty that it expressly forbids polygamy and generally prescribes monogamy (see K. Barth). Consequently, the church in Africa should imitate the patient pedagogy of the God of the Old Testament.

2.2. *The church and modern polygamy in Africa.* Today there is a new form of polygamy in Africa which perverts the traditions of the ancestors. In this form the wife or wives following the first are taken against the will of, or unknown to, the first. A wife who is not the first generally has no contact with the kinship group of her husband and is practically kept like a concubine. This practice exists also among Christians.

As a rule, the church counters this practice with strict insistence on monogamous marriage and with appeals to the New Testament. But it would be pastorally more effective, as a first step, to oblige modern polygamists to follow the more demanding form of traditional polygamy. Among other things, this involved as quite decisive factors both that the first wife give her consent and that all wives and children live in harmony together. However, the increasing emancipation of women in modern Africa has put pressure on the ideals and demands of the native African traditions associated with polygamy, just as it puts pressure on modern polygamy.

It should be pointed out — precisely with reference to the emancipation of women — that polygamy is a male institution. When appeals are made today for official recognition of this institution, it is men who make them, hardly ever women. With progressive literacy and professional possibilities, women are less and less dependent on men.

In any case, instead of threatening excommunication, the churches should accompany polygamists with a more sympathetic pastoral ministry and, with sound catechesis, change the consciousness of the population at the grassroots level.

BÉNÉZET BUJO

Bibliography

Barth, K., *CD* 3/4 (1961) 198–99. Boka-di-Mpasi-Londi, "Inculturation chrétienne du mariage," *Telema* 17 (1979) 3–4. Bühlmann, W., "Fragen zu Ehe und Familie: Bringt 'Familiaris Consortio' die Antwort?" *TGA* 25 (1982) 159–71. Bujo, B., *African Theology in Its Social Context* (1992). Idem, *Les Dix Commandements pour quoi faire? Actualité du problème en Afrique* (1985). Idem, "Die pastoral-ethische Beurteilung der Polygamie in Afrika," *FZPhTh* 31 (1984) 795–804. Cazeles, H., "Mariage (NT)," *DBS,* 926–35. De Cleen, N., "Contribution à l'étude de la polygamie admise par la philosophie," *RCA* 27 (1970) 49–73. Grelot, P., *Le couple humain dans l'écriture* (1962). Idem, "Die Entwicklung der Ehe als Institution im Alten Testament," *Concilium* 6 (1970) 320–25. Hillman, E., *Polygamy Reconsidered: African Plural Marriage and the Christian Churches* (1975). Kalanda, P., "Christian Marriage and Widow Inheritance in Africa," in *Church and Marriage in Eastern Africa* (1975). Kisembo, B., L. Magesa, and L. Shorter, *African Christian Marriage* (1977). Kornfeld, W., "Mariage (AT)," *DBSup,* 5:905–26. Lamburn, R., "Polygamy," in *Church and Marriage in Eastern Africa* (1975) 89–118. Legrain, M., *Mariage chrétien, modele unique? Questions venues d'Afrique* (1978). Mariama Bâ, *Ein so langer Brief: Ein afrikanisches Frauenschicksal* (1980). Mbiti, J. S., *Love and Marriage in Africa* (1973). Mulago, V., *Mariage traditionnel africain et mariage chrétien* (1981). Radcliffe-Brown, A. R., and D. Forde, *African Systems of Kinship and Marriage* (1962). Ritzer, K., *Formen, Riten und religiöses Brauchtum der Eheschließung in den christlichen Kirchen des ersten Jahrtausends* (1962). Schillebeeckx, E., *Le mariage: Réalité terrestre et mystère de salut* (1966). Urruntia, F., "Can Polygamy Be Compatible with Christianity?" *AfER* 23 (1981) 275–91.

℞ POPULAR RELIGION ℞

1. Concept.   2. Causes.   3. Contents.   4. Structures.   5. Pastoral-Theological Approach.

1.   The concept "popular religion" is derived from the discrepancy between an official Christian (also non-Christian) proclamation of faith and religion (→religion, religions) as lived by the "people" (→"people" [*Volk*], "nation"), that is, the general mass of the faithful. Popular religion is a response of the faithful to decrees, prescriptions, and behavioral requirements transmitted by an elitist circle of religious "initiates" to those who are religiously "uninitiated." A latent tension arises between these two groups because, on the one hand, the ecclesiastically legitimate institution is inclined to hold on to its monopoly over the administration and application of the means of salvation and prevent other religious practices, while, on the other hand, the people do not see why this or that has been prescribed and intuitively seek a space in which their own symbols (→symbol) and rites can become comprehensible and effective. Thus popular religion represents an unconscious, collective protest against the elitist rationalization of religion by trying, on a symbolic level, to assert the image and realization of an unbroken world in the life of the faithful. Here lies its enormous potential for change which, despite inherent elements of passivity and fatalism, has given rise in the course of history to messianic movements whose spiritual source and social location can be traced to agents of popular religion. Popular religion is a component of popular culture that mediates vitality, endurance, and meaning to human beings threatened by elitist cultural elements. It expresses a deep faith in God's power and salvific will, a trust in the power of the supernatural and in the possibility of human influence on it. It regards the world and →God as one and wants to experience God's →salvation concretely here and now. Fatalism combines with a faith-filled trust to form a complex whole which puts popular religion in an ambiguous light.

2. The roots of popular religion can be traced to the specific claim of the Christian proclamation, apart from general religious needs, to make the mystery of the person of Jesus Christ in his incarnation, death, and resurrection the focal point of religious praxis. Already at the beginnings of Christian proclamation this turned out to be a basic assumption: Paul (→Paul the apostle as missionary) came to Athens, saw the many temples and altars of the Greeks, and praised their piety. But the altar "to the unknown God" was a welcome opportunity to reproach the Athenians for their "religious ignorance" (Acts 17:23), to criticize their "religious materialism" (Acts 17:29), and to present a new image of God incarnationally and soteriologically centered in Christ (Acts 17:30–31).

For the Christian proclamation is not indigenous to a naturally developed and culturally integrated religiosity that could legitimate it within one culture or one religious sphere. On the contrary, at any one time Christian proclamation involves a secondary penetration into a preexisting religious system through which the culturally safeguarded religiosity of the people is questioned, subjected to radical criticism, and restructured from the angle of the christological event. The fact that Christianity arose out of the Jewish–Old Testament religion and thus incorporated elements of this religious culture does not contradict this. The break with Judaism was just as inevitable as that with Greco-Roman "heathenism."

Later this phenomenon repeated itself under different cultural preconditions so that up to today it is recognizable even in centuries-old Christian cultures. A. Gramsci pointed out in the first half of the twentieth century that the piety of the Italian people in no way tallied with that propagated by the official church of Rome; rather, the people possessed their own forms of faith and religious ways of behavior corresponding to their social position and anti-intellectual →culture. The geographical and social sphere seized by Christianity was and is maintained by a solidly institutionalized and unconscious use of violence which, from the vantage point of the dominating, central, and intellectual culture, does not allow the popular, peripheral culture a chance to express itself.

3. As regards contents, popular religion is nourished from the context of the respective culture — ethnicity, public and private sex roles, type of employment of a social class, and its geographical location in the countryside or in the city. It is considerably molded by the living tradition of the family, which, as the location of primary socialization, mediates religious perceptions, motivations, patterns of behavior, and religious convictions that become anchored in the subconscious of the person. These are not first and foremost transmitted by formal catechetical instruction but rather penetrate the souls of individuals by means of images, symbols, mythological elements, and stories which are identified with the figure of the mother and father. This primary religious experience takes a central position which it asserts against all later intellectual rationalization.

Despite the great diversity of the symbols, images, and rites of the individual cultures of humanity, they are everywhere based on the same elements which touch the great questions of human existence: death, life, fertility, afterlife, unity and community, the meaning of human existence, suffering and sickness, guilt and punishment. These elements form the unconscious and symbolic foundation of popular religion and have been appropriated by and assimilated into Christian ideas over the course of centuries. From this assimilation has resulted the people's conception of world and God which instinctively regards diverging worldviews with skepticism and feelings of rejection.

The figure of God the Father recedes into the background. God is the distant governor of the universe and the almighty (also arbitrary) lord of human destiny. It is possible to make God mercifully disposed with the help of the saints, who perform a mediating function between God and humankind. The image of Christ is strongly stamped by Monophysitism. God has appeared on earth in the humanity of →Jesus, worked miracles through his omnipotence, healed the sick, expelled the evil powers, and raised the dead. Popular religion expects similar manifestations of God's power. The life and death of Jesus were unalterably fixed by the fact of divine providence. In the same way human destiny cannot be changed. At the most it can in individual cases be rescinded by the direct intervention of divine power. The life of Jesus ended definitively on the cross. His death stands under the sign of the scapegoat which, by reason of divine commission, had to take all guilt upon itself. God's just claim to compensation by blood was thus fulfilled. The human being remains a prisoner of the eternal law of guilt and compensation. Resurrection in this world as →liberation for a new and creative humanness is unknown to popular religion. The resurrection of Jesus remains on the level of that of a miraculous holy man — proof of his divinity and at the same time of his inability to be really man. The role of the →Holy Spirit is without importance since human action and divine providence are worlds apart. There is hardly any consciousness of the new life in the Holy Spirit which is responsible for the progress of this world and which should bear witness to the saving event.

So it is logically consistent that the ecclesiological dimension of salvation is missing. The outpouring of the Spirit on all humankind (Jl 3:1–5), the establishment of the final covenant between God and humanity (Heb 8–10), the new creation of cosmos and humanity in the person of the firstborn (Col 1:12–20), as well as the hope for the fulfillment of human history in the fullness of the risen Lord (Eph 1:3–14) are given little room in the salvation expected by popular religion. Consequently popular religion is not sufficiently conscious of the horizontal dimension of the new divine relationship, solidarity, and fellowship in Jesus Christ.

4. With a view to the specific mediation of salvation, three characteristic structures of popular religion stand out. First, the relationship between the human being and the hereafter is characterized by direct contact. By means of religious practices a direct relationship is established with a saint which assumes the form of a covenant and is supposed to mediate salvation (devotional structure). Second, the relationship between believer and saint assumes the nature of a contract limited as to time and circumstances which is sealed by a so-called promise or vow. When the petition has been granted, the promise has to be kept so that the beneficiary does not become indebted to the supernatural power (protective structure). Third, there is the privatized mediation of salvation which dispenses from an ecclesial-sacramental mediation. In this way the believer evades ecclesiastical control over the means of salvation and their ethical-religious requirements (autonomous structure). These basic traits of popular religion are not necessarily contrary to participation in the official cult. Although the mediation of salvation is regarded as individual and vertical, much time is devoted to the social aspect of participation in religious celebrations.

5. Elements for a pastoral-theological appraisal of popular religion can be found in its deep piety; its sense of the holy and transcendent; its ability to pray and make sacrifices, suffer, and heal; its willingness to put up with hopeless situations; its feeling for friendship, love, and family solidarity. It is necessary to bring these values of popular religion into a genuine and honest dialogue with the demands of the official Christian proclamation.

JOACHIM G. PIEPKE, SVD

Bibliography

Ahrens, T., *Volkschristentum und Volksreligion im Pazifik: Wiederentdeckung des Mythos für den christlichen Glauben* (1976). Argyle, M., and B. Brei-Hallahmi, *The Social Psychology of Religion* (1975). Arias, M., "Religiosidad popular en America Latina," in *Iglesia y religiosidad popular en America Latina* (1977) 17–37. Baumgartern, J., *Wiederentdeckung der Volksreligiosität* (1979). Bediako, K., "The Roots of African Theology," *IBMR* 13/2 (1989) 58–65. Bleyler, K. E., *Religion und Gesellschaft in Schwarzafrika: Sozial-Religiöse Bewegungen und Koloniale Situation* (1981). Brandão, C. R., *Os Deuses do povo: Um estudo sobre a religião popular* (1980). Büntig, A. J., *El catolicismo popular en la Argentina*, 6 vols. (1969–1972). Castillo, F., *Theologie aus der Praxis des Volkes* (1978). Cohen, A. P., "Bibliography of Writings Contributory to the Study of Chinese Folk Religion," *JAAR* 43 (1973) 238–365. CNBB, *Bibliografia sobre religiosidade popular* (1981). Equipo SELADOC, *Religiosidad popular* (1976). Espín, O., *Faith of the People* (1997). Exeler, A., and N. Metter, *Theologie des Volkes* (1978). Geertz, C., *Local Knowledge: Further Essays in Interpretive Anthropology* (1985). Idem, "Religion as a Cultural System," in *Interpretation of Cultures* (1973) 87–124. Goizueta, R. S., *Caminemos con Jesús: Toward a Hispanic Latino Theology of Accompaniment* (1995). González-Galarza, F., *Mexican Popular Religion: A Way of Spirituality* (1990). Hiebert, P. G., "Popular Religions," in *Toward the 21st Century in Christian Mission* (1993) 253–68. Huber, W., "Ökumenische Perspektiven zum Thema 'Religion des Volkes,'" in *Volksreligion* (1978) 165–73. Lancaster, R. N., *Thanks to God and the Revolution: Popular Religion and Class Consciousness in the New Nicaragua* (1988). Lück, W., *Die Volkskirche: Kirchenverständnis als Norm kirchlichen Handelns* (1980). Mbiti, J. S., *Concepts of God in Africa* (1982). Morande, P., *Synkretismus und offizielles Christentum in Lateinamerika* (1982). Mouw, R. J., *Consulting the Faithful: What Christian Intellectuals Can Learn from Popular Religion* (1994). Rahner, K., *Volksreligion — Religion des Volkes* (1979). Sartori, L., *Religiosità popolare e cammino di liberazione* (1978). Schreiter, R. J., *Constructing Local Theologies* (1985). Suss, G. P., *Volkskatholizismus in Brasilien* (1978). Turner, H. W., "Religious Movement in Primal (or Tribal) Societies," *MissF* 9 (1981) 45–55. Vrijhof, P. H., and J. Waardenburg, *Official and Popular Religion* (1979). Westermann, D., *Africa and Christianity* (1937).

❧ PRAYER ❧

1. Christian Prayer. 2. Prayer in the Religions of the World. 3. The Act of Praying. 4. Prayer and Mission.

"Prayer and mission are only a part of the diversity of prayer found in holy scripture and in the prayer books of the church" (F. G. Vicedom). Through prayer we participate in God's dealings with the world and humankind. In the New Testament there is special mention of prayer for missions (Acts 4:23–31; 12:5–12). Down through the ages the great missionary figures have always turned to the people in their homelands to pray for the success of their labors. Thus in the writings of St. Boniface we observe a careful attention to prayer. "For him prayer was the be-all and end-all of mission aid" (F. Flaskamp).

Hand in hand with the new missionary movements in the early nineteenth century, prayer associations were founded for special missionary intentions, special mission fields, people in special positions, and particular religions (missions to Muslims and Jews).

1. In the Protestant church, the idea of special prayer for mission efforts was particularly cultivated by the British and American missionary societies. In their monthly publications, special prayer requests were recommended to readers. Many mission groups and associations met on certain days to pray for the missions. A number of mission associations, apart from collecting money and offering practical help, made prayer for missions their main preoccupation. In the Catholic Church, papal encyclicals on mission always mention the importance of prayer to ensure God's blessing on missionary work. For this purpose the apostleship of prayer is highly recommended (*Maximum Illud* and later texts). Since 1927 the monthly prayer requests of the Apostleship of Prayer (founded in 1844) have been published together with general prayer requests. The relationship between mission and prayer was emphasized in a concrete manner when the French Carmelite Thérèse of Lisieux was declared principal patron of all missions (December 14, 1927; →mission patrons). In the Protestant world, this theological connection was made clear by making "Rogate" Sunday (the Sunday before Ascension Day) a day of prayer for missions.

2. Each religion has a knowledge and awareness of a relationship of humanity to God, of the turning of the Absolute to humanity, and of humanity's response and turning to the Absolute in prayer. Basically, prayer is the affirmation and consciousness of one's created condition. Through prayer the whole of humanity is involved in an exchange with God — even if the phenomena and processes are differently named and described. Ultimately, they all have the same purpose. In prayer all individuals and communities move toward God. This demonstrates a common feature of all religious traditions and transcends all theological differences. Prayer could be described as a knowledge of God, a vital inner awareness coming from the Spirit of God. It is revelation and the voice of God. In the whole history of humanity and in all religions there is an uninterrupted tradition of prayer. Were evangelization and the Christian proclamation to turn a blind eye to these common forms, tendencies, and aspirations of human beings, they would be disdaining "the noblest faculty that peoples — including the heathen — possess" (F. Heiler).

Prayer constitutes the decisive foundation for dialogue between religions. Every person's prayer is possible only by the operation of the →Holy Spirit. The Spirit is the essential condition for salvific action and prayer. The religions are the teachers of prayer for "generations of people" (*EN* 53) and thus prepare the foundation for dialogue and the work of the Holy Spirit "in the world before Christ was glorified" (Acts 10:44–47; *AG* 4;13; *DV* 5).

3. Consequently, answers to the question of differences between Christian and non-Christian prayer are to be looked for not in the religions and their distinctive notions of God but rather in different human attitudes. The dividing line runs through all religions, including Christianity, and concerns the attitude of the individual to his or her limitedness and to God. Trust and freedom are the characteristics of genuine Christian prayer. Their norm is the prayer of Jesus, which involves profound trust and an all-embracing turning to community and world. The reality of the world, responsibility for the world, and fraternal solidarity with all people are the characteristics of genuine and Christian prayer. Being Christian implies a tension between "prayer and loyalty to the earth" (D. Bonhoeffer).

4.   Church documents rightly emphasize that, before all organization, prayer is the most important driving force of missionary work. Prayer has been described as the missionary activity par excellence, and the mission of the church and the missionary community is always and primarily "a mission to pray for the salvation of the world" (K. Rahner). In a sense prayer for missions is a test of whether the community is working for the mission of God or for itself. Prayer for mission can be related only to "the sacrifice of the Son for the salvation of the world" (Rahner). In this way it reminds us that mission is theologically anchored in the center of the divine mission. In all phases of the actual missionary activity prayer is absolutely necessary for the genuine preparation for evangelization. Missionary work and prayer must always go hand in hand. For missionary existence prayer is not only the foundation of but also the linkage with the *missio Dei*.

HORST RZEPKOWSKI, SVD

Bibliography

Archer, J. C., "Missionary Education and the Local Parish," *IRM* 14 (1925) 333–43. Arens, B., *Die katholischen Missionsvereine: Darstellung ihres Werdens und Wirkens, ihrer Sätzungen und Vorrechts* (1922). Barth, H. M., *Wohin — Woher mein Rufen? Zur Theologie des Bittgebetes* (1981). Bieder, W., *Das Mysterium Christi und die Mission* (1964). Bryant, D., *With Concerts of Prayer: Christians Join for Spiritual Awakening and World Evangelism* (1984). Cabral, J., "A oração ao serviço das missiôes," in *Actas do I congresso Nacional da UMC* (1948) 148–58. Carmody, D. L., *Prayer in World Religions* (1990). Cragg, K., *Alive to God: Muslims and Christian Prayer* (1970). Dhavamony, M., *Prayer in Christianity and Other Religions* (1975). Dresden, J. L., *The Ministry of Prayer and Praise: Spiritual and Catechetical Sessions on Prayer* (1994). Feldkämpfer, L., *Der betende Jesus als heilsmittler nach Lukas* (1978). Flaskamp, F., "Die Missionsmethode des hl. Bonifatius," *ZMRW* 15 (1925): 18–100. Handmann, R., *Das Gebet als Missionsmacht* (1912). Heiler, F., *Prayer* (1937). Higgins, J. J., *Thomas Merton on Prayer* (1975). Kornke, H., *Die Kranken im Dienste der kath. Heidenmissionen: Die Missionshilfe der Kranken* (1935). Lenchak, T. A., J. Kodell, and A. F. Detscher, "Prayer," *CPDBT* 756–65. Luzarraga, J., *Oración y misión en el Evangelio de Juan* (1978). Monloubou, L., *Saint Paul et la Prière: Prière et évangélisation* (1982). Montgomery, H. B., *Prayer and Missions* (n.d.). Nilles, P., "Apostolisches Beten," *PM* 20 (1936) 27–51. Origin, *Prayer: Exhortation to Martyrdom*. Plathow, M., "Geist und Gebet," *KuD* 29 (1983) 47–65. Rahner, K., "Sendung zum Gebet," *Schriften zu Theologie*, 3:249–61. Rzepkowski, H., "Die Sicht der nichtchristlichen Religionen nach 'Evangelii Nuntiandi,'" in "*. . . denn Ich bin bei euch*" (1978) 339–50. Schaller, H., *Das Bittgebet* (1979). Scherer, G., *Reflexion, Meditation, Gebet: Ein philosophischer Versuch* (1973). Schilling, D., "De oratione pro infidelium conversione," *PCL* 31 (1935) 72–74. Seumois, A. V., "Missionary Prayer in the Early Church," *Worldmission* 4 (1953) 282–308. Spindler, M., *La mission, combat pour le salut du monde* (1967). Thielike, H., *Das Gebet, das die Welt umspannt* (1961). Ulrich, F., *Gebet als schöpferischer Grundakt* (1973). Underhill, M. M., "Women's Work for Mission: Three Home Base Studies," *IRM* 14 (1925) 379–99. Vicedom, F. G., *Gebet für die Welt: Das Vaterunser als Missionsgebet* (1965).

❧ PREACHING ❧

1. Missionary Preaching at Home and Abroad.   2. Contextual Preaching in the Third World.   3. Ecumenical Preaching in Industrialized Western Societies.

Preaching is the oral mode of proclaiming the word of God in the church of Jesus Christ. Its form is thereby tied to the conditions of both time and place. It puts the kerygma into words for a particular group and within a particular situation and context. Preaching, therefore, happens in the wake of the communication sought by God with humankind. It uses language as a means by which God reveals Godself to people (Traber 1983, 684; see Jn 1:14).

1. In the nineteenth and up until the mid–twentieth century, missionary preaching was understood as the prerogative of missionaries both at home and abroad. Their preaching at home often functioned to present their mission activity overseas and raise support in associations and church congregations. Preaching on the mission field served to pass on the biblical message and make converts to Christianity. Thus preaching lost its biblical richness, that is, that all preaching should aim at gathering the congregation and sending it out on the eschatological mission of the people of God (→"people" [*Volk*], "nation"). So missionary preaching was poised between faith in God's mission and the organized work of missionary societies and support groups. Protestants, in particular, tended to see it as a secondary matter for the churches, and overseas, too, it was not directly aimed at founding churches. We can immediately see the dangers inherent in missionary preaching from the very beginning: pragmatism and the business of running a mission; the cleft between inwardness and outwardness, between Christians and "heathens"; moralizing legalism; excluding the daily lives of the hearers from the sermon; the individualization of the hearer through personal appeals instead of addressing the local community and acknowledging its context; and glorifying the historical facts that had brought about the mission. Missionary preaching thus became a "special sermon" or an address tied to special occasions, and so by definition jeopardized its testimonial character.

There have been few attempts at defining an explicit "missionary homiletics"; nevertheless, the importance accorded to preaching within organized mission work is quite remarkable. N. L. von Zinzendorf (1700–1760) was skeptical about public proclamation of the gospel in the mission field in the form of sermons, not believing it would have any effect. He wanted to confine himself to collecting "first-timers," individuals to be told about salvation in private conversations, not public sermons. The kerygma was to be replaced by a textual exposition; when proclaiming the gospel, the tone was not to be loud but soft, "where we think the Holy Spirit has prepared souls to listen quietly" (Richter 1928, 97 n. 2).

The first approach to missionary homiletics was made by R. Stier in 1830 when he was teaching at the Basler Mission College. His *Outline of Biblical Proclamation, or Guide to the Art of Preaching by the Word of God* (1844) stresses the missionary task of congregational preaching and thus the close link between congregational and missionary preaching (see 5). The purpose of both was, according to Acts 20:20–21, to proclaim, teach, and testify (4). The precondition for this goal was that "natural man in his blindness and sinfulness" (3) was the hearer of the sermon and that the Bible had to be understood as a "textbook" from which the sermon was to be drawn (39). Yet this precondition presupposes that the preacher is already "a man of God" (46–47) and thus on a different plane from the "natural" person.

It is noteworthy that Stier thought that "simple addresses," the prime form of missionary witness, had to be accompanied by conversation, being "the most appropriate form of continuing mission" (142–43). Questions and answers arising in conversation enable the acceptance or rejection of the gospel. The simple conversation Jesus had with the Samaritan woman in John 4 is exemplary for him here.

The character of living witness in contrast to preaching was repeatedly expressed around the turn of the century by C. Blumhardt Jr. in his letters to his son-in-law, R. Wilhelm, a missionary in China. "When you arrive at a strange village never preach...until you have got socially warmed up.... Get to know them, gain their trust.... Then preach but cautiously even then. It is our life, not our preaching, that must give the people light" (Blumhardt 1958, 5.6).

Another who sought the "special sermon" in the late nineteenth century was G. Warneck, the first German professor of missiology in Halle (1896–1908). Warneck stressed the special nature of missionary preaching. It had to achieve two things: (a) introduce the biblical notion of mission and thereby educate for missionary activity; and (b) publicize mission history, since the end-time was fast approaching. In a series of articles on Mt 28:19 (Warneck 1874), Warneck offered a combination of scripture and experience in order to give biblical legitimation to the Christianizing of the people and thus to discover a "predisposition" of world history toward mission (Holsten 1953, 159). Preaching was thus to be proclamation echoing through the whole population (Warneck 1874, 185–94). His exposition of Mt 28:29–30 again shows that the "fullness of time" does not have a purely eschatological meaning (Warneck 1892–93, 3:1, 258). Developments in world history will provide a place for the kerygma, but Warneck uncovers a sore spot of his age: that missionary activity only has a future where it takes account of the whole historical and cultural life of a people and aims to build up Christian communities.

Early twentieth-century approaches are more strongly related to the content of missionary preaching, but still with very few references to missionary outreach. In 1929 A. Schlatter particularly pointed to the danger of legalism in missionary preaching which "inevitably distorts the image of God" (1929, 263). He called for a unity in the preaching of gospel and law, which would sharpen the conscience in the sense of Rom 12:2 and lead to real freedom. "The question, 'What shall I do?' is placed in their own consciences; the law of God seizes them and moves them through the gospel" (263). An approach still much followed today was taken by H. Kraemer in 1938 at the World Mission Conference in Tambaram, Madras. In *The Christian Message in a Non-Christian World,* he called for "reading" and interpreting the context, that is, the political, social and religious factors. Like the International Mission Council's meeting ten years earlier in Jerusalem, Kraemer strove for a "comprehensive approach," appealing to the whole person and also opening one to an awareness of the social parameters to be considered in setting up a Christian community. It is clear that Protestant missions, despite their strength in methodological proclamation, intensive social welfare, and intercultural dialogue, have exposed their greatest weakness at this point, in contrast with Catholic missions and their large congregations (K. Latourette).

W. Holsten's concern was to deliberately subordinate "missionary facts and experiences" to hearing the text and to understand mission as the essence of the kerygma, or as an "article of faith" (Holsten 1953). W. Trillhaas distinguished missionary preaching "in the mission field" from that "at home." The former was more catechism and baptismal instruction than preaching in the European sense, and the latter was preaching to waken the congregation from their sleep (Trillhaas 1947–48, 17–18). New, exciting, and exotic elements were to be "brought in," as it were, as elements intrinsically belonging to the familiar and traditional. Although not explicitly, Trillhaas hoped that missionary preaching would enrich the speaker's own theology and that of the "mother churches."

W. Freytag outlined the beginnings of an intercultural understanding of preaching when he assigned proclamation to the ecumenical church, "the congregation of Jesus from all peoples" and judged the "authenticity" of witness by the church's "conformity with its Lord" and participation in his suffering. "As long as we as church are not prepared to follow in the way of suffering, our witness is not genuine and does not have the approval of the Lord, who sends us out" (Freytag 1961, 1:217). Freytag, however, averts a misunderstanding that is often linked with definitions of witness which focus on its exemplary character. It is not a matter of our Christian life nor a matter of things in our lives "turning out well," but "what the Lord does to us when we let him be the Lord — *that* is what bears witness to him" (1:219).

2. Schlatter, Kraemer, and Freytag anticipated the contextual emphasis of preaching which has developed in the churches of the Third World. For these churches contextual preaching means the following: (*a*) witnessing to God's reconciliation with the world and God's liberating action in history so that the earth would become more inhabitable and life together more humane (ecumenicity of preaching); (*b*) opening up and testifying to the church's social, religious, cultural, economic, and political context with a view to critical correction (contextuality of preaching); and (*c*) acknowledging that people experience God's loving presence in doing God's will (ethical aspect of preaching). All this constitutes a rejection of preaching devoted to denominationalism, individual conversion, and the separation between the history of salvation and that of the world. This shift to the contextual emphasis was a matter not of "missionary facts" but of the future of God's mission. The eschatological orientation gained new importance.

The best-known approach to contextual homiletics is that of the Reformed theologian Allan Boesak. A "colored" who has spent most of his life in the repressive apartheid system of South Africa, he endows preaching with the form of ethical challenge. The liberation of the black and colored population from oppression is the decisive criterion for assessing the proclamation of reconciliation (Boesak 1982). Boesak defines a sermon as the proclamation of the gospel in comprehensible language to people in a specific situation. A comprehensible, context-related sermon can become "relevant" to the congregation. He does not consider a mere analysis of the context as adequate, the point being to proclaim the text "prophetically" as the present word of God and place the hearer before a decision through pointing out the ethical dimension. This can only be "authentic" if the person is "genuine." Anyone who has experienced the liberating action of God can give convincing testimony to God's working in specific conflicts, thus firmly linking preaching to its context. This aspect is found in many contextualized approaches, for example, in Melanesia, where preachers are warned against a lack of credibility. They must live their own sermons, or their words will be a stumbling block to the congregation.

Authentic witness is also sought by three forms of preaching that have become increasingly widespread in Latin America and Asia as part of a hermeneutical reorientation: the discussion sermon, the narrative, and the contextual Bible study. *The Gospel in Solentiname*, by E. Cardenal, and *Peasant Theology*, by C. Avila, are two vivid examples of how the biblical stories become relevant to the often dispossessed peasants and can also be understood in the rich churches, which also means they show how life can be changed: "We pray, 'Your will be done.' But what is God's will referring to the land? . . . If he is our father, then all goods are the goods of one family and must be shared among all." Social-historical exegesis focuses on stories and interpretations such as those by Carmelite C. Mesters (originally from Holland), derived from Brazilian base communities after "twenty years of wandering the roads of the Bible and Brazil" (Mesters). The theological premise of his work is that God is a God of the suffering and the dispossessed and takes their side in history, that is, for their liberation and in all their steps toward justice. Methodologically, this means expressing the conflict that arises when one suspects that reality and its dominating forces are not as they should be before God, listening to God's liberating word, and acting in obedience to it. God's history of liberation of humankind must not be passed over in silence. It wants to come to life: "from life to Bible — from Bible to life," according to the title of Mesters's major book. The hermeneutical triangle used to narrate and interpret the Bible is also geared to this emphasis: to see reality, to reach an ethical judgment from the Bible, and then to act for change. Mesters's work is a Latin American example of allowing the "ordinary" people to speak, the people of God (→"people" [*Volk*], "nation"). Their lives are written into the biblical liberation story, and the wealthy are shown how God gives voiceless people a clear, vivid language, literally bringing about the →reign of God.

Similar trends are apparent in Asia in minjung theology and an Asian theology of the people. Picture-meditations, poems, and biblical reflection, chiefly in the grassroots urban and rural mission and with the support of sympathetic groups and theologians (K. Koyama, Choan-Seng Song, R. Fung, M. Takenaka, P. Niles), tell of sufferings and hope — and of a liberated Asia, whose renewal is to start not from the "crusading mind" of Western control and dominance but from the "crucified mind" (Koyama, Kim Chi Ha, E. de la Torre, M. Katoppo). It is particularly characteristic that the preacher walks in solidarity with the suffering people — the people who are blessed with bearing their mission. The reason for the people's missionary "task" is repeatedly expressed. This narrative style, the turning away from preaching removed from history and life, is reflected in consciousness-raising Bible studies like those done by theologian and sociologist R. Macin in Mexico City with factory workers and farmworkers, under the influence of P. Freire's pedagogy of the oppressed. A word or theme is brought out in its existential, even conflictual meaning. For example, the term "sin" might be defined as loving goods more than our fellow people; this is a sign that we are dominated by Cain. "Cain," says Macin, means "to purchase." To purchase something is good, as long as it is not done with egoism, in order to hurt someone else. In that case, it is bad and a crime against creation (Macin 1976, 6–7).

H. Bürkle has observed the entwinement of biblical tradition and the present in African preaching. Biblical characters are contemporaries, and past events take on immediacy. Application in the form of directly speaking to the congregation sometimes leads to responses like those known in black U.S. churches. Sermons are necessarily lengthened thereby, and also through the elements of cyclical repetition, illustrations, allegory, and symbolic language (Löytty 1971, 113). This process presupposes familiarity between the congregation and the preacher along with their sharing in common everyday experience, a sharing proper to the role of the preacher as the "mouthpiece" of Jesus and teacher of the community. The text is primarily understood as a teaching text and Jesus is very "present": for example,

"Jesus says today that we here..." Through the almost timeless continuity, the historical character of the gospel recedes and the eschatological passages of the New Testament have little or no meaning.

3. Preaching in industrialized, materially rich countries is not made ecumenical when the congregation simply observes the situation of others with its own eyes or judges it by its own scales of values and religious customs. Western industrialized society tends to usurp and absorb in order to maintain its own power and also to marginalize its critics.

The preaching of God incarnate, who reconciles all humanity by bringing justice and turns without compromise to the poor — this kind of preaching is difficult, both because it calls society to a self-critique, and because it seeks to overcome the economic and military spirit by God's Holy Spirit. This kind of preaching does not originate from a spirit of contradiction, but from the righteousness of God which desires to become incarnate. This means that a justice that is not accessible to all of humankind is not God's justice. Thus God needs people who allow themselves to accept this justice which reconciles the whole of humanity. The task of ecumenical preaching is to call and arouse people who are willing to accept it.

As a part of ecumenical life, preaching aims at learning to see one's own reality with the eyes of others. This sensitivity presupposes the willingness to become someone else and to conceive of changes in oneself and others as genuine ecumenical sharing. The point of such sermons will be not only to call the congregation to see and hear others but also to learn to see, hear, and discover more with them — through their Bible reading, through their discussions, through their obedience, and, above all, through their view of our hearing and seeing, of our understanding of obedience and discipleship. Ecumenical preaching, then, does not express what can be said about others, but what they say themselves and what it means for the church of Jesus Christ in an industrialized society to take in the thought, action, and admonitions of others, indeed, anything strange, unfamiliar, and new.

Ecumenical preaching serves "theological decolonization." It seeks discipleship at the local level and does not presume to swallow up other places and continents or take them over in a spirit of theological, cultural, or political arrogance. It is aware of the danger of hollow, clerical posturing where partnership, "ecumenical exchange," and "worldwide reconciliation" are evoked but where there is impenitent neglect of the political and economic tension arising from the dominance of the rich Western industrialized countries at the international level. A well-meaning sermon that seals harmony in what it leaves unsaid and that glosses over the sufferings of others and our lack of responsibility and solidarity subjects any ecumenical encounter to the spiritually colonialist stranglehold of a "smiling mission" and will create additional distance and distrust, instead of the desired ecumenical closeness. Preaching that embraces the whole of human life is thus the test of our credibility (Mt 25:31–46; 1 Cor 8:14). The more it perseveres in the cause of the weak and suffering, whether at home or abroad, and uncompromisingly allows biblical witness to point out the weaknesses of the local community and its own society, the more the listening congregation will understand that it is really with its Lord and that the preacher is talking about the things that really matter. Consequently, concerns for keeping people entertained or emotionally engaged are only secondary to the task of relating the congregation to the everyday encounter with and care and support for others, for strangers and outcasts in our own society. "Anyone able to show compassion discovers the meaning of life, true life grounded in God. Such people obtain a share in the new world of God, along with those they have helped" (K. Scharf). Wolfgang Gern

Bibliography

Anderson, G., et al., eds., *Mission Legacies: Biographical Studies of Leaders of the Modern Missionary Movement* (1994). Avila, C., *Fische, Vögel und die Gerechtigkeit Gottes* (1981). Bedouelle, G., *Saint Dominic: The Grace of the Word* (1987). Blumhardt, C., Jr., *Christus in der Welt: Briefe an Richard Wilhelm* (1958). Boesak, A., *The Finger of God: Sermons on Faith and Socio-Political Responsibility* (1982). Bürkle, H., "Predigt in Afrika: Anmerkungen zu ihrer Hermeneutik," *VF* 26 (1981) 72–84. Cardenal, E., "Die Dritte Welt als Thema der Gemeinde," *WPKG* 67 (1978). Idem, *The Gospel in Solentiname*, 4 vols. (1976–1982). Idem, *Die Mülltonnen der Reichen und der arme Lazarus: 15 Predigten über Arme und Reiche in der Mission* (1982). *Concise Encyclopedia of Preaching* (1995). Davis, G. L., *I Got the World in Me and I Can Sing It, You Know: A Study of the Performed African-American Sermon* (1983). Duke, R. W., *The Sermon as God's Word: Theologies for Preaching* (1980). Dürr, H., "Heidenpredigt," *RGG* 5:537–39. Freytag, W., *Reden und Aufsätze*, 2 vols. (1961). Grafe, H., *Die volkstümliche Predigt des Ludwig Harms* (1965). Graham, B., *A Biblical Standard for Evangelists* (1984). Holsten, W., "Missionspredigt," in *Das Kerygma und der Mensche* (1953) 155–63. Idem, "Möglichkeit und Sinn einer heimatlichen Missionspredigt," *EvTh* 6 (1946–47) 115–42. Kraemer, H., *Die christliche Botschaft in einer nichtchristlichen Welt* (1940). Löytty, S., *The Ovambo Sermon* (1971). Macin, R., *Bibelkunde für Arbeiter und Bauern* (1976). Maier, C. T., *Preaching the Crusades: Mendicant Friars and the Cross in the 13th Century* (1994). Mesters, C., *Abraham und Sara* (1984). Idem, *Die Botschaft des leidenden Volkes* (1982). Idem, *Defenseless Flower: A New Reading of the Bible* (1989). Idem, *God Where Are You? Rediscovering the Bible* (1995). Idem, *Vom Leben zur Bibel, Von der Bibel zum Leben*, 2 vols. (1983). Idem, *Das Wort Gottes in der Geschichte der Menscheit* (1984). Ratzinger, J., *Dogma and Preaching* (1987). Richter, M., *Der Missionsgedanke im evangelischen Deutschland des XVIII. Jahrhunderts* (1928). Schlatter, A., "Das Gesetz und das Evangelium in der Heidenpredigt und in der Christengemeinde," in *Gesunde Lehre* (1929) 254–65. Stier, R., *Outline of Biblical Proclamation, or Guide to the Art of Preaching by the Word of God* (1844). Traber, M., "Kommunikation," in *ÖL* (1983) 682–85. Trillhaas, W., "Grundsätzliches zur Aufgabe der Missionspredigt," *Jahrbuch für Mission* (1947–48) 16–20. Uttendörfer, O., *Die wichtigsten Missionsstrukturen Zinzendorfs* (1913). Waida, G., "Communication through Preaching in Melanesia," *Catalyst* 2 (1981) 18–35. Warneck, G., *Evangelische Missionslehre*, 3 vols. (1892–93). Idem, "Der Missionsbefehl als Missionsinstruction," *AMZ* 1 (1874) 41–42. Idem, *Warum hat unsere Predigt nicht mehr Erfolg?* (1880). Wegener, R., "Das Gesetz in der missionarischen Verkündigung," *EMM* 61 (1917) 6–18. Wilson, P. S., *A Concise History of Preaching* (1992). Wohlrab, K., "Schöpfung, Sünde und Gnade in der afrikanischen Heidenpredigt," *Die deutsche evangelische heidenmission Jahrbuch* (1936) 28–35. Zahn, F., "Die evangelische Heidenpredigt," *AMZ* 22 (1895) 26–37.

❧ PROPHECY ❧

1. In the Old Testament. 2. In the New Testament. 3. In Later Church History. 4. Theological Assessment of Prophecy.

Prophets appear in most religions. Both the biblical prophets and other prophets within and outside Christianity deliver their prophecies either in a state of trance or in normal wakefulness. Thus the phenomenological criterion of ecstasy is not suitable as a theological criterion for a critical examination, whether positive or negative. The phenomenon is more widely spread than is generally accepted, especially in the →African independent churches (C. Baeta, D. B. Barrett, H. J. Greschat, G. Guariglia, K. Schlosser, B. Sundkler), in India (W. Hoerschelmann, P. S. Raj), in Korea, in Indonesia (T. Müller-Krüger), in Afro-Brazilian (M. Gerbert, D. Bento) and Afro-Caribbean (G. M. Mulrain) popular religion, and in Korean and north and central Asian shamanism (G. Schüttler). It was also known in the religion of the Greeks, Romans, Celts, Germans, and North American Indians. Recurring parallels can be shown between Israelite prophets and those outside Israel, between Hellenistic and Christian prophets, and between traditional African and Christian-African prophets, between pre-Christian and Christian prophets in Latin America. Prophecy appears as a form of prediction, as a pastoral instrument of counseling, and as proclamation on social issues. Real prediction, pastoral help, and social-critical analysis, as well as the misuse of prophecy for the purpose of extending the prophet's power, are all to be observed. In the following paragraphs the concentration will be on the prophets of the biblical tradition.

1. In the Old Testament, the borders between true and false prophets are fluid. The distinction was drawn between true and false prophecy generally in this way: what was recognized as true prophecy was handed down. This process of reception parallels T. Kuhn's model of the reception of a new paradigm by a community of scholars. False prophecy (with a few significant exceptions — see 1 Kings 22) was not accepted in the Old Testament tradition. True prophecy was always controversial at first. Examples are the economic, political controversy generated by Amos, Isaiah's criticism of the Jerusalem politics of alliances, and Jeremiah's demand that the exiles should make themselves at home in Babylon.

2. Prophecy in the New Testament has little in common with the prophecy handed down in the Old Testament. The great political, social, and theological themes of Old Testament prophecy are hardly articulated in New Testament prophecy. An exception is apparently found in Revelation, which takes up the religious heritage of Hellenism and late Jewish apocalyptic and processes them independently. Generally, prophecy was built into the liturgy and was understood as an instrument of proclamation for the whole community. Paul gives some minimal criteria for liturgical operation in 1 Corinthians 12–14. Prophecy should, like all other gifts of the Spirit, serve the "common use." It should not be opposed to the revelation of the word become flesh and should be open to judgment by others. Put in modern terms: prophecy must not destroy the relationship between the tradition and Jesus of Nazareth. It must edify the congregation (or society?), and it must submit to ecumenical criticism. It is a matter of indifference to Paul whether prophecy exists under ecstatic-enthusiastic conditions or whether it contains a precognitive element. Of note in this regard is Acts 21:4, 10–14, where Paul (or Luke?) does not contest the genuineness of prophecy (though he does not follow the advice of the prophet himself). That means for us, for whom an "altered state of consciousness" is suspect, that ecstatic and intuitive →communication (and not only what is rational and analytical) can have a prophetic content. Such communication must, however, be submitted to the same criteria as every other human opinion. It must be in harmony with the spirit of the gospel, responsible to the whole congregation, intelligible to the world (1 Cor 14:14–15), and useful, even if not necessarily accepted, proclamation.

3. In the early church, prophetic utterances occurred occasionally. Generally it is maintained that, nevertheless, prophecy was pushed aside more and more to the realm of schismatics and heretics (e.g., the Montanists). D. Hill, D. E. Aune, and others show convincingly that the prophetic role, which originally could be filled by any member of the congregation, was taken over very early on by "catechists, preachers, the educated, and the theologians." Its authority was based on the declaration and extrapolation of an existing tradition, especially the scriptures.

We find prophecy displaced to fringe church groups in the further history of the church: to the Albigensians, the Cathars, the Baptists, the Prophets of the Cevennes, and those involved in early Pietism, the Pentecostal movements, and the free churches (independent churches). The Reformers, especially Zwingli and Calvin, bound the prophetic gift to the preaching ministry, which, above all with Zwingli, was the responsibility not of a single pastor but of the whole congregation. The instrument for this was the *Prophezei,* a theological institute where lay people and theologians argued with each other about the practical applications of the biblical message — for example, economic and military-political implications.

Two prophets in church history can be particularly helpful to us in understanding the prophetic movements of the Third World: Blaise Pascal and George Fox. Pascal kept his ecstatic initiation into Christianity a secret all his life. He kept the record of his ecstatic experience in a memorial which was found after his death, sewn into his jacket. Pascal succeeded in communicating this experience of a prophetic call cognitively, without speaking of his personal experience at all.

George Fox is more important for us because he was the founder of a prophetic community in Europe (the Quakers). The Quakers (Society of Friends) have prophesied in important instances against the text of scriptures but in the spirit of the gospel. I mention only their policy of peace (for which they won the Nobel Peace Prize in 1947) and their fights against slavery (against such passages as 1 Cor 7:21; Eph 6:5; Col 3:22; Ti 2:9; Philemon 1; 1 Pt 2:28), against the death penalty (many texts in Exodus), against the corporal punishment of children (Prv 13:24), against the exclusion of girls from schools, against economic exploitation of American Indians, and against persecution of those of other faiths (as evidenced by William Penn and the founding of Pennsylvania). Their prophecy occurred because of a lifelong practice of silence in worship. Until recently, the Quakers were condemned as fanatics because their principle of "inner light" put them in conflict with the teachers and preachers of the institutional churches. Today, however, it has been increasingly recognized that the principle of "inner light" should be judged not in the abstract but by what it has taught the Quakers. We should recognize that in all important points of controversy the Quakers were in the right against the "Bible theologians."

4. Prophecy seems to be absent in Western churches today. The lexicon *Religion der Geschichte und Gegenwart,* for example, provides under the heading "Prophets" a great deal of material from the Bible and the history of religion but hardly any contributions from church history, practical theology, or systematic theology. One might conclude from this that prophecy in the Western churches is limited to the ordained ministry. However, this statement does not apply to many newly emerging churches of the Third World. It is an open question how far the prophetic phenomena of these churches are valid and applicable to the West. The ministerial proclamation of the church can hardly cover the whole spectrum of the prophetic legitimately. That proposition is already shipwrecked on the fact that the biblical prophets were seldom paid for their prophecy. The question becomes even more complicated when we consider that today a wide range of persons — for example, E. F. Schumacher ("Small is beautiful"), Einstein, and Bonhoeffer — are sometimes referred to as prophets.

This problem, along with contact with prophets from the Third World, makes it urgent to work out criteria for true prophecy. The following criteria are discussed in the literature:

- The true prophet agrees with scripture. This is a generally useless criterion because the true prophet will on occasion prophesy against the text of scriptures (see the above discussion of the Quakers), just as many banal or false prophets mouth Bible sayings with ease. In this respect, it makes no difference whether the prophecy is uttered in a trance or when awake.

- Matthew 7:16 states: "You will know them by their fruits." If this is a criterion of judgment and not (as applies to the prophet him- or herself) a criterion of action, then it is problematical. There are those who interpret the word "fruits" in terms of the prevailing morality. This association of the fruits of faith with the status quo and belittlement of controversial proclamation or faith as "superstition" has been commented upon by G. Theissen: "'Superstition' is...the faith rejected in a society. 'Faith' could ironically be defined as the officially recognized superstition. Where the line is to be drawn is determined by those wielding power" (Theissen 1974, 230). In his commentary on Matthew, U. Luz notes the problem of taking "fruits" as the deciding factor and proves this from the history of the effect of the text: "It was used so often because it was applicable to everything and against everything" (Luz 1985). The reduction of prophetic activity to what is acceptable is also responsible for the trivialities in many prophetic communications, including those from the other world.

- Deuteronomic theology suggests that a genuine precognition is a criterion of prophecy (Dt 18:22). This is not, however, appropriate as a criterion since precognition is a natural human gift, like singing, dancing, or dreaming. "The human soul possesses the ability, if one presupposes parapsychological talent, to read the past and the future" (A. Köberle). These gifts can be used "prophetically" as well as "physically."

- It is often said that true prophecy comes from God, false prophecy from human beings. This is a tautology, however. Whether one prophet speaks "from God" or not is indeed a matter for dispute. In addition, all prophets, including the great canonical prophets of the Old Testament, are influenced by their biographical, psychological, and cultural contexts. Even less useful is the statement that discerning the spirits is a pure "spiritual" gift.

- A "lived theology of the cross" is the most preferable "spiritual" criterion. Theissen describes the Jesus movement in the New Testament as "unstable" because it had within its ranks resistance fighters as well as collaborators with the Roman occupying power. The latent aggression against the Romans was "transferred," especially in the reworking of the death of the movement's leader. "The guilt of the Romans is not publicized here, but their own guilt....Jesus must die for our sins. The failed Messiah became the bringer of salvation" (Theissen 1974). That the guilt was projected onto a "scapegoat," the Messiah, was nothing special. However, that the Jesus movement identified itself with this scapegoat and celebrated him in the →Eucharist (Lord's Supper) turned human relationships upside down from within. "This reworking of aggression created space for the new vision of love and reconciliation, whose central point was the new command to love one's enemies. The existence of the 'vision' is itself an enigma. For the reverse conclusion is also possible: the presupposition of the different forms of reworking aggression was a basic agreement free of anxiety, a renewed basic trust in the reality which radiates from the figure of Jesus until today" (Theissen 1974).

A prophetic ministry is possible in a contemporary church that (in theological terms) is a lived theology of the cross and that (in psychological terms) fosters a reworking of aggression.

Instead of understanding themselves as censors of the prophets, church institutions should understand themselves as hosts for the reworking of aggression for a new vision of love and reconciliation. To demand prophecy from church leadership, bishops, or the World Council of Churches is an illusion. Whoever expects this misjudges the sociological reality of the upper echelons of church organizations, which, in the first place, defend their organization and, only in the second place, defend their gospel. What we can expect is that these ecclesiastical and ecumenical authorities will not in principle suppress criticism of themselves and of the social and church structures for which they are responsible and will leave it to others to determine whether such criticism is prophetic.

WALTER J. HOLLENWEGER

Bibliography

Amaladoss, M., "Mission as Prophecy," in *New Directions in Mission and Evangelization,* vol. 2 (1994) 64–72. Aune, D. E., *Prophecy in Early Christianity and the Ancient Mediterranean World* (1983). Baëta, C., *Prophetism in Ghana: A Study of Some "Spiritual" Churches* (1962). Barrett, D. B., *Schism and Renewal in Africa: An Analysis of Six Thousand Contemporary Religious Movements* (1968). Bento, D., *Malungo: Decodificação da Umbanda: Contribuicão à historia des religões* (1979). Brinton, H., *Friends for 300 Years: Beliefs and Practice of the Society of Friends* (1953). Buber, M., *The Prophetic Faith* (1949). Cavendish, R., *Encyclopedia of the Unexplained: Magic, Occultism, and Parapsychology* (1974). Dautzenberg, H., *Urchristliche Prophetie* (1975). Gagg, R., *Kirche im Feuer: Das Leben der südfranzösischen Hugenottenkirche nach dem Todesurtail durch Ludwig XIV* (1961). Gerbert, M., *Religionen in Brasilien* (1970). Gill, R., *Prophecy and Praxis* (1981). Greschat, H. J., *Westafrikanische Propheten: Morphologie einer religiösen Spezialisierung* (1974). Guariglia, G., *Prophetismus und Heilserwartungs-Bewegungen als völkerkundliches und religionsgeschichtliches Problem* (1959). Heschel, A., *The Prophets,* vol. 2 (1962). Hill, D., *New Testament Prophecy* (1979). Hoerschelmann, W., *Christliche Gurus: Darstellung von Selbstverständnis und Funktion indigenen Christseins durch unabhängige chrismatisch geführte Gruppen in Südindien,* Studien zur interkulturellen Geschichte des Christentums 12 (1977). Kelsey, M. T., *Prophetic Ministry: The Psychology and Spirituality of Pastoral Care* (1982). Köberle, A., "Okkultismus," *RGG* 3/4: 1614–19. Kuhn, T., *The Structure of Scientific Revolutions* (1970). Lindblom, J., *Prophecy in Ancient Israel* (1962). Luz, U., "Das Evangelium nach Matthäus (Mt 1–7)," *EKK* 1/1 (1985). Monloubou, L., *Los profetas del Antiguo Testamento* (1991). Müller-Krüger, T., *Der Protestantismus in Indonesien: Geschichte und Gestalt* (1968). Mulrain, G. M., *Theology in Folk Culture: The Theological Significance of Haitian Folk Religion* (1984). Overholt, T. W., *Channels of Prophecy: The Social Dynamics of Prophetic Activity* (1989). Idem, *Prophecy in Cross-cultural Perspective: A Sourcebook for Biblical Researchers* (1986). Raj, P. S., "A Christian Folk-Religion in India: A Study of the Small Church Movement in Andhra Pradesh, with a Special Reference to the Bible Mission of Devadas," *SDGSTh* 40 (1985). Schlosser, K., "Propheten in Afrika," *KGF* 3 (1949). Schüttler, G., *Die letzten tibetischen Orakelpriester: Psychiatrisch-neurologische Aspekte* (1971). Sullivan, F. A., *Charisms and Charismatic Renewal* (1982). Sundkler, B., *Bantu Prophets in South Africa* (1961). Sundkler, B., et al., "Propheten," *RGG* 3/5:608–35. Theissen, G., *Urchristliche Wundergeschichten* (1974). Yoccum, B., *Prophecy: Exercising the Prophetic Gifts of the Spirit in the Church Today* (1976).

❧ PROSELYTISM ❧

1. Development of the Term. 2. Proselytism as an Interconfessional Problem. 3. Mutual Respect and Cooperation. 4. The Present Situation.

1. The Greek term *proselytos* was used in the Septuagint to translate the Hebrew *gher,* meaning a stranger who resided for a long time or permanently in the country, stood in a certain relationship of bondage with the Israelite people, and consequently also entered into a religious relationship with Yahweh as the God of the covenant people. In the course of time the word took on a purely religious meaning and meant the crossing over from non-Jewish ("heathen") to Jewish society and the affirmation of Jewish monotheism ("God-fearing"), or it even implied full incorporation into the Jewish religious community by means of circumcision and commitment to the whole Torah (proselytism in the narrow sense). The New Testament mentions the fact of proselytism (Acts 2:11; 6:5; 13:43) and disapproves of the making of converts by any possible means (Mt 23:15). According to the scriptures (Old Testament and New Testament), the "proselyte" was a non-Jew who became a "Jew" by accepting the Jewish faith. Christianity took over the term analogically, so that proselytizing and the spread of the Christian faith (Christianizing, evangelizing, missionizing) were identical terms right up to recent times. But in Protestant circles M. Kähler already began to differentiate the concepts: "One makes proselytes, that is: imitations of what one is oneself." He did not, however, question the justification of offering the "missionary" message.

2. Mutual "sheep-stealing" within Christianity led to tensions. The first Protestant missionaries in the Middle East (P. Fisk and L. Parsons) were expressly instructed to work within the old Eastern churches but not to found Protestant communities of their own. But, since the mission to Muslims remained closed to them, very soon they began to found Protestant communities with Orthodox Christians. The missionaries tried to justify this on the grounds that the Orthodox communities were lethargic and corrupt. But the Orthodox church leaders condemned this as a dishonest practice, as proselytism in the negative sense. This conflict between the Eastern and Western churches has not yet quite come to an end. The Papal Secretary of State, Cardinal A. Casaroli, said that "proselytism" was one of the main problems between the Roman Catholic and Orthodox churches.

Similar clashes occurred as Protestant missionaries came to Latin America. In the beginning they were mainly interested in the dissemination of the Bible in the different vernaculars, then in pastoral ministry in the foreign and immigrant communities, and finally in the proclamation of the Protestant message in general and in community-building. The discontinuation of the monopoly of the Catholic Church in Latin America was desirable also from the Catholic point of view, but the way the struggle was carried on was no compliment to either side. Neither the rigid insistence of the Catholics on their historically inherited rights nor the "one-sided anti-Catholic orientation" of the Protestants (H.-J. Prien) reflect a Christian frame of mind. At the moment even the term "mission," used with regard to the relationship of the churches to each other, is frowned upon; and even more disagreeable is any kind of wooing away of each other's members by dishonest means and methods, that is, by proselytizing in the modern sense.

3. Mutual distrust and anathemization have considerably diminished during the past decades, and mutual respect and cooperation have developed in stages over the period.

3.1. The question of unity was urgent for the World Council of Churches from the beginning. The first plenary assembly at Amsterdam (1948) emphasized that common faith in Jesus Christ as God and savior is the real bond which must articulate itself in life and work. The so-called Toronto Declaration (1950) called the confession of Christ as the Divine Head of the Body the foundation for conversation, cooperation, and common witness. Evanston (1954) decided to make a study on the topic "proselytism and religious freedom," and the resulting document, *Christian Witness, Proselytism and Religious Liberty,* was accepted and published by the assembly in New Delhi (1961).

3.2. Religious liberty was a very difficult and hotly debated question at Vatican II. The decree *Dignitatis Humanae (DH)* was sent back for revision and subjected to correction several times. Eventually, on December 7, 1965, it was adopted by 2,308 "yes" to 70 "no" votes (8 invalid) and solemnly promulgated.

3.3. These fundamental declarations of the Catholic Church and the World Council of Churches led to a "joint working group" of Protestants, Orthodox, and Catholics to tackle the question of proselytism. The group began its work in 1965 and presented its first reports in 1966 and 1967. After churches and experts had carefully studied the matter and concluded that the issue was not only the elimination of incorrect attitudes but the promotion of positive cooperation, the document was reworked and published in May 1970 under the title *Common Witness and Proselytism* (text in: *ER* 23 [1971] 9–20).

3.4. This document begins with the basic statement: "Unity in witness and witness in unity...is the will of Christ for his people." The divisions of Christianity lasting for centuries are a counterwitness to the Christian message. Whereas the concepts apostolate, mission, confession, evangelism, kerygma, message, witness, common witness, and so on, are positively evaluated, the word "proselytism" comprises all improper attitudes and behavior in the practice of Christian witness that violate the right of the individual to be free from external coercion in religious matters. Without trying to deny the factors that divide the churches, we should acknowledge the riches which all have in common and bear common witness to them. On the one hand, the document appeals for these practical attitudes:

- the source of witness must be love;
- the main concern of witness must be the glory of God and the salvation of human beings and not the prestige of individual communities;
- witness must be nourished by the conviction that it is ultimately the Holy Spirit who brings about the response of faith to witness;
- witness must respect the free will and personal decision of the individual;
- witness must respect the rights of every person and community to witness to his or her own convictions, including religious convictions.

On the other hand, the following behavior is rejected:

- every type of physical coercion, moral constraint, or psychological pressure, including abuse of mass communications;
- every open or disguised offer of temporal or material benefits in return for change in religious adherence;
- every exploitation of need or weakness or lack of education in view of inducing adherence to a church;
- anything raising suspicion about the others' intentions;

- all political, social, or economic pressure in order to bring about conversions or to prevent others — minorities in particular — from exercising their right to religious freedom;

- every unjust or uncharitable reference to the beliefs or practices of others including spiteful condemnations: "In general, one should compare the good qualities and ideals or the weaknesses and practices of one community with those of the others, not one's ideals with the other's practice" (27).

4. The document *Common Witness and Proselytism,* as a product of Protestant, Orthodox, and Catholic teamwork, constitutes a high point in basic ecumenical declarations. But documents alone do not remove all practical difficulties. Renunciation of subjective convictions and inherited prejudices cannot be prescribed but is a process that comes about in patient searching, humble listening, common prayer and action, and a confidence in the grace of God. The realization that God wills unity and that no church possesses an absolute and exclusive monopoly on the truth facilitates an encounter. The further realization that individual conversions are perfectly reasonable and merit respect but will not bring about unity makes us more serene and provides sufficient space for organic growth and gradual maturation toward one another. We hope the times of bitter confrontation are gone forever. Mutual respect, dialogue in love, community in truth — including common witness — are the greatest needs of the moment. Christians divided among themselves are no genuine witness to the non-Christian world.

KARL MÜLLER, SVD

Bibliography

Armstrong, R. S., "Christian Witness, Proselytism and Religious Liberty," *ER* 13 (1960) 79–89. Idem, *Common Witness: A Study Document of the Joint Working Group of the Roman Catholic Church and the World Council of Churches* (1981). Idem, "Common Witness and Proselytism: A Study Document," *ER* 23 (1971). Idem, "The Integrity of Evangelism," *PSB* 3 (1981). Glassman, R. B., "An Evolutionary Hypothesis about Teaching and Proselytizing Behaviors," *Zygon* 15 (1980). Greenspahn, F. E., and M. Marty, *Pushing the Faith: Proselytism and Civility in a Pluralistic World* (1988). Hammer, R. J., "Proslytismus," in *Lexikon zur Weltmission* (1975) 446–47. Hanigan, J. P., "Conversion and Christian Ethics," *ThTo* 40 (April 1983) 25–35. Horner, N. A., "The Problem of Intra-Christian Proselytism," *IRM* 70 (1981) 304–13. Kähler, M., *Schriften zu Christologie und Mission* 28 (1971) n. 45. Loffler, P., "Proslytismus," in *Lexikon für Ökumene* 984–85. Míguez-Bonino, J., "A Mirror for the Ecumenical Movement? Ecumenism in Latin America," in *Voices of Unity* (1981) 41–56. Neuhausler, E., "Proselyten," *LThK* 8:810–11. Schreiter, R. J., "Changes in Roman Catholic Attitudes toward Proselytism," in *New Directions in Mission and Evangelization,* vol. 2 (1994). Triebel, J., *Bekehrung als Ziel der missionarischen Verkündigung* (1976). Valderrey, J., "Sekten in Mittelamerika," *PMVB* 100 (1985). Vatican II, "Decree on Ecumenism: Unitatis Redintegratio" (November 21, 1964). Idem, "Declaration on Religious Liberty: Dignitatis Humanae" (December 7, 1965). Idem, "Declaration on the Relation of the Church to Non-Christian Religions: Nostra Aetate" (October 28, 1965). World Council of Churches, *Christian Witness: Proselytism and Religious Liberty* (1961) Idem, "Common Witness and Proselytism," *ER* 23 (1971) 9–20.

✎ PROTESTANT COMMUNITIES AND ORDERS ✎

1. Origin. 2. Examples.

1. The same historical impulses, models, and influences of Anglican England that led to the emergence of →missionary societies also stimulated the development of Protestant communities. Pietism developed new forms of common life and the idea of communities (e.g., the Labadists, the Society of Women in the Wilderness, and the Ephrata Cloister in the United States). Some of the communities undertook responsibilities and tasks in foreign missions whereas others concentrated on home mission. The primary concern of all these movements was not the revival of the religious life but new forms of the apostolate. The social shock waves of World War II led to a new movement, so that throughout the whole Protestant world orders and communities, often quite unconnected, sprang up in the different denominations. They are to be compared not so much with the religious orders and congregations in the Catholic Church as with the secular institutes or the Little Sisters and Brothers of Jesus.

2. The external and internal ferment in the Protestant churches after World Wars I and II prepared the ground for the foundation of a new wave of religious communities. One could almost speak of a revival of Christian communities in the Protestant churches during this time, not least in the countries where the Reformation originated. The Evangelical-Ecumenical Brotherhood of St. John was originally founded in 1929 by F. Heiler (1892–1967) as the Protestant-Catholic Eucharistic Community. It is a High Church movement that aims at helping its members lead a deeper liturgical and Christian life. It had been preceded by the Evangelical Order of Humiliati (1921), a High Church movement with temporal vows. Together with G. A. Glinz, Heiler also founded a Protestant Franciscan third order (Evangelical Franciscan Brotherhood of the Following of Christ, 1927 Marburg). K. B. Ritter, W. Stählin, and others founded the Evangelical Michael Brotherhood (1931 Marburg) with the aim of renewing the liturgical and theological aspects of the Protestant church. The Jesus Brotherhood (1961) was an attempt to realize the common life within the Lutheran Church. Pastor E. Weschke founded the Gabriel Guild in 1958 as a Lutheran movement whose members would lead a religious life in their everyday environment. The Christus Brotherhood was founded in 1949 by H. and W. Hümmer in Selbnitz as a mixed Protestant brotherhood. The community of Imshausen (1949) is also a mixed community, with vows in the manner of Taizé (the first vows were taken in 1955). The Sydow Brotherhood (1922) is a union of Lutheran pastors, the Timotheus Brotherhood is a community of former church youth workers; and the Cornelius Brothers (or Brotherhood) is an association of former military officers. Of course, these communities are to be distinguished from groups that lead a common life in monastery-like foundations.

As early as 1936 young women came together in Darmstadt to form a prayer and Bible circle, and from this arose the community of the Evangelical (until 1964, Ecumenical) Marian Sisterhood under the leadership of P. Rieding and Sisters Basilea (Klara) Schlink and Martyria (Erika) Madauß. The Sisterhood of Prayer (1944) and the Irenenring Sisterhood are communities of faith and life for single women over twenty-one. A large circle of friends is associated with the Irenenring. The Society of Brothers incorporates the experiences of the common life of the Hutterites, including community of goods. Founded by E. Arnold (1883–1935) in 1920 in Germany, it has foundations today in Germany, Liechtenstein, Great Britain, Paraguay, Uruguay, and the United States (one reason for its spread was that in 1934 it was banned by the national socialists in Germany). Arnold was ordained by Hutterite ministers in 1930.

N. Söderblom (1866–1931) founded a number of communities in Scandinavia:

the Society of St. Birgitta, founded in 1920 for the promotion of liturgical life among pastors and laypeople (women and men) in the Lutheran Church of Sweden; and the Order of the Cross in Norway, founded in 1933 for pastors and laymen. Other communities in northern Europe are the Theological Oratorium (1926), founded by T. Lonborg-Jensen; the Fraternity of St. Ansgar (1933) in Denmark, since 1946 with a female branch; the Ecumenical Minor Sisters and the Daughters of Mary of Kollund (Denmark), inspired in 1936 by G. Norman (then Mother Paulina) and in 1958 officially founded with the help of Pastor Harritsoe. They live in small groups observing the three vows. The Holy Spirit Sisters (1954) take religious vows and live as a Lutheran community according to the Benedictine rule. Another community is the Swedish Sodality of Apostolic Confession (Sodalitium confessionis apostolicae).

In connection with the High Church movement, since 1841, 114 religious houses and communities have been founded. Of these 57 still exist today, for instance, the Society of the Sacred Mission (founded in Kelham in 1894) and the Community of the Resurrection (Mirfield, 1892). In Scotland, G. MacLeod founded the Iona Community in 1938. It includes pastors and laity, men and women. They follow a rule but have no perpetual vows and withdraw from time to time to a former monastic settlement on an island. There is no obligation to follow a common life — their "religious life" is the conscious Christian witness of life in their normal milieu.

In the French-speaking countries there are a number of communities which have an influence on the whole Protestant world. Les Veilleurs (the Watchers) was founded in 1923 by W. Monod for the cultivation of the Christian life in a kind of Franciscan third order. The Community of Pomeyrol is composed of sisters in the Reformed Church; the community was founded toward the end of the 1920s in Paris by A. Butte and then moved to Pomeyrol. They have perpetual vows, were intensely promoted by W. Monod, and enjoy the constant guidance of the Theological Faculty of Montpellier. The beginnings of the community of Taizé go back to 1939, to the Grande Communauté in Lausanne, an association of students under R. Schutz formed for the purpose of study and prayer. Taizé was founded in 1944; in 1949 the first vows were taken; and in 1952–53 the rule was worked out. In Switzerland there is the Community of Grandchamp. In 1931 a number of women gathered for a period of spiritual recollection. As a result of the constant contact and the service for others there arose a community of sisters under the superior Sister G. Micheli. The sisters are guided and directed by Taizé. The first vows were taken in 1952, and the rule of Taizé was adopted in 1953. In 1954 the Community of Villemétrie was founded. No vows are taken so that there will be no restriction of the Protestant liberty of Christian living, but the community does have a rule for common life. The task of the community is research in modern theology and ethics.

In Italy the Waldensian Agape Community was founded by T. Vinay in 1961, but its beginnings go back to 1946–47. The members living in community follow a rule. In the United States there are, among others, the Koinonia Farm and the Fellowship of St. Augustine, and in South Africa the Transvaal Mission Brotherhood. Since 1923 brotherhoods have been increasingly developing in churches around the world — for example, in China, Japan, Nigeria, and India (the Christian Ashram Fellowship).

Today there are about sixty communities of various sizes and organizational principles. Crises, divisions, and dissolutions form part of the picture of this dynamic movement in the Protestant world today.

The goal of all these communities is the thorough Christianization of life by means of missionary witness and service. Furthermore, some groups dedicate themselves to serving churches overseas.

HORST RZEPKOWSKI, SVD

Bibliography

Alvárez, J. "La vida religiosa en las iglesias protestantes," *VidRel* 36 (1974) 227–38. Barrie, W., *The Franciscan Revival in the Anglican Communion* (1982). Bracht, H., "Luthers Urteil über die Mönchsgelübde in ökumensicher Betrachtung," *Catholica* (Münster) 21 (1967). Biot, F., *The Rise of Protestant Monasticism* (1963). Edel, G., "Die evangelische Brüderschaftsbewegung in Europa,"*ARGG* 12 (1960) 302–22. Halkenhauser, J., *Kirche und Kommunität: Ein Beitrag zur Geschichte und zum Auftag der Kommunitären Bewegungen in den Kirchen der Reformation* (1978). Ispert, B., "Mönchtum und Protestantismus," *EuA* 49 (1973) 312–19. Lohse, B., *Mönchtum und Reformation: Luthers Auseinandersetzung mit dem Mönchsideal des Mittelalters* (1963). Mudge, B., "Monastic Spirituality in Anglicanism," *RevRel* 37 (1978) 505–15. Mumm, R., *Ökumene in brüderschaftlichen Leben* (1971). Reiner, I., *Alternativ leben in verbindlichter Gemeinschaft: Evangelische Kommunitäten, Lebensgemeinschaften, Junge Bewegungen* (1979). Roger, F., *Living Today for God* (1962). Scharffenorth, G., *Schwestern: Leben und arbeiten evangelischer Schwesterngemeinschaft: Absage an Vorurteile* 1984). Schreiter, W., *Evangelisches Mönchtum, Entwicklung und Aufgabe der Brüder- und Schwesternschaften in der Kirche* (1964). Stökl, A., *Taizé: Geschichte und Leben der Brüder von Taizé* (1980).

R

♔ RECONCILIATION ♕

1. Biblical and Theological Meaning. 2. Theology of Reconciliation in Mission.

The term "reconciliation" is used to convey a wide variety of contemporary meanings. In situations of arbitration, it means the cessation of hostility. In the language of the divorce court, it means the end of the separation of an estranged couple. In a highly ideologically charged manner in contemporary Latin America, it has been proposed as a conservative alternative to liberation theology, a usage begun in the Los Andes Statement of 1985 and continued in the Santo Domingo documents of the Fourth General Conference of CELAM, the organization of the episcopal conferences of Latin America. In recent times, reconciliation has become the byword for getting beyond the tragedies and atrocities of war, dictatorship, and apartheid in Latin America and South Africa or for the healing of the European continent after the collapse of the Berlin Wall in 1989. It was, for example, the theme of the Second European Ecumenical Assembly in 1997. In some instances, reconciliation as a concept has been conflated with forgiveness, justice, reparation, and expiation. In other instances, it has been seen as the end point of a process that includes all of these. It is also used by others as a codeword for granting amnesty to wrongdoers, repressing memories of atrocity, and returning to some semblance of a normal way of life. Theologically, "reconciliation" has traditionally had more specific usages. It was one of several words, used already in the New Testament, for God's saving activity in the world through Christ. For Roman Catholics the term has been associated especially with the sacrament of the same name, whereby the penitent is absolved of sin and brought back to harmonious relationship with God. For twentieth-century Protestants, it is associated especially with the fourth part of K. Barth's monumental *Church Dogmatics,* where God's purposes for the world are explored.

Because of the dramatic events of the end of the twentieth century — a time when a number of wars and dictatorships came to an end — reconciliation has taken on a missiological significance, not only as a way of speaking of God's good news for the world but as a way of doing mission itself.

1. Reconciliation in the broad senses outlined above can be found throughout the Bible, in stories such as the reunion of Isaac and Esau (Genesis 33) or of Joseph and his brothers (Genesis 45) and in the parables such as that of the lost sheep or the prodigal son (Luke 15). The Day of Atonement, which is mirrored in Christ's expiatory death, is seen by some as a model of reconciliation. The word *katallassein* (to reconcile) is used, however, only thirteen times in the New Testament, and then exclusively in the Pauline and Deutero-Pauline correspondence. J. Comblin has suggested that the concept of reconciliation in Paul (the term itself meaning in Greek to make peace after a time of war) functions on three levels: a christological level, of God reconciling the world through Christ (Rom 5:11); an ecclesiological level, with Christ reconciling Jew and Gentile (Eph 2:12–16); and a cosmic level, where Christ reconciles all the spirit and powers of the universe, whether in heaven, on earth, or under the earth (Col 1:19–20). The reconciling work of Christ is now entrusted to the church in a ministry of reconciliation (2 Cor 5:11–21).

The Christian teaching on reconciliation, based on Paul, can be summarized in five points. First, reconciliation is the work of God, who initiates and completes reconciliation in Christ. Reconciliation is not, therefore, a human work, but the work of God within us. Paul's point is important to remember since the experience of the need for reconciliation invariably carries with it the sense of the enormity, the complexity, and the near impossibility of the task. That reconciliation is quintessentially the work of God is evidenced in the fact that reconciliation is experienced typically first in the life of the victim and not in the repentance of the wrongdoer. It can be characterized as the experience of grace — the restoration of one's damaged humanity to the life-giving relationship with God. While some literature on reconciliation focuses on the important matter of repentance and forgiveness, it should not be forgotten that reconciliation as understood here is a prior condition, not a result of repentance and forgiveness.

Second, because reconciliation is principally God's work for which we are but "ambassadors for Christ's sake" (2 Cor 5:20), it could be characterized more as a spirituality than a strategy. There can be strategies in the sense of step-by-step procedures in the arbitration of grievances, but reconciliation in this theological sense is a way of living that creates the space for new possibilities. Again, it is usually the reconciled victim who takes the lead, experiencing the grace of reconciliation as a vocation to heal the situation and the wrongdoer. That spirituality includes truth-telling, where lies had created the atmosphere that made wrongdoing the rule of the day; creation of community, especially in situations of dictatorship where middle-level and communal social structures had been dismantled for the sake of control; and safety, that trust might be reestablished.

Third, the experience of reconciliation makes of both victim and wrongdoer a new creation (2 Cor 5:17). The experience of God's reconciling work in Christ is not a restoration to our former state but, through the resurrection, is the dawning of a new humanity. This is corroborated in the experience of reconciled victims: the experience is not what they had imagined it to be, but rather finds them led to a new place. Here one encounters also the difficult area of justice and forgiveness. Seen in this light, justice cannot be equated with a form of restitution, since restitution is in so many instances impossible (as in the case of those who have died) or has no demonstrable equivalent (as in the case of punishment). What will constitute justice therefore is best proposed by those who have experienced reconciliation. Similarly, the complexities of forgiveness and the healing of memories must also be seen from the perspective of a new creation rather than the restoration of the old. Forgiving and healing are not matters of forgetting, as in the adage "Forgive and forget." One can never forget, but one can remember in a different way; that is, a memory can now give life to the future rather than dwelling on the undeniable hurt of the past. The model here is Christ's appearance to Thomas in John 20: the glorified body of Christ still bears the scars of his torture, but they are now sources of healing for Thomas.

Fourth, the process of reconciliation that creates the new humanity is the narrative of the passion, death, and resurrection of Christ. The passion and death are remembered not for the gruesome and unjust torture they were but as a "dangerous memory" (J. B. Metz) that subverts the power of injustice that estranges humanity and the world from God. The resurrection is the confirmation and the manifestation of God's power over evil. The stories of the appearances of the risen Christ are stories of God's healing and forgiving power in the world. At the center of all of this stands the cross, at once a symbol of powerlessness, the abuse of power, and God's power. Its paradoxical quality reaches down into the mystery of violence and of healing. To come to understand the meaning of the cross is to plumb the meaning of reconciliation.

Fifth, reconciliation reveals the complexity of the world to be reconciled. The challenge of reconciliation is always a daunting one, but its eventual dimensions are usually not able to be grasped until the process is well along the way. For that reason the final state of reconciliation cannot be described at the outset, nor can its course be programmed at the beginning. For the reasons mentioned above — it is the work of God, it is more spirituality than strategy, it is a new creation, it is encompassed in the mystery of the cross — it ultimately can only be grasped cosmically and perhaps eschatologically.

2.   Given this understanding of reconciliation, can it be a form of mission? Some, with D. Bosch, have argued that the end of the twentieth century needs a new paradigm for mission. If one looks at the situations which framed — for better or for worse — earlier notions of mission, one might be able to go beyond the somewhat general proposal of an ecumenical paradigm that Bosch offered. If much of nineteenth- and twentieth-century mission occurred in the framework of colonialism and was often characterized as bringing civilization, education, and health to benighted peoples, and if the next phase occurred in the postcolonial period of nation-building, where mission was expressed in terms of solidarity with struggling people (embodied in dialogue, liberation, and inculturation), then perhaps the dramatic events that frame the end of the century point in another direction. That direction is reconciliation. Given the tumultuous events of the twentieth century, the lingering wounds of colonialism, and the yawning gap created by the relentless march of technology and capitalism, reconciliation recommends itself as a suitable frame for mission and expression of the good news of Jesus Christ. Reconciliation acknowledges the enormity of the task created by the consequences of history and the centrifugal powers of the present. It also provides a new frame for considering dialogue, liberation, and inculturation that moves beyond the optimism that spawned those approaches but does not give up their deepest intentions. Dialogue takes on a new form as it looks to a kind of reconciliation that brings all partners to a new place. Liberation continues the struggle for justice but can acknowledge that the justice it seeks may not come as quickly as had once been anticipated. Inculturation can be understood as an affirmation of memory and identity without collapsing into a divisive and dangerous factionalism. Reconciliation as a form of mission acknowledges the centrality of truth in a world enmeshed in lies, seeks safety and security as the basis for trust, and works toward community in situations of displacement and isolation. Its profoundly paradoxical view of the world helps it balance the ironies and complexities of a world of violence without sacrificing the dream of a new humanity.

Robert J. Schreiter, CPPS

Bibliography

Barth, K., *CD,* pt. 4, "The Doctrine of Reconciliation" (1956). Bosch, D., *Transforming Mission* (1991). Comblin, J., "O tema de reçonciliação e a teologia na América Latina," *REB* 46/192 (1986)

272–314. Duchrow, U., *Versöhnung im Kontext der Nicht-Versöhnung* (1996). Metz, J., *Befreiendes Gedächtnis Jesu Christi* (1970). Müller-Fahrenholz, G., *Vergebung macht frei: Vorschläge für eine Theologie der Versöhnung* (1996). Schreiter, R. J., *Reconciliation: Mission and Ministry in a Changing Social Order* (1992). Idem, "Reconciliation as a Model of Mission," *NZM* 52/4 (1996) 1–8. Weckel, L., "Menschenrechtsverbrechen und Versöhnung: Zum Gebrauch des Versöhnungsbegriffs in Kirche und Theologie," *ZMR* 79 (1995) 305–12.

❧ REIGN OF GOD ❧

1. The Reign of God and the Missionary Movement. 2. Present and Future of the Reign of God. 3. The Reign of God as New Creation. 4. The Reign of God and the Poor. 5. The Reign of God in the Sign of the Cross. 6. The Signs of the Reign of God. 7. The Reign of Reconciliation. 8. Thy Kingdom Come!

1. In the West, until modern times, the biblical picture of the world and history, stamped by apocalyptic (→apocalyptic and mission), was the frame of reference for all expectations regarding the future; the immortality of the soul was also included in this premodern understanding. The Enlightenment and the modern critique of religion, however, criticized what they perceived as the devaluation of the "here and now," a false consolation in the next world, and any vision of the world to come that was a mere projection of this world as people experienced it. Nevertheless, since →eschatology is a basic element of the Christian message and faith (A. Schweitzer, J. Weiss), there have been a number of attempts to reestablish the value of the biblical symbol which best expresses the essence of Christian hope: the reign of God. These attempts can be reduced to four basic types, which, singly or in combination, have significance for mission and ecumenism today.

a. The reign of God is the reign of morality. Hope for the future belongs to the realm of personal certainty and trust. "Nothing can separate us from the love of God" (Rom 8:38).

b. The reign of God is the reign of messianic peace, righteousness, and reconciliation. It is for the poor and the oppressed. "Behold, I make all things new" (Rv 21:5).

c. The reign of God is the reign of the Judge. In the face of secularism and modern tendencies of salvation through self-help, one should remember the coming judgment on human sins and the salvation of believers. "Since we must all appear before Christ's judgment seat, so that each one may receive good or evil, according to what he has done in the body..." (1 Cor 5:10).

d. The reign of God is God's mission to the world and the active mission of people in the world, who are directed to the coming reign of God and proclaim it. Traditional concepts of church and mission must constantly be revised in the light of this: "And this gospel of God's reign will be preached throughout the whole world, as a testimony to all nations; and then the end will come" (Mt 24:14).

The modern missionary movement therefore asks social questions regarding the reign of God. It has always been the church's concern to advance the reign of God on earth, although the abandonment of missionary activity because of fanatical chiliastic assumptions or apocalyptic expectations would also be within the realm of possibility for some church traditions. Mission — following the messianic prophecies ("The hand on the clock of the reign of God" [J. H. Jung-Stilling]) —

is *praxis pietatis* and, as such, the work of the reign of God. Even when mission was understood primarily as saving souls as well as a contribution to social discipline (H. Lehmann), the theology of the reign of God included the possibility of a purification of the missionary motive and of the critique of missionary theory and practice. So the impetus for the emancipation of slaves and the reestablishment of human dignity could originate from the pietist revival movement.

Mission in the twentieth century, understood as participation in God's mission in and to the world, nourishes itself in the same way as the struggle for justice for the poor and bases itself on the message of the reign of God that was preached by Jesus and the early church. This theology of mission has been influenced by — and influences in turn — intensive exegetical, hermeneutical, and dogmatic concerns. These will be discussed below, with some problems which are also important for the →theology of mission.

2. The biblical expectation of the reign of God emerges from the tensions created between the Hebrew tradition of liberation and justice and the actual situation of Israel as unfaithful to its covenant responsibilities. Yahweh's coming and the messianic hope of all-embracing *shalom* (→peace and mission) in history and in nature underwent significant development before the appearance of Jesus, whose message can be summarized in the Marcan proclamation: "The reign of God is at hand, repent and believe in the gospel" (Mk 1:15). Transmitted in various forms and formulated against an apocalyptic background, this central statement functions as the criterion of Jesus' messianic behavior. As the Christian community formulated it, the reign of God appeared in person in →Jesus. Such a statement expresses the basic certainty of faith, without ignoring its difference from all other experiences. →God is still hidden; God's sovereignty is still confessed; but it is a sovereignty that reaches out to the world. Time receives direction through the reign of God, and history is given a meaning. Existence becomes a struggle for enduring love and justice. And yet that which is to come is already immersed in history. The reign of God already has a history in the mission of Jesus. The time of the "not-yet" stands under the sign of "no-more" and within the sign of "now-already." This makes hope realistic and reality full of hope (J. Moltmann).

Since Kant, the modern person has viewed the hope of the reign of God as suspect. The "last things" are not in the next world but in the present one. In fact, what the Bible teaches about history and the end of history is not to be understood as referring chronologically to the "present world" and the "next world," or spatially to "within the world" and "beyond the world," or metaphysically to "time" and "eternity"; rather, the biblical worldview of apocalyptic understands the announcement of the reign of God as the proclamation of the future as a power determining the present, even though that reign is hidden.

Modern experience teaches us also that another age must break into the present to give hope. We know from the Christian message of the reign of God that →salvation is near and that freedom, even in the midst of the misery of the present, is possible. In the longing of faith, in the obedience of the body, in liberation, and in new beginnings, the reign begins in the midst of history but remains hidden in the present. Therefore one may not play off common sense against →eschatology. The reign of peace is also eminently necessary for reason, since eschatology must be secularized in order that the "genesis of rights" (E. Bloch) can begin. Thus the God of hope and God's reign, which has become present in Jesus, help create justice for the poor, love for the weak, community for those without God, and integrity in nature.

3. The opposite of inwardness and materialism, individualism and collectivism, the reign of God means a new way of understanding the material world and inaugurates attitudes not of passive resignation but of genuine hope. The tradition of modernity localizes the "last things" in the activity of the human spirit. Such a view should be seen not as a resistance to the Christian hope of God's reign but as the striving of a life that wants authentic freedom — "the spirit of life because of righteousness" (Rom 8:11). The eschatological Spirit of God is at work under conditions of righteousness and protects life by renewing it. The presence of the Spirit inaugurates a new creation. As the spirit of resurrection, God's Spirit is the spirit of life; to know that the Spirit creates life and maintains it helps to sustain a spirit of life in the face of death. The word of God's reign gives even the dead a future. It is a word of justice and resistance, therefore, and stands against any attempt to push ultimate human fulfillment into a vague hope of "pie in the sky when we die."

The expectation of the reign of God as new creation assimilates the experience of negative reactions to projects of hope and to hopeful pictures and images. We can speak of a new heaven and new earth only in parables, and speech in metaphors is a sign that Jesus as Christ is not yet made manifest. Parables make possible the vision of what should be (M. Buber). To disqualify them from the very beginning as improper is mistaken. Although their images are often remote from the realities of today's world, they repay study because through them are presented the alternatives of salvation and damnation, and urgent questions are asked about human hope and meaning.

4. Today's theology of mission strongly emphasizes the close connection between the reign of God and the poor, connection made both in the Old Testament (Leviticus 25) and in the New Testament (Matthew 5; Lk 4:18). Connections are also made to the understanding of the reign of God which has been developed in the tradition of Christian socialism. The encounter with the poor peoples of the Third World and with the "church of the poor" has given a face to oppression, deprivation, suffering, and loss of rights but also to redemption and promise. Jesus preached the gospel of God's reign to the poor: that is, the ruined, the imprisoned, the blind, the lame, the lepers, and the dead. Biblically, poverty extends from economic, social, and physical marginalization to psychological, moral, and religious deprivation. The poor are those who have nothing to live for and receive nothing from life. "Wealth," therefore, is multidimensional, and its meaning stretches from economic exploitation by social domination to the self-satisfaction of those who are in power. The good news preached to the poor brings *both* rich and poor, healthy and ill, powerful and powerless into a community of the poverty of all people before God, but the concrete form of the coming rule of God is the community of the poor and converted, whose redemption is promised. Jesus' mercy is for groups who lack bread and respect in society. They are blessed because they are helpless and rely only on hope. Following Christ consists of leading a life of love and solidarity with the poor and outcast. However, the decisive aid to the poor takes place in God's invitation to them to full participation in God's reign. The assertion that Christ is present in the poor is important in this connection (Mt 25:31–46). The coming judge of the world is present in his lowliest brothers; what one does to them, one does to him. Solidarity with the poor takes place, however, also in the cross and resurrection of Jesus. In the context of the breaking in of the reign of God, the cross is the confrontation with the ruling powers of enslavement; this situation of oppression appears to triumph now, but in reality it is already defeated. The reign of God will be resisted by the established powers; it makes them poor and leads to suffering, but as the cross of those awakened by God, it is an alternative to the domination of the mighty and also the "power of the powerless."

The messianic role of the poor, of course, can be ideologically misused. Hence the christological anchoring in the marginalized existence of Jesus "crucified outside the gate" (Heb 13:12) is even more important.

5. The hidden reign of God is already present in Jesus and his actions. Christ, therefore, is our hope (1 Tm 1:1; Col 1:27). This is the key statement of all hopes and at the same time the essence of a reflective interpretation of the message of the reign of God. Eschatology without →christology is blind, and vice versa. The story of Jesus, his death, and his resurrection have revealed what will come to be. Therefore, Christians' hope and struggle are hope and struggle for the foundations of a new humanity and the new world. Faith in God's reign knows of no society free of suffering and guilt; it uncovers the "anonymous history of the suffering of the world" (J. B. Metz) and opposes it. German theologian J. B. Metz criticizes the "pseudo-religious symbol of evolution," which dreams of an eternity free of surprises and in which all and everything are included without grace. The symbols of God's reign, communicated by the cross, mean instead "interruption."

6. The church takes its identity from its mission to preach, serve, and witness to the reign of God. It is an anticipatory sign, living by the standard of God's reign and the righteousness of that reign. It prays on behalf of the human community. It celebrates the coming of God's reign and proclaims and serves it as God's missionary people (C. van Engen). Catholicity and unity are understood as eschatological goals, although present in mystery. Word and sacrament, ministry and charisms are understood as agencies of God's reign with which the church demonstrates its hope as messianic community; through these it translates this hope into action aimed at structuring the present in terms of the eschatological spirit of God in history. "But if we hope for what we do not see, we wait for it in patience" (Rom 8:25). Waiting, however, does not happen without confirmatory signs. In →baptism, the church displays faith in its origin and celebrates the secret of its awakening. In the Lord's Supper, it displays hope in the future and receives the gifts of creation as provisions for the journey (E. Jüngel). The sacraments bring the history of God together with the reality of our life. They are food for missionaries. The signs of God's reign are, therefore, not mere signs of remembrance of the crucified and resurrected one; they are also signs of his future. Because the Spirit is tied to concrete institutions, one can justifiably identify God's presence in the signs. As long as God does not confirm the meaning which the signs bear, however, everything remains open and is therefore exposed to contradictions and rejection. Faith counts on the hope proclaimed and represented by the signs of God's reign-becoming-reality. That God keeps faithful to what is right (Psalm 50) is the reason for all hope. The reign's truth remains open and is nothing other than having hope. Ecclesiocentricity and naive sacramentalism are unthinkable within such an understanding. That God preserves what is right and so advances the reign is, then, the basis of the promise and conviction over which faith rejoices.

7. "In Christ, God was...entrusting the message of reconciliation to us" (2 Cor 5:19). The goal of the reign of God is reconciliation, the removal of the difference between faith and knowledge, nature and grace, hope and experience — a difference we have already become conscious of through the promise. If the reign of God — and God as such as its content — is reconciliation and →communication, that is, the removal of ambiguity and contradiction, then the reign is not a reconciliation constructed by insidious means or by mere piety in the face of the horrors and terrors in the world. The word of reconciliation says: reconciliation is something different from anything hitherto experienced. Precisely because the Christian community is turned toward the "future of reconciliation," it maintains that reconciliation does not belong to the present situation but lies in the future as a utopia, which has to be outlined and realized. Conflicts that belong to the present situation are transcended in the act of reconciliation and are overcome by courageous and creative interventions. So the moment of imminence cannot be lost, but the moment of division should not be extinguished, lest the word of reconciliation become a cynical reactionary promise. God's truth is reconciliation, but its ultimate form is not yet accomplished. One may neither leap over the difference nor consign all reconciliation to the future. Otherwise the new thing is lost, and the difference between the realization of the hope now possible and the leaven which makes this possible is abandoned. The concerns of →black theology and →liberation theology teach us such distinctions. There is no real reconciliation if it is not preceded by actual historical liberation. The on-the-road character of Christian and church existence within the horizon of God's reign has been a part of ecumenical conviction since Vatican II. It belongs to missionary experience.

8. Just as in the entire biblical tradition the active effort for the reign of God and its righteousness is connected with patient waiting for its coming, so action and patient waiting find their way into the language of →prayer. "Thy kingdom come" (Mt 6:10) and "Maranatha" (1 Cor 16:22; Rv 22:20) provide the evidence for this. Against all hope, the reality of evil can make itself felt. Set against its crushing weight, talk of the reign of God appears once again as idealistic prattle. The hope of God's reign takes up the prayer of the reign against evil. As redemption from evil is no accomplished fact, neither is the reign: redemption and salvation ultimately constitute a hope that is expressed in prayer. Contrary to widespread opinion, and in spite of all admirable "works of the reign," prayer acknowledges a final dependence on God. The reign of God is not the reign of human beings, although it involves people in its coming to fulfillment. All missionary work is eschatologically directed. It begins with prayer for the reign. Because the reign of God is in our midst (Lk 17:21), hope for it can no longer be without worldly dimensions — so much remains within our power to move closer to love. This obliges us to analyze reality more intensely. The prayer "Thy kingdom come" is reason enough. In no way do we build God's reign, yet it is in part based on the human community in the light of our hopes for the future. The "Maranatha" takes care that the prayer for God's reign does not secretly degenerate ideologically. We pray for the coming of the Lord, whose presence, when completely revealed, will make prayer for God's reign unnecessary because then God will be all in all (1 Cor 15:28). At that time, the aim and goal of mission will have been attained.

KLAUSPETER BLASER

Bibliography

Barth, K., *The Christian Life: Lecture Fragments* (1981). Blaser, K., "Mission und Erweckungsbewegung," in *Pietismus und Neuzeit: Jahrbuch zur Geschichte des neueren Protestantismus,* vol. 7 (1982) 128–46. Bornkamm, G., *Jesus of Nazareth* (1960). Bright, J., *Kingdom of God in Bible and Church* (1953). Buess, E., *Gottes Reich für diese Erde* (1981). Castro, E., *Freedom in Mission: The Perspective of the Kingdom of God* (1985). Coppens, J., *La relève apocalyptique du messianisme royal* (1979). Cornehl, P., *Die Zukunft der Versöhnung* (1971). Cullmann, O., *Christ and Time* (1946). Freytag, W., "Mission im Blick aufs Ende," in *Reden und Aufsätze* 2 (1961). Füllenbach, J., *The Kingdom of God* (1995). John Paul II, Pope, *Redemptoris Missio* (1990). Kasper, W., *Jesus the Christ* (1976). Kraus, H. J., *Reich Gottes — Reich der Freiheit* (1975). Küng, H., *The Church* (1967). Ladd, G. E., *The Presence of the Future: The Eschatology of Biblical Realism* (1974). Magaña, A. Q., *Eclesiología en la teología de la liberación* (1983). McBrien, R. P., *Do We Need the Church?* (1969). Metz, J. B., *Faith in History and Society: Towards a Practical Fundamental Theology* (1980). *Mission and Evangelism — an Ecumenical Affirmation* (1982). Moltmann, J., *The Church in the Power of the Spirit* (1975). Idem, *Theology of Hope* (1967). Idem, *The Trinity and the Kingdom of God* (1981). Newbigin, L., *Sign of the Kingdom* (1981). Idem, *Your Kingdom Come* (1980). Nordsieck, R., *Reich Gottes — Hoffnung der Welt* (1980). Osthatios, M. G., *Theology of a Classless Society* (1980). Pannenberg, W., *Theology and the Kingdom of God* (1969). Paul VI, Pope, *Evangelii Nuntiandi* (1975). Pernia, A. M., *God's Kingdom and Human Liberation* (1990). Pixley, G., *God's Kingdom* (1981). Rahner, K., "The Hermeneutics of Eschatological Assertions," in *TI,* vol. 4 (1966) 323–46. Schnackenburg, R., *God's Rule and Kingdom* (1963). Schreiter, R. J., *Reconciliation: Mission and Ministry in a Changing Social Order* (1992). Snyder, H. A., *The Community of the King* (1977). Idem, *A Kingdom Manifesto* (1985). Idem, *Liberating the Church: The Ecology of Church and Kingdom* (1983). Idem, *Models of the Kingdom* (1991). Sobrino, J., *Christology at the Crossroads* (1976). Song, C. S., *The Compassionate God* (1982). Tillich, P., *Systematic Theology,* vol. 3 (1963). Van Engen, C., *God's Missionary People: Rethinking the Purpose of the Local Church* (1991). Verkuyl, J., *Contemporary Missiology* (1978). Visser't Hooft, W. A., *The Kingship of Christ* (1948). Viviano, B., *The Kingdom of God in History* (1986). Walther, C., *Typen des Reich Gottes Verständnisses* (1961).

❧ RELIGION, RELIGIONS ❧

1. Problems of Definition. 2. The Essence of Religion. 3. Types of Religion. 4. The History of Religion. 5. Syncretism. 6. A Critique of Religion. 7. Models of the Theological Assessment of Religion.

1. The question What is religion? betrays its Western origin. Such a question is possible only where there is a difference between the totality of a culture and its religion. In cultures where religion is an integral part of the whole way of life and is not shunted out to the margins, where it is understood as the total way of life of the community and the individuals within it (as in Eastern cultures) or as the basis of all the institutions of life (as in tribal societies), this question is not asked. There is a complete absence of any specific term that is applicable only to religion. It is significant that the problem of defining religion was urgent in the Roman state. In the Roman state one's entire life was ordered and controlled by a comprehensive legal system, and religion also had to be defined as part of public life and manageable within a legal framework.

The derivation of the word "religion" leads us no further forward, especially as the Latin offers a great variety of meanings. Should *religio* be derived from *relegere* (= to reunite, from *religere* = to observe cautiously) or from *religare* (= to bind up, to bind fast, to be led away)? The problem is intensified by our having to define a phenomenon which, on the one hand, possesses universal validity and dimension but, on the other hand, must bring within one term such differing realities as Hinduism (even describing that as one religion creates its own difficulties), Islam, Shintoism, and Tibetan Buddhism.

Maximum and minimum definitions (e.g., "Religion is intimacy with the holy") can be understood in either an inclusive or an exclusive sense. On the one hand, they could include Marxism, but, on the other hand, they might not apply to Buddhism because it appears to exclude the conception of God. Moreover, there are the various goals and interests within the different branches of the discipline called history of religion. It makes a great difference whether religion is defined functionally from the sociological point of view; from that of psychology, which confines itself mainly to religiosity; from the viewpoint of philosophers of religion who see a system of direction in religion; or from that of students of the phenomenology of religion who advocate a substantial or real definition and to a large extent refrain from value judgments.

2. The essence of religion is a complex matter that must be examined in terms of a number of elements.

2.1. There is no religion without experience of the transcendent. Such experiences take so many forms that they cannot be reduced to one common denominator. The variety seems to be infinite. In most religions the entry of God into the life of a group or an individual is formative. This experience takes on central importance and defines a person's relationship to the world and to himself or herself. The prerequisite of this experience is the separation of heaven and earth; it is the basic experience of human beings and the mythological preface of all tribal religions. Ultimately it is a difference only of degree whether the experience of God is conceived more in relation to human beings and their bodies (as in African tribal religions), to nature (Indian religions), to the cosmos (Chinese religions), or to categories of personal histories (the "prophetic" religions), or is formulated so abstractly that God is no longer even included (early Buddhism). The enlightenment of the Buddha must be mentioned at this point. In spite of his long preparation, it was the sudden experience of enlightenment that radically changed the Buddha's life, his ethics, and his thinking. Buddha called that which he had recognized in the enlightenment experience the "Unconditional, the Unchangeable, the Unapproachable." With this "knowing," salvation is possible, and he taught his disciples that they could partake of it now insofar as they achieve enlightenment. Buddha denied the actual existence of God, yet he filled the "god-shaped gap," on the one hand, with ideas of Nirvana and dharma (the eternal law which controls everything of a transitory nature) and, on the other hand, with concepts which in other religions are predicates of God.

At this point it is important to remember that one cannot, in terms of the history of religion, recognize any "development" in the experience of God (i.e., from vague spirits in animism, through polytheism to monotheism), as an earlier generation of scholars believed, but that behind every monotheistic or polytheistic experience of God there stands the tribal religion's knowledge of one all-embracing and all-conditioning reality, called God, and this knowledge is its precondition (Pettazzoni 1960, 81).

2.2. Experiences need to take form, to be capable of ritualistic repetition — otherwise they will have a destructive effect. They must be capable of being handed down — otherwise they sink into oblivion. Ritual is the most elementary response to the breaking in of the transcendent. People are involved in ritual with their whole being — emotionally, cognitively, aesthetically, and ethically. Where the breaking in of the Other presents itself primarily in terms of nature and is experienced as directly life-threatening, the ritual will center around those areas that are the most dangerous, the times of transition in the annual cycle and the life-cycle (→initiation in diverse contexts). Ritual and myth stand in a reciprocal relationship. Myth is the interpretation of ritual, which for its part can be seen as giving form to myth. In myth, which is the symbolic narration of the unutterable and otherwise inexpressible, the experience of the transcendent becomes teachable and learnable.

2.3. The ethical dimension belongs to the basic event of religion. There is no experience of the transcendent without ethical consequences. Every ethical code is ultimately based in the religious and remains closely linked to this origin, however far it tries to separate itself from it or indeed has to distance itself from it and restate itself by the segmentation of its sphere of activity. Piety is the aspect of ethics that is permanently assigned to religion; action which is bound to conscience is the second aspect; and that which is sanctioned and controlled by society and law is the third. Insofar as it recognizes any meaning and function for religion, the sociology of religion holds that religion is the "cement" that holds ethical action together (see the works of E. Durkheim, among others).

2.4. Religion arises from the experience of the transcendent and answers the question of the "transcendence" of a human being, that is, after death. It secures life and gives form to the problem of death at its central point. Where the continuity of life and the succession of generations is of vital importance, as in tribal religions, death is understood as the passage to life with the ancestors. Where deliverance from the transitory world and the sufferings of existence is a central doctrine (as in Hinduism and Buddhism), the passage to the "other side" is understood as the destruction of the circle of rebirths, as entry into the Absolute or into Nirvana. Where God is the center of religion, →salvation is imparted in the shape of a savior, and death must be understood as the doorway to life with God, however this may be described, whether as a material or a spiritual paradise.

2.5. The experience of the transcendent may be individual, but it always contains meaning for others, for the social group. There is no religion without a community. Ritual, worship, and ethics exist in community and have no validity outside community. This holds good whether the community existed naturally beforehand or was created afresh as a religious order, sect, or church.

2.6. The doctrine of the faith is one of the component parts of religion, even if in a derivative sense. The experience of transcendence is communicated by ritual and by word. Insofar as ritual speaks to the cognitive level of communal human life, it contains a doctrine *in nuce,* whether it is verbalized or not and in whatever form it occurs, whether as a confession of faith, as instructions for performing ritual, as songs of praise, or as wise proverbial sayings which contain the predicate of God and make it ethically relevant.

To summarize: religion becomes real only in the concrete forms of religions. In spite of all the weighty and convincing arguments against a definition of religion, we venture to offer the following phenomenological expression: religion is the human response to the experience of the transcendent which takes form within a community through ritual, worship, and ethics.

3. Research into the history of religion has given attention to the synchronous as well as more intensively to the diachronic understanding of religion. It looks for types, for basic structures; it attempts to show differences and agreements, to clarify "chosen relationships," and to explain why affinities exist between certain religions and why others are so far apart. The danger in this procedure lies in leveling the differences between religions, each of which ultimately has a significance *sui generis,* in overlooking the specific peculiarities of each and fitting them into a framework which is not appropriate to the history, center, and meta-center of each. In spite of this, the diachronic procedure has its justification and is relevant to the history of religion. It has a definite religious and political significance, for example, in Islam, which distinguishes between "book" religions and those religions which have no "book" and therefore, according to Islamic teaching, no valid revelation. Islam adopts a positive attitude to book religions because it includes them within its understanding of the history of salvation, while other religions are subject to its massive missionary onslaught. The State of Indonesia, with its Islamic majority, has followed the consequences of this attitude and has required the adherents of tribal religions to convert to one of the book religions (Islam, Christianity, Hinduism, or Buddhism).

The distinction, derived from sociological criteria, between tribal and world religions (in other words, popular and universal religions) draws attention to one important difference. Tribal religions have value only in their existing sociopolitical contexts and are in principle not missionary. They determine the entire social life of the vital community of a people, and their aim is the well-being of this group. Those who belong to the "in-group" are strengthened by it, so long as they conform to the norms; outsiders are regarded as enemies. Agreements and trading relationships can overcome enmity and regulate a common life. This does not include the transmission of religious and ethical attitudes. Religious transgressions are regarded as transgressions against the group, so that ritual (especially as pastoral care) has as its aim the reestablishment of the social community, of which the ancestors (also the various levels of deities, but not God, who transcends everything) are an integral part. A popular (or tribal) religion into which one is born is focused ultimately on the present life, not the life to come. In contrast to this, universal religions press for a decision for or against; they want to expand their sphere of influence. Religion, community, and territory are no longer identical. The segmentation of life demands concessions from ethical convictions. The claim of a universal religion is, however, total. Therefore, such a religion is intolerant in its outside relations but must summon up a certain tolerance inwards, while popular religions are intolerant toward their own adherents but are outwardly tolerant in matters of religion, because what is outside does not concern them. In universal religions the striving for salvation is directed more to the next world than to this. God — or God's substitute — becomes its guarantee.

The same differentiation, seen from the point of view of cultural anthropology, marks the distinction between nature and culture religions or, from the point of view of the history of religion, the distinction between animistic and theistic religions. Even though this classification has found widespread acceptance on the basis of its apparent plausibility, it is false, in spite of individual correct observations. It presents an evolutionary model of religion which cannot be maintained in historical terms. Moreover, the conceptualization is unclear, and the contrasts are artificial and cannot be found in the reality of religion.

A sense of superiority, linked with a latent racism, is obvious in this mode of thinking.

The distinction between mystical and prophetic religion, derived by N. Söderblom from the viewpoint of the history of religion, which is ultimately based on insights from the psychology of religion and which was strengthened by F. Heiler (see Heiler 1921, 248ff.), is aimed at the Zoroastrian/Old Testament and Greek mystery religions, and also at Indian piety. It has proved its worth as a fruitful heuristic principle. Mystical piety is concerned with union with God; the body is mortified, and the soul seeks its rest. In contrast, faith stands at the center of prophetic religion; it seeks to shape life. Piety lives from hope, which cannot be shaken. Ecstasy is of little importance here; rational consideration is all-important. In mystical religion God is eternal majesty and serenity. God is over the world and immanent at the same time. God acts — if at all — outside time rather than in history, as the theology of prophetic religion maintains. In this case, revelations do not possess the historical burdens of the world, as in prophetic traditions; history lays no claim to truth. On the contrary, the religious person must overcome history in order to grant it validity. Mystical devotion is individualistic — overcoming sin serves only to purify the soul; it is a stage on the long road to fulfillment. The prophetic assertion of the forgiveness of sin opens up instead free space for action, for social involvement, for the unbroken lifelong commitment to the service of good and one's neighbor. In the former case, everything is directed toward the esoteric, in the latter, toward the community and congregation. In the former, one is tolerant toward other religions because they are regarded at the most as lower stages on the way to enlightenment. Prophetic religion, in contrast, has a dualistic way of thinking and makes a sharp distinction between good and evil. One is intolerant of evil and untruth; truth must be spread over all the world with a missionary awareness of the message. The goal of religion, transcending death, is, in the mystical tradition, union with the highest good (*summum bonum*), which can be attained now in ecstasy, visions, and enlightenment, so that the transition is rapid. In prophetic religion, people focus upon the destruction of this world and at the same time upon its fulfillment, to which they are committed. Mystics long for eternal bliss; members of prophetic religions for the fulfillment of the kingdom of righteousness. Both traditions can, however, come together in thoughts of love, however differently they are colored.

It would be a misunderstanding of the nature of these ideal types if one saw in them irreconcilable opposites. On the contrary, they should help to bring about understanding and make dialogue between religions even more urgent. In fact, in the real world of living religions, the types overlap many times. John's Gospel, with its christologies of mission, for which it is indebted to the prophetic tradition, and its ethic of love moving toward unity, is the most profound example showing that both traditions merge into each other in full maturity.

4. The question of the origin of religion, which kept research into the history of religion in the last century in a state of suspense, is rarely posed today. It cannot be answered historically. We know of no society without religion. Religion is apparently a constituent part of being human. Even the new way of formulating that question, whether religion is endogenous or exogenous in origin, proves that it is an unreal question. The understanding that has taken root in Protestant theology since W. Herrman, that religion is to be explained by the deficit experience, the questionableness of life (R. Bultmann, K. Barth, P. Tillich, but also compare Augustine), is too simple.

The sociological models of the interpretation of religion do not ask the question of the origin of religion; neither do they seek to answer this question in any way, because they are not interested in posing historical questions. The question is, however, implicit and is revealed in retrospect in the conclusions reached. The integration model, advanced mainly by E. Durkheim, which has found many disciples since his time, sees religion as the most important integrative factor in society. It provides a value system by which society can measure itself and punishes behavior that does not conform to the norm. These values are externalized in rituals at the same time as they are internalized as communal events through myth and participation. Society encounters itself in religion in a sublimated, objectivized, and idealized form. That means, however, that religion is a product of society itself. Society needs a teacher and a disciplinarian and has created them in religion.

The compensation or projection model is ultimately aligned with psychology and sees religion as a substitute for unfulfilled wishes, as an escape route from the misery of the world, as a haven where one forgets the storms of life. People project those wishes that are not fulfilled on earth onto heaven. Looked at positively, this means that religion has a consoling function — it provides meaning and the ability to endure. In both cases, however, it is true that it is a false awareness in a false situation, that is, a situation that alienates people. The origin of religion is the human. Humanity "makes" religion; religion does not make humanity (K. Marx).

The secularization model, first advanced by M. Weber, assumes the three-stage model of A. Comte and states that religion had a meaning in an earlier stage of humanity but that it has now been overthrown by the reasoning and understanding of human beings. With the segmentation of life, religion frees space for secular activities. It withdraws into the private sphere until it becomes superfluous and is superseded by secularization. Religion can give meaning and social cohesion in the childlike stages of human development. But even in this respect humanity is seen as the ultimate origin of religion. Religion is not a deception, not a substitute, not a projection, but a necessary transition stage. As noted, this model is incapable of verification in terms of the history of religion.

Similarly unverifiable is the assumption of a development in religions such as that held in the eighteenth and nineteenth centuries, an assumption which was essentially molded by the theory of social Darwinism. A development from a primitive stage (e.g., magic), via a diffuse religion (animism and polytheism), to the pure form of the so-called higher religions cannot be demonstrated historically. Every religion, even those of tribal societies, is a highly complex whole which includes all facets of life. There is no development of religion from a primitive to a higher level but only transformations (G. Mensching). This poses a new question: In what relation do tribal religions stand to world religions, and how is this relationship to be interpreted in terms of the history of religion?

We must distinguish the constitutive factors of the primary religious experience, still accessible to us in tribal religions, from the secondary religious experiences of world religions. The primary religious experience, the basis of all piety, is directed to vital life. It is oriented toward the cycle of life and the seasons and is basically defined as the participation of human beings in their world. "Participation" is to be understood ontologically as sharing, dynamically as taking part, and socially as joining in. The →symbol is an elementary means of communication of the primary religious experience, which is seen in its totality in ritual. The ethic of the experience is determined by reverence for life, which, transcendentally understood, is anchored in God. God is here conceived as the One, even though it would not be correct to speak of monotheism. God is spoken of very loosely as the One in many facets and connections. Experience of the one world corresponds to knowledge of the origin of life in the One, and experience of the manifold nature of this world is reflected in the manifold nature of the opportunities to overcome it transcendentally. In primary religious experience, monotheism and polytheism are not opposites but present different opportunities to encounter reality. Increasing and stabilizing life — preventing a diminishment of it or an interruption in the succession of generations — are the aims of the structure of primary religion in a small society, a structure which has validity only within its respective societal setting. One is born into this structure, just as one is born into the society. One cannot make a decision in favor of it, any more than one can in the last resort withdraw from it. To do so would be to cut the tribal bond. The problem of changing one's religion does not exist. Even when slaves are accepted into the community, or enemies become partners in business or marriage through a covenant, there is still no question of changing one's faith or adopting another faith but only of observing new laws and taboos.

Cultural contact and change, trading relations, and the enlargement of territory, as well as natural catastrophes, defeats in war, and epidemics, have often revealed the limitations of traditional religion, which can be seen no longer to cover the newly separated areas of life. The new is initiated by prophets, seers, reformers, founders of religions. Secondary religious experience takes these into consideration. It replaces sense intuition by comprehensive rational conceptualization. Now there is a doctrine that helps one to look at the unity of the world in a new way and teaches one to understand transcendence, God as Godself. Now one can and must make a decision for what is new. The performance of ritual no longer satisfies; it is now also a question of inner fulfillment. Faith and discipleship are demanded, and truth must be distinguished from falsehood. The individual relationship is more important than the collective. Religion no longer serves the integration of a natural group but differentiation from other groupings. The individual's freedom of choice and room for action grow. Religion no longer covers all spheres of life, so the room for secularism grows. Mission is possible; it is necessary.

The course of the history of religion does not run in a simple straight line so that the new, introduced by seers and founders, (in other words, the secondary religious experience), replaces the primary experience. Rather, in a third phase, the vital elements of the secondary experience are integrated into the primary experience in a complex process of rejection and symbolic reintegration and form a new synthesis. This leads to a growth in syncretism, which is unavoidable and which is to be evaluated positively. The deeper this synthesis, the more vigorously will the new religion be able to establish itself as a national religion (e.g., the integration of the Jerusalem cult into the Davidic and Solomonic temple worship, the integration of the pre-Meccan tradition into the pilgrimage cult of Muhammad, and the integration of the Germanic midwinter festival into Christmas). We can recognize the "progress" of the history of religion in these three stages. It is not to be understood as "development" but as change and accommodation.

Whether the history of religion can deduce from this process one goal to which all religions are moving cannot, by its very nature, be foreseen. This would be a postulate from the realms of theology and the philosophy of religion, a postulate which — up to now at any rate — cannot be verified historically. Rather we can recognize a process in which every religion tends to distance itself from its origins and is then forced by reform movements or schisms to reaffirm its origins. In other words, the three steps in the history of religion — basic experience, reestablishment, and integration — are often brought about under different circumstances and conditions, often coupled with political goals.

5. The problem of syncretism has its origin in the need to integrate primary and secondary religious experiences, which at the same time is the necessary condition for the possibility of the →inculturation and indigenization of a religion. This process of integration can proceed on a narrow or a wide basis, radically or tolerantly. The tolerance threshold of any particular religion is determined by its central axiom. Where alien infiltration by the new threatens what already exists, the argument between them is sharper (see the criticism of foreign gods by the Israelite prophets). This argument is unavoidable because every religion tends toward inclusive, absolute authority, if not in the exclusive sense, then in the inclusive sense. Tribal religions make this claim internally, world religions, in varying degrees, externally.

A conscious syncretism (G. Mensching) is then to be distinguished from the syncretism that develops naturally and is immanent in every religious change. Conscious syncretism has various origins and motives — legal, political, and those that arise from the philosophy of religion. Because treaties between nations in antiquity could be concluded only in the name of the gods, it was necessary to draw up lists of equivalent deities who could guarantee the validity of the treaty (as, e.g., in Sumeria). When land areas were incorporated into a foreign state, the foreign gods were either subjected to the local ones or treated as equals so that they could be identified with them. New formations of a dual or even a triple nature were possible. Where, however, an earnest striving for a unified religion predominates, because of the conviction (as in the mystical tradition) of an original essential unity, elements of different religions are molded together and a new entity is formed, though one which often claims to be a return to the original form. The new religious formations and the new religious movements of the twentieth century belong here. In their radical selection of what they adopt they pose questions to the established religions and challenge them to move forward to a new consciousness. Whether new religions with worldwide validity will develop out of them cannot be determined but is in any case unlikely. Possibly they are an indication that the image of the history of modern religion will be stamped by a diffuse form of popular, subjective vagabond piety.

6. Since every religion tends to distance itself from its center, to grow shallow, or to be perverted, criticism of religion is immanent in every religion. Where claims and reality are wide apart, criticism has its place. Tribal religions have often ritualized it. The festival of the renewal of the covenant in the Old Testament provides such a ritual opportunity for criticism. The Herero of Namibia extinguish the ancestral fire and renew it when the power of religion, as believed, and the power of the ancestors, as experienced, are no longer congruent. Criticism is incumbent on seers, prophets, and priests. Every reform of religion and every new founda-

tion begins with immanent criticism of religion. Politically motivated criticism of religion in antiquity and in modern times (e.g., as an aspect of colonialism) must be included here. Other peoples and their religions are presented in a negative light through comparisons as a way of strengthening one's own religious identity. Criticism of religion of this kind serves to sanction in religious terms the political overthrow of others or their extermination. We must distinguish from this activity the criticism of religion in modern times, which, by sociological, psychological, and philosophical means, tries to adopt a position outside all religion in order to rob religion of its all-embracing claims of giving meaning to life and itself replace these claims. Where external criticism of religion is politically inspired, it takes the place of religion itself and initiates a "religion outside religion" (H. R. Schlette).

Certain currents in Protestant theology have — via L. Feuerbach — taken up the external criticism of religion and radicalized it to purify the motivation and doctrine of their own religion. Secularization has been legitimized in this way. This could happen only while the "nonessentials of religion rather than its essentials" were fixed (H. Fries). The theological price has been high. Christianity, in freeing itself from entanglement with other religions, denied its own historical past and cut its ties to the primary religious experience and its natural (though not its theological) connection with its mother religion, Judaism. This historical disconnection has resulted in a far-reaching loss in the understanding of the first article of faith. An ethical cognitive rigorism is the result. We are still looking for the proof that a theology that is relevant in the context of the non-Christian world can be advanced on this theological basis.

7. The relationship of Christianity to other religions (→theology of religions) has been defined in various ways in the course of the history of the church. A total of five different models have been worked out. The basic model developed by the early church, accepted by and large by Protestant orthodoxy and still the authoritative model in the Roman Catholic Church today, is the "fulfillment model." The classical statement is presented in Vatican II. The non-Christian religions are classified and judged in relation to the church. This approach is justified in various ways. God has revealed Godself in non-Christian religions (Rom 1:19; Acts 14:17). This revelation is still valid, even if it is corrupted by human beings. The revelation of Christ fulfills the knowledge that is locked up within other religions. The doctrine of *logos spermatikos* opens up another line of argument and in a special way makes it possible for the ancient time of the pre-Christian philosophers to bear fruit in Christian teaching without a breach. K. Rahner's concept of "the anonymous Christian," which includes deeper christological considerations, should be brought in here. According to Rahner, human beings have been given not only a natural knowledge of God but also, through the work of Christ, some measure of grace. A "supernatural existential" is created, so that after the death and resurrection of Christ nobody any longer lives outside the realm of Christ, and everybody can be spoken of as a hidden Christian.

How strongly this train of thought affects the diametrically opposed "diastatic model" of dialectic theology becomes clear in that K. Barth speaks of an "ontological connection" between Christ and all people which is the "legal justification" of the proclamation, so that all people can be spoken of *de jure* in terms of their designated existence as Christians (*CD* 4/2, 511). This model must be called diastatic because in its approach it judges religion as the "concentrated expression of human unbelief" and every "natural revelation" as false. Christianity is classified, on the one hand, among the *massa perditionis* of all religions and, on the other hand, as the religion to which grace has been granted and which has been radically set aside from the total collection of religions. It is only in the dialectical step forward of the new christological beginning that the other religions can be brought back again into the system and brought under and within Christianity or, more precisely, Christ.

The dualistic model — seen in the early Middle Ages, during the period of intense debate with Islam in the colonial period, and once again today in evangelical, fundamentalist circles — sees in non-Christian religions the hand of evil, if not viewing them as the creations of Satan. There is no connection with the Christian faith. The other religions must be overthrown. They are condemned to die because people must be transferred from the kingdom of darkness into the kingdom of light (1 Pt 2:9). This task is taken on by mission, which thereby acquires the dignity of salvation history. In this model one can hear overtones which have their origin in Western feelings of superiority.

The progress model is focused on history, which is understood dialectically as a self-expression of the absolute Spirit, and sees in Christianity the point of convergence of all religions (W. Pannenberg). In the liberal tradition of E. Troeltsch, Christianity is explained as the highest development of all religions. In this model the concept of the absolute claim of Christianity finds a home, even if not in the harsh form it takes in the dualistic model.

In the same way, the dialectical model takes the history of religion seriously, as it is at home with trinitarian faith. It turns round the Barthian model (see Ratschow 1979; Sundermeier 1979). The finding of the history of religion that "God always stands at the beginning" (W. F. Otto) is taken seriously theologically. The existence of the religions stands under the blessing of God (C. Westermann). The primary religious experiences, the basis of all religions, are God the creator's means of sustaining human life and of protecting people in their humanity. They are among the means through which God works creatively to sustain the world. Jesus' advent in the midst of the Jewish religion belongs to the area of secondary religious experiences. That God has made Godself known in Jesus in a unique, unrepeatable fashion separates the Christian faith from all other religions and is a truth that cannot be proved, only attested. Jesus' death and resurrection as the end of all religious forms are equally the grounds for the possibility of a convivial coexistence of all religions, so that the Holy Spirit as the Spirit of Christ can lead everyone into all truth. Just as this truth prevails in the integration of other primary religious experiences into that of Abraham, Moses, and David and prevails against all error and obscurantism in Judaism and Christianity, so it will become reality for everyone and in all religions.

THEO SUNDERMEIER

Bibliography

Asmussen, J. P., J. Laessøe, and C. Colpe, *Handbuch der Religionsgeschichte,* vol. 3 (1974). Barth, K., *CD* 1/2 (1956) 280–361. Bianchi, U., *Probleme der Religionsgechichte* (1964). Bürkle, H., *Einführung in die Theologie der Religionen* (1977). Colpe C., "Theologie, Ideologie, Religionswissenschaft," *ThB* 68 (1980). Eliade, M., *History of Religious Ideas* (1978). Idem, *The Sacred and the Profane: The Nature of Religion* (1959). Idem, *Patterns in Comparative Religion* (1958). Idem, "The Quest for the 'Origins' of Religion," in *The Quest: History and Meaning in Religion* (1969) 37–53. Goldammer, K., *Die Formenwelt der Religionen* (1960). Heiler, F., *Erscheinungsformen und*

Wesen der Religion (1961). Idem, *Das Gebet* (1921). James, W., *Varieties of Religious Experience* (1923). King, W. L., *Introduction to Religion: A Phenomenological Approach* (1968). Küng, H., *Christianity and World Religions* (1986). Lamper, D., and C. Wulf, *Das Heilige: Seine Spur in der Moderne* (1987). Lanczkowski, G., *Einführung in die Religionsphänomenologie* (1978). Idem, *Einführung in die Religionswissenschaft* (1980). Mensching, G., *Die Religion: Erscheinungsformen, Strukturtypen und Lebensgesetze* (1959). Oelmüller, W., *Wahrheitsansprüche der Religionen heute* (1986). Idem, *Wiederkehr von Religion? Perspektiven, Argumente, Fragen* (1984). Otto, R., *The Idea of the Holy* (1926). Pannenberg, W., *Systematic Theology*, vol. 1 (1988) 119–88. Pettazzoni, A. *Der allwissende Gott: Zur Geschichte der Gottesidee* (1960). Preus, J. S., *Explaining Religion: Criticism and Theory from Bodin to Freud* (1987). Ratschow, C. H., "Die Religionen," *HST* 16 (1979). Ritschl, D., *Zur Logik der Theologie* (1984). Schlette, H. R., *Einführung in das Studium der Religionen* (1971). Sundermeier, T., "Die Einzigkeit Christi und andere Glaubenssysteme: Die Frage nach dem Dialog der Religionen," *ÖR* (1979) 26–35. Idem, "Warum sollte, nein, muß der Theologiestudent auch Religionsgeschichte studieren?" in *Kirchlicher Dienst und Theologische Ausbildung* (1985) 35–42. Troeltsch, E., *The Absoluteness of Christianity and the History of Religions* (German, 1902; English, 1971). Van der Leeuw, G., *Religion in Essence and Manifestation* (1963). Waardenburg, J., *Classical Approaches to the Study of Religion*, 2 vols. (1973–74). Idem, *Religionen und Religion* (1986).

❧ RITES CONTROVERSY ❧

1. Rites Controversy in General. 2. Definition. 3. The Rites Controversy in China. 4. The Problem of Rites Today. 5. The Rites Controversy in India.

1. The rites controversy, which concerned the admissibility and suitability of native religious customs and linguistic forms and which raged in the seventeenth and eighteenth centuries in India and China, is a thing of the past. As a result of both modernization and secularization, the ecclesiastical bans of 1742 and 1744 were lifted in 1940.

2. In India, the controversy concerned the so-called Malabar Rites, that is, the lifestyle adapted to the religious life of the Brahmans introduced by R. de Nobili. The biggest problems centered on the wearing of the holy thread, the hair-tuft, the ablutions, and the use of sandalwood. In China, where the controversy assumed much greater proportions, it concerned missionary methods introduced by M. Ricci which made concessions to the official state-supported Confucianism. There were differences of opinion concerning a number of questions: the aptness of Chinese philosophy as a preparation for the Christian faith, application of the Chinese words corresponding to "heaven" and "supreme ruler" to the God of the Christian revelation, toleration by Christians of the cult of Confucius and of ancestor worship, the permissibility for Christians of ancestor tablets regarded as the residence of the dead, the dropping of ceremonies objectionable to Chinese in the Christian sacraments, and the extent to which European church laws were binding on the Chinese.

3. The Jesuits, who followed Ricci's method, were motivated by the best intentions, wishing to help Christianity to assert itself quickly in China. They were convinced that the Chinese educated classes would not become Christian unless at least the cult of Confucius and ancestor worship were allowed. The Holy See, however — as early as 1704, then officially in 1710, and definitely in 1742 — made a negative decision which had a very unfortunate effect on the further development of the mission. But it would be wrong to claim that in doing so it condemned all Chinese culture. The Roman commission of theologians was well aware of the instructions of 1659 which said that under no pretext should any people be advised to change their rites, customs, and practices — provided they were not explicitly contrary to the true religion and good morals.

The Holy See did not even forbid everything about which misgivings had been expressed but only those rites which it felt were superstitious per se and therefore incompatible with the Christian religion. Hence "heaven" and "supreme ruler" were rejected as misleading, and the name "Lord of Heaven," which Ricci had already introduced, was made obligatory. The sacrificial rites in honor of Confucius performed on such occasions as the solstice and the inauguration of officials, as well as the sacrifice to ancestors in the family, were condemned as un-Christian because in practice they could not be separated from superstition. But the ban was kept within reasonable bounds. Mere physical presence at these ceremonies was not forbidden. The ancestor tablets were banned only when they were described as the residence of the soul. If it was only a question of having the name of the deceased written on them, they could also be used by Christians.

So the rites were not rejected merely because they were national customs and practices nor simply because they were different but rather in order to guarantee the purity of the faith. From the perspective of the theology of the times, it was regarded as prudent simply to characterize certain rites as incompatible with the Christian faith. The Protestant missionaries were confronted with similar problems. As late as 1890 at a conference in China it was stated that idolatry was still an essential part of ancestor worship, and in choosing the name for God there was so much divergence of opinion that even today there is no agreement about the matter. In 1940 the bans were rescinded in the Catholic Church on the grounds that, through the secularization of religious thought both in India and in East Asia, the controversial rites had become just neutral popular customs. Furthermore, theological thinking in the West has changed so much that there is general agreement today that the position of the Holy See vis-à-vis the rites was unnecessarily strict. With the help of comparative religion we have a better understanding of the religions (→religion, religions) and the meaning of their rites.

4. The study of cultures has shown that non-Christian religions manifest important values and centuries-old cultures (→culture) and possess their own profound mentality and religiosity anchored in tradition. Modern theology has taken this into account. Since the end of colonialism, indigenous peoples exhibit a stronger consciousness of their own culture and insist on more →inculturation, that is, the generous incorporation of their cultural values into the life of their churches. If the modern church is to preserve a unity that encompasses the whole world, then a great measure of tolerance has to be shown and these values must be recognized. But, even though it is considered fitting today that individual peoples formulate the Christian faith according to their culture and develop liturgy and theology in their own way, the question must be asked whether there are limits that ought to be maintained in order to safeguard the faith. It seems that the problem of rites is even more relevant today than formerly, for today too there are differences of opinion, and in some places this has led to open confrontation. It is certainly true that many forms of Christian piety are products of European culture and should not be imposed on other peoples, but there are undoubtedly basic elements of Christian faith that are universally accessible in God's revelation in all human cultures. Here we come up against limits to inculturation. It is the task of theology to point out these limits, which are often hard to determine. Cultural differences will remain, of course. But pluralism is no longer justified where the cohesion of the community of the faithful is in danger. According to K. Rahner, the moment a regional church, the church of a certain culture or a certain theology, barricades itself behind its special characteristics, the will to truth and the universal revelation of God are betrayed. While preserving their individuality, the churches of the world must nevertheless relate to one another in loving openness and be willing to learn from one another. The church and the theologians must not go so far as to allow every practice out of a sentimental kind of love and tolerance. The revelation of God passed down to us must be the final standard (→Chinese theology).

5.   The rites controversy was triggered and fought out in the country which then regarded itself as the hub of the world: China. There M. Ricci was the central figure. But the Chinese rites controversy caused a parallel phenomenon at the same time in India. Here it was R. de Nobili, inspired by Ricci, who became the key figure. Although the problems and the methods used by the opposing parties were not identical, the crucial issue, which was decided once and for all in a struggle lasting two hundred years, was the same: the insertion of the Christian mission and churches into the existing →culture.

Whereas the rites controversy in China is a thing of the past, the problem in India is still very much alive. Perhaps it could even give decisive impulses to the Christian mission and its churches.

In regard to the Indian context, inculturation means that Christianity, while preserving its transcendent character, must adapt itself to the form of Indian culture. This is an insight that we take for granted today. However, as a matter of fact, this insight was the result of two hundred years of theological debate and even more so of the progressive secularization of life in India. It was only slowly that customs that seemed inseparably intertwined with Hinduism, the religion of South India, were disentangled and modified and then came to be regarded as religiously neutral forms of Indian culture.

Together with this religious transformation of the problem, the attitude of the Catholic Church, the theologians, and the Christian people also changed — from the ecclesiastical edicts which condemned the adoption of these "rites" with increasing severity in the decrees of 1704, 1710, and finally of 1742, until the lifting of the bans in 1940. In this situation the followers and opponents of de Nobili could be found just as much among Indian as among European Christians and missionaries, even if the leading Portuguese classes, especially the hierarchy, bitterly opposed him. These latter knew only a Christianity which identified with Portuguese culture, and for them the negative attitude of the Roman curia was the voice of God.

The rites controversy of the Latin church had no parallel in the mission of the Syrian church. The reason for this was, first, that all Syrian Christians belonged to higher castes, and lower castes were not allowed into their church until recent times. This helped insulate Syrian Christianity from many of the sources that fostered the rites controversy. Second, the Syrian Christians rejected any form of religious connection with Hinduism. Even entering a Hindu temple was forbidden, not to mention taking part in any Hindu rite. They drew from Syrian and, consequently, early Christian sources for their liturgy, particularly its language, and their theology. Fears about the orthodoxy of the Christians, such as those resulting from the methods of de Nobili, did not exist among the Syrians. Third, since they did not want to make converts among the Hindus and even less to integrate diverse cultural and caste elements into their church, a missionary experiment like that of de Nobili had neither interest nor relevance for them. Therefore, the debate about de Nobili and his methods remained confined to Indians of the Latin church. It was only during the last fifty years that the situation changed, and by then the dispute was already resolved.

One might have expected the Protestant missionaries and the churches founded by them to take a stand regarding de Nobili. But this was not the case. Far-sighted missionaries like B. Ziegenbalg often adapted to the Indian culture where they deemed it advisable. But there was no ecclesiastical authority outside the country which — however little acquainted with the real problems — forced them to take up a specific position about this decisive missionary problem in the name of the faith.

After de Nobili's missionary method had been rejected by the Roman authorities, the great central theme of the Christian mission advocated by him, namely, adaptation to Indian culture, receded into the background. This development resulted from a number of factors: the temporary dissolution of the Jesuits and the collapse of their missions in India, the increasingly stronger missionary efforts of Protestant groups, the bitter civil war of the Padroado and Propaganda churches, the development of a strong neo-Hinduism, and the progressive secularization of Indian life. In the literature of the time it is hard to find a reference to de Nobili. Occasionally new missionary attempts which went in the same direction appealed to de Nobili. For example, Brahmabandhab Upadhyaya (b. 1907), the most well-known and most radical reformer, who was seeking a new direction for church and mission and to justify himself against his opponents, referred to de Nobili, but without going into the theological background.

Today de Nobili's ideas are being given greater attention. To begin, the increasing necessity of "Indianizing" the Indian church and mission gives fundamental importance to "inculturation," the object of de Nobili's whole lifework — even if there are still opponents in India who describe this method as "Hinduization" rather than "Indianization."

What makes de Nobili so relevant today, however, is the continuation and completion of his idea of totally incorporating Christianity into Indian reality, that is, not only into Indian culture but also into Hindu religion itself. Certainly de Nobili never thought of establishing a theological and vital connection with Hinduism or of regarding Hinduism as a vehicle of salvation for the Indian. The Indian mission today not only is concerned with adopting ideals and values of Hindu culture but is asking the fundamental question which is shocking for some and disturbing for all: To what extent is Hinduism a vessel and vehicle of salvation? When the question could be discussed theologically for the first time after Vatican II, more and more Indian theologians (such as D. S. Amalorpavadass, M. Amaladoss, F. X. D'Sa, I. Hirudayam, K. Kunumpuram, S. Rayan, G. Soares-Prabhu, and in particular R. Panikkar, who is partly following the vision of Swami Abhishiktananda [H. Le Saux]) looked for new ways to view the relation between Hinduism and salvation. De Nobili himself, whose vision these theologians want to pursue logically to its religious conclusions, would have vigorously rejected this approach since, with the premises at his disposal at the time, he could only come to the conclusion that Hinduism was inescapably and irredeemably monistic. In spite of his high esteem for Indian culture and religious values, de Nobili would never have tried to build an Indian Christian theology (→Indian theology) on them. But developments have outpaced de Nobili and have opened new perspectives for us. Many Indian theologians hold that Hinduism, which is incarnated in Indian culture, has been for the overwhelming majority of Indians of all times the way leading to →salvation and even today remains the only concrete way to God in their religious and social situation — a situation that will not change until perhaps one day the full light of the divine word which enlightens every person reveals itself to them. Naturally, the saving power does not come from Hinduism itself but from the "unknown Christ in Hinduism" (Panikkar). We are only now making the first faltering attempts to solve a problem that will occupy Indian theology for the coming decades.

Since the new missionary situation in India forces us to create alternatives to the traditional missionary methods, de Nobili's vision will have decisive consequences for practical missionary work in the future. After de Nobili's time this type of innovation was limited almost exclusively to the outcastes (Harijans, Pariahs) and the aboriginals (Adivasis), who alone were accessible for experimental mission work. But these two groups, which were the chief missionary objective of the Christian mission during the past hundred years, are opposed to the Brahmanistic form of Christianity inspired by de Nobili. The alternative, however, the big breakthrough to the higher castes, is not yet in sight. Although officially abolished, the caste system still constitutes a decisive force which determines the future of Indian life.

Nevertheless, in recent times the concept of Indianization promoted by de Nobili has triumphed in an area least expected: in the liturgy of the Catholic Church.

The ideas of de Nobili (and others, especially Amalorpavadass) triumphed when a twelve-point program was accepted for the official liturgy of the Catholic Church. However, as a result of the great cultural diversity of India, concrete implementation always rests in the hands of the Indian regional conferences (subject to Rome's approval) and of the local bishop. Implementation is not prescribed, simply permitted. These innovations, rather unique in modern liturgy, were not rescinded even through the later instructions of the Holy See on the liturgy (*Inaestimabile Donum*, April 3, 1980). The twelve points can also be integrated into the celebration of the Eucharist to give it visually a completely new "Indian" character (e.g., worshipers sitting on the floor around a small table instead of an altar; a saffron shawl as priestly dress instead of the Roman vestments; use of oil lamps instead of candles, incense sticks instead of thuribles, and flowers in symbolic arrangements; and Indian gestures which are used liturgically for the first time). But expressly forbidden in this "Indian Mass" is the Indian *anaphora* with Hindu texts, mostly from the Vedas and Upanishads (this was never formally allowed), and the use of non-Christian holy books within the liturgy (their use is not forbidden outside the liturgy). The wise limitation of these permissions assures that Indian cultural heritage is gaining access to the Roman liturgy for the first time, but at the same time it avoids offending older Christians who have not yet come to terms with these innovations.

In this way de Nobili has stimulated reflection and action even in our time. This has manifold consequences, which in turn will have to keep in step with the changing situations.

BERNARD WILLEKE, OFM, AND ENGELBERT ZEITLER, SVD

Bibliography

Amalorpavadass, D. S., *Gospel and Culture: Evangelization, Inculturation, and "Hinduization"* (1978). Idem, *Post-Vatican Liturgical Renewal in India* (1968). Idem, *Research Seminar on Non-Biblical Scriptures* (1974). Bachmann, B., *Roberto Nobili: Ein Missionsgeschichtlicher Beitrag zum christlichen Dialog mit dem Hinduismus* (1972). Beckmann, J., "Ritenstreit," in *LThK* 8:1322–24. Berentsen, J. M., "The Ancestral Rites: Barrier or Bridge?" in *JCQ* 49 (1983) 160–68. Beyreuther, E., *Bartholomäus Ziegenbalg: Bahnbrecher der Weltmission* (1956). Bonalumi, L., *The Chinese Rites Controversy and the Post-Vatican Shift to Liturgical Inculturation* (1989). Bosch, D., *Transforming Mission* (1991) 447–50. Boyd, R. H. S., *An Introduction to Indian Christian Theology* (1979). Griffiths, B., *Christ in India: Essays toward a Hindu-Christian Dialogue* (1967). Idem, *Vedanta and Christian Faith* (1978). Kulanday, V. J. F., *The Paganized Church in India* (1985). Le Saux, H. (Abhishiktananda), *Hindu-Christian Meeting Point* (1969). Minamiki, G., *The Chinese Rites Controversy from Its Beginnings to Modern Times* (1985). Mookenthottam, A., *Indian Theological Tendencies: Approaches and Problems...in the Works of Some Leading Indian Theologians* (1978). Mundadan, M., *Sixteenth Century Traditions of St. Thomas Christians* (1970). Ntetem, M., *Die Negro-afrikanische Stammesinitiation: Religionsgeschichtliche Darstellung, theologische Wertung und Möglichkeit der Christianisierrung* (1983). Panikkar, R., *The Unknown Christ of Hinduism* (1981). Idem, *The Vedic Experience* (1983). Rahner, K., "Ritenstreit: Neue Aufgaben für die Kirche," *STh*, vol. 16 (1984) 178–84. Thauren, J., *Die Akkommodation im katholischen Heidenapostolat* (1927). Thomas, M. M., *The Acknowledged Christ of the Indian Renaissance* (1976). Uzukwu, E., "Africa's Right to Be Different: Christian Liturgical Rites and African Rites," *BThA* 4 (1982). Verstraelen, F. J., et al., *Missiology: Texts and Contexts of Global Christianity* (1995) 53–54, 218–19, 229, 236. Ziegenbalg, B., *Malabarisches Heidentum*, ed. W. Caland (1926).

S

❧ SACRIFICE ☙

1. Definition. 2. Broadening of the Concept in the Study of Religion. 3. Theories about the Origin of Sacrifice. 4. Problems in Mission Practice. 5. More Recent Theological Discussions.

1. According to a theological tradition which has its starting point in the Old Testament and New Testament, sacrifice is a ritual action in which God is brought a visible gift as recognition of God's sovereignty. The motives of thanks, expiation, and petition are also bound up with this homage. Through the ritual, which, in a more or less festive form, represents the separation of the gift from the profane domain and its consecration, the sacrifice is distinguished from other religiously motivated gifts. A farewell meal can emphasize more strongly the community between those presenting the sacrifice and the recipient. Destruction of the sacrificial gift is frequently an enduring part of the ritual but does not belong to the essence of the sacrifice as such. Since acknowledgment of sovereignty is paid only to the true God, sacrifices to other beings that are falsely held to be gods must be condemned as sacrilegious aberrations. Therefore, in the Old Testament sacrifices to strange gods or to demons are expressly forbidden and branded as apostasy from Yahweh, the more so in that the sacrificial feasts of the Canaanite fertility cults were connected to sexual orgies as well (see e.g., Ex 22:19; 34:13–15; Lv 17:7; Nm 25:1–5; Dt 32:16–17; Jgs 6:25; 1 Kgs 11:4–9; 16:31–32; 18:16–40; 2 Kgs 10:18–27; Hos 2:8–21; 4:12–14; 13:1–4; Is 57:1–3; Jer 7:13; 44:15–25; Ez 6:4, 13; 8:8–11; 16:18–21; 23:37–39; Bar 4:7; Ps 106:28, 36–38). In the same way Paul prohibits the faithful from taking part in heathen sacrificial meals (1 Cor 10:14–22).

2. Since today other forms of religion are known to us apart from monotheism and polytheism, the definition of sacrifice must be broadened as well.

2.1. The receiver of the sacrifice can be not only God or "the gods" but also other beings whose religious veneration is recommended, for example, spirits of nature, ancestors, or saints (in syncretistic popular religion).

2.2. The intention of the sacrifice does not necessarily include the acknowledgment of absolute sovereignty; it can be directed to a being of superhuman but limited power and amoral character and hence can be an attempt at bribery (e.g., regarding commercial activity, *do ut des,* or appeasement of malevolent or capricious beings). Often the assumption that bribery is possible is linked to the idea that the sacrifice (i.e., the "soul" of the visible gift) serves the recipient as nourishment and that the recipient needs this nourishment.

3. In the study of religion, other nuances have emerged (apart from the traditional understanding of sacrifice as gift) which negate this character of gift, minimize it, or treat it as a secondary, mistaken development or mistaken interpretation. Thus the original purpose of sacrifice is considered to be only release of magical power through destruction (killing a living being), without there necessarily being a personal recipient. According to other interpretations, the ritual now designated as a sacrifice was at first only the dramatic presentation of a mythical primeval event (the killing of a divine or semidivine being with which the present cosmic order began) or the projection of aggression to a marginal object — "sacralized violence." Nearly all these theories take into account only bloody sacrifices (the killing of animals or humans) and so cannot explain the phenomenon of sacrifice in its totality, especially the offering of firstlings or firstfruits.

4. In the encounter with non-Christian religions in the context of missionary activity, the first question is what presuppositions and intentions the adherents of these religions ascribe to the sacrifices they practice. There are three possibilities for missionary practice: (*a*) Sacrifice can be condemned as morally reprehensible (because of its *do ut des* character or the orgies associated with it or simply because it is not directed to the true God) and therefore completely suppressed. But such a response pays little heed to the need for visible, symbolic actions and has little chance of success; the result has often been that the rites continue to be carried on secretly. (*b*) Sacrifice can be transformed or reinterpreted into ordinary feasts, symbolic rites with social significance but without the previous religious content (see Pope Gregory's instructions to the Anglo-Saxon missionaries concerning harvest festivals; or, in Papua New Guinea, the changing of the "swine feast" from a slaughter for the ancestors to a popular feast at the close of the Eucharist). (*c*) The traditional offerings (gifts of vegetables and slaughtered animals) can be incorporated into Christian worship as paraliturgical forms of popular religion. This was most easily carried out with reference to the custom of offering firstlings or firstfruits in thanksgiving to the creator god. But such offerings are found among only a few non-Christian peoples (and especially not among those with whom mission has had special difficulties, e.g., nomadic hunters and gatherers). To many non-Christian people, the creator god plays only a very limited role in worship, even when they believe in the existence of such a god. In such cases sacrifices are generally made to completely different beings, for example, lesser deities, ancestors, or spirits of nature (→inculturation).

5. In the theological controversies over the Christian understanding of sacrifice since the sixteenth century, polemic about restrictions against sacrifice by both Roman Catholic and Protestant authors has been more prominent than the intention of making a clear explanation of the basic issues. What does it mean to describe Jesus' death as a sacrifice? How can Christ's sacrifice, made once and for all according to biblical testimony, be seen in the same light as the continually repeated celebrations of the Eucharist, insofar as these are given the character of a sacrifice? In the 1980s, for the first time, an ecumenical consensus was reached as to the impropriety of applying concepts of sacrifice from the history of religions to →christology and the doctrine of the sacraments. In this important process of dialogue, theologians from the Orthodox Church as well have come to a new understanding of Christ's sacrifice and the →liturgy, especially the Eucharist (→Eucharist [Lord's Supper]). It all hinges on the exegetical, dogmatic, and systematic theological explanations of the following categories of questions.

5.1. The basic conversion of ancient concepts of sacrifice through the proclamation of the "sacrifice" of Jesus Christ brought about by God needed an explanation in exegesis and in the history of religion. To what extent is the death of Jesus to be understood as "sacrifice"? God (the Father) is here the one making the offering; human beings are the recipients. At any rate there are parallels to this "about-face" in pre- and extra-Christian traditions. They are found particularly in the Hebrew Bible, and that is not without significance. Recent ecumenical studies (e.g., by K. Lehmann, E. Schlink, and T. Schneider) unequivocally describe as mistaken the attempt to "convert" the understanding of sacrifice in the history of religion through New Testament testimony. This is admittedly important not only in terms of history but also in terms of the theology of mission, since through this insight cherished assumptions that extra-Christian sacrificial practices could be a suitable spiritual preparation for understanding Christ's sacrifice, or that of the Eucharist, are consigned to the region of theological naïveté and missiological opportunism.

5.2. The classical satisfaction theory of atonement (especially that of Anselm of Canterbury) requires a clearly defined and careful interpretation. If an angry, wrathful God is conciliated by human sacrifice here, is not the whole scope of the argument determined by the statement that God is the giver of this sacrifice? The many learned analyses of the classical Christian satisfaction-reconciliation doctrine carry new weight in modern ecumenical discussion.

5.3. Reformation theology made a clear distinction between propitiatory sacrifice (*sacrificium propitiatorium*) and sacrifice of praise and thanksgiving (*sacrificium "eucharistikon"*) and thereby between *sacrificium* and *sacramentum*. Only the death of Jesus could serve as a propitiatory sacrifice. The situation in the sixteenth century required the condemnation of the sacrifice of the Mass as a human act by the performance of which people could justify themselves, because the uniqueness of Christ's sacrifice appeared to be fundamentally threatened. At the Council of Trent also, the connection between the death of Jesus and the sacrifice of the Mass could not be set out with final clarity. The condemnations of Trent (e.g., "Whoever says that the sacrifice of the Mass is only one of praise and thanksgiving or the mere memorial of the sacrifice of the Cross, but not a propitiatory sacrifice; or that it only avails the one who communicates, and one may not offer it on behalf of the living and the dead, for sins, punishment, satisfaction and for other needs, let them be anathema" [DS 1753]) show a remarkable lack of precision. Today looking back with a historical-critical eye, as well as emphasizing the ecumenical dimension, we can describe both judgments as limited to their period and so not relevant for us today. So also the more recent Roman Catholic pronouncements (e.g., →Vatican II's document on the liturgy) have set the concept of sacrifice at the heart of the discussion about the death of Jesus and the Lord's Supper/Eucharist, which comprehensively or totally repudiates the former condemnations. Admittedly doubts have not been fully removed, as the letter of John Paul II on the Eucharist (1980) would have us think. Statements published by K. Lehmann and E. Schlink (1983) and by K. Lehmann and W. Pannenberg (1980) argue against such a confident consensus. In these writings the concepts of the *repraesentatio* of the unique (self-)sacrifice of Christ and the *participatio* of the faithful have a central significance. In this way, on the basis of the New Testament, the sacrifice of Christ is understood as a personal self-gift and becomes completely separated from previous assumptions about sacrifice. The meaning has now changed from an autonomous act (e.g., as gift to a deity, to God) to one of participation in Christ's sacrifice.

5.4. Nevertheless, there remains the double meaning of a "descending" (*kataba-sis*) and "ascending" (*anabasis*) understanding of sacrifice. The latter is the participation in Christ's obedience and self-sacrifice: this is the christological jus-tification of the Christians' sacrifice and that of the church, a concept in which the true humanity ("human nature") of Christ is of great significance, as the whole christology of the early church emphasized. Those who understand their lives as worship ("spiritual sacrifice" [1 Pt 2:5]) and present their bodies as an "acceptable sacrifice to God" (Rom 12:1) do not present God with something new but partic-ipate in Jesus Christ's offering of himself and so unite the ascending with the descending sacrifice. This sacrifice in no way effects salvation but is the expression of salvation already received. The application of this understanding to the Roman Catholic as well as to the Protestant understanding of worship (in daily life and in the liturgy) and of the Eucharist/Lord's Supper in particular is the basic tendency of the consensus just outlined.

5.5. Admittedly, in the evolving interdenominational consensus there remains the systematic-theological (and linguistic) question as to how the concept of sac-rifice can be used in the interpretation of Jesus' death and of the offering of Christians (the church) in service and obedience. Does the connection to the gen-eral concept of sacrifice, known from the history of religion, no longer exist? How then can the concept be used? And does it not become, through the complete "con-version" (see above, 5.1), a statement without analogy? Whoever affirms this can find support in the liberal theologians of the nineteenth century, who found the sacrifice to a God who *accepted* it as suspect as sacrifice to a God who *gives* it. Also those who do not want to include this (morally justified) evaluation must ask themselves to what extent talk of the "sacrifice of Christ" is not ultimately only a *modus loquendi* for another statement that does not stand in antithesis to a sacrificial gift given by God. This question is not completely modern, since the New Testament authors (including Paul) already permit consideration of whether the terminology of sacrifice derived from the Old Testament is unassailable, if it concerns the proclamation of what has happened in the advent, work, death, and resurrection of Jesus.

JOSEPH HENNINGER, SVD, AND DIETRICH RITSCHL

Bibliography

Anderson, G. A., *Sacrifices and Offerings in Ancient Israel: Studies in Their Social and Political Importance* (1987). Arinze, F. A., *Sacrifice in Ibo Religion* (1970). Barth, K., *CD* 4/1 (1956) 277–83. Barth, M., "Was Christ's Death a Sacrifice?" *SJTh—OP* 9 (1961). Chilton, B., *The Temple of Jesus: His Sacrificial Program within a Cultural History of Sacrifice* (1992). Daly, R. J., *Christian Sac-rifice: The Judeo-Christian Background before Origen* (1978). Dunnill, J., *Covenant and Sacrifice in the Letter to the Hebrews* (1992). Francis, M., *The Origins of the Christian Doctrine of Sacrifice and the Use of the Metaphor of Sacrifice in the Eucharistic Theology* (1982). Girard, R., *Things Hidden since the Foundation of the World* (1987). Idem, *Violence and the Sacred* (1977). Gray, G. B., *Sacrifice in the Old Testament: Its Theory and Practice* (1971). Haas, O., *Paulus der Mis-sionar* (1971) 30–34. Henninger, J., *Les fêtes de printemps chez les Sémites et la Pâque israélite: Études Bibliques* (1975). Idem, "Sacrifice," in *EncRel* 12 (1987). Heusch, L., *Sacrifice in Africa* (1985). Horvath, T., *The Sacrificial Interpretation of Jesus' Achievement in the New Testament: Historical Development and Its Reasons* (1979). Kurtz, J. H., *Sacrificial Worship of the Old Tes-tament* (1980). Lehmann, K., and E. Schlink, *Le sacrifice, Systèmes de pensée en Afrique noire*, Cahiers 2–6 (1976–83). Marx, A., *Les offrandes vegetales dans l'Ancien Testament: Du tribute d'hommage au repas eschatologique* (1994). Perelmuter, H. G., D. J. Harrington, and M. G. Witzak, "Sacrifice," *CPDBT* 856–63. Schlink, E., *Ökumenische Dogmatik* (1983). Stevenson, K., *Accept This Offering: The Eucharist as Sacrifice Today* (1989). Idem, *Eucharist and Offering* (1986).

Willi-Plein, I., *Opfer und Kult im alttestamentlichen Israel: Textbefragungen und Zwischenergebnisse* (1993). Yerkes, R. K., *Sacrifice in Greek and Roman Religions and Early Judaism* (1952). Young, F. M., *The Use of Sacrificial Ideas in Greek Christian Writers from the New Testament to John Chrysostom* (1979).

❧ SALVATION ❧

1. Salvation in the Bible. 2. Salvation in the History of Theology. 3. Modern Understanding.

According to the liturgical creeds, we confess that God's only-begotten Son "for us and for our salvation" came down from heaven and was "crucified for us under Pontius Pilate." For those who prayed those words in the past the meaning was quite clear: salvation according to the →Bible can come only from God in the form of →liberation, deliverance, peace (→peace and mission), and justice. Today the word "salvation" has disappeared almost entirely from everyday speech, and for this reason any preaching on salvation encounters many difficulties.

1. In the Old Testament, God was the deliverer and helper of a people that God had adopted through a covenant. For this reason the Israelites felt justified in calling upon their covenant partner, and the latter was obliged to go to the aid of the troubled people. In the course of the history of Israel these statements were confirmed in the wonderful acts of liberation that the people experienced: liberation from Egyptian slavery; assistance while wandering through the desert; help against the Philistines and all other hostile neighboring peoples, especially the Assyrians under Sennacherib; and finally liberation from Babylonian captivity. It was God alone who did these things, not tiny Israel. In this way God has glorified God's own name. Wherever the need arose, great men and women came forward who affirmed their hope in divine help. Increasingly, expectation shifted to the end of time in which God alone would prevail and peace would be enjoyed by all, including the heathen. However, not only the people but also individuals could present their expectations before God and expect salvation, healing, rescue, and preservation from death. This appears especially in the Psalms, where Yahweh appears as "the God of my salvation" (Ps 50:16).

The New Testament understood the coming of Jesus Christ as the fullness of time in which definitive salvation was accomplished. It consisted of the establishment of the reign of God (→reign of God), the liberation from the destructiveness of sin, the disarming of all powers hostile to God, and the outpouring of the →Holy Spirit as a community-building force. All this is expressed in the term "good news," the good news being meant above all for those deprived of salvation, that is, the poor, outcasts, in short, all who suffer physically, socially, or spiritually. Salvation is brought to them through →Jesus. This salvation means holistic redemption in body and soul, in the here and now, and at the end of time. It comes about when human beings turn in faith to Jesus, who becomes their savior. In the same way all who follow him will experience salvation. For salvation was merited on the cross for all people and for all times. Sinners were made children of God. These ideas were further developed by Paul (→Paul the apostle as missionary), who understands salvation as new creation, justice, and eternal life or resurrection (→justification). The salvation expected at the end of time is even now experienced as present. To sum up, it must be asserted that salvation constitutes a complex statement about God's saving humankind; it is both liberation and pacification in the present and an eschatological hope for blessedness and the restoration of creation.

2. In patristic times the community of the faithful regarded itself as the ark of salvation in the general deluge of time. *Extra ecclesiam nulla salus* (Outside the church there is no salvation) was the formula used. In its own way it continued the old idea of the people of God which alone is chosen. For only in the covenant with God can salvation be found. It was Origen and Cyprian of Carthage in particular who used this proposition as a weapon against the heretics. The church mediated salvation through baptism and the eucharistic community. Accordingly, whoever did not seek this remained outside of salvation. Afterwards the formula was extended to all nonbelievers. This meant that all "heathens" (without baptism of desire) were consigned to hell. This thought became one of the most powerful missionary motives (→theology of mission). The teaching of baptism of desire and the *votum ecclesiae,* which was also taken up by Vatican II, represented a great step forward. The council not only considered the goodwill of the individual as a way of salvation but also regarded the great religions as orientation to the people of God and its salvation (*LG* 11–16). Henceforth the church is regarded as a sign or sacrament of salvation for the peoples of the earth. And all the good and truth they possess is regarded as *praeparatio evangelica* (→inculturation; culture; religion, religions).

The Reformation placed special emphasis on faith in God's saving word and action (justification of the sinner). Salvation is to be found only in God, in the gospel of Jesus Christ, and as unmerited grace. The human situation as such remains sinful. Change comes about through the acceptance of the sinner who experiences him- or herself as both loved and able to return this love. In this way people, anxious about their fate, find their merciful God and God's gift of salvation.

3. Right up to the present times the concept of salvation was understood as "salvation of souls" without regard for the physical, social, cultural, and historical dimensions of the individual. It was only through the more accurate examination of the scriptures that the perspective of the whole person was exposed and salvation appeared in its full worldliness. The decolonization of whole continents (→colonialism) also revealed the economic dimension of salvation. This explained why so many people placed their hopes in Marxism. In the free West the belief in progress spread. According to the notion of progress, salvation consists in the accumulation of consumer goods and people's insurance against the crises of life. In this situation Christians have the task of unmasking materialistic ideas of salvation and pointing out the principal source of all evil — namely, the heart oblivious to God and neighbor. Evil and alienation are, in the last analysis, overcome only in the discipleship of the poor, merciful, and crucified Jesus, whose death and resurrection brought about the salvation of the whole world.

To come to grips with the situation of evil, Christians of the Third World take different approaches. Liberation theology arose in response to intolerable economic and political pressure on the Latin American continent (→liberation theology, →Latin American theology). Since their humanity is endangered by such an oppressive situation, Latin American Christians hope for God's help to overcome structural sin and set their hopes on a humanized world as a way to salvation. In Africa, Christians are distancing themselves from the theology of their for-

mer masters and attempting to build on the religiosity of the old tribal culture
(→African theology; initiation in diverse contexts). Salvation is present in the
family, in community with the ancestors (→ancestor worship II [in Africa]), and
in forms of worship emphasizing the spiritual world, which integrates the people
with their environment. Asian Christians live to a great extent with structural
poverty (→Filipino theology; Indian theology; Korean theology). Those who choose
poverty are not looking for economic solutions but rather for a spirituality which
is possible only with a freely accepted, simple lifestyle. For the followers of Buddha, salvation is inner peace and the cessation of desire. Wealth corrupts and robs
a person of "full humanity."

By way of summary let us consider the World Missionary Conference in Bangkok, Thailand (1973) (→world missionary conferences), with its theme "Salvation
Today." Here the christological aspect of salvation (redemption and sanctification)
was emphasized, but great stress was also laid on the anthropological dimension.
Salvation is always an issue of the whole person in his or her society and culture. Efforts for liberation, justice, and equality of the races and sexes constitute
ways of obtaining salvation. The conference at Melbourne, Australia (1980), endorsed these statements and placed special emphasis on the salvation of the poor
and oppressed. Churches and individual believers are now called upon to make
this a reality.

HEINRICH DUMONT, SVD

Bibliography

Bergant, D., M. A. Getty, and R. J. Schreiter, "Salvation," *CPDBT* 867–71. Best, E., *The Temptation and the Passion: The Markan Soteriology* (1990). Bosch, D. J., *Transforming Mission* (1991)
393–99. Farris, T. V., *Mighty to Save: A Study in Old Testament Soteriology* (1993). *Gaudium
et Spes* (1965). Gutiérrez, G., *A Theology of Liberation*, rev. ed. (1988). Hultgren, A. J., *Christ
and His Benefits: Christology and Redemption in the New Testament* (1987). Jeremias, J., *New
Testament Theology* (1971). Khoury, A., and P. Hünermann, *Was ist Erlösung? Die Antwort der
Weltreligionen* (1985). Moyd, O. P., *Redemption in Black Theology* (1979). Potter, P., *Das Heil der
Welt Heute* (1973). Rahner, K., *Schriften zur Theologie*, vol. 8 (1967). Rogers, J. B., *Case Studies
in Christ and Salvation* (1977). Snook, L. E., *The Anonymous Christ: Jesus as Savior in Modern
Theology* (1986). Stott, J. R. W., *Christian Mission in the Modern World* (1975). Thomas, N. E.,
Classic Texts in Mission and World Christianity (1995) 122–35. Weiss, J., *Jesus' Proclamation of
the Kingdom of God* (1971). Werbick, J., *Soteriologie* (1990). Williams, S. K., *Jesus' Death as Sav-
ing Event: The Background and Origin of a Concept* (1975). World Council of Churches, *Bangkok
Assembly 1973: Minutes and Report of the Assembly of the Commission on World Mission and
Evangelism of the World Council of Churches* (1973). Idem, *Salvation Today and Contemporary
Experience: A Collection of Texts for Critical Study and Reflection* (1972).

∽ SPIRITUAL RENEWAL ∼

**1. Catechumenate for the Baptized. 2. Conversion Liturgy. 3. Parish
Renewal. 4. Mission and Charisms.**

1. After a phase of decolonization and depoliticization of the missionary activity of the church and in the course of the new relationship between the world
religions, there is need to return to the deeper spiritual sources of all missionary work and evangelization. Missionary spirituality grows out of the personal,
joyful, and decisive encounter of the evangelist with God; it is basically personal
witness of this encounter. The modern world "is calling for evangelizers to speak
to it of a God whom the evangelists themselves should know and be familiar with
as if they could see the invisible" (*EN* 76; see Heb 11:27). The whole church has

been given "a mandate to evangelize" and consequently "needs constant conversion and renewal, in order to evangelize the world with credibility" (*EN* 15, 60). Encounter with God and the certitude that Jesus lives (see Acts 2:32, 36) are not the result of methodical efforts; this certitude grows, according to different life-situations, every time the recipient reaffirms acceptance of the sacramental and charismatic offer of God's grace. A document published by three central European bishops titled *Erneuerung aus dem Geist Gottes* (Renewal in God's Spirit) (→Holy Spirit) describes the theological and pastoral foundations of such a comprehensive spiritual renewal of the church from the background of the different epochs of Christian and mission history.

Baptism is the basic sacrament of conversion and the new beginning in Christ. The spiritual life bestowed through it grows only to the extent that the basic option for God and the church is from time to time renewed and deepened (e.g., through the renewal of baptismal and confirmation promises). Through the praxis of infant baptism the church testifies that God makes the first move, that the grace of baptism is not a reward for our efforts. But the first living encounter with God takes place when the person expressly and consciously accepts the offer of God's grace, for it takes effect "according to the individual's preparation and cooperation" (DS 1529). This is the reason why, since the introduction of the New Order of Baptism in 1969, the parents and godparents do not answer in the name of the child but rather confess their own faith in God because of the baptism they themselves received and undertake the responsibility of helping the child to make its own personal decision later on. Whereas adults prepare themselves for →baptism through a catechumenate, there is no such instruction for Christians who were baptized early in their lives but who know little about the faith. It is becoming increasingly clear that many persons who "were born in a Christian country or in sociologically Christian surroundings have never been educated in their faith and, as adults, are really catechumens" (*Catechesi Tradendae* 44). A catechumenate for baptized adults invites all to follow consciously and personally that path along which they were conducted in their youth by catechesis and sacraments. In more recent religious movements various forms have developed which are mutually complementary. The *cursillo* is a short course of three days; the "Catholic Charismatic Renewal" offers seven-week seminars; and the "neocatechumenate" goes on for eight to ten years.

2. From various liturgical elements a "conversion liturgy" has developed. It is an expression of the church in a changed historical situation involving all the basic processes of the faith, integrating the individual more closely into his or her parish or the religious community in which he or she lives.

The liturgy of baptism is the public and symbolic reenactment of the death and resurrection of Jesus. When the water is poured over the candidate (or the candidate is immersed) and the accompanying baptismal formula is pronounced, it is Jesus himself who baptizes (*opus operatum*). The response necessary for effectiveness (*opus operantis*) in the case of the baptism of adults is expressed in the baptismal confession of faith and in the laying-on of hands by the godparent. The baptismal confession of faith and the laying on of hands belong to the liturgical core of the response of the candidate and the church to the offer of God's grace. It is fitting therefore that the decision of the adult Christian who has been baptized as a child be expressed in a similar way. After a suitable preparation (e.g., in a catechumenate for the baptized, in seminars and retreats), the individual stands before the group and asks God in a prayer, usually spontaneous, for a new outpouring of the Holy Spirit. While saying prayers of praise, thanksgiving, and intercession, those present lay hands on the head of the candidate. "When persons are being blessed the laying on or extending of hands gives more powerful expression to the petition for God's blessing and the mediation of the blessing by the Church" (*Benedictionale* 31).

This rite can be celebrated in connection with the celebration of the sacraments, within the Mass before the Offertory and after the Communion, or within the framework of a eucharistic adoration. But it can also be done in the "house church," during a pastoral visit, or wherever two or three are gathered in the name of Jesus.

Depending on the individual's life-situation and spiritual maturity, the conversion liturgy can be experienced in different ways.

- *Personal option for God and the church in faith.* Conversion begins by listening to the word of God handed down in the tradition of the church. This fundamental option leads to the acceptance of the sacramental graces and the gifts of the Spirit. Turning to God is inseparably linked to turning to the church present in the actual community of word and worship. Frequently the relationship to the actual church needs sanctification by the Spirit of God. The fundamental option for God also includes the rejection of Satan, neoheathen cults, and pseudoreligious experiences.

- *Reaffirming the acceptance of the offer of God's grace in the sacraments.* An essential aspect of the sacraments that the individual receives only once in a lifetime (baptism, confirmation, holy orders) is that from time to time he or she expressly accepts the grace offered by God in them. Consequently the liturgical expression of a conscious or more profound response to the reception of these sacraments can occur at a later time. The important point is not the age at which a person is baptized or confirmed but the process of growing in the response to God's offer of grace. The reaffirmation of loyalty to God enables husbands and wives to renew their marriage vows and to reaffirm each other. In a similar way religious renew their religious vows.

- *Openness for the gifts of the Spirit.* God respects human freedom so much that God waits for our request for the Holy Spirit (Lk 11:9–13; Jn 14:13–16). As Christians grow more mature in the spiritual life they realize more and more which gifts God wishes to give them for service in church and society.

During the celebration of the conversion liturgy many have an experience of the nearness of God and the church, an "experience of the Spirit." This depends on the seriousness of the individual's preparation by the power of the prevenient grace of God, on the individual life-situation and character, and ultimately on the free action of God's grace. For many the total experience is similar to that of adult baptism. The Holy Spirit disposes human experience toward Jesus Christ (1 Cor 12:2–3) and toward activity in church and society. The Spirit liberates from the overestimation of the rationality of life and from interest in the offerings of the entertainment industry and pseudoreligious experiences.

The conversion liturgy is the concretization of the relationship of an individual to God and the church bestowed in baptism as well as the concretization of the relationship of the church to this person. Consequently, while having a spiritual structure different from that of the liturgy of baptism itself, the conversion liturgy nevertheless grows out of it. It has an importance which transcends culture, religion, and race and is also "missionary liturgy" in the sense of 1 Cor 14:23ff., since all present share in this event. It is a kind of reevangelization, a way of intensifying the common →spirituality of the whole church. Consequently, it is not the expression of any definite spiritual movement.

3. The conversion liturgy is a form of spiritual renewal that has grown out of the impulses of →Vatican Council II and is a continual process of renewal, a way of becoming Christian accessible to all. It is open for all manifestations of the Holy Spirit, no matter where they are found: in spiritual movements, in the separated churches, in society. When these impulses are taken over and integrated, the following factors are crucial:

- By its nature the parish must be open for the whole range of spiritual experiences and ways — for the nonpracticing just as much as for those who practice the faith intensively. Consequently, no group can be permitted to impose its own ideas on the parish to the exclusion of others.

- Each spiritual movement makes an indispensable contribution to parish renewal, but the parish cannot be monopolized by any one movement and its goals, methods, charisms, and dimensions of pastoral psychology.

4. Evangelization is "the essential mission of the church," "the vocation proper to it," and "its deepest identity" (*EN* 14). Consequently, the common spirituality of the whole church and of all pastoral ministries is missionary by its very nature with regard to Christians and non-Christians alike. For the individual, spirituality is an attitude to God under the movement of the Spirit which embraces one's whole existence. This spirituality is perceptible to others and has an effect in the church and the world. The spirituality of the individual too is essentially missionary: "It is unthinkable that a person should accept the Word and give himself to the Kingdom without becoming a person who bears witness to it and proclaims it in his turn" (*EN* 24). Hence evangelization (→evangelism, evangelization) is the basic charism of the whole church and of each individual Christian, a charism which sustains all other charisms, penetrates them, and fits them into an organic whole. A charism is a grace (*charis*), a special capacity an individual receives from the Spirit for life and service in the church and world. Charisms frequently correspond to natural human abilities. But charisms cannot be deduced from these; they arise from the free choice of God. Natural abilities are purified, developed, and taken into service by the Holy Spirit. Charisms are related to the word, the sacraments, and ministries. Nevertheless, being manifestations of the Holy Spirit closely related to experience and individual situations, they are not "handed down" in the tradition of the church in the same sense. They can be received and exercised only by the individual's actual surrender to God.

The basic charism of evangelization has various forms.

- The "wordless witness" of a life lived in the power of the Spirit is generally the first step in evangelization (*EN* 21; 41). But this "indirect" mission in the long run proves ineffective if it is not explained and developed through an explicit proclamation of the Lord Jesus Christ.

- This proclamation happens not only in sermons and catechesis but also in a "person-to-person" communication of one's own experience of faith (*EN* 21–22, 46–47). In such a "personal witness" the individual speaks "with courtesy and respect" (1 Pt 3:16), briefly, and objectively about his or her own journey in faith (see Lk 1:49; Mk 5:19). Through such a witness the Spirit of God can touch the hearts of listeners to accept the saving offer of God's salvation (see Acts 2:37). This means more than an intellectual assent to the truths of the faith (see *EN* 23). To some is given in a special way the charism of "first proclamation," which awakens the initial faith and is the precondition for catechesis.

- The catechumenate is "a period of formation in the whole Christian life, an apprenticeship of sufficient duration" (*AG* 14) and flows from the charisms of faith and the prophetic word, of prayer and teaching, of healing and liberation, of guidance and discernment.

HERIBERT MÜHLEN

Bibliography

Bakole, W. L., *Paths of Liberation: A Third World Spirituality* (1984). Barbour, C. M., "Jesus, Shalom, and Rites of Passage: A Journey toward Global Mission and Spirituality," *Missiol* 3 (1987) 299–313. Bosch, D., *A Spirituality for the Road* (1979). Cordes, P. J., *In the Midst of Our World: Forces of Spiritual Renewal* (1988). Fischer, K., *Women at the Well: Feminist Perspectives on Spiritual Direction* (1988). Gittins, A., *Bread for the Journey* (1993). Gutiérrez, G., *We Drink from Our Own Wells: The Spiritual Journey of a People* (1984). Jones, C., G. Wainwright, and E. Yarnold, *The Study of Spirituality* (1986). Larsen, E., *Spiritual Growth: Key to Parish Renewal* (1978). Lovelace, R. F., *Renewal as a Way of Life: A Guidebook for Spiritual Renewal* (1985). Marcoux, M., *Cursillo, Anatomy of a Movement: The Experience of Spiritual Renewal* (1982). Merton, T., *The School of Charity: The Letters of Thomas Merton on Religious Renewal and Spiritual Direction* (1993). Parry, D., *This Promise Is for You: Spiritual Renewal and the Charismatic Movement* (1982). Paul VI, Pope, *Evangelii Nuntiandi* (1975). Raguin, Y., *I Am Sending You: Spirituality of the Missioner* (1973). Reilly, M. C., *Spirituality for Mission* (1978). Scherer, J. A., and S. Bevans, *New Directions in Mission and Evangelization,* vol. 1, *Basic Statements 1974–1991* (1992). Shorter, A., *African Christian Spirituality* (1978). Sobrino, J., *Spirituality of Liberation: Toward Political Holiness* (1988). Thomas, N., *Classic Texts in Mission and World Christianity* (1995). Wallis, J., *A Call to Conversion* (1981).

✥ SPIRITUALITY ✥

1. Missionary Dimension of Christian Spirituality. 2. Concrete Expressions. 3. Dialogue with the Religions. 4. Spirituality for a Just World.

The word "spirituality" can be translated as "life according to the Spirit" or "life in the Spirit." It means the relationship of a person or a community to God. Although traditionally the more personal aspect of the relationship was emphasized, today there is a stronger stress on the reference of spirituality to the revelation event in the mystery of creation and the mystery of Christ. We can distinguish various types of spirituality: spiritualities centered around the passion, the Eucharist, or Mary; Pauline, Johannine, Benedictine, Ignatian spirituality; and so on. "Missionary spirituality" is not one among many but an essential feature of every genuine spirituality.

1. The objection is often advanced that in the process of conversion the real concern of individuals — how they are to understand themselves before God — must not be overshadowed too soon by the dimension of the world; people, it is said, react negatively if they are distracted from their personal problems by world mission. Nevertheless, we must insist that every →conversion is always a conversion to a God who cares for the whole world, who has intervened in history, and who always calls people for a mission.

The classical God-experience occurred on Mount Horeb in the incident of the burning bush. Moses said to himself: "I must go and look at this strange sight." He wanted to linger in this mystical experience. But the Lord shook him out of his reverie and there and then gave him a missionary task: "Come not nearer!...Now go!...I send you to Pharaoh to bring the children of Israel, my people, out of Egypt!...I shall be with you; I have sent you" (Ex 3:3–14). The inner relationship between vocation and mission could hardly be more clearly expressed.

The call of Isaiah occurred in the same way. Faced with the overwhelming experience of the holiness of God on the high throne, he suddenly realized: "What a wretched state I am in! I am lost, for I am a person of unclean lips." But the Lord did not let him dwell very long on his sinfulness; God said: "Your sin is taken away; your iniquity is purged;...go, and say to this people..." (Is 6:5–9). The call and sending of Jeremiah (Jeremiah 1) and most of the prophets happened in a similar way.

And so too in the case of →Jesus. The "Spirit led him" into the desert. The same Spirit led him to Galilee, where he appeared in the synagogue on the Sabbath and read the text from Isaiah: "The Spirit of the Lord has been given to me....God has sent me to bring the good news to the poor" (Lk 4:14–21; Mk 1:12). This happened too in the case of the disciples: Jesus called them with a power that could only come to him from God, who has authority over the lives of all people; and he called them not so that they would remain with him in rapt contemplation but rather to send them out with the same authority: "Follow me and I will make you fishers of people" (Mk 1:17). "After this the Lord appointed seventy-two others and sent them out ahead of him, in pairs, to all the towns and places" (Lk 10:1). Then after they had been with him for three years and were witnesses of his resurrection, some of them still "doubted," so that Jesus "reproached them for their incredulity and obstinacy." But the best way of overcoming this doubt was to entrust them with a great commission: "Go out to the whole world; proclaim the good news to all creation" (Mk 16:14–15; Mt 28:17–20).

In the first Christian communities the close relationship between vocation and mission was also obvious. The Holy Spirit did not allow the people of the community of Antioch to develop a spirituality which only involved "offering worship to the Lord and keeping a fast" but said to them: "'I want Barnabas and Paul set apart for the work to which I have called them.'...So these two, sent on their mission by the Holy Spirit, went down to Seleucia and from there sailed to Cyprus" (Acts 13:2–4).

And so it was a return to the authentic biblical message when →Vatican Council II reintegrated mission with the church, when it was emphasized that the missionary activity could not be subdelegated to the missionary societies but that the "Church is by its very nature missionary" (*AG* 2; *LG* 1); that a nonmissionary church would not be the church of Christ but a caricature; that, consequently, all in the church should feel themselves sent to evangelize the world. It can be put this way: all the evangelized must evangelize, for only the evangelized are capable of evangelizing. So a person is baptized not only to "save his or her soul" but to become a full member of the church and to take a full part in the mission of the church. All this can also be found in the document *Evangelii Nuntiandi* (1975) of Paul VI, in John Paul II's *Redemptoris Missio* (1990), in the statements by evangelicals at Lausanne (1975) and Manila (1989), and in all the assemblies and →world missionary conferences of the World Council of Churches.

2. The concrete expression of spirituality takes a number of forms, some of which are discussed below.

2.1. *Zeal for the reign of God.* The first missionary task is not to bring all people by hook or by crook into the church but to proclaim the reign of God to all people without exception, especially the poor and the weak, the downtrodden and marginalized, to assure them of God's all-embracing and unconditional love. This is the essence of salvation history, the core of Jesus' message to us. The axiom "Outside the church there is no salvation" would be better formulated today as "The church is the universal sacrament of salvation" (Y. Congar). Proclaiming salvation means "to evangelize," to proclaim the good news, "to shalomize," to bring healing and peace. After the churches have for so long split the world and antagonized the Jews, the "heathen," and other non-Christians, and even waged war against them, today they must make common cause with all and promote the unity of the human race. For "the Church, in Christ, is in the nature of a sacrament — a sign and instrument, that is, of communion with God and of unity among all peoples" (*LG 1*).

2.2. *Zeal for the church.* When individuals are called to the →reign of God, into a closer companionship with Jesus by →baptism and the other sacraments, they enter the church not just to indulge in pious singing in the company of like-minded people, not to make the church stronger and more powerful, but to make it a more meaningful, more credible "seed of the beginning [of the] reign of God" (*LG 5*); and furthermore, as a second task, to expressly proclaim to the world the message about Jesus.

After the Western churches have for centuries carried out the task of evangelization with zeal, if not always with the best missionary methods, today they display unmistakable symptoms of fatigue. In contrast, the churches of Asia, Africa, and Latin America have recognized that they should no longer remain just objects of evangelization but become subjects of mission themselves. The awakening of missionary consciousness in the Third World is one of the most gratifying aspects of the present situation of the church. The task of the churches of Europe and North America is now to accompany sympathetically their one-time "missions" as sister churches; from them they can perhaps regain their missionary impulse. Mission today must be "mission in six continents" (formulated thus for the first time at the World Missionary Conference in Mexico City, 1963) because Europe and North America, with so many people who neither practice nor believe anymore, have themselves become the most difficult mission territory.

3. Formerly, the aim of mission was to wipe out the religions and make all people into Christians. Today genuine evangelization takes place in the tension between dialogue and witness. In the meantime we have also developed a new →theology of religions (even though this is not completely accepted by many Christians and many churches). On the basis of the new mutual understanding and to strengthen it and make it effective, the World Conference of Religions for Peace was organized and has been meeting regularly since 1970 in Kyoto, Japan. A whole series of congresses, often jointly sponsored by Rome and Geneva, have taken place, involving participation by representatives of the Christian churches and other religious ways. In addition, in 1993 in Chicago, the week-long Parliament of the World's Religions took place. Much of this activity has taken place at an academic or official level and is only beginning to have an effect on ordinary Christians. Nevertheless, it is clear that we are at the beginning of a new era of religious understanding.

4. Since the church does not exist "for itself" but always "for others," on its path to the future it faces, apart from the challenge of dialogue with other religions, another challenge with what has been called the "dialogue with the poor." What is meant is not just a dialogue of words, but a dialogue of life, a dialogue based on real understanding combined with the commitment for a just world, for peace and disarmament, ecology and alternative lifestyles, human dignity and human rights, a commitment against hunger and disease, poverty and oppression. This is the express concern of political theology and →liberation theology. These efforts have shown that mysticism and politics are related not only biblically but also in our contemporary praxis. On the one hand, a mysticism without politics would probably not even be genuine and would remain a rather cheap indulgence in loving God. Politics without mysticism, on the other hand, risks engendering a gigantic state with the capacity for brutal domination by the powerful. For that reason there should be cultivated not just a vertical mysticism for the redemption of individual souls but also a horizontal mysticism-in-solidarity for the →liberation of the whole world.

WALBERT BÜHLMANN, OFM CAP

Bibliography

Auer, A., "Frömmigkeit," in *LThK* 4:403–5. Balthasar, H. U. von, *Christlich Meditieren* (1984). Combes, A., *Saint Thérèse and Her Mission: The Basic Principles of Theresian Spirituality* (1955). Crosby, M., *Spirituality of the Beatitudes* (1981). Degrijse, O., *Der missionarische Aufbruch in den jungen Kirchen* (1984). Dupre, L., and D. Saliers, *Christian Spirituality,* vol. 3, *Post-Reformation and Modern* (1991). Fisher, J., *Society of the Divine Word Mission Spirituality* (1993). Gittins, A. J., *Bread for the Journey: The Mission of Transformation and the Transformation of Mission* (1993). Henkel, W., *Bibliografia missionaria* (1984, 1985) 136–40. Gutiérrez, G., *We Drink from Our Own Wells* (1988). Idem, *A Theology of Liberation,* rev. ed. (1988). Kamphaus, F., and J. Bours, *Gelebte Spiritualität* (1979). Kenney, K., *Prophetic Witness in Luke-Acts: Aspects of a Contemporary Spirituality for Mission* (1981). Kraft, M. G., *Understanding Spiritual Power: A Forgotten Dimension of Cross-cultural Ministry* (1995). Magnkey, J., *A Model for the Mission of the Missionaries of the Sacred Heart in the Light of the Spirituality of the Heart* (1986). McGinn, B., and J. Meyendorff, *Christian Spirituality,* vol. 1, *Origins to the Twelfth Century* (1988). Metz, J. B., *Zeit der Orden? Zur Mystik und Politik der Nachfolge* (1977). Mieth, D., *Gotteserfahrung und Weltverantwortung: Über die christliche Spiritualität des Handelns* (1982). Paris, P., *The Spirituality of African Peoples: The Search for a Common Moral Discourse* (1995). Raitt, J., *Christian Spirituality,* vol. 2, *High Middle Ages and Reformation* (1989). Reilly, M. C., *Spirituality for Mission: Historical, Theological and Cultural Factors for a Present-day Missionary Spirituality* (1978). Rotzetter, A., *Seminar Spiritualität,* 4 vols. (1979–82). Sobrino, J., "Spirituality and the Following of Jesus," *ML* 677–701.

❧ STATE, CHURCH, AND MISSION ❧

1. Concept and Characteristics of the State.   2. Theory of the State.   3. Alliances of Mission and State Religion.   4. Conflicts between Mission and State.

1. As a derivative of the Latin *status* (condition) via the Italian *lo stato* (Machiavelli), the concept "state" has passed into most cultural-linguistic usages with the meaning of the ordered condition of a definite, geographically circumscribed territory. According to the present usage in political science, "state" refers to a political unit or a politically organized society that is regarded as fully or partially self-governing (e.g., a state within a federal state) within definite and internationally recognized geographical boundaries. In other words, a state enjoys autonomy (Gr.: *autonomos,* sc. *demos:* a people that makes its own laws) or sovereignty (Fr.: *souverain:* without foreign control).

2. Philosophical investigations concerning the phenomenon of "the state" can be classified according to two basic ideas: that of Plato (the state as a supratemporal phenomenon) and that of Aristotle (the state as a real combination of forces). In both philosophical traditions the state is understood as an organizational form inherent in human nature. In contrast, Marxist-Leninist thinking sees in the state a historically conditioned political tool of the economically ruling class which has to be overcome and which will disappear with the classless communist society.

It is generally assumed that for a political unit or community to be regarded as a state the following elements are essential and constitutive:

- a population, the size of which vary greatly (the Republic of Nauru has 8,421 inhabitants, the People's Republic of China 1.05 billion);
- a territory permanently occupied by this population (the Republic of Nauru has 8 square miles, the People's Republic of China 3.7 million square miles);
- some form of independent public system of order possessing ultimate sovereignty or authority both internally (e.g., a legislature and judiciary) and externally (e.g., a system of defense);
- the existence of a collective will extending over generations, independent of a concrete constitution (i.e., an identity).

These elements apply to politically organized groups which transcend the extended family or clan, independent of their organizational forms (monarchy, aristocracy, democracy, and their variations) and their designation (empire, kingdom, state).

State and nation — the latter being understood as a group of people of common descent, language, culture, history, and homeland — are not necessarily congruent, even in the case of larger tribal units (e.g., the Zulus at the beginning of the nineteenth century).

The approval of a specific state by the population living within its territory and under its laws — whether that approval is by a whole or a part (minorities) — is of importance for the theory of state (the common good, internal and external peace as the goal of the state) and political philosophy (*societas perfecta:* a perfect community completely claiming the individual in his social disposition and completely fulfilling him as a social being, the realization of the "moral idea" [Hegel]). Yet this approval bears hardly any importance in political reality.

3. The unity of one religion and state as an actual reality (state religion) or, in the past, as a goal (established or state church with discrimination against religious minorities as shown, e.g., in the Bill of Rights in England, 1689, excluding a Catholic from the succession to the throne) still plays a certain role today in a number of forms.

In the interests of such a unity, Christians in antiquity were persecuted as enemies of the state (see Diocletian's decree about offering sacrifice: edicts 2–4, 303, and 304), and later in Christian states heretics were similarly treated by the Inquisition. By exercising a protectorate over mission personnel and property, the colonial powers acquired considerable influence even outside the territories annexed by them (Portugal, France in East Asia, for a short time also Germany in China).

As a result of the close connection in certain places between the state and the prophetic universal religions, Christianity and Islam, these religions have used the state for their missionary work.

Whereas in Islam, especially in the Caliphate Period (661–1258), religion and the state were regarded as inseparable and the Koran became the code of law (at the moment this idea is experiencing a renaissance), the theology of empire beginning with the time of Constantine I (306–37) saw the idea of a world Christianity realized in the Christian emperor. This was exemplified, for instance, by the convocation of the Council of Nicea (325) by Constantine. Both emperor and pope were in the service of this world Christianity. This was the basis for the development of the Spanish-Portuguese *padroado,* that is, the pope's obliging the state to take responsibility for the propagation of the faith in the countries already discovered or to be discovered (see the bull of Alexander VI, *Inter Caetera,* May 3, 1493). Missionaries became servants of both majesties — of God and of the emperor (or king), that is, of the state. The moral obligation of the Protestant colonial powers to missionize was realized especially in Calvinism (see *Confessio Belgica,* 1561). The change of colonial power in a particular territory occasionally resulted in the complete replacement of missionaries or the change of confession of the Christian population (e.g., in Sri Lanka). The frequent incompatibility between the goals of church and state (in America the founding of an Indian church was prevented by the state) led to the foundation of the Congregation for the Propagation of the Faith in the Catholic Church (*Propaganda Fide,* 1622) and of independent missionary societies in the Protestant churches. There were also conflicts between representatives of the colonial powers and individual missionaries (B. de Las Casas, Francis Xavier, W. Penn, C. Lavigerie, etc.).

4. In states closely allied with a particular religion, attempts at evangelization will lead to conflicts even when no "protectorate" stands behind the missionaries. The attempt to replace religious values considered fundamental to the stability of the state is regarded as a threat. This has led to a general ban on missionary work in, for instance, Israel and Saudi Arabia, and sanctions against missionaries, today mostly by denying entry and work permits or expelling missionaries already there, as, for example, in India and Burundi.

Freedom of religion is officially fixed in most modern constitutions and in many cases is internationally guaranteed by UN membership. However, the limits of freedom of religion and its scope, including the change of religion, are interpreted and put into practice in widely different ways.

OTHMAR NOGGLER

Bibliography

Beckmann, J., "The Propagation of the Faith in Africa," *HCH(J)* 6 (1981) 270–79. Idem, "The Propagation of the Faith in America," *HCH(J)* 6 (1981) 232–70. Idem, "The Propagation of the Faith in Asia," *HCH(J)* 6 (1981) 279–325. Dharmaraj, J. S., *Colonialism and Christian Mission: Postcolonial Reflections* (1993). Dussel, E. D., *Historia de la Iglesia en América Latina: Coloniaje y Liberación 1492–1972* (1972). Ehler, S. Z., *20 Jahrhunderte Staat und Kirche* (1962). Escobar, S., and J. Driver, *Christian Mission and Social Justice* (1978). Forsyth, P. T., *Missions in State and Church: Sermons and Addresses* (1908). Hopkins, D., *Black Theology USA and South Africa: Politics, Culture, and Liberation* (1989). Latourette, K. S., *A History of the Expansion of Christianity,* 7 vols. (1971) Lehmann, P., *The Transfiguration of Politics* (1975). Lernoux, P., *People of God: The Struggle for World Catholicism* (1989). Mirbt, K., *Mission und Kolonialpolitik in den deutschen Schutzgebieten* (1910). Neill, S., *Colonialism and Christian Missions* (1966). Niles, P. *Resisting the Threats to Life: Covenanting for Justice, Peace, and the Integrity of Creation* (1989). Okullu, H., *Church and State in Nation Building and Human Development* (1984). Raab, H. *Kirche und Staat von der Mitte des 15. Jahrhunderts bis zur Gegenwart* (1986). Rivinius, K. J., *Weltlicher Schutz und Mission: Das deutsche Protektorat über die Katholische Mission von Süd-Shantung* (1987). Robertson, R. "Church-State Relations and the World System," in *Church-State Relations: Tensions and Transitions* (1987). Schilling. W., "Staat II: Religion und Staat in der ausserchristlichen Welt," *RGG* 6:295–305. Schweitzer, W., "Staat III: Staat in der christlichen Lehre," *RGG* 6:297–305. Tutu, D., *Crying in the Wilderness: The Struggle for Justice in South Africa* (1982). Van der Bent, A. J., *Between Christ and Caesar: Classic and Contemporary Texts on Church and State* (1986). Idem, *Christian Response in a World of Crisis* (1986). World Council of Churches, *Churches and State: Opening a New Ecumenical Discussion,* Faith and Order Paper 85 (1978).

❧ THE STUDY OF RELIGION ❧

1. The Roots of the Study of Religion. 2. Methods. 3. Comparative Religion. 4. Significance for Mission and Mission Studies.

1. The roots of the study of religion are to be found in three streams of Western intellectual history: namely, in the Enlightenment, in the romantic movement and in the field of historical theology. The modern Enlightenment, which had its antecedents in the Enlightenment of antiquity with its criticism and reinterpretation of myth, made possible the distancing of oneself from the subject of research, something which academic work on religion has to maintain in contrast to theological reflection. Admittedly, this distancing has all too commonly been overvalued, especially when the world of religions is delivered up to the critical dissecting knife of reason. Today, it is clear that this attitude toward research must be expanded to include a hermeneutic that listens to the content of religious messages. As heir to the Enlightenment, rationalism exalted itself as a judge of religious mythology, which it believed it could interpret according to its own rules. Then the realization developed that there is no direct path from mythos to *logos* and that the content of myth cannot be recast in rational truths without sacrificing its substance. Even the process of "demythologizing," which is by no means peculiar to theology and which, it is believed, can put the "kerygmatic form" of a religious message into a concept, has had to recognize its limitations in dealing with religious content. F. Schleiermacher, whose thought marks the transition from rationalism to romanticism, stressed that the spirit of religion (→religion, religions) can only be understood on its own terms and cannot be forced into rational frameworks. If today a new consciousness of myth and its irreducibility holds sway in philosophy, then the inadequacy of a purely Enlightenment attitude in the study of religion has already been discovered.

This leads to the second root of the study of religion: romanticism. Romanticism fostered the yearning for an experiential, pure, and primal faith. It was the romantic movement which gave the greatest inspiration to the study of religious folklore as well as to research into Oriental religions. It was believed that one could find one's way back to the sources of religious life in long-past and far-distant cultures. Questions were asked with great enthusiasm about the historical and then later the social and psychological roots of religion. It was believed then that the "essence" of religion could be discovered in its origins, whether this origin was to be found in a common religious background or in a specific form of belief in God (e.g., monotheism).

The more recent question — raised particularly in the twentieth century in sociological and psychological approaches — regarding the function (i.e., the functional effect) of religion continues the question of origins. It does this insofar as it seeks to explain religion not per se but rather in light of its background/context. Indeed, instead of inquiring into the origins of religion, questions are asked about its effects. Such inquiry, of course, is no longer inspired by romanticism but by a pragmatism which operates with numbers and objective measurements. Romantic impulses, however, have continued to leave their mark on the image of research into religion, along with sociological and psychological ones.

The third root of the modern study of religion is to be found in theology and above all in the field of historical theology. Historical theology drew ever-widening circles around the Old Testament and New Testament and thereby contributed to research into the history of religion in the ancient Near East and classical late antiquity. Biblical studies, as well as the study of the early church, have given vital stimulus to research into the history of ancient religions. Ever since Schleiermacher, however, systematic theology has questioned the nature of the "sacred," and without doubt there is a direct line leading from Schleiermacher to R. Otto, who, in his analysis of the "holy," or, more precisely, the "numinous," believed that he could get to the heart of all religions. If the numinous in Otto's writings is yet another category which can only be looked for and descriptively evoked in the religious experience of humanity, then for G. Mensching it becomes an ontological quantity, whose encounter with people constitutes the character of religion. For phenomenologists, the holy is a quantity presupposed in the history of religion which is experienced as a holy force (see, e.g., G. van der Leeuw) or as a quality of being which stands in opposition to the profane (see, e.g., M. Eliade). Undoubtedly, one is dealing here with an extension of theological thought into the study of religion. However, the study of religion begins by first developing its own hermeneutic which will justify its unique position as an academic discipline, so that today we can see a multiplicity of new approaches which fight for an appropriate understanding of their own and other faiths. It is clear from all this that complete objectivity is impossible and that latent prejudgments and conscious perspectives will always leave their mark on the historian of religion.

2. It is generally agreed that the study of religion, as opposed to the philosophy of religion, is possible primarily on the basis of research into the history of religion. This must be carried out according to the criteria of secular history, fully applying historical-critical methods. These, however, need to be supplemented by a hermeneutic, because not only must facts be established and historical connections described but a living faith must also be made visible (W. C. Smith). For this reason, research into the history of religion must reach beyond objectively ascertainable facts, since it must lead to an understanding of how and why particular forms of belief have been preserved — or not, as the case may be.

The second stage of all work in the history of religion is the systematic comparison of religions. The purpose of this systematic research is the drawing up of general structures and the demonstration of recurring basic patterns and "archetypes" (M. Eliade). The phenomenology of religion has seen its main task above all as drawing attention to such constant features. In so doing, it has, in many ways, failed to show the conditions under which this or that form of belief in God, of the image of the human person, and experience of the world were revealed. In this connection, the comparative study of cultures has taken a further hesitant step forward in showing under which conditions certain manifestations, such as nativism and messianism, occur.

3. In the study of comparative religion three types of procedures can be distinguished. First, there is the "nonreligious interpretation of religious concepts" (a concept, by the way, already used on the religious side — see D. Bonhoeffer and G. Ebeling). The common desire of these research concerns, which in themselves are very different, is to understand religion in dimensions which are basically not religious. Thus religious research which is rooted in social science is in many ways concerned with understanding religious phenomena against a matrix of social phenomena and with partially reducing the former to the latter. The psychology of religion can be a kind of game of reductionism. This furthers the concern that religion is classified as a cultural manifestation in the general picture of culture, rather than being considered as an independent quantity. Whereas certain procedures purportedly interpret religious facts without making value judgments about them (such interpretations are always derived from latent criteria), the study of religion which criticizes ideology (e.g., C. Colpe) proceeds from a given standard, namely, the emancipation of men and women in the modern sense of autonomy. From this point of view, religion must be judged according to its "potential for emancipation." In this way the standard which is brought to bear on religion is molded by human understanding.

The second approach to the study of religion is concerned with an interpretation of religious phenomena themselves, determined by the unique quality of what is "religious." As already indicated above, this particular approach sees as the point of reference the holy or the transcendent. In this way, the various religions can be understood as different experiences of the one holy, or they can be described as different mythological expressions of a reference to the transcendent. In the last resort, it is the one — ultimately the Christian — God who works through all religions (F. Heiler). The study of religion takes this kind of fundamental interpretation into consideration but can never accept such positions as dogma.

A third possible approach, deriving from a line of scholars that runs from W. Dilthey to O. Bollnow, regards religions as forms of expression of the religious life. According to this approach, religion should be interpreted both critically and sympathetically.

4. The significance of the study of religion for mission and mission studies lies in the way it portrays the historical context in which missionary work takes place. The dialogue partners addressed in mission cannot be understood apart from the cultural and religious tradition in which they stand. The first element of such dialogue is language, followed by the particular properties of the tradition to which they belong. A Bible translation must be clear about which terms it uses for basic religious concepts, beginning with the term for God and including the terms for religious qualities such as grace, love, humility, and sin and for anthropological concepts such as sense, heart, and soul. An explicitly Christian proclamation must be clear about the basic concepts of the religious tradition of those who are being addressed. Research into the study of religion can enable one to understand unfamiliar concepts and basic assumptions and so create the right conditions for missiological reflections on how these can be connected to the categories given by other religions, even when these categories deviate from the parallel Christian concepts. This holds true not only for linguistic concepts but also for basic religious assumptions, some of which diverge considerably from Christian parallels, while others reveal unexpected parallels. Thus, one will find many expressions, especially in the ethical proverbs of various peoples, which resemble in form and content those of the Book of Proverbs, which itself has taken over many elements of ancient Near Eastern wisdom. The proverbs of peoples are often discovered to be treasure houses in which one finds many analogies with the moral teaching of the New Testament. Obviously, divergences from the biblical message are encountered where the local religion, by reason of a long self-contained development, has produced a different autochthonous system of concepts, which must, above all, be understood as such. The question of establishing a relationship between the far-reaching Western Christian tradition stamped by Hellenism and Greco-Roman philosophy and the religious tradition being addressed is then a missionary task (→theology of mission).

The study of religion can, however, not only help in grasping the uniqueness of other religious traditions. If phenomenology has demonstrated the fundamental religious thoughts which are always reappearing and "archetypes" which exhibit (admittedly more in structure than in content) the same factors throughout the history of religion, then the study of mission cannot ignore this knowledge (→theology of religion).

Hans-Joachim Klimkeit

Bibliography

Colpe, C., *Theologie, Ideologie, Religionswissenschaft: Demonstrationen ihrer Unterscheidung* (1980). Eliade, M., *History of Religious Ideas* (1978). Idem, *Patterns in Comparative Religion* (1958). Idem, *The Quest: History and Meaning in Religion* (1969). Gensichen, H. W., "Religionswissenschaft und Theologie," in *Theologie: Was ist das?* (1977) 107–25. Glock, C. Y., and P. E. Hammond, *Beyond the Classics? Essays in the Scientific Study of Religion* (1973). King, W. L., *Introduction to Religion: A Phenomenological Approach* (1968). Lanczkowski, G., "Science of Religion," *SM* 5:259–62. Martin, H. L., *Essays on Jung and the Study of Religion* (1985). Morris, J., *The Study of Religion* (1981). Otto, R., *The Idea of the Holy* (1926). Preus, J. S., *Explaining Religion: Criticism and Theory from Bodin to Freud* (1987). Schlette, H. R., "Theology of Religions," *SM* 5:282–84. Idem, *Towards a Theology of Religions* (1966). Sharma, A., *Our Religions* (1993). Smith, W. C., *The Meaning and End of Religion* (1962). Idem, *Toward a World Theology: Faith and the Comparative History of Religions* (1981). Sundermeier, T., "Zur Verhältnisbestimmung von Religionswissenschaft und Theologie aus protestantischer Sicht," *ZMRW* 64 (1980) 241–58. Swidler, L., *Toward a Universal Theology of Religion* (1988). Tillich, P., *Christianity and the Encounter of the World Religions* (1963). Van der Leeuw, G., *Religion in Essence and Manifestation: A Study in Phenomenology* (1963). Waardenburg, J. J., *Classical Approaches to the Study of Religion: Aims, Methods, and Theories of Research* (1973). Idem, *Reflections on the Study of Religion: Including an Essay on the Work of Gerardus van der Leeuw* (1978).

❧ SYMBOL ❧

1. The Notion of Symbol. 2. Symbol in the Life of the Church. 3. Missionary Adaptation of Symbol.

1. Contemporary anthropological usage distinguishes symbol from sign. "Sign" is the generic term to express the relationship between a signifier and its object. "Symbol" is a specific term that includes a certain presence of the reality signified, even if such a reality is only partially perceived or communicated. In this sense, sacraments, whether in their ritual totality of words, action, and material elements or in their particular material aspect, can be called symbols. The notion of symbol includes also a relationship of connaturality between the signifier and its object. Such a connaturality stems from the ability of the signifier to evoke the reality it signifies, thanks to the former's natural quality to serve as image, icon, emblem, and so on, of the latter. In this sense symbols have a universal acceptance, as opposed to conventional signs. Thus, washing with water, eating and drinking in community, and anointing the sick with oil are symbols founded on the nature of things and the experience of peoples.

Symbols acquire fuller expression in the realm of religion, insofar as this is ordained to the experience of a divine presence or intervention in the life of a community. The principal type of symbol employed by religion is rite, which can be described as an activity consisting of a formulary accompanying a gesture and/or the application of a material element. By nature a rite is institutional and is traditional to the community which celebrates and repeats it at various moments of its life or the life of its members. Such moments refer especially to fundamental human situations such as birth, growth, marriage, sickness, and so on. The rites of passage symbolize, that is to say, indicate, the presence of the divine in the turning points in human life. A symbol, however, does not merely signify the presence of a reality; it also establishes and fosters relationship with that reality, a relationship of awe, admiration, gratitude, and alliance.

This notion of symbol differs from the broad concept which defines symbol as the stylization or spiritualization of a sign. Such, for example, would be a balance symbolizing justice, or incense symbolizing the efficacy of prayer. In these cases, the signifier does not point to the presence of the reality it signifies and hence differs from the anthropological understanding of symbol.

2. The church, as a community of faith, has the mission to proclaim and celebrate its faith. Faith is proclaimed through the preaching of the word of God and professed principally through the "symbol" of faith which is the solemn declaration of the church's creed. Faith which is proclaimed through spoken symbol is celebrated through ritual symbols or rites. Foremost among these are the sacraments in which both the spoken and ritual symbols converge to form a liturgical celebration. Thus, the full liturgy of the sacraments consists of the proclamation of the word of God and the performance of the ritual symbol. The →word of God brings about faith and conversion and leads the assembly to the reality signified by the sacramental symbol.

The sacramental rite consists of a spoken formulary accompanying and explaining a ritual gesture. In some sacraments the formulary and gesture involve the use of material elements, such as water, bread and wine, and oil. Sacraments as symbols are thus primarily an activity rather than a material element. The church believes that the subject of this activity is Christ himself, since "by his power he is present in the sacraments, so that when a man baptizes it is really Christ himself who baptizes" (*SC* 7). The same is said of the proclamation of the word, "since it is he himself who speaks when the holy Scriptures are read in church" (*SC* 7). The presence of Christ, and consequently, of his paschal mystery, in both the proclamation of the word of God and the performance of the ritual symbol puts the sacraments in the category of symbol. Indeed, in the sacraments the conditions imposed by contemporary anthropology on symbol are fulfilled: presence of the reality signified, connaturality of the signifier with its object, and relationship of the community with the reality signified by the symbol. Sacraments establish and foster relationship between Christ and the community; they are symbols of encounter with Christ; they make his paschal mystery present in ritual symbol and communicate it to the community.

Besides the sacraments the church possesses other symbols. These are best understood in their relationship with the proclamation of the word of God and the performance of the ritual symbol. Their function is to prepare the community to celebrate God's word and the sacrament, to remind them of the reality signified by the sacraments, and to illustrate or explain this reality. It is in this sense that they are called symbols, for they exist in function of the primary symbols from which they derive their meaning. Some examples of these symbols are found in sacramental celebrations and are called explanatory rites. The postbaptismal anointing, the giving of marriage rings, and so on, are meant to illustrate certain aspects of the sacrament. Outside of sacramental celebrations but in relation to the liturgy one can name such symbols as holy water, icons, palm branches, and so on. In their use the church recognizes a certain virtual presence of Christ's mystery because of their relationship with the sacraments.

3. The symbols employed by the church originate to a large extent from the biblical world and from various cultures with which the church was in contact. In the West the prominent ones are the Greco-Roman and the Franco-Germanic cultures. Although a large number of symbols are transcultural and, therefore, are able to be shared by people from different cultures, many of the church's symbols are specific to certain cultures or epochs. The question of adaptation thus becomes a necessity, because of the diversity of cultures in the church. This is especially true of the missions, to which Vatican II has given great attention in such documents as *Lumen Gentium, Sacrosanctum Concilium,* and *Ad Gentes.* Sacramental symbols like washing with water, eating and drinking, and anointing are transcultural. However, each culture has its specific form or mode of performing these symbols. Cultural adaptation in these cases involves not necessarily a change of the symbolic element but rather a change in the mode of performing it in accord with the people's cultural form. Liturgy experts, with the assistance of cultural anthropologists, will have to study how the washing in baptism, for example, could be performed employing the mode used by a given culture for a parallel activity. Asian and African cultures are rich in such ritual activities, some of which form part of the religious observance. The process of adaptation by the method of either acculturation or inculturation should avoid syncretism in the process. This can be done by paying attention to the transcultural quality of the symbols and by infusing the cultural element with Christian meaning through biblical typology.

Other symbols, especially the explanatory rites of liturgical celebrations, are often not transculturally transparent. The giving of white vestments at baptism does not manifest the joy and dignity of the neophyte in those cultures where white is the color of mourning. Symbols like the gestures of standing, kneeling, or processing and objects like the insignia of authority are not always cultural constants. In these cases, adaptation could be done through dynamic cultural equivalents or through substitution, provided the norms of faith and liturgical adaptation are observed. In some cases, dynamic equivalent or substitution may not be sufficient to satisfy the demand for symbols that are rooted in the cultural experience of the people. Hence, the need for creativity.

Symbols abound in the liturgical year. These symbols are often connected with the seasons of the year and the cosmic elements like spring, equinox, and full moon and with human activities like planting and harvesting. Examples of feasts with this connection are Easter, Pentecost, Christmas, Epiphany, the birth of John the Baptist, and rotation and ember days. Adaptation of these feasts can mean a change of date to suit the calendar of human activity, as in rotation days, or the introduction of cosmic symbolism to illustrate the meaning of the feast. Easter, which falls during summer in the tropics and in autumn in the Southern Hemisphere, can be celebrated with texts and symbols that are evocative of any given season of the year.

There are also symbols connected with place: the place of gathering, the place reserved to the leaders of the assembly, the place for proclamation and prayer, and so on. These have cultural underpinnings. The adaptation of the church edifice, for example, as the symbol of the assembled community (the church edifice was originally called *domus Ecclesiae*) can take into account the architectonic structure and the function of community centers found among peoples of particular cultures. The baptistery, sanctuary, lectern, and altar are places which possess strong symbolic meaning in the liturgy. However, they have also a cultural significance. The adaptation of such places is necessary in order to provide a coherent and culturally appropriate space for the proclamation of the word of God and the celebration of the sacramental symbols.

ANSCAR J. CHUPUNGCO, OSB

Bibliography

Ayo, N., *The Creed as Symbol* (1989). Benjamin, R., *African Religions: Symbol, Ritual, and Community* (1976). Chauvet, L. M., *Symbol and Sacrament: A Sacramental Reinterpretation of Christian Existence* (1993). Chupungco, A., *Cultural Adaptation of the Liturgy* (1982). Cooke, B. J., *The Distancing of God: The Ambiguity of Symbol in History and Theology* (1990). Douglas, M., *Natural Symbols: Explorations in Cosmology* (1970). Dulles, A., *The Craft of Theology: From Symbol to System* (1992). Eliade, M., *Images and Symbols* (1952). Hendricks, W. L., "Symbol," in *A New Handbook of Christian Theology* (1992) 467–68. *The Herder Symbol Dictionary* (1986). Johnson, F. E., *Religious Symbolism* (1969). Jung, C. G., *Man and His Symbols* (1968). Motzko, M. E., *Karl Rahner's Theology: A Theology of Symbol* (1976). Perrin, N., *Jesus and the Language of the Kingdom: Symbol and Metaphor in New Testament Interpretation* (1980). Rahner, K., "The Theology of Symbol," *TI* 4 (1966) 221–52. Ricoeur, P., *Figuring the Sacred: Religion, Narrative, and Imagination* (1995). Idem, *Interpretation Theory: Discourse and the Surplus of Meaning* (1976). Idem, *The Symbolism of Evil* (1967). Tillich, P., *The Dynamics of Faith* (1958). Idem, *Theology of Culture* (1959). Turner, V., *The Ritual Process: Structure and Anti-Structure* (1969).

T

❧ THEOLOGICAL EDUCATION ❧

1. Definition. 2. Founding Phase and Building Up. 3. Crises. 4. Changes in Theological Education. 5. Exchange of Experiences.

1. The term "theological education" is understood here as education for church service in Asia, the Near East, Africa, Central and Latin America, the Caribbean, and the Pacific region. As a rule, theological education takes place under church auspices, in theological colleges, seminaries, Bible schools, and so on. In the post-colonial period in many places theological faculties or departments of religious studies have been created in which Roman Catholic and Protestant theology is taught along with non-Christian religions.

2. In the founding and expansion phases of educational institutions, the most important task of theological education was understood mainly as the training of indigenous pastors and theologians to prepare them to replace the large number of foreign workers in the higher offices of mission churches. Obviously, in doing this, plans were laid according to patterns of education known in Western countries. Instruction took place in the languages of the colonial countries, and teaching materials originated from the mother churches and propagated their denominational slants. Residential educational centers were expanded. One basic problem of theological education in the initial period was that the resources available did not stretch far enough for a system of education which could meet the academic standards of theological education in North America and Europe.

3. In the course of reorganizing the mission churches into structurally self-sufficient churches, and through the unexpectedly rapid growth of Christianity in areas of the Third World, a profound change in theological education was introduced at the beginning of the 1960s. Shortcomings in the ideas of education known up until this period developed in some places into a crisis in theological education. Especially on the Roman Catholic side — but not only there — the discrepancy between the limited number of fully educated priests and the steadily growing congregations was alarmingly high. Doubts emerged concerning the relevance of the content of this education to church and society. Institutions of theological education had been created in isolation, so they were seen as foreign bodies by the indigenous churches and were criticized by the universities for backwardness and indifferent levels of education. This problem was intensified on the Protestant side by a denominationally self-inflicted isolation.

4. Change in theological education is a long-term process which is by no means finished today, and the educational institutions, churches, missionary organizations, and overall ecumenical programs (World Council of Churches, Lutheran World Federation) are jointly concerned with this task. The picture of theological education has become extremely diverse in the course of this change; one finds traditional patterns, reforms built into the system, and innovative alternatives running partly parallel to each other and partly mixed together. The basic trends of this change since the beginning of the 1960s can be summarized under five points.

4.1. Before the preparation for changes occurred, ministry was largely restricted to courses of instruction for candidates for ordination. The emphasis since then has been placed more strongly on the education of lay preachers, catechists, part-time pastors, deacons, elders, religious education teachers, social workers, kindergarten teachers, Sunday school instructors, church musicians, and so on. Since their restructuring, institutions of theological education have taken over more functions; they are now frequently a theological seminary, a religious education and social-science training school, a center for further education of elders and ministers, and a lay training center, all in one. Behind this concept lies a comprehensive understanding of ministry which links its theological approach to the Reformation tradition of the priesthood of all believers. Conducting more study courses in one center and contact among students from all areas of study — for example, during the holding of shared worship — give visible expression to an understanding of theological education as preparation for the whole ministry of the church. For the rest, the conventional distinction between "theological education" and "Christian education" is being blurred because of the new orientation of theological education.

4.2. The alienation of theological education from the reality of life in the younger churches and from the conditions of existence in countries of the Third World is being countered by measures of indigenization. Instruction now takes place partly in the local languages. Teaching materials are translated or produced directly by local authors in the national languages. Practically everywhere there is an observable turning away from the academic system of teaching to a more strongly vocational and practically oriented education. "Ministerial formation" has become the model, replacing theological education. Consequently, there is a concern to orient the contents of teaching more strongly than before on the vital questions of the life of the local churches. Attempts are made to enter into the challenges conditioning the context which these churches encounter. In this respect, some educational institutions take on a sort of innovative role in their churches. The so-called contextualization (→contextual theology) of theological education is reflected in the fact that themes such as local popular piety, religious pluralism, cultural identity, illiteracy, poverty, human rights abuses, and political authoritarianism are dealt with in the teaching programs.

4.3. One theme has recently preoccupied many institutions of theological education in all regions of the Third World, a theme which could be regarded as an index of a radical new direction of theological education and the structure of church ministry: "theology by the people" and "ministry by the people." Hidden behind these concepts is a concern to give back the responsibility for theological education to the Christian congregation as a whole, to remind people that, in the beginnings of Christianity, responsibility for instruction in the faith was accepted and carried out by the congregation. The criticism lying behind this new approach is that proclamation and instruction in the faith have been delegated to a small circle of people who have developed into a select professional group and have often enough stood in spiritual and academic isolation from the congregation. The reproach is made as much of the elitist system of theological education as of the traditional way of church life, that they both take place in an ivory tower, that is, with no relation to the people, who are "outside, in front of the door," and who must daily struggle for survival in dehumanizing conditions. "Theology by the people" and "ministry by the people" are expressions of an attempt to describe new forms of community life "outside, in front of the door," and — in a pictorial and in a literal sense — to open the doors of institutions of theological education to the upholders of living church communities. The presentation of such primary experiences of Christian existence is recognized as an indisputable first step in theological education, to be followed only secondarily by reflection on comprehensive connections and recourse to the great theological traditions.

4.4. So-called Theological Education by Extension (TEE) is a special attempt at indigenization in which the greatest possible increase in student numbers and the most comprehensive adaptation of study courses to the previous knowledge and conditions of life of students have been significantly and successfully realized. TEE can be characterized as a kind of extramural studies which is augmented by regular instruction and which takes place in small groups with tutors and lecturers. The study material is prepared as far as possible in readers that suit those studying by themselves (programmed texts). TEE is based on a system of courses in which the student individually decides the length of his or her studies and the date of completion. TEE has proved effective especially in the formal theological education of long-serving lay preachers, of leading workers in the →African independent churches, of women involved in church work, as well as of workers in thinly settled areas. According to a rough estimate (Kinsler 1983), at the end of the 1970s there were about three hundred to four hundred TEE centers worldwide with about one hundred thousand students altogether. Today some estimate that these numbers have more than doubled. By far the greatest number of these centers are found in Third World countries.

4.5. Academic theological research has advanced parallel to the popularizing of theological education in the last several decades. So in the countries of the Third World, structures exist for research work that are in tune with the particular local circumstances. This work is supported by the linking up of a number of educational institutions in interregional theological unions which have set themselves the aim of conducting joint research projects, publishing theological journals, holding consultations on contemporary questions of theology, and creating a forum for the exchange of information among teachers. By the early 1980s there were already ten unions of theological institutions in Africa, nineteen in Asia and the Middle East, six in Latin America, and three in the Pacific region. Postgraduate studies (masters and doctoral programs) are offered jointly by some institutions in Asia and Africa. An example is the South East Asia Graduate School of Theology (an institution in which all the larger centers of theological education in South East Asia are involved), which offers facilities for research with a clearly formulated relationship to the Asian context.

5. Many initiatives for overcoming the problems of educational structures alienated from their context flow from the Program for Theological Education (PTE) of the World Council of Churches. Founded as the Theological Education Fund (1958–77), the PTE is an important forum for the exchange of experience and information about theological education "in six continents," for working out new directions in education, and not least for the transfer of experiences and knowledge of theological education from the Third World to the theological establishments of Europe and North America. Teachers in the Third World use the opportunity of regular, and at times very intensive, exchanges through the PTE to link their concern for the grounding of theological education in the local context with an opening for the mutual concern that transcends context.

CHRISTINE LIENEMANN-PERRIN

Bibliography

Bauer, A. O. F., *Being in Mission* (1987). Buchwalter King, G., *Globalization: Tracing the Journey, Charting the Course / Theological Education* (1993). Conn, H. M., and S. F. Rowen, *Missions and Theological Education in World Perspective* (1984). Freire, P., *Pedagogy of the Oppressed* (1970). Haar, G. T., "Religious Education in Africa," in *Exch* 50 (1988). Hopewell, J. E., "Theological Education," *CDCW* (1971) 591–92. Kinsler, F. R., *Ministry by the People: Theological Education by Extension* (1983). Lienemann-Perrin, C., *Training for a Relevant Ministry: A Study of the Work of the Theological Education Fund* (1981). Myklebust, O. G., "Missiology in Contemporary Theological Education: A Factual Survey," *MissS* 12 (1989) 87–107. Idem, *The Study of Missions in Theological Education,* vol. 1 (1955). Neely, A., "The Teaching of Missions," in *Toward the 21st Century in Christian Mission* (1993). Peterson, S. L., *Mission Study Resources for the Future* (1995). Program for Theological Education/WCC, *Ministerial Formation* (1979–). Schwartz, G., *An American Directory of Schools and Colleges Offering Missionary Courses* (1973). Sutcliffe, J. M., *A Dictionary of Religious Education* (1984). Ward, T., "Educational Preparation of Missionaries: A Look Ahead," *EMQ* 23 (October 1987) 398. Whiteman, D., ed., "Mission Studies: Taking Stock, Charting the Course," *Missiol* 24 (1996).

✎ THEOLOGY OF MISSION ❧

1. Theological Models of Mission. 2. Renewed Reflections on Mission Theology. 3. The Contemporary Situation.

1. The fact that Christianity is a missionary religion unites it with Buddhism and Islam and differentiates it from traditional religions such as Shintoism and the tribal religions of Africa, which claim validity only for a tribe or a people. Mission belongs to the essence of Christianity and the churches, as burning does to fire (E. Brunner). It is, however, a gift and also a task. As a "city set on a hill," the church is missionary in its very existence (Matthew 5) and at the same time is sent into the world by a special command (Jn 20:21). Both descriptions provide equally valid grounds for mission and are developed in a variety of ways by the New Testament witnesses. Since then they have played a variety of roles in church history. Wherever the church preached the gospel and lived by it, it was missionary. It obeyed the commission to go into the world of nations only in periodic bursts of activity. Very soon in the early church, people believed that the missionary commission had been fulfilled by the apostles (Rom 10:18) and that it was no longer incumbent upon the church as a whole, a view which the churches of the Reformation adopted. Considerations of a theology of mission in the narrower sense were, therefore, not important and only rarely proposed. The new awakening of interest in mission in modern times led to a new appreciation of the essential nature of the missionary task of the church. It was especially important because this new awakening coincided with the expansion of Western domination and apparently sprang from the same origins. This influenced missionary work in many ways, but also harmed it.

1.1. *Warneck's doctrine of mission.* A theological purification of the missionary motive and a new appreciation of appropriate missionary methods and aims became necessary. G. Warneck, a pastor in Rothschirmbach who after his retirement in 1896 became honorary professor of mission at the University of Halle, was the first to tackle this task thoroughly and wrote a Protestant doctrine of mission (Warneck 1892–1905, vol. 1). This book remained in use up to World War II, both within and far beyond the limits of the German-speaking world, and had no small influence on the Catholic theology of mission (Schmidlin 1923). Even today, there is no theology of mission on the Protestant side comparable in extent and influence. Warneck's five-fold justification for mission serves as an apologetic both for establishing as broad a foundation of mission as possible and for ensuring a place for the study of mission in the ranks of the classical theological disciplines. The important branches of theology, dogmatics, ethics, ecclesiology, church history, and even ethnology demonstrate with one accord that Christianity must carry out mission and that the church must have a missionary direction. But Warneck's study also carries within it a triumphalistic note. The world of religions, he argues, waits for Christianity, which puts itself at the disposal of the modern world as a spiritual basis because of its flexibility and adaptability. "It is, therefore, certain to become the general religion of humanity" (1:96). "Because Christianity is not form and law but spirit and life, it may pervade the whole of human personal and social life, which may also take on the same popular, civic, social, and cultural forms" (1:292). Warneck rejects the identification of "Europeanization" with "Christianization" because of Christianity's universal dimension: Christianity is for humanity and humanity for Christianity (1:319).

Warneck is indebted to the pietist heritage of mission but also learns from the denominational conflicts of the nineteenth century that there cannot be mission without the church. The mission of the church must be spared denominational wrangling as far as possible. His definition of mission, which has been widely disseminated, is, therefore, very open and states: "By Christian mission we understand the entire activity of Christendom that is directed to the planting and organization of the church of Christ among non-Christians" (1:1). The subject of mission is Christianity. Therefore, the instruments of mission are individual Christians, especially those who are committed and called. Mission requires a special vocation through the Holy Spirit and the church. The aim of mission is the planting of churches. If the church is founded in a non-Christian environment, mission has achieved its aim. According to Warneck, mission in the Christian West would be a contradiction in terms and should be called proselytism, not mission. Mission aims at the conversion and baptism of non-Christians.

Warneck is indebted to the history of romantic thought, according to which God not only works in nature but is also present in history, which is recognized as the sphere of divine activity. Nations have their prescribed place in history, as well as their special destination. They come into being through the means of God's revelation. Mission, therefore, must apply itself to the conversion of nations and to the founding of national churches. In practical terms, this means that it must turn to the middle class of a people, since the "middle position is the healthy core of the people" (3:279). Warneck believes that with this premise he is aligning himself with Jesus, who was poor but not destitute (*pauvre* in the original [1:108]). It is significant here how experience in one's own country is projected onto distant peoples. One seeks to build churches after one's own model, whether they are national churches, as per Warneck, or denominational churches, as per other theologians of mission (e.g., K. Graul and L. Harms).

Warneck unites the different strands of the missionary movement in his design for a theology of mission. He speaks of individual conversion but also speaks of the conversion of whole peoples. He wants the establishment of Christian churches, but at the same time he sees all humanity being shaped by Christianity and formed anew.

1.2. *The conversion and church-planting models.* The elements that are united in Warneck's theology have been separated, however, especially in Catholic theology of mission. J. Schmidlin, who is generally recognized as the first Catholic missiologist and the father of the conversion model, does link these elements together under Warneck's influence. Changes of emphasis should not be overlooked, however. They are found, above all, in this: in Schmidlin's work there is no discussion of the organizational structures of the church. The picture of the hierarchically organized Roman Catholic Church is not analyzed. On the contrary, it is elevated through identification with the reign of God (Schmidlin 1923, intro., 22). The ultimate goal of mission, argues Schmidlin, can only be induction into the organized church; conversion is only the preliminary goal. A change of heart and baptism are the signs of conversion, which is a religious act through and through but which has social and cultural consequences — leaving the old social and cultural connections and integrating into a new religious and cultural environment, that of the Christian West, with its "moral concepts" and "better methods of work," its "higher culture" and civilization.

The church-planting of the Louvain school (P. Charles, J. Masson) can be distinguished from the conversion model in that in the former, conversion or being born again as a child of God (i.e., "saving souls") is not seen as the goal of mission. Mission begins on the doorstep of every congregation. Conversion can only be the means; the goal is the extension of the visible church. "Mission goes out from the church; it is led by the church for the church, and its goal is the church in this world" (J. Masson). One cannot escape from the horizon of a legalistically constituted church. There are no goals for mission beyond the visible church because the invisible church is mediated through the faith which the church imparts, through the sacraments and structured ministry. The church is the "sacrament of the world"; it is the "meaning of the earth"; it is the reign of God (P. Charles).

The problem with both the conversion and church-planting models lies not only in their identification of the institutional church with the reign of God (a position rarely held today) and in their Eurocentric starting point and reference points but also in the fact that according to these ideas, the person of another faith is seen purely as the *object* of mission. People are divided into the categories of "the damned" and "the saved," mere objects of head-counting in an ecclesiastical inventory. This betrays the essence of the gospel, which addresses people in their subjectivity. The human person is made part of the unchangeable and inexchangeable "I-ness" of God's word of love.

In their pure forms, neither model is used today. Nevertheless, the conversion model is strongly reflected in evangelical circles, especially the →faith missions, that is, when detached from its explicit ecclesiological connections. Mission here has the single aim of converting people, who should for their part become missionaries in order to bring others to Christ. Mission progresses from conversion to conversion. If a community is created by the proclamation of the gospel, it is considered, so to speak, as a by-product, the theological importance of which is hardly considered, but whose form is for that very reason often the object of the most violent controversies and the cause of divisions.

The church growth model (→Church Growth movement) should be included here. In this school, detailed sociological, ethnological, and precise statistical plans are devised in order to make possible strategies aimed at the efficient deployment of missionaries for the growth of congregations. The ecclesiastical and theological presuppositions of this procedure are rarely, if ever, considered. The fact that evangelical missions can appropriate both models shows that, in a different situation, they are not as diametrically opposed to each other as they appeared to be in discussions within the Catholic Church. Their unity was, after all, postulated by Warneck, as well as Schmidlin.

1.3. *The salvation history model.* World War II, with its political and spiritual repercussions, made a rethinking of mission necessary. The colonial era was coming to an end; the West could no longer with any justification regard itself as the center of the world. The churches of the Third World emerged strengthened by the crises which were caused by the war and could no longer be kept in dependence or as "daughter churches." The International Missionary Conference at Whitby, Ontario (1948), attempted to put things right and used a concept summed up in the slogan "partnership in obedience." This concept sought to define the relationships between the "older" and "younger" churches in such a way that the common goal of the one mission remained in sight. At the same time, with the slogan "expectant evangelism," it opened up a perspective toward new directions in the theology of mission. Eschatology came to the fore. From then on, in conjunction with Western awareness of history, eschatology defined the theology of mission. But which history was meant, and which understanding of history was to be used for the interpretation of missionary events? These were questions that resulted in differences of opinion, without the reasons for these differences ever being fully recognized. Conflicts often arose over subsidiary issues, and causes were confused with secondary symptoms and consequences.

The salvation history model of mission was the most widespread and, up to the present, is the most influential in the circles of those active in mission. The theological span of its representatives is broad, among which W. Freytag, G. Vicedom, J. Blauw, and D. Bosch are to be counted as chief representatives. Documents of the World Council of Churches and the Lutheran World Federation also reflect this view. Furthermore, texts like *Ad Gentes, Evangelii Nuntiandi,* and *Redemptoris Missio* from the Roman Catholic side should also be included here.

Theology of mission, which is oriented by the salvation history concept, derives its exegetical justification from the work of O. Cullmann, above all from *Christ and Time* (1946). This view of mission receives its classic presentation in B. Sundkler's theology of mission; Sundkler offers the most self-contained plan and has put his stamp on a range of terms which have found wide acceptance without their origin being acknowledged. According to Sundkler, the history of mission begins with an event which is decisive for salvation history, the call of Abraham. It is God's answer to the lost state of humanity since Adam's fall and to their revolt in building the Tower of Babel. God works in a double fashion: God chooses people and treats them as examples, as "substitutionary" examples. Sundkler acknowledges the law of "progressive reduction" in the course of the history of salvation (the election of a people, of a "faithful remnant," of the Son of Man), which finds its high point and turning point in the cross. From this point, the remnant continues according to the law of "progressive expansion": the election of the apostles and the founding of the church, which spreads throughout the world to announce the message of salvation to humanity. The universality of the New Testament has its inverse counterpart in the particularism of the Old Testament but is grounded in it, since this is the only way for the meaning of history, which is mission, to be made plain. The length of time between the first and second coming of Christ is determined by the announcement of the Lordship of Christ. Mission fills this period. It becomes the measure by which the end of history can be determined. According to Cullmann, Mk 13:10 and 2 Thes 2:5–7 are key texts for the theology of mission. The church may not stand still; it must venture into the world. Time and geography stand in a close relationship to each other. The longer the time before the return of Christ, the greater the chances for the geographical expansion of the proclamation of the gospel. According to Sundkler, mission is "crossing frontiers," and that is as much in the geographical sense as in the broader sense of "translation" into other languages, cultures and social settings. The centripetal and centrifugal movements of mission are related to each other. Only the person who stands firm at the center can reach the periphery. The "ministry of crossing frontiers," the office of a missionary, alone serves the purpose of the people setting out on a popular pilgrimage (Mt 8:11–12) to participate in the great feast, which is anticipated in the Lord's Supper (→Eucharist [Lord's Supper]). The Lord's Supper is a sacrament of mission.

Mission takes place "with a view to the end" (W. Freytag); it prepares for it. The end will break in when all peoples have heard the gospel. The missionary movement of the twentieth century has received a tremendous amount of energy from this theology of mission, which dominated the World Missionary Conference in Edinburgh in 1910. J. R. Mott believed that this goal of reaching all peoples was possible "in this generation."

Responsibility for the world clearly has no place in this concept. Mission calls people out of this (sinful) world. The difference between the church and the world widens to a chasm in the view of many representatives of this model. The service of love, *diakonia,* which is to be carried out by the church, becomes oriented more toward an individual ethic. It has no meaning in itself but merely serves the proclamation by preparing the ground for it. It accompanies or is the fruit of →faith. Mission's proper work is, according to general opinion, the proclamation of the gospel to non-Christians, a spiritual salvation service. Individual missiologists, such as Sundkler, try to draw out another line of thought, which is embedded in the idea of Christ's Lordship. The "royal rule of the love of Christ" is to be understood as absolute and must be lived out absolutely! In the salvation history model, in contrast to the teachings of Vatican II, for example, other religions are described as ways which lead to damnation. That view applies even to those representatives of this model who do not wish to deny non-Christian religions anthropological or cultural value and who guard against any general condemnation of them. In both cases, however, conversion is regarded as essential; it is sealed by baptism, which is both a question of being led out of the old religion and of being grafted onto the Body of Christ, the church. Baptism is also understood, in the original meaning of the word, as a sacrament of mission.

The church has its origin in the preaching of the word in the context of and surrounded by other religions. But the church is not the goal of mission; its goal is the reign of God. The church is the pilgrim people of God, which strives to reach this goal. The church points to this goal, is its image, and communicates it in God's name; it can be described as the "sacrament of salvation" (*LG* 1, 48). Mission is not called, says Sundkler, to build "fortresses" on this earth but "thresholds which lead to the temple of the Lord." Mission, therefore, does not build the reign of God, as one still sang in the nineteenth century, but only "colonies of the reign of God." These "colonies" differ from one another but have an unmistakable Christian identity. The church always maintains a link with a culture, but it always and in all circumstances maintains a certain countercultural character. Its first commitment must be to what is countercultural, in order that a higher degree of indigenization can be achieved. The missionary task is a "task of interpretation." "Interpreter" is another name for missionary (Sundkler).

At the International Missionary Conference at Willingen (1952), K. Hartenstein, a director of the Basel Mission, introduced the concept of *missio Dei,* which quickly found wide acceptance (through the agency of G. Vicedom), without distinguishing the different ways in which he applied it. That brought considerable confusion into the theology of mission. In the salvation history model of mission, the meaning of this concept is unequivocal: mission takes its origin not from human beings, not from the church, but from God. It is God who sends Jesus, who is the first, the archetypal, the "real" missionary. His mission continues in the mission of the church. In spite of this model's trinitarian approach, it remains unclear how the *missio Dei* relates to the *missio hominum.* H.-W. Gensichen makes the tension between God's purpose in salvation and human witness the starting point and basic structural principle of his theology of mission. He attempts to make that theology stand beside the somewhat multifaceted concepts of "dimension" and "intention," which for the most part go back to L. Newbigin.

1.4. *The history of the promise model.* Objections to the salvation history model have been advanced from different sides. One criticism is that the model downplays the world and history. History fades out if it is divided into salvation and world history, and one ends up concentrating on those small extracts which concern Israel and the church. One no longer has the whole world in view, seeing humanity largely as a *massa perditionis* since one is chiefly concerned only with the rescue of the few. If apocalyptic thought gains the upper hand over eschatology, then the church stands alone in the center of all thought, plans, and action. Mission as mission to the world falls out of sight. J. C. Hoekendijk first advanced this criticism during the preparatory work for the International Missionary Conference at Willingen (1952). This criticism attracted worldwide attention and gained wide acceptance through a study entitled "The Missionary Structure of the Congregation," which was commissioned at the World Assembly of the World Council of Churches at New Delhi (1961) and which gave a central place to Hoekendijk's thesis. On the Roman Catholic side, the new model, now under the influence of J. B. Metz and J. Moltmann, was represented above all by L. Rütti; and on the Protestant side, with varying degrees of emphasis, it was identified with H.-J. Margull, W. J. Hollenweger, M. Linz, and others. In the history-of-the-promise model, just as in the salvation history model, the concept of the *missio Dei* is a point of departure for considering a theology of mission. In contrast to the salvation history model, here it is not the mission of the Son and the mission of the church, initiated by the Holy Spirit, which are considered but the mission of God as such. Mission is understood as the predicate of God. "God is a missionary God" (Hoekendijk). God makes Godself known. The goal of God's all-embracing work of salvation is the world. Atonement is not for the church and is not solely found in the church. It is for the world. Therefore, the sequence runs: God — world — church; not God — church — world (as was reflected in the salvation history model). Mission is not a function of the church; the church is a function of mission. Salvation is not presented in the church; the church does not lead an exemplary life; it does not distribute salvation through preaching and sacrament. It exists only in the experience of its ex-centricity. It is here that it realizes its "pro-existence." It must be the "church for others" (D. Bonhoeffer).

The content of the *missio Dei* is history in a comprehensive sense. In sharp antithesis to the hierophantic image of God, which is assigned to Hellenism and the Baal faith system, God is conceived as being the One who makes Godself known in *promissio* to the world. There is no "resident" God, but only the God of the Exodus, who enters into history and reconstitutes it through the word of promise and so brings about the divine purpose. The world, apart from God, does not exist. It is not static. It has no being in itself but is "simply a stage in history in which one lives with God, no longer an inflexible framework . . . but a malleable, transformable one" (Hoekendijk). The world discovers itself in progressive movement. If, in the salvation history model, history exists only for the sake of mission, in this case the phrase is inverted: mission, even the church, exists only for the sake of history. The church is at the service of history; it is both challenged and put into question by it. The church must be converted to the all-embracing service of liberation. If the church is in any sense universal, as it is called in Latin American liberation theology (→Latin American theology), then it can exist only for the universal →liberation of the poor (J. Comblin).

This starting point for mission theology takes concrete form in solidarity with the poor and the oppressed. This is set out in the history-of-the-promise concept, which was first fully stated at the Melbourne World Mission Conference in 1980. Hoekenkijk and his allies, however, remained generally opposed to this concept and argued against it, however vaguely. They spoke of a "messianic lifestyle," by which mission is understood as "creating a relation of shalom" with the world. Mission is "hope in action" (H.-J. Margull).

K. Barth's theology had an influence on the salvation history understanding of mission through K. Hartenstein's work. (In 1932, Barth became the first person to remind us that mission is an internal trinitarian concept within dogmatic theology.) It is, however, false, though understandable, to describe the history-of-the-promise theology of mission as an offspring of Barthian theology. Barth's theology of mission does share two weaknesses with this latter theology: the difference between law and gospel is blurred, and the inner-trinitarian distinction between God the creator and God the reconciler is reduced to a mere verbal distinction. The resurrection of Jesus is universalized. It has so changed the world that, according to Barth, for all people, whether they realize it or not, God has willed to be fulfilled only together with them and they can be fulfilled themselves only together with God. "That Jesus Christ lives means" that the union between God and each and every one of us exists "in an inviolable and indissoluble coexistence and conjunction" (*CD* 4/3:39, 40). This conviction leaps out of every sentence of the history-of-the-promise model. Religions become a negligible factor; social questions take precedence. Religion signals conservatism, the status quo, the Baalization of the world. God has abolished all religions. Religion deflects one from liberating the world; it hinders the movement of universal hope in the historical process. Missionary preaching has not made any connections with the "gods" because it dethrones them. The gospel creates its own connections, the sphere of its activity. Missionary proclamation has revealed how God is at work also in those secular movements which work for liberation, in order to bring the world to universal peace. It does not announce salvation but discovers that salvation is "involved with the world and is of the world, that it involves a reality which we call the world" (Rütti 1972, 178). The question of eternal salvation is no longer raised, or only incidentally, since creation is already saved; history as a whole is the implicit history of salvation.

The meaning of this model in practical terms for missionary work is that it is not a question of going from the center to the periphery, from the church to the world, but from the world to the world. The missionary is not the one with a special call, not the priest or minister, but first and foremost laypersons. The others, the bystanders, are not called to become members of the church (that would be proselytism). They should let themselves be brought into God's mission in the world and into the future, which will put everything right. Only in this way can a human being find his or her true humanity. True humanity is itself hidden in mission, and its true nature will be revealed above all in mission, which leads it into the future (Moltmann). Mission thus moves from sending to sending. Sending leads into the future, and the future leads to a new sending.

1.5. *The communication model.* Since H. Kraemer addressed himself to the problem of the →communication of the Christian faith, the question of communication has received great attention in the theology of mission. Kraemer showed that the real problem was not the methods of proclamation and rhetoric (communication "of") but the definition of the relationship between people (communication "between"). The new definition, however, often merely replaces the former fact. This is not the case in the work of E. A. Nida (1960), for whom the mission and communication models are the same (H. Balz). Just as in the history-of-the-promise model, for Nida there is no existence for Christians for themselves, except in the sense that human beings are the receivers of God's message and are at the same time its relay-stations and transmitters. There is only movement, the act of communication. Being a Christian consists of receiving and passing on the gospel, which means, of course, to those who are not yet Christians. Communication means, then, the missionary going out to non-Christians. How the communication of the faith is carried out by Christians is not something that Nida considers. It has no place in his system, because in the last resort there is no place for the church in his scheme. Nida analyzes very carefully the anthropological and transcultural problems of communication from one cultural setting to another. The difference between the sender and receiver of the message is crucial. This difference has its origin ultimately in the infinite difference between the eternal God and humanity. But as God, through the kenosis of the Son, established communication with humanity, so the senders must involve themselves in the limitations of space and the →culture of others and even adopt their language and culture, without giving up their identity in any way. It is, therefore, more than a question of translating the words of the Bible into another language. Every culture is a closed value system in itself, the four pillars of which — religion, language, society, and culture — completely determine one's worldview and philosophy. Missionaries translate their message into this other system and link it to its existing thought and knowledge. This process is essential, although the identity of the message must not be endangered. Authoritative revelation is not adjustable. Nida does not pursue the idea that knowledge and even the understanding of revelation can change, can be broadened or reformulated. He is only concerned with communication as such. Nevertheless, since revelation proceeds from God and is effective today through God's Spirit, these difficulties can be overcome.

Nida is a linguist and a Bible translator by trade. His model is susceptible to considerable problems of form. It is, therefore, reasonable to combine it with others and thereby give it substance. However, there has been little sign of this in the past. There is, for example, G. Collet's starting point for a theology of mission, with its concept taken from the epistemology of "communicative freedom," but Collet does not give any recognition to Nida. H. Balz has put forward an important explanation in which he takes note of the fact that mission is a matter not only of rooting the faith but also of defending it: for example, if the faith in a "younger church" threatens "to become old." For this aspect of the issue he turns to the concept of "hermeneutics," as addressed in the New Testament. The two together complement each other and so make up the whole of the missionary proclamation and theology.

2. The theology of mission is defined by four basic premises which stand in correlation to one another: the holy scriptures as the foundational text; the tradition of mission history and theology, which prevents any unhistorical ways of thinking; ecumenical discussion, in which particular attention is given to Third World theologies; and, finally, the world situation and the particular context in which a theology is articulated. For various reasons — internal and external, theological and situational — mission today is being questioned, so that a new awareness of its basis, form, and goal is required. The challenges coming from without are: the process of secularization in traditionally Christian countries; the end of the domination of the West and its culture (→culture of modernity); the strengthening of the self-awareness of other religions and their political influence; and the creation of new religious and quasi-religious movements which offer plausible explanations of life and which determine the ethical direction of many people (→new religious movements). The North-South economic divide belongs here as a circumstance which threatens the very existence of many Third World countries and which presents a theological challenge of the first order (→development). Among the inner, theological causes for questioning mission are: certain exegetical insights and also, on the Catholic side, certain pronouncements of Vatican II on the possibility of salvation in other religions (e.g., *LG* 16; *NA* 2). The discernible discrepancy between the message which the church proclaims and the life and lifestyle of its members, even the un-Christian nature of the life of many Christians, has made it clear that the missionary situation now begins right in the heart of the West. "Mission in six continents" was the response of the World Missionary Conference in Mexico City in 1963. With this call it signaled a profound change in the concept of mission: where the church is, it is missionary in its being and in its proclamation. Everywhere the church is concerned with overcoming disbelief and awakening faith, with overcoming enmity with love, with transforming social despair with hope. Everywhere "the whole church" is responsible for bringing "the whole message to the whole world." This was the message of the Mexico City conference.

The debate within Protestantism on the theology of mission consists essentially of a dispute between the proponents of the salvation history model and those of the history-of-the-promise model. In a slightly different form, the same debate can be seen among Catholics. The debate is more intense on the evangelical side because the first model mentioned is converted into eschatological dualism by apocalyptic thought (P. Beyerhaus). These two models thus have come to stand in diametrical opposition to each other. This opposition came to a head because certain marginal features of the history-of-the-promise model were emphasized, giving it a one-sided interpretation, in the sense of a revitalized "social gospel." Some charged that the model betrays mission in favor of a process of humanizing the world into the reign of God. This controversy, and also the one over the understanding of universal salvation, as mentioned at Vatican II, led eventually to various consensus papers (*Evangelii Nuntiandi;* "Mission and Evangelization: An Ecumenical Declaration," from the WCC; "Die Frage nach dem Missionsverständnis heute," from the EMW [Evangelisches Missionswerkes] and the EKD [Evangelical-Protestant Church of Germany]; the declarations on mission and ecumenism of the World Assembly of the Lutheran World Federation in Budapest in 1984; and so on). A universally valid understanding of mission cannot be derived from these publications, even if the manifold agreements are helpful. The significance of the actual context for which a theology of mission is designed must not be undervalued.

Below we extract important elements from these texts and relate them to one another with insights from biblical exegesis and Third World theologies.

2.1. *Present-day problems.* "The earth is the Lord's and the fullness thereof" (Ps 24:1). "Let the people praise you, O God, let all the people praise you" (Ps 67:5). The Psalter contains a theology of mission in a nutshell. The earth is God's, and God wills that the earth remain and render the all-embracing praise for which it was created. God calls the earth and all peoples to unite in the eternal, inaudible song of creation, the cosmos. In Israel this praise rings out, clear and unmistakable. Israel praises God, and all peoples are invited to join Israel in its praise. God sends forth the word to creation, just as dew and rain and frost are sent upon the earth (Ps 147:15ff.). The earth is created and sustained through God's word; through this word, Israel too is created. The whole world belongs to God, and the world can recognize this in Israel. God gives justice to all peoples and exercises judgment over them, but in Israel, God does this directly and unambiguously through the law and the commandments. All peoples belong to God, but God makes this claim clear to Abraham (Genesis 12). *Pars pro toto:* in speaking to a part of creation, righteousness is declared to all. This declaration is in accordance with what was right formerly and agrees with symbolic thought in all religions. Abraham's presence in the midst of other peoples and religions acts as a model. Abraham is called forth; he leaves the country. But his exodus has no meaning in itself; the purpose is living in the land in the presence of God. In Canaan, Abraham calls on God. He does not destroy a "holy oak tree" but builds an altar to God near an existing holy place (Gn 12:6). He does not disturb the other inhabitants;

he lives in the midst of them. According to this text, it is through his neighbors that he comes to know of the messianic kingdom that was to have such a vital significance for salvation, for the faith of his people, and for all nations (Gn 14:18ff.; Psalm 110). Abraham's knowledge of God is widened by his living in the midst of other religions, but he maintains his own identity among them. So God's "own people" are created, in whom and through whom God makes the divine purpose of →salvation for all people visible and attainable (→"people" [*Volk*], "nation"). In the experiences of Abraham and Israel lay the foundation of all Christian knowledge of God. Israel's relation to God in praise, intercession, and lamentation shows how people live with God.

Whether one should describe God's path with the chosen people up to the birth of Christ as "salvation history" or whether one should define it as a "plan of salvation," as in much Catholic theology, is irrelevant. It is much more important that every story of the Old Testament and New Testament be told over and over again, so that they become a part of one's life. In this way, the continuity and unity of God's saving actions become real, which is what matters. This is more important than a systematic definition, which can easily destroy the living unity of God's inclusive activity.

Jesus' coming places the story of Abraham and also the existence of his descendants within the law, while Jesus proclaims the new law of the reign of God in Israel and calls the twelve disciples as representatives of the old Israel. Jesus comes to his own, which is at the same time Israel and the world. Both Israel and the world reject him in the same way. Therefore, after Easter the way of mission begins again in Israel and leads to the nations. For Paul the idea of preaching first to Israel and then to the nations implies no sense of a time sequence but rather implies a "principle": God treats all the people in all the nations just as God treats people in Israel. As God has turned to Israel, so God turns to all. The mission to the nations does not become the model for the mission to Israel (in 1983, in addressing the question of Israel, the regional synod of the Evangelical Church in the Rhineland rightly distanced itself from such linkage, one that had provoked much violent discussion beforehand), but the reverse is true: the mission of Jesus and his disciples to Israel is the abiding model for the mission to the Gentiles. The unity with Israel is fundamental to the unity of the churches with one another, and Christianity's relationship to the religion of Israel, in spite of the unique nature of this tie, forms the prototype for the relationships to other religions.

2.2. *Biblical aspects.* The sending of Jesus, the *missio filii*, happened in such a way that the word "dwelt among people" (Jn 1:14). Jesus lived with people, ate with them, was happy and sad like them. He was among them not as a stranger among strangers but as somebody who was trusted, who spoke their language, and who talked to them as one who came from them and was one of them. He lived not only *for*, but *with*, people. *Pro*-existence (life *for* others) was not the mark of his life, but con-vivence (life *with* others).

His convivence is seen above all in the festive fellowship of the table, which went far beyond everyday fellowship. Where Jesus enters in, there is festival, daily life is exalted, and life is raised to a new level: it is fulfilled. By his coming, Jesus intended that people should have life, more abundant life (Jn 10:10). Nowhere is life in its fullness more available than in fellowship-creating common meals. Here people realize themselves to the full because they are with others; all are treated the same; they eat the same food and rejoice in the same way over its careful preparation. There is agreement in discussion. It is no coincidence that Jesus made the communal supper the basic integrating activity of his community. In his proclamation, Jesus presented the reign of God as a feast to which the master of the house extends an invitation (Lk 14:15–16). It is Jesus' mission to invite people to this feast. All who are invited to a feast are changed because they rejoice in what is to come. If it is a courteous invitation, one will do everything possible to accept it: one prepares for it a long time in advance. This change is not a condition but a consequence of the invitation. This is true of Jesus' call to repentance, which is a call to joy (see Mt 13:44ff.).

One cannot hold a feast on one's own; it must be a community event. God wants communion with people. This is where the message of the reign of God comes in. It is realized in Jesus' life with people (Lk 17:21). Jesus' call to discipleship is an invitation to the community of those who are going together to the feast. It is an invitation to join the pilgrim people of God. The reign of God is in the future, but it is nevertheless already attainable. The festal community of the Lord's Supper celebrates him who has come and is to come: this festal supper is the feast of the church in mission; it is, as the Melbourne conference said, "food for missionaries."

→Liberation theology has made us aware of Jesus' preferential option for the poor. Poverty in the Old Testament and New Testament is an ambiguous term (though ecumenical texts sometimes suggest it has a clear and unequivocal meaning in the Bible). In the Old Testament, poverty is even presented as the consequence of idleness (Prv 10:4, 13, 20). It is precisely for this reason that Jesus' unconditional turning to the poor attracts attention across social and moral boundaries. He turns to the poor, not to help them in a condescending manner but in order to be "with them," to eat the bread of the poor with the poor, so as to recognize and reestablish their identity and value. Because Jesus crossed over the borders, his presence has made nearness to God's reign available and has brought liberation and healing (→healing and medical missions). This shows, in contrast to the traditional presuppositions which were as much a part of ancient Israel as they were a part of traditional religions of Asia and Africa, that God does not desert the poor and sick, that the promises of the Old Testament are valid, that God pays attention to the rights of the poor and widows, and that God is their advocate (Psalm 146; Amos; Isaiah, etc.).

Jesus has not left the rich standing at the door but is concerned that all, rich and poor, should be together at the table (Prv 22:2). For him it is a case of the *communio oppositorum:* whoever eats and celebrates together changes his or her attitude to others and is influenced by them. (One should also notice that later on Paul blames the Corinthians not because they let the rich come to the Lord's Supper but because the rich did not wait for their food until the slaves and laborers had come, so that they could all eat together [1 Cor 11:17ff.]).

One of the fundamentals of Jesus' life and teaching is a thoroughgoing crossing of frontiers to reach people, frontiers erected by law, by moral, social, and political differences, and by religion. Jesus interprets the Mosaic law with regard to people. It is given for the sake of people, and the ideas current at that time about cleanness and uncleanness and about observance of the Sabbath are reinterpreted and set out anew on the basis of humanity (Mk 2:27; 7:15–16). For mission to conclude from this that the humanization of humankind depends on it alone is to lose the way of Jesus. Anyone who wants to pursue a matter for its own sake, even if it be life, loses it (Mt 10:39; 16–25). Jesus does not seek the assent of the bystander. On the contrary, one misses the point about Jesus precisely when mission is not really concerned about human beings and when their worth and freedom are abused (whether it be on racial, national, cultural, religious, or social grounds). In fact, mission is concerned with regaining the humanity of human beings, redeeming their alienated lives. That means, however, that mission produces transformation, changes, and a turning back toward the life that comes from God. Mission aims at liberation because of the joy in the one who is coming. It follows, therefore, that whoever loses her/his life, finds it (Mk 8:35; Lk 17:33).

Jesus maintains his presence among men and women right up to death on the cross. We should note that the resurrection first becomes real to the disciples the moment that Jesus sits down with them at table (Lk 24:13ff.) and gives them bread and fish (John 21). Jesus is not "the man for others" (Bonhoeffer) but the man "with" others. Therefore, the church must not avoid living out its mission in convivence.

The problem of other religions is not a subject of Jesus' teaching. That may be surprising, but it corresponds with the range of his encounters with people. He is sent to Israel. All people, *pars pro toto,* are thereby meant. During the institution of the Lord's Supper, the first interpretation of his death, he explains that it is "given for many" ("many" = inclusive, i.e., "all" [Mt 26:28]). Because his mission involves not only God but also humanity, the commandment of love stands at the heart of his →ethics. God's love and human love are not thereby made identical, but they cannot be separated. They are "separate but undivided" because, according to Hebrew understanding, in the countenance of the other person, the other is illuminated, even God (*Slav. Enoch* 44; Jas 3:9). One's relationship to the least of one's fellow human beings will be the measure by which the eternal judge will judge (Mt 25:31). Here also Jesus pushes his way through the outer layers and formal structures of religions to humanity. The truth of human beings can be found in every religion; the question of their religious truth is secondary in comparison. It is a question that Jesus does not ask.

The evangelists interpreted the mission of Jesus in their own ways and so gave different foundations for the mission of the church. Anyone who looks for only one justification for mission or acknowledges only one misses the richness of the biblical theology of mission.

Matthew has the Gentiles in view right from the outset (2:1ff.; etc.). According to Matthew, the church is missionary in its being, not only when it starts its mission activity. The church is the salt of the earth, the city set on a hill (Matthew 5). If the church loses its missionary dimension, it forfeits its being as church, and vice versa. Matthew does not, therefore, challenge the church to become missionary; he challenges it to really be the church. It achieves this goal (*a*) when it is a learning church (Mt 11:29 is the center point of the Gospel), that is, when it learns from Jesus; and (*b*) while it is the teaching church (Mt 28:20 is the conclusion of the Gospel), that is, while it spreads Jesus' teaching and accepts into the community through baptism those people who listen to Jesus' word and are governed by him. At the time that Jesus was on earth, he and his disciples taught only in Israel (Mt 10:5–6). Death and resurrection, however, unleashed the full power of Jesus, and henceforth the whole world has become the field for the church's proclamation. Matthew 28 does not relate to Daniel 7, in spite of earlier exegesis, and so does not refer to the enthronement of Jesus as Lord of the world; rather, it sums up the whole gospel and links the authority of the disciples to the proclamation to the living and the resurrected. The disciples heard the command to teach. Matthew, however, writes his gospel in such a way that teachers have a summary of Jesus' teaching from which they can learn and teach, that is, a handbook for catechists, community leaders, and missionaries.

The Gospel of Mark describes in an exemplary way the training of missionaries by Jesus. Mark 1:17 has a programmatic character. The intrinsic meaning is brought together by Mark in the concept "gospel," which for him explicitly involves christology (see 8:31ff., which forms the center of the Gospel together with the story of the Transfiguration [9:2ff.]). Mark develops a "Son of God" christology. It is relevant for all people. "This is my beloved Son, listen to him," declares the introductory formula. At the end of the Gospel, the Roman(!) centurion confesses at the foot of the cross: "Truly, this man was the Son of God" (15:39). The believer recognizes the Son of God, who is hidden from the unbeliever. Therefore, the secret of this man must be proclaimed in all the world (Mk 13:10; 14:9). So that this proclamation can happen, Jesus calls the disciples, prepares them for their task, and even sends them out on a "trial run" in preparation for later ministry.

It is noticeable that in Mark those addressed by the disciples' preaching are not named. Israel is not meant in any special sense. Mark apparently had another group in mind. The minjung theology of Korea (→Korean theology) draws attention to the fact that Mark uses the term *ochlos* instead of *laos,* in the sense suggested by the LXX. Jesus, according to Mark, stood in a special relation to the people (→"people" [*Volk*], "nation"). Even if some of the minjung theses are exegetically overdone, it is true that, according to Mark, Jesus accepts the people unconditionally; they are healed by him and are present with him. Judgment is proclaimed to the leaders, the upper classes. Mark 2:13 teaches us by example. Jesus teaches the people and eats with them. The joy that a certain type of person is called to be a disciple is the reason for the joy at the meal. The missionary situation does not arise in Mark through other religions, but the social context is relevant for missionary proclamation and joyful existence.

Luke's work is conceived from the outset as a history of the primitive church and mission in such a way that the path is depicted from the periphery to the center, from Galilee to Jerusalem, from Jerusalem to Rome. Luke is a historian. Ordering, sorting, schematizing, classifying: these are the methods of historiography. He turns the eschatological events surrounding Jesus of Nazareth into history and shows how Jesus was a missionary to the Jews and how his path led to his death, resurrection, and ascension. The Spirit creates a new beginning and is the real missionary to the nations. The Spirit seeks a sphere for itself, chooses its tools through which to work. The foremost tool is Paul (→Paul the apostle as missionary). Luke's work is not only a history of the early church but a narrative of examples for missionaries laid out on a large scale. Those who let themselves be led by the Spirit, like Paul and the apostles, will find the same things happening to them. The same miracles and signs will happen for them as in the early church. This is what Luke affirms. It is consistent with this affirmation that Luke's work, especially the Acts of the Apostles, has proven its worth in the recent history of missions as a textbook in which missionaries can find themselves. However, Luke's thoroughgoing social criticism is often overlooked. According to Luke, the missionary church is a small band of the poor, of the weak in social terms, of those who sell what they have and become strong in hope. The few rich people in the missionary church are encouraged to divide their possessions. In this way, the community becomes a light, shining in the world (Lk 2:32–35).

While Matthew speaks of the proclamation of Jesus being brought out into the open and makes clear that it must be taught everywhere and at all times, Mark is concerned with "people" mission in a precise sense. It is only in Luke that one can speak of mission to the Gentiles in the strict sense. Luke describes religions in a very open, almost liberal, way (Acts 17). The Gentiles seek God, even when they do not know God. In all their religious activity, they worship the one who is God, and they build altars to God, in spite of their ignorance. The proclamation of Jesus and joining the church not only cause a complete break with former things but create new bridges, new points of contact. The gospel is the fulfillment of their secret longings and hopes. It is the fulfillment of that which is unfulfilled. The life of Jesus is at the heart of Luke's writings, as he is in the writings of the other evangelists. Central to this teaching is the reference to God, the message of the joy of the Lord. God wants to rejoice over and with all creation. The gospel serves to bring God's creatures back home; mission exists for this purpose. All are invited, but only the poor, those in bondage, the oppressed, and those on the fringes of society come (Lk 14:23; 4:18ff.). To be a Christian means for Luke to share the eschatological joy (1:14, 47; 15; Acts 2:26, 46–47). Christians are "the first set free in creation" (J. Herder); their life is the "feast of the liberated" (Hoekendijk). For those who are sent to announce the invitation it means being a witness, "participating in the story of Jesus," and this is a story of obedient suffering (J. Kremer) (see Acts 14:22; Lk 24:26).

John's Gospel, often described as a "mission text" par excellence, speaks of the *missio hominum* only in the second place. It is interested in the *missio filii*. The meaning of Jesus' coming is summarized under the concept of sending. Being sent is a christological concept in John's Gospel. The task and the nature of the disciples and of the community of the church can be described by it, but only in a derivative sense. The term stems from the Jewish system of law as handed down by the LXX and means allowing oneself to be represented. The messenger is a fully accredited representative of the one who has sent him (Jn 14:9–10); the messenger's words represent those of the one who has sent him. John takes up the prophetic tradition of the Old Testament and forms a christology of the Son out of the prophetic mission. The one who is sent directs his words to the world; it is a word of judgment. It causes division. (It is described in John almost in dualistic terms.) Sins are forgiven and retained (20:22–23). Yet the goal is not damnation but deliverance, since the reason for mission is God's love for the world (3:16–17).

There is no mission without authorization. As Jesus' authorization derives directly from the Father, so the disciples' authorization derives directly from Jesus. The commission for mission is the founding act of the church (20:21–22) and is bound up with the bestowal of the Spirit. The Johannine congregation knows persecution (9:22) and suffers the problem of church divisions. The question of church unity is coupled with the question of its mission (John 17). Mission and unity belong to the essence of the church because both are grounded in love. Love knows no separation but seeks unity. Divided love is counterproductive; it does not gather in but destroys. A divided church cannot convince others. Love and witness must be one. Love is whole, or it is nothing.

The evangelists tell of the suffering, death, and resurrection of Jesus; Paul (→Paul the apostle as missionary) interprets what has happened and makes it the basis of his theology (→justification). The world, alienated from God, is reconciled to God through Jesus' expiatory death. That is an objective, inclusive event which is valid for all. "Valid" does not, however, mean "automatically effective" for all. God does not force or overwhelm people but calls and invites them. The freedom of God is preserved in →faith, as is that of each person. →Reconciliation seeks faith. Faith, however, comes from hearing (Romans 10). Therefore, the word of reconciliation must be proclaimed to all people, as far as the ends of the earth (Rom 1:5; 2 Cor 5:19–20). Paul also refers to the Israelite system of law as it pertains to those sent to advance the faith, but he applies it exclusively to the ministry of preaching. The ministry of →preaching is a missionary office by definition because God turns to all through the word, through which the "obedience of faith" was established among the Gentiles (Rom 1:5; 15:18). The reconciliation offered to all must be announced, both locally and globally. The new creation of humanity is the goal of proclamation, so that all people, the whole of creation, offer God the praise that is due (Phil 2:10–11). The idea of the Lordship of Christ belongs in Paul to the realm of doxology, rather than to theological argument or to ethics.

This idea is treated in the Deutero-Pauline writings, especially in Ephesians 1, where it is used for the justification of mission. Because Christ is Lord of all powers and dominions, his Lordship must be announced. Mission leads people into the realm of the Lordship of Christ, who is represented by the church. There is a great danger of mission becoming an instrument of the expansion of a church which gives itself sovereignty and demands obedience. Throughout the history of the church, church and mission have often succumbed to this danger. This, however, betrays not only Paul's theology of mission but equally that of the evangelists.

3. Three core problems in the contemporary theology of mission are consequences arising from both the above biblical insights and current discussions and ecumenical debate on the topic.

3.1. *Mission and other religions.* Arriving at some kind of judgment concerning other religious traditions (→theology of religions) is intrinsic to the theology of mission because it determines not only the question of missionary methods but also the relationship of the churches to the indigenous culture which bears the deep imprint of the previous religion.

We must make a distinction between the Roman Catholic and Protestant responses to this problem. In the Catholic tradition, from the early church up to the present time, the doctrine of *logos spermatikos* in its various shades and variations has been expounded and maintained. Vatican II also referred to it. The council was less innovative in its pronouncements than is often maintained and was also less united than later interpretations have claimed.

Lumen Gentium 8 says that outside the church "elements of sanctification and truth" are to be found; these are "forces impelling toward Catholic unity." God had a universal plan for the salvation of humanity from the beginning of time. God is not far from any one and so should be sought by every person. But the religious efforts of the other religions still need to be "enlightened and corrected," as *AG* 3 expresses it in a very guarded manner. To conclude from this, however, that the non-Christian religions are the "ordinary" way to salvation, as H. R. Schlette puts it in a significant extension of K. Rahner's thought, means emphasizing only one side of the intentions of Vatican II.

Evangelii Nuntiandi explains these same issues in a completely different way.

In any Roman Catholic evaluation, the non-Christian religions are nothing but a "preparation for the gospel," according to Eusebius of Caesarea. "Our religion effectively establishes with God an authentic and living relationship which the other religions do not succeed in doing, even though they have, as it were, their arms stretched out toward heaven" (*EN* 53).

On the Protestant side, the criticism of other religions moves within a field marked out by a number of extremes: the position, still advanced on the evangelical wing, that non-Christian religions are a demonic concoction and lead to damnation; the opposing position that all religions are attempts in their own terms to reach God (the stance advanced by the early Barth); the position that when one sees and values those elements which make a religion a religion, one will recognize "in the contingency of [any religion's] salvation event — whether it be the manifestation of the deity, the coming of the bodhi, or the going out of the inspired one — the rule of the God and Father of Jesus" (C. H. Ratschow). A definite consensus exists today that all religions involve the creator God who protects the humanity of human beings. All religions, including Christianity, are liable to pervert their task and, instead of advancing life and helping to make it human, destroy it and disregard human worth. There is also agreement that the religions keep alive in humankind the question of God and have "taught generations of people how to pray" (*EN* 53). The question, however, of how far genuine salvation is offered through these religions must be asked anew. The biblical insight that "God our Savior, who desires all men to be saved and to come to the knowledge of the truth" (1 Tm 2:4) must be taken more seriously on the Protestant side, because with God "to will" and "to act" are identical and do not work at variance with each other. Jesus' teaching must, however, also be thought out afresh: love toward the eternal Son of Man is expressed in love toward people, precisely at the time when the loved one is not aware of it and is not known (Matthew 25). Jesus breaks through the barriers which religions erect. He redefines the relationships between what is clean and unclean and interprets them on the basis of human values (Mt 15:7). Those who slam shut the door to the religions endanger their own faith. They then deny the truth rooted in Hebrew thought (e.g., Isaiah 53) and strengthened by Jesus that the countenance of God also shines forth to us through other people; or expressed in another way, that every aspect of our life has something to do with the relationship to God and that this is true in all religions. Furthermore, the dialectic in the evaluation of religions must be rethought, as shown in the Epistle to the Romans. Next, the relationship of Christianity to other religions must be understood as analogous to the relationship between →Judaism and Christianity, without disturbing its special and unique historical bond with Israel. Christ is the end of the law — that is, the form of religion — only in the sense that he fulfills it. He does not render the law and religion superfluous or abolish them because, says Paul, the religious shaping of law and life by God are holy and good (Rom 7:12). Without religion, salvation would be given by God alone. But it is precisely for this reason that the form of the religions can be evaluated afresh. They will be accepted afresh in faith and be established (Rom 3:31). The final conclusion is unavoidable: there is the possibility of salvation in the other religions. Anyone who denies this basic affirmation narrows the comprehensive purpose of salvation and denies the gospel of Jesus. However, anyone who wishes to speak out as a Christian in those places where salvation is actually offered and obtained through religions which are still foreign to us should not overlook the fact that people in all religions can be guilty, shipwrecked on their own religious forms. Such people attempt to put themselves beyond the law and the gospel. So long as we are in this life, we live here within the law and the gospel and must put up with the tension which is rooted in the two-sided judgment of the religions, which implies the judgment of the law in Paul. The conviction, however, that salvation is offered through the words of the gospel and through the sacraments is a confession grounded in faith. Christians cannot put themselves beyond faith. This is a further reason why a Christian cannot say in which religion and under which conditions salvation is offered.

The consequences of this understanding of other religions, in regard to its attitude toward a →culture shaped by a former religion, are great. They raise considerable concerns on the part of the indigenous churches as they attempt to achieve a positive and clearly thought out relationship with their own cultures. We can distinguish three models of ways of looking at this relationship which have so far been worked out in mission. The first model is based on the Old Testament prophetic command "to root out, and to pull down, and to destroy and to throw down" the old in order to build up the new and to plant (Jer 1:10). The missionary fells the holy oak tree, destroys the temple of the idols, and starts with a clean slate. The second model of selective acceptance takes its line from Paul (1 Thes 5:21), taking the elements corresponding to Christian worship and everything which is not contrary to it and incorporating them into Christian worship. The third model follows the incarnation: Christianity becomes incarnate in the new environment and adopts the color and form of the existing surroundings. The former feast days and festivals are taken over but renamed and celebrated as feast days for Christ and the saints. Crosses are erected in the old places of worship. The former things are "baptized." This is the model which is most strongly advocated ecumenically today.

Let us take seriously the idea that in proclamation that which is addressed is not the object but the subject of the proclamation event. Let us go further and take seriously the idea that all religions belong to God's action in the world and that God is present in them, so that God reveals Godself to us in these other religions and that the encounter illustrates interdependence, since the former bondage of Christianity to Western tradition and culture must not be treated as essential but as accidental (→intercultural theology). In the theological evaluation of intercultural and interfaith encounters, the subject-character of the other culture must be observed and respected. That means that an about-face must take place in the encounter; the churches must learn to think from the point of view of the other culture, to understand the Christian faith from that point of view, to verbalize this understanding, and to give it shape. In other words, the churches must encounter other religions from the posture of convivial existence, as was seen in the case of Abraham. The fear that the Christian faith will sink into a quagmire of the foreign culture is as groundless as the exaggerated fear of syncretistic infiltration (a danger which one must naturally guard against), since every encounter of this type takes place through the working of the Holy Spirit, who effects a new creation. This does not happen out of "nothing"—the Spirit works as the one who makes the work of the creator holy!

3.2. *Mission and dialogue.* In contemporary ecumenical discussions, the relationship of the church to other religions is often brought under the twin heading "witness and dialogue." It is never reported in the course of this discussion that dialogue replaces witness, despite indications to the contrary. Those involved in the dialogue realize that a completely free discussion without commitment, in which everybody can speak without regard to the consequences, contradicts the essence of religions with their claims on the whole lives of their adherents. The real problem is in what relation witness and dialogue stand to each other. Four propositions crystallize this problem: (a) Dialogue precedes witness. It is practiced in listening. Through dialogue, missionaries get to know "the other," so that they can direct their witness more effectively. Dialogue is preparation for witness. This model is advocated above all by the evangelicals. (b) Dialogue broadens witness and serves to enrich one's own faith. Those who witness are aware of their own faith. At the same time they are convinced that "God has not left Godself without a witness" (Acts 17) in the other religions. Therefore, they approach the other religions in order to get to know not only what is strange and new in them but also what is in tune with the Christian faith, so as to take it over and incorporate it (1 Thes 5:21). In this sense dialogue does not mean replacing what is foreign but assimilating it to oneself in order to be able to take it over. The pronouncements of Vatican II are formed on this model. (c) Dialogue and witness proceed on parallel lines close to each other but do not intersect, although they are interchangeable, and can thereby inspire and limit each other. In dialogue one really enters into what is foreign and different. No attempt is made to bridge the contradictions in the different kinds of faith, although horizons of understanding are opened up. For a while one enters entirely into the other religion. It is only when it becomes an actual temptation that one begins to understand the other religion (W. Freytag). When one returns to the world of one's own faith, this experience is seen as an enrichment, because it leads to a deeper understanding of one's own faith and its truth. K. Cragg and large parts of the WCC dialogue program can be included in this model. (d) In spite of some similarity, the following model differs significantly from the previous ones. Dialogue and witness are closely interwoven here in such a way that witness is seen as an integral part of dialogue. The possibility of mutual testimony is the indication of real dialogue. The truth, as the partners in dialogue recognize it, may not be silenced. On the contrary, dialogue presupposes it, because it is only on this basis that new truth can be found. This concept of dialogue proceeds from the presupposition that finding the truth is not yet finished, even when believers, in spite of their vulnerability, are sure of their God's necessity for salvation. The Spirit, however, will lead one into all truth (Jn 16:13). In the words of the Uppsala World Assembly of the WCC (1968), Christ himself, through the encounter with other religions, wishes to "correct the limited and distorted knowledge of those who know him."

On the basis of the insights above, this model must be deepened and broadened in two respects. Because mission is an invitation to a feast which God prepares, this invitation can be issued only in the context of convivial existence. It was pointed out previously that convivence is the condition for the possibility of missionary witness. Jesus lived in this way among people; so did Peter in the midst of the deplorable environment of the socially and religiously untouchable tanner "caste" (Acts 9:43). The Spirit led him there to insights about people of other faiths, insights which had been hidden from him until then. Dialogue is not the casual intellectual discussion of individual representatives of different religions, but can only take place in lived community; it is "dialogue in community," as it was called in the Consultation on Dialogue in Chiang May (Thailand, 1977).

A frequently expressed question has its justification in this context. The question is this: Why doesn't missionary witness, that is, the invitation to travel together along the path to the feast that God has prepared for us in Christ, suffice? Why must it be embedded in dialogue? The dogmatic reason for this lies with God as such. Dialogue between religions is rooted in God's communication with all creation. It began with the creation of humanity and will not be finished until humanity comes home to the "Father's house" (Lk 15:17–18). The simple reality is that there are different religions, and analogies exist among them. Indeed, there is no part of the form of Christian religion, however small, which does not have analogies in other religions, and there is hardly one which has not been derived from them or shaped by them. The integration of Christianity in the general history of religion does not lessen its anchoring in the Christ-event but is its given historical-universal horizon.

Just as Christianity cannot live in the discipleship of Jesus and according to the model given by the apostles without the most intense convivial dialogue with Israel, so it must not break off conversation with other religions, even though it has often done this with high-handed haughtiness. Whereas, however, dialogue with Israel is like a conversation between a daughter and the mother from whom she has been estranged, the dialogue with other religions is like a conversation among siblings who, while getting reacquainted with one another, must overcome alienation or even enmity.

To sum up, the model of convivence has its center in witness. This witness is surrounded on all sides by dialogue. The right to mutual witness makes dialogue honest and true. Dialogue, however, cannot be used as a mere means for witness, as is proposed in the first model discussed above. The principle of keeping an open end to the dialogue must not be precluded. In the model of convivence one is confident that by means of God's conversation with all people, conducted by the Spirit, they — all people — will be led into the fullness of truth. Dialogue is a positive turning to others. Because Jesus of Nazareth reveals to us God's epiphany in the countenance of the Jew in incomparable clarity, we are fitted for and called to the life of dialogue.

3.3. *Mission and development.* In the salvation history model, world history is traced out around mission. In the history-of-the-promise school, in contrast, mission serves history. In the former, the world (to which no constitutive meaning is attached) is the accidental background to missionary activity. In the latter, the world defines the agenda of church and mission. In the first case, development-related activity (→development) can only be complementary to the real task of proclamation; it is merely the good works which follow faith. In the second model, development can become, at least in extreme extensions of this approach, a work in its own right to which preaching is added, where necessary, as an "explanatory postscript" (Hoekendijk). Today, almost no one defends this extreme position. The intense discussions over the barricades of opposing opinions have led to new insights. The unity of proclamation and worldwide social action, witness and interventions to ensure justice and →peace, has been shown to be essentially Christian. The commitment of the International Congress for World Evangelization (→evangelical mission theology II [Lausanne movement]) in 1974 speaks a language just as clear as the memorandum of the Evangelical Church in Germany entitled "The Development Service of the Church: A Contribution to Peace and Justice" (1973) or the World Mission Conference in Melbourne (1980). Yet the discussion breaks down, on the Catholic side as well, over the question of how the ordering of development activity and missionary proclamation is to be settled. The reason for the uncertainty lies in the fact that hitherto nobody sought to clarify how the "world," the primary context of mission, was to be understood and what value was to be placed upon it. The concept remains vague in discussions and is closely linked to every abstraction that is typical of Western theology.

The experiences of the liberation theologians in Latin America, South Africa, and Korea have decisively altered the background of this discussion (→Latin American theology; Korean theology; black theology). These theologians have brought theology out of its ivory tower and into actual, concrete situations: they have turned the attention of the church to the world, a world in which the majority of humanity is poor, exploited, and oppressed, a world in which vast numbers of people are at enmity with one another. God loves them. God came into their midst and lived with them. Liberation theologians have learned the depth of this truth which had been lost to established Western theologians. The concept of convivence, stemming from the experience of base communities, which have offered us various aids to interpretation as outlined above, can contribute to a way out of the cul-de-sac of theoretical interpretation of "the world." This way begins in the milieu of neighborly help in urban and small-village groups in Brazil and finds expression in communities for aid, education, and celebration. The experience of convivence brings the recognition that there is no contradiction between the preaching subject and the listening object of mission, between the sending church and the receiving world. This experience means that the teacher is also the learner, that teaching and learning are a reciprocal event. In the same way, the subject-object division in the concept of aid has been overcome. Aid, in the Western understanding of the term, moved from above to below, from the rich to the poor, from the haves to the have-nots. It had to do with condescension and power and demanded from the recipients humility and gratitude. The experience of convivence, however, teaches that to help is a reciprocal event in which both sides always give and receive. Convivence implies mutual participation. Righteousness is here lived in its true sense, since each person grants to the other the right to life and living space, the right to existence, and the unconditional recognition of the other's human value. Each retains her or his own identity; the loss of self is not required. The idea of pro-existence, stemming from the helper-syndrome, with its many consequences, is overcome. Free space, in order to live with others, is granted, and freedom is won.

Latin American liberation theology speaks from the perspective of the poor and has thus regained the perspective of the early church. The early Christian community lived in imitation of Jesus so that Christians learned from each other, shared their possessions equally with each other, celebrated together, and gave expression to their joy over their redemption (Acts 2:4ff.). Proclamation of the word and service, understood in the sense of convivence, are not alternatives. If they are seen as opposites, that means stepping out of convivence. It means driving asunder what God has joined together. Mission and development belong together, though they should not be confused with each other. Mission without development activity is empty; development activity without mission is blind. Both, however, are totally incomplete without the common celebration of life, which gives thanks to God.

Just as there can be no dialogue with people of other faiths if it is not preceded by a common life, so there can be no effective church development aid and no worldwide social involvement without our first being with people from far away places and without their becoming neighbors through the shared life. Once more it must not be denied that this also holds good for proclamation. Only in this way will the subject-object division practiced by Western theology be overcome; only in this way will the tangible form of faith as Jesus lived it be regained; only so will the life-threatening inequality of the North-South divide be broken down.

Biblical insights and realizations derived from the ecumenical discussions, together with the traditions and theologies of the Third World, have led us by the hand to a new model of the theology of mission.

Its starting point is Abraham, *initium est principium*. It is established anew by Jesus, takes its direction from the community of the early church, finds its forerunners in the practice of the first missionary outreach of the Moravians, and today is realized in the life of, for example, the Little Brothers and Sisters of Jesus of Charles de Foucauld and of the Taizé brothers. If we bring the characteristics of the model together as key phrases, then we must mention the following: being present; being the city set upon a hill and the salt of the earth; being with the poor; issuing an invitation to the feast of convivial existence; and giving an account of the hope that is in us (1 Pt 3:15). We can call that the model of Abraham for mission.

THEO SUNDERMEIER

Bibliography

Anderson, G., "American Protestants in Pursuit of Mission," *IBMR* 12 (July 1988) 98–109. Idem, *The Theology of the Christian Mission* (1961). Idem, "Theology of Mission," *CDCW* (1971) 594–95. Barth, K., "Die Theologie und die Mission in der Gegenwart," *ZZ* (1932) 189–215. Bevans, S. B., and J. A. Scherer, *New Directions in Mission and Evangelism*, vol. 1, *Basic Statements, 1974–91* (1992). Idem, *New Directions in Mission and Evangelism*, vol. 2, *Theological Foundations* (1994). Blauw, J., *The Missionary Nature of the Church: A Survey of the Biblical Theology of Mission* (1974). Bohren, R., *Mission und Gemeinde* (1962). Bosch, D. J., *Transforming Mission: Paradigm Shifts in Theology of Mission* (1991). Idem, *Witness to the World: The Christian Mission in Theological Perspective* (1980). Braaten, C. E., *The Flaming Center: A Theology of the Christian Mission* (1977). Castro, E., *Freedom in Mission: The Perspective of the Kingdom of God* (1985). Coote, R. T., and J. M. Phillips, *Toward the 21st Century in Christian Mission* (1993). Cragg, K., *Christianity in World Perspective* (1969). Gensichen, H.-W., "Akzente und Problemstellungen in der gegenwärtigen Missionstheologie," *ZM* 70 (1986) 112–27. Idem, *Glaube für die Welt: Theologische Aspekte der Mission* (1971). Harnack, A., *The Mission and Expansion of Christianity in the First Three Centuries* (1962 — trans. of vol. 1 of 1908 edition). Hiebert, P. G., *Anthropological Reflections on Missiological Issues* (1994). Hoekendijk, J. C., *The Church Inside Out* (1967). Idem, *Kirche und Volk in der deutschen Missionswissenschaft* (1967). Jongeneel, J. A. B., *Missiologie: Het christendom als wereldzendingsgodsdienst* (1986). Knitter, P. F., *No Other Name?* (1985). Kraemer, H., "The Missionary Implications of the End of Western Colonialism and the Collapse of Western Christendom," in *History's Lessons for Tomorrow's Mission* (1960). Küng, H., *Christianity and the World Religions: Paths of Dialogue with Islam, Hinduism, and Buddhism* (1986). Lenchak, J. A., C. Osiek, and R. J. Schreiter, "Mission," *CPDBT* 630–38. McGavran, D. A., *Understanding Church Growth* (1980). Idem, "What Is Mission?" in *Contemporary Theologies of Mission* (1983) 15–29. Müller, K., *Mission Theology: An Introduction* (1987). Newbigin, L., *Mission in Christ's Way* (1987). Idem, *One Body, One Gospel, One World: The Christian Mission Today* (1958). Idem, *The Open Secret: Sketches for a Missionary Theology* (1994). Idem, *A Word in Season* (1994). Niles, D. T., *Upon the Earth: The Mission of God and the Missionary Enterprise of the Churches* (1962). Nürnberger, K., *Die Relevanz des Wortes im Entwicklungsprozess* (1982). Rahner, K., "Grundprinzipien zur heutigen Mission der Kirche," *HPTh* 2/2 (1966) 46–80. Rütti, L., *Zur Theologie der Mission* (1972). Scherer, J. A., *Gospel, Church, and Kingdom: Comparative Studies in World Mission Theology* (1987). Idem, *That the Gospel May Be Sincerely Preached throughout the World: A Lutheran Perspective on Mission and Evangelism in the 20th*

Century (1982). Schmidlin, J., *Katholische Missionslehre im Grundriß* (1923). Senior, D., *The Biblical Foundations for Mission* (1983). Sundermeier, T., *Konvivenz und Diffenenz* (1995). Idem, "Convivence: The Concept and Origin," *Scriptura* 510 (1992) 68–80. Thomas, N. E., *Classic Texts in Mission and World Christianity* (1995). Verkuyl, J., *Contemporary Missiology: An Introduction* (1978). Verstraelen, F. J., et al., *Missiology: An Ecumenical Introduction* (1995). Vicedom, G. F., *The Mission of God: An Introduction to a Theology of Mission* (1965). Warneck, G., *Evangelische Missionslehre: Ein missionstheologischer Versuch,* 5 vols. (1892–1905).

❧ THEOLOGY OF RELIGIONS ❧

1. Background and Meaning. 2. "Conscientization" as Criterion for Christian Theology of Religion. 3. A Postmodern Christian Theology of Religion.

While it is common for Christian theology of religion to enter immediately into a treatment of the theological implications of the many religions, to do so risks missing critical issues. If one believes that the central question of a theology of religion involves the "salvation" value of other religious ways, it is relatively easy to approach theology of religion. If one realizes that a theology of religion involves appraising how complex traditions — embedded in history and embodied in culture — diversely envision the character of the Whole and fashion praxes consistent with these visions, the matter is much more complex. Many Christians do take the first course, and then the central question is narrowed to how one construes certain biblical passages to account for the salvation of non-Christians. In this article, however, the attempt is to shape an approach that considers religious traditions as total ways of life, often marked by as much internal plurality and syncretism as is Christianity itself.

1. As commonly used, the term "theology of religion" is so freighted with unexamined presuppositions as to raise questions whether it is useful. First, the term is biased toward Jewish, Christian, and Muslim construals of reality because the word "God" (*theos*), designating the author of existence, rises out of these Semitic traditions. Second, through its reference to a search for interpretation or understanding (*logos*), the term assumes a Western way of seeking theoretical clarity. This is true of K. Barth's argument that *as religion* Christianity has no advantage over other religions. It is also true of J. Hick's claim that all religions are diverse ways of naming a single God.

Concretely, as used by Christians, theology of religion is based on the presuppositions (*a*) that the character of the divine is such that God *can* reveal Godself definitively; and (*b*) that God has indeed been decisively revealed in Jesus of Nazareth, who is called the Christ in the New Testament. This raises perspectival and commensurability questions, since this Christian revelational base means that non-Semitic religious traditions must play the "theology of religion" game by rules that put them at a disadvantage from the start.

At another level, as humanity has become aware of how diverse and rich are the world's religious ways, it has become immensely difficult to define the term "religion." Hundreds of definitions have been put forward, but two scholars' cautions suffice to show how precarious will be a theology of religion done from a merely Western or even a biblical point of view.

First, historian of religion J. M. Kitagawa notes that "religion" is a Western word used in ways that presume religion is a distinct, private, "spiritual" dimension of life, even though that understanding is often quite without parallel in other cultural traditions. As a corrective, Kitagawa recommends that one think of "religious-cultural-sociopolitical syntheses" instead of "religions."

Second, against common perceptions of a fundamental unity of religious experience among all peoples, anthropologist C. Geertz notes that religion functions as *"(1) a system of symbols which acts to (2) establish powerful, pervasive, and long-lasting moods and motivations in men by (3) formulating conceptions of a general order of existence and (4) clothing these conceptions with such an aura of factuality that (5) the moods and motivations seem uniquely realistic"* (Geertz 1973, 90; italics in original). One implication of this position should complicate the life of theologians. According to Geertz, religions are no mere set of beliefs conceptualizing locally matters experienced universally. Rather, they are the a priori lenses that engender experiences and insights that warrant and back visions of the "general order of existence."

In the theological realm, the perspective of a G. Lindbeck, as opposed to that of a W. C. Smith, captures the significance of this insight. Those persuaded by Smith's view will believe that there is a fundamental unity in religious experience and that, if we develop the proper habits of mind and heart, we will overcome the barriers that divide us from one another. Such persons see in the various religious traditions diverse ways to *express* common but ineffable experiences. Those inclined to Lindbeck's views — for example, J. DiNoia — distrust "expressivist" theories that religions are diverse ways of speaking about the same ultimate reality.

When one grasps the point that Kitagawa, DiNoia, and Geertz make quite differently in their respective disciplines, the problem of theology of religion deepens. It may be stated as follows: given the unverifiable nature of the revelation or fundamental intuition of the character of the Whole in *every* religious tradition, can *any* tradition justify a judgment on the truth and values of another tradition?

This, then, is the context for articulating a *Christian* theology of religion. Anyone convinced of the relativity of religious traditions revealed by historical, social-science, or philosophical insights is led inexorably to what L. Gilkey has called a judgment of "rough parity" among them. Without naively asserting absoluteness, can Christians legitimately make *theological* appraisals of other traditions? Can this theology remain humble and open to new insights when the mystery of the cosmos indicates humility, and yet anchor full Christian conviction, identity, and praxis?

2. We attempt here to show, first, that the term "conscientization" is a candidate for describing religious growth and for being a criterion for evaluating what religious traditions — including the Christian — are ultimately about. The goal is to offer a metaphor for the religious growth or appropriation process that will serve the needs of both inner-Christian and cross-tradition discussions. Second, we hope to offer a detour around the sterile repetition of truisms that besets discussions today. Having done this, we will take christological bearings on conscientization, since one's construal of Christian identity is key to one's theology of religion.

By the term "conscientization" is meant a process whereby the total consciousness of a person and culture is formed and appropriated. The term itself is borrowed from P. Freire's work on pedagogy but here denotes the way in which an individual and a culture participate in, construct, and effect "reality." This involves a process of both grasping and appropriating a tradition's vision of the Whole and the responses indicated by this vision. And it takes for granted that such a conscientization process differs greatly for individuals and groups within each tradition and that it differs enormously among traditions — for example, in Christianity and Buddhism, but also in "local religions" such as Melanesian or Native American.

Becoming Christian involves a community and individuals undergoing a *Christian* form of conscientization. An analogous process occurs when persons become Buddhists or appropriate local religions. Religious traditions, by a combination of means, help shape the strata of consciousness and conscience. Since we deal here mainly with Christian theology, we concentrate here on the Christian process of being transformed in a structure of life marked by faith, hope, and love mediated in and through Jesus of Nazareth. The goal of Christic conscientization is sanctity transformed by grace enabling the follower to exemplify the divine, self-giving love of *agape* manifested in Jesus. The reality, of course, is that Christians vary greatly in the degree to which they allow grace to transform them. Similarly, Buddhists vary greatly in the degree to which they achieve enlightenment. And not every Sioux is lifted up by the Great Spirit. Indeed, helping one cope with falling short of ideals is one of the most important wisdoms a tradition can impart.

Although the New Testament presents a kaleidoscope of christologies, the narratives in which they are embedded fall into several basic patterns, each of which must be viewed in the light of the Hebrew Testament doctrine of God as creator, initiator of covenant, redeemer, and lawgiver. The New Testament offers pictures of Jesus as a decisive figure for the future of all humankind by designating him as a latter-day Isaian suffering but liberating servant, as savior, as Messiah (*christos*), as a new David and Moses, as Lord, as Son of God, and as eschatological king. Taken together, these titles indicate the "christomorphic" (*morphism* comes from the Greek word *morphe,* "shape") claim of Christians: *that God relates to the cosmos in a way analogous to God's relation to Jesus as the Christ — particularly in the paschal mystery where love transforms death.* Good Friday and Easter reveal the trinitarian structure of christomorphic existence and that the destiny of the cosmos and human beings is shaped by the life, teaching, death, and resurrection of Jesus of Nazareth, who is called the Christ.

It is tempting to limit the debate on theology of religion to whether "exclusivists" (who take literally such texts as Jn 14:6 and Acts 4:12) are right in saying that the explicit act of faith in Jesus as Christ and incorporation into the church are necessary and alone sufficient for salvation. Alternatives then become those associated with "inclusivists" (Catholics following Vatican Council II and ecumenical Protestants and the Orthodox following WCC positions — see especially J. Dupuis and G. D'Costa) and with "pluralists" (who believe each religion is a valid way to God — see especially the work of P. Knitter and J. Hick). While this is an important discussion, it is not central to a Christian theology of religion.

The thrust of a christomorphic religious-cultural-sociopolitical synthesis is toward the ideal of agapaic existence aimed at realizing the reign of God. And as the thrust of the life of Jesus was toward realizing this reign by purifying both "religious" and "political" structures of first-century Israel, so should Christian conscientization carry the followers of Jesus in both directions. Analogously, the thrust of Buddhist conscientization is enlightenment and the compassionate existence of the bodhisattva. Are the terms "kingdom of God" and "Nirvana" truly commensurable, so that the analogy in process (i.e., at the level of conscientization) carries forward into true analogy in finality? This is the object of dialogue, and the questions admit no easy answers.

Following L. Newbigin, if one has been touched by the seriousness of the previous question, the ultimate issue becomes whether the gospel that Jesus is the Christ (personally and as messenger) is still "good news" of final importance for all the world. Given today's appreciation of religious diversity and philosophical relativity, should one continue to have confidence in the gospel? Does the dialogic relationship with God in Jesus that the New Testament portrays as the walk of faith, hope, and love put individuals and the body of Jesus' followers in a dimension of life altered *ontologically* for the better by the "good news" of the gospel? Is this orientation a way toward achieving the cosmic-level reconciliation *necessary* to overcome the problems humankind and the environment face? And how does this mode of existence relate to other religious traditions in areas like the comparability of goals such as the Nirvana of Buddhists, the vision-quest of Native Americans, and the integration of Chinese religions?

The careful reader will first ask: Exactly how is Jesus good news? Must one not put more detailed content into the question, take a stand on whether Jesus is God? the sole means or mediator of salvation? the sole valid *revealer* of God? the founder of the church that embodies and teaches his message? the sole path to salvation? In Christian history, the question why one should have confidence in the gospel has, after all, been answered by saying yes to these questions. Is it not disingenuous to sidestep them now just because the traditional answers are "implausible" to moderns? Possibly so, but the impasse at which theology has arrived and the grave situation of a world in darkness may also indicate the need to bracket textbook answers that yield truisms and cut off dialogue.

Learning from R. Panikkar and A. Pieris, in other words, the position adopted here is one that questions whether narrower versions of christology and the religious problem do justice to the depths of our cosmic predicament, to Christian revelation, or to other religious visions. The question then becomes threefold. What should comprise a basic Christian theology of religion in the contemporary context of (a) the richness of other religious traditions; (b) valid criticisms of Christianity and other religious traditions raised by modern thought; and (c) the many traditions' sincere criticisms of one another?

Having paid attention to these questions, can Christians articulate a theology of religion without the failure of nerve L. Sanneh and L. Newbigin call a loss of confidence in the gospel? Is one to agree with Nietzsche, for example, that Christianity is a slave religion and therefore ought to be abandoned? These questions go far beyond the limits of the present article, but they form the context in which Christians must take their bearings at the turn of the third millennium.

When all this is absorbed, to the extent that Christians are persuaded that hope in a christomorphic destiny for the cosmos is grounded hope and not mere arrogance, they will assume a humble posture in regard to other traditions. For confidence in the gospel is not confidence in Christian superiority but in the mercy of God manifested in Jesus — *hope* that in Jesus, God reveals the measure and end of cosmic life and the means to attain it. The gospel is a challenge to follow Jesus and to participate in the divine plan (or *mysterion*) for creation (Rom 16:25; Eph 1:9–23), not a path to superiority.

At another level, learning from other religious ways, Christians can accept in them what is compatible with a christomorphic construction of the origin and destiny of the cosmos in God's kingdom. But, in asserting this, one must quickly insist also that knowledge of what this means and judgments based on it are deeply mythic and mysterious — like what one sees looking through a dark mirror (1 Cor 13:12) into an unknown future.

The teaching of the central authority of the Catholic Church at and subsequent to Vatican II, while not universally accepted by Christians, is instructive as a position marked by "irenic ambivalence" toward other religious ways. In addition Conciliar Protestants and the Orthodox, on the whole, have accepted these texts as relatively adequate construals of Christian identity. And evangelical Protestants, even when they disagree with them, have tended to consider them worthy of discussion.

The four major texts in question in Vatican II teaching are *Gaudium et Spes* 22; *Lumen Gentium* 16; *Ad Gentes* 3, 7, and 9; and the whole of *Nostra Aetate*. This teaching is extended in subsequent papal teaching by Paul VI (in *Ecclesiam Suam* 96–106 and virtually the whole of *Evangelii Nuntiandi*) and by John Paul II (in *Redemptor Hominis* and *Redemptoris Missio*). At the outset, it should be said that one finds in Roman Catholic teaching scant recognition of the ambiguities of the Christian tradition.

Passages from *Redemptoris Missio* (December 7, 1990, arts. 5, 43, 55) illustrate well the Catholic combination of irenicism and ambivalence toward other faiths and traditions. The irenicism springs from a conviction that there are reservoirs of spiritual riches in other traditions. The ambivalence springs from a conviction that the Christ and his gospel are *the* measure and revelation of the divine will, as well as the means for obtaining it. Overall, however, papal and conciliar teaching exemplifies the tendency of Christian theology to treat other traditions' "truths" as *myths* and to treat its own "myths" as *objective truths*. This in spite of historical studies of religious traditions showing that every religion we know — including Christianity — originates in mythic narratives (which describe the transcendent character of the Whole in this-worldly stories).

While his viewpoint is not attractive to those convinced of the absoluteness of Christianity, in his 1903 masterpiece on the problem of claiming the superiority of Christianity, *The Absoluteness of Christianity and the History of Religions*, E. Troeltsch casts serious doubt on standard Christian attempts to claim objective absoluteness or supernaturality for Christianity over against other philosophical and religious visions. His conclusion was that seeking a position from which one could judge others led, first of all, to an extinction of genuinely *Christian* religiosity:

> To wish to possess the absolute in an absolute way at a particular point in history is a delusion. It shatters not only because of its impracticability but also because it runs counter to the nature of every historical expression of religion. Wherever this delusion has crystallized into serious theories, there has swept over religion a doctrinaire rigidity and a deathlike chill that dispel the mysterious semidarkness in which alone the animating power of religion is communicated, in which [one] first becomes aware of [one's] pettiness and meanness, and in which — through intuition and faith — [one] first senses [one's] true dimensions. (Troeltsch 1971 [1903], 122–23)

Is Christianity, then, to give up belief in the universality and finality of Jesus as the Christ? That is not the point of the discussion. Rather, as W. O'Flaherty has reminded us, dealing equitably with both one's own and other people's myths may provide a way out of the impasse created by sterile repetitions of one's own and other people's confessional dogmas, as well as a way to overcome one-dimensional academic relativism.

Once one understands that the Christian structure of existence entails appropriating habits of mind and heart nurtured by the experiences prayed for in Eph 1:16–19, the criteria for both authentic Christian conscientization and a Christian theology of religion become clearer. In love, hope, and faith, the Christian gains confidence in the gospel news of God's promise of salvation. The center of the gospel is not the superiority, righteousness, or privilege of Christians, but God — Abba/Theos, Word/Wisdom, and Spirit paradigmatically revealed in Jesus. And just as the meaning of the resurrection of Jesus is not exhausted by a category such as resuscitation, neither may the way God's promise will work out in the cosmic and eschatological scope be adequately conceptualized in terms such as the finality and universality of Christ when they are interpreted *restrictively*.

The truth that the follower of Jesus knows is a message about divine love, tempered by the message that humans are responsible to act in accord with conscience and that God is also judge. The Vatican II teaching that the salvation of those who do not know Christ is a mystery known to God states also that God's grace works invisibly in the heart of all persons of goodwill (*GS* 22). When one understands that habits of mind and heart formed in the conscientization process are not abstract but guided by the concrete religious and cultural practices that comprise traditions, it is not a long step to theorize that the same Spirit who works in syncretistic Christian traditions works also through non-Christian traditions and practices to help their followers appropriate the one vocation of all: to enter into contact with the mystery of transition from death to life, which Christians see as the paschal mystery of Jesus.

3. Perhaps paradoxically, the proper perspective on which to found a theology of religions is a reprise of our construal of Christian identity above, a construal based on the biblical narratives regarding the basic characteristics of the Christian myth. At a first level, these stories, as "premodern" myths, invite persons and cultures universally to appropriate as good news a message about the God who promises to deal with humans and the cosmos as Jesus was dealt with in the resurrection, where he became the firstborn of all creation from the dead (Col 1:15; Acts 26:23). Conviction that this is no mere imaginary fancy is mediated by the Spirit (2 Cor 1:22), thus anchoring the trinitarian structure of Christian life.

At a second level, in the formation of Christian doctrines such as "Outside the church [or 'Aside from Christ'] there is no salvation," Christians, to be sure, draw upon and elaborate aspects of biblical texts. Exclusivist texts do exist (e.g., Eph 2:11ff.). A more adequate way of dealing with them than making them the center of a theology of religion, however, is to see them as dramatic witness to the light the believer experiences in accepting the Christ. The author of Ephesians was not, after all, writing to pagans but to Christians, trying to help them better understand what depths and riches God was offering them in the Christ. Yet texts such as this have been interpreted *restrictively*, the assumption of theologians, apparently, being that only in Christ could one gain light on the mystery of existence.

In the premodern period in the West, in a world where no other religious

THEOLOGY OF RELIGIONS ✌ 457

choices but the Christian were socially legitimated, theological doctrines restricting salvation to believing members of the church (and, as a sort of escape clause, persons such as the imagined boy in the wilderness who had no chance to know Christ) were plausible. Then the only two non-Christian religious options in reasonable proximity to Christians were the Jewish and the Muslim, both of which fair-minded historians judge were demonized by Christians (a treatment they reciprocated).

As modernity dawned and the greatest expansion of Christianity in history began, seeds of contemporary change were sown. Among them, insights from historical and scientific studies cast doubts on the absoluteness of Christianity, both morally and intellectually. In a first response to historical and literary insights into the stratiography of the Bible and the insights of physical science studies into the stratiography of the universe, major revisions were made in the doctrine of creation. In large part, the revisions came about in response to the assaults of the new science, but they also represented a retrieval of older spiritual and allegorical methods of interpreting the Bible and tradition.

The issues posed by many Christians today, in recognizing positive value in other religious traditions, represent an analogous challenge to Christian doctrines of the value of other religious ways, soteriology, and mission. A second response to modernity is required. Religious plurality — viewed in a positive light — has become for this generation what the new history, philosophy, and science were for an earlier one. The issues, however, go far deeper. The apparently contradictory and competing visions, "truths," ethics, and practices that exist among the world religions and local religions raise deeper questions than those posed by, for example, the new science to the doctrine of creation. As has been said: *if any religious tradition is "seriously right" about the character and destiny of the cosmos, then the others appear to be "seriously wrong" — unless some point of higher integration can provide a comprehensive horizon that resolves the apparent contradictions.*

A comprehensive horizon is not readily apparent, and the crisis resulting from the lack of such a "metavision" comprises the so-called postmodern problem. The term "postmodern" indicates a shift in consciousness from that of liberal modernism, which had enormous confidence in the capacities of human reason to comprehend reality and solve problems. In postmodernity's many forms and apparent inability to reach a grand unified vision, however, one element favorable to religious ways of knowing stands out. In the light of the failure of scientism, politics, and social engineering to create utopia, religious ways of knowing "reality" have gained respect for their depth, texture, and richness. These elements go far beyond the doctrines one can extract from their mythic narratives and metaphors. Indeed, the best of postmodern science, in the analysis of L. Gilkey and F. Ferré, itself is marked by a deeply "religious" character.

And so, one arrives at the postmodern state where world-envisioning religious-cultural-sociopolitical syntheses exist in a state of philosophical rough parity, but also where that philosophical judgment of parity should not be taken as a warrant for relativism or indifference. World-envisioning religious-cultural-sociopolitical syntheses are the best compasses we have to work out our location in the cosmos.

Following Jesus of Nazareth, more than simply following a teacher in this context, entails accepting a *love* relationship initiated by God, leading to profound *hope* in which one's heart is transformed and strengthened to put the message of Jesus into practice. One participates through *faith* in the "proleptic" structure of

Christian existence — anticipating the reconciliation of all things in the manner that it has already occurred in the death and resurrection of the Christ.

The Christian structure of existence is ultimately eschatological, hoping for the fulfillment of all things in God. Its eschatological structure also grounds the necessity of dialogue and collaboration with all persons of goodwill in an *interim ethic* compatible with and productive of the vision of universal fellowship in love. For the eschatological myth in which Christians live, breathe, and take up being anticipates *universal* fellowship, not salvation *only* for Christians. And Christian history gives absolute, incontrovertible, and unambiguous testimony to the ambiguity of the capacity of Christians to realize that vision, thus fatally wounding any Christian moral ground for claiming superiority. Likewise, there is little chance things will change dramatically in the near term. History, then, is a Socratic tutor, whose lessons impart the truth that whatever else Christianity has been, it stands in need of correction even as it tries to witness to its pearl of great price, revelation of a future that no other religious or secular tradition has been able to realize either.

If it learns to appropriate conscientized ethics built around the submission to Allah taught by Islam; liberation from illusion taught in Indian religions; the integration of Confucianism; the letting go that leads to compassion in Buddhism; and awareness of the mystery of the life-force in local traditions, Christianity can only grow. Other traditions may grow in dialogue with Christianity as well. One need not believe that there is complete compatibility between the Christian vision and that of other religious traditions to learn from them. Nor does learning from them preclude faith in the ultimacy of Jesus as Christ. For in the interim period between creation and final realization of the kingdom, there is the paradox of completeness yet sufficient incompleteness in every religious tradition that each can profit from all the others in the dialogue of life. This incompleteness precludes neither Christian proclamation of faith in Jesus nor hope that non-Christians might believe in him and convert to him. But it does leave itself open to the probability that mutual transformation will occur in and through the process of dialogue.

A postmodern Christian theology of religion that acknowledges the paradox of absoluteness mediated in and through conscientization by means of the relative, while it awaits God's eschatological reconciliation of opposites in the kingdom, loses nothing if it enters into dialogue with other traditions, anticipating analogous completeness and incompleteness in them. They, after all, are part of the brokenness that the doctrine of original sin leads us to anticipate everywhere, including Christianity in its many forms.

WILLIAM R. BURROWS

Bibliography

Barth, K., *CD,* vol. I/2 (1956). D'Costa, G., *Theology and Religious Pluralism* (1986). D'Costa, G., ed., *Christian Uniqueness Reconsidered* (1990). DiNoia, J., *The Diversity of Religions: A Christian Perspective* (1992). Dupuis, J., *Toward a Christian Theology of Religious Pluralism* (1997). Ferré, F., *Hellfire and Lightning Rods: Liberating Science, Technology, and Religion* (1993). Geertz, C., *The Interpretation of Cultures* (1973). Gilkey, L., "Plurality in Its Theological Implications," in J. Hick and P. Knitter, eds., *The Myth of Christian Uniqueness: Toward a Pluralistic Theology of Religions* (1987). Idem, *Reaping the Whirlwind: A Christian Interpretation of History* (1976). Kitagawa, J., *The Quest for Human Unity: A Religious History* (1990). Knitter, P., *Jesus and the Other Names* (1996). Idem, *No Other Name?* (1985). Idem, "Toward a Liberation Theology of Religions," in J. Hick and P. Knitter, eds., *The Myth of Christian Uniqueness: Toward a Pluralistic Theology of Religions* (1987). Lindbeck, G., *The Nature of Doctrine: Religion and Theology in a Postliberal Age* (1984). Newbigin, L., *The Gospel in a Pluralist Society* (1989). O'Flaherty, W., *Other Peoples' Myths: The Cave of Echoes* (1988). Panikkar, R., *The Cosmotheandric Experience: Emerging Religious Experience* (1993). Pieris, A., *An Asian Theology of Liberation* (1988). Idem, *Love Meets Wisdom: A Christian Experience of Buddhism* (1988). Ruokanen, M., *The Catholic Doctrine of Non-Christian Religions: According to the Second Vatican Council* (1992). Sanneh, L., *Encountering the West: Christianity and the Global Cultural Process* (1993). Schineller, J., "Christ and Church: A Spectrum of Views," *TS* 37 (1976). Smith, W. C., *Towards a World Theology: Faith and the Comparative History of Religion* (1981). Toulmin, S., *Cosmopolis: The Hidden Agenda of Modernity* (1990). Idem, *The Return to Cosmology: Postmodern Science and the Return to Modernity* (1982). Tracy, D., *Analogical Imagination: Christian Theology and the Culture of Pluralism* (1981). Idem, *Dialogue with the Other: The Inter-religious Dialogue* (1990). Troeltsch, E., *The Absoluteness of Christianity and the History of Religions* (1971; Germ. orig. 1903). Waardenburg, J., *Classical Approaches to the Study of Religion: Aims, Methods, and Theories of Research*, 2 vols. (1973).

❧ TOLERANCE AND RELIGIOUS LIBERTY ❧

1. Scope of the Concepts. 2. The Classical Teaching of the Church. 3. History. 4. Theological Principles.

1. Tolerance, meaning an attitude of more or less grudging sufferance of other religions (with religious liberty — the free exercise of religion — as its consequence), has different dimensions: state and society can/should practice it in relation to churches and religions; churches exercise it toward one another and grant it to other religions (→religion, religions); and it is also the attitude of individuals toward members of another faith. Tolerance and religious liberty can be the object of civil law, social ethics, and psychology. Here we are concerned with the relationship of tolerance and religious liberty to the evangelization of those who either are not yet or are no longer believers and, consequently, with tolerance of Christians and Christian churches toward other religions and worldviews.

2. The classical teaching of the Catholic Church, as expounded by Pope Leo XIII in the encyclical *Immortale Dei* (1885) and previously taught as the accepted doctrine of the church by eminent theologians like Augustine and Thomas Aquinas, agrees, in a rare case of unanimity, against the demand for "unlimited freedom of religion" made, for instance, by the French Revolution. Leo considered it "not permissible to put the different cults on the same legal level as the true religion." "In such a view," according to the *LThK*, "the question what freedom can be allowed to other religions, confessions and cults apart from the true religion coincides with the question of the tolerance of an evil in society.... It is traditional teaching that the *bonum commune* can in certain circumstances induce the public authorities not to prevent an evil (since God does not)" (10:243). According to this view, tolerance is a compromise that arises out of a concession to external circumstances, and only in this way is tolerance legitimate. A more fundamental affirmation would be a mistake in expressing a false understanding of the truth. Since the time of the Scholastics and their teaching on universals, the axiom *ens et verum et bonum (et pulchrum) convertuntur* has prevailed: truth is indivisible; it is universal and comprehensive (→the absoluteness of Christianity). The revealed truth of the Christian faith presupposes natural reason; it corresponds with it, elevates its insight, and gives it unsurpassable certainty. Hence tolerance as a generous attitude toward a pluriformity of opinions is not possible and not allowed. However, a distinction must be made between this severity toward the error expressed in a diversity of views and tolerance for the person who is in error. People can quite possibly have subjective reasons for their behavior in which they are so entangled that they may not be guilty. For this reason Augustine insisted that "error should be hated, but the person in error loved"; moreover, we should never cease loving those who are in error in order to bring them back to the right path.

3. This position has deep historical roots: the Roman state, liberal for political reasons, allowed subject peoples to practice their cults but persecuted Christians because, in the interest of the one truth and the one God on which Christianity was based, Christians rejected the cult of the emperor. Appealing to the rights and liberties to which all people are entitled, the persecuted Christians demanded internal and external freedom of religion (see especially Tertullian). After the promulgation of the Edict of Milan (313), the Roman emperors, now Christian, out of political necessity like their pagan predecessors, tried to consolidate the unity of the empire by means of the unity of religion. Leaders of the church such as Leo the Great and Augustine henceforth justified the preferential treatment of Christians as opposed to the claims of the heathen and heretics. The *compelle intrare* (Lk 14:23) became a basic axiom that justified the role of the state as protector of Christian truth. As late as the nineteenth century, this view was still held in the churches.

In the Middle Ages a distinction was made. The Thomistic axiom became paramount: *Accipere fidem est voluntatis, sed tenere fidem iam acceptam est necessitatis.* "Whereas the unity of the church and the empire, the absoluteness of the truth and the duties transmitted by baptism were regarded as a justification for acting also with force against heretics, . . . concerning non-Christians the principle was that they must not be forced to believe. Hence, hand in hand with the persecution of heretics . . . there was the policy of converting heathen peoples through nonviolent mission" (Schlette 1970).

This claim experienced a final intensification in the Reformation and Counter-Reformation: the wars of religion, the cooperation of church and state according to the principle *cuius regio, eius religio,* or the compelling of people to emigrate instead of giving them religious liberty led to the counter-reaction of the Enlightenment.

4. We can see then that in the "success story" of Christianity (in the major communions) tolerance and religious liberty are not recognized as basic theological categories. This is also the case with the other religions of the "prophetic type," with the monotheistic religions of Islam and Judaism: as a rule they reject other claims to truth, pity those in error, and attempt to make converts; at most, they tolerate to some extent those who approximate their own formulation of truth. It was not until theologians were forced by opposition (for instance, by the Enlightenment) to engage in dialogue that they began to rethink fundamental principles and thus to gain deeper insight into broader theological contexts. These contexts now show that the theological principles were always such "that they would have had to lead to tolerance and liberty if historical conditions had not dictated a different interpretation" (Schlette 1970).

These are some of the pertinent theological principles:

- The Christian lives out of the conviction that God in Jesus once and for all and in an unsurpassable manner brought the salvation for which humanity had been waiting. This finality and universality are guaranteed by God and mediated and interpreted by the ecclesial community; Christianity's truth is revealed truth and salvific truth for all. Hence the Christian has no reason to relativize the faith.

- The dignity of the person, freedom of conscience, and humanity itself are based on the connection of the human being with God's absoluteness and truth, which are manifested in truth and love — the most human characteristics of the human community. Humanity is always ordered to the Absolute. But people can realize truth and love only in a relative way. Experience has made the modern Christian more realistic. History is not only a never-ending stream mediating truth but also the ugly "ditch" (G. Lessing) impeding it. Community as a worldwide "ideal communication community" (J. Habermas) is an ideology: cultures, languages, and thought-categories create a diversity of reality and a plurality of its interpretations. This plurality is not only an inescapable reality but also an index of human creatureliness (K. Rahner). All people, Christians and non-Christians alike, share this common lot.

- All this must have consequences. One is that the diversity of insight into truth is founded in God's creation; all people of all religions share in it. Hence the religions "are searching for truth," and their teachings contain "traces of salvation and truth" (*NA*). Furthermore, the realization of the limitation of our own faith statements (dogmas, creeds) and of most ecclesiastical institutions obliges us to be modest. In addition, the realization that grace is unmerited and that love is commanded forbids any kind of intolerance. We are obliged, rather, to help each other in the search for truth and love.

- This demands fundamental readiness for dialogue, mutual respect, and readiness to learn (acceptance). But it also enables Christians (like all others) to assert their claim and justify it through "performance" in word and deed (→theology of religions).

- There is something correct in the assertion of G. Sauter that only faith — under the above assumptions and not as something specifically Christian alone (all religious people live in this "myth" of a common seeking for God) — is tolerant. For the term "tolerant" always contains the basic meaning of *tolerare:* to endure, to suffer under the experience of wanting the Absolute and being able to realize only the finite. Consequently, the tolerance that awakens humility, willingness to understand, and solidarity is ultimately a mirror of God's tolerance with us, the people who have been accepted and "redeemed" in the incarnation of the Son (G. Ebeling).

- The Bible, which proclaims a "history of relationships" between God and humans as good news (J. Blettner), knows this fact in the many theologies of its books. It does not see it only as an expression of human incapacity for truth but as an expression of fullness and enrichment. The Bible is the *norma normans* of our faith, not in one single definition but in the diversity of its theologies. Can Christians be less open-minded than the Bible?

FRANZ WOLFINGER

Bibliography

Albornoz, A. F. C., *The Basis of Religious Liberty* (1963). Idem, *Freedom of Religion and Belief, Basis of Peace* (1984). Blettner, J., *Toleranz als Strukturprinzip* (1985). Koshy, N., "Religious Liberty," *DEM* (1991) 859–63. Lecler, J., *Geschichte der Religionsfreiheit im Zeitalter der Reformation,*

2 vols. (1965). Linnan, J., "Declaration on Religious Liberty, *Dignitatis humanae* (12 December, 1965)," in T. E. O'Connell, ed., *Vatican II and Its Documents: An American Reappraisal* (1986) 167–79. Littell, F. H., *Religious Liberty in the Crossfire of Creeds* (1978). Lutz, H., *Zur Geschichte der Toleranz und Religionsfreiheit* (1977). Mitscherlich, A., *Toleranz: Überprüfung eines Begriffs* (1974). Murray, J. C., "The Declaration on Religious Freedom," in J. H. Miller, ed., *Vatican II: An Interfaith Appraisal* (1966) 565–85. Idem, *Religious Liberty, an End and a Beginning: The Declaration on Religious Freedom: An Ecumenical Discussion* (1966). Panikkar, R., "Toleranz, Ideologie und Mythos," in *Rückkehr zum Mythos* (1985). Pavan, P., "Declaration on Religious Freedom," in H. Vorgrimler, ed., *Commentary on the Documents of Vatican II,* vol. 4 (1969) 49–86. Rahner, K., "Dialogue and Tolerance as the Foundation of a Humane Society," *TI* 22 (1991) 14–25. Idem, "Reflections on Dialogue within a Pluralistic Society," *TI* 6 (1969). Idem, *Religious Freedom: Main Statements by the WCC (1948–75)* (1976). Schlette, H. R., "Toleranz," *HthG* 4 (1970) 245–53. Splett, J., "Ideologie und Toleranz," in *Weltverständnis im Glauben* (1965) 269–86. *Statements on Religious Rights and Related Rights from 1937 to 1955 Made by the Commission of Churches on International Affairs and Related Ecumenical Agencies* (1955). Swidler, L. J., *Religious Liberty and Human Rights in Nations and Religions* (1986). Wolfinger, F., "Pluralität und Toleranz: Christliche Grundprinzipien und ihre Bedeutung für den Rechtsstaat," in *Rechtsstaat und Christentum,* vol. 2 (1982) 13–30.

❧ TRADITION ❧

1. Tradition as Phenomenon. 2. Tradition as an Identity Problem of the Church. 3. Tradition as Task. 4. Tradition and Mission.

1.   Tradition as a phenomenon can be viewed under a number of different headings. Here we will discuss it briefly in general terms; in religious terms; and in relation to the Old and New Testaments.

1.1.   *In general.* Tradition (Lat.: *traditio* = passing on, handing down) is ultimately identical with human life. Not only is life itself passed on, but its dimensions of culture (stamped by language and customs), society (organized in structures and functions), and politics (protected by laws and organizations) are determined by transmitted experience and so by growth and maturation but also paralysis and death. Tradition links the generations in a process of physical and intellectual communication in which the process itself, the persons concerned in it, and the meanings imparted must be distinguished. It has a group-forming effect, enabling individuals to identify with their history and culminating in a philosophy of history (G. W. F. Hegel, M. Scheler). This in turn acts as a critique of tradition by recognizing and rejecting obsolete ideas which are obstacles to the progress of humanity. Hence, in the radical Enlightenment, tradition becomes the epitome of everything that impedes the advance to autonomous reason (F. Bacon, R. Descartes). This view had repercussions in classical social criticism (K. Marx) and psychoanalysis (S. Freud). The belief in progress thus developed and the emergence of the technological world have to a great extent resulted in a break with tradition. In contrast, modern social criticism has rediscovered tradition with its necessary functions of "liberation" and the critique of ideology (T. Adorno, H. Marcuse, E. Bloch).

1.2.   *In religion.* No matter whether religion (→religion, religions) is understood as a part of →culture or (by believers) as culture's link with the transcendent, it too contains the above-mentioned, easily recognizable aspects of tradition. On the one hand, tradition is subject to the aforementioned human conditions which are, in turn, believed to be influenced by →God. This easily makes tradition (as something absolutely protected) rigid. On the other hand, religion favors a prophetic criticism of tradition (understood as revelation). In religions with written traditions we can detect the same tension between text and interpretation which is itself in turn recorded (e.g., in the Talmud of the Jews and the Sunna of Islam). This is especially significant in the universal religions which arose as something new out of protest.

1.3. *In the Old Testament.* Here the tension was clearly seen. As historical revelation, tradition was characterized by the promise of Yahweh to the patriarchs. This was passed on by word of mouth and later recorded in the scriptures, especially in the Torah. In addition, oral traditions became important which interpreted the law and were judged according to it. These lines of tradition were recorded in the Mishnah and Talmud. The protest of the prophets, in contrast, was characterized by a criticism of tradition which exposed the real tradition of revelation as an ever-new promise pointing to the future, for which reason its written record has been regarded as holy scripture.

1.4. *In the New Testament.* The message and history of →Jesus (the result of a prophetic protest), understood as the final fulfillment of salvation by God, were retold as the once and for all valid message (Rom 6:10; Heb 10:10), until they were, at first sporadically, written down in the Pauline letters and then in the Gospels. Here we find tradition clearly recorded as legitimation of the truth, especially in Paul's letters (Galatians 1 and 2 Corinthians) and in Luke (Lk 1:1–4; Acts 1:1–3). The legitimation by Jesus and the apostles preserved the connection with the dawning of salvation which is understood in the Holy Spirit, witnessed to in writing in the holy scripture, and as such distinguished clearly from noncanonical texts.

2. In the history of the church the question about unfalsified proclamation becomes a consciously reflected question about the identity of the church. For this reason three clearly defined positions are typical and decisive:

2.1. Irenaeus of Lyons (d. ca. 202), in his work *Adversus Haereses,* upholds the tradition of the apostolic church against the secret traditions of the Gnostics and their alleged immediacy with God. The church watches over the genuine tradition because the true faith is entrusted to it by Jesus by way of the apostles (3, *praefatio*). This is understood quite pragmatically and historically: the teaching of the apostles is assured by the succession of the bishops (3.3.1–4). It is preserved in the church as the real *gnosis* — to which the scriptures and their interpretation also belong (4.33.8). For this reason in the search for truth the link with the church must be preserved and, if necessary, recourse must be made to the communities founded by the apostles and particularly — because of greater convenience and its greater apostolicity — to the community in Rome (3.3,1–3). This pragmatic perspective is grounded in the believing conviction that the same charism of truth prevails in the bishops as in the apostles (4.26.2, 5). Hence tradition is the transmission of truth through the apostles and the church; it is tangible in the scriptures and in the witness of the bishops and is sustained by the power of the Holy Spirit, who lives in the church and keeps it young (3.24.1).

2.2. The decree of the Council of Trent on holy scripture and traditions (1546) introduces a much more restricted view of the problem and the concept of tradition. Since Irenaeus's time it had been recognized that tradition has a wider scope than does scripture. This led to the church's acceptance of truths of the faith that had been transmitted only by oral means (a position earlier advanced by Tertullian, Augustine, Vincent of Lérins). Opposing the rejection by Luther of certain traditions as merely human and so to be discarded and his limitation of tradition to scripture alone, the council wanted to preserve the comprehensive right of the church to live the truth and pass it on. Hence it teaches that the pure gospel is preserved in the church and defines as dogma that its truth and order are contained in the scriptures and in nonwritten traditions (DS 1501–5). Even if it establishes in this way a sphere of doctrine apart from the scriptures it nevertheless places greater emphasis on the relationship of church and scriptures, both sustained by the same power, than on an exact definition of oral traditions (J. Geiselmann, J. Ratzinger). In the concept "pure gospel" (DS 1501), the position of Irenaeus is maintained, even if the concept of tradition is used only in the plural and is limited to oral traditions. In the future, therefore, the confessional controversy would concentrate on the existence and contents of such traditions, and this increasingly became a debate about the completeness of the scriptures.

2.3. In the dogmatic constitution *Dei Verbum* (*DV*; 1965), Vatican II expressly stressed the comprehensive view of Irenaeus and came to a dynamic understanding of tradition, even if the old Scholastic theology had led to some compromises; the council stated that the fullness of the revelation in Jesus Christ is, by his commission and in the power of the Holy Spirit, transmitted through the apostles in preaching, example, and institutions. This also embraces the scriptures, which were composed in the power of the same Spirit, and the tradition is passed on as a heritage by the bishops (7). This tradition — and within it the scriptures as its most tangible expression — constitutes by means of its doctrine, life, and worship all that the church is and believes. Hence tradition is identical with the church in all its members and functions, sustained by a continual dialogue with God and by the power of the Holy Spirit, who leads it to the truth (8). Tradition and scripture together are the one wellspring (9), the one deposit of the word of God, the teaching office serving this word through authoritative interpretation. In this way, tradition, scripture, and the magisterium contribute effectively to the salvation of souls under the action of the one Holy Spirit (10). In a departure from the narrowness of apologetic theology, tradition now becomes another name for the church understood as sacrament. Even if *Dei Verbum* contains no sign of criticism of tradition — of particular importance for ecumenism — it arrives at an understanding of tradition which, by its reference to the scriptures, should really be acceptable to all churches. In the dialogue between the churches, the basic divisive problem still remaining is the sacramentality of the church and the magisterium.

3. The phenomenon and Christian interpretation of tradition reveal its essential function. This has four main consequences.

3.1. *Tradition and trust.* The fact of life and history as the basic data of tradition (in the Christian understanding, the salvation of God breaks into human history) calls for the trusting acceptance of reality, also described as faith. For this reason, any attempt to bring about salvation oneself would mean death. This is true whether the reliance on what is technically or politically feasible leads to a break with tradition or the enthusiastic impatience of some religious movements results in the flight into a new *gnosis*.

3.2. *Tradition and criticism.* As an accepted reality, tradition involves a twofold criticism: on the one hand, the given reality itself must be laid bare in the historical forms in which it is expressed; on the other, the critically exposed tradition — as "dangerous memory" (J. B. Metz, H. Marcuse) — must examine these forms concerning their life-transmitting function for today and tomorrow and, if necessary, identify them as dead or alien. In the sphere of faith this criticism is the task of a hermeneutic theology which, as language about God, must echo God's word given to it. Every refusal to take such a critical stance leads to ideology and utopia.

3.3. *Tradition and community.* The "group-forming" function of tradition means that tradition is imbedded in and controlled by the interrelationships within the community. Besides, in the Christian religion this brings into play the power of the Holy Spirit who guides the community. Hence faith and critical theology are possible only in the church and its concrete structures; but these too are subject to criticism. Where theologians experiment without conscious relationship to the church, they easily find propaganda instead of promise in hermeneutical theology, revolt instead of reform in political theology, a new third force instead of unity in ecumenical theology, and pure humanism instead of proclamation in mission.

3.4. *Tradition and the future.* The "freeing" function of tradition shows its liberating power oriented to the future, and in the Christian message of redemption it presses on to absolute fulfillment. It is the real driving force of the mission of the church — no matter whether this is realized hermeneutically in ever-new formulations of the old message, politically in striving for liberty, ecumenically in seeking the full truth, or, in the sphere of mission, in the proclamation to all peoples. Where this power, straining toward the Lord who will come again, is not taken into account, the forward-flowing stream of tradition is blocked. This results dogmatically in preserving empty formulas, politically and ecumenically in quarreling about status and power, and in mission in a presentation of the gospel to humanity merely out of a sense of duty.

4. The message of the gospel encounters the tradition of a people not as an abstract quantity but in the living form of a community stamped and determined by it. It is holistic, comprehensive, and complex. It comprises the understanding of existence as such and is active as a power which in the encounter with other cultures, ideas, and traditions compares, classifies, and judges. In this encounter the irrevocable unity of religious traditions with the cultures and their mutual dependence have to be taken into account. A pedagogical or liturgical adaptation merely out of psychological necessity does not do justice to this living relationship of culture and religion and the challenge of religion to culture; this requires a more profound process. In this connection, *EN* 20 speaks of the evangelization of culture and cultures. The evangelization of cultures points to a process that goes far beyond the idea of adaptation. The dependence of individuals and of the whole of society on culture and tradition is taken seriously, and the renewal of a people is intimately linked with the evangelization of culture. Theology is here understood as the culturally determined and stamped response to the voice of Christ. On a theoretical, systematic level this corresponds to the concept of →inculturation, which, in its dialogical structure, is something new compared with accommodation. In this dialogical reference between tradition and Christian message, culture and religion are offered the possibility of a new creation and of permanence for the future; and Christianity grows to its fullness and experiences an enrichment on the way to its comprehensive universality.

The relationship between the Old Testament and the New Testament can be seen as a model for the relationship between the Christian message and the traditions. In this relationship a new dimension opens up. By describing the scriptures of Israel as "old" and the message of Christ as "new," Christianity relativizes the previous tradition. With respect to the Old Covenant, the New Testament exercises the function of interpreter. The gospel has a judging and prophetic function with regard to the traditions. Apart from this relativization, the previous message of the Old Testament is enhanced in value. It is universalized through the new people of God. The sphere of validity of the previous traditions gains a more comprehensive and broader scope through the Christian message. But this in itself does not answer the question how the old tradition is to be understood. That is interpreted theologically in the New Testament only through the idea of "fulfillment." That is the essential task of traditional theology and mission theology in particular: finding an adequate place for the traditions within a Christian theology.

VIKTOR HAHN, CSSR, AND HORST RZEPKOWSKI, SVD

Bibliography

Bevans, S., *Models of Contextual Theology* (1992). Bishofberger, O., "Die Evangelisierung der Kulturen: Zur Frage der Anpassung in Evangelii Nuntiandi," *NZM* 32 (1976) 315–23. Childs, B. S., *Biblical Theology of the Old and New Testaments* (1992). Cook, G., *New Face of the Church in Latin America: Between Tradition and Change* (1994). Congar, Y., "Christianisme comme foi et comme culture," in *Evangelizzazione e culture: Atti del congresso internazionale scientifico di missiologica,* vol. 1 (1975, 1976) 976–84. Idem, *Die Tradition und die Traditionen,* vol. 1 (1965). Ebeling, G., "Tradition VII," *RGG* 3/6:976–84. Idem, *Wort Gottes und Tradition: Studien zu einer Hermeneutik der Konfessionen* (1964). Gensichen, H.-W., "Evangelium und Kultur: Neue Variationen über ein Altes Thema," *ZfM* 4 (1978) 134–49. Gerrish, B., *Tradition and the Modern World: Reformed Theology in the Nineteenth Century* (1978). Goldammer, K., "Tradition II," in *RGG* 3/6:967–68. Gremillion, J., *The Church and Culture since Vatican II* (1985). Grey, M. C., *Feminism, Redemption and the Christian Tradition* (1990). Hilberath, B. I., *Theologie zwischen Tradition und Kritik: Die philosophische Hermeneutik H.-G. Gadamers als Herausforderung der theologischen Selbstverständnisses* (1978). Hinze, B. E., "Reclaiming Rhetoric in the Christian Tradition," *TS* 57 (1996) 481–99. Hoeckmann, R. A., "A Missiological Understanding of Tradition," *Angelicum* (Rome) 61 (1984) 649–70. Hünermann, P., "Evangelisierung und Kultur: Eine systematische Reflexion," *ThQ* 166 (1986) 82–91. Langan, T., *Tradition and Authenticity in the Search for Ecumenic Wisdom* (1991). Martin, F., *The Feminist Question: Feminist Theology in the Light of Christian Tradition* (1994). McCarthy, R., *The Catholic Tradition: Before and after Vatican II (1878–1993)* (1994). O'Malley, J. W., *Tradition and Transition: Historical Perspectives on Vatican II* (1989). Paul VI, Pope, *Evangelization in the Modern World (Evangelii Nuntiandi)* (1975). Ratzinger, J., "Tradition III," *LThK* 2/10:293–99. Reid, S. B., *Experience and Tradition* (1990). Roest, C. A. "What Is So New about Inculturation and the Meaning of Culture?" *Gregorianum* (Rome) 61 (1980) 253–73. Shorter, A., *Toward a Theology of Inculturation* (1988). Waldenfels, H., *Kontextuelle Fundamentaltheologie* (1985) 437–48. Ware, K., "Tradition and Traditions," *DEM* (1991) 1013–17. Wiedenhofer, S., "A Growing Tradition, Not a Fixed Revelation," in F. X. D'Sa and R. Mesquita, eds., *Hermeneutics of Encounter* (1994) 247–59.

❧ UNIFICATION OF CHURCHES ❧

1. Preconditions. 2. Existing Church Unions (Chronologically Arranged). 3. Union Negotiations (by Area).

1. Although, as recently as a few years ago, the twentieth century could still be described as the "great century of Christian unity" in comparison with the nineteenth century, today it would be better to speak of an era of making ecclesiological distinctions. The more the Roman Catholic and Orthodox churches join in ecumenical discussion (→ecumenism), the more the accent on organic union as the real goal of the efforts for unity has given way to other models of church unity — models which are primarily intended not to bring about an effective overcoming of church divisions but rather to allow the actually existing pluriform church traditions to function together in a more advantageous way. Concepts such as "conciliar unity" are certainly not designed to force the question of visible church unity into the background. The fact is that in ecumenical church discussions and in actual practice the earlier concentration on organizational union has given way to another order of priorities. The churches of the Third World are particularly affected by this development. They have known — at least since the Tranquebar Statement of 1919 — and still know that they have been harmed by the "unholy" denominational divisions within clear geographical frontiers: divisions "for which we were not responsible, and which were at the same time imposed upon us from outside" (Bishop V. C. Azariah of Dornakal); divisions which in their experience must flagrantly injure not only the visible unity of the Body of Christ but also the credibility of the evangelistic witness of Christianity in a minority situation.

However those changes are to be judged which ever since that time have determined the state of the ecumenical discussion, for the majority of non-Catholic and non-Orthodox churches in countries of the Third World the question of union in the sense of an interdenominational visible church union within a geographical area has not yet been resolved.

2. The following survey of unions and union negotiations in the Third World does not claim to give the complete number of such cases but is limited to particularly characteristic examples. Unions involving fewer than three different denominations are not mentioned, nor are older union plans which must be regarded as suspended (e.g., those in East Africa and Nigeria). An up-to-date summary is produced by the *Ecumenical Review* every two years.

2.1. *Japan.* The Church of Christ in Japan (Nippon Kirisuto Kyodan) was created by a union of Protestant church groups imposed in 1940 by a state decree. In spite of the withdrawal of the Lutherans, most Anglicans, and some other churches at the end of the war, the Kyodan continued to be the strongest Protestant church (→Japanese theology).

2.2. *South India.* The Church of South India (CSI), constituted on September 27, 1947 — that is, practically at the same time as the independence of India as a united national state — was formed with Anglican and Methodist components as well as an existing Presbyterian-Congregational-Reformed federal community (the South India United Church, founded in 1908) after a time of preparation that had lasted for decades. The Lutherans, the Baptists, and the Methodist Episcopal churches did not take part in the formation of this union and still remain separate churches today. With about 1.5 million members today (1 million at the time of its foundation), the CSI is the strongest Protestant church in India. The decisive factor in its coming into existence was the conviction that only in unity would the fullness of truth be accessible and that the fulfillment of union could be only the first step on the way to comprehensive unity. Two factors were significant here: the full integration of spiritual ministries on the basis of the historical episcopate and the establishment of liturgical unity envisaged for a definite point in time after the achievement of union. The question of formulating a new confession of faith was left open because, in the opinion of the churches entering into the union, this pre-supposed a longer experience of church communion. The dialogue with the South Indian Lutheran churches on doctrine, which lasted for years, has helped the CSI in this respect to clarify some questions left open, even if it has proved impossible until now for the Lutherans to enter the union, nontheological factors obviously being stronger than doctrinal agreement. While individual Western churches de-nied the CSI full recognition, the union functions today widely throughout India and Asia as a unique model of unity.

2.3. *The Philippines.* Among the many Protestant communities which together make up only a fraction of the Christians in the Philippines, the United Church of Christ, constituted in 1948, includes only a minority of mainly Presbyterian and Congregational groups. The continuous influx of nonecumenical, mainly American missions and the growth of their congregations have put an additional strain on efforts for wider church unity.

2.4. *North India.* On November 29, 1970, the Church of North India (CNI) was formed. The partners came mainly from the same traditions as those in the South India union but included in addition the Baptists, the Church of the Brethren, and the Disciples of Christ. The Methodist Episcopal Church remained outside the union. Today the CNI numbers about five hundred thousand members in twenty-two dioceses. The principle of growing together has proved itself in the CNI. However, it followed its own path on the question of the integration of min-istries. The CNI has recently come closer together with the Methodist Church on this question in separate talks, so that an extension of the union appears possible in the foreseeable future.

2.5. *Pakistan.* After a common prehistory with the North India union, the in-dependent Church of Pakistan was formed in 1970 as a minority church in predominantly Islamic surroundings. It is structurally different from the Church of North India in that Lutherans are also involved in the union.

3. The paragraphs that follow (3.1–3.5) sketch the state of union negotiations according to area.

3.1. *India.* After the foundation of the CSI and the CNI, it was obvious that they should go further with the process of unification on another level, this time for all India. In 1973 a joint theological commission was assembled from the two union churches together with the Mar Thoma Church (MTC). The commission's work was fostered by the fact that on the one side the MTC and the Anglican Church and on the other side the CSI and the CNI already considered themselves to be in full communion with each other. A joint council was constituted on the basis of a newly worked out model of union at Nagpur in 1978. It consists of thirty members from each of the three churches, made up of five bishops, ten ministers, and fifteen laypeople (of whom at least five are to be women). On the second Sunday in November in each year, the "Festival of Union" is celebrated in the three churches. Three regional joint councils have the task of the common responsibility of making a future organic union come alive, through intercession as well as shared missionary and social work down to the congregational level. A book with the liturgies of the three cooperating churches, which can also be used in the most important regional languages, should strengthen the sense of community in liturgical life.

3.2. *Malaysia.* During World War II, the idea of a church union occurred to Protestant church leaders of the then colony of Malaya interned by the Japanese in Singapore. In the 1970s the result was a union plan designed on the North Indian example and including the Lutherans, the Anglicans, the Methodists, and the Mar Thoma Church. After many years of negotiations, an ecumenical theological college was opened in 1979. The Lutherans meanwhile have withdrawn their cooperation. In 1985 the Christian Federation of Malaysia was formed in which the Roman Catholic Church also takes part. It should serve the purpose, among other things, of all Christian groups finding themselves together, in order to create true unity of the churches in Malaysia.

3.3. *Sri Lanka.* Union negotiations in Sri Lanka have been going on since 1940 between the Anglicans, Methodists, and Baptists and after 1947 also with the Jaffna diocese of the CSI. The Plan of Union presented long ago is very similar to that of North India and is chiefly distinguishable from the South India union in that the Baptists are also involved. Recently, the conflicts between the Singhalese majority of the population and the Tamil minority have hindered the work for church unity.

3.4. *Ghana.* Two Presbyterian churches, two Methodist churches, and the Mennonite Church prepared for unification as the Church of Christ in Ghana. The union, however, did not take place on the assigned date in 1981 or 1983. The decentralized process of preparation for the union through union committees in each of the proposed dioceses proved to be so demanding and time-consuming that the central committee had to postpone the date again and again. Subcommittees stayed at work for years, one of them even to prepare the festivities at the inauguration of the new church, especially the regulation of vestments for the celebration service. For the union of ministries they wanted to follow the South India example, and they had the support of the Anglicans for this goal, in spite of the fact that the Anglicans had left the union committee. In 1983 the plan had to be abandoned, and the union committee dissolved because one of the most powerful partners, the Presbyterian Church of Ghana, suddenly decided to withdraw. The Christian Council of Ghana must now keep together and, if possible, reactivate those elements in the churches that have remained ready for union.

3.5. *South Africa.* For a long time the multiplicity of denominations as much as the race problem has made the question of church union as urgent as it is difficult. After limited beginnings, a church unity commission was formed in 1968 in which the Anglicans, the Methodists, the Presbyterians, and the Congregationalists now work together, but with only minimal participation from the coloreds and the blacks. The commission itself describes the plan of union it has worked out, remarkably enough, as a "boring document, which is mainly of interest to church bureaucrats and committees." Nevertheless, there are already union orders of service in use on a trial basis in congregations, and the commission tries to awaken understanding of the necessity of church unity in wider circles.

HANS-WERNER GENSICHEN

Bibliography

Blake, E. C., *A Proposal toward the Reunion of Christ's Church* (1961). Burbidge, J., *One in Hope and Doctrine: A Study in the Theology of Church Union* (1968). Crow, P. A., *A Bibliography of the Consultation on Church Union* (1967). Fey, H., *A History of the Ecumenical Movement,* vol. 2, *1948–1968* (1970). Grant, J. W., *The Canadian Experience of Church Union* (1967). Groscurth, R., *Kirchenunionen und Kirchengemeinschaft* (1971). Lee, R., *The Social Sources of Church Unity: An Interpretation of Unitive Movements in American Protestantism* (1960). Meyer, H., "Einheit der Kirche I: Einigungsbestrebungen," *ÖL* (1983) 1192–1200. Idem, *Unity in Each Place . . . in All Places,* Faith and Order Paper 118 (1983). Neill, S., *Towards Church Union, 1937–1952: A Survey of Approaches to Closer Union among the Churches* (1952). Idem, "Union Movements," *CDCW* (1971) 618–20. Rouse, R., and S. Neil, *A History of the Ecumenical Movement,* vol. 1, *1517–1948* (1954). Sundkler, B. G. M., *The Church of South India* (1954). World Council of Churches, *Survey of Church Union Negotiations* (appearing biennially since 1957).

V

❧ VATICAN COUNCIL II ❧

1. The Importance of Mission in the Council as a Whole. 2. Concept and Theological Foundation of Mission. 3. Structure of Missionary Activity. 4. "Young Churches." 5. Possibility of Salvation for Non-Christians and Esteem for Non-Christian Religions. 6. Understanding of the Missionary and of Missionary Institutes. 7. Organizational Questions. 8. Flaws in Vatican II's Understanding of Mission. 9. Further Developments after Vatican II.

1. Vatican II (1962–65) revealed a missionary orientation in the broadest sense of the term, beginning with the basic program of *aggiornamento,* that is, a self-understanding of the church appropriate to the modern situation of the world. But the council was also concerned with mission in the specific sense. In spite of a new esteem for non-Christian religions and the recognition of the possibility of salvation for all people of goodwill, the council wanted to emphasize the meaning and necessity of missionary activity. Consequently, the missionary dimension is present in most of the conciliar documents but more particularly in the missionary decree *Ad Gentes (AG).* The relationship of the different council documents to each other is complicated because they were worked out at different times. In the commission responsible for preparing the mission decree, enormous difficulties arose concerning the definition of mission. The first draft had to be drastically cut down because much of the material was supposed to be integrated into other documents, especially into *Lumen Gentium (LG).* However, the remainder was rejected by the council members, and so, relatively late in the council, a new draft had to be worked out. This draft formed the basis for the mission decree, which was promulgated on December 7, 1965. There had not been enough time to rework the document into a coherent whole. On the one hand, the different origins of individual parts are evident, and unnecessary repetitions can be found. On the other hand, results from other documents already worked out could be fitted in, although of course, the influence of *Ad Gentes* itself on the rest of the conciliar texts is minimal. *Ad Gentes* is no innovative draft; neither is it a repetition of old theses or a mere confirmation of traditional missionary work. It is rather a valuable transition document taking account of previous theories and results without committing itself to one side or the other. In some important passages too it gives pointers for the future without blocking possible developments. It would be arbitrary to look for the "real" missionary statements of the council in other documents, for instance, in the pastoral constitution *Gaudium et Spes (GS).*

2. The council wanted to do away with the idea that mission is a peripheral phenomenon of the church, constituting a sphere of activity reserved to specialists. While wanting to understand mission as an ecclesiastical reality, it also wanted to comprehend the church as a missionary entity. And so *Ad Gentes* is anchored in the ecclesiology of *Lumen Gentium.* The church is, especially as the pilgrim people of God, missionary per se, destined to extend to all regions of the earth (*LG* 9–17). As universal sacrament of →salvation, the church must be present to all people in

471

order to bring them into contact with the saving message of Christ and to incorporate them into his body. But what is aimed at is not a naive Christianization of the world but a renewal of the world in the spirit of the gospel. *Ad Gentes* 2–9 elaborates still further the theological justification for mission. The basis of mission lies in the missions of the Son and the →Holy Spirit motivated by the love of God. The incarnation of God in Jesus Christ, God's decision to enter into history in a new and final manner, constitutes the basis for the mission of the church (see also *Dei Verbum* [*DV*]: the Christian economy "will never pass away"). The mission of the church is the continuation of the mission of Christ and his disciples and the fuller blossoming of what was inaugurated in the Pentecost event. Furthermore, mission is an eschatological event, the implementation of God's plan in history; it terminates only with the Second Coming of the Lord. But mission also means a fulfillment of the striving of human nature. In this theological reasoning, traditional elements of missiological thinking are taken up, but influences from the more recent Protestant missiology are also evident, especially with reference to the eschatological perspective.

Ad Gentes 6 tries to clarify the concept of mission. While in principle the missionary task of the church always remains the same, it changes as a result of changing circumstances and conditions. For actual mission work, *Ad Gentes* uses the term "missionary activity" (*activitas missionalis*) or "missions." On the one hand, in the description of this missionary activity the council endeavored to distance itself from an outdated geographical understanding of mission. On the other hand, the practical historical developments could not be ignored. The definition of "missions" was obviously geared to the Congregation for the Propagation of the Faith: "'Missions' is the term usually given to those particular undertakings by which the heralds of the gospel are sent out by the Church and go forth into the whole world to carry out the task of preaching the gospel and planting the Church among peoples or groups who do not yet believe in Christ. These undertakings are brought to completion by missionary activity and are commonly exercised in certain territories recognized by the Holy See" (*AG* 6). It should be noted that the expressions "generally" and "for the most part" tone down the absoluteness of this definition. Consequently, the postconciliar interpretation is not always unambiguous; thus some regard the need for "re-evangelization" (e.g., in Europe and North America) as mission in this sense, but others do not.

3. *Ad Gentes* 10–18 describes the different but closely related elements of missionary activity, such as Christian witness, the proclamation of the gospel, the gathering of the people of God, and the building up of the Christian community. Christian witness means faith in action open to and in solidarity with the environment and attentive to God's activity even outside the church. Without the basic witness of Christian love all missionary undertakings are meaningless. However, a wordless witness is not enough. In *AG* 13, →conversion is understood in the biblical sense as a continual growing toward the Christian message of salvation and is distinguished from incorporation into the ecclesiastical community. In accordance with the declaration on religious liberty, *Dignitatis Humanae* (*DH*), *AG* 13 condemns coercion and all unworthy devices in missionary work. In connection with missionary proclamation, the catechumenate is treated in detail (*AG* 14). Missionary activity does not come to an end until the "young church" is established in its social and cultural milieu as a viable community. That is to be considered to be the case only when a local clergy and local catechists, orders, and congregations and an apostolically active laity are present. *Ad Gentes* 15 demands an ecumenical orientation for the "young churches." This passage alludes to the theme of mission and unity so important in the ecumenical movement. The council did not address directly the controversy of the different missiological schools (especially of Münster and Louvain) over the specific goal of missionary activity, especially since by then the confrontation had lost its former intensity. *Ad Gentes* 6 brings the two trends together in a synthesis: "The special end of this missionary activity is the evangelization and the implanting of the Church among peoples or groups in which it has not yet taken root. All over the world indigenous particular churches ought to grow from the seed of the word of God, churches which would be adequately organized and would possess their own proper strength and maturity."

4. A topic of the most vital interest to conciliar missiology was that of the "young churches" or particular churches of the so-called mission countries. The goal of missionary activity as understood by the council is not just the conversion of individuals but the establishment of viable particular churches. Though these are the fruit of the missionary work of the older churches, they are no longer simply the objects of mission but now themselves have become also the subjects of mission. In this way the council parted company with a colonialist and paternalistic understanding of mission. It was an advantage that before and during the council the →local church was, in a certain sense, rediscovered, and so ecclesiology could provide reasons for the autonomy of the "young churches." The particular or local church is an image of the whole church and must as such be taken seriously. The young churches must attain full maturity. As long as help from outside is still necessary for this purpose, this maturity must not be stifled but rather promoted. Apart from those elements of a complete particular church concerning personnel (bishops, priests, →laity), *AG* 22 demands a large degree of →inculturation. In metaphorical language the text describes a church that does not consist of imported Christianity but builds itself up anew — needless to say, on the basis of the word of God and ecclesiastical tradition but taking into account all possibilities of expression that the local →culture can offer. In this way the council opted for an ecclesiastical pluralism with respect to culture; this is one of the conditions for the development of a really universal church.

5. Although the council wanted to reaffirm the necessity of missionary activity, it also stressed the possibility of salvation for non-Christians that had already been established in preconciliar theology (e.g., *LG* 16; *AG* 7), though it refrained from putting forward a theory about the consistency of the two principles. Whereas some representatives of a traditional missiology saw a danger for the missionary spirit in the optimistic view of Vatican II, the tendency of the council was to see missionary activity as an active response to what God is accomplishing outside the church (*AG* 6, 11). In this context the non-Christian religions were not seen so much as possible channels of salvation. The main concern of *Nostra Aetate* (*NA*), in contrast to the past, was to see the religions (→religion, religions) in a positive light and thus as open avenues for dialogue and cooperation with their followers without, however, playing down the missionary consciousness of the church in any way (*NA* 2). The apparently conflicting statements of the council are not contradictions; they are reactions to the complex reality.

6. *Ad Gentes* devotes a special chapter (4) to the missionary. Here the missionary is to a great extent still understood according to the long-standing model as a person who leaves his or her home country to engage in missionary work elsewhere. As a rule the missionary vocation is a lifetime commitment. But in the council there were also votes against this conception, and some passages imply that no geographical "exodus" is required for missionary activity. But the council was concerned about supporting traditional missionary work also. For this purpose the missionary institutes (orders, congregations, and missionary societies) are as necessary as ever. Nevertheless, the council realized that mission is in a period of transition: the *Ius Commissionis,* according to which a territory is entrusted to a missionary institute, is coming to an end. Consequently, the missionary institutes and the missionaries must understand their work as collaboration in the particular church under the local bishop.

7. Although Vatican II refused to regard mission mainly in an institutional and juridical light, it nevertheless had to take up numerous questions of missionary praxis. Here it pointed in the appropriate direction rather than lay down patent solutions. To ensure that the proclamation of the gospel is carried out in unity and order, missionary activity is subject (apart from the Uniate churches) to the Congregation for the Propagation of the Faith (founded in 1622, now called the Congregation for the Evangelization of Peoples). However, this central institution was supposed to become a dynamic instrument of leadership. Furthermore, the council demanded that all those participating in missionary activity (bishops, bishops' conferences, clergy, laity, missionary institutes) cooperate and coordinate all their undertakings. The council also emphasized the scientific investigation of questions connected with mission. While Vatican II based worldwide mission involvement on the fundamental missionary obligation of all the baptized, it formulated it with regard to particular groups in more specific ways: for example, the bishops (*AG* 38). The dioceses must make an annual contribution on behalf of the mission work of the church. Because of the theology of *communio,* help for the disadvantaged local churches in the form of personnel and funds is taken for granted.

8. The ecclesiocentrism of which traditional missionary thinking is often accused applies to the council only in a limited way. Certainly its understanding of mission has an ecclesiological basis, but the church itself is not regarded as a self-contained entity concentrated on itself. It is rather the sacrament and instrument of salvation for the world and the pilgrim people of God. As such the church is "on the way" and remains oriented to service in the world. There are, however, some deficiencies in the council's understanding of mission. A greater self-criticism with regard to mission history, in particular regarding the Eurocentrism of mission and its uncritical link with →colonialism, would have been in order. The sociopolitical dimension of missionary activity is indeed included in the council's understanding of mission; but it could have been more strongly stressed. We must, however, take into account that themes such as →development in the Third World and →liberation were not taken up or discussed in greater depth until after the council. In this respect *Ad Gentes* must really be supplemented by *Gaudium et Spes.*

9. On August 6, 1966, *Ecclesiae Sanctae,* the *motu proprio* containing norms for the implementation of some conciliar decrees, was promulgated. The regulations regarding *Ad Gentes* urge especially the implementation of the practical instructions of the council. Of theological importance is the demand that the →theology of mission be incorporated into theological courses in order to bring out quite clearly the missionary nature of the church. In the sphere of mission law, in 1969 the *Ius Commissionis* was replaced by the *Ius Mandati,* according to which missionary work is to be understood as contractually regulated cooperation. The local bishops, the missionary institutes, and the Congregation for the Evangelization of Peoples are parties to this contract. In the following years the missionary theme has been further developed and worked out through the synods of bishops (1971, on justice in the world; 1974, on evangelization; 1977, on catechesis). The results of the synod of 1974 were expounded — according to the mind of Pope Paul VI — in the apostolic letter *Evangelii Nuntiandi* in 1975. From a terminological angle this document deals more with evangelization (→evangelism, evangelization) than with mission. The understanding of mission has become considerably more comprehensive; parts of the de-Christianized West are described as in need of reevangelization. New themes such as liberation and basic communities are positively approached. The council's understanding of mission has found its way into the new canon law (CIC of 1983). Canons 781 to 792 deal with the missionary activity of the church (*de actione ecclesiae missionali*). Canon 781 emphasizes that the whole church is by its nature missionary and that the work of evangelization must be regarded as a basic task of the people of God. But the further missiological development is not reflected any more in the new Code of Canon Law. Neither does the basically Western conception of canon law provide the conditions under which the universal church could inculturate itself pluralistically.

FRITZ KOLLBRUNNER, SMB

Bibliography

Achutegui, P. S., *Ecumenism and Vatican II: Select Perspectives* (1972). Alberigo, G., and J. Komonchak, *History of Vatican II: 1959–1965,* 5 vols. (1996–). Alexander, C., *The Missionary Dimension: Vatican II and the World Apostolate* (1967). Dulles, A., and P. Granfield, *The Church: A Bibliography* (1985) 48–51. Jaeger, L., *The Ecumenical Council, the Church and Christendom* (1961). Küng, H., *The Living Church: Reflection on the Second Vatican Council* (1963). Lindebeck, G. A., *Dialogue on the Way: Protestants Report from Rome on the Vatican Council* (1965). Lindell, C. G., *The Concept of Mission in the Roman Catholic Church in the Light of Vatican II* (1967). Miller, J. H., ed., *Vatican II: An Interfaith Appraisal* (1966). O'Connell, T. E., *Vatican II and Its Documents: An American Reappraisal* (1986). Schütte, J., *Mission nach dem Konzil* (1967). Sheard, R. B., *Interreligious Dialogue in the Catholic Church since Vatican II: An Historical and Theological Study* (1987). Tholens, C. P., "Monastische Missionsinitiativen im Lichte des Zweiten Vatikanischen Konzils," *ZMRW* 49 (1965) 156–60. Vorgrimler, H., ed., *Community on the Documents of Vatican II,* 5 vols. (1967–69).

❧ WOMEN ❧

1. The Women's Question Today. 2. Women and the Church. 3. Women in the Ecumenical Movement and in the Third World. 4. Evaluation.

1.   The contemporary discussion on the question of women takes place against a background of far-reaching changes that have happened since the Enlightenment, particularly in the last century. Church and society in the West proceeded from the assumption that the inborn nature of women differs from that of men and, bound up with that, that women are inferior to men. Dualistic thought assigned to women the realm of body/nature, while men were seen as being in the realm of spirit/culture. The status of women was denoted by their biological state of health in motherhood and by their supportive role and obedience to men. Decisive changes first took place through the admission of women to education and study (e.g., admittance to university) and through the struggle for women's right to vote. With this struggle "the exit of women from the 'imposed status of legal incapacity' began." Second, changes took place as a result of the entry of women, especially those of the lower classes, into the industrial workplace. Peasant and middle-class family structures broke up and made a new organization of housework necessary. This development mainly resulted in a double burden for women with a family and a profession but at the same time led to at least partial economic independence. Third, with medical advances in obstetrics (I. P. Semmelwiese discovered the cause of puerperal fever) and developments in contraception ("the pill") the fatal element was removed from women's biological fate and a greater degree of self-determination was made possible.

In the first phase of the women's movement of the twentieth century the priority was equality (equal education, equal pay, equal opportunities, and equal rights). In the second phase, the feminist phase, women no longer wanted simply to adopt the same aims and values as male culture (patriarchy) but desired to discover and postulate their own scale of values, identity, and culture. Here the women's movement found itself in the company of other movements for autonomy (the struggle against racism in the United Nations and South Africa, the decolonization of the Third World, movements among various minority groups) insofar as acquiescence in "foreign values" and "domination" was questioned and rejected. The women's movement shares with other protest movements (e.g., the ecological movement and the peace movement) the questioning of the dominant cultural inequality, but sees as its special contribution that it considers the crises of the present age (the environment, armaments, injustice) as the result of patriarchy and the value it places on power, hierarchy, and violence. The movement analyzes violence as a means of domination over women, nature, and minority groups and as the consequence of the patriarchal assumption of power in which power is practiced first and foremost "over" them and not with them. It advocates a radical "paradigm shift" away from the rigid hierarchical model to models of empathy and of sympathetic and enabling sharing. Exposure of the oppression of women and female identity occurred around the subjects of the body, menstruation, birth, sexuality, the understanding of nature, symbols, and myths, but also in relation to the family, violence against women, rape, women's language, art, historiography, literature, research, and so on. The Western women's movement was influenced by the writings of S. de Beauvoir (*The Second Sex*), B. Friedan (*The Feminine Mystique*), and K. Millet (*Sexuality and Domination*) and through the rediscovery of Virginia Woolf. This growth of literature on women and feminist literature shows how many hidden talents and untouched fields of research there are still to be developed.

2. The secular women's movement admonishes the churches, especially the Roman Catholic Church, for their considerable share of guilt in the justification of the oppression of women in practice and criticizes the Christian tradition as the expression of patriarchy: "When God is male, the male is God" (M. Daly). As a matter of fact, the ordination of women is one of the few areas of professional life in which at least nominal equality has not yet been generally established. The theological and traditional arguments advanced for this state of affairs are labeled by these women as part of antifeminist ideology. The feminist critique of theology concentrates on the following points. (*a*) *The image of God:* exclusively male images of God give women no possibility of positive identification without their having to deny in part their feminine identity. Masculine images of God such as king, judge, lord, and warrior are rejected as projections of masculine power complexes. (*b*) *Sexuality:* the devaluation of feminine sexuality and its association with original sin, as well as its reduction to functions of propagation of the species, hinder a healthy development of female sexuality. (*c*) *Patriarchal language and images:* the →liturgy and spirituality of the churches are characterized by language that excludes women (brother, father, son). The use of military language is particularly criticized (weapons of faith, heavenly hosts, soldier of Christ, etc.). (*d*) *Understanding of the cross:* it is increasingly difficult for women to gain access to an acceptable understanding of the symbolism of the cross, which many women see as a symbol of a negative approach to life with a "sadomasochistic character" (E. Sorge). (*e*) *The structure of the church:* the structure is hierarchical and anti-women insofar as there are hardly any women in its decision-making bodies and it chiefly allocates a subordinate function to women. A clear division of Christian tradition is recognizable here among women, between those who see themselves entering a "post-Christian era" (M. Daly) and those who seek new possibilities of identification and inspiration in the goddess movement.

Women have to make it their first priority to respond to these challenges. Within men's theology there are, with a few exceptions, no disputes with the feminist critique. Feminist theology attempts to take the critique of the secular women's movement seriously and divides it into broad sections. At any rate, it does not see the wholesale rejection of the Christian tradition and the re-creation of the cult of the goddess as alternatives. Different approaches to a new understanding of the →Bible from women's points of view are attempted: new interpretations of biblical texts which speak of women, new evaluations of central biblical themes in the light of the feminist critique, and the development of a feminist hermeneutic that makes visible the patriarchal control of Christian tradition and demands its restoration in the spirit of the gospel. E. Schüssler Fiorenza, R. R. Ruether, L. Russell, V. Mollenkott, and others have devoted themselves to this task in the United States; in Europe, leading voices include E. Moltmann-Wendel and K. Halkes. L. Schottroff and D. Sölle represent feminist critique and exegesis directed toward social criticism. Central theological take-off points are the *imago Dei* nature of man and woman, the exodus story, women around Jesus, and the Pauline text Gal 3:28: "In Christ there is neither male nor female."

3. The situation of women in the Third World is characterized by double and triple oppression: through poverty, racism, and sexism. Typical examples of such oppression are prostitution tourism, the lowest wages for working in industry, domestic violence, rape and incest, lack of education and health care, economic dependence, poverty, and the burden of work in the fields and maintaining the home. With few exceptions, women are assigned a subordinate role in most cultures; in India, for example, they are completely at the disposal of men, first their fathers, then their husbands, and then their sons. As a rule, Christian missions have not questioned the subordinate position of women, as they have done with other cultural values, but strengthened it. In certain matriarchal societies, Christian missions have broken up the leading role of women as priestesses. At least general achievements in the fields of education and health have brought progress and liberation also to many women. In many churches of the Third World, the subordinate position of women is still unbroken and justified by men and women.

Since its foundation in 1948 the →World Council of Churches (WCC) has put the question of the role and status of women on the agenda of the churches and has initiated many studies of these questions in member churches. Questions of women and the ordination of women are highly controversial ecumenical themes, especially in discussions with Orthodox churches and the Roman Catholic Church. The WCC conference "Sexism in the Seventies," held in 1974 in Berlin, spelled out the disadvantaged role of women in the member churches in the most pointed way but at the same time initiated the dialogue of the Western women's movement with women in the Second and Third Worlds. The "Study of the Community of Men and Women in the Church," which grew out of it, encouraged dialogue in the churches between men and women on questions of identity, ecclesiology, and the understanding of the Bible. The experiences of this dialogue, brought together in the Sheffield conference in 1981, made it clear that women in the Third World gave a different priority to the question of women, placing it behind the pressing problems of survival. The web of oppression, as it is described, is woven from racism, class structures, and sexism.

The Sixth World Assembly of the WCC (Vancouver, 1983) achieved a significant measure of participation from women delegates (a third of all delegates), and women contributed substantially on all themes of the world assembly, not just those concerning women. At the much-acclaimed preparatory conference for women, the issues of a "universal sisterhood" and "leaving a woman's place" were raised. Third World women complained of a lack of sensitivity on the part of the Western women's movement to social and political oppression, while Western women often bemoaned a lack of consciousness over the question of sexism. Under the slogan "universal sisterhood," women of the Third World countries have begun to make their own analyses of the situation of women and oppression. Already in the course of "community studies" of the WCC, this subject came up at regional conferences in Asia, Africa, Latin America, and the Middle East. Within the framework of the →Ecumenical Association of Third World Theologians (EAT-WOT), regional women's conferences were planned and finally conducted with the aim of holding a world conference of women, which took place in Costa Rica in

December 1995. Asian women have created their own organ of feminist theology and spirituality (*In God's Image*), and publications critical of the role of women in churches in the Third World are appearing in increasing numbers (e.g., *The Emerging Christian Women* in India). The Women's Department of the WCC has published a collection of prayers, Bible studies, and feminist texts by Third World women. E. Tamez (Costa Rica), M. Katoppo (Indonesia), M. Oduyoye (Nigeria), Sun Ai Park (Korea), A. Gnadadason (India), and M.-T. Parcile (Uruguay) are some of the names to be noted here.

If there remained any doubt of the relevance of feminism for women of the Third World, it was erased as women gathered from all parts of the world for the UN-sponsored conference on women in Beijing, China, in 1995, the largest meeting of its kind ever to be held.

4. The question of women is a crucial touchstone for the churches' readiness for renewal and missionary activity. Are the churches open to the questions of women? Do they take criticism of structures, language, and theology seriously? Are they losing women in the twentieth century just as they lost workers in the nineteenth century? Will the dialogue among women of the First, Second, and Third Worlds save the women's movement from sectarian narrowness and the fate of marginalization? Mission and →development are promoted by the rich countries without the input of those concerned, especially women. The women's question will remain a persistent, if controversial, matter for discussion in ecumenical dialogue in the future. Because this question cannot be easily resolved by itself, it is better when the churches address it willingly and in complete honesty.

BARBARA VON WARTENBERG-POTTER

Bibliography

Beaver, R. P., *American Protestant Women in World Mission: A History of the First Feminist Movement in North America* (1980). Carr, A., *Transforming Grace: Women's Experience and Christian Tradition* (1988). Case-Winters, A., *God's Power* (1990). Chopp, R., *The Power to Speak: Feminism, Language, God* (1989). Daly, M., *Beyond God the Father* (1973). Eck, D., and J. Devaki, eds., *Speaking the Faith: Global Perspectives on Women, Religion, and Social Change* (1987). Fabella, V., and M. A. Oduyoye, *Third World Women Doing Theology* (1988). Fiorenza, E. Schüssler, *In Memory of Her: A Feminist Theological Reconstruction of Christian Origins* (1983). Grant, J., *White Women's Christ, Black Women's Jesus: Feminist Christology and Womanist Response* (1989). Halkes, C. H. M., *Gott hat nicht nur starke Söhne: Grundzüge einer feministischen Theologie* (1980). Hersel, S., *A Voice for Women: The Women's Department of the World Council of Churches* (1981). Johnson, E. A., *She Who Is* (1993). McFague, S., *Metaphorical Theology: Models of God in Religious Language* (1982). Mollenkott, V., *The Divine Feminine: The Biblical Imagery of God as Female* (1984). Moltmann-Wendel, E., *Ein eigener Mensch werden: Frauen um Jesus* (1980). Idem, *Frauenbefreiung: Biblische und theologische Argumente* (1982). Idem, *Frau und Religion, Gotteserfahrung im Patriarchat* (1983). Idem, *Freiheit, Gleichheit, Schwesterlichkeit* (1977). Idem, *Das Land, wo Milch und Honig fließt. Perspektiven einer Feministischen Theologie* (1985). Plaskow, J., *Sex, Sin, and Grace: Women's Experience and the Theologies of Reinhold Niebuhr and Paul Tillich* (1980). Proctor-Smith, M., *In Her Own Rite: Constructing Feminist Liturgical Tradition* (1990). Ruether, R. R., *Sexism and God-Talk: Toward a Feminist Theology* (1983). Idem, *Women-Church: Theology and Practice of Feminist Liturgical Communities* (1985). Ruether, R. R., and R. S. Keller, eds., *Women and Religion in America: A Documentary History*, 3 vols. (1981, 1983, 1986). Russell, L., *Feminist Interpretation of the Bible* (1985). Idem, *Household of Freedom: Authority in Feminist Theology* (1987). Russell, L., et al., *Inheriting Our Mothers' Gardens* (1988). Schneider, S., *Beyond Patching: Faith and Feminism in the Catholic Church* (1991). Schottroff, L., "Maria Magdalena und die Frauen am Brage Jesu," *EvTh* 42 (1982). Idem, *Traditionen der Befreiung II: Frauen in der Bibel* (1980). Sharma, A., *Religion and Women* (1993). Idem, *Today's Women in World Religions* (1993). Idem, *Women in World Religions* (1987). Sölle, D., *Sympathie* (1978). Idem, *The Strength of the Weak: Toward a Christian Feminist Identity* (1984). Townes, E., *Womanist Justice, Womanist Hope* (1993). Tucker, R. A., and W. L. Liefeld, *Daughters of the Church: Woman and Ministry from New Testament Times to the Present* (1987). Idem, "Female Mission Strategists: A Historical and Contemporary Perspective," *Missiol* 15 (1987) 73–89. Idem, "Women in Mission," in *Toward the 21st Century in Christian Mission* (1993). Wartenberg-Potter, B., *Wir werden unsere Harfen nicht an die Weiden hängen: Engagement und Spiritualitität* (1986). Wartenberg-Potter, B., and J. Pobee, *New Eyes for Reading: Biblical and Theological Reflections by Women from the Third World* (1986). Welch, S., *Communities of Resistance and Solidarity: A Feminist Theology of Liberation* (1985). Williams, D., *Sisters in the Wilderness: The Challenge of Womanist God Talk* (1993). Wolf, C., *Macht und Ohnmacht der Frauen in der Kirche* (1983).

❧ WOMEN IN THE NEW TESTAMENT ❧

1. The Pauline Letters.   2. The Post-Pauline Letters.   3. The Gospel of Mark.   4. The Gospel of Matthew.   5. The Gospel of Luke.   6. The Acts of the Apostles.   7. The Gospel of John.

Women disciples and missionaries are clearly present in all four Gospels and in the Pauline letters. However, the portrait of women's involvement in the mission is far from uniform. That women participated in a wide variety of ministries, including leadership, in the early church is apparent; that some New Testament authors sought to restrict women's ministry to the private sphere with behind-the-scenes supportive roles is also evident.

1.   The letters of Paul provide the earliest canonical evidence for women's involvement in the Christian mission. They also supply the most names of women ministers in the early church. There were as yet no job descriptions for Christian ministers. The terminology and roles were still very fluid in the first century.

1.1.   *Co-workers.* The term Paul uses most frequently of those who minister with him is *synergós,* "co-worker." Paul speaks of "co-workers with God" (1 Cor 3:9; 1 Thes 3:2), "co-workers in Christ" (Rom 16:3, 9), and "my co-workers" (Rom 16:21; 2 Cor 8:23; Phil 2:25; Philemon 24). Among those so designated is one woman: Prisca along with her husband, Aquila, (Rom 16:3). That she is mentioned before her husband indicates her higher status. Paul elaborates on their importance not only to him personally but to "all the churches of the Gentiles" (Rom 16:4). Furthermore, they are heads of a house church (Rom 16:5; 1 Cor 16:19). Paul states that co-workers in the mission are equal (1 Cor 3:8–9).

In Philippians 4:3, Paul names Euodia and Syntyche, who "have struggled [*synēthlēsán*] at my side in promoting the gospel, along with Clement and my other co-workers [συνεργῶν]." With the term *synathléō* (to contend or struggle along with someone), Paul likens the tremendous exertion of these women on behalf of the gospel to that of an athlete who strains every muscle in a contest. They are not peripheral to the mission but have been working right at Paul's side. These two may have been a missionary team, as were Paul and Barnabas (Acts 13:2), Prisca and Aquila (Rom 16:3), Junia and Andronicus (Rom 16:7), and perhaps Tryphaena and Tryphosa (Rom 16:12). If such were the case, Paul's urging Euodia and Syntyche to "come to a mutual understanding in the Lord" (Phil 4:2) expresses his desire that their team ministry not end in dissolution as did his own partnership with Barnabas after their dispute over John Mark (Acts 15:36–40). Alternately, Euodia and Syntyche may have been leaders of separate house churches in Philippi. Whatever their dispute, perhaps over a theological difference, it is openly expressed and has an effect on all the members. Because of their prominent leadership in Philippi, Paul is anxious that they resolve their disagreement speedily.

1.2. *Laborers*. Four women in Romans 16 are named as "laborers," that is, for the gospel. Paul sends greetings to Mary, "who has worked hard [*ekopíasen*] for you" (Rom 16:6); to Tryphaena and Tryphosa, "workers [*tàs kopiósas*] in the Lord"; and to "beloved Persis, who has worked hard in the Lord" (Rom 16:12). Paul uses the same verb, *kopiáō*, to speak of his own intense apostolic work (1 Cor 15:10; Gal 4:11). Like himself, "co-workers" and "laborers" hold positions of authority. Paul urges the Corinthians, "be subject to every co-worker and laborer [*synergounti kai kopiōnti*]" (1 Cor 16:16).

1.3. *Ministers*. Romans 16 begins as a letter of recommendation for Phoebe, who is "deacon" (*diákonos*) at the church in Cenchrae (Rom 16:1). Twice Paul uses the term *diakonos* in tandem with "co-worker" (1 Cor 3:5, 9; 2 Cor 6:1, 4). Paul describes the ministry of *diákonos* in terms of toil and suffering in the service of the gospel (2 Cor 6:3–10; 11:23–29) and recognizes that there are various kinds of service (*diakonía;* 1 Cor 12:5). According to Eph 4:11–12, apostles, prophets, evangelists, pastors, and teachers do "the work of ministry." Preaching the gospel is *diakonia* (2 Cor 11:7–8), as is financial assistance (Rom 15:25; 2 Cor 8:4; 9:1, 12, 13; see also Lk 8:3). Paul speaks of himself as a "minister [*diakonos*] of God" (2 Cor 6:4), "of Christ" (2 Cor 11:23), "of the gospel" (Col 1:23; Eph 3:7), "of a new covenant" (2 Cor 3:6), and "of reconciliation" (2 Cor 5:18). He asserts that this ministry (*diakonía*) is a gift from God (2 Cor 4:1; see also 2 Cor 3:5; Eph 3:7; Col 1:25).

Paul also notes that Phoebe "has been a benefactor [*prostáti*] of many and of myself as well" (Rom 16:2). The term *prostáti* implies that she was the patron and host of the house church at Cenchrae, providing for the community financially and probably presiding over its gatherings. That she is in need of a letter of introduction to another community attests that she was a traveling missionary, much like Paul himself.

1.4. *Apostles*. Among those Paul names as apostle is the woman Junia (Rom 16:7). Although he recognizes the Twelve as apostles (1 Cor 15:5), Paul also uses the term of himself (Rom 1:1; 11:13; 1 Cor 1:1; 9:1, 2; 15:9; 2 Cor 1:1; 12:12; Gal 1:1; Eph 1:1; Col 1:1; 1 Tm 1:1; 2:7; 2 Tm 1:1, 11; Ti 1:1), Apollos (1 Cor 4:6, 9), Barnabas (1 Cor 9:5–6), Epaphroditus (Phil 2:25), Silvanus and Timothy (1 Thes 1:1; 2:7), James (Gal 1:19), and Andronicus and Junia (Rom 16:7). In defense of his own ministry, Paul says that an apostle is one who has "seen Jesus our Lord" and whose "work in the Lord" is visible in bringing others to faith (1 Cor 9:1). The root meaning of *apóstolos* is "one sent," that is, to proclaim the gospel. In contrast to those disciples who ministered in their own home context, apostles were traveling missionaries. In his greeting to Andronicus and Junia in Rom 16:7, Paul also notes that they are relatives of his who were in prison with him and that they are "prominent among the apostles," having been "in Christ" before he was.

1.5. *Heads of house churches*. In Paul's greetings to heads of house churches, it is notable that a number of women are named: Prisca, along with her husband, Aquila (Rom 16:5; 1 Cor 16:19); and Nympha (Col 4:15). Most likely Phoebe (Rom 16:7) also served in this capacity. Chloe, whose people brought Paul information about the dissension in Corinth (1 Cor 1:11), may also have been the head of a house church. The Acts of the Apostles names two others: Mary, the mother of John Mark (Acts 12:12), and Lydia (16:40). Most probably Martha, who welcomed Jesus "into her home" (Lk 10:38), and the "elect lady" to whom 2 John is addressed were also heads of house churches. For the first two centuries the Christian communities gathered in private homes. Ministries carried out in this context mirrored the functions typical of the Greco-Roman household. With a woman's usual role being internal household management, it was a logical development for women to preside over the gatherings of believers in their homes.

1.6. *Women greeted by Paul.* There are three other women mentioned in Paul's letters about whom little more than their names is known. The letter to Philemon is addressed as well to Apphia, "our sister" (Philemon 2). The designation "sister" is also used of Phoebe (Rom 16:1) and may have been a title with ministerial connotations beyond the usual address of Christians toward female members of the community. Another woman to whom Paul sends greetings is Rufus's mother, who he says has been "a mother to me also" (Rom 16:13). Nothing further is known about Julia and Nereus's sister, whom Paul greets in Rom 16:15. That they play an important role in the community can be inferred from Paul's singling them out for public recognition. It is notable that one-third of those greeted by Paul in Romans 16 are women.

1.7. *Egalitarian statements about women.* In addition to those Pauline texts that name women ministers there are a number of passages in which Paul speaks in an egalitarian way of women. The most well known is Gal 3:28, "There is neither Jew nor Greek; there is neither slave nor free person; there is not male and female; for you are all one in Christ Jesus." This baptismal formula asserts that incorporation into the Christian community makes distinctions of ethnicity, social status, and gender no longer significant. Alluding to Gn 1:27, to the creation of male and female in God's image, the statement asserts that regardless of differing procreative capacities and social roles assigned men and women in a patriarchal society, all persons become full members of the Christian community through baptism.

There is also a very egalitarian view of the relations between husband and wife in 1 Cor 7:3–5. Responding to a problem about which the community has written, seemingly about sexual abstinence within marriage, Paul concedes that members do practice such abstinence for a time, but only on condition that it be by mutual consent. This is surprising in a patriarchal milieu such as that of first-century Judaism and Christianity, where the husband would normally exercise his right to make decisions unilaterally. In addition, Paul asserts that both husband and wife have their duty toward the other (v. 3) and that each has authority over the body of the other (v. 4).

In the same letter Paul also addresses questions about spouses who are not believers. In this context he states, "The unbelieving husband is made holy through his wife, and the unbelieving wife is made holy through her husband" (1 Cor 7:14; similarly 7:16). In Paul's estimation both wives and husbands are instruments of holiness for their spouses; each can lead her or his partner to salvation.

Paul also speaks highly of unmarried women and virgins. He says that such a woman is "anxious about the things of the Lord, so that she may be holy in both body and spirit" (1 Cor 7:34). A woman free from the care of husband and family could more easily devote herself to ministry in the church.

Another significant passage is 1 Cor 11:11–12, "Woman is not independent of man or man of woman in the Lord. For just as woman came from man, so man is born of woman; but all things are from God." Paul seems to argue here for equality and mutual dependence for women and men in general, not only for husbands and wives. He observes how the order of creation in Genesis 2, to which he alludes, is reversed in the natural order. Since all things have their origin in God, there can be no more superiority or inferiority based on precedence.

1.8. *Restrictions on women.* Although these egalitarian statements exist in Paul's letters, there are other passages that contradict them. The same pericope that offers an egalitarian vision of the relationship between women and men (1 Cor 11:11–12) undercuts it with, "But I want you to understand that Christ is the head of every man, and the husband is the head of his wife, and God is the head of Christ" (v. 3); and, "Man is the image and glory of God, but woman is the glory of man. Indeed, man was not made from woman, but woman from man. Neither was man created for the sake of woman, but woman for the sake of man" (1 Cor 11:7–9).

The same letter in which Paul speaks approvingly of both men and women praying and prophesying in the liturgical assembly (1 Cor 11:4–5) contains the admonition, "As in all the churches of the saints, women should be silent in the churches. For they are not permitted to speak, but should be subordinate, as the law also says. If there is anything they desire to know, let them ask their husbands at home. For it is shameful for a woman to speak in church" (1 Cor 14:33–36).

1.9. *Liberationist or chauvinist?* In trying to resolve these contradictions in Paul, scholars propose various solutions. Some see him as revolutionary, with liberated attitudes toward women, rooted in the boundary-crossing praxis of Jesus. For them, the passages that attempt to silence women are non-Pauline interpolations. Others find ways to reinterpret apparently sexist statements in a way that makes Paul consistently egalitarian. Still others see Paul as neither completely sexist nor egalitarian, allowing that he himself was still working out the ambiguities in diverse and changing situations. Another possibility is that Paul championed equality for women, as well as for Gentiles and slaves, on the level of religious understanding, but not in the social sphere. In 1 Cor 7:17–40, Paul advises believers not to make changes in their social situation with regard to circumcision, slavery, or marriage. He asserts that the time until the parousia is short (7:29–31), that one's state in life is a gift from God (7:17), and that "the slave called in the Lord is a freed person in the Lord, just as the free person who has been called is a slave of Christ" (7:22). By the same reasoning, it may be said that Paul considered men and women no different "in the Lord," but he did not advocate revision of patriarchal structures in the social sphere.

However one understands Paul's attitudes toward women, his egalitarian statements do open a space for Christian communities to configure relations between women and men in patterns of genuine equality, mutuality, and collaboration in all spheres.

2. If statements about women in Paul's own letters are ambiguous, such is not the case with those who wrote subsequently in his name and with the mantle of his authority. There is a clear movement in the post-Pauline letters toward subordination of women to men and increasing restrictions on women's ministry.

In three different letters (Col 3:18–4:1; Eph 5:22–6:9; and 1 Pt 3:1–7) there appear similar versions of a Christianized household code advising submission of wives to husbands, children to parents, and slaves to masters. The most fully developed treatise on subordination of wives to husbands is found in Eph 5:21–33. These codes reinforce the rule of the husband/father/master according to the patriarchal household structure advocated from the time of Aristotle on. These New Testament texts are prescriptive, rather than descriptive. They portray an ideal, already outmoded in many Greco-Roman households. They clash entirely with texts such as Gal 3:28 and those that portray women as heads of households and in other independent, decision-making positions. The adoption of these codes would have consequences far beyond the family, as faith communities saw themselves as the "household of God" (Eph 2:19; 1 Tm 3:15) and so patterned their relationships.

The Pastoral Letters (1–2 Timothy, Titus) give witness to an even greater effort at reinforcing patriarchal structures in the church at the turn of the first century. Qualities desired in those who serve as overseers (*epískopoi*), ministers (*diákonoi*), and elders (*prebýteroi*) are those of the ideal male head of a household (1 Tm 3:1–13; Ti 1:5–9). That women also exercised the ministry of *diákonos* is clear from 1 Tm 3:11, where they are addressed directly.

Although the author of the Pastorals lauds Timothy's mother and grandmother, Eunice and Lois (2 Tm 1:5), for their having transmitted "sincere faith" to Timothy, he is no advocate of women preaching, teaching, or holding positions of authority. In 1 Tm 2:11–12 he advises that women "receive instruction silently under complete control," and he forbids "a woman to teach or have authority over a man." For him the way to salvation for women is through childbearing (1 Tm 2:15) and occupation with domestic concerns. His ideal older woman is one who teaches younger women to love their husbands and children and be good homemakers (Ti 2:3–5).

That many women had devoted themselves, instead, to public ministry in the church is evident from the long section that restricts their activities (1 Tm 5:3–16). Celibate women, often living in groups, were dedicated to prayer, charitable works, and teaching, with compensation for their ministry coming from the church. In an attempt to contain their growing numbers and influence, the Pastor sets forth qualifications for those who would aspire to the order of widows. A woman who has children and grandchildren is to be supported by her family and not the church (1 Tm 5:3–4). To be enrolled as a widow a woman must be sixty years old and married only once (1 Tm 5:9). Very few women in the early church would fulfill these qualifications. According to the Pastor, a widow is to dedicate herself to prayer and charitable works rather than teaching (1 Tm 5:5, 10). And "women who have widows" (1 Tm 5:16), that is, those who sponsor houses of widows, are to assume their financial support rather than look to the church for compensation for their ministry.

3. In the Gospel traditions the portrait of women is no less ambiguous. In the Gospel of Mark women are most frequently portrayed as recipients of Jesus' compassion. In the course of the Galilean ministry Jesus heals Simon's mother-in-law (1:29–31), Jairus's daughter (5:21–24, 35–43), a woman afflicted with hemorrhages (5:25–34), and a Syrophoenician woman's daughter (7:24–30). One negative tradition about women is found in Mk 6:17–29, where Herodias and her daughter effect the beheading of John the Baptist. No women are listed among those called as disciples (1:16–20; 2:13–17; 3:13–19), yet women play a crucial role in the passion narrative.

As Jesus' ministry in Jerusalem moves to its climax, he lauds a widow who put two small coins into the temple treasury (12:41–44). Jesus' remark that "she, from her poverty, has contributed all she had, her whole life" (12:44), interprets her action as one that mirrors Jesus' own pouring out of his life. In the prelude to the passion a nameless woman anoints Jesus' head (14:3–9), the action of a prophet identifying the king (see 1 Sm 10:1; 16:13). In contrast to the followers of Jesus who "left him and fled" at his arrest in Gethsemane (14:51), women disciples witness his crucifixion, death, and burial. Mark 15:40–41 names "Mary Magdalene, and Mary the mother of James the younger and of Joses, and Salome" among the many women who "used to follow him and ministered to him when he was in Galilee" and who had come up with him to Jerusalem. Those who saw where the body was laid were "Mary Magdalene and Mary the mother of Joses" (15:47).

In the concluding episode of the Gospel (16:1–8), Mary Magdalene, Mary, the mother of James, and Salome find the tomb empty and are the first to receive the news of Christ's resurrection. They are commissioned to go and tell the disciples and Peter, but the Gospel ends, "They said nothing to anyone, for they were afraid" (16:8). In this Gospel all are portrayed as fallible followers, including the women. Yet they become the indispensable link between the historical Jesus and risen Jesus.

4. Many of the same traditions involving women are taken over by Matthew from Mark. Matthew recounts the healing of Simon's mother-in-law (8:14–15), the official's daughter, the woman with a hemorrhage (9:18–26), and the Canaanite woman's daughter (15:21–28). He tells of Herodias and her daughter's complicity in the death of John the Baptist (14:3–12). Matthew likewise preserves the traditions about the woman who anointed Jesus before his passion (26:6–13) and the Galilean women witnesses of his crucifixion (27:55–56) and burial (27:61). He names Mary Magdalene, Mary the mother of James and Joseph, and the mother of the sons of Zebedee among the "many women...who had followed Jesus from Galilee, ministering to him" (27:55–56). Mary Magdalene and "the other Mary" are the ones who remain to see the place of burial (27:61) and who come back after the Sabbath to see the tomb (28:1). Different from Mark's account, Matthew narrates that as they "ran to announce" the news of the resurrection to the disciples, Jesus himself appeared to the women and greeted them. He reassures them and reiterates the commission to tell the others to go to Galilee, where they will see him (28:8–10).

Several traditions about women are unique to Matthew. In his opening verses he includes in the genealogy of Jesus: Tamar (1:3), Rahab (1:5), Ruth (1:5), and the wife of Uriah (1:6). Each of these four women is in an anomalous situation; each is outside the boundaries of a regular patriarchal marriage. As such, each represents a threat to the patriarchal order. Each acts in an unconventional manner that ends in furthering God's purposes for Israel. This points forward to the unusual situation of Mary's conception of Jesus (Mt 1:16) and prepares the reader to see God's purposes come to fruition in another extraordinary way.

Also unique to Matthew is that in the account of the ambition of Zebedee's sons, it is their mother who asks Jesus to let them sit at his right and left in his kingdom (20:20–21). In addition, only Matthew recounts that Pilate's wife sent Pilate a message during the trial of Jesus, "Have nothing to do with that righteous man. I suffered much in a dream today because of him" (27:19). Matthew alone preserves the parable of the ten virgins (25:1–13), challenging disciples to readiness for the coming reign of God.

From traditions Matthew shares with Luke comes the parable in which Jesus likens the kingdom of heaven to the work of a woman mixing bread dough (Mt 13:33; Lk 13:20–21). And as Jesus approaches the holy city he uses the feminine image of a mother hen wanting to gather her brood under her wings to describe his own desire to gather together the children of Jerusalem (Mt 23:37; Lk 13:34; see Ps 91:4).

5. The Third Gospel retains many of the same traditions of women who are healed by Jesus: Simon's mother-in-law (4:38–39), Jairus's daughter, and the woman with a hemorrhage (8:40–56). Luke omits the account of the Syrophoenician woman and that of Herodias and her daughter but includes unique stories of Jesus' compassion toward a widow in Nain whose only son had died (7:11–17) and toward a woman who had been bent over for eighteen years (13:10–17). The tradition of the woman who anointed Jesus for burial becomes quite another story in Lk 7:36–50. Placed in the midst of the Galilean ministry, the focus of this account is the lavish love poured out on Jesus by a woman who had been forgiven many sins. Luke retains the story of the widow who gave her whole life (21:1–4) in much the same form as Mark.

Luke's opening two chapters preserve traditions unique to him that profile three prophetic women. Elizabeth is portrayed as "righteous in the eyes of God, observing all the commandments and ordinances of the Lord blamelessly" (1:6). She is the sign of encouragement to Mary (1:36) and mentor to her (1:39–45) when both women become pregnant under extraordinary circumstances. Her naming of John opens the way to faith and praise of God for her husband and relatives and all those "throughout the hill country of Judea" (1:57–66).

The annunciation to Mary (1:26–38) portrays her as a woman of faith and courage in the most unusual and difficult circumstances. Filled with the Holy Spirit (1:35), she prefigures the ideal disciple who hears the word of God and acts on it (8:21; 11:28). Mary's canticle (1:46–55) prophesies the lifting up of all the lowly, words that typify the mission of her son (4:18–19). Mary is shown to be faithful in observing Torah as she presents her son in the temple (2:22) and annually journeys with her family to Jerusalem for the Passover feast (2:41). She searches to understand God's ways, "pondering on them in her heart" (2:19, 51). Two further allusions to Mary (8:19–21; 11:27–28) emphasize that discipleship is dependent not on blood relationship to Jesus but rather on hearing and acting on the word of God. Mary only appears among the disciples in the postresurrection setting of the gathering of the women and men who await the coming of the Spirit (Acts 1:14).

Luke 2:36–38 features the prophet Anna, a widow advanced in years who has dedicated herself to prayer and fasting in the temple. As one of the first Lucan characters to recognize Jesus, she speaks about him "to all who were awaiting the redemption of Jerusalem" (2:38).

These powerfully prophetic women in Luke 1–2 are cast in the mold of the female prophets of the First Testament such as Miriam, Deborah, Huldah, and Judith. But such portraits of women are not to be found in the remainder of the Third Gospel. Taking a position similar to that of the author of the Pastoral Letters, Luke's portraits of women followers of Jesus reinforce silent, passive roles for them. In the story of Martha and Mary (10:38–42) it is receptive listening that is exemplary for a woman, not active leadership in ministry (10:40).

The Galilean women disciples appear much earlier in this Gospel (8:1–3). Luke names Mary Magdalene, Joanna, the wife of Herod's steward Chuza, and Susanna among the many other women who accompanied Jesus and the Twelve on the itinerant mission. However, they are portrayed not as preaching but rather as wealthy patrons giving financial backing to the mission (8:3). The silencing of the women reaches its apex in the empty tomb narrative. After having witnessed the death of Jesus (23:49) and his burial (23:55–56), Mary Magdalene, Joanna, Mary the mother of James, and the other women who accompanied them proclaim the message of the resurrection to the "apostles." But, as Luke relates, "their story seemed like nonsense, and they did not believe them" (24:11).

Three parables, two of them unique to Luke, undermine the portrait of silent, passive women that Luke attempts to reinforce. The parable of the baker woman hiding leaven in the dough (Lk 13:20–21) likens her action to that of God in the divine realm. The woman searching diligently for a lost coin portrays God's extravagant search for those who are lost (15:8–10). And the insistent widow exemplifies God's persistent pursuit of justice and divine power in seeming weakness (18:1–8).

6. In Luke's second volume women wait along with the men in the upper room (1:14) and likewise receive the gift of the Spirit (2:1–4). Both women and men become believers (5:14; 8:12). Many of the women are of high status (17:4, 12). The name of one woman convert from Athens, Damaris, is preserved in Acts 17:34. Women as well as men are persecuted for their faith (8:3; 9:2). Philip's "four virgin daughters gifted with prophecy" receive brief mention (21:9). A negative example of one who threatens the unity of the fledgling community by lying is Sapphira along with her husband, Ananias (5:1–11).

Tabitha, a disciple at Joppa, is "completely occupied with good deeds and almsgiving" (9:36), in particular, making tunics and cloaks (9:39). She is a leader among the widows (9:39) and is resuscitated by Peter. Lydia, a dealer in purple cloth, from the city of Thyatira, is baptized by Paul along with her household. She prevails upon Paul to accept her hospitality (16:13–15). It is to her house that Paul returns after his release from prison following the uproar over the slave girl from whom he cast out an oracular spirit (16:16–24). That Lydia's home had become the meeting place for the Christian community is evident in Acts 16:40.

Luke recounts Paul's relations with Prisca and her husband, Aquila, in Acts 18. Paul stays with them in Corinth and works in the same trade with them (18:2–3). The missionary couple sails with Paul to Ephesus, where he leaves them to minister. The importance of the leadership of both is evident from the episode in which Apollos, a Jew from Alexandria, "an eloquent speaker" and "an authority on the scriptures" (18:24), arrives in Ephesus and begins preaching in the synagogue. When Prisca and Aquila recognized that he was in need of further instruction, together they "took him aside and explained to him the Way of God more accurately" (18:26). Although these women are given brief mention in Acts, the primary focus is on Peter and Paul as the apostles who carry forth the mission in ways that closely parallel the actions of Jesus.

7. Preserving traditions different from those of the Synoptics, the Fourth Evangelist conveys very strong portraits of ministering women. Jesus' mother is a catalyst for the inauguration of Jesus' public ministry at Cana (2:1–12) and is a witness at his death (19:25–27). A woman in Samaria is portrayed as the first missionary (Jn 4:4–42). She engages in a deep theological discussion with Jesus, which leads to her belief in him as Messiah (4:29). In a gesture parallel to that of the first fishermen called (Mk 1:18, 20), she leaves behind her water jar (4:28) and goes to testify to her whole town, who also come to faith (4:39).

In the Fourth Gospel it is Martha who makes the most complete confession of faith. In her discussion with Jesus about resurrection, prior to his resuscitation of Lazarus, Martha proclaims, "Yes, Lord. I have come to believe that you are the Messiah, the Son of God, the one who is coming into the world" (Jn 11:27; cf. Mk 8:29 and pars., where it is Peter who makes such a proclamation). In John's version of the burial anointing, it is Mary of Bethany who performs the action, while Martha serves (12:1–8).

As in the other three Gospels, Mary Magdalene is a witness of the crucifixion. In John's account she is joined by Jesus' mother; his mother's sister, Mary the wife of Clopas (19:25); and the Beloved Disciple (19:26). But in Jn 20:1–2, 11–18 she goes alone to the empty tomb. She is the first one to whom Jesus appears, and he himself commissions her to tell the news of the resurrection to the rest of the community. In this account there is no hint that her word is not believed.

From this brief survey of New Testament texts concerning women it is evident that there are conflicting and ambiguous traditions. Women disciples are clearly present and are often mentioned alone, without reference to their husbands or fathers. From the traces of women believers and ministers mentioned in the Gospels and in the Pauline letters, one can surmise that women's participation in the mission was not unusual, nor was it marginal. But it is clear that the early church and the New Testament writers were not of one mind about the propriety of women exercising public ministries and taking leadership positions. The most telling illustration comes from comparing the differences in the four Gospel accounts of the women's witness about the resurrection along with 1 Corinthians 15, where Paul omits any mention of women in the list of resurrection witnesses.

In evaluating the New Testament evidence for women's participation in the mission of the early church it is important to recognize that the traditions have been written predominantly by men, for men, and about men. One should not presume, then, that if women are not mentioned in the text that they were not present. Nor should those women mentioned in the texts be regarded as unique; rather they should be thought of as representative. Interpreters must also evaluate the patriarchal biases of New Testament authors and distinguish between what is prescriptive and what is descriptive. Finally, the canonical traditions preserve only part of the story. Other versions are found in apocryphal works; still others are lost to us forever.

BARBARA E. REID, OP

Bibliography

Pauline and Post-Pauline Letters

Bassler, J., "1 Corinthians," *WBC* 321–29. Bowman Thurston, B., *The Widows: A Women's Ministry in the Early Church* (1989). Branick, V., *The House Church in the Writings of Paul* (1989). Briggs, S., "Galatians," in E. Schüssler Fiorenza, ed., *Searching the Scriptures,* vol. 2. (1994) 218–36. Brooten, B., " 'Junia . . . Outstanding among the Apostles' (Romans 16:7)," in *Women Priests: A Catholic Commentary on the Vatican Declaration* (1977) 141–44. Idem, *Women Leaders in the Ancient Synagogue: Inscriptional Evidence and Background Issues* (1982). Cantarella, E., *Pandora's Daughter: The Role and Status of Women in Greek and Roman Antiquity* (1987). Castelli, E., "Romans," in E. Schüssler Fiorenza, ed., *Searching the Scriptures,* vol. 2 (1994) 272–300. Collins,

J. N., *DIAKONIA: Re-interpreting the Ancient Sources* (1990). D'Angelo, M. R., "Colossians," in E. Schüssler Fiorenza, ed., *Searching the Scriptures,* vol. 2. (1994) 313–24. Idem, "Women Partners in the New Testament," *Journal of Feminist Studies in Religion* 6 (1990) 65–86. Davies, S., *The Revolt of the Widows: The Social World of the Apocryphal Acts* (1980). Dewey, J., "1 Timothy," "2 Timothy," "Titus," *WBC* 353–61. Ellis, E., "Paul and His Co-workers," *NTS* 17 (1970–71) 437–52. Fiorenza, E. Schüssler, *Discipleship of Equals: A Critical Feminist Ekklesia-logy of Liberation* (1993). Idem, *In Memory of Her: A Feminist Theological Reconstruction of Christian Origins* (1984). Idem, "'Waiting at Table': A Critical Feminist Theological Reflection on Diakonia," *Concilium* 198 (1988) 84–94. Fiorenza, E. Schüssler, ed., *Searching the Scriptures,* 2 vols. (1993, 1994). Gaventa, B. R., "Romans," *WBC* (1992) 313–20. Irvin, D., "The Ministry of Women in the Early Church: The Archaeological Evidence," *Duke Divinity School Review,* 45 (1980) 76–86. Johnson, E. E., "Colossians" and "Ephesians," *WBC* 338–42; 346–48. Kraemer, R. S., *Her Share of the Blessings: Women's Religions among Pagans, Jews, and Christians in the Greco-Roman World* (1992). MacDonald, D. R., *There Is No Male and Female: The Fate of a Dominical Saying in Paul and Gnosticism* (1987). Maloney, L., "The Pastoral Epistles," in E. Schüssler Fiorenza, ed., *Searching the Scriptures,* vol. 2. (1994) 361–80. Murphy-O'Connor, J., "St. Paul: Promoter of the Ministry of Women," *Priests and People* 6 (1992) 307–11. Osiek, C., "Galatians," *WBC* 333–37. Idem, "Philippians," in E. Schüssler Fiorenza, ed., *Searching the Scriptures,* vol. 2. (1994) 237–49. Perkins, P., "Philippians," *WBC* 343–45. Portefaix, L., *Sisters Rejoice: Paul's Letter to the Philippians and Luke-Acts as Seen by First-Century Philippian Women* (1988). Reid, B., "Problematic Paul on Women," *NTR* 5 (1992) 40–51. Schottroff, L., *Lydia's Impatient Sisters: A Feminist Social History of Early Christianity* (1995). Tanzer, S., "Ephesians," in E. Schüssler Fiorenza, ed., *Searching the Scriptures,* vol. 2 (1994) 325–48. Wire, A. C., *The Corinthian Women Prophets: A Reconstruction through Paul's Rhetoric* (1990).

The Gospel of Mark
Anderson, J. C., and S. D. Moore, eds., *Mark and Method: New Approaches in Biblical Studies* (1992). Beavis, M. A., "Women as Models of Faith in Mark," *BTB* 18 (1988) 3–9. Dewey, J., "The Gospel of Mark," in E. Schüssler Fiorenza, ed., *Searching the Scriptures,* vol. 2 (1994) 470–509. Gill, A., "Women Ministers in the Gospel of Mark," *AusBR* 35 (1987) 14–21. Graham, S. L., "Silent Voices: Women in the Gospel of Mark," *Semeia* 54 (1991) 145–58. Grassi, J. A., "The Secret Heroine of Mark's Drama," *BTB* 18 (1988) 10–15. Kinukawa, H., *Women and Jesus in Mark: A Japanese Feminist Perspective* (1994). Kopas, J., "Jesus and Women in Mark's Gospel," *RevRel* 44 (1985) 912–20. Malbon, E. S., "Fallible Followers: Women and Men in the Gospel of Mark," *Semeia* 28 (1983) 29–48. Munro, W., "Women Disciples in Mark?" *CBQ* 44 (1982) 225–41. Ricci, C., *Mary Magdalene and Many Others: Women Who Followed Jesus* (1994). Schmidt, J. J., "Women in Mark's Gospel," *TBT* 19 (1981) 228–33. Selvidge, M., "'And Those Who Followed Feared' (Mark 10:32)," *CBQ* 45 (1983) 396–400. Sugirtharajah, R. S., "The Syrophoenician Woman," *ExT* 99 (1986) 13–15. Tolbert, M. A., "Mark," *WBC* 263–74.

The Gospel of Matthew
Anderson, J. C., "Matthew: Gender and Reading," *Semeia* 28 (1983) 3–27. Kopas, J., "Jesus and Women in Matthew," *ThTo* 47 (1990) 13–21. Levine, A. J., "Matthew," *WBC* 252–62. Schaberg, J., *The Illegitimacy of Jesus: A Feminist Theological Interpretation of the Infancy Narratives* (1987). Wainwright, E., "The Gospel of Matthew," in E. Schüssler Fiorenza, ed., *Searching the Scriptures,* vol. 2 (1994) 635–77. Idem, *Towards a Feminist Critical Reading of the Gospel according to Matthew* (1991).

The Gospel of Luke and Acts of the Apostles
Corley, K., *Private Women: Public Meals* (1993). D'Angelo, M. R., "Women in Luke-Acts: A Redactional View," *JBL* 109 (1990) 441–61. Durber, S., "The Female Reader of the Parables of the Lost," *JSNT* 45 (1992) 59–78. Fiorenza, E. Schüssler, "A Feminist Critical Interpretation for Liberation: Martha and Mary: Lk. 10:38–42," *RIL* 3 (1986) 21–36. Hamm, D., "The Freeing of the Bent Woman and the Restoration of Israel: Luke 13:10–17 as Narrative Theology," *JSNT* 31 (1987) 23–44. Haskins, S., *Mary Magdalene: Myth and Metaphor* (1993). Jervell, J., "The Daughters of Abraham: Women in Acts," in *The Unknown Paul: Essays on Luke-Acts and Early Christian History* (1984) 146–57. Karris, R. J., "Missionary Communities: A New Paradigm for the Study of Luke-Acts," *CBQ* 41 (1979) 80–97. Idem, "Women and Discipleship in Luke," *CBQ* 56 (1994) 1–20. Kopas, J., "Woman in Luke's Gospel," *ThT* 43 (1986) 192–202. LaHurd, C. S., "Rediscovering the Lost Women in Luke 15," *BTB* 24 (1994) 66–76. Martin, C., "The Acts of the Apostles," in E. Schüssler Fiorenza, ed., *Searching the Scriptures,* vol. 2 (1994) 763–99. Moltmann Wendel, E., *The Women around Jesus* (1987). Parvey, C., "The Theology and Leadership of Women in the New Testament," in *Religion and Sexism* (1974) 139–46. O'Day, G., "Acts," *WBC* 305–12. Osiek, C., "The Women at the Tomb: What Are They Doing There?" *ExAud* 9 (1993) 97–107. Reid, B., *Choosing the Better Part? Women in the Gospel of Luke* (1996). Idem, "Luke: The Gospel for Women?"

CTM 21 (1994) 405–14. Reimer, I. R., *Women in the Acts of the Apostles: A Feminist Liberation Perspective* (1995). Ryan, R., "The Women from Galilee and Discipleship in Luke," *BTB* 15 (1985) 56–59. Schaberg, J., "Luke," *WBC* 275–92. Seim, T. K., *The Double Message: Patterns of Gender in Luke-Acts* (1994). Idem, "The Gospel of Luke," in E. Schüssler Fiorenza, ed., *Searching the Scriptures,* vol. 2 (1994) 728–62. Senior, D., and C. Stuhlmueller, eds., "The Mission Perspective of Luke-Acts," in *The Biblical Foundations for Mission* (1983) 255–79. Via, E. J., "Women in the Gospel of Luke," in *Women in the World's Religions, Past and Present* (1987).

The Gospel of John

Brown, R. E., "Role of Women in the Fourth Gospel," in *The Community of the Beloved Disciple* (1979) 183–98. Brown, R. E., et al., *Mary in the New Testament* (1978) 179–218. Collins, R. F., "Mary in the Fourth Gospel: A Decade of Johannine Studies," *LouvStud* 3 (1970) 99–142. Dollar, S. E., *The Significance of Women in the Fourth Gospel* (1983). Grassi, J. A., *The Hidden Heroes of the Gospels* (1989) 113–35. Moloney, F., *Woman First among the Faithful* (1986) 84–102. O'Day, G. R., "John," *WBC* 293–304. Reinhartz, A., "The Gospel of John," in E. Schüssler Fiorenza, ed., *Searching the Scriptures,* vol. 2 (1994) 561–600. Rena, J., "Women in the Gospel of John," *ExT* 17 (1986) 131–47. Schneiders, S., *The Revelatory Text* (1991). Idem, "Women in the Fourth Gospel and the Role of Women in the Contemporary Church," *BTB* 12 (1982) 35–45. Scott, M., *Sophia and the Johannine Jesus* (1992).

❧ WORD OF GOD ❧

1. Historical Survey. 2. Systematic Theology Alternatives.

1. This article will first survey the topic of the word of God from a historical perspective, discussing the Old and New Testaments and then addressing the major successive attempts to deal with the subject.

1.1. In the Old Testament the word is essentially a word about the way one should live (Torah). It is rooted in the covenant between Yahweh and Israel and is proclaimed by the priesthood at the shrine: Yahweh is Israel's God; Israel is Yahweh's people. As such, Yahweh is shown as the true God before other peoples and also before their gods. The people are promised victory over their enemies, prosperity, and peace if they obey the commandments.

Next to the priestly word of command comes the word of the prophets. This word assumes the tradition of the saving action of Yahweh in favor of Israel, as well as the covenant and the law, but also proclaims the will of Yahweh now relevant to the historical situation of the people of the covenant. In contrast to the priest, who holds a fixed office at the shrine, the prophet — excepting the institutionalized cultic prophets — is charismatic, spontaneously called to a task of fixed duration. Therefore, the prophet's authority is easily challenged, especially if his or her message is not acceptable to the elite. The lack of a recognizable authority for his or her office is made good by the prophet's claim to being called, directly and inescapably and despite his or her own resistance, and to having been entrusted with an urgent message from Yahweh which is valid in absolute terms. The word of the prophets receives unqualified recognition for the first time after the national catastrophes of 720 and 586 B.C.E., when Jeremiah's message of damnation, for example, appeared to have been fulfilled. The classic word of the prophets dries up with the loss of independent statehood, that is, is transposed gradually into apocalyptic (→apocalyptic and mission). We see already here breaking out the tension between office and spirit that has accompanied the history of the concept of the word of God ever since. The word of Yahweh is a word with the power to create. The determining factor is the confrontation of faith in Yahweh with the cults of its environment. The giver of fertility is not the Canaanite Baal but Yahweh.

Yahweh is the Lord of nature and of history. Yahweh's control over salvation and damnation presupposes the reality of Yahweh's power.

The word of God in the Old Testament is in the first place a spoken, proclaimed word. Nevertheless, it was set down in writing very early on. The Ark of the Covenant tradition knows of a decalogue written on tablets of stone. The later prophets wrote down their proclamation, or it was written down for them. There is the idea of heavenly scrolls. During and after the exile, the time of collecting, checking, editing, and forming the canon of the holy scriptures began. The desire for certainty of salvation led to the postulation of the verbal inspiration of the text of the law, conscientious obedience to which can alone bring hope of participation in Yahweh's future. Judaism becomes a religion of scripture and doctrine. In apocalyptic texts charismatic immediacy is retained, but the writers of these texts present their works as infallible revelation and impose the curse of God on omissions or alterations to their text.

1.2. The turning point of the New Testament begins with Jesus' proclamation (→Jesus) that the →reign of God is near; his assuring the penitent, the afflicted, and the rejected of God's concern; and his warning the self-righteous of the incorruptibility of God's judgment. Jesus' preaching put in question the religious self-understanding of the Jewish elite and the social order based on it; this eventually led to his being rejected and condemned to death. The disciples' testimony regarding their encounter with the resurrected Jesus and with the Spirit led to the gathering of the Christian congregation. The words of Jesus and the recollections of his days were handed down and collected; through this process, the "words of the Lord" that the resurrected one, through the gift of the spirit of →prophecy, proclaimed to his community flowed into the tradition.

Through the apostolic witness, Jesus, the proclaimer and communicator of the →reign of God, becomes the proclaimed Christ. With this development the word of God is turned into gospel, into joyful message: the eschatological future is anticipated in Jesus as the Christ and in faith becomes accessible to everyone through the →Holy Spirit. Jesus' death on the cross effects atonement, his resurrection new life with God. Because the Spirit creates faith through the proclamation itself, the missionary word becomes the basic event of the community of Christ. According to John's Gospel, God in God's fullness is contained in the person, the word, and the work of Jesus. In the Prologue, Jesus is the eternal word of God become flesh. The concept of Logos, appropriated from early Judaism/Hellenism, plays a paramount role in the subsequent history of christology and the doctrine of the word of God. This development implies also that faith in the creative power of the word of God is carried over to Jesus Christ (Jn 1:3), that, for example, this creative power is ascribed to the word of Jesus (Heb 1:3). It is significant that in New Testament times the word of God is chiefly preached and accepted in faith. The word is the existential →communication of the gracious but also judging presence of God, which one accepts in faith and responds to in →prayer. In the debate with Judaism the Old Testament was used as a source of proof-texts, and the original sense of the words of the text was applied very freely. At first scope was given for the communication of the word and the response of prayer within a fullness of spiritual gifts. A few basic offices were crystallized out of this, which were further reduced under the impact of syncretistic false doctrine. So the word was withdrawn from the itinerant prophets and was reserved to the overseer (*episkopos*), from which eventually the office of bishop was developed. With the formulation of a rule of faith (*regula fidei*), which served as a baptismal confession, the content of the word was regulated. Scriptures which were held to be normative — for example, the Pauline Epistles — became the normal lectionary readings in the congregations. The oral tradition of Jesus was gradually submerged in the individual writings, which then served as sources for our Gospels. The process of collecting, checking, editing, and forming the canon of the New Testament writings began. Attributing the origin of the writings to the apostles played a considerable role in the selection. The doctrine of inspiration in early Judaism finds a certain response in the Christian communities, at least as far as prophetic predictions of the Christ-event in the Old Testament are concerned. Moreover, one is obviously aware that the proclamation of Christ and the witness to Christ are effected by the Spirit.

1.3. The use of the concept of Logos by the Gnostics led to a very close connection in the early church between the concept of the word of God and the scriptures. Influenced by the content of the truth of the Hellenistic philosophical inheritance, the apologists spoke of the *logos spermatikos,* to which the truth of pre-Christian thought was ascribed. In the East tension continued between the word of God as scripture and proclamation, on the one hand, and, on the other hand, the word of God as the incarnate Logos, ascertainable through intuitive, speculative "vision." Mystical theory and the epiphany in worship were preferred to the written sense of the word. In the West, the concept of the word of God remained more historical, more personal, and more closely tied to the written word. However, the "word of God" became increasingly a doctrinal term, protected and developed by dogma and tradition. Alongside this tradition there developed a spiritual, mystic line which placed apocalyptic revelation, that is, inner illumination (Joachim of Fiore) (→apocalyptic and mission), above the actual words of the scriptures. Scholasticism, influenced by Aristotle, recognized the scriptures as the norm of revelation, without seeing a tension between tradition and scripture. Reacting to the Reformation principle of *sola scriptura,* the Council of Trent finally established scripture and tradition on an equal footing by making christology serve as a basis for both.

1.4. In the time of the Reformation, the call of the Renaissance, "back to the sources" (*ad fontes*), becomes important for opposing the predominance of the suspect church tradition. In contrast, for Luther the word of God is above all a proclaimed word, the living voice of the gospel (*viva vox Evangelii*). The gospel is also the criterion of the word: the encouraging word of the justifying grace of God in dialectical opposition to the law, which demands righteousness. Law and gospel are distinguished not by their content but by their function. The law demands new life in Christ; the gospel gives assurance of it as participation in an alien righteousness. The law kills the old Adam; the gospel awakens to new life. Both are also necessary for the believer, who in this life is simultaneously justified and yet a sinner. The same word of scripture can be effective as law or gospel as God wills. The gospel, in dialectic contrast to the law, is the criterion of the word also in scripture: "What leads to Christ!" No matter how intransigent a "Bible-thumper" Luther is, he can deal with scripture critically and freely where, in his opinion, the clear message of the gospel cannot be heard. Because the Catholic tradition had, in Luther's judgment, become legalistic, he invokes the scriptures for the sake of the gospel. But against the left wing of the Reformation (the Enthusiasts), Luther imposes the criterion of the apostolic witness. The word of God reaches me not through inner illumination of the Spirit but from without, through the preaching of what God has done for us (*verbum externum*). The sovereign word, which creates faith, speaks of the grace of God to the sinner. By this means, the inner witness of the Spirit corresponds to the external content of the word.

Melanchthon links Luther's concept of the word to the humanistic principles of sources, defines faith as assent to the word, and reflects on the relationship between self-knowledge and knowledge of the work of Christ. Calvin holds to the proclaimed word which demands faith, emphasizing strongly, however, the didactic element. The sum of all teaching is knowledge of God and of oneself. God is to be known from creation but also speaks through the scriptures, whose authority is derived from this source. Calvin's strongly biblically oriented theology has remained the norm until today in many Reformed churches.

1.5. The move toward the didactic, which we can observe in the approach of Melanchthon and Calvin, was taken to its logical conclusion in the time of controversies over dogma. Protestant Orthodoxy developed doctrinal structures by deduction and definition which needed an axiomatic foundation. One finds such a foundation in the doctrine of the infallibility of scripture as the verbally inspired word of God. Pietism, which emphasized the neglected direct devotion of the heart, heard the living God speak in the verbal inspiration of scripture. The doctrine of the inspiration of scripture became the bastion of true belief in times of Enlightenment, historical criticism, and liberalism, and through the revival movements and mission came to maturity as such in the modern evangelical wing of world Protestantism.

The Enlightenment revolted against the dead doctrinal structures of orthodoxy with its demand for a rational basis for and criticism of the content of faith. The Copernican turning point had placed humanity irreversibly in the center of the universe as the measure of all things. Idealism constructed a philosophical concept of God, who was then unmasked by the materialistic reaction. Feuerbach saw in the objects of religious veneration either abstractions of empirical reality or the projection of unfulfilled wishes. Marx interpreted religion in sociopathological terms; Freud viewed it in psychopathological terms. Historical criticism placed Christianity into categories of the history of religion and thereby relativized it. It became more and more difficult to speak meaningfully of God or the word of God.

1.6. K. Barth starts from the postulate of faith in an objective revelation-event. The fundamental givenness of the divine revelation shakes the foundations of all human experience, including human religion. In Barth's dialectic the "thesis" of the absolute and holy word of God is followed by the "antithesis" of the nullifying and sinful human word, which, however, becomes graciously enveloped in the "synthesis" of God's word and is used for the revelation-event. On the basis of this christologically applied dialectic, Barth opens up the possibility for countless preachers to speak again of the word of God and to proclaim this word. At the same time one finds the Lutheran Renaissance going back to the depths of the Lutheran concept of the word of God. In this way the harsh controversy between Barth and the conservative Lutherans was worked out in the Confessing Church struggle. In contrast to W. Elert, who understood the Lutheran dialectic between law and gospel as a diastasis of "two words of God," Barth emphasizes that there can be only one word of God, which is grace and gospel in every case. The law is a form of the gospel and emerges from the gospel.

The existentialism of R. Bultmann put its stamp on the middle decades of the twentieth century differently from Barth's dialectic. Bultmann links historical-critical research into the New Testament with a radical hermeneutic in which the mythological forms of expression of the biblical tradition are translated into an existentially understood "kerygma" (demythologizing program). Through encounter with the word, the human being is brought to a decision about the authenticity or inauthenticity of his or her existence. Like Barth, Bultmann emphasizes the inaccessibility of God: to speak about God has absolutely no meaning; one can only speak of God (i.e., as one affected by God). The radical nature of the exegesis of historical criticism and the existential interpretation of New Testament texts provoked vehement reaction from conservative circles (with cries of "no other gospel"), especially where the demythologizing program apparently led to the even more radical conclusions of the "God is dead" school of theology.

1.7. The massive and compelling problems of social ethics no longer produce theology. In Bultmann there is historicity, but no history; futuricity, but no future; fulfilling existence, but no social structures or processes; inauthenticity, but no injustice, oppression, or misery. In light of decolonization, problems of development, Marxist-inspired liberation struggles, and ecological hazards and nuclear threat, it has become clear that the theology of the word abbreviated the biblical message in individualistic terms, on a personalized, spiritualized, and existentialized level, and thus diminished it. To counter Barth's "revelational positivism," W. Pannenberg attempts to anchor theology in history and thereby to get a grip on the unresolved problems of the nineteenth century. But the "political theology" of J. Moltmann and J. B. Metz contains more inflammatory material. Under the influence of the neo-Marxist futurologist E. Bloch, the social questions of the future become a central theme of theology. Radicalized unevenly, this development is carried through into Latin American liberation theology (→Latin American theology; liberation theology).

Liberation theology presents a theology, formerly measured out in Western terms, with a revolution. The path of knowledge does not proceed from the intention of the text, reconstructed by historical criticism, to its application to the situation, but the situation is the point of departure, and the text (read unhistorically) is then asked if it can illuminate the situation. The concern to make the oppressed conscious of their situation and of the possibility of changing it (conscientization) takes the place of proclamation of the word. A new canon appears within the canon, according to which the scriptures are read and interpreted selectively. So Exodus becomes the center point of the Old Testament, but without the possession of the land (in which the so-called liberated people subject other peoples to their yoke and rob them of their land). Jesus' sermon in Nazareth (Lk 4:16–18) becomes the key to the understanding of Jesus: he ignores the ruling classes or attacks them while he actively shows his solidarity with the oppressed. The theology of Paul or of John sinks into the background. Law and gospel are applied according to the class system; judgment is pronounced on the oppressors, grace for the oppressed. Moreover, the theory-praxis dialectic takes the place of the hermeneutical circles of Western theology. Theory is legitimate only as a reflection on the liberating process. The consequence is action-reflection, not theory-application. Because salvation is seen as liberation in sociopolitical terms, God's saving action in history is seen wherever liberating acts take place. The great achievement of liberation theology is that it has shoved roughly into the light dimensions that were overlooked or neglected by conventional theology: the biblical faith is applied not to the salvation of the individual but to the culmination of the whole of history in the reign of God. The reign of God is characterized by social justice, for example, by a bias toward the poor. The poor's lack of necessities of life is an evil, and overcoming such deprivation belongs at the center of a soteriological theology. Reconciliation with God and one's neighbor cannot shut out the social dimension: life is indivisible. This brings the significance of social structures and historical processes into view. Ideology as collective self-justification of the devices of vested interests must be denounced. The Bible condemns the pious legitimation or whitewashing of the misuse of power and exploitation. These are insights from which no theology can any longer retreat if it is not to fall short of the comprehensive outlook of the Bible. Admittedly, the question arises whether liberation theology does not present itself as ideology in theological garb. It too is the legitimation of the devices of collective interests, and its hermeneutic makes it immune to the demands of the *verbum externum* of the scriptures. But one can apply criticism only when one is in a position to work out the abiding problems properly from one's own fundamentals. The theology of the word is presented with the task of fully developing its potential in this direction.

1.8. Feminism is the critique of patriarchy in its sociological, psychological, linguistic, literary, and religious-mythic-symbolic manifestations. Patriarchy may be defined as a system of social relations in which the male is normative and in which the male-female relationship is one of domination and subordination. The feminist critique of Christianity is that by its symbols, myths, doctrines, worship, and thought-forms the Christian tradition serves to maintain the patriarchal oppression of women in the world.

This feminist critique is extended to Christian scripture in such a way as to expose the Bible's male-centeredness and its use as a source of patriarchy and oppression. Feminist biblical scholars have produced an enormous corpus of writings from this perspective, although these writings are by no means monolithic. Though there is room for disagreement in principles, goals, and strategy, feminist biblical hermeneutics can be roughly divided into two types: revolutionary and reformist.

Revolutionary feminism views Christianity as hopelessly corrupted by the patriarchy that produced its sacred texts and nourished its social world. The biblical texts are viewed not only with suspicion but with fundamental distrust. Reformist feminism, in contrast, desires to maintain continuity with the Christian tradition while criticizing and reforming it from within. Some within this group search for an uncontaminated core of Christian truth, "a canon within a canon" (such as Gal 3:28), from which to interpret the word of God. Others articulate a "hermeneutic of suspicion" and warn against any attempt to determine a timeless essence of revelation. They urge us to admit and wrestle with the fact that the Old Testament and New Testament are both a source of revelatory and liberating truth and a resource for patriarchal culture and thought.

Much like →liberation theology, feminist biblical hermeneutics expresses a strong critique of any historical interpretation of the biblical text that does not serve the liberation of women and oppressed minorities. Conversely, its focus is on a restoration of biblical interpretation in the spirit of the gospel.

1.9. The churches of Africa and Asia directly continue the tradition of the missionaries, which stems practically without exception from pietist circles and the revival movements. The sermon (→preaching) is related to the Bible; routines, ministries, competence, and moral direction, however, are placed in the foreground. This situation has developed because of a feeling of uncertainty within the establishment resulting from cultural discontinuity and a loss of identity and moral constraints through modernization and urbanization. The affliction of cultural alienation from the Christian faith communicated from the West leads especially in Africa to "independent churches" (→African independent churches), which create a connection between biblical piety and traditional forms of life and thought. Often offended by missionaries of the third generation, young theologians demand inculturation or indigenization (→inculturation) of the message and Christian forms of life, and occasionally a *confessio Africana*. These attempts, however, frequently remain isolated and elitist. That does not exclude the fact that, perhaps unconsciously, a certain amount of cultural exchange takes place in the sermons, which are given overwhelmingly by laypeople. Another phenomenon is the experience of oppression, of economic misery, and of a generally critical social situation, to which the narrow pietistic sermon cannot do justice. In the most recent times the demand for "contextualization" has become increasingly loud. The Christian message and the Christian way of life should be applicable to the situation of the socially disadvantaged, who, in the Third World, are the overwhelming majority of the population. In South Africa there have been attempts to develop a black theology, rejecting North American models. But the project has seldom gone further than the demand for a new hermeneutic. It appears as if a local interpretation of liberation theology in South Africa has a better chance of finding a wide audience than do the attempts to construct a black theology.

2. Our historical survey has brought to light a number of questions and alternatives in the area of problems concerning the word of God.

2.1. Does the word of God reach people through the institutionalized care of a tradition anchored in history or through direct charismatic contact? On the one hand, one should observe that nowhere does the charismatic line emerge without the precondition of tradition. On the other hand, tradition becomes ossified if it does not guarantee space for the charismatic element.

2.2. Is the word of God the living salutation in a proclamation which appeals to the biblical witness, or is it a verbally inspired scripture which need only be exegeted? Whoever has once seen the historical character of the scriptures and discovered their depth and relevance will regard the doctrine of verbal inspiration as an unnecessary and counterproductive burden. It appears to contradict the incarnation of the word in human historical reality in order to deify something human and relative. The character of the word must be preserved as God's direct form of address and as encouragement and demand specifically directed to individuals.

2.3. Is there a dialectic within the word of God between the law that judges and the gospel that saves, or is there only "one" word of God? The two statements are not coterminous, but neither are they mutually exclusive. One must take care in this that law and gospel differ only in function and not in content. If one resolves this dialectic, the sermon either becomes legalistic or suppresses the seriousness of the divine claim as purely a communication of grace.

2.4. Is the content of the word of God limited to the salvation of the individual soul or to the comprehensively conceived eschatological reign of God in which the believer obtains a share by anticipation? There is no question that the first view presents the New Testament message in abbreviated form and does grave harm to the relevance of the word in concrete times of trouble in history. The existentialist narrowing of the kerygma cannot be maintained either.

2.5. Today the weightiest question in hermeneutics is whether the form of the text, defined by historical criticism, should be translated into the modern situation — obviously in accordance with the presuppositions of the hermeneutical circle — or whether one can enlist a text used purely as a paradigm to illuminate a situation which has already been interpreted. Just as questions posed by the situation can bring new dimensions into the historical exposition of the text and just as one must go beyond the original exposition of the text in translating the word in order to put the whole range of problems of the situation under the word, so one must not depart from the outwardness of the biblical witness as demand and encouragement. If one makes such a departure, one is only reinforcing one's own prejudices and ideological credentials with the word of scripture.

2.6. Should the message be translated into the hearers' forms of thinking and living (through inculturation, indigenization, and contextualization), even if syncretistic hybrids cannot be avoided in doing this, or should one strive to pass on as "pure" a doctrine as possible? A pure doctrine does not exist and never has existed. Even what Protestantism supposed to be a "pure gospel" was colored by the culture in which it developed. One must beware of syncretism, but one cannot exclude it in a purist way. A living, less orthodox faith is in any case preferable to an alienated and alienating message that can only be taken over and maintained by piety.

2.7. What counts: the word or the deed? The word of God is →communication, communication as meaning which indicates a reality. Without the lived word, the clarity of meaning is lacking. Without the lived word, the reality of the eschatological message in this world is lacking. Finally, the lived word can also be illusion, utopia, deception. On the one hand, the life of the community and the new ethics lived out by Christians had a powerful impact in the early church and substantiated the proclamation, and it has often been repeated in the history of mission that the deed has undergirded the preached word. On the other hand, the word of God is God's message to the world which the church is commissioned to communicate. Without this awareness of a commission there is no mission, and without mission the church has lost its raison d'être.

Klaus Nürnberger

Bibliography

Barth, K., *CD* 1/1, 1/2 (1960, 1956). Idem, *The Word of God and the Word of Man* (1957). Bimwanyi-Kweshi, O., "Alle Dinge Erzählen von Gott: Grundlegung Afrikanischer Theologie," in *Theologie der Dritten Welt* 3 (1982). Bouyer, L., *The Eternal Son: A Theology of the Word of God and Christology* (1978). Brunner, E., *Man in Revolt* (1947). Callow, K., *Discourse Considerations in Translating the Word of God* (1974). Elert, W., *The Structure of Lutheranism* (1962). Kittel, G., "Word," *ThWNT* 4 (1967) 68–143. Nowell, I., W. G. Thompson, and G. S. Sloyan, "Word," *CPDBT*

1095–1101. Nürnberger, K., *Affluence, Poverty and the Word of God: An Interdisciplinary Study of the Programme of the Missiological Institute* (1978). Idem, "Die Relevanz des Wortes im Entwicklungsprozess: Eine Systematisch-theologische Besinnung zum Verhältnis zwischen Theologie und Entwicklungsstrategie," *EHS* 200 (1982). Idem, "Das Wort Gottes in einer sozialpolitischen Konfliktsituation," *EvTh* 35 (1975) 249–66. Pannenberg, W., *Revelation and History* (1963). Walther, C. F. W., *Law and Gospel* (1928). Wendland, E. R., *The Cultural Factor in Bible Translation: A Study of Communicating the Word of God in a Central African Cult* (1987).

ᕫ WORLD COUNCIL OF CHURCHES ᕬ

1. The Nature and Unity of the Church in Mission. 2. Mission and Evangelism. 3. The Importance of the Laity for Mission. 4. Mission and the Renewal of the Church. 5. Commitment to Justice. 6. Missionary Life Style. 7. Mission to the Poor.

1. The World Council of Churches (WCC) owes its existence largely to the modern Protestant missionary movement. According to its own understanding of purpose, it has always been a movement for the promotion of the unity of the church in its mission. Since the incorporation of the International Missionary Council it has a special responsibility to interpret mission as part of the task of the church. Inevitably topics such as "Mission and the Church" and "Mission and Unity" occupy the most prominent place in the mission-oriented thinking and statements of the WCC. In this connection, the Johannine words of sending and commissioning (Jn 17:21; 20:21) take on a vital significance. The WCC is committed to the unity of the church. Meanwhile, it has become increasingly evident that mission is integral to the nature and work of the church (→theology of mission). The form and nature of the church are determined above all by the fact that it is sent into the world to continue Christ's mission. Thus, to speak of the church means to speak of its mission, by which it shares in the salvific work of the triune God in this world. When in 1982 the Central Committee of the WCC adopted the document "Ecumenical Affirmation: Mission and Evangelism" (ME), this understanding of mission was confirmed. The document put forward seven ecumenical convictions, which were affirmed as the basis of the common ecumenical understanding of Christian mission. One of these has to do with "the church and its unity in God's mission" (20–27). At Lund in 1952, the Faith and Order Commission also related the tasks of mission and unity closely together, clearly stating that such a link was in accordance with the New Testament. Incidentally, the role of the representatives of churches of the Third World was decisive here. They brought from their missionary situation the idea that the task of promoting church unity can be fully understood only when it is focused on the gospel. In fact, the regional ecumenical bodies for East Asia and Africa made a considerable contribution to the discussion on mission and unity. The Central Committee of the WCC had already, in the previous year at Rolle (1951), marked an important stage with a definition of the term "ecumenical." Henceforth, "This word . . . is properly used to describe everything that relates to the whole task of the whole Church to bring the gospel to the whole world." In 1971 at Louvain the Faith and Order Commission took up several aspects of the missionary dimension of the church: the church is defined as a missionary community; the missionary dimension of the Eucharist (→Eucharist [Lord's Supper]) is defined in the light of the nature and task of the church; the apostolicity of the church is described as participation in the mission of Christ.

Since the Fifth General Assembly of the WCC (Nairobi, 1975) its constitution speaks of its functions and purposes: "To facilitate the common witness of the churches in each place and in all places"; "to support the churches in their world-wide missionary and evangelistic task"; and "to foster the renewal of the churches in unity, worship, mission, and service." The General Assembly stressed the necessity of promoting more strongly the dimensions of witness and evangelism in all the programs of the WCC (section 1), and this was confirmed by the Sixth General Assembly at Vancouver in 1983.

2. The question of definition now arises. How are the terms "mission," "evangelism," "witness," and "confessing Christ" (Nairobi) understood by the WCC? Clearly the last three are synonyms, but the question of the relation of mission and evangelism to each other remains. Both occur together in the nomenclature of the Commission on World Mission and Evangelism. They belong together. The spreading of the good news through word and deed forms the heart of the church's mission. Within the commission, it was the representatives of the Third World churches who most strongly declared the two terms to be identical. The introduction of the term "world mission" was intended to emphasize that mission was no longer understood as an undertaking of the Western churches in other continents (mission by the West) but was viewed as a universal task of the whole church. Behind this lies the concept of "mission in six continents," which was put forward at the World Missionary Conference at Mexico City in 1963. It ascribes the responsibility for the mission of the universal church first and foremost to the local church at any particular time and removes the distinction between overseas and home mission. This, in turn, derives from the theological concept of the *missio Dei*. It concerns God's mission in and with the world, a mission which the church shares with the Son of God under the guidance of the →Holy Spirit. The obedience of the church to the mission of its Lord is authenticated through mission by the local congregation at home. The congregation's awareness of its participation in worldwide mission must be complementary to this. While participating in world mission by its interest, the congregation becomes aware of its catholicity through seeking information, through →prayer, and through the sharing of persons and resources (ME 37; →partnership in mission). In ME 6 and 20, one can detect nuances of a difference in the meanings of mission and evangelism. Mission involves the church's awareness of and spreading of its apostolicity ("the action of the Body of Christ in the history of mankind"). Evangelism forms the innermost heart of this sending and is concerned with the proclamation of the →reign of God, as it is made manifest in the life, work, suffering, death, and resurrection of Jesus Christ. Admittedly this proclamation is fulfilled not just in the preaching of the word but also in the outward expression of the life of a church, which is aware of its mission. The "total" understanding of evangelism which finds its expression in this concept takes into account the fact that "the gospel always speaks to people in their totality" (Bangkok). The dynamic force that it contains imposes itself as a promise and as a claim on the sovereignty of God in all aspects of human life. A joint publication of the WCC and the Vatican, "Common Witness," develops this position. "Mission and Evangelism" deals with it under the heading "The Gospel to All Realms of Life" (14–19).

3. The significance of the →laity for mission is of great importance for the WCC. In the ecumenical concept of mission, the laity become the decisive bearers of the gospel. In Mexico City three of the four sections dealt with the witness of Christians and the local congregation. As long ago as 1954 the Second General Assembly at Evanston had devoted a whole subgroup ("The Witnessing Laity") of Section II to the witness of the laity. Their importance was stressed ("The laity stand in the outposts of the Kingdom of God"), and the necessity for educating the laity was emphasized. The most important contribution to this topic was the study on the missionary structure of the congregation. The apostolate of the laity, the missionary renewal of the congregation (moving from the "coming-structure" to the "going-structure"), as well as the complete reappraisal of the church's understanding of its role ("the church for the world" — borrowing from D. Bonhoeffer's "the church for others") were Evanston's most important contributions.

4. Evanston's study on the missionary structure of the congregation contributed to its other major theme, "mission and renewal," the idea being that renewal does not come before mission but is fulfilled in mission. Uppsala had called its Section II "Renewal in Mission" and had thereby numbered the church among the urgent mission fields. Section III at Bangkok was called "Renewal of the Churches in Mission." This makes it clear that reflecting on mission means reflecting on whether the church is remaining true to its purpose, that is, to the commission given to it by its Lord. This necessarily leads to a growing impetus for church renewal and reform. "Mission and Evangelism" devotes article 13 ("Conversion") to this topic and declares that the call to →conversion should begin with the repentance of those who do the calling and issue the invitation. The congregation renews itself while it carries out its mission task. Thus mission is not only a sign by which we recognize the church, but also a sign of its life. A particular case of the refusal of renewal occurs in the structures of power and dependency which exist between the churches and missionary organizations of the former sending countries and the churches of the Third World. This issue was discussed at Bangkok (Section III) under the moratorium proposal. The resulting power gap was declared to be irreconcilable with a true understanding of the church and its unity. Section IV of the Melbourne World Mission Conference (1980) identified the power of the self-sacrificing love of the crucified Christ as the moving force of mission. Church structures and methods of evangelism likewise take their direction from the crucified one. The mission of the church, therefore, is conducted on the "frontiers," where the Lord, who was crucified outside the city gates, leads it. Power and money, to which the church has access, must be used in mission in solidarity with the poor and powerless. Churches who do this will realize both God's mission and authentic renewal.

5. An obedient church will be brought into the human struggle for justice because its mission compels it to stand beside the powerless, the victims of social, political and economic injustice. Bangkok (Section II), Nairobi (Section V), and Melbourne (Section II) have spoken out clearly to this effect: whoever preaches the message of the →reign of God must confront the powers of injustice and oppression. The way in which this happens has been mapped out in the work and suffering of Jesus Christ, with whom the reign of God has been inaugurated. The commitment to justice and →human rights is an integral part of the proclamation of the love of God and of the conquest of the power of sin in the world.

Whoever preaches this message of liberation must be ready to take up the cross (→liberation; liberation theology).

6. Mission, seen as a following of the way of Jesus, demands an appropriate missionary lifestyle, to which the churches must turn in renewal. "Mission calls for a serving church in every land, a church which is willing to be marked with the stigmata (nail marks) of the crucified and risen Lord" (ME 30). The church must serve the gospel and, while doing so, must above all serve those to whom it applies most of all, namely, the poor. The church's life, forms, and structures must be such that they promote this work and do not hinder it. For this reason Melbourne (Section II) declared it to be an anomaly for a church to be part of the establishment of any society. Melbourne (Section IV) called a church in which power is exercised with humility and love a sign of the reign of God for the world. This naturally requires participatory procedures: for example, church leaders must seek the judgment of the community as to whether their exercise of power really serves the poor and oppressed.

7. The major new theme since Melbourne is the role of the poor in mission. The poor must be included as participants in church-missionary activity, not merely as recipients of welfare. This is where we find the greatest challenge to renewal and a changed lifestyle. The christological foundations in Phil 2:5–11; 2 Cor 8:8; and Lk 4:18–19, and the recollection of Jesus' proclamation of the reign of God as good news for the poor — these led Melbourne to the declaration that following Jesus involves an obligation to the poor (Section IV). Consequently, it is important for the church to include the poor as bearers of the message and to hear the good news in new and authentic ways from them. "Mission and Evangelism" reminds us that God's universal purpose of salvation manifests itself always in particular ways, today through the downtrodden, the oppressed, the tortured, the poor of the earth. The church is called to find salvation again among them, to relearn life in emulating them, and to rediscover hidden and forgotten dimensions of the gospel when it begins to read the Bible with the eyes of the poor (ME 35–36). This is where the future of mission lies, with the churches of the poor.

MARTIN LEHMANN-HABECK

Bibliography

Anderson, G. H., ed., *Witnessing to the Kingdom: Melbourne and Beyond* (1982). *Bangkok Assembly 1973: Minutes and Report of the Assembly of the Commission on World Mission and Evangelism of the World Council of Churches, December 31, 1972, and January 9–12, 1973* (n.d.). Castro, E., *Freedom in Mission: The Perspective of the Kingdom of God* (1985). Gill, E., ed., *Gathered for Life: Official Report, VI Assembly, World Council of Churches, Vancouver, Canada, 24 July–10 August 1983* (1983). Goodall, N., ed., *The Uppsala Report 1968: Official Report of the Fourth Assembly of the World Council of Churches Uppsala, July 4–20, 1968* (1968). Lehmann-Habeck, M., "Evangelisation im umfassenden Sinne — eine ÖRK-Position," *EvMiss* (1984) 25–38. Neve, H. T., ed., *Sources for Change: Searching for Flexible Church Structures: A Contribution to the Ecumenical Discussion on the Structures of the Missionary Congregation by the Commission on Stewardship and Evangelism of the Lutheran World Federation* (1968). Orchard, R. K., ed., *Witness in Six Continents: Records of the Meeting of the Commission on World Mission and Evangelism of the World Council of Churches Held in Mexico City, December 8th to 19th, 1963* (1964). Paton, D., ed., *Breaking Barriers, Nairobi 1975: The Official Report of the Fourth Assembly of the World Council of Churches, Nairobi, 23 November–10 December 1975* (1976). Rouse, R., and S. C. Neill, *A History of the Ecumenical Movement*, 2 vols. (1957). Scherer, J. A., *Gospel, Church, and Kingdom: Comparative Studies in World Mission Theology* (1978) 93–163. Scherer, J. A., and S. B. Bevans, *New Directions in Mission and Evangelization*, vol. 1, *Basic Statements, 1974–1991* (1992). Van der Bent, A. J., *Vital Ecumenical Concerns: Sixteen Documentary Surveys*

(1986). Visser't Hooft, W. A., ed., *The New Delhi Report: The Third Assembly of the World Council of Churches, 1961* (1962). Wieser, T., ed., *Planning for Mission: Working Papers on the New Quest for Missionary Communities* (1966). Wietzke, J., *Mission Erklärt: Ökumenische Dokumente von 1972 bis 1992* (1993). Wilson, F. R. ed., *The San Antonio Report* (1990). World Council of Churches, *From Mexico City to Bangkok: Report of the Commission on World Mission and Evangelism, 1963–1972* (1972). Idem, *The Church for Others and the Church for the World: A Quest for Structures for Missionary Congregations: Final Report of the Western European Working Group and North American Working Group of the Department of Studies on Evangelism* (1968). Yates, T., *Christian Mission in the Twentieth Century* (1994). *Your Kingdom Come: Mission Perspectives: Report on the World Conference on Mission and Evangelism, Melbourne, Australia, 12–25 May, 1980* (1980).

❧ WORLD MISSIONARY CONFERENCES ❧

1. Definition and Significance. 2. Edinburgh, 1910. 3. Jerusalem, 1928. 4. Tambaram/Madras, 1938. 5. Whitby/Toronto, 1947. 6. Willingen, 1952. 7. Achimota/Accra, 1957/58. 8. Mexico City, 1963. 9. Bangkok, 1973. 10. Melbourne, 1980. 11. San Antonio, 1989. 12. Salvador, Bahia, 1996.

1. "World missionary conferences" is the name given to the eleven gatherings held so far in the twentieth century at which Protestant Christianity, meeting on a representative basis, took as its theme its participation in God's mission to the world. If the first world missionary conference in Edinburgh in 1910 took place thanks to the outstanding organizational talent of J. R. Mott, the succeeding conferences were regular assemblies of the International Missionary Council (IMC) which arose out of this first conference. Since the integration of the IMC and the →World Council of Churches (WCC) in 1961, the conferences have been held under the auspices of the WCC's Commission for World Mission and Evangelism, whose birthplace is also considered to be Edinburgh. Thus from the beginning the world missionary conferences were linked up as part of the ecumenical movement (→ecumenism), in many cases involved the same people (among others, J. R. Mott, C. Brent, V. S. Azariah, W. Temple, J. H. Oldham, W. Paton, P. S. Minear), and were programmatically influenced to an increasing extent by the ecumenical movement. It is to the credit of the world missionary conferences that they gave a considerable place at an early date to the leaders of the younger churches at the international and interdenominational level.

Insofar as the world missionary conferences reflected the abiding mission of the church (→theology of mission) with ecumenical and intercultural breadth and also within the context of changing times, they focused on the tensions and solutions of their particular age. At the same time they directed the consensus they achieved into the institutions and churches involved so that, although they lacked any legislative authority, their influence was considerable. They have brought together important material on virtually all aspects of missionary work and stimulated various significant developments. The contribution which the conferences made toward clearing up the relationships between the →missionary societies and the younger churches, which had been full of difficulties and tension, has had important consequences. On the ecumenical level, it led to the integration of the IMC and the WCC (1961). At the local level, overseas as well as in the former "sending" churches, it gave a decisive impetus toward the effective constitutional integration of mission and church, a move whose theological implications had long been unresolved. This led, *inter alia,* to the handing over of missionary property to the younger churches. Since 1973 the "repentance" of the rich churches under the slogan "The gospel [only?] for the Poor" has taken a prominent place in discussions. This commitment of the more recent world conferences, which were castigated as being "too political," led to evangelical circles distancing themselves and developing their own structures. Evangelical conferences were held practically simultaneously (Lausanne, 1974, Pattaya, 1980) with the world conferences — a move already intimated in the evangelicals' rejection of the integration of the IMC and WCC.

2. *Edinburgh, 1910.* No essential questions of content were put before the 1,365 authorized representatives of the various missionary societies — only the Orthodox and Roman Catholics were missing — as they came together to make plans for the critical coming years for the missionary onslaught of the Christian West on the non-Christian East and at the same time to mobilize the reserves of the home bases for this task. In the light of the "receptive nature" of the awakening people of the East (the seventeen Asians present were seen as signs of that); in the light of the growing unity of the world and its →culture under Western leadership; in the light of rapid and convenient means of transportation, the delegates came to the common conviction that they were meeting in "the decisive hour" of world mission. All energies were to be concentrated on exploiting this auspicious moment for the "evangelization of the world in this generation" (the phrase shows the influence of the Student Volunteer movement). The goal of the Christianization of the world could be achieved only if the churches coming into existence as the result of mission work in the mission field now became bearers of mission in the non-Christian world, with the help and leadership of the "older" Christian communities. The missionary consciousness of the white man remained unbroken, however; the concepts of "mission" and "colonization" and the extension of the "kingdom of God" and of (Western) "civilization" were naively confused.

3. *Jerusalem, 1928.* In the Anglo-Saxon missionary world, to which the great majority of the 231 participants belonged, World War I had produced nothing like the feeling of uncertainty that it had in Continental missionary circles. Inspired by the vision of a "world transformed by Christ," and under the influence of the "social gospel," the conference pressed for opposition to everything that limited the value of humanity and its self-development. Sections were assigned to race conflict, industrialization, the problems of land settlement. Secularism was discovered to be the opponent of mission. World religions were viewed as possible allies in the development of a better world. Because the Continental delegates, for all their agreement over individual matters, would not give up their suspicions that the Americans and the younger churches under their influence "wished to transform our poor earth into the Kingdom of Heaven by their own strength" (M. Schlunk) and were for their part suspected of fleeing the world with their calling on the savior who saves sinners, the tensions at the conference were great. They succeeded in avoiding a breach, of which there were already indications in the preparatory work of the conference, only by strict concentration on christology in the final message. Some commentators have seen the position of →Vatican Council II presaged in the invitation extended to non-Christians as well as to Christians "to study Jesus Christ in the Holy Scriptures, . . . [though] to come to Him means to surrender oneself." A significant difference from Edinburgh was seen in the far greater weight given to the younger churches, who were now represented by seventy delegates and who with a paper of their own raised the question of the unity of the church. Their self-awareness, which was partly connected with their aspirations for national churches, made it plain that missionary work had to proceed from the younger churches as its center (later known as the church-centric conception of mission). The relation between the younger and older churches thus became the all-important question of mission.

4. *Tambaram/Madras, 1938.* At this "first really and truly worldwide ecumenical conference of Christianity in its almost 2,000 years of history," the representatives of the younger churches, including for the first time people from Africa and South America, made up a narrow majority of the 471 delegates. The general theme, "the building up of the younger churches as a part of the historic universal Christian community," continued the church-centered setting of mission, taking up the momentum from the ecumenical conferences of Oxford and Edinburgh in 1937 with a special emphasis on the local congregation. Mission was logically seen as the work of the whole church in the whole world, the work of a church which was now seen as the greatest hope of the world. In the face of an imminent second world war, the continuing war between China and Japan, and the "new political religions" such as communism, nationalism, and scientific skepticism (which demand their own ungodly sacrifices), the euphoria of Jerusalem had disappeared. The delegates, who worked as an intimate community, declared that the church "is experienced...as the model of [the] redeemed people of God, to which [God] will bring the whole of humanity." Among the preparatory studies (on topics such as theological education, Christian literature, and structures of the younger churches), H. Kraemer's work *The Christian Message in a Non-Christian World* (1938) let loose a debate which is still worth reading today. The IMC, in fact, was employing Kraemer to reject the liberalism of the history-of-religions position found in the much-read *Re-thinking Missions: A Layman's Inquiry after 100 Years* (1932) and the interpretation of W. E. Hocking's position in that report. A scarcely expected but again topical emergency resolution came at the end from the German delegation, advocating an eschatological orientation for the concept of the church. The church must oppose "injustice and social evil," but because it stands "between the times," it has "no social program" for a "new world order."

5. *Whitby/Toronto, 1947.* The 112 delegates from forty countries at the first representative ecumenical meeting after World War II thankfully declared that "the spiritual unity which binds us in the one Body of Christ...has not been broken in the wars." The renewed experience of this unity in an atmosphere which was nothing short of Pentecostal, in contrast to a "world in upheaval," made possible a declaration on the supranationality of mission which was a signpost to the future. But more importantly, the experience of the →Holy Spirit, together with the expectation that the next ten years would be decisive for mission, brought the conference, under the slogan "expectant evangelism," close to the Edinburgh conference of 1910. The call for revival became thereby at the same time as a call for a really missionary church. Because of this call, the relationship, full of tension, between the "younger" and "older" churches, and their common responsibility for mission in obedience to the living →word of God, can be described by the phrase (always disputed but never bettered) "partners in obedience."

6. *Willingen, 1952.* When the 181 delegates met, they were reeling from the shock (and this time the Americans were included) of the closing of China to mission. The end of colonial empires in Asia, moreover, which was becoming apparent at the same time, marked the end of the "Vasco da Gama epoch" (R. Panikkar) of mission history. The forcing into line of the Chinese church, without any resistance, and the outburst of hostility toward missionaries in other places released an "orgy of self-criticism" (M. A. C. Warren) in missionary thought. "Missions under the Cross" was the title of the official conference report. Not only was a purification of missionary motives announced, but the justification of mission had to be completely set out afresh. The response was only partially successful. Because of their differences over the significance of history and its relation to salvation history (*Heilsgeschichte*), the delegates could agree only on a compromise declaration, which in a deliberately eschatological formulation clumsily set out side by side elements of the preparatory studies with their fully integrated contemporary theology. While this declaration set mission in the broadest conceivable context of *Heilsgeschichte* and the activity of the triune God (→Vatican Council II) and thereby broke away from its former church-centered model, it can be considered in the light of its consequences as one of the most significant declarations of a world missionary conference. The understanding of mission as participation in the mission of the triune God, as expressed in the phrase *missio Dei,* led to a new foundation for mission which is summed up in the works of J. Blauw and D. T. Niles.

7. *Achimota/Accra, 1957/58.* The theological integration of mission and church worked out as a consequence of Willingen deepened the crisis in mission once more since this theological solution had to lead to the creation of new structures and the breaking up of old forms. Above all, the pressure of the younger churches, meeting in the newly independent Ghana with their 68 delegates and total of 180 registered participants, influenced the conference over the question of the integration of the IMC and the WCC far more than the record of the vote in favor would lead one to think. Furthermore, the concern of the younger churches for a direct connection with the older churches and the world denominational bodies, bypassing the →missionary societies, indicated a revolutionary change which reminded the participants of the passage in which Paul (→Paul the apostle as missionary) sees his missionary work in Asia as finished and leaves its continuance to the congregations there. Achimota thus shows something of the need of the former bearers of the Western mission to see a new hope and opportunity in the theologically acceptable but yet willingly avoided structural integration of mission and church in the younger as well as the older churches.

8. *Mexico City, 1963.* At this first world missionary conference held after the integration of the IMC and the WCC in New Delhi in 1961, about two hundred representatives of churches came together from all over the world, among them for the first time delegates from the Orthodox churches and Roman Catholic observers. With the overarching theme "God's Mission and Our Task," the topic "The Witness of the Congregation in Its Neighborhood" stood at the heart of the conference, together with the witness of Christians to those of other religions and to the secular world. The cooperation of the →laity as an expression of the missionary understanding of the local congregation was also a central consideration. Further suggestions for a joint supradenominational and supranational action in mission were sought. There was no longer a question of crisis. Thus this conference marked the end of a development. No longer do representatives of missionaries from the West take counsel with representatives of the younger churches of the non-Christian East about the most effective way to build up missionary younger churches. Instead, churches from all over the world, represented by their special-ists in home and overseas mission, encourage each other to participate in the *missio Dei,* in the knowledge that nearly everywhere "mission in six continents" faces a non-Christian or post-Christian majority. Mission is the task not of a few awakened people but of everybody who is of the church.

9. *Bangkok, 1973.* This strongly emotional "nonconference" with its 320 partici-pants (including observers and the press) pushed the question of poverty into the center of the debate on the theology of mission under the theme "The Salvation of the World Today." Under pressure over the bias of the churches and rejecting a consensus on the eternal truths (thus avoiding definite conflicts of opinion), the conference documented the growing influence of →contextual theology. Never be-fore had the representatives of the rich churches found themselves in the dock in this way. Individual conversion was demanded of them and of their churches, in order for them to free themselves from complicity with institutional injustice. It was also demanded that they participate in setting aside the recognized causes of evil in the world. Dialogue was sought with other religions in order to estab-lish the foundations of a common struggle for a more humane world. The concern of the Third World churches with their own identity also found expression in the consideration of the question of temporarily eliminating the sending of Western colleagues and financial aid to areas where the churches had not yet worked out their own priorities (the moratorium). On the one hand, the controversy, which the conference brought to the attention of Christians in the rich Northern Hemi-sphere, brought home the suspicion that the readiness to admit shared guilt in the exploitation of the Third World, like the ability to make a distinction between the end of mission altogether and the temporary shrinking of Western missions, had not developed very far. On the other hand, the conference delegates had to ask whether in their voting for fundamental change — reminiscent of Jerusalem — they had made it sufficiently clear that God's salvation is more than social justice.

10. *Melbourne, 1980.* In contrast to the hopes expressed at Bangkok, by the time of the Melbourne Conference the oppression of the powerless by the powerful had grown in practically all areas of life. The conference pushed the churches even more decisively toward solidarity with the poor and their →liberation. Some five hundred participants from eighty-five countries took as their theme "Thy Kingdom Come." Because God had identified with the poor in Christ and assures them that he is with them and for them, the gospel is good news for the poor. For the rich this means thoroughgoing repentance and renunciation. Challenged once more to liberate itself from complicity with the powerful in oppression and exploitation and to become the church of the poor, the church must point to the good news of the coming of the →reign of God in the conflicts of this world and give signs of the reign of God. Allowance will be consciously made for theological partiality in order to clarify the challenges. The majority of the delegates gave up the attempt to distinguish between spiritual and material poverty in order to avoid promoting a new spirituality and thus curtailing the message which is valid for the whole of humanity (holism). Similarly, the concern with reference to the "not-yet" to pre-vent a definite identification of the struggles of the poor with the contemporary signs of the reign of God proved unavailing. The fear was too great that an "eschatological reservation" could be used as an excuse not to do everything humanly possible to bear witness to the coming reign as being already present. Therefore, the same criticism must be leveled against the conference as against →liberation theology, by which it was so extensively influenced.

11. *San Antonio, 1989.* Following Bangkok and Melbourne, one might gain the impression that, as a counterweight to a tradition of mission which in a one-sided way saw its main focus in the conversion of the individual and in individual salvation, the WCC had, equally one-sidedly, given prominence to the social and political involvement of mission. San Antonio corrected that impression. Some 700 participants met in this strongly multicultural city in the southwestern United States, 269 of them being delegates, among them 43 percent women. The theme was "Your Will Be Done — Mission in Christ's Way." In its message, which proceeded from a trinitarian starting point (see the contribution of the Lutheran World Federation to the understanding of mission in its statement, "God's Mission as a Common Task"), the conference emphasized the "fullness of the gospel" in the "living tension" between "spiritual and material needs, between prayer and action, between evangelism and social responsibility, between dialogue and witness, between power and vulnerability, between local and universal aspects." There was a call to the true fullness of mission (holism) in the closing ecumenical declaration of the Central Committee of the WCC in 1982, "Mission and Evangelization," which served this conference in many ways as a theological foundation. The first section of this declaration, with its "holistic understanding of mission," challenged the member churches "to come to an agreement and to lend concrete expression" in "acts of faithfulness." The holistic understanding of mission of San Antonio and "many good experiences" were attested in a letter which about two hundred participants at San Antonio "who were interested in evangelical concerns" sent to the International Congress for World Evangelization of the Lausanne movement. The latter was meeting in Manila under the slogans "Preach Christ until He Comes" and "The Whole Congregation Is Called to Bring the Whole Gospel to the Whole World." The request was expressed that the next world missionary conferences of the WCC and the evangelicals should take place "simultaneously, in the same place, with a series of joint sessions." If that were to happen, the scandalous division of the missionary movement, which has given such a considerable impulse to the search for church unity (Jn 17:20–21) would be at least partially overcome.

12. *Salvador, Bahia, 1996.* The most recent conference on world mission and evangelism took place in Salvador, Bahia, Brazil, from November 24 to December 3, 1996. The theme of the conference was "Called to One Hope: The Gospel in Diverse Cultures."

The topic — the relation between the gospel and cultures — was chosen in response to the WCC assembly in Canberra, where difficulties became apparent regarding how the relationship between the gospel and culture will shape the form of Christian witness as we enter the twenty-first century. The more that churches around the world begin to articulate their faith in terms of their particular cultures, the sharper becomes the issue of catholicity and contextuality. The Bahia conference addressed issues related to the cross-cultural sharing of the richness of the gospel, including the shape of an ecumenical, intercultural hermeneutics.

A total of 574 people (247 voting members) from over a hundred countries met for ten days in the third-largest city in Brazil. Once the capital of the far-flung Portuguese empire, Salvador then stood at the heart of the colonial slave culture. As a result, according to the conference message, Brazil today "has the second largest population of people of African origin of any nation." It is a country renowned for its multicultural richness and religious pluralism — grassroots Afro-Brazilian, Pentecostal, and Catholic communities. In Salvador, the see of the Catholic primate of Brazil, which reputedly has a church for every day in the year, many Catholics practice Candomblé, a religion with roots deep in West African spirituality.

The flow of the conference program — exposure, encounter, exploration, and engagement — encouraged maximum involvement. Participants were confronted with the richness and variety of local cultures and expressions of the faith at the "Rainbow of Gospel and Cultures" — an exposition of cultural artifacts and religious symbols brought by participants to Salvador. A major block of time was devoted to *encontros* (encounters), where each major region of the world, as well as women, youth, and both Native and Afro-Brazilians, had an opportunity to present their cultures and spirituality. Only after encountering this reality did participants settle down in sections, subsections, and small groups to explore the conference theme. A number of consultations around the world — part of the WCC's three-year Gospel and Cultures study process — had provided volumes of raw material. From that material, regional representatives had met to craft the conference's preparatory papers. The conference theme itself was divided into four sections: (*a*) authentic witness within each culture; (*b*) gospel and identity in community; (*c*) local congregations in pluralistic societies; and (*d*) one gospel, diverse expressions. A total of eleven subsections enabled the participants to address specific issues, and numerous small-group sessions gave delegates an opportunity to have a voice. In the end, four section documents were produced, as well as a "message" and the "acts of commitment."

Two daily activities served to bind the program together. The richly symbolic worship, which took place every morning in a beautiful spot overlooking the "Bay of All Saints," served what one delegate called "a variety of delicious meals rather than a seven-course banquet." The Slave Dock remembrance service — at the place where African slaves were disembarked, baptized en masse, branded, and sold — was a highlight of the conference. Thirty or more small Bible study groups gathered daily to reflect on the missiological implications of the conference theme based upon Acts 1–17.

The Salvador Conference could have been a time of confrontation — given the very different understandings among the churches of the content of the gospel and its relationship to culture. Issues such as proselytism (a concern of the Eastern and Orthodox churches), syncretism (an evangelical preoccupation), the oppressive imposition of Christianity upon subject peoples (indigenous peoples, slaves), and religious pluralism were on the agenda. The diverse perspectives of ecclesiastical representatives and professional theologians and the determined interaction of grassroots people made this conference an event where, in the words of a mission executive, "the cultural context was described by everybody." A significant input came from eighty "frontiers of mission" voting members. They had been selected by churches and conference organizers to represent the perspectives of "feet-on-the-ground" Christians. The significant contribution of laity (52 percent), women (39 percent), and youth (14 percent), as well as of Native and Afro-Brazilian peoples, was felt throughout the conference.

Other groups participated as well. Among them were Roman Catholics, including Vatican observers, who shared their experience and struggles with the conference theme. Although the wish expressed at the San Antonio conference in 1989 that future WCC and evangelical mission conferences take place simultaneously and adjacently remained unfulfilled, evangelicals and Pentecostals made a positive and significant contribution at the conference, though it must be noted that evangelicals at Salvador addressed their concerns primarily to fellow evangelicals and not to the WCC.

The closing "message" expresses the hope of participants that "this last great mission conference of the twentieth century has clearly illuminated that the gospel to be most fruitful needs to be both true to itself, and incarnated or rooted in the culture of a people."

WOLFGANG GÜNTHER AND GUILLERMO COOK

Bibliography

Anderson, G. H., *Witnessing to the Kingdom: Melbourne and Beyond* (1982). Bell, G. K. A., *Documents on Christian Unity* (1924, 1930, 1939–58). Douglas, J. D., *Let the Earth Hear His Voice: International Congress on World Evangelization, Lausanne, Switzerland, Official Reference Volume* (1975). *Ecumenical Letter on Evangelism, "Conference Message," and "Acts of Commitment"* (1997). Gill, D., *Gathered for Life: Official Report, VI Assembly, World Council of Churches, Vancouver, Canada, 24 July to 10 August, 1983* (1983). Goodall, N., ed., *Missions under the Cross* (1953). Idem, ed., *The Uppsala Report 1968: Official Report of the Fourth Assembly of the World Council of Churches, Uppsala, July 4–20, 1968* (1969). Hogg, W. R., *Ecumenical Foundations: A History of the International Missionary Council and Its Nineteenth Century Background* (1952). *International Congress on Mission (IMC), Manila, 2–7 December 1979* (1981). Latourette, K. S., *Christianity in a Revolutionary Age: A History of Christianity in the Nineteenth and Twentieth Centuries*, vols. 3 and 5 (1961, 1962). Lausanne Committee for World Evangelization, *Lausanne Occasional Papers (LOP)* (1978–82). Mott, J. R., *Addresses and Papers* (1946–47). Motte, M., and J. R. Lang, *Mission in Dialogue: The SEDOS Research Seminar on the Future of Mission, March 8–19, 1981* (1982). Neill, S., *Towards Church Union* (1952). Newbigin, L., *One Body, One Gospel, One World: The Christian Mission Today* (1958). Orchard, R. K., *The Ghana Assembly of the International Missionary Council, 28th December 1957 to 8th January 1958: Selected Papers* (1958). Idem, *Witness in Six Continents: Records of the Meeting of the Commission on World Mission and Evangelism of the World Council of Churches Held in Mexico City, December 8 to 19th, 1963* (1964). Padilla, C. R., *The New Face of Evangelicalism: An International Symposium on the Lausanne Covenant* (1976). Paton, D. M., *Breaking Barriers, Nairobi, 1975: The Official Report of the Fourth Assembly of the World Council of Churches, Nairobi, 23 November–10 December 1975* (1976). Payne, E. A., and D. G. Moses, *Why Integration? An Explanation of the Proposal before the World Council of Churches and the International Missionary Council* (1958). Ranson, C. W., *Renewal and Advance: Christian Witness in a Revolutionary World: The Whitby Meeting of the IMC, July 1947* (1948). Rouse, R., and S. C. Neill, *A History of the Ecumenical Movement*, vols. 1 and 2 (1957). Schreiber, A. W., *Die Edinburgher Welt Missions Konferenz 1910*, the Tambaram (Madras) series 1-7 (1939). Visser't Hooft, W. A., *The New Delhi Report: The Third Assembly of the World Council of Churches 1961* (1962). Wilson, F. R., *The San Antonio Report* (1990). World Council of Churches, *Conference on World Mission and Evangelism: Salvador Report* (1997). Idem, *The Missionary Obligation of the Church: Willingen, Germany, July 5–17, 1952* (1952). Idem, *Spirit, Gospel, Cultures: Bible Studies on the Acts of the Apostles* (1995). Idem, *Toward a New Age in Mission: The Good News of God's Kingdom to the Peoples of Asia*. Idem, *Your Kingdom Come: Mission Perspectives: Report on the World Conference on Mission and Evangelism, Melbourne, Australia, 12–25 May, 1980* (1980). *World Missionary Conference, 1910*, 9 vols. (n.d.). Yates, T., *Christian Mission in the Twentieth Century* (1994).

❧ YOUTH AND MISSION ❧

**1. The Sociological Concept of Youth. 2. Youth in Theological Context.
3. Youth in Evangelization.**

1.   In nontechnical, informal usage, "youth" means that age between childhood and adulthood characterized by maturing processes and qualification stages (toward marriage and a profession); the vitality and beauty of youth provide the basis for the often-commercialized "youth myth." But the more the suggestive-emotional dimensions of this informal understanding are analyzed, the more its lack of precision becomes apparent. It turns out to be simply a stereotype for youthfulness as such, totally removed from the concrete, particularly the social, conditions of its surroundings.

The sociological category "youth" was easy to define in smaller, more simply structured societies, for instance, among preliterate peoples. It embraced the period between the end of childhood and the beginning of an adulthood of full responsibility, entrance to adulthood often being emphasized by rites of initiation (→initiation in diverse cultures). In highly complicated industrial Western societies, which have abandoned many of the structures that used to give order and meaning to life, it is no longer possible to delimit the term "youth" chronologically. Roles, values, and patterns of behavior are no longer so fixed that they can be exclusively attributed to definite age-groups. In adolescent psychology the new term "postadolescence" indicates the difficulties of chronological delimitation, for, on the one hand, postadolescents have appropriated all the privileges of adulthood (vacations, holidays, spending, private accommodations, intimate relations), while, on the other hand, despite their great independence, they are dependent on the resources of their parents (or on government grants and allowances) for the financing of such a lifestyle.

The open concept of youth suggested by this situation only shows up the extremely complex situation of young people within society as a whole. Accordingly, only the problems of young people's daily lives are reflected in the sociological theory of adolescence. These difficulties in theory and praxis may not yet exist in those countries in which the proportion of young people (up to twenty-five years) constitutes about 50 percent of the total population, in which traditional patriarchal structures still determine the self-understanding of individuals as well as of age-groups, and in which the individual is still supported by the cohesion of the joint family (clan). But one can expect that in proportion to the penetration of Western civilization and its values into such countries the above-mentioned problems will arise.

2.   The concept of youth in a theological context gains importance when we reflect on the special responsiveness of young people to religious issues. Especially within religious pedagogy, the model of a "theological anthropology of adolescence" (G. Biemer) provides the first impulses for a theological penetration of the many-sided phenomenon of youth. This model is based on the correlation of E. H. Erikson's psychology of identity with K. Rahner's basic model of theological anthropology. This correlation has produced the following theologically relevant criteria for adolescence: a strong relation to mystery, the development of physiological liberty and freedom of choice, intercommunication, and orientation to the future. We should probably also add readiness for action. What is common to all these categories is that they are open to both success and failure. Consequently, they constitute experiences that are particularly typical for the lives of young people. According to these categories, the following leadership roles might be assigned to adults: that of mystagogue, liberator, advocate, representative, companion, and cooperator. By means of these individual criteria a religious profile specific to youth can be elucidated. The uniqueness of youth is that it is the time during which freedom is first realized, the time the burden and joy of anticipating the future is first felt, and the time happiness and problems of sexuality and love are first understood.

This theological anthropology of adolescence helps to free young people from their role as objects in the church — for a long time they were interesting and important only as objects of instruction, conversion, and recruitment. Young people are *subjects* of and in the church. In the same way, such an anthropology overcomes that (unreflected) puerilism which assigns young people, because of their age, a specific "charism" or a special power of "prophecy." At the same time, such statements as "The youth are the hope of the church" are unmasked as theologically unreflected, for the "Spirit-given hope" of the church can never rest in a primarily biologically defined condition. With D. Bonhoeffer we can say that "the spirit of youth is not the Holy Spirit, that the future of the church is not the youth, but the Lord Jesus Christ alone" (Bonhoeffer, *Acht Thesen über Jugendarbeit der Kirche* [Eight Theses on Youth Work in the Church], 1933). To this clear distinction might be added that something can be of meaning for the church as a "spiritual community" only insofar as it lives in and comes about through the Holy Spirit. If a clear limit is drawn in this way against a fashionable overestimation of "youth," young people can nevertheless be, precisely because of their youthfulness, a spiritual challenge to an adult-centered church. Because they embody new values, speak another language, question what is traditional and taken for granted, they thus contribute (sometimes patiently, sometimes less so) to a reform of that church which is not a stranger to them but always has a place for them in its living community.

If young people are seen in this way — in their responsiveness to the essential questions of life, in their sensitivity to the needs of others, in their interest in great figures of salvation and church history — then it will be possible to accept them when they disturb the status quo and are full of passionate criticism. Young people today, everywhere in the world, want to live their faith in their own way; they also want to help build up their church and to share responsibility for it. These are some concrete conclusions emerging from this theological anthropology of adolescence.

3. All over the world the church encounters young people in the most varied religious situations. Whereas in countries of Western civilization it meets young people who are sometimes baptized and attending church but do not understand the relevance of the Christian faith, in countries where the church is persecuted it encounters young people for whom the church is a unique refuge of human freedom, and in countries of the Third World the church serves young people whose daily life it safeguards, whose everyday questions it takes seriously because of its commitment to truth. No matter how different their experiences with faith and church may be, youth will open themselves to Jesus Christ and his truth where this faith gives meaning to their lives, where the community of faith makes people feel at home and awakens responsibility for the world, where faith liberates people for the service of peace, freedom, and social justice. A "civilization of love" could take shape in the commitment of those young people who take Jesus Christ as a model because his lifestyle is uniquely valid today, because there is no more relevant message than his gospel, because he is recognizable in the faces of the poor, and because his beatitudes constitute for them a motive and program of action.

ROMAN BLEISTEIN, SJ

Bibliography

Aden, L., D. G. Benner, and J. H. Ellens, *Christian Perspectives on Human Development* (1992). Biemer, G., *Der Dienst der Kirche an der Jugend* (1985). Bleistein, R., *Jung Sein Heute* (1986). Bonhoeffer, D., *Acht Thesen über Jugendarbeit der Kirche* (1933). Fowler, J., *Stages of Faith: The Psychology of Human Development and the Quest for Meaning* (1981). Gillespie, V. B., *The Experience of Faith* (1988). Griese, H. M., *Sozialwissenschaftliche Jugendtheorien* (1982). Harris, M., *Portrait of Youth Ministry* (1981). Myers, W., *Theological Themes of Youth Ministry* (1987). Nelson, C. E., *Helping Teenagers Grow Morally* (1992). Robert, D. L., "The Origin of the Student Volunteer Watchword: 'The Evangelization of the World in This Generation,'" *IBMR* 10/4 (1986) 146–49. Strommen, M. P., *Five Cries of Youth* (1988). Warren, M., *Reading and Resources in Youth Ministry* (1987).

CONTRIBUTORS

Byung-Mu Ahn. Professor of New Testament, Hankuk Theological Seminary, Seoul, Korea (Korean Theology).

Peter Antes. Professor of History of Religions, University of Hanover, Germany (Mission in Non-Christian Religions [with H. Waldenfels]).

Catalino G. Arévalo, SJ. Professor of Systematic Theology, Loyola School of Theology, Ateneo de Manila University, Manila, Philippines (Filipino Theology).

Horst Balz. Professor of New Testament, Ruhr-Universität, Bochum, Germany (Ancestor Worship II [in Africa]).

Hans-Jürgen Becken. Consultant at Evangelisches Missionswerk, Stuttgart, Germany (African Independent Churches).

Heribert Bettscheider, SVD. Professor of Pastoral Theology, Philosophisch-Theologische Hochschule SVD, Sankt Augustin, Germany (Faith; Liberation).

Stephen B. Bevans, SVD. Professor of Doctrinal Theology, Catholic Theological Union; Director of the Chicago Center for Global Ministries, Chicago (coeditor of the English edition; Common Witness).

Klauspeter Blaser. Professor of Systematic Theology and Missiology, University of Lausanne, Switzerland (Reign of God).

Roman Bleistein, SJ. Professor, University of Munich, Germany (Youth and Mission).

Richard H. Bliese. Assistant Professor of Mission and Evangelism, Lutheran School of Theology at Chicago; Associate Director, Chicago Center for Global Ministries, Chicago (coeditor of the English edition; Confession [with L. Schreiner]; Evangelical Mission Theology II [Lausanne Movement] [with J. Scherer and J. W. Nyquist]; Globalization; Missionary Societies [with H. Rzepkowski]).

David J. Bosch. Deceased. Formerly Professor of Missiology, University of South Africa, Pretoria, South Africa (Evangelism, Evangelization).

Jon Bria. World Council of Churches, Geneva, Switzerland (Martyrdom).

Walbert Bühlmann, OFM Cap. Former Secretary General of the Capuchin Missions (Spirituality).

Bénézet Bujo, Professor of Moral Theology, University of Fribourg, Switzerland (Polygamy).

William R. Burrows. Managing Editor, Orbis Books, Maryknoll, New York (The Absoluteness of Christianity; Theology of Religions).

Arnulf Camps, OFM. Professor Emeritus of Missiology, Catholic University of Nijmegen, The Netherlands (Local Church).

Anscar J. Chupungco, OSB. Director, Paul VI Liturgical Institute, Malabalay, Philippines (Symbol).

Guillermo Cook. Directed planning for the Salvador de Bahia Conference on World Mission and Evangelism; a member of the Latin American Theological Fraternity (World Missionary Conferences [with W. Günther]).

Ernst Dammann. Professor Emeritus of History of Religion and African Studies, University of Marburg, Germany (Language and Translation).

Heinrich Dumont, SVD. Professor Emeritus, Philosophisch-Theologische Hochschule SVD, Sankt Augustin, Germany (European Theology; Salvation).

Franz-Josef Eilers, SVD. Professor of Communications at Divine Word Seminary, Tagaytay City, Philippines; Lecturer in Communications at the Gregorian University; Secretary for Social Communications of the Federation of Asian Bishops' Conferences (Communication).

Virginia Fabella, MM. Dean, Sister Formation Institute, Manila, Philippines (Ecumenical Association of Third World Theologians [EATWOT]).

Klaus Fiedler. Professor of Missiology, Chancellor College, University of Malawi, Zomba, Malawi (Evangelical Mission Theology I; Faith Missions).

Hans-Jürgen Findeis. Professor of New Testament, Catholic Theological Faculty, Bonn, Germany (Missiology).

Edward Foley, OFM Cap. Professor of Liturgy, Catholic Theological Union, Chicago (Art).

Mark R. Francis, CSV. Associate Professor of Liturgy, Catholic Theological Union, Chicago (Baptism; Liturgy).

Richard Friedli. Professor and Director, Institute of Mission and Science of Religion, University of Fribourg, Switzerland (Intercultural Theology).

Mary Frohlich. Assistant Professor of Spirituality, Catholic Theological Union, Chicago (Mission Patrons).

Hans-Werner Gensichen. Professor Emeritus of History of Religions and Missiology, University of Heidelberg, Germany (History of Mission; Peace and Mission; Unification of Churches).

Wolfgang Gern. Director, Gossner Mission, Mainz, Germany (Development; Preaching).

Anthony J. Gittins, CSSP. Professor of Theological Anthropology, Catholic Theological Union, Chicago (Anthropology; Conversion).

Hans-Jürgen Greschat. Professor Emeritus of History of Religions, University of Marburg, Germany (New Religious Movements).

Horst Gründer. Professor of Modern History, University of Münster, Germany (Colonialism).

Christoffer Grundmann. Lecturer, University of Hamburg, Germany (Healing and Medical Missions).

Andreas Grünschloß. Lecturer, University of Mainz, Germany (Initiation in Diverse Contexts)

Margaret E. Guider, OSF. Associate Professor of Systematic Theology, Weston Jesuit School of Theology, Weston, Mass. (Children and Mission).

Wolfgang Günther. Lecturer, Hermannsburg, Germany (World Missionary Conferences [with G. Cook]).

Louis Gutheinz, SJ. Professor of Systematic Theology, Theological Faculty of Fu Jen University, Taipei, Taiwan (Chinese Theology).

Heidi Hadsell. Director, Ecumenical Institute, Bossey, Switzerland (Ecology and Mission).

Ferdinand Hahn. Professor Emeritus of New Testament, University of Munich (Justification).

Viktor Hahn, CSSR. Professor, Philosophisch-Theologische Hochschule SVD, Sankt Augustin, Germany (Tradition [with H. Rzepkowski]).

Willi Henkel, OMI. Director of the Pontifical Missionary Library of the Congregation for the Evangelization of Peoples; Director of the Urban University Library and Associate Professor of Mission History, Pontifical Urban University, Rome (Mission Statistics).

Joseph Henninger, SVD. Professor Emeritus, University of Fribourg, Switzerland (Sacrifice [with D. Ritschl]).

Walter J. Hollenweger. Professor Emeritus of Missiology, University of Birmingham, England (Prophecy).

Leslie J. Hoppe, OFM. Professor of Old Testament, Catholic Theological Union, Chicago (Fundamentalism).

Wolfgang Huber. Professor Emeritus of Systematic Theology (Ethics), University of Heidelberg, Germany (Human Rights).

Leo Karrer. Professor and Director of the Institute of Pastoral Theology, University of Fribourg, Switzerland (Laity).

Karl Kertelge. Professor of New Testament, Catholic Faculty of the University of Münster, Germany (Paul the Apostle as Missionary).

Georg Kirchberger, SVD. Professor of Dogmatic Theology, Divine Word Seminary, Ledalero, Indonesia (Ministry, Office of).

Norbert Klaes. Professor of History of Religions, University of Würzburg, Germany (Christology).

Hans-Joachim Klimkeit. Professor and Director of the Institute for the History of Religions, University of Bonn, Germany (The Study of Religion).

Fritz Kollbrunner, SMB. Editor of *Neue Zeitschrift für Missionswissenschaft* (Vatican Council II).

Martin Lehmann-Habeck. Berlin, Germany (World Council of Churches).

J. B. Libânio. Professor of Dogmatic Theology, Istituto Santo Inacio, Belo Horizonte, Brazil (Latin American Theology; Liberation Theology).

Christine Lienemann-Perrin. Professor, University of Basel, Switzerland (Theological Education).

Louis J. Luzbetak, SVD. Mission Researcher, Techny, Ill. (Anthropology and Mission).

Simon S. Maimela. Professor of Systematic Theology, University of South Africa, Pretoria, South Africa (Black Theology).

Roman Malek, SVD. Director, Institute Monumenta Serica, Sankt Augustin, Germany (Ancestor Worship I [General]).

Gustav Menzel. Retired Missions Director, Wuppertal, Germany (Partnership in Mission [with K. Müller]).

Dionisio Miranda, SVD. Professor of Ethics, Divine Word Seminary, Tagaytay City, Philippines (Ethics).

Heribert Mühlen. Professor Emeritus of Dogmatic Theology, Paderborn, Germany (Spiritual Renewal).

Karl Müller, SVD. Professor Emeritus of Missiology, Philosophisch-Theologische Hochschule SVD, Sankt Augustin, Germany (coeditor of the German edition; Inculturation; Partnership in Mission [with G. Menzel]; Proselytism).

Lesslie Newbigin. Retired bishop of the Church of South India; Birmingham, England (Culture of Modernity).

Othmar Noggler, OFM Cap. MISSIO, Munich, Germany (State, Church, and Mission).

Eugen Nunnenmacher, SVD. Professor of Missiology, Philosophisch-Theologische Hochschule SVD, Sankt Augustin, Germany (Culture).

Klaus Nürnberger. Professor, University of Pietermaritzburg, Pietermaritzburg, South Africa (Word of God).

John W. Nyquist. Associate Professor of Evangelism, Trinity Evangelical Divinity School, Dearfield, Ill. (Evangelical Mission Theology II [with J. A. Scherer and R. H. Bliese]).

James C. Okoye, CSSP. Associate Professor of Old Testament, Catholic Theological Union, Chicago (African Theology).

John Pawlikowski, OSM. Professor of Ethics, Catholic Theological Union, Chicago (Judaism).

Joachim G. Piepke, SVD. Director of the Anthropos Institute, Sankt Augustin, Germany (Popular Religion).

Felix Porsch, CSSP. Professor, Philosophisch-Theologische Hochschule SVD, Sankt Augustin, Germany (Holy Spirit).

Barbara E. Reid, OP. Associate Professor of New Testament, Catholic Theological Union, Chicago (Women in the New Testament).

Dietrich Ritschl. Professor Emeritus, University of Heidelberg, Germany (Ecumenism; Sacrifice [with J. Henninger]).

Heribert Rücker. Bochum, Germany (God).

Christopher Rowland. Dean of Jesus College, Cambridge University, England (Apocalyptic and Mission).

Horst Rzepkowski, SVD. Deceased. Formerly, Professor of Missiology at the Philosophisch-Theologische Hochschule SVD, Sankt Augustin, Germany (Creation Theology and Missiology; Missionary Methods [with J. Schmitz]; Missionary Societies [with R. Bliese]; Prayer; Protestant Communities and Orders; Tradition [with V. Hahn]).

Leo Scheffczyk. Professor Emeritus of Dogmatic Theology, University of Munich, Germany (Eucharist [Lord's Supper]).

James A. Scherer. Professor Emeritus of Missiology, Lutheran School of Theology at Chicago (Evangelical Mission Theology II [Lausanne Movement] [with R. Bliese and J. W. Nyquist]).

Josef Schmitz, SVD. Professor, Philosophisch-Theologische Hochschule SVD, Sankt Augustin, Germany (Missionary Methods [with H. Rzepkowski]).

Ulrich Schoen. Professor Emeritus, University of Mainz.

Lothar Schreiner. Professor of History of Religions and Missiology, Kirchliche Hochschule, Wuppertal, Germany (Confession [with R. Bliese]).

Robert J. Schreiter, CPPS. Professor of Doctrinal Theology and Director of Joseph Cardinal Bernardin Center for Theology and Ministry, Catholic Theological Union, Chicago (North American Mission Theology; Reconciliation).

Ulrich Schoen. Professor Emeritus, University of Mainz.

Donald Senior, CP. Professor of New Testament, Catholic Theological Union, Chicago (Bible).

Wolfgang Stegemann. Professor of New Testament, Augustana-Hochschule, Neuendettelsau, Germany (Jesus).

Theo Sundermeier. Professor of Mission and History of Religions, University of Heidelberg, Germany (coeditor of the German edition; Religion, Religions; Theology of Mission).

Yoshiki Terazono. Professor, Fukuoka, Japan (Japanese Theology).

M. M. Thomas. Deceased. Formerly of Kerala, India (Indian Theology).

Werner Ustorf. Professor of Missiology, University of Birmingham, England ("People" [*Volk*], "Nation").

Elias Voulgarakis. Professor, Athens, Greece (Orthodox Mission).

Herwig Wagner. Professor Emeritus, Neuendettelsau, Germany (Church Growth Movement).

Hans Waldenfels, SJ. Professor and Director of the Institute of Fundamental Theology, University of Bonn, Germany (Contextual Theology; Mission in Non-Christian Religions [with P. Antes]).

Barbara von Wartenberg-Potter. Pastor, General Secretary of the Christian Council of Germany, Stuttgart, Germany (Women).

Dietrich Wiederkehr. Professor of Dogmatic Theology, University of Lucerne, Switzerland (Eschatology).

Bernard Willeke, OFM. Professor Emeritus of Missiology, University of Würzburg, Germany (Rites Controversy [with E. Zeitler]).

Franz Wolfinger. Director, Study Center, Munich, Germany (Tolerance and Religious Liberty).

Engelbert Zeitler, SVD. Founder and former Director of Ishvani Kendra [Missiological Institute], Pune, India (Rites Controversy [with B. Willeke]).

Paul Zepp, SVD. Professor Emeritus of Canon Law, Philosophisch-Theologische Hochschule SVD, Sankt Augustin, Germany (Mission Law).